BEFORE THE MAST:

Life and Death Aboard the *Mary Rose*

edited by Julie Gardiner
with Michael J. Allen

The Mary Rose Trust acknowledges with gratitude the contribution made by the HMS Edinburgh Trust, towards the cost of preparing this volume reflecting life on board a Tudor warship. HMS *Edinburgh*, like the *Mary Rose*, was on active service when she was lost with all hands off the coast of Russia in 1942.

This work is published as a tribute to the men who lost their lives in both vessels

BEFORE THE MAST:

Life and Death Aboard the *Mary Rose*

edited by Julie Gardiner
with Michael J. Allen

with contributions from

Mary-Anne Alburger, Michael J. Allen, Edward Besly, Duncan H. Brown, Kirstie Buckland,
Esther Cameron, Jo Castle, Victor Chinnery, Juliet Clutton-Brock, Mike Cowham, Jennie Coy,
Diana Crawforth-Hitchins, Brian Daley, Brendan Derham, A. Elkerton, Nick Evans,
R.W. Evans, Rachel Every, Marian Forster, Charles Foster, Ian Frame, Julie Gardiner,
Emma Green, F.J. Green, James Greig, Erika Hagelberg, Sheila Hamilton-Dyer,
Jon Hather, Robert E.M. Hedges, Robert Hicks, Linda Hurcombe, Rob Janaway,
Stephen Johnson, John Kirkup, Kirran Louise Klein, Linda Lemieux, Colin McKewan,
Lorraine Mepham, Jeremy Montagu, E. David Morgan, Quita Mould, Ian Oxley,
Mark Redknap, Maggie Richards, Mark Robinson, Jen Rodrigues, Robert Scaife, Wendy Smith,
Alan Stimson, Ann Stirland, Robert Thomson, Rosemary Weinstein, Michael J. Williams
and Robin Wood

The Archaeology of the *Mary Rose*
Volume 4

First published 2005 by The Mary Rose Trust Ltd
College Road, HM Naval Base, Portsmouth, England PO1 3LX

This edition published 2013 by Oxbow Books Ltd, 10 Hythe Bridge Street, Oxford OX1 2EW, on behalf of the Mary Rose Trust

British Library Cataloguing in Publication Data
A catalogue record for this book is available from the British Library

ISBN 978-1-78297-387-4

Series Editor: Julie Gardiner
Series Editor (graphics): Peter Crossman

Designed by Julie Gardiner and Peter Crossman
Produced by Wessex Archaeology

Printed by Printworks International

**The publishers acknowledge with gratitude a grant from the
Heritage Lottery Fund towards the cost of publishing this volume**

Cover illustration: An interpretation of the crew having a meal. A still taken during filming of the BBC *Timewatch* programme *The Secrets of the* Mary Rose. Photograph: Ben Lawrie. © Ben Lawrie 2004

Contents

PART 2: SCIENTIFIC STUDIES: CREW, CONDITIONS AND ENVIRONMENT,
edited by Michael J. Allen

12. Acquiring the Data: introduction to the palaeo-environmental and scientific analyses
Underwater environmental archaeology and the *Mary Rose*, by Michael J. Allen and Ian Oxley 501
Sampling, processing and assessment, by Ian Oxley and Michael J. Allen 503
Taphonomy, by Michael J. Allen 508
Sea-bed environment: processes and effects . . .511
Analyses conducted .514

13. The Crew of the *Mary Rose*
Human remains, by Ann Stirland 516
The 'burials' 516
Numbers of individuals 519
Sexing the remains 519
Age at death 519
Stature 520
Skeletal indices 520
Skeletal morphology 521
Dentition 523
Pathology 523
Activity and occupation 532
Anomalies 542
Conclusions 543
Dentistry, by R.W. Evans 544
Condition of the bone and teeth 544
Matching the jaws and skulls 547
Comparison of the skulls with modern groups 549
Tooth decay (caries) 552
Gum (periodontol) disease 554
Other observations 555
Concluding comment 557
The genetic affinities of the *Mary Rose* crew: DNA analysis of the skeletal remains, by Erika Hagelberg and Ian Frame 557
Maternal and paternal DNA markers 558
Mitochondrial DNA and human history . . .558
The present study .559
DNA analysis 559
Results 560
Outlook 562
Human remains: other scientific analyses, by Michael J. Allen and Andrew Elkerton 563

14. Provisions for Board and Lodging: the animal and plant remains
Introduction, by Michael J. Allen 564
Meat and fish: the bone evidence, by Jennie Coy and Sheila Hamilton-Dyer with Ian Oxley .564

Origins and recovery of the animal bone assemblage 564
Evidence of meals .567
Casked beef 569
Casked pork 574
Orlop deck pork store 574
Scattered pork, beef and mutton 577
Fish 577
Haunches of venison 584
Other possible food species and animals present 585
Size and type of food mammals and fish . . .585
The significance of the *Mary Rose* animal bone assemblage 586
Food, packing and plants: the archaeobotanical remains, by Wendy Smith and F.J. Green . .588
Background and introduction, by F.J. Green 588
The history of the plant remains study 589
Condition of the plant remains, location and quantification, Wendy Smith with F.J. Green 591
Foodstuffs and seasoning 593
Recovery of foodstuffs 597
Other plant material on board 598
Weed/wild plant remains 599
Discussion: food, packing/bedding materials and plants on board 600
Overview 602
'Flesh, fish, biscuit and beer': victuals for the ship, by Jennie Coy and Sheila Hamilton-Dyer 602
Reconstructing the menu 603
Fish in the menu .604
Serving and sharing 605
The Tudor naval diet in its historical context 607
Reconstructing the provisioning 608
Reconstructing the victualling, by Jennie Coy with Julie Gardiner 609
Sources of supply on the *Mary Rose*, by Jennie Coy 611
The animal bone and victualling evidence; a summary discussion, by Jennie Coy . . .612

15. Conditions on Board: pests, parasites and pollen
The ship rat, by Jennie Coy 613
Domestic dog, by Juliet Clutton-Brock 614
Insects, by Mark Robinson with Michael J. Allen .614

A view overboard: pollen analysis, by Robert
    Scaife with Michael J. Allen 617
  Pollen assessment of chests and
    containers, by James Grieg 629
  Summary 629

16. Science and the *Mary Rose*
Scientific studies, by Michael J. Allen 630
Science for the *Mary Rose* 630
  Analysis of animal fats, by E.David Morgan
    and Michael J.Williams 631
  Analysis of glue from arrows, by
    Michael J. Allen 632
  Chemical analysis of medicines, ointments and
    related items, by Brendan Derham 633
  Human remains .641
  Other science 641
The *Mary Rose* as a source of scientific study 641
  Palynological trials, by James Grieg 642
  Absolute dating on the *Mary Rose*, by
    Robert E.M. Hedges 642
  DNA history and the *Mary Rose*, by Erica
    Hagelberg 643
  Other analyses, by Michael J. Allen 648

PART 3: LOOKING TO THE FUTURE

**17. Concluding Comments and Avenues
for Future Research**, by Julie Gardiner and
Michael J. Allen
Use of space and the operation of the ship . .653
Provisioning the ship 656
Welfare 657
The crew 657
Science and technology 658
Spatial analysis of the ship 658
Closing the chapter 658

Appendix 1: Chest contents 661
Appendix 2: Catalogue of textile remains 671
Appendix 3: Plant remains 677
Bibliography 696
Index, by Barbara Hird 713

List of Figures

Fig. 12.1 Isometric of samples taken from the Carpenters' cabin

Fig. 12.2 Reconstruction of diver taking samples underwater

Fig. 12.3 Taking samples from the hull in the shiphall during cleaning

Fig. 12.4 Sampling a column monolith

Fig. 12.5 Numbers of samples taken per year 1976–84

Fig. 12.6 A sample being separated out into component elements

Fig. 12.7 Processing a sample

Fig. 12.8 Sorting material

Fig. 12.9 The ship as she arrived on the sea-bed, with guns and artefacts in disarray

Fig. 12.10 Model of the erosion and sedimentation of the wreck site

Fig. 13.1 Locations of individual skeletal elements within the ship

Fig. 13.2 Human bones on collapsed boxes on the sea-bed

Fig. 13.3 Commingled bones from the Hold and Orlop decks

Fig. 13.4 A pair of matched femora with prominent entheses

Fig. 13.5 The human skeleton

Fig. 13.6 A femur showing probable healed childhood rickets

Fig. 13.7 A pair of matched tibiae showing healed childhood rickets

Fig. 13.8 A fused, bowed and expanded sternum

Fig. 13.9 A fused, angulated sacrum

Fig. 13.10 Probable scorbutic changes from adolescence

Fig. 13.11 Probable adolescent scorbutic changes in a tibia

Fig. 13.12 Possible healed scorbutic lesions on a cranial surface

Fig. 13.13 SEMs of new bone formation

Fig. 13.14 Old healed fracture at nasion

Fig. 13.15 Unreduced spiral fractures of a paired tibia and fibula

Fig. 13.16 Severely traumatised right elbow

Fig. 13.17 A right femur with an old, bowing fracture

Fig. 13.18 Avulsion fracture of tibial tubercle in a pair of tibiae

Fig. 13.19 Avulsion of the tuberosity of a fifth metatarsal

Fig. 13.20 Bilateral osteochondritis dissecans of femoral condyles

Fig. 13.21 Posterior fracture-dislocation of acetabular rim

Fig. 13.22 Bilateral necrotic femoral head pits

Fig. 13.23 Healed depressed cranial fracture

Fig. 13.24 Probable healing cranial arrow wound

Fig. 13.25 (left) The human scapula; (right) bilateral os acromiale

Fig. 13.26 An archer shooting a standard arrow from a replica war

Fig. 13.27 Simon Stanley at full draw with a replica war bow

Fig. 13.28 Laying the body into a replica bow

Fig. 13.29 Enthesophytes on a distal fibula

Fig. 13.30 Enthesophytes on a matched pair of clavicles

Fig. 13.31 Distribution of the Fairly Complete Skeletons

Fig. 13.32 Twisting left apophyseal joints of matching vertebrae

Fig. 13.33 Osteoarthritis and marginal osteophytes

Fig. 13.34 Schmorl's nodes

Fig. 13.35 Ossification into the ligamentum flavum

Fig. 13.36 Spondylolysis

Fig. 13.37 Initial sacrilisation of a vertebra

Fig. 13.38 Large bronze culverin found in M3

Fig. 13.39 Bilateral Perthes disease

Fig. 13.40 Bipartite inca bone in the occipital

Fig. 13.41 Simplified views of the skull

Fig. 13.42 The main external features of a molar tooth

Fig. 13.43 a) the right side of the skull b) part of a maxilla

Fig. 13.44 Occipital aspect of skull with three inca bones

Fig. 13.45 a) part of a mandible showing large bony swelling; b) dental pantomograph

Fig. 13.46 a) unerupted third molars and other feaures b) palate and upper dentition showing sockets for supplemental lateral incisors; c) edentulous lower molar regions due to ante-mortem molar loss

Fig. 13.47 Right side of matched skull and mandible

Fig. 13.48 a) matched skull and mandible; b) occlusal view of mandibular dental arch; c) buccal teeth

Fig. 13.49 Section through a molar, premolar and jaw

Fig. 13.50 a) good maxillary dental arch with minimal signs of malocclusion; b) maxillary dentition from an older person

Fig. 13.51 Intra-oral radiograph of three molars

Fig. 13.52 How the location of caries (decay) has changed through time

Fig. 13.53 a) Periodontal disease; b) effects of caries

Fig. 13.54 Styloid processes, cystic radiolucencies, gross caries

Fig. 13.55 Dental pantomograph showing gross caries

Fig, 13.56 How attrition reduces the teeth

Fig. 13.57 Human mitochondrial DNA

Fig. 14.1 Articulated fish bone embedded in silt

Fig. 14.2 Main distribution of animal and fish bones

Fig. 14.3 Cattle bones represented in beef cask 81A2610/2702

Fig. 14.4 The best preserved casked salt beef collection

Fig. 14.5 Cattle midline butchery

Fig. 14.6 Typical cattle butchery

Fig. 14.7 Bones pulled off during butchery of cattle

Fig. 14.8 Pig bones represented in cask 81A3346

Fig. 14.9 Pig bones from cask 81A3346

Fig. 14.10 (top) Disposition of pig bone in O2; (bottom) pig bones and adipocere from the Orlop deposit

Fig. 14.11 Pig bones represented in the Orlop deposit

Fig. 14.12 Whole bones from the Orlop pig deposit

Fig. 14.13 Diagrammatic skeleton of a cod

Fig. 14.14 (left) Cod vertebrae and (right) fin rays
Fig. 14.15 Two obliquely chopped cod vertebrae
Fig. 14.16 Butchered cod cleithra and postcleithra
Fig. 14.17 Butchery of conger eel
Fig. 14.18 Fallow deer bones
Fig. 14.19 (top) Measurements of the centrum length of abdominal vertebrae; (bottom) measurements of the width of the cleithra
Fig. 14.20 Location of archaeobotanical samples
Fig. 14.21 Plant remains by deck and sector
Fig. 14.22 Distribution of cereal grain
Fig. 14.23 Distribution of fruit
Fig. 14.24 (left) Plums/greengages (right) grape
Fig. 14.25 Distributions of chaff, grain and weeds
Fig. 14.26 (left) possible clover; (right) agrimony
Fig. 14.27 Seventeenth century painting of a pig being butchered
Fig. 14.28 Eighteenth century depiction of cod butchery
Fig. 15.1 Rat bones
Fig. 15.2 The dog skull

Fig. 15.3 The flea and the human flea *Pulex irritans*
Fig. 15.4 Puparia of the seaweed fly *Thoracochaeta zosterae*
Fig. 15.5 Location of pollen samples
Fig. 15.6 Pollen diagram
Fig. 16.1 Structure of chemicals found in medicaments
Fig. 16.2 Oxcal distribution of radiocarbon dates
Fig. 16.3 The polymerase chain reaction (PCR), a method for the amplification of a specific DNA sequence
Fig. 16.4. Bone specimens from which DNA was recovered
Fig. 16.5. Alignment of the published sequences of the human and pig mitochondrial DNA *cytochrome b* genes
Fig. 16.6. Direct sequencing of a fragment of the mitochondrial *cytochrome b* gene, amplified from an extract of a *Mary Rose* pig bone
Fig. 16.7 Location of the human jawbones examined for microstructual changes
Fig. 17.1 The *Mary Rose* as depicted on the *Anthony Roll*
Fig. 17.2 The *Mary Rose* as she is today

List of Tables

Table 12.1 Taphonomic considerations effecting the loss or decay of biological and non-artefactual assemblages

Table 12.2 Marine Mollusca recorded by Culley

Table 13.1 Number of skulls and mandibles

Table 13.2 Total numbers of bones occurring in pairs

Table 13.3 Number of individuals in each age category

Table 13.4 Stature based on the femur

Table 13.5 Cranial index

Table 13.6 Orbital index

Table 13.7 Total facial index

Table 13.8 Number of skulls, jaws and teeth recovered

Table 13.9 Comparison of *Mary Rose* skulls with Eastman Standard cephalometric data

Table 13.10 Comparison of cephalometric data from six racial groups

Table 13.11 Numbers and % of teeth present, unerupted, missing and carious

Table 13.12 Carious sites on teeth

Table 13.13 Classification of attrition

Table 13.14 Numbers and % of skulls within attrition groups

Table 13.15 Numbers and % of individuals in attrition groups correlated with decks

Table 13.16 Average number of carious molars per skull correlated for teeth lost post-mortem by location on ship

Table 13.17 Human bone submitted for DNA analysis

Table 13.18 Mitochondrial DNA sequences of nine crew members

Table 13.19 Samples examined for brain tissue

Table 14.1 Number of animal bone samples and total fragments

Table 14.2 Fragment numbers examined from Tudor contexts

Table 14.3 Animal bones by deck and sector

Table 14.4 Cask contents

Table 14.5 Anatomical elements of cattle in the three main casks

Table 14.6 Anatomical remains of pig in cask 81A3346 and the Orlop deck deposit

Table 14.7 Summary of fish records by sector

Table 14.8 Fish in casks and baskets

Table 14.9 Frequency of butchery marks on fish remains

Table 14.10 Comparison of anatomical distribution of fish

Table 14.11 Habitats of weeds/wild taxa

Table 14.12 Records of peppercorns

Table 14.13 Possible rations per man

Table 15.1 Insect remains

Table 15.2 Insect remains

Table 15.3 Pollen samples

Table 15.4 Pollen

Table 15.5 Pollen

Table 15.6 Pollen from caulking and sailcloth

Table 15.7 Pollen from assessed samples

Table 16.1 Analysis of pig and beef fat

Table 16.2 Compounds identified in a sample of glue from a *Mary Rose* arrow and beeswax

Table 16.3 Samples submitted for chemical analysis

Table 16.4 Basic identification of samples

Table 16.5 Results of CHN elemental analysis

Table 16.6 Radiocarbon determinations

Table 16.7 Human jaws analysed for microstructural changes

List of Colour Plates

Plate 50 Carved wooden panel

Plate 51 Nail-boarded stool

Plate 52 Chest 81A1429

Plate 53 Chest as recovered but emptied of contents

Plate 54 Large fragment of wicker basket as recovered

Plate 55 Selection of the pewter objects

Plate 56 Selection of pottery vessels

Plate 57 Selection of wooden bowls, dishes and spoons

Plate 58 Reconstructed wooden drinking tankard

Plate 59 Wooden bowl with internal graffiti

Plate 60 Dish bearing the 'H' brand denoting official issue

Plate 61 Fine, large wooden bowl

Plate 62 Selection of wooden and leather vessels

Plate 63 White slipped storage jar and small cooking pot

Plate 64 Wicker-covered pottery flask

Plate 65 Small wooden canister and peppercorns

Plate 66 Wine flagon

Plate 67 Wooden and pewter spoons

Plate 68 DNA sequencing of nine amplification products from *Mary Rose* human bone extracts.

Plate 69 Fragments of hypnoid moss from possible bedding

Plate 70 Articulated cod vertebrae

Plate 71 Articulated pig bones from cask 81A3346

PART 2. SCIENTIFIC STUDIES: CREW, CONDITIONS AND ENVIRONMENT

edited by Michael J. Allen

12. Acquiring the Data: Introduction to the Palaeo-environmental and Scientific Analyses

Underwater Environmental Archaeology and the *Mary Rose*

Michael J. Allen and Ian Oxley

The obligations of any archaeologist are clear: to examine and analyse the remains of the activities of man in the past. It must be accepted that the analysis of all *archaeological* material should aim to contribute to the sum of archaeological knowledge. Such an aim overrides the mere collection or salvage of objects. Information on how people actually lived, and the conditions in which they lived, can be gleaned from even the most unprepossessing deposits. Evidence of a non-artefactual nature is as important as the safe recovery and conservation of material items and it should be universally regarded as such. It appears that, at the time when excavations were conducted on the *Mary Rose*, the primary objective of many sites in the sphere of underwater archaeology was the salvage of objects and ship's structure (Firth 2002, chap. 2). Unfortunately, over two decades later, this still remains the case for many projects. What is presented in the following chapters not only significantly enriches our understanding of life on board the *Mary Rose* and in Tudor England, but we hope will also serve to demonstrate the wealth, depth and diversity of interpretative information that can be lost without such a study. The Mary Rose Trust was actively involved with those working within the field of environmental archaeology in order to redefine the methods of collection, processing, and analysis of non-artefactual material of all types (Oxley 1984). Consequently, what is published in the following chapters constitutes some of the first full analyses of organic non-artefactual remains from *within* an underwater wreck itself, rather than of the sediments *in which* it was found.

A vast array of non-artefactual organic remains was preserved with the *Mary Rose*, either as a result of burial in essentially constant anaerobic conditions beneath fine-grained waterlogged silts, or by impregnation with, or replacement by, metal corrosion products, especially of iron or copper. These rare preservational conditions, combined with a single-event 'life-assemblage', provide the potential to study remains that are specific to life

aboard a Tudor ship. The non-artefactual evidence is indispensable in understanding the working of the ship, life aboard her, and aspects of the economy and society of the time that supported the burgeoning navy (eg, Kenchington *et al*. 1989). Preserved materials include waterlogged plant remains, animal and human bone and biological tissue (animal fat and human brain), which are rarely preserved so well and uniformly on more familiar dryland sites.

Although the last three to four decades have seen great progress in the practice of underwater archaeology, that relating to the recovery, retrieval and study of non-artefactual remains (plant macrofossils, pollen, etc) has not been so evident, nor has the application of other scientific methods to these remarkably preserved assemblages (eg, chemical analysis, mtDNA, etc). This source of data has often been overlooked, particularly in relation to environmental and other non-artefactual remains (Oxley 1991), and the potential of environmental archaeology and archaeological science in underwater conditions is often not fully appreciated (Oxley 1984).

The Mary Rose Trust was one of the first to embrace environmental archaeology wholesale. Although a few other projects have also undertaken sampling and recovery of plant remains and pollen (eg, Haldane 1986; 1991; 1993; Ward 2001), the immense task of their analysis has meant that, until now, few have been published in any detail. Several individual statements and interim comments appear in the annual reports of the *VOC-ship Amsterdam* Foundation, such as the identification of tobacco leaves (Magedans 1987). Armitage provides an interesting overview of the study of faunal remains from shipwrecks of the period AD 1500–1880 (1989) and Reilly (1984) reports on the few animal remains from the almost contemporaneous Cattewater wreck (*c.* 1530). The range and quality of the materials recovered from the *Mary Rose* can be gauged by popular texts (Rule 1982) and by the discourse presented in this volume.

All too often on previous underwater wreck-site excavations, acceptable standards of sampling and analysis were abandoned because the environmental work was seen to be slow, difficult and tedious; the results from scientific and specialist analysis were not as immediately available as those of the recovery of, for instance, a cannon or other recognisable object. On the *Mary Rose* excavations, however, there was a commitment to the recovery of environmental data and most of the practical difficulties experienced underwater were overcome with time and patience combined with good planning, disciplined methods and the guidance of an in-house environmental archaeologist. Here, the work on the *Mary Rose* was undoubtedly ahead of its time (cf. Oxley 1984; 1991; A. Elkerton and C. Dobbs, pers. comm.).

The recovery and analysis of this wealth of information does not, however, come without its own problems. Environmental evidence is often destroyed or missed, because it is not looked for. On underwater shipwreck sites in particular it has often been the case that disproportionate care and attention has been paid primarily to the artefacts and, after that, to the ship structure, to the detriment of other kinds of evidence (cf. Lavery 1988). On the *Mary Rose* controlled samples were taken and valiant efforts made to process, assess and analyse those remains. The divers took a large very number of samples to recover as much 'evidence' as they could, even if they did not fully comprehend what could be obtained from them.

Margaret Rule realised the possibilities and potential of palaeo-environmental material and was instrumental in making the initial approaches to local specialists and inviting them to advise her. Thus, during the main excavation phase (1979–82), environmental science in many of its manifestations was a considerable component of understanding the wreck site, and obtaining further information about the site, the vessel, the materials and the people aboard, once they had been brought ashore. Jennie Coy and Frank Green, two environmental archaeologists then at Southampton University, were 'on board' and advising the project soon after the raising of the wreck. Subsequently, individuals on the *Mary Rose* team were delegated responsibility to deal with the material and liaise with the specialists.

In the latter part of the excavation, however, the emphasis of the project concentrated on the recording of the hull, and on the recovery and removal of objects within it, in preparation for the lift. Once the form of the vessel had been determined in the muds, the hull and objects were recorded, recovered, identified, and curated as accessions to a museum rather than as an integral part of a larger *archaeological assemblage*, as on dryland sites. Following the lifting of the hull, the archaeological diving team was essentially disbanded. This was the key moment when the project moved from archaeological excavation to one of the conservation and study of the hull by maritime and nautical experts, and to the study of the objects essentially within a museum environment. Research became specifically object and, to some degree, ship oriented, rather than

'site' oriented. In the post-lift and latter stages of fieldwork, the unwritten and unvoiced ethos of the Mary Rose project was undoubtedly driven by the desire to preserve and record the vessel itself and the accompanying objects. In this respect the whole post-lift ethos of the project differed from that of the excavation phase and certainly from that of a dryland archaeological excavation where relationships between site, object, and context (locations and distributions) are prime concerns.

Apart from the dive- and shorelogs, one of the main immediate post-excavation products was the generation and maintenance of numerous independent lists of artefacts, samples, timbers, etc. Objects and their associated samples were categorised into essentially functional groups such as 'domestic: container', 'personal: accessory', 'stowage: staved container', for objects or 'cultural: faunal', 'marine: sediment' for samples (see Chapter 1 for more detail). This form of cataloguing, which is, again, much more museum than archaeologically oriented, was hugely helpful in making initial sense of the 26,000 or so objects, samples and timbers that were recovered. However, its effect, was to fragment the spatial and contextual elements, isolating items as individual objects of study, rather than as integral components of a single 'life' assemblage, whose location, association and spatial distribution (plan) was crucial to any reconstruction of how the ship was organised and operated. Admittedly, the assemblage was not pristine, nor fossilised; items had been disarrayed and moved significantly (see taphonomy, below), but the object-based ethos did not help the final analysis of many of the biological assemblages, in particular, where precise context, confirmed association, and exact, rather than generic, location were not always immediately, if at all, available. Although the records make it possible to locate the sector of almost every find and sample individually, it is less easy for a researcher to compile composite information from the paper archive about groups of different categories of artefacts and items found in both specific and general locations, or to establish their direct relationship with one another or with elements of the ship structure. Even plans of objects and their association with environmental remains are not present as the DSM data (*AMR* Vol. 1 and Chapter 1, above) have yet to be processed.

It is undeniable that this 'object and ship' philosophy drove both the acquisition of items for museum and exhibition display which is inextricably linked to fund raising and also, to a large extent, the archaeological research programme – the Trust's advisors advocated the approach as did early decisions regarding the form and content of intended publication (A. Elkerton, pers. comm.). Unfortunately, one result has been that it left some of the scientific and environmental analyses somewhat sidelined; considered to be of lower priority and significance than many of the delicate objects and fragile timbers. This is, to some extent, understandable,

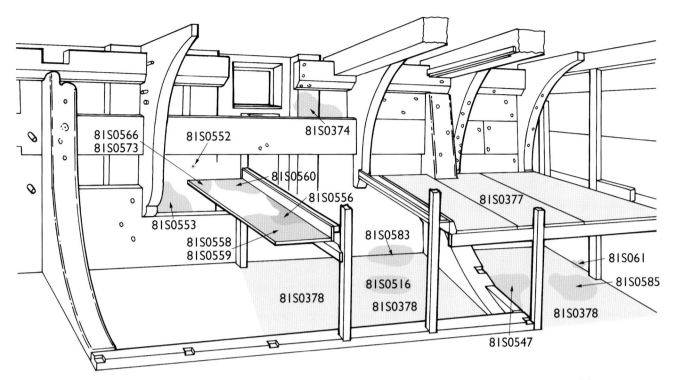

Figure 12.1 Isometric showing samples taken from the M9 Carpenters' cabin (as recorded). 81S0566: seeds, hay (see insect report); 81S0573: straw/sediment (see Table 14.12); 81S0553: straw ?matting; 81S0558: hay/textile; 81S0559: hay; 81S0560: hay/sediment ?radiocarbon date (see Table 14.15a); 81S0556: ?hay; 81S0378: sediment (associated with 81S0377 = plant material); 81S0394: sediment and ?seaweed; 81S0583: basket; 81S0516: hay/rope; 81S0547: plant material/hay (see Table 14.12); 81S0377: plant material (Reay records upper leg frags of insect); 81S0585: sediment and seeds

especially since palaeo-environmental research is expensive in its post-excavation treatment and its results less immediate. Following recovery from the wreck, it required heavy investment of post-excavation resources merely to process and retrieve items, many of which are microscopic and required the help of the few (and potentially expensive) specialists who had extensive relevant experience, and reference collections, necessary to identify and analyse them. Even at the best of times results were never as quickly available, nor readily presentable, to an eagerly waiting public as were the stunning, reconstructable objects which could capture their immediate imagination.

This approach was not unique to the Trust, and Firth (2002) demonstrates that this preoccupation with the intrinsic relevance of 'finds' is enshrined in the *Protection of Wrecks Act* 1973, and pre-eminent in the publication of many other historic wrecks such as the *Kennemerland* (Price and Muckelroy 1974; 1977; 1979; Price *et al.* 1980; Dobbs and Price 1991), *Dartmouth* (Holman 1975; McBride 1976; Martin, P. 1977; Martin C. 1978), *Amsterdam* (Marsden 1972), *Anne* (Marsden and Lyon 1977) and *Invincible* (Bingeman 1985). Although there are a few published accounts of underwater wrecks attempting to interpret 'life' and 'life style', they have tended to emphasise the potential (eg, Cattewater wreck, Redknap 1984), rather than demonstrate it.

Sampling, Processing and Assessment
Ian Oxley and Michael J. Allen

Sampling

Despite exceptional conditions of preservation, material was not collected and raised blindly, simply because it was recognised as being different, unusual or well preserved. Samples of materials recovered from the sea-bed were taken from the outset of the *Mary Rose* research in 1971. However, from the establishment of the main excavation (1979–82) a more structured programme of sampling was considered within the whole excavation rationale. The sampling was not, however, primarily for the recovery of palaeo-environmental remains. The conditions permitted the preservation of many fragile and delicate items, and of material that would decay on removal from the controlled conditions of the sea-bed environment. Any object, substance, or deposit which was not an 'artefact', 'timber', or obviously 'human bone' was designated as a sample. Thus, 'Sample' was essentially a generic term for many of the items observed on the sea-bed that were recovered within a block or mass of sediment. These items had to be recovered from the sediment by washing, sieving or washover flotation (see below). As such, 'samples' included a diverse range of objects, such as fragments of clothing (eg, jerkins),

Figure 12.2 Reconstruction of diver taking samples underwater

textiles and chest contents, and not just 'environmental and non-artefactual remains'.

Some sampling was principally conducted as good practice to minimise physical damage to objects and the deleterious decay caused by the change of environment during and after recovery. Essentially this was done by attempting to maintain the burial environment until controlled recovery, removal or extraction from the sediment could be achieved. Other samples were of masses of material or fine fish bones which were known, or assumed, to contain micro- or macroscopic remains that needed appropriate land-based recovery methods (processing by sieving or flotation and sorting and extraction under low magnification). Where possible, containers such as chests were raised with their contents intact and then excavated and sampled on the deck of the *Sleipner* or in the laboratory.

Samples were taken by the divers, largely of recognisable items or remains (Fig. 12.1), but also of sea-bed sediment etc. These were normally lifted in 10 litre plastic containers with close-fitting lids, such as ice cream boxes

Figure 12.3 Taking samples from the hull in the shiphall during cleaning

(Fig. 12.2). Bones and groups of bones were similarly sampled, but a number of factors came into play. These included visibility of the material (size, integrity, associated objects or deposits, adhered material), weather and sea conditions and time of day, as well as operational factors such as the competence and experience of the diver, strategic decision-making imposed on the dive, the excavation season or year, dive deadlines and time constraints. The duration of an individual dive was limited, typically only 45–57 minutes, during which excavation, recording, DSM measurement and samples had to be taken, although each dive shift would have comprised a number of dives over the day. Many of the later samples each season (81 and 82 with 'S' numbers in excess of about 1000) were taken by finds assistants during shore excavations. There is, generally, no corresponding Shorelog that deals specifically with the non-artefactual remains – and little information on the actual relationships between the sample material and the original artefacts, unless an entire object was being emptied (eg, a chest). Yet further samples were taken from the hull during cleaning in the first few years after the ship was raised (Fig. 12.3).

Many 'samples' were recorded as being associated with an object or item. These 'associations' however varied from being clear and direct, such as fragments of textile or the contents of chests, to the much more general, such as where a tub of sediment was collected from amongst a jumble of objects. In such cases it is often not possible to determine which specific object (if any) had a direct relationship with the material sampled.

In addition, a further programme of sampling was undertaken aimed at the understanding and interpretation of the stratigraphy. A series of 'column samples'

was taken, principally in 1980 and 1981, to provide information about the conditions under which the sediments accumulated. Questions driven largely by Andrew Fielding, Jon Adams, Chris Dobbs, Ian Oxley and Bob Stewart were addressed by taking series of undisturbed sediment samples. These included samples taken vertically through exposed stratigraphic sections in 2-litre ice cream-type tubs, so that undisturbed blocks of the stratigraphy could be removed (Fig. 12.4), or in cut-open plastic tubes or gutter that had been driven into the sediment, allowing more detailed on-shore examination of the sediment profile and its structure. About 35 samples were taken through the main and key stratigraphic units: the hard shelly layer sealing the wreck site, the grey clays and seaweed lenses forming the main sediments, and the grey clays and sands beneath them. Unfortunately there was no-one locally who, independently of the Trust, came forward with expertise and skills in marine sedimentation to advise and lead analysis of the sediments. Nevertheless, these column samples facilitated student analyses of particle size and the contained macrofossils (for example Bettley 1985/6; Dassow 1984). These data can be combined with that conducted for conservation criteria (published in *AMR* Vol. 5, 24–5).

Much of sampling was question-oriented (from general to highly specific) but many of those questions were not formally articulated, nor transferred to sample sheets or cards. As there was no formal assessment stage, such as is now ubiquitous in land-based archaeology, some of the processing and resultant analysis may not have addressed the original questions posed by the divers or environmental team at the time of recovery.

Post-excavation history
Michael J. Allen

By 1979 a number of samples (excluding animal bone) had been taken that were considered useful for environmental scientific analysis (plant remains, fish bones, sediment samples, etc) and these were stored pending further examination and the development of a programme for their various processing, assessment and analysis requirements. In 1979 one of the archaeological supervisors, R.G. (Bob) Stewart (1979–80), was given the responsibility for sampling and in 1980 he set up the first proper sampling and processing programme including paraffin and froth flotation and simple wet sieving. He reviewed the stored samples taken in 1971–9 and outlined the requirements for dealing with these potential data (Stewart 1980; archive). This was timely as, in fact, only a small proportion of the final total of samples had been taken during that period; the majority were recovered during the main excavations that commenced that year. By the end of 1988 over 1800 samples had been recorded (Fig. 12.5).

Figure 12.4 Sampling a column monolith; after divelog sketch by Oxley, June 1981 (divelog 81/2/282) and Dean et al. 1995, fig 106

This ultimately led to the appointment, in 1981, of Peter Boyd, the first non-diving member of the team dedicated to environmental archaeology. Practical processing began in earnest and continued until 1988, apart from the excavation season of 1982. During this time Boyd was assisted by Ian Oxley, who acted as his diving assistant, taking most of the samples and co-ordinating and implementing their agreed, evolving sampling strategy. Following Boyd's departure in 1982, the full responsibility for archaeological science fell to Oxley, who had been a member of the diving team since 1980. It was apparent (to Oxley) that the processing of the sample material required a very heavy investment of time, money and personnel. The processing programme was extended to include other categories of samples in order that an assessment of the entire collection might be attempted.

During this time assistance was provided by a number of volunteers and by helpers on Manpower Service Commission schemes. Some of the more capable and those who showed specific aptitude or had been trained (eg, graduates of biological science) took on specific and designated responsibilities (eg, John Buglass and Alex Naylor). The aid and advice of a range of external specialists, in particular Coy and Green, continued to be enlisted. Other leading environmental archaeologists gave advice or identified items from time to time. Despite an almost complete lack of funds for environmental research, Oxley ensured that the processing programme continued in some form. Many of the analytical programmes were set up, largely by inviting specialists to investigate the unique material that had been recovered, and also by passing material to students for dissertations and course projects. By 1983, for instance, analysis of animal bones was underway with Coy and Oxley working entirely at weekends at the Faunal Remains Unit at Southampton University. This analytical programme was assisted by the enthusiastic

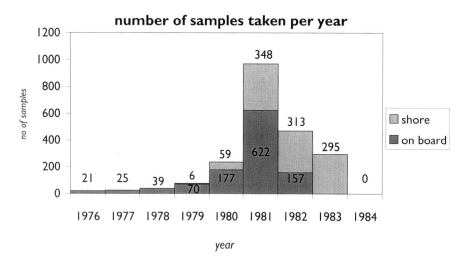

number of samples taken per year

and unpaid research into relevant historical sources by Jennifer Bourdillon, a faunal expert in her own right.

Some of the other major classes of material were reviewed at the Trust in June 1984, by Frank Green, James Greig, Mark Robinson, Phillipa Tomlinson, Ian Oxley, Rob Scaife, and Peter Dodd, and in seminars held jointly with the Association for Environmental Archaeology (November 1985). This led to pilot studies on pollen preservation in underwater wreck contexts by Greig (Chapter 16), later pursued by Scaife in 2001–2 (Chapter 15 and *AMR* Vol. 2), and also to some specific analyses on the botanical remains by Dodd (plums) and detailed microscopic work, by Tomlinson, confirming macro-morphological identifications made by Green (Chapter 14). The initial major analyses of plant remains, animal and fish bones were conducted voluntarily by established environmental archaeologists outside their normal working hours.

Following Oxley's departure in 1988, the programme of processing, analysis and reporting lost its impetus and essentially became moribund. Several attempts were made to encourage and revitalise this programme but the final reporting was ultimately driven by the receipt of HLF funding for this publication (2001) and the management of the programme by Wessex Archaeology. One of the most significant contributions in this final phase was that of English Heritage in providing Wendy Smith for three months of analytical work and reporting to assist Frank Green in the completion of the contribution on the plant remains.

Numbering and processing
Ian Oxley

All samples were allocated a sample number prefixed by the year and 'S'. This system conformed with that used for artefacts (A), timbers (T) and human bone (H) (see also Chapter 1, above). A complex nomenclature of suffixed numbers (xxxx/1.2) was devised defining components and subdivisions of samples (archive). In many cases, only part of a sample was processed; this may then have been either subdivided (ie, after processing) and/or individual items removed, each being given a unique suffix identifier. Thus any one sample, for instance 81S0319 (shown in Fig. 12.6), recorded initially as 'flora: plant remains', could be subdivided for processing (81S0319/1 and 81S0319/2). An item or component separated from that sample was again individually numbered and identified (eg, 81S0319/1.3: broom (*Cystis scoparius*) and 81S0319/1.7: insect aphid). All sample numbers, with details of their provenances, were entered into the *Mary Rose* database in dBase.

Most samples were processed by some form of wash-over flotation. The precise methods evolved and developed through time and experience, but samples were generally immersed in a tank with a continuous flow of fresh water (Fig. 12.7). During immersion larger, more significant and recognisable items were picked out, whilst the flot was washed onto a 63 micron mesh sieve. In many cases samples were left for two days under continuous running water and sediment in suspension was removed via the overflow leaving the plant and other material in clear water. The residues were sorted by volunteers for recognisable remains (Fig. 12.8). Paraffin flotation was occasionally employed from earliest times to recover insects, but the potential for their recovery was not always recognised and no systematic approach was taken. Decisions as to which should be treated in this way were, of necessity, largely informed by irregular visits from Dr R. Reay and Graham Bremmer (Biological Sciences, Portsmouth Polytechnic) and Frank Green.

Animal and human bones
The majority of the bones were systematically cleaned and samples of materials or deposits associated with them taken where necessary. Air-drying followed an intensive cascade wash in fresh water (see *AMR* Vol. 5 for details) and subsequent storage has taken place within an environmentally controlled area. No obvious visible deterioration in the condition of the bone was recorded during processing, drying or analysis (see *AMR* Vol. 5, 48, 100).

Fish bones
Major fish bone concentrations were sampled and wet-sieved in their entirety on 1mm mesh sieves to facilitate retrieval. Material which passed through this sieve has been retained by the Trust for future analysis. All of the

Fig. 12.6 Sample 81S0319 from O2 being separated out into component elements

larger bones were retrieved from the 1mm residue by hand sorting, but a proportion of each residue remained unsorted. After sorting, the bones were air-dried and stored in a controlled environment.

Straw/plants

Samples included seeds, pods, flower heads, straw, hay, grass, and wicker fragments from disintegrated baskets which were recognised at the time of excavation. The term 'straw' was often applied to plant-like material because of its appearance, regardless of its actual content. Oak leaves recovered from the Hold (80S0029, 80S0057 and 81S0093) remained flexible when stored in distilled water.

Plant remains and insects

On the whole, sediment samples for the recovery of organic plant remains were processed by laboratory wash-over flotation (Fig 12.7 and 12.8) with the flots collected on a 250 micron mesh sieve. The flot was transferred to sample tubes containing 50–100% industrial methylated spirit (IMS). Storage in a solution of less than 50% resulted in the expansion and growth of a black, slimy organic product and the release of hydrogen sulphide (rotten egg smell). A solution much above 50% IMS caused leaching of the colour (chlorophyll) surviving in, for example, moss (Plate 69) that was still pale green when recovered in the sample. Most of the flots, whether assessed, partially or wholly sorted or unsorted, are retained in archive.

The residues were water-sieved on a 250 micron mesh to clean and disaggregate them. These were sorted and the archaeobotanical and other material transferred to plastic boxes. From 1984 some of this botanical material was stored in alcohol-glycerine formalin solution (AGF) (Kenward *et al.* 1980). The AGF solution, however, had to be removed before identification and analysis could be undertaken. Botanical material extracted for analysis after 1996/7 has been stored in IMS. Some seed pods (such as peppercorns and broom) and fruit stones were successfully air or freeze dried for display purposes.

Figure 12.7 Processing sample 82S0115; possible 'sack' of straw from O9

Insects were noted in some samples (Chapter 15), and were decanted and removed into 100% IMS for storage. A few were successfully air dried for display purposes.

Chest contents

Samples were taken and processed because of the known organic contents of the chests. Initially priority was given to constituents which may have been in danger of deterioration (fruit stones, peppercorns, textiles, etc.).

Artefact associated

A number of samples associated with artefacts were taken and assessed. These included large quantities of materials such as leather, textile and wood fragments.

Study

Michael J. Allen

At no time during the major processing phases was there an internal team of palaeo-botanists, archaeo-zoologists or other trained specialists. Although assessment and advice was intermittently given by external specialists, some of the original identification of material was made by the divers, other members of the Mary Rose Trust or by visitors. Consequently preliminary, and sometimes incorrect, identifications

*Figure 12.8 Alex Naylor sorting material and 'hay',
sample 82S0024 from H4*

were made in the early days, have become enshrined in
the popular literature (eg, Rule 1982; and the *Mary
Rose* website), and remain in the archive files. These
include the 'identification' of peas in pods (Rule 1983b,
197) which are in fact broom pods (see Smith and
Green, Chapter 14) and of ginger root (unidentifiable
plant root) from chest 81A2099 (archive). As this chest
also contained peppercorns and a small set of balance
and weights it was assumed that the chest belonged to
an apothecary (see, for instance, Richards 1997;
Gaimster 2003). In fact, the latter is a fine and rare
survival of a coin balance (see Chapter 6). Further, a
number of specific remains were studied because of
their unique preservation and the opportunities offered
by the assemblage. These occasionally resulted in *ad hoc*
verbal identifications, such as of flea fragments from
O2, a full record of which was not always made; some
identifications in archive have no formal record of the
identification, nor who originally made them. It is,
therefore, often difficult to discern which are correct,
and which were made by divers or teams members and
may be more speculative (eg, *Zostera*, eel grass: see
below).

With hindsight it seems apparent that the material
archive was, to a certain extent, 'plundered' by a range
of analysts: in some cases simply taking the scientific
opportunity to work on such rare material. Most of the
specialist programmes were not directly funded or
managed by the Trust, and the analytical timescales
were not under its control or jurisdiction. As analyses
were conducted free-of-charge, timetables were often
extremely elastic or vague, making it difficult for the
Trust to co-ordinate and manage a cohesive post-
excavation and reporting programme and some
material loaned out many years ago has yet to be
reported on or returned to the archive. In the case of
student-based analyses, the value of the final product
was unpredictable; dependent to a great deal upon the
academic supervisors involved, and the ability and
tenacity of the individual students. That is not to say, of
course, that much good work was not successfully
undertaken.

Aims of analysis

The principal aim of analysis, as presented here, was to
elicit information about life on board the *Mary Rose*:
Tudor society and economy at war. Analyses of animal
and fish bones allow reconstruction of the diet, the
menus, the packaging and processing of the food and its
origin. The plant remains provide evidence of food and
seasoning, packing and bedding, giving hints about
Tudor economy and lifestyle. Evidence and interpretation pertaining to these aims are presented below
(Chapter 14), with those concerning conditions and live
animals on board in Chapter 15. The remains of the
crew themselves are discussed in Chapter 13.

Beyond this conventional archaeological aim, the
material from the *Mary Rose* provided opportunities for
a series of applied archaeological and purely scientific
investigations. These included the examination for the
presence of pollen in marine contexts (applied
archaeological science) and the survival of various
chemical isotopes and mtDNA in archaeological (ie,
ancient) bone samples (biological and forensic science).
The results of some of these studies had little or no
direct relevance to our interpretation of the *Mary Rose*
and her crew. Nevertheless, the assemblages recovered
from the ship have, in these circumstances, aided the
advancement of other scientific disciplines. As such they
are summarised in Chapter 16.

Taphonomy
Michael J. Allen

Key to the interpretation of many of the biological
assemblages (bone and plant remains in particular) is
the complex relationship between the original materials
'in life' on board the ship, and their presence and

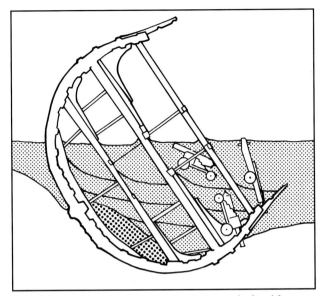

Figure 12.9 The ship as she arrived on sea-bed, with guns and artefacts in disarray

survival in their final resting place within the sea-bed sediments that encapsulated them. These site formation processes are collectively referred to as *taphonomy*. It is clear that the presence and locations of material were radically altered during the sinking of the vessel, and by her impact with the sea-bed, as well as during the post-sinking history of the vessel, including decomposition on the sea-bed, consumption by marine life and, ultimately, by excavation and selective recovery. This study of taphonomy entails disentangling a complex history of changes to, and movement of, materials during and since the sinking, of the many biases of survival on the wreck site, and of recovery from the sea-bed. The specific study of site formation processes relating to the biological remains is integral to the interpretation of their original composition and location (see Coy *et al.* Chapter 14). Although the non-artefactual organic assemblages are very rich, diverse and well-preserved, we must not allow this to distract us from the fact that they represent only a portion of those that originally existed on board. Furthermore, we can be sure that this portion is, like every artefact assemblage, a biased one.

Although many remains were well-preserved on the sea-bed and within the vessel, the wreck did not survive as a fossil of the floating ship. The sinking was a catastrophic and violent event. Considerable disarray of a large number of minor objects occurred as the *Mary Rose* started to sink. Many items were smashed to pieces as heavy objects, such as guns and rigging, crashed across the decks. On sinking, there was a chaotic movement of objects; many items especially on the Upper deck and castles would have been spilled into the sea to float off or sink independently of the vessel. Other lightweight and, in particular, airtight containers will have broken free from lower decks (the Main deck and Orlop), and either become trapped until they were

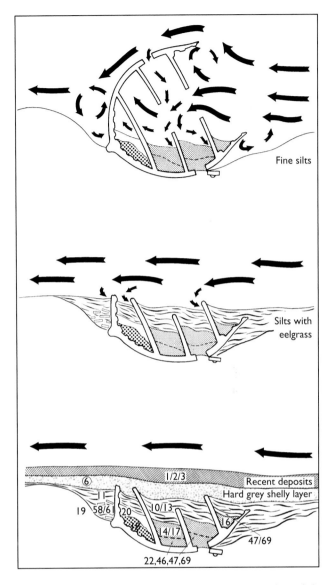

Figure 12.10 Model of the erosion and sedimentation of the wreck site

waterlogged and sank, or floated off during her progress to the sea-bed some 14m below the surface. The greatest loss would have been from the open decks at bow and stern. People and objects were trapped in the open waist of the ship by horizontal anti-boarding netting and presumably also by falling rigging and guns.

The vessel hit the relatively soft sea-bed with more than a jolt, creating an impact crater in the clay, and potentially throwing some items to both port and starboard, away from the hull. As she lay on the sea-bed (Fig. 12.9), sediment slowly started to accrete, and many items started to decay. Human bodies that had not floated away became disassembled as flesh, muscle and ligaments decayed, leaving bones independent of each other. No whole or fully articulated skeletons were recovered. Animal flesh from the ship's provisions and cooked flour- or cereal-based products will have rotted or been eaten, though ingredients in the raw form may have been less prone to decay by marine organisms.

Table 12.1 Taphonomic considerations mainly effecting the loss or decay of biological and non-artefactual assemblages

Event	Action	Consequence	Examples of loss & decay
1. Listing	Small & untethered items & rigging fall to the deck & lurch to starboard, or are flung overboard	Many items displaced, some broken. Some items & crew go overboard	Items, especially from the castle decks (eg, casks, biscuit); some crew lost
2. Sinking	Items displaced, some dislodged & part company with the vessel	All unsecured objects move to starboard, smaller items & personal belongings lost from castle decks & through gunports	Mainly personal items
3. Collision with sea-bed	Hull crashes into sea-bed; major jolt, structural damage to vessel, many larger items dislodged	Guns and large items dislodged to starboard (see Fig. 12.9), other items dispersed from hull	Smaller items lost on sea-bed to decay; many items work free of the wreck & float away, others trapped below decks eaten by fish etc, and/or decompose
4a. Scouring, decay, collapse & burial	Depositon of sediment internally, sealife invades vessel. Scourpits erosion of superstructure; erosion of external structure; hull starts to collapse	Fish & other organisms consume edible material, organic material starts to decay, human bodies start to decay and disarticulate	Organic items, biscuit, human flesh, meat & vegetable matter eaten, decays or rots. Trapped bodies decompose and disarticulate
4b. Futher decay, burial and sealing	*In situ* organic decay; physical damage & gribbling, etc, some further dispersal of loose items	Some physical displacement & continued decay (as above), damage by gribble, teredo worm & marine worms (eg, *Arenicola*)	Exposed wood (hull & objects) decay & rot

As the vessel itself began to decay and collapse (Fig. 12.10), many more objects were dispersed from the hull and fell into the starboard side. Within all of this process, the larger wooden and non-organic objects that had already come to rest are likely to have moved little and any deterioration occurred *in situ*. Smaller items, such as the biological remains and masses of fish(bones) that were not already buried and sealed, would have been subject to considerable local movement and removal. Even when parts of the hull were well sealed and deeply buried, those parts on the surface of the sea-bed were subject to currents, scouring, dispersal and decay.

Large current-formed scourpits developed on either side of the hull. Mud, sediments and objects were re-exposed and redistributed and laid open to further physical and biological decay, destruction and dispersal. Fine grey silts and clays covered the wreck. Eventually the site was slighted and a horizontal 'hard shelly layer' (see sea-bed environment, below) sealed the whole site. This underlay the biologically active black oxidised clay and shingle of the present sea-bed.

Thus, the final location, presence or absence of material, was determined by a wide range of variables whose individual contribution to the site formation process is extremely difficult to assess. Nevertheless, some biological items could be seen clearly to have been concentrated in specific areas. Broom, for instance, was primarily recovered from the foreward section of the Orlop and Main decks, but whether this relates to its storage and use or to any subsequent movement of materials between decks during sinking cannot be determined. Similarly, many provisions that are poorly represented may have floated away or been spilled as casks were broken open. In other cases, plant material within artefacts was simply not recovered. For instance wadding from some of the great guns was lost when the contents were washed out during post-excavation research (A. Hildred pers. comm.; *AMR* Vol. 3); also, skulls were washed out before it was realised that possible brain tissue survived in some. As such, although the remains recovered are diverse and represent a unique assemblage, the interpretations put forward of their original use on board have to be, in some cases, speculative.

Some taphonomic considerations, mainly affecting biological and non-artefactual assemblages during the sinking, are summarised in Table 12.1.

Sea-bed Environment: Processes and Effects

The sediment history presented in *AMR* Vol. 1, chapter 9, is a generalised site-wide scheme that is not specific to any part of the vessel. Each location within the wreck created its own unique current and flows, and consequently produced an individual sediment record, each of which falls within the general pattern of the whole site. Those details are not presented here. Nevertheless we are able to make some comments about the principal consequences of taphonomy and site sedimentary history for categories of organic non-artefactual remains.

It is clear that the ultimate state of preservation and survival of some of the assemblages was largely due to the nature of the sea-bed environment. The modern sea-bed is described in *AMR* Vol. 1, chapter 8, and other effects of the preservation, or lack of them, are given in *AMR* Vol. 5, chapter 2, largely relating to artefacts and the hull itself. Here we consider the nature of the sea-bed in historic times, post-sinking, and the potential deleterious and preservational effects to the vessel, her contents and, in particular, to the non-artefactual organic assemblages.

The Tudor and post-Tudor sea-bed environment

We have little evidence of the nature of the Tudor sea-bed environment, except that the *Mary Rose* came to rest on hard, very pale grey, Eocene Barton Clays. Rapid colonisation of parts of the structure towards the bow by oysters and oyster spat (*Ostrea edulis*) indicates a comparatively immobile Tudor sea-bottom, probably of the exposed hard clay surface. Apart from these glimpses we have little further *evidence* of the sea-bed at the time of sinking, but comparisons with the present sea-bed seem justified (see *AMR* Vol. 1, chapter 8). The sedimentation history can be used to *infer* the sea-bed environment and the possible effects on the biological and environmental assemblages.

Marsden presents a rationalised numbering scheme for the stratigraphic units encountered during the excavation (*AMR* Vol. 1, 77–82) but the original deposit numbers are used here, as these can be directly related to the archive. On colliding forcibly with the sea-bed, the vessel created a shallow impact crater within the Barton Clays (deposit 19). The first 'sediment' within the hull, however, was already on board; the shingle ballast comprising flint gravel of pebbles and shells (deposit 18) quarried from beaches around the Portsmouth harbour environs, and possibly also dark grey to yellowish brown sand (deposit 25). The ballast was displaced to starboard, and it is possible that the sand, a former component of the sandy beach gravel, was washed out as a distinctly separate deposit of 10–15mm thickness against the port side ceiling planking of the listing vessel. If the sand could be separated from the shingle gravel, so too could a number of other items or assemblages have been segregated and detached. Stuffing in mattresses may have partially dissagregated, and buoyant items, including bodies, became trapped against deck beams within the vessel. When they became waterlogged, or trapped gases were released, they fell to the sloping deck below. Gentle but subtle changes occurred in the original composition of the material and of assemblages. Bodies will have cooled rapidly at a depth of 14m and, after only 2–4 weeks, those that were not eaten would have started to disarticulate and skin and flesh separate from the bones (Simpson and Knight 1985, 6–18, 94–8; Smith 1986). During this decay the bodies would have 'floated' relatively freely within a compartment unless pinned down by debris, thus scattering the remains (see Chapter 13).

Initially the hull was a relatively sealed structure that protected the interior from the tidal flow and strong currents. The first sediment to settle within the hull was clean, soft, slightly sticky grey clay (deposit 20) that was probably deposited within a matter of weeks. It was found to be almost devoid of artefacts, suggesting the very gentle settling of fine muds. This first sediment collected against the hull and partitions, in corners and in any cavities and recesses, on each deck within the structure. Gentle currents would have aided the dispersal of some of the lighter items on board, 'winnowing' them away from the wreck site. There is little evidence of any sessile sea life (seaweeds, marine molluscs, etc, that are permanently attached to the sea-bed) at this stage, apart from the oysters and spat mentioned above. Occasional records of fragments of crabs, again especially in the scourpits, indicate some of the benthic (sea-bed) fauna. Certainly fish and other marine life are likely to have feasted well.

Many of these initial deposits were thixotrophic (an immobile 'emulsion' that becomes fluid upon disturbance) suggesting well-sorted, gentle-current deposited sediments of moderately coarse (coarse silt and fine sand) matrix. These primary sediments are not very deep (though specific depths vary greatly) but accumulated rapidly. We know that, for instance, fine sediment 100–250mm thick can accumulate in present conditions on the wreck site in a single winter (recorded in archive by Dobbs in 1980). In this submarine environment, objects and organic matter were rapidly covered and sealed by a thin coat of unconsolidated anaerobic, alumino-silicate dominated mud (a silty clay loam; see *AMR* Vol. 5, chapter 2).

Scourpits

Initially most of vessel stood proud of the sea-bed creating a considerable barrier to tidal flow; the most powerful being east to west. Any object impeding a strong flow of water will generate turbulence leading to erosive scouring. Consequently, current deflected by the hull became turbulent and vortices were created, scouring the contemporaneous sea-bed sediments and cutting into the more resilient natural clay. The resulting erosive action formed large scourpits alongside the hull. The scour exposed and undercut the keel and, at the Sterncastle, undercut at least 8m outboard. Thus the *Mary Rose* literally scoured herself, thereby lowering the hull deeper into the natural sea-bed. While this occurred, inside the protected cavity of the hull, clean, well-sorted silt and clay particles continued to drop out of suspension and accumulate rapidly over many of the waterlogged objects strewn within the vessel. The weight of sediment on decks, or more significantly, on the more flimsy internal partition walls, caused them to buckle, bow and collapse.

Collapse of the port side

The upper, port side of the listing vessel was exposed to the full onslaught of the tidal current and infestation by benthic marine life such as gribble (*Limnoria* sp.) and *Teredo* (see *AMR* Vol. 5, chapter 2). The wooden structure of the vessel itself started to disintegrate. Corrosion and rusting of metal fittings resulted in their failure and separation of major structural elements. This, combined with the weight of sediment, led to the collapse of the superstructure; many items dropped into the muds and scourpits, some were buried and preserved, others disintegrated or were washed away. Currents penetrated the disintegrating structure accelerating the collapse of the port side. Although some of the major timbers became embedded within the unconsolidated sediment, others lay on the sea-bed and were dispersed by currents. The disintegration of the protective superstructure removed the main obstacle to fast running tides across the site and objects thus exposed would not have survived for long (Fig. 12.10). Most of the lighter organic remains had already been long sealed beneath the fine muds and were either preserved, or were slowly degrading *in situ*.

Change in the sea-bed sedimentation

With a now 'open' sea-bed, punctuated by exposed deck and hull timbers, more normal sea-bed sedimentation occurred (deposit 10). The sediment matrix remained essentially similar to the main Tudor deposit. It is described as a soft pale grey clay, often creamy in texture, which averaged 2.5m thick and was characterised by laminae or discontinuous lenses of organic matter. They lay not as horizontal bedded layers, but as warped and bowed organic 'strings' within the grey clay. The form of this deposit, vegetation lens – silt – shells – silt – vegetation lens, with as many as 12

cycles in 0.6m in some locations, has been taken to suggest rapid precipitation and burial. Relatively thick deposits prevented disruption and bioturbation of the lenses of 'weed' and crushed shell by boring molluscs and worms, etc. The duration of such sedimentation can be suggested to be as little as about 20 years. However, the organic lenses define minor scour hollows created by vortexes reeling through exposed broken hull and partitions within the wreck, providing shallow scoops and eddy pools into which plant detritus could accumulate in drifts (Fig 12.10). The organic lenses were initially described as 'grass and straw' in a brown or black organic deposit or 'goo' but, from about 1980 onwards, they are consistently recorded as 'seaweed' lenses, layers or laminae. There is no detailed description of them nor any confirmed identification of the species(s) present but, in his review of the stratigraphic data in 1988, Jon Adams refers to them as being lenses of *Zostera* (eel grass) rather than seaweed. Bettley, an undergraduate student at the time also reported *Zostera* from some very specific deposits in casks, chests, and on the floor of the Carpenters' cabin in M9 (Bettley 1985/6).

Zostera or eel grass/sea grass is not an algal seaweed, but a marine flowering emergent plant, ie, one that thrives in shallow water of the intertidal zone rather than the sea-bed location (15m) in which the *Mary Rose* sank. At this depth in the Solent there is too little light for algal seaweed to survive, and the soft clay did not provide a suitable substrate to which it could attach. The wreck itself would, however, have offered both firm substrate and height so could well have supported kelps (*Laminaria* spp.) and red algae (eg, *Ceramium* sp.) on its upper timbers soon after it sank, and prior to its collapse (Mallinson pers. comm.). Rafts of *Zostera* can be torn up from the intertidal zone in storms and drift considerable distances. Drift algae can inundate any obstruction or hollow on the sea-bed from mid to late summer. Vast quantities of seaweed drift around as fallen leaves do in autumn on land. These drifts are often dominated by one species but that can change from one year to the next. It is probable, that algal seaweeds would not have survived in a recognisable form, and the identification of these lenses as principally comprising *Zostera* is most likely correct.

Relatively large complete oyster valves (reported as being in excess of 100mm and 130mm diameter) were also noted within the grey clay, as was one larger band of 'seaweed' (deposit 13). This was variously described as a thick band of compressed seaweed; a layer of black organic matter with vegetation; thick organic lens extremely rich and with visible weed; and as containing brown fibrous remains. This seems to be an episode when larger drifts than usual of *Zostera*, but also possibly kelp, were deposited across the wreck and sealed by further grey silts.

In terms of the relevance to the organic non-artefactual and artefactual remains, we can see that the open conditions of the hull allowed rapid sedimentation incorporating few finds but some structural timbers. In this sedimentary environment remains became more deeply buried and better-sealed, and only material exposed on the sediment surface suffered degradation and dispersal.

Levelling of the site

The open, largely infilled, wreck enabled fast-running currents to erode and plane the site, stripping it of the uppermost sediment and dispersing remains and timbers within it. This whole episode is evidenced by the sharp and level contact between deposit 10 (silt and 'seaweed' layer), and the overlying hard shelly layer (deposit 6; see Fig.12.10).

Shelly Layer

Although it was only an average of 0.3m thick, much attention has been paid to the hard grey shelly layer (deposit 6), as it essentially sealed the wreck site and had to be penetrated to gain access to the *Mary Rose*. It was thicker where it infilled scour features or other disturbances. The dense, compacted clay was more solid than the deposits beneath and above it and covered the tops of most of the hull frames (Fig 12.10). It seemed to comprise numerous laminae of crushed shells, sand and silty clay (see *AMR* Vol. 1, 79). In general terms this layer divides the post-Tudor from the Tudor deposits. The majority of finds within it are post-Tudor, though the presence of some Tudor finds indicates the widely scattered nature of artefacts within the area, and the delayed decay of the exposed port side structure. It represents a sea-bed environment that contrasts with those indicated by the sediments above and below it. A variety of shells was identified, including easily recognisable species such as oyster and slipper limpet, but also *Spisula* sp., and *Anomia ephippum*, saddle oyster (but only one record of the latter by Boyd (1982)). The only quantitative and objective analysis was performed by Dr Culley, then of Portsmouth Polytechnic (Culley 1985 *contra* Marsden in *AMR* Vol 1, 79–80 who assigned it to Norman Tebble).

A single sample (80S16) from M6 was examined from which Culley identified eleven species/taxa (Table 12.2). He concluded that they originated from mud or muddy sand substrates that were soft and organic enough for worms of *Audouinia* and *Amphitrite* to inhabit, upon which the pyramidellid gastropod *Turbonilla elegantissima* parasitises. Certainly the components of the shelly layer contain lenses of both mud and sand, but we cannot be certain if the species recorded were living on and in this layer, or whether all

Table 12.2 Marine Mollusca recorded by Culley from sample 80S0016 from the 'shelly' layer

Species	No. recorded
Spisula subtruncata, cut through shell	61
Spisula subtruncata, cut through shell	++
Ostrea edulis, common oyster	3 (MNI = 3)
Crepidula fornicata, slipper limpet	2
Rissoa guerini, rissoid gastropod	2
Buccinum undatum, common whelk	1 with 6 barnacles (*Semibalanus balanoides*) attached
Chlamys varia (valves), variegated scallop	1
Nucula turgida, nut shell	1
Nucula cf. *turgida*, nut shell	1+
Thracia phaseolina (valves) a bivalve	2 (MNI = 1)
Thracia phaseolina (valves) a bivalve	++
Turbonilla elegantissima, pyramidellid gastropod	1
Barnia candida, white piddock	1
cf. *Cerastoderma* sp., cockle	+

MNI = Minimum Number of Individuals;
sample size 10 litres

these species, and the matrix itself, were washed in from other locations.

The presence of *Crepidula fornicata* (slipper limpet) is of particular chronological interest. It did not arrive in England until 1880 (Barrett and Yonge 1958) when it was accidentally introduced with oyster spat from North America (McMillan 1968), and probably did not arrive in the Solent before 1900. Although two shells (<2.7%) were present in this sample there is some possibility that the layer was disturbed by trawling at this location (*AMR* Vol. 1, 77). The two main species recorded by the divers were oyster and slipper limpet; two of the largest and most easily recognisable, not necessarily the most common (see Table 12.2). Although we cannot discount the possibility that this layer was still forming in the twentieth century, the low numbers of slipper limpet may indicate either that they were only present in the later and upper part, or were intrusive into its upper disturbed surface. The general grab sample does not have enough stratigraphic control to examine the potential chronological development through the lenses that comprise this layer, and do not allow this ambiguity to be resolved from the current data.

Whatever the precise date or duration of this layer, it represents coarser sea-bed sedimentation and created aerobic deposits in which little or no ancient organic matter could survive. This, in turn, was sealed with the black, oily, mobile mud and shingle currently present on the sea-bed.

Analyses Conducted

The major programmes of biological and chemical analysis conducted were those on the human skeletal remains (Stirland 2000; Chapter 13) and teeth (Evans, Chapter 13), mammal bones (Coy with Oxley, Chapter 14), fish bones (Hamilton-Dyer 1995; Chapter 14) and plant remains (Smith and Green, Chapter 14). These investigations embraced previous smaller analytical projects including that of the plums (Dodd 1986), and identifications of grapes and broom by Phillipa Tomlinson. Together, the animal and plant remains provide the major source of data for interpreting the diet of the crew and provisioning for the ship (Chapter 14).

A number of other studies were conducted at a variety of differing levels. These included single identifications (bracket fungus by E.B. Gareth Jones, Chapter 8), the listing of remains (insects by Dr D.C. Reay), limited analysis programmes (insects by Robinson, Chapter 15), and pollen assessment and analysis (eg, Scaife, Chapter 15; Grieg, Chapter 16).

More detailed analytical studies, such as those of the animal fats (Morgan and Williams, Chapter 16), chemical studies including chromatography of tar, pitch and dye (J. Evans, Chapter 16), chemical analyses of the medicaments (Dereham, Chapter 4), examination of brain tissue (see Chapter 13), and DNA analyses (Hagelberg et al. 1989; Hagelberg and Clegg 1991; and Chapters 13 and 16), were also conducted. Other studies conducted for undergraduate and postgraduate theses included analyses of the sediments (ie, Bettley 1985/6; Dassow 1984), but also post-graduate research into isotopes in human bones (Bell 1995). This study, in particular, led to further detailed scientific analysis of oxygen isotopes which, although begun before 2000 (Stirland 2000, 154–5; Chapter 12), has yet to be completed or reported on (see Chapter 16). In contrast, analysis such as the mtDNA (Hagelberg, Chapter 13), pollen (Scaife, Chapter 15) and the insects (Robinson, Chapter 15) were 'commissioned' as late as 2004 in order to 'mop up' some of the outstanding analyses and are included in the chapters that follow.

13. The Crew of the *Mary Rose*

It is difficult to comprehend the scale of the human tragedy caused by the loss of the *Mary Rose*. We do not have exact figures for either the number of men on board, or the number lost, but if the contemporary accounts are accurate, somewhere around 380 men out of a possible 415 died. That is 90% or more of the crew, most of whom had no chance to escape as the ship sank.

To put a modern perspective on those figures, the combined death toll from the ships HMS *Sheffield* and RFA *Sir Galahad*, both lost during the Falklands war in 1982, was 75 men, amounting to less than 15% of each ship's complement (HM Naval Records, info. J. Lippiett). In terms of the nature of the sinking, perhaps a more apt comparison is with that of the *Herald of Free Enterprise*, the 'roll-on-roll-off' ferry that capsized as she left Zeebrugge Harbour in March 1986. Her bow doors had not been secured and water flooded the car decks, in much the same way as it would have poured in through the *Mary Rose*'s open gunports, sinking the *Herald* in less than three minutes. Even so, nearly 60% of the more than 450 people on board the *Herald* survived (www.plimsoll.org/WrecksAndAccidents).

Of the possible 380 fatalities, the remains of 179 were recovered from the wreck of the *Mary Rose*, amounting to 45% of the entire crew. The collection is an unparalleled assemblage of Tudor human remains. While other individuals have been examined archaeologically, there are no comparably large

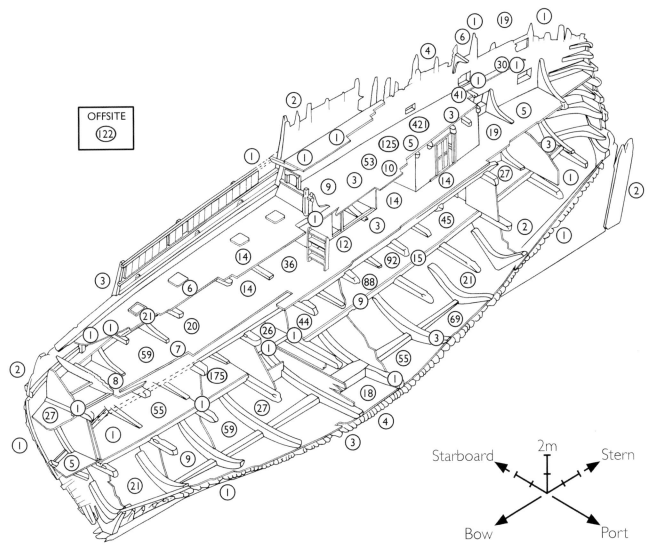

Figure 13.1 Distribution of individual skeletal elements within the hull (no. of bones)

assemblages from terrestrial sites and no war cemeteries of this date. The closest parallel is the 'war' cemetery or battle grave of 1461 at Towton, near Tadcaster, north Yorkshire (Fiorato *et al.* 2000). Where Tudor graves have been excavated, the preservation and survival is rarely as good as it is for the *Mary Rose* crew, even though these remains had become disarticulated.

The *Mary Rose* assemblage is of great importance for the study of human remains from post-medieval and Tudor England generally, as well as for the specific information it provides about the individuals concerned. The remains of over 150 men have provided the opportunity to study details of the age, health, lifetime stresses and dental health of a very selective population. Some of the particular strains, stresses, injuries and illnesses that affected the crew of a Tudor warship have been revealed, indicating the hard life already led by this group of young men, most of whom were under 30 years of age when they died. The unique preservation conditions have also offered the opportunity to examine other, non-osteological, aspects of these burials. Most unusually, some soft tissue survived and though, sadly, most of it could not be conserved, it was possible to undertake a brief examination. DNA analysis has recently begun and, although we are only able to report on preliminary results here, this work will continue. Already there are indications that not all the crew may have been British.

This chapter presents what we know to date about the men themselves. Medical, forensic and archaeological science will develop the potential for study of many further aspects of the human remains. Thus, our knowledge will undoubtedly increase and, although we shall never know their names or histories, this knowledge will bring us ever closer to the men who lived and died on the *Mary Rose*.

Human Remains

Ann Stirland

When the *Mary Rose* sank only about three dozen of her documented crew of 415 men escaped drowning (*Anthony Roll*). The Cowdray engraving suggests that the men who did escape were probably in the fighting tops. The rest were trapped by the anti-boarding netting which covered all exposed decks; this netting, and the speed of the sinking, sealed their fate.

Men were trapped at all levels in the ship when she sank. However, the distribution of human skeletal material as it was found within the hull shows large numbers of bones in certain areas. Figure 13.1 demonstrates this point. Here, the numbers represent individual skeletal elements and where they were found. It can be seen, for example, that there was a lot of material on the Upper deck (groups of 421 and 125 bones) and other large groups in certain areas of the other decks. This distribution probably does not

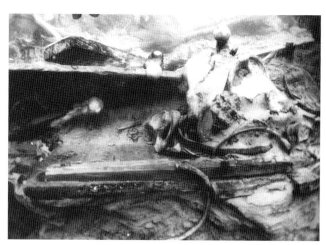

Figure 13.2 Human bones on collapsed boxes on the sea-bed in U9

represent the positions of most of the men when they died. The angle at which the ship lay, the movement of water within the wreck and the activities of marine predators, who probably removed parts of decomposing bodies, all contributed to the mixing of the remains. Damage to, and movement of, some of the decks further compounded this mixing. For example, the area between sectors 7 and 8 of the Hold and Orlop decks showed evidence of some movement and damage and there were large groups of bones found here (Fig.13.1). This mixing was very apparent when human bone was found during the excavation (Fig. 13.2).

The human remains were excavated sector by sector throughout the ship, recorded and placed in crates to be raised to the surface. At the surface, groups of bones which were found together were given the same number and put into net bags, apart from the skulls and mandibles, which were kept separate. All the nets of bones were washed in a cascade of clean, fresh water, which ran through four baths (see *AMR* Vol. 5 for details). The bones were finally dried and numbered individually.

When received by the author in 1984, three of the skulls were missing. It was thought that they might still contain some brain matter and had been sent to Bristol University for CT scanning (see Allen, below). The rest of the bones arrived in their nets, apart from the skulls and mandibles, which were in individual boxes. The nets containing the rest of the bones were mostly packed into very large boxes, apart from some of the unassociated femora, which were in separate, long boxes. It quickly became clear that they were all still completely mixed (Fig. 13.3).

The 'burials'

Since the sea-bed silts had provided an anaerobic environment, which had considerably slowed the processes of decomposition, the human bone, like much organic material from the wreck, was in a superb state

Figure 13.3 Commingled bones from the Hold and Orlop decks, sectors 7 and 8

of preservation. Some bone was heavily stained with iron oxides and a small amount of material had become exposed on the sea-bed and was somewhat eroded, but the majority of the bones were extremely well preserved and with very well marked entheses (Fig. 13.4). Given the uniqueness of the collection and the quality of most of the surviving bone, it was decided to try and match bones into some semblance of individuals. Two excellent students assisted in this and the re-sorting took place over a year. The amounts of bone from each sector were variable (Fig. 13.1), so the sorting was very time-consuming. The bones from each sector of the ship were examined separately and the matching was done morphologically, starting with the femur (Fig. 13.5). Having matched pairs of femora, we paired the tibiae and fibulae, and matched the three leg bones at the knee. This was possible because of the superb quality of the surviving bone. Innominates were then paired and, where possible, a femur was fitted into its matching acetabulum. If there was a matching sacrum, we could assemble the vertebral column and, assuming that the first cervical vertebra was present, a cranium could be fitted on to that. Generally, however, this was as far as we got. Although humeri, radii, ulnae, scapulae, clavicles, patellae and hands and feet were sorted into pairs they could not, of course, be added to individual skeletons, because of the nature of the shoulder, wrist and ankle joints. Although the femoral head fits snugly into the acetabulum, allowing a hip joint to be reassembled, the same is not true for the shoulder, wrist and ankle whose joints are much looser, articulating in a different manner to the hip. Equally, the patella 'floats', sliding up and down the femur as the knee articulates, and a collection of mixed ribs cannot be fitted to an individual sternum. There were examples where there had been a close archaeological association on the sea-bed between bones that obviously came from the same individual, and some of these included arms, hands and feet, scapulae, clavicles and even ribs. Where this occurred, they were left as one individual.

All the re-sorting of the human skeletal material yielded a total of 92 Fairly Complete Skeletons (FCS),

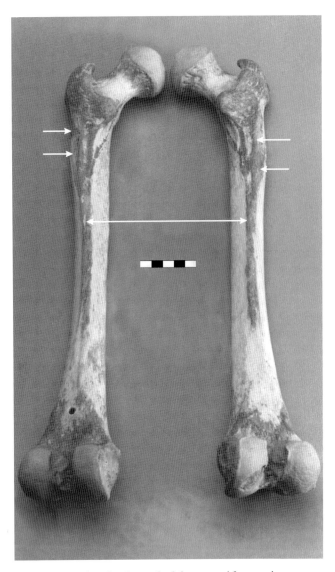

Figure 13.4 A pair of matched femora with prominent entheses (arrows)

some of which were more complete than others. In a number of cases, the bones making up a single individual came from more than one sector of the ship. The skulls and mandibles were matched by a team from Birmingham University Dental School who also found some separation of these elements across the ship. Some individuals, however, appeared not to have moved far from where they had died and these were among the most complete in the FCS group. The Fairly Complete Skeletons were distinguished from the mass of the rest of the bone by giving them a special FCS number. This number, prefixed by a #, was marked on every bone in a group that belonged to a putative individual. Originally, the numbers began at #100 and ran sequentially to #191. Subsequently, however, these numbers were simplified by starting at #1 (#100) and running to #92 (#191). The groups to which each number applied either consisted of large collections of bones belonging to one probable individual, or of collections of paired and matched bones which

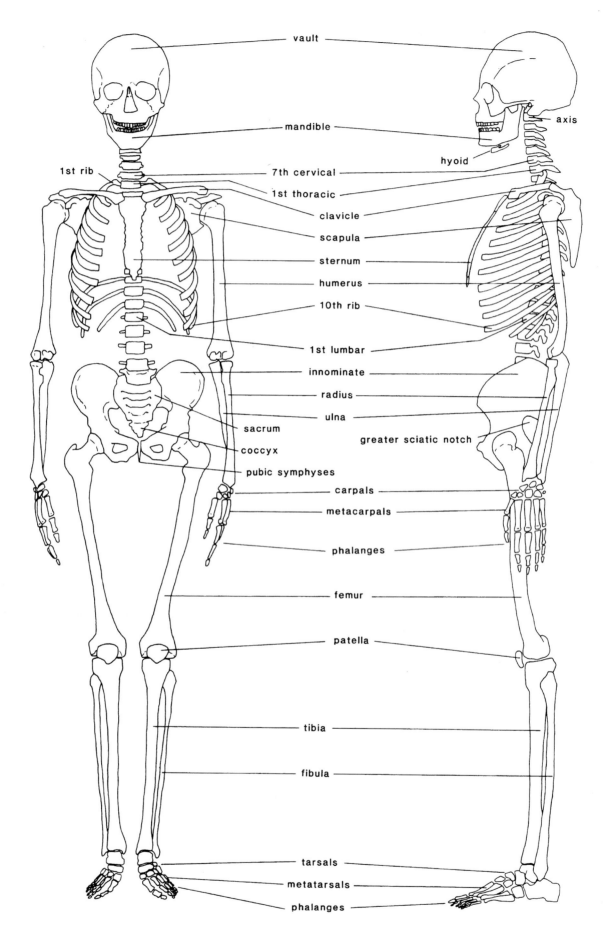

vault

mandible

axis

hyoid

1st rib

7th cervical

1st thoracic

clavicle

scapula

sternum

humerus

10th rib

1st lumbar

innominate

radius

ulna

sacrum

coccyx

greater sciatic notch

pubic symphyses

carpals

metacarpals

phalanges

femur

patella

tibia

fibula

tarsals

metatarsals

phalanges

Figure 13.5 The human skeleton (courtesy of Jacqueline I. McKinley)

Table 13.1 Number of skulls and mandibles

Matched skulls with mandibles	68
Unmatched skulls	58
Unmatched mandibles	48
Matched maxillas with mandibles	2
Skulls from Bristol	3
Total	179

Table 13.2 Total numbers of bones occurring in pairs

	Left	Right
Pelvis	107	108
Femur	114	110
Tibia	108	117
Fibula	105	96
Scapula	102	105
Clavicle	84	90
Humerus	119*	99
Radius**	107	98
Ulna**	105	92
Total	951	915

* highest individual score; ** there are 2 broken radii & 2 broken ulnae that could not be given a side. These are omitted from totals

Note: The above are bones that always occur in pairs in the human body. However, here they have been counted for each side wherever they occurred in the sample; they were not necessarily in pairs, hence the discrepancy in the totals for each side

probably contributed to a single individual but which had many different archaeological numbers. As well as these FCS individuals, there were also small groups of bones that were paired and matched and, of course, a large mass of undifferentiated bone. This material remained mixed and unmatched into individuals, and was recorded as such by bone and by sector.

Numbers of individuals

The number of individuals represented in the sample was determined by counting the number of the most frequently occurring individual bone. The skulls and mandibles, both matched and unmatched, yielded one total (Table 13.1) and the pairs of bone another (Table 13.2). Table 13.1 shows that the minimum number of individuals present, based on the skull and mandible count, was 179. In Table 13.2, the most frequently occurring bone is the left humerus, which scored 119. Thus, the minimum number present was taken as 179. If there were 415 men on the ship when she sank, 179 would represent about 43% of that total. This figure is probably fairly accurate, given that the skeletal remains were excavated from roughly half the ship. There is considerable confusion, however, with regard to the number of men who were actually on board the *Mary Rose* when she sank. The *Anthony Roll* gives the crew list as 185 soldiers, 200 mariners and 30 gunners – a total of 415 (Rule, 1982, 27; *AMR* Vol. 1). Other figures have been suggested, however, including the idea that there were an extra 300 archers on board when she sank. This seems to have come from Sir Peter Carew whose brother, Sir George, was the Vice Admiral on board the *Mary Rose* and who drowned with her. Sir Peter is reported to have said that the '*sayde Mary Roose, thus heelinge more and more, was drowned, with 700 men wiche were in here*'. Since he also goes on to say, however, that '*he had in the shipp a hundrith maryners*' the report may not be very accurate (Philips 1839, 109–11). Neither figure tallies with those in the *Anthony Roll*.

If there were an extra 300 on board when she sank, it would make the ship's complement about 715 men and change the surviving sample size to 25%. However, since the majority of the men were trapped under the netting when the ship went down, and since she silted up very quickly, trapping them further, it seems probable that, had there been an extra 300 on board, the excavation would have found many more human

skeletal remains. It has, therefore, been assumed that the sample size is 179 individuals, and represents about 43% of the whole crew.

Sexing the remains

Although some recent work does suggest that it will be possible to accurately assign a sex to children's skeletons using DNA (Stone *et al.* 1996) this is not the case at present. It is only possible to sex an individual skeleton, using present techniques, if the individual was either an adolescent or an adult. The relevant bones that may be used to discriminate between the sexes must also be present. Those most commonly used are the skull, plus the mandible, and the pelvis. Measurements of the humeral and femoral joints are also used, as are the lengths of the clavicles (Krogman 1973, 143–8; Ubelaker 1984, 41–4). The unassociated long bones from the ship were sexed using measurements of the humeral and femoral heads and of the length of the clavicle. Since they had been re-sorted and matched, the FCS group was sexed using all surviving appropriate bones for each skeleton.

Five categories were used to sex all these remains. They were: F (female); ?F (probable female); ? (undetermined); ?M (probable male); M (male). Not surprisingly, using the techniques described and the above categories, all skeletons examined were of males or probable males.

Age at death

The approximate age of an individual at death is easier to determine from the skeleton for juveniles, adolescents and young adults in their twenties than it is for older individuals. The patterns of eruption both of the

Table 13.3 Numbers of individuals in each age category

Juveniles	1*
Adolescents	17
Young adults	54
Middle-aged adults	15
Old adults	1**
Total	88

* There is probably more than 1 child. The FCS juvenile is *c.* 12–13 yrs old, but there were other bones (not in the FCS group) with unfused epiphyses suggesting a child of about 10 yrs

** There are some non-FCS odd bones with a degree of osteoarthritis which could have belonged to other old adult individuals in the group

Note: 4 FCS could only be aged as 'adult' & have not been included

deciduous and the permanent teeth and the stage of closure of the epiphyses are used to assign age to the skeleton of a young individual. All these features occur within specific time spans thus enabling us to assign an approximate, although not a specific, age to a younger skeleton. As individuals age, however, the above indicators disappear, although there are other features which may be employed in ageing an older skeleton. All techniques do require a skeleton to be both fairly complete and discrete, a situation that clearly did not apply to the burials from the *Mary Rose*. Given the commingled state of most of the material, therefore, it was obvious that only the FCS group could be aged with any accuracy, since they were the only skeletons that had been re-sorted and matched.

All possible criteria were used in assigning age to the FCS group of skeletons. As well as the techniques discussed above for ageing younger individuals, age changes at the pubic symphysis of the pelvis (Suchey and Brooks 1988) and, where applicable, changes that occur at the sternal ends of the ribs with age (Işcan *et al.* 1984) were also used. The application of all the techniques produced rather a wide range of ages, many of which overlapped, and it was necessary to simplify these. The majority of the individuals in the FCS group were, therefore, placed in one of three categories, which were called Young, Middle or Old Adults. There were a small number of juveniles, who were pre-adolescent, in the group and some adolescents who were less than about 18 years. The majority, however, fell into the following categories:

- Young Adults, aged from about 18 to 29–30 years
- Middle Adults, aged from about 30 to about 39–40 years
- Old Adults, aged over about 40 years.

Table 13.3 shows that the largest number of individuals were in the Young Adult group, followed by the adolescents, a result that is probably predictable for a warship's crew.

Table 13.4 Stature based on the femur

Left femur	Right femur	Combined FCS femurs
N = 82	N = 92	N = 104
X = 170.9	X = 171.2	X = 170.6
SD = 4.5	SD = 5.0	SD = 4.6
(5′7"±1.8")	(5′7.5"±2")	(5′6"±1.8")

Key: measurements in cm; N = number; SD = standard deviation
The results from both sides & from using the combined FCS bones are the same

Stature

Stature was calculated only for individuals whose growth had ceased and whose epiphyses were fused. The formulae most frequently used are those devised by Trotter, particularly in her 1970 work. This study showed that greater accuracy was achieved when the combined lengths of the femur and tibia were used, rather than the humerus or other arm bones. More recent work (Waldron 1998, 77), however, has demonstrated that the best estimate of stature for British skeletal material, at least for males, is achieved by using only the femur. Following Waldron, therefore, the stature of the *Mary Rose* men was calculated using the femur only. There were 82 left and 92 right femora that could be measured. Using Trotter's formula (Trotter 1970, table xxviii), mean stature was calculated for both bones and compared with the combined left and right results for the FCS group (Table 13.4). The mean stature for the group was 1.71m (5′7") with a range of 1.59m (5′3") to 1.80m (5′11") and a standard deviation (SD) of between 40 and 50mm (~ 2"); about two-thirds of the men will have had heights within ± 1 SD of the mean. Comparison with historical and conscription data (Kunitz 1987, 271; Floud *et al.* 1990, 22–3) demonstrated that the stature of the *Mary Rose* men fell within the same range as those of other European males over the last 200 years. While not as tall as the tallest modern men, they were no shorter than most of their other modern counterparts.

Skeletal indices

A total of four indices were derived for this group. This is fairly common practice among anthropologists, since these indicies can yield valuable information about a group. The three taken on the skull describe how an individual will have looked when all the soft tissue was in place in life. They are useful when comparing how a group of individuals is similar to or different from comparable groups today.

The Cranial Index was derived following Bass (1971, 54–69). A total of 99 skulls were measured and Table 13.5 shows the results. The majority of the men were either dolicho- or mesocranic (long- or medium-

Table 13.5 Cranial index

	Category	No. crania
X★–74.9	Dolichocranic (narrow /long-headed)	44
75.0–79.9	Mesocranic (average/medium headed)	44
80.0–84.9	Brachycranic (broad/round-headed)	10
85.0–X★	Hyperbrachycranic (very broad headed)	1
Total		99

★ where X is unknown

headed). Four individuals had very long, narrow heads (with cranial indexes in the range 67.5– 69.9) however, and one was hyperbrachycranic, with a skull that was rather inflated and round.

The Orbital Index was derived also following Bass (1971). Eighty-five skulls had sockets intact enough to take the necessary measurements and Table 13.6 shows the results. The majority of the men had either wide or medium orbits. Eight individuals had rather narrow sockets, however, and one had very narrow sockets.

The ratio of the height to the breadth of the face, including the teeth, is expressed as the Total Facial Index. It can only be derived if the relevant bones are intact and include nasion, gnathion and both zygomatic arches (see Fig 13.41 and dental glossary). It was derived following Bass (1971) and a total of 50 matched skulls and mandibles were measured (Table 13.7). There was an even spread of face shapes across the broad, average and narrow forms.

All the above indices showed a normal distribution. It is, therefore, likely that the whole crew will have had similar head and face shapes to those measured, and statistically unlikely that the distribution would be skewed by the addition of the remainder of the sample. Clearly, the crew was a group of men with faces and heads that would fit into the modern population, without appearing in any way bizarre.

The Robusticity Index compares the length of the shaft of a long bone with its mid-shaft diameter, describing the strength or robusticity of a long bone. The probable use of the specific limb is then inferred. This index was derived for all the humeri and femora from the *Mary Rose* that could be matched in pairs, and

Table 13.6 Orbital index

	Category	No. individuals
X★ –82.9	Chamaeconchy (wide orbits)	32
83.0–89.9	Mesoconchy (average/medium orbits)	33
90.0–X★	Hypsiconchy (narrow orbits)	20
Total	85	

★ where X is unknown

Table 13.7 Total facial index

	Category	No. individuals
X★–79.9	Hypereuryprosopy (v. broad face)	6
80.0–84.9	Euryprosopy (broad face)	13
85.0–89.9	Mesoprosopy (average/medium face)	12
90.0–94.9	Leptoprosopy (slender/narrow face)	12
95.0–X★	Hyperleptoprosopy (very narrow face)	7
Total		50

★where X is unknown

the right and left sides were compared. The bones appeared to be very strong and robust but, in order to determine if this was really so, the results were compared with those of the males from a medieval parish cemetery in Norwich (Stirland 1992, 127, table 5.5.2). The femur showed no significant differences between the sides in either group of men. However, while the *Mary Rose* men showed no significant differences between the sides in the robusticity of their humeri, this was not the case with the men from Norwich. Here, the right humerus was significantly more robust than the left (Stirland 1992). These results imply that the men from Norwich were tending to use their right arms more than their left, while those from the ship's crew were using their arms more equally. The right arm is used preferentially by 90% of the human species and the results from Norwich reflect this trend. However, the ship's crew would seem to have been using their arms rather differently, and much more equally, than is usually the case. Various shipboard activities, such as raising and lowering the sails, and operating as part of a gun crew, would have entailed the equal use of both arms a lot of the time. For this to have significantly altered the results of the robusticity index, however, these activities would have to have been engaged in over a long period of time.

Other indices were derived for the femora from the ship's crew and these are discussed in Stirland (1992, 101 and 196). Their usefulness, other than in the description of the general size and shape of a bone, is at present unclear.

Skeletal morphology

There are a number of discontinuous morphological traits that have been recorded and described for the human skeleton. Sometimes they have been used to infer genetic relationships within groups of skeletons. Usually, however, the environmental or other pressures on the expression of such traits are unknown and their presence or absence in a group should be treated with caution.

A group of six traits that are often recorded occur at the proximal end of the femur (Finnegan 1978). They

Glossary of terms relating to human bone

ABDUCTION - movement of a limb or part of the body away from the mid-line.

ACETABULUM - the socket for the head of the femur that forms the hip joint in the pelvis.

ACROMIAL PROCESS - the bar of bone along the back of the scapula. The lateral end articulates with the clavicle and helps to form the shoulder joint.

ADDUCTION - movement of a limb or part of the body towards the mid-line.

AETIOLOGY - the study of the causes of a disease.

ALLEN'S FOSSA, POIRIER'S FACET AND PLAQUE - variations on the neck of the femur which appear as pits or raised areas of bone. A discontinuous morphological trait (see below).

CONDYLES/EPICONDYLE - condyles: the articular (joint) surfaces of the femur, mandible, occipital and tibia; epicondyle: the bulbous areas of bone proximal (see later) to the distal joint surfaces of the femur and humerus. Tendons and ligaments attach to the bone in these areas.

DIAGENETIC - Post deposition physical and chemical alteration of mineral and sediment components

DISCONTINUOUS MORPHOLOGICAL TRAITS - a group of six variations on the neck of the femur which may or may not express genetic relationships between individuals.

DISTAL - the part of a bone that is furthest from the skull.

EBURNATION - polishing of the joint surface caused by bone-on-bone movement when the cartilage has disappeared.

ENTHESES - areas where muscles attach to bone.

ENTHESOPATHIES; ENTHESOPHYTES - inflammation with lesions and/or a build up of new bone on the entheses.

EPIPHYSES - the articular joint surfaces in the long and short bones and at the edges of the flat bones. They are attached to the main part of the bone by a thin layer of cartilage, allowing the bone to continue growth, and fusing to the main bone when growth ceases (see growth plate).

EXOSTOSES IN THE TROCHANTERIC FOSSA - spicules of bone occurring in the trochanteric fossa behind the greater trochanter of the femur. A discontinuous morphological trait.

FOSSA - a depressed area of a bone sometimes, as in the hip, forming part of the joint.

GLUTEAL RIDGE - the area on the proximal posterior femur where large muscles attach. In some individuals, the ridge is so developed that it becomes a tuberosity (see below).

GROWTH PLATE - the area of a long or a flat bone where growth occurs in the juvenile. The area is attached to the bone by cartilage that allows growth to continue. When growth ceases, the cartilage turns to bone.

HYPOPLASTIC BANDS - pits or bands on the permanent teeth. They indicate where growth was disrupted in the child allowing the unerupted permanent teeth to stop growing. When growth starts again, the band or pit is left.

HYPOTROCHANTERIC FOSSA - a depressed area on the posterior femur, associated with the third trochanter.

LESION - an area on bone where disease, damage or injury has occurred in life. The bone has healed but the evidence remains.

MALLEOLUS - the medial and lateral edges of both tibia and fibula which form part of the ankle joint. Each malleolus has large, stabilising, ligaments attached to it.

OCCIPITAL - the rear part of the skull.

OSTEOPHYTES - new bone growth at joint margins or other areas away from the entheses.

PERIOSTEUM - a membrane that covers all bone, apart from the joint surfaces. When subjected to infection or trauma, it can become inflamed and, eventually, produce areas of new bone on top of the original surface.

PERIMORTEM - around the time of death. If an event is said to be perimortem, it is not usually possible to say whether or not it was the cause of death.

PERTHES DISEASE - a childhood condition in which part of the growth plate of the femoral head is damaged and dies (necrosis), often causing the head to become deformed for life.

PROXIMAL - the part of the bone that is nearest to the skull.

PUBIC SYMPHYSIS - the area of the pelvis at the front which forms the pubis.

RACHITIC - of rickets.

SEM - scanning electron microscopy.

THIRD TROCHANTER - a nodule of bone sometimes present at the top of the hypotrochanteric fossa (see above). It is not a true trochanter, having no epiphysis.

TROCHANTERS - the large nodule which forms the femur behind the head and neck (greater trochanter). The lesser trochanter is a nodule on the posterior part of the bone.

TUBERCLE - a small, rounded projection of bone.

TUBEROSITY - as above, but larger, forming a protuberance of bone.

are: the third trochanter; hypotrochanteric fossa; Allen's fossa; Poirier's facet; plaque on the femoral neck; and exostoses in the trochanteric fossa (see glossary).

Again, the degree to which these traits are genetically controlled is unknown and recent work has demonstrated that their expression is probably related to environmental and ageing factors (Stirland 1996, 249–52). The results demonstrated that the traits on the head and neck of the femur (Allen's fossa and plaque) are related to age, with the former having a higher frequency in young males and the latter in older ones. Poirier's facet appears to be sexually dimorphic, revealing differences between males and females occurring as a result of increased muscle function in males. Exostoses in the trochanteric fossa are enthesopathies. They occur with increased frequency in the ageing skeleton, but may also be related to activity. On the femoral shaft, the hypotrochanteric fossa occurs predominantly in the young, while the so-called third trochanter is not really a trochanter at all, having no epiphysis, but is related to activity and an increased size of the gluteal ridge. It occurred with increased frequency in the *Mary Rose* crew when compared with the Norwich men, suggesting an increase of activity involving the former (Stirland 1996).

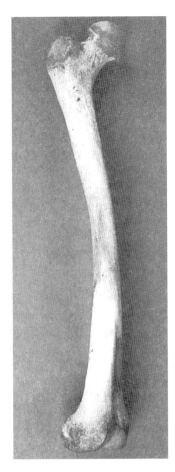

Figure 13.6 A femur bowed anteroposteriorally, probably as a result of healed childhood rickets

When the work was originally done in the mid-1980s, other morphological traits were recorded for these skeletons. However, the degree of mixing of individuals and the unclear meaning of many of these traits means that no further analysis has been done on them.

Dentition

All the information on the teeth is provided by Evans (below).

Pathology

Many diseases do not leave any trace on the skeleton, since they kill too quickly, but there are a number that can be detected from changes in the bones. They include chronic conditions such as osteoarthritis, chronic infectious diseases such as syphilis and tuberculosis, and some that are related to diet, such as scurvy and rickets. Fractures, particularly in pre-twentieth century skeletons, may also leave very clear indications on the skeleton as, in the past, they were usually inadequately treated.

Malnutrition

Since the burials are so mixed and represent a little less than half the ship's complement, it is not possible to calculate frequencies for the following categories of pathological lesions in the whole group. They have, therefore, been reported on as separate examples.

Dietary deficiency may range from a lack of some essential nutrients to total starvation, and any imbalance in diet, including excess, can lead to problems. A prolonged lack of essential nutrients may lead to deficiency diseases, some of which may affect the skeleton.

Although it may have been better than that of an agricultural worker in the sixteenth century, the diet of a mariner in 1545 was restricted (Stirland 2005, chapter 3; see also Chapter 14), at least by modern standards.

Oppenheim states that the rate for victualling a mariner in 1545 was 18 Tudor pence (d) a week

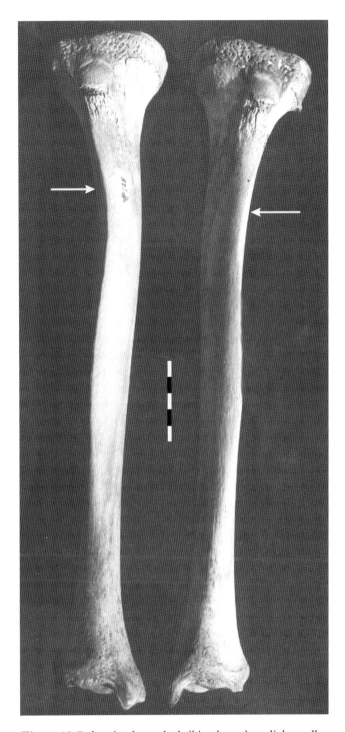

Figure 13.7 A pair of matched tibiae bowed mediolaterally: healed childhood rickets (arrows)

(1896b, 82). This allowed for a pound of biscuit and a gallon of beer for each man per day, plus '*200 pieces of flesh*' for every 100 men on four days of the week (Oppenheim 1896b). Other evidence for 1565 states that a standard ration was based on 4½d a day in port and 5d a day at sea. This provided a gallon of beer and a pound of bread (fresh or biscuit) plus four flesh days. On these days, either two pounds of fresh beef or half-a-pound of salt beef or bacon were provided. The other three days were fish days when either a quarter of a stockfish or four herrings were available. Half a pound

Figure 13.8 (Top) a fused, bowed and expanded sternum: probable osteomalacia, compared with a normal sternum (below)

of cheese and four ounces of butter were also included (Rodger 1997, 235). Other authors (Anon 1731; Davies 1964; Maybray King 1968) indicate only slight variations to these quantities and proportions, with the most significant addition being peas, enabling us to suggest typical rations (see Chapter 14). The men will have supplemented the diet when they could with fresh foods, including fruit and vegetables. Evidence for some of these victuals, and for peppercorns, was found during the excavation of the hull (Chapter 14).

Apart from any problems of availability, the chief difficulty with all the fresh foods, including the beer that was brewed without hops, was one of preservation. Short-term preservation was accomplished by dry-salting, drying and packing in salt pickle but the lack of any long-term method of keeping food fresh and good led to sickness, enfeeblement and scurvy (Kemp 1970, 5). For example, the outbreak of dysentery in the Portsmouth ships in August 1545 was said to have been caused by corrupted food (Rodger 1997, 234). Thus, the crew of the *Mary Rose* will have subsisted on a diet that was composed of some fresh but mostly preserved foods, at least whilst on board ship. The preserved foods will have been variable in their quality. The crew members' subsistence whilst away from the ship is unknown.

Rickets and osteomalacia

Rickets in children and osteomalacia in adults are caused by a lack of vitamin D in the diet. The main source of this vitamin is from the action of sunlight on dehydrocholesterol in the skin (Sharman 1981, 25). The effect of a lack of vitamin D on a growing child's skeleton leads to bones that are incompletely mineral-ised. If these are weight-bearing long bones, they can develop bending deformities which persist in the adult skeleton. In the adult, the demineralised skeleton of osteomalacia can become deformed under the load-bearing stresses that affect the ribs, vertebrae, sternum and pelvis, although not the long bones.

Some members of the crew of the *Mary Rose* appear to have suffered from dietary deficiencies as children and others when they were adults. Healed childhood rickets is suggested by two femora bowed antero-posteriorly (Fig. 13.6) and twelve tibias bowed medio-laterally (Fig 13.7). One bowed and expanded sternum (Fig. 13.8) and two angulated sacrums (Fig. 13.9) imply the presence of osteomalacia in some adults.

Scurvy and anaemia

Scurvy is a serious disease, which is caused by a prolonged deficiency in vitamin C. If left untreated, it can kill. It mainly affects the connective tissues of the body and can cause haemorrhage in many areas, as well as affecting the immune system. Because the immune system is compromised by scurvy, the disease can occur along with other conditions, such as dysentery. There are records of scurvy occurring in such association in

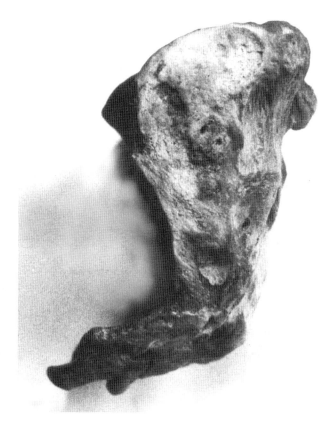

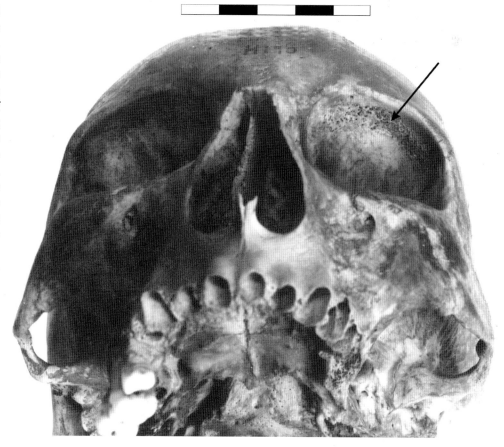

Figure 13.9 A fused, angulated sacrum: probable osteomalacia

fied in skeletons. Recent work suggests that chronic bleeding in children also can occur at multiple sites on the cranium (Ortner *et. al.* 1999), including at areas of attachment of the muscles that are associated with chewing (Ortner and Eriksen 1997). Some changes that may affect adults include haemorrhaging along long bone shafts (Steinbock 1976, 256–8), and it is possible that the skeletal changes associated with scurvy occurring in adolescence may be retained in the adult (D.J. Ortner, pers. comm. 2000).

It is possible that the evidence of attacks of adolescent scurvy may be retained in some of the skeletons from the ship. There are lesions of the eye sockets, where new bone appears to have been laid down on old (Fig. 13.10) and evidence of healed haematomas along some long bones (Fig. 13.11). There is also pitting of the surface of a number of skulls, such as that seen in Figure 13.12, which may represent the healed lesions of scurvy. It is important to emphasise, however, that scurvy is difficult to diagnose in dry bone, since various conditions produce similar changes. For example, varicose veins, or localised trauma to bones such as the tibia, can produce new bone along the shafts. Similarly, lesions on the skull and in the orbits are controversial, since there are claims that other forms of malnutrition can produce similar changes. These

some of the long sea voyages of the past (Watt 1981, 58–9) and scurvy was, for centuries, the scourge both of sailors and, at times, of the general population. A diet that mainly consists of cooked foods, or one that is low in fresh fruit and vegetables, will cause the disease to appear. Haemorrhage (scorbutic bleeding) will occur in the skin, the gums and the periosteum. The results of chronic haemorrhaging into the periosteum are particularly clear on the bones of young children and are considered to be the most important single sign of scurvy (Steinbock 1976, 254). If the disease reaches a healing phase, the haematomas that form can ossify or calcify, producing characteristic new bone along the shafts of long bones, which sometimes can be identi-

Figure 13.10 Probable scorbutic changes from adolescence: new bone laid down in the orbits

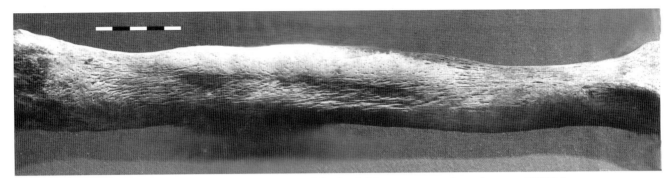

Figure 13.11 Probable adolescent scorbutic changes in a tibia: healed haematomas along the crest: FCS14

include iron deficiency, the commonest form of anaemia today. Since an inadequate intake of dietary iron, or a loss of iron through persistent diarrhoea or blood loss from gut parasites causes iron deficiency anaemia, it is likely to have been common in the past. While some consider that cranial and orbital lesions are associated with this disease, this is not now a generally held view. Other metabolic or infectious diseases can also produce similar lesions.

It is not possible to discriminate between scurvy and iron deficiency anaemia in dry bone. All the diseases of malnutrition can, and usually do, occur together in a population and in an individual. Clearly, there is evidence for some malnutrition, both childhood and adult, amongst the crew of the *Mary Rose*. Famine was a persistent problem in the first half of the sixteenth century (Stirland 2005, chapter 3), particularly in the 1520s. Given their ages at death, a lot of the men will have been infants or young children during this decade, and evidence that they suffered dietary stress persists in their bones. A number of them had suffered from rickets and probably from scurvy as young children, and some seem to have had osteomalacia as adults. From

this study, it is not possible to say whether they suffered from any other deficiency diseases as well.

Infectious disease

Common acute viral infections, such as measles and mumps, are too short-lived to leave markers on children's bones although, because they cause disrupted growth, they may leave characteristic hypoplastic bands or pits on the teeth. Some chronic infections, however, such as leprosy, syphilis and tuberculosis, may affect the skeleton. While there is no evidence for either leprosy or syphilis among the crew, there is some evidence for an infectious respiratory condition.

The visceral surfaces of the ribs are in contact with the pleural membrane covering the lungs. Recent work has discovered lesions on these visceral surfaces in a number of ribs and, when examined using a scanning electron microscope (SEM), these lesions are formed by new bone laid down in the periosteum covering the rib (Wakely *et al.* 1991). The new bone is highly vascular, the channels becoming roofed-over and thus creating the new bone surface. The presence of a common respiratory infection is suggested by the position of these lesions and their frequency in both Old and New World skeletons. Where the cause of death is known and the lesions occur in the New World collections, chronic pulmonary tuberculosis has been suggested as the agent (Wakely *et al.* 1991). SEM pictures clearly show similar lesions, with the formation of vascular new bone, on two adult ribs from the ship's crew. Figure 13.13 (top) shows the new bone formation, where channels are forming. These channels have incipient roofs which eventually become complete new bone (Fig. 13.13 (bottom)). The SEM appearance of these channels is similar to those on other ribs (Wakely *et. al.* 1991, pers. comm., 2000). If the formation of this new bone is caused by a chronic lung infection, possibly tuberculosis, then someone on the *Mary Rose* was suffering from it.

Fractures

In the past, fractures were usually unreduced and untreated, so that the evidence for the trauma is retained on the healed bone. There is evidence for only a small number of fractures for this group of skeletons,

Figure 13.12 Possible healed scorbutic lesions on a cranial surface

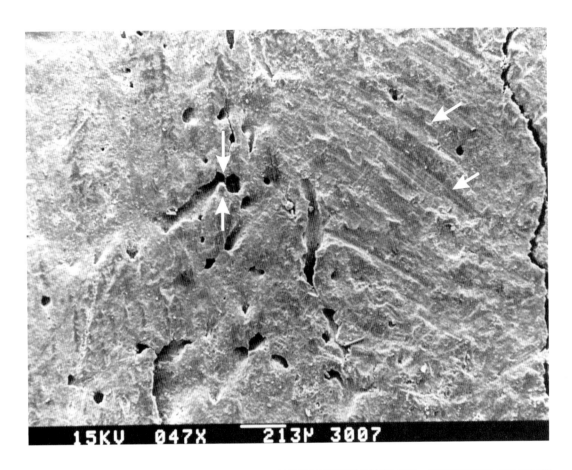

Figure 13.13 (top) SEM of new bone forming on a visceral rib surface; the left-hand arrows indicate a new channel with an incipient roof and the right-hand arrows indicate areas of sand abrasion; (bottom) SEM of a new, completely roofed channel in the same rib (left-hand arrow) and an area of new bone formation (right-hand arrow)

528

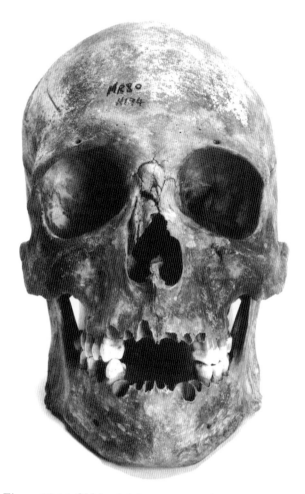

Figure 13.14 Old healed fracture at nasion

although they represent a group of fighting men from a
Tudor warship.

There are three probable nasal fractures, although
one of them may have been a perimortem trauma.
Figure 13.14 shows a well-healed example. There are
two healed traumatised sternums. One has a fracture,
together with an old, healed fracture at the sternal end
of a right rib, suggesting some trauma to his upper right
abdomen. The other sternum is completely perforated
by an old lesion. Altogether, only seven ribs have healed
fractures, four of them from one man. Either few of the
men suffered from chest injuries, or they were wearing
half-armour or padded jerkins (see *AMR* Vol. 3). Some
breastplate fragments found on excavation lend support
to this idea, although even breastplates would not have
saved them from severe injury by penetration from a
war arrow (S. Stanley, pers. comm. 2000). Such
protection would, however, have been effective against
blows to the rib cage.

There are three fractured and one severely strained
ankle. All fractures are of the left fibula, while the strain
involves the lateral ligaments of both a left tibia and
fibula and was probably caused by an adduction force
applied to the ankle. The fractures were caused by
abduction of the distal fibula, leading to shearing of the
lateral malleolus. A paired right tibia and fibula both

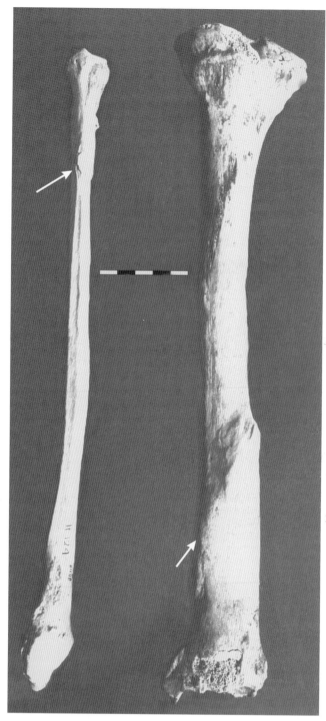

*Figure 13.15 Unreduced spiral fractures of a paired tibia
and fibula (arrows)*

have an unreduced spiral fracture, affecting the distal
tibia and the proximal fibula (Fig. 13.15). This kind of
fracture is caused when a twisting force is applied to the
bone. FCS75 has evidence of a severely traumatised
right elbow with consequent osteoarthritis (Fig. 13.16).
The damaged joint looks as if the trauma occurred in
adolescence when the epiphyses were fusing; it may
have been an epiphyseal fracture. One young adult
femur shows evidence of a childhood bowing fracture.
The bone is twisted and flattened and the femoral head

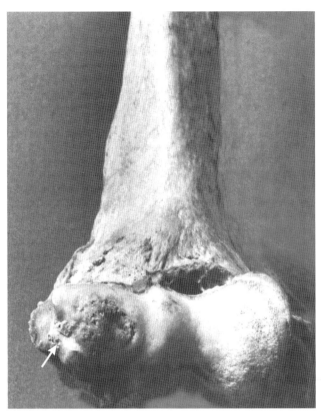

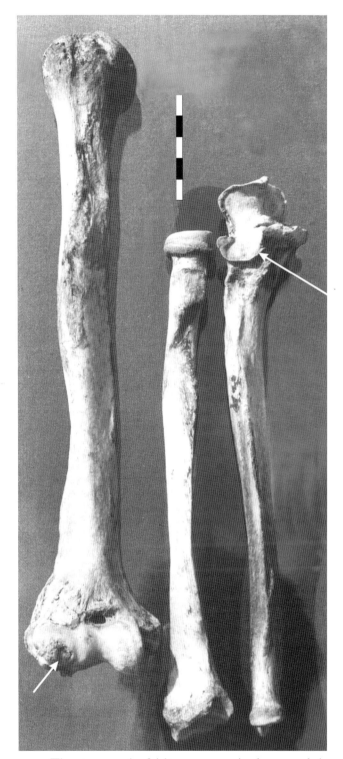

Figure 13.16 (Above and right) Severely traumatised right elbow with some osteoarthritis: FCS75

is dropped (Fig. 13.17). Old, healed fractures are also evident on an ulna, a calcaneus and part of a spine.

Avulsion fractures, where the attached ligament traumatically tears away a piece of bone leaving an unhealed lesion, can occur at various epiphyseal sites on the skeleton. These include on the tibial tubercle, the distal humerus and the tuberosity on the proximal fifth metatarsal. Six examples of avulsion of the tibial tubercle occur in this group of men (Fig. 13.18) and three fifth metatarsals have avulsion fractures of the tuberosity (Fig. 13.19). Figure 13.19 demonstrates a metatarsal where this trauma had occurred fairly recently before the man died, since healing of the opposing fragments of bone has begun and would have been completed had the man not drowned. A bad jump or fall can cause such injuries if the foot is sharply adducted. A ship like the *Mary Rose* will have provided an unstable environment in which the crew had to live and work. Avulsion injuries of the knee and foot are uncommon in other medieval groups and the ones present in this group may represent the remains of some of the mariners, where climbing, jumping, slipping and falling were probably common occurrences.

Osteochondritis dissecans (transchondral fracturing) can affect the immature growth plate of some convex joint surfaces. It is caused by traumatically induced shearing side impact or rotation forces (Resnick and Niwayama 1981, 2257–8). A fragment of the growth plate becomes necrotic and dies, leaving a characteristic

scar. The trauma is fairly common in boys and is associated with some sports, such as football. The preferential site is the distal femur although other sites may also be involved (Resnick and Niwayama 1981, 2261–72). Although there are six cases of the condition on the distal femoral condyles in these men, some occurring bilaterally (Fig. 13.20), the distal humerus and the first metatarsal are the most commonly affected areas. Some of the humeral examples may be related to the use of the longbow and those of the feet may have a similar aetiology to the avulsion injuries discussed

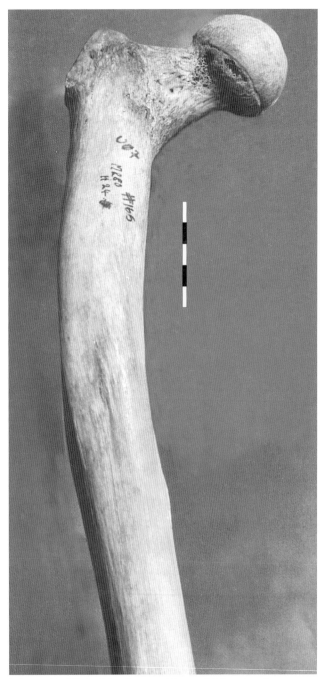

Figure 13.17 A right femur with an old, bowing fracture

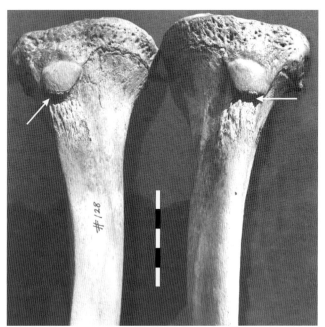

Figure 13.18 Avulsion fracture of the tibial tubercle in a pair of tibiae (arrows)

femoral head, some bilaterally, (Fig. 13.22) and some unilaterally. In two cases, FCS9 and FCS39, there are also the acetabular rim fractures discussed above. In both cases, these fractures are matched by femoral head pits, FCS9 on the left and FCS39 on the right. This is the first reported example of these matching lesions. It

above. It is interesting that, in the remains of those individuals available for study (about 43% of the crew), the distal femur was not the site of preference.

Posterior fracture-dislocation of the hip can occur when the head of the femur is traumatically forced out of the posterior acetabulum. The femoral head frequently carries a fragment of the posterior acetabulum with it (Fig. 13.21). This kind of injury is caused when severe violence is applied to the flexed knee, causing it to hit a fixed object, such as the dashboard of a car during a collision. Five examples occur in the crew of the *Mary Rose*, two bilaterally, two on the right side and one on the left (Fig. 13.21). There are also six examples of necrotic pits in the top of the

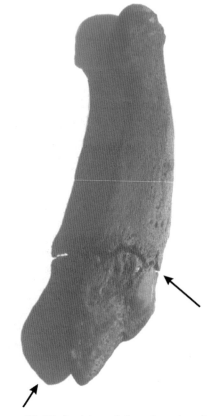

Figure 13.19 Avulsion of the tuberosity of a fifth metatarsal (arrow)

Figure 13.20 Bilateral osteochondritis dissecans of the femoral condyles (arrows)

may be another indication of the instability of the ship's environment.

Another category of trauma apparent in these men is that of head wounds. There are fourteen cases of these, some representing healed depressed cranial fractures and some other kinds of head wounds. The fractures leave shallow depressions on the surface of the skull (Fig. 13.23) and are often caused by a blunt, rather than a sharp, instrument. One skull, however, has evidence of a fairly recent penetrating wound, which is not a fracture. The wound, which would have been caused by a sharp missile such as a bodkin point (a type of arrowhead), was in the process of healing when the man drowned (Fig. 13.24). The form of the wound and the angle of penetration suggest that it was probably caused by an arrowshot from above and, since the victim survived the attack, it is likely that he was wearing some kind of protective headgear. Remnants of helmets were found during the excavations, supporting this possibility. An alternative suggestion is that the wound could have been caused by a practice arrow at the butts. In this case, however, the point would have been wrapped in order to prevent serious injury, although it clearly penetrated the man's helmet and skull! If the incident had occurred during battle, the arrow would have been naked and would have penetrated the helmet and been more likely to cause a fatal wound (S. Stanley, pers. comm. 2000), which this clearly was not.

Figure 13.21 Posterior fracture-dislocation of the acetabular rim (arrow)

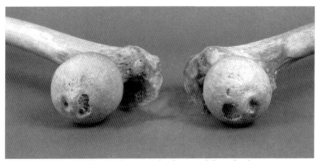

Figure 13.22 Bilateral necrotic femoral head pits

Osteoarthritis

Osteoarthritis is the disease which is most prevalent in both modern populations and in archaeological groups (Rogers and Waldron 1995, 32). It becomes active when cartilage is lost at the surface of a joint, causing the bone to react on this exposed surface and at the joint margins. It only affects the synovial joints of the skeleton, some more than others, including the joints of the hip, knee, hands and feet. Its prevalence increases with age and its presence in an individual does not necessarily indicate the practise of a particular activity or occupation, contrary to popular belief.

The literature is littered with examples of the mis-diagnosis of osteoarthritis in archaeological material. In dry bone, the disease is characterised by eburnation on a joint surface. There may also be new bone or pitting on the joint surface, the contours of which may be altered, as well as marginal osteophytes at the joint edge. Recent work has provided a firm basis for the diagnosis of osteoarthritis in a skeleton (Rogers and Waldron 1995, 44). Either eburnation or at least two of

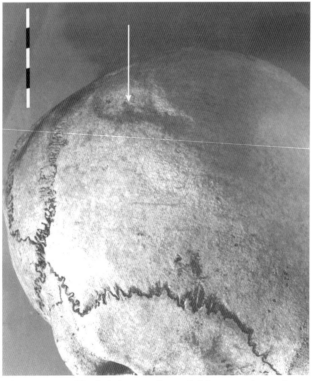

Figure 13.23 Healed depressed cranial fracture (arrow)

the other characteristics must be present. The spine and the rest of the skeleton will be discussed separately for the *Mary Rose* men, with the spines being dealt with in the next section of this report.

The fractured elbow of FCS75, discussed above, was already showing signs of developing osteoarthritis. One other pathological right elbow, that of FCS44, has the classic changes already mentioned, with eburnation and pitting, marginal osteophytes and altered joint contours. There are another 63 cases of non-vertebral osteoarthritis in the crew. Most of it occurred in men over the age of 30 and the majority of it affected the articular surfaces of ribs. Some of this may be related to patterns of activity, but it is not possible to be certain.

Activity and occupation

Identification of the probable activities or occupations engaged in by the living and recorded on their skeletons is sometimes undertaken by researchers. This is often attempted by considering a combination of factors, including significant changes to the bones, artefacts excavated from the site and ethnographic or documentary information. The problem with any archaeological sample, however, is that so little is usually known about the people interred in the burial ground since, by definition, there are usually no documentary records about them. This includes a lack of information about the activities or occupations in which they were involved. Some comparisons have been made with observed skeletal changes in trauma and in sports medicine in the living, and these can be useful sources of information. There has also been a substantial body of research undertaken to identify problems that may occur as a result of patterns of work. These include those associated with persistent long-term keyboard use, known as Repetitive Strain Injury (RSI). Too often, however, such studies on archaeological samples have not taken into account three important factors which will affect the identification and diagnosis of occupational or activity-related skeletal change. These are:

- The fundamental asymmetry which is present in the human skeleton;
- The ages of individuals having particular skeletal changes that may be related to activity;
- The method by which muscles function, not singly but together in groups.

These factors must always be considered when attempts are made to identify what people were doing from the changes to their bones which occurred during life.

The human skeletal remains from the *Mary Rose* are very well preserved because of their rapid burial in anaerobic sea-bed silts. The bones are hard and non-

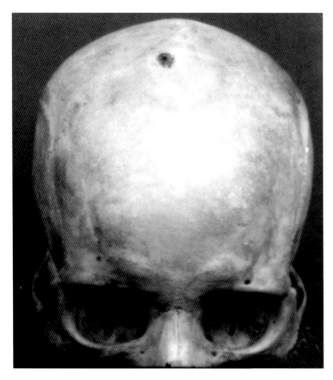

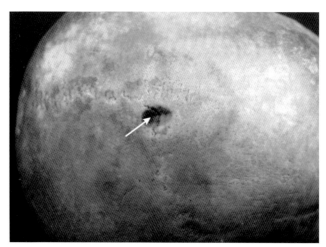

Figure 13.24 (Left and above) probable cranial arrow wound, in the process of healing (arrow)

friable, unlike many cemetery burials. They are much better preserved, for example, than many of the burials from the medieval parish site of St Margaret Fyebridgegate, Norwich (AD 1240–1468). Many of the *Mary Rose* bones are complete and undamaged with very clear markings for tendon and ligament attachments (Fig. 13.4, above). Furthermore, the *Anthony Roll* provides us with a record both of the numbers of men on board and of their occupations: 200 mariners, 185 soldiers and 30 gunners. When the examination and recording of the burials was in progress, therefore, it seemed that it might be possible to identify at least some of the activities or occupations followed by the men.

Os acromiale

As the examination, matching and recording of the bones proceeded it became clear that there were marked changes to many of them that were not merely a function of their preservation. In particular, there was a high frequency of an unusual anomaly of the scapula, known as *os acromiale*. In this condition, the final epiphyseal element of the acromial process fails to unite to the bone (Fig. 13.25, top), leaving a characteristic incomplete bone or pair of bones (Fig. 13.25, bottom). In the example shown here, both the ununited fragments were also recovered. The epiphysis normally unites to the bones in males by 18–19 years of age. This union does not occur, however, in about 3–6% of individuals (Stirland 1984).

Of the 207 scapulae from the wreck, 26 (12.5%) have os acromiale. Since many of these are single bones, however, lacking their matching partner, it is unclear whether the anomaly affected both bones of a pair or

only one. However, there are 52 complete pairs of scapulae in this sample of 207 and, of these, ten pairs have os acromiale. Therefore, the prevalence for the pairs of scapulae is 19%, much higher than the modern frequency. Six pairs have the anomaly bilaterally (Fig. 13.25), three on the left side only and one on the right side only. Looking at the ten pairs with os acromiale as a group, therefore, nine scapulae have it on the left and seven on the right. Looking at the 26 scapulae with the condition from the whole group of 207, however, 15 (14.7%) have the anomaly on the left and 11 (10.5%) have it on the right. Thus, there is not only a considerably increased prevalence of os acromiale in the group when compared with the modern incidence but there is also an increased prevalence of the condition on the left side. Although os acromiale affects an epiphysis, all the affected bones belong to fully adult men, so the high prevalence is not simply caused by immature bones, and a further explanation is needed. Os acromiale has often been considered as a developmental anomaly, the epiphysis failing to unite to the main bone. There have been suggestions, however, that it can be caused by a trauma to the shoulder (Miles 1994), and that it is more common bilaterally (Liberson 1937; Sterling *et al.* 1995). It is certainly more common bilaterally among the *Mary Rose* men, although its cause was unclear. Accidental shoulder trauma is unlikely to affect so many men in the same way but a common pattern of activity might do so.

Shooting the bow

It was a legal requirement during the medieval and early post-medieval period for all fit males under the age of 60, excluding the Clergy, Judges and all who were 'lame, decrepit or maimed', to practise in the use of the longbow. From the ages of 7–17 every boy had to be provided with a bow and two arrows by his father and, after the age of 17, had to provide a bow and four arrows for himself (Hardy 1995, 9). In order that all men could practise, butts were provided in every town

534

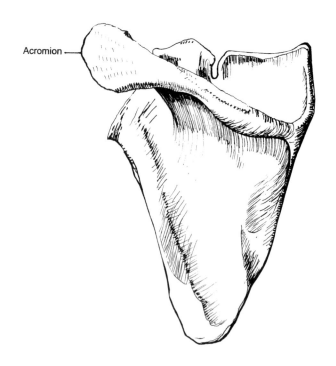

Figure 13.25 (right) The human scapula; (below) bilateral os acromiale from FCS7, excavated from the Hold. This man had other changes as well as the os acromiale, suggesting he might well have been a war bow man

Acromion

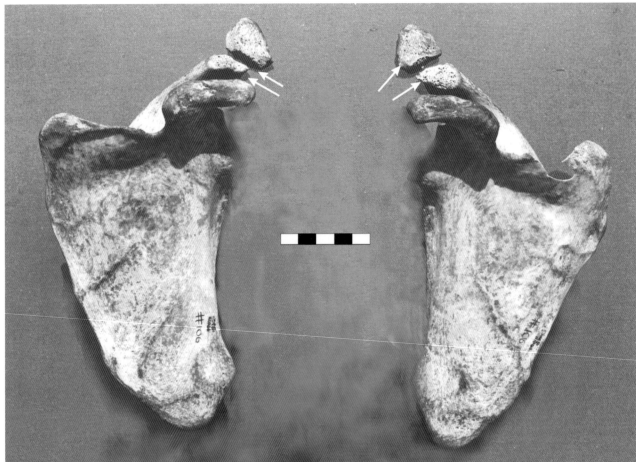

and, to be accepted for military service in 1542, all men aged 24 and more were required to shoot to a mark 200m away (Hardy 1995). Although archers are not specifically mentioned in the *Anthony Roll*, 250 yew longbows, 400 sheaves of livery arrows and six gross of bowstrings are listed in the inventory for the *Mary Rose*. The excavation yielded the remains of 172 longbows, approximately 4000 arrows, up to 18 leather spacers for either 24 or 36 arrows, and bracers (wristguards), many of which were stamped with a variety of marks. Some longbows were also stamped and these, together with the livery arrows, suggest that there could have been a personal retinue on the ship. Such stamps could also have been put on the bows by the bowyer. Since war

Figure 13.26 A modern archer shooting a standard arrow from a replica war bow of 54.5kg (120lb) draw weight: a) at full draw and b) after the arrow is released. © H. M. Greenland

longbows (war bows) were made to a specific standard, each bowyer needed to be identifiable (S. Stanley pers. comm., 2000). Some of the soldiers on board will probably have been war bow men although every ship in the *Anthony Roll* is listed as having longbows, suggesting that many mariners also used the bow (A. Hildred, pers. comm. 2000).

Technique and draw weights
The technique used by the medieval archer to shoot the longbow was different from that used by a modern archer. Where the modern archer draws the bow back to a fixed point on the chin or face under the leading eye, the longbow man drew to the ear or breast using an instinctive aim and no fixed reference point (Bartlett and Embleton 1995, 32). Figure 13.26 demonstrates the technique and stance adopted by the modern longbow man shooting a replica war bow; the arrow travelled 216m (H.D. Hewitt Soar, pers. comm. 1999). Using this technique, the arrow is shot from the bow at

an angle of 45° from the horizontal to give maximum range. The archer in Figure 13.27, Simon Stanley, is drawing a replica war bow of 75kg (165lb) draw weight at a 45° angle. The replica war bows have very heavy draw weights and it is thought that the medieval war bows were of a similar weight. This assumption is supported by the experimental work done to test the draw weights both of excavated bows from the ship and of modern replicas of the same bows (Hardy 1995, 212–216; and see *AMR* vol. 3, chapter 8). Computer modelling of the bows from the ship had predicted they would have draw weights of 45.5kg (100lb) to 78kg (172lb) at a 30 inch (760mm) draw. Although these bows were so degraded that they could not be drawn properly to test their weights, the replica bows (MRA, Mary Rose Approximations), made of Oregon yew, yielded draw weights which were very close to the predictions for the ones from the ship. Persistent drawing of such heavy war bows would have a significant effect on the archer.

Figure 13.27 Simon Stanley at full draw with a replica war bow of 75kg (165lb) draw weight. (Note the 45° angle at which the archer is drawing). © Roy King

An archer uses the major muscles of the arm, spine and shoulder in drawing a longbow. The bow arm is fully extended while the drawing arm is tightly flexed across the chest with the middle two or three fingers exerting the same pull on the bow string as the draw weight of the bow.

> *'The effect of the natural elasticity of the bow is to swing the bow arm across the chest so, to counteract this, the shoulder muscles have to develop a pull of about 300lb [136kg] force to draw a 60lb [27.2kg] bow, which is five times as great as the pull exerted on the arrow. The resulting forces across each shoulder joint, for the draw of a 60lb bow, is greater than three hundredweight [152.4kg]'.* (Hardy 1995, 150–1)

The much heavier war bows would require even more strength to draw properly and they were, of course, used on a regular basis for practise as well as in battle. The shooting technique consisted of 'laying [the] body in the bow' (Hardy 1995, 135) and 'press [ing] the whole weight of his body into the horns of his bow' (Trevelyan 1947, 18n). Given that the majority of

Figure 13.28 Laying the body into a replica bow of 63.5kg (140lb) draw weight © H.D.H. Soar

archers would be right-handed, then this technique of leaning into the bow using the whole strength and weight of the body (Fig. 13.28) would put a greater stress on the left shoulder (the bow arm) than on the right. It seems likely, therefore, that the high frequency of os acromiale in the crew of the *Mary Rose* might be related to the long term use of the heavy war bow and that the technique employed in the shooting of this bow could account for the left-sided dominance of the anomaly. The lack of substantial numbers of males with os acromiale in other medieval burial groups suggests that the men with the condition may have been specialist or professional archers. Thus, the non-union of the acromion in these cases may have been caused by the persistent use of a heavy war bow, probably from adolescence. Some men will have been more proficient with the bow than others leading, perhaps, to their selection into an elite group for their skill. Such a group could be considered as composed of specialist or professional archers and may have been present on the ship.

Other research

A research project, undertaken during the 1990s, compared pairs of humeri and femora from the *Mary Rose* and from the males buried in the Norwich medieval parish cemetery. The research attempted to determine whether there were any detectable differences, in the paired bones between the two groups, which could be attributed to patterns of activity (Stirland 1992). It was based on the statistical analysis of a series of measurements, one of which was that of the area of the humeral head where the muscles involved in abduction attach. The results demonstrated that the dimensions of the left shoulder were greater in the *Mary Rose* men than they were in the men from Norwich and it was concluded that this increase in size was probably due to the presence of a group of specialist archers among the remains of the crew (Stirland 1993, 105–13). Since all males were required to shoot the bow, archers will have been present also in the Norwich group and will have served their time as part of retinues. Os acromiale was present among the Norwich men, but at a lower prevalence (6%) than in the ship's crew and occurring predominantly on the right side, suggesting a lack of specialist war bow men in the group. Another study of modern elite Olympic archers demonstrated evidence for increased dimensions of the shoulder of the bow arm, usually the left (Mann and Littke 1989, 85–92). This was attributed to the repeated pulling of a bow and the consequent loading (1545kg over a four-day event) of the shoulders.

Clearly, all the research projects discussed above do not allow us to identify an individual archer from changes to his shoulders. Rather, they suggest that, when two or more groups of skeletons are compared, the presence of a cluster of changes, including an increased prevalence of os acromiale, may indicate the presence of specialist war bow men in one group rather than the other.

Other changes to bone

Comparisons of entheses on the proximal femur were made for the same two groups of skeletons. These included both measurements of the trochanters and scoring of the entheses on a 0–4 basis, according to development (Stirland 1992). The gluteus medius and minimus muscles attach on the greater trochanter, which was bigger on both sides in the men from the ship than it was in the Norwich men. The enthesis for gluteus maximus, on the gluteal tuberosity, was also more developed in the ship's group, particularly on the right, than it was in the Norwich group. The gluteal group of muscles is used to keep the pelvis stable so that it doesn't slip sideways. Gluteus maximus is used both in climbing and balancing

and to keep the trunk steady while throwing or while shooting a longbow (Stirland 1992).

There are areas of the pelvis where certain muscles attach, which also show signs of stress in young men from the crew. This applies in particular to the pubis, where the large muscles that adduct the thigh attach proximally. These muscles are also involved, with others such as the hamstrings, in flexion and extension of the hip and the thigh. While they attach on the pubic area of the pelvis, these muscles also attach distally on the posterior femur, forming a large fan (Kapandji 1983, vol. 2, 59, and fig. 137). Out of a total of nineteen men who have such changes in the FCS group, nine belong to young individuals, five of whom have signs of muscle stress on the pubis. These thigh muscles that attach on the pelvis can also be used in flexion and extension of the hip and thigh. When the body is supported on both limbs, the adductors are used to stabilise the pelvis. They are also essential in maintaining certain postures in some sports (Kapandji 1983, vol. 2, 61, fig. 142). A longbow archer uses them when at full draw and shooting at a 45° angle. Their increased size in some of the *Mary Rose* crew supports the idea of the presence of a group of young men using a heavy war bow. Many femora in this group have extremely well developed muscle attachment sites on the posterior femur, as elsewhere (see above). The development of these sites suggests an increased use of the adductors, the flexors and the extensors of the hips and thigh. A similar development of the attachment sites of these muscles on the pubis supports this view.

Enthesophytes (Fig. 13.29) can develop at muscle attachment sites both as a function of age, and of chronic repetitive stresses at any age (Waldron 1994, 101). The latter is clearly the case in young individuals. Since only the FCS numbers could be aged with accuracy, enthesophytes were only analysed for this group. Enthesophytes were present in 39 (42%) of the FCS group and, of these, 23 (25%) were young men. The humerus was the most affected bone. Fifteen of the 23 young men had enthesophytes on the upper humerus at the attachments of muscles involved in adduction; they were probably related to patterns of activity. Enthesophytes may also develop at the site of the attachment for the costoclavicular ligament on the clavicle (Fig. 13.30). This ligament is involved, together with others, in elevation of the humerus and

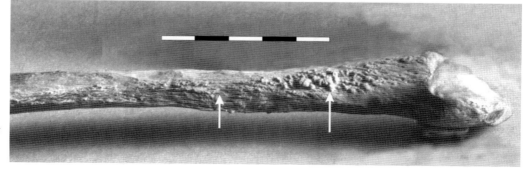

Figure 13.29 Enthesophytes on a distal fibula (arrows)

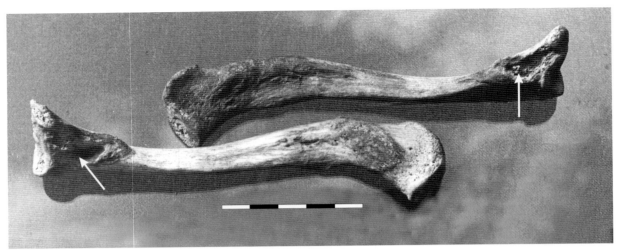

Figure 13.30 Enthesophytes on a matched pair of clavicles, at the attachment for the costoclavicular ligament (arrows)

stabilisation of the scapula. In the FCS group, seven of the pairs of clavicles have enthesophytes at this site on both bones and two on the right side only.

Possible archers on the Mary Rose
A number of the FCS skeletons have some of the changes discussed above and these may indicate the presence of archers. Three skeletons in particular should be discussed here.

Two skeletons, FCS82 and FCS83, were found in M2, aft of the so-called Pilot's cabin and across a 'knee' (Fig. 13.31). Archery equipment was associated with these two including arrows, some loose and some in a spacer, a wristbracer and a slashed jerkin thought to be worn by archers. Both were stained brown and had crystals of haematite and vivianite growing on them. Because of all the associated equipment, it was assumed by the archaeologists that FCS82 and FCS83 were archers. Although they were both young adults, FCS82 was a little older than FCS83. He was also considerably shorter at about 1.68m (5´6"), compared with FCS83 who was about 1.82m (5´11"). The best evidence for an archer is on the bones of FCS83. All muscle attachments are very well developed and the spine is noticeably stressed in the mid-section. Both clavicles have deep impressions for the costoclavicular ligament which is particularly severe on the right side. The left clavicle has very strong attachment areas for other ligaments. Simon Stanley (pers. comm., 2000) reports sore clavicles after shooting the bow for some time and it may be that FCS83 was an archer. FCS7, who was found in H2, may also have been an archer. This skeleton is one of the most complete of the FCS group. The individual was probably in his mid-twenties and about 1.76m (5´9") tall. There is os acromiale of both scapulae and strong development of humeral entheses. The left humerus has an avulsion of the medial epicondyle. A similar avulsion fracture of the left elbow occurred in a skeleton with os acromiale from the battle of Towton who was also assumed to be an archer

(Boylston *et al.* 1997, 38). FCS7 also has some spinal changes, particularly affecting the thoracic-lumbar junction. Lumbar 1 has no left transverse process and a poorly formed left superior articulation for the matching thoracic 12, which is also twisted out of alignment. The articulations of lumbar 4 and 5 are twisted in a similar manner and the left articulations are flattened. Such twisting of articulations occurs in other lower thoracic spines in the group (Fig. 13.32) and may be associated with the use of the heavy war bow.

The combination of all the above evidence strongly suggests the presence of a group of specialist archers on the *Mary Rose*, skilled in the use of the very heavy war bow. While it is extremely difficult, if not impossible, to identify an individual archer from the pathological changes to his skeleton, the presence of a group of such men may be inferred when two groups are compared and shown to differ in the manner demonstrated.

Other occupations
Armament
It is clear, both from the *Anthony Roll* illustration and from the excavation, that the *Mary Rose* was heavily armed. This armament consisted of two main types of large gun – wrought iron breech-loaders and bronze muzzle-loaders (see *AMR* Vol. 3 for a full description and discussion of the guns). The breech-loaders were fired by using a 205.5kg (450lb) breech block, which needed four men to lift it on top of the gun every time it was fired (A. Hildred, pers. comm. 2000). These guns fired iron anti-ship or stone anti-personnel shot (*AMR* Vol. 3). The bronze muzzle-loaders were large, fired iron shot and were used on the main gundeck. There were three such guns on each side of the Main deck, in the bow, amidships and astern, and between them were four iron guns on each side. The headroom on this deck varies from 1.83m to 1.96m, away from the main beams. The mean height of the measurable men was 1.71m and the tallest was about 1.80m, so there would have been sufficient headroom for them to operate the

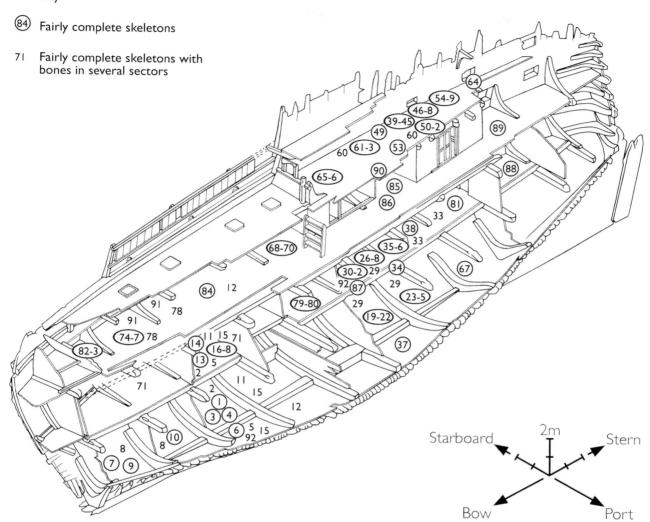

Key

(84) Fairly complete skeletons

71 Fairly complete skeletons with
bones in several sectors

Figure 13.31 Distribution of the Fairly Complete Skeletons (FCS)

big guns, although the working space may have been cramped.

A gun crew on the *Mary Rose* probably consisted of five or six men, who will have been necessary to move

Figure 13.32 Twisting of the left apophyseal joints of a matching T12 and L1 that may be associated with persistent shooting of the heavy war bow (arrows)

the bronze guns backwards and forwards. One of them will have been a master gunner and 30 gunners are listed in the *Anthony Roll*. The ship had a total of 91 guns altogether and a master gunner and his crew may have worked on more than one gun. Four men will have been required to lift the very heavy breech blocks onto and off the wrought iron guns. Thus, the moving and operation of the heavy ordnance would have placed a lot of strain on the men involved, particularly on their vertebrae.

Vertebral pathology

Recent work compared the four common types of vertebral pathology between the columns of the ship's crew and those of the Norwich men (Stirland and Waldron 1997). These are:

* Osteoarthritis of the apophyseal joints (pitting and marginal osteophytes; Fig. 13.33, top);
* Marginal osteophytes (Fig. 13.33, bottom);
* Schmorl's nodes (Fig. 13.34);

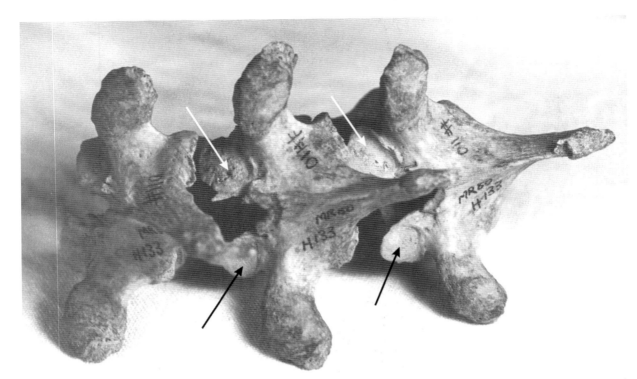

Figure 13.33 (top) Osteoarthritis of the apophyseal joints (arrows); (bottom) marginal osteophytes (arrow)

- Ossification into the ligamentum flavum (Fig. 13.35).

There were also high frequencies of spondylolysis (Fig. 13.36) and of cranial or caudal shift (Fig. 13.37).

The age distribution between the two groups is quite different. Eighty-five per cent of the vertebrae from the *Mary Rose* were from adolescents or young adults, while a fairly equal split of 54% from young adults or adolescents and 46% from mature or old men occurred with the vertebrae from Norwich. There was little osteoarthritis in the ship's crew but the amount and distribution of the other three types of pathology was quite similar between the two groups (Stirland and Waldron 1997, figs 4–6). However, there was an increase in ossification into the ligamentum flavum in the ship's crew and this was so extreme in some cases that the adjoining vertebrae were almost locked (Fig. 13.35).

The results of this research demonstrated that, although the ages of the two groups of men are different, with the men from the *Mary Rose* being predominantly young, the results of the comparison of the spinal pathology showed many similarities between them. It appears that, in the younger ship's crew, there has been an acceleration of the spinal lesions that are usually associated with ageing. This acceleration is probably related to the activities of the crew, many of which would have involved heavy manual work in fairly confined spaces, particularly with the gun crews.

A possible gun crew

A large bronze culverin, 3.3m long and weighing 2.13 tonnes, was found in M3 (Fig. 13.38). A group of six FCS skeletons, FCS74–78 and FCS91, were found in close association with this gun and, from the deposits on the bones, they seemed to have been in this area for a long time. All were in their early to mid-twenties and, apart from FCS78, all of them had strong, robust skeletons, with very well-marked entheses. Some of the

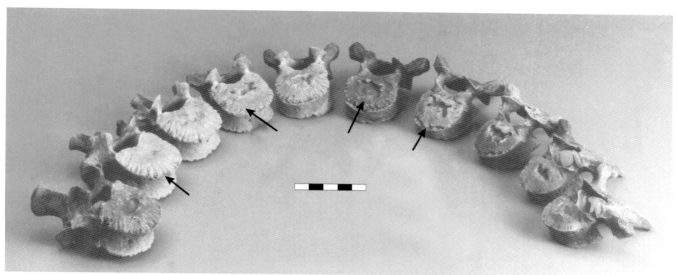

Figure 13.34 Schmorl's nodes (arrows) FCS21

spines show high levels of pathology, particularly FCS74, FCS75 and FCS77. The spine of FCS74 is that shown in Figures 13.33 (bottom) and 13.35 while FCS75 has similar, although less dramatic, vertebral pathology and also an osteoarthritic right elbow. A lot of

this skeleton is darkly stained and there are crystals of iron oxide in the form of haematite and vivianite on many of the bones. FCS76 also has stained and encrusted bones and rachitic tibiae. There is evidence of some vertebral stress and there are well-developed entheses. FCS77 has a very stressed spine with osteophytes at the sacroiliac joints and enthesophytes on the pelvis. The whole lower back appears to have been subjected to extreme pulling, pushing and lifting forces and the vertebrae appear like those of a much older man. FCS91 was the tallest of the group with a very strong and robust skeleton, large bones and well-developed entheses. Unlike the other five skeletons, FCS78 had a gracile skeleton and was the shortest of the group. There is no entheseal development and very little vertebral pathology although some of the bones are stained in a similar way to those of FCS74 and FCS76, implying that this man lay in the same area as the others for a long time.

Some of the vertebral pathology discussed above is present in five of the skeletons that were found with the large culverin in M3; all are young. Three of the five have marked spinal changes, especially FCS74, and all have well-developed entheses and strong, robust bones. They all appear to have been in the same area of the ship for a long period of time and may represent the remains of a gun crew.

Figure 13.35 Ossification into the ligamentum flavum (arrows)

Figure 13.36 Spondylolysis

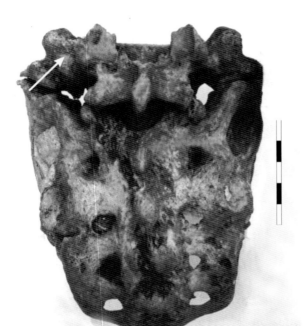

Figure 13.37 Initial sacrilisation of an L5: caudal shift

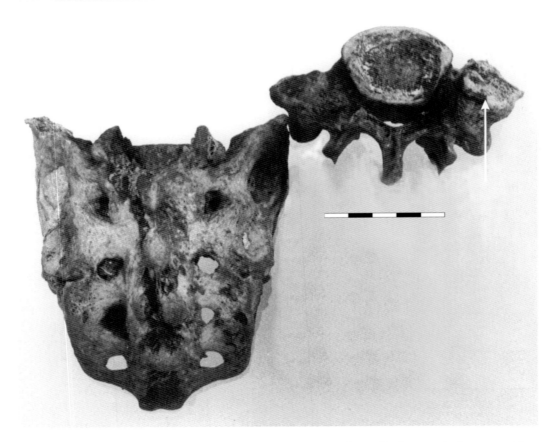

Anomalies

FCS88

The skeleton of FCS88 is particularly interesting, given the nature of the group as a whole and the fact that they represent the remnants of the crew of a fighting ship. FCS88 was probably in his late twenties or early thirties when he drowned and his femoral heads and acetabulae are anomalous. Both acetabulae are wide and shallow and both femoral heads are flattened and dropped (Fig. 13.39). This is not an example of bilateral congenital dislocation of the hip, since there is no evidence for new hip joints formed above or near the normal one. It is much more likely to be a case of bilateral Perthes disease or necrosis of the femoral head. The bones have healed well, suggesting that this disease was a childhood

Figure 13.38 Large bronze culverin found in M3

event. The consequence for the adult may have been some impairment of mobility or agility and his role on the ship may not have been strictly that of a fighting man. The skeleton was found in O10, one of the main storage areas of the ship. There were many valuable and attractive artefacts in this area, including a number of chests and most of the total coinage found in the wreck – 45 or more silver and seven gold coins representing well over a month's wages for a captain, never mind an ordinary mariner. Given his disabilities, and his presence in this area, it may be that FCS 88 was the Purser.

Inca bones

Inca bones occur in the occipital, where a separate bone is created by a transverse suture that runs across the whole width of the bone from asterion to asterion. They are more prevalent in South American populations and rare in European ones. They may be a familial trait.

Three skulls from the ship's crew have inca bones, two of which are bipartite (Fig. 13.40). These men may possibly have been related to each other.

Conclusions

The human skeletal remains from the *Mary Rose* comprise a group of men who were largely young, strong and fit and who, in appearance, would fit into a modern population. In the main they had large bones and strongly developed entheses. Many of them may have suffered from childhood diseases and some of them from diseases as adults. Starvation was probably prevalent, at least in England, during the 1520s and adult deficiency diseases also seem to have been present later. Much of the skeletal development that we see in these men probably resulted from their activities and occupations on board the ship and suggests that some

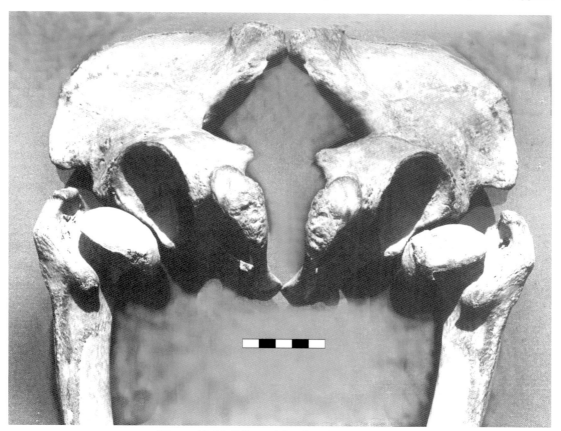

Figure 13.39 Bilateral Perthes disease: FCS88

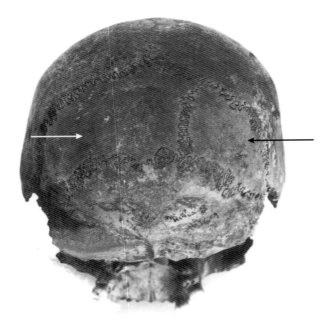

Figure 13.40 Bipartite inca bone in the occipital: FCS70

of them, at least, were professionals. It is not unreasonable to assume that there was a group of specialist war bow men present and it is likely also that some of the men were regular members of a gun crew. Some of the pelvis, leg and foot bones indicate that certain individuals had worked for some time in an unstable physical environment, perhaps as mariners. It is probable that there was a core of professional mariners in the group, since a small number would be needed both as shipkeepers and as officers, such as the master and the boatswain. There is, of course, very little documentary evidence for any of this and few records of any professionals in the navy at this time. It would, however, be an irresponsible misuse of manpower if known good men, whether archers, soldiers or mariners were just dismissed after each voyage or campaign. It is, surely, more reasonable to assume that they would be a valuable resource and, therefore, used continuously particularly when manpower was so short in the navy.

We know for certain the name of only one member of the *Mary Rose*'s crew: Sir George Carew, the Vice Admiral, though Roger Grenville was probably the Captain. The only information we have about the crew is that contained within their skeletal remains. This study has sought to give some idea of what kind of men they were. Where they came from (and recent oxygen isotope work suggests some of them may have come from southern Europe, L. Bell, pers. comm 2000) and who they were is quite another matter.

Dentistry
R.I.W. Evans

The human remains from the *Mary Rose* provided an unparalleled opportunity to study the dentition of group of Tudor men of varying age. The wreck yielded 126 crania, or parts thereof, 116 mandibular elements and many individual loose teeth representing the remains of a maximum of 179 individuals. In addition to straightforward macroscopic observations made on the skulls, jaws and teeth, a series of more detailed examinations was undertaken in order to provide comparative data with the modern population. The bones of the skull and jaw are complex; explanatory diagrams are presented in Figure 13.41, with the parts of the teeth annotated in Figure 13.42. The distribution of the skeletal remains about the ship has been discussed by Stirland, above, and is illustrated in Figures 13.1 and 13.31.

Condition of the bone and teeth

The skulls, jaws and teeth recovered from the *Mary Rose* proved to be remarkably well preserved. Many skulls still had delicate structures such as styloid processes and pterygoid hamuli (Fig. 13.43), the undamaged presence of which demonstrate the care taken by the divers during excavation.

Three skulls were still coated with sediment, and on one this had hardened into a concretion which was impossible to remove without risk of damaging the underlying bone. Some bones had been stained dark brown by iron pigments leaching from nearby objects whilst on others the smooth, hard shiny surface had changed into a chalky surface texture, probably due to the action of minute marine creatures (Bell *et al.* 1991).

The junctions between the bones of the skull are called sutures. These usually have a fairly regular pattern. At the back of the skull this pattern is like an inverted 'Y' where three bones, the occipital and right and left parietal bones, come together at the lambdoid suture. In the *Mary Rose* crew extra bones, known as Inca bones (Fig. 13.44, see also Fig. 13.40, above), were present in the sutures of three skulls. The forehead of a child forms from two bones which join together in the midline of the skull at the metopic suture. This suture usually disappears as the two bones fuse together between 2 and 6 years of age to create the single frontal bone of the adult forehead. Several of the adult crew had metopic sutures still present but the incidence of this feature was similar to that expected in other groups, ancient and modern. Small depressions were present on fourteen vaults, suggestive of healed, depressed, fractures (eg, Fig. 13.23, above). One skull bore traces of a helmet liner.

Without antibiotic medicines Tudor people suffered more from infections than we do today and there is evidence within the crew that some had severe suppurative disease in the regions of the ears and jaw joints, particularly mastoiditis and temporo-mandibular joint disease. Some people may have had difficulty breathing through their noses as several skulls had de-

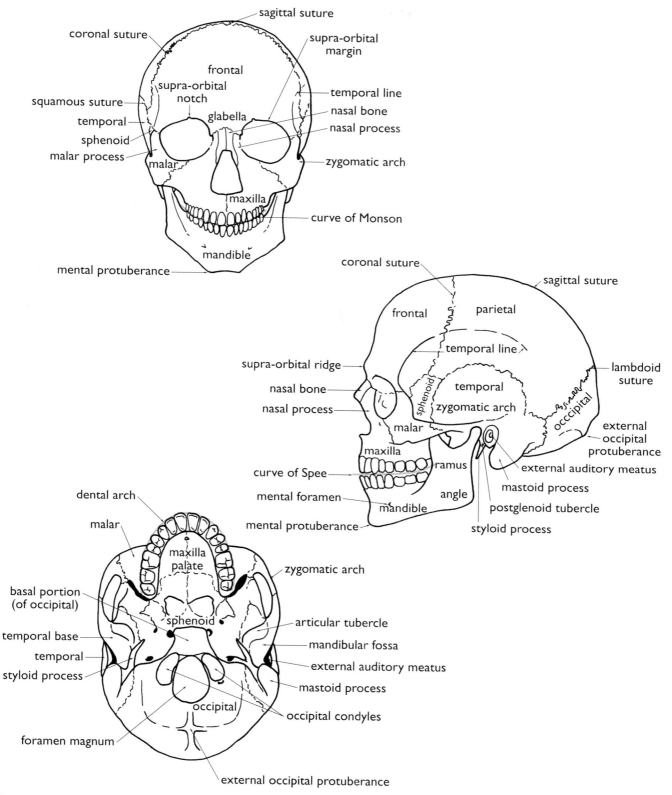

Figure 13.41 Three simplified views of the skull showing the various bones

viated nasal septae, the midline wall between the right and left sides of the nasal airway being bent. Several mandibles were misshapen and had lost the usual symmetry between the right and left sides either of the mandibular body (Fig. 13.45a) or of the right and left condylar necks and condyles. Radiographs (Fig. 13.45b) failed to help diagnose the causes of the bony swellings.

In the living person bone creating cells (osteoblasts) and bone removing cells (osteoclasts) work in harmony

SIDE VIEW

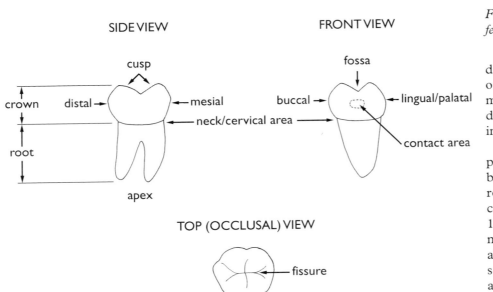

cusp

crown — distal → ← mesial

neck/cervical area

root

apex

FRONT VIEW

fossa

buccal → ← lingual/palatal

contact area

TOP (OCCLUSAL) VIEW

fissure

Figure 13.42 The main external features of a molar tooth

dento-alveolar complex so osteoclastic action removes much of the overall bone. After death bone remodelling is impossible by these means.

Empty tooth sockets were present within the jaw assemblage, especially those of single-rooted teeth, incisors and canines, (Figs 13.45a and 13.46a) indicating post-mortem loss. Teeth were also absent from jaws where no socket remained, indicating ante-mortem tooth loss with subsequent socket healing (Figs 13.45a, 13.46b–c). Possible causes of ante-mortem loss were tooth decay (dental caries), gum (periodontal) disease, trauma or surgical treatment. Single rooted teeth are more easily lost post-mortem than multi-rooted teeth. Individual teeth were also recovered separately, unassociated with any jaw.

to reshape the skeleton during growth, and heal fractures. When a tooth is removed the socket which once held the root of the tooth is filled in with new bone and the bone remodelled to a degree. When several teeth in a row are removed this remodelling can be quite marked and, in extreme cases, when all the teeth are absent, only the basal bone of the original mandible remains. As, in such circumstances, the body has no teeth, it no longer needs the alveolar bone of the original

Figure 13.43 Photographs of a) the right side of the skull showing styloid processes (superimposed), pterygoid hamuli and staining on the parietal and zygomatic bones; b) part of a maxilla showing gross caries on buccal surfaces of molars, calculus on tooth surfaces, unerupted third molar, pterygiod hamulus, post-mortem loss of central incisor and canine

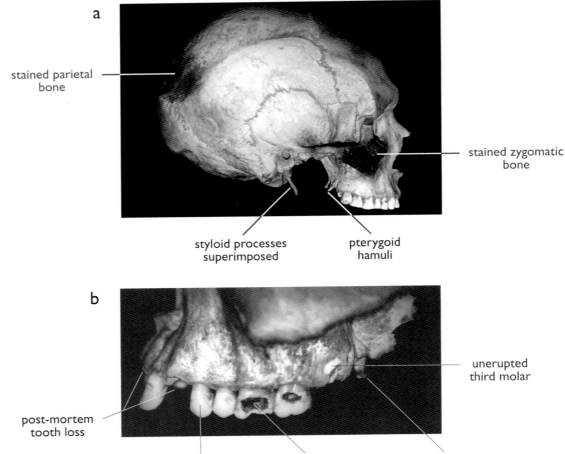

a

stained parietal bone

stained zygomatic bone

styloid processes superimposed

pterygoid hamuli

b

post-mortem tooth loss

unerupted third molar

calculus

buccal caries

pterygoid hamulus

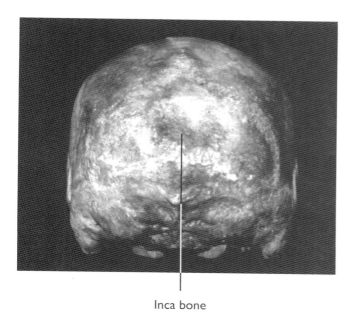

Inca bone

Figure 13.44 Photograph of occipital aspect of skull with three Inca bones in the region of the occipito-parietal suture

This chalky nature to the exposed root surface seems to be a feature of marine submersion.

Matching the jaws and skulls

Although 126 cranial and 116 mandibular elements were recovered, along with many individual teeth, their disarticulation meant that, unless individual mandibles could be matched to skulls, only limited analysis could be carried out. Having made the initial observations that the shape of the bones and dental arches were similar to those of a modern British group, but that the degree of dental irregularity (malocclusion) was less, four experienced dentists (the author, the late Professor R.J.Anderson, the late Dr M.E.Corbett, and Professor T.D.Foster) studied the remains with a view to matching skulls and jaws.

For a match to be taken as correct at least three of the four dentists had to agree the pairing on at least two separate occasions. No proven method for such work

An interesting feature of many tooth roots was that, macroscopically, the exposed dentine surface between the enamel and alveolar bone margins, had lost its normal texture and colour and assumed a matt, chalky appearance. One such tooth has been examined in a scanning electron microscope (Bell *et al.* 1991). This showed that the topographical change is due to diagenetic alteration and had a different distribution on the root surface to that found in earth burials. A similar appearance is seen on teeth recovered from another wreck, the *Earl of Abergavenny*, sunk in 1820 (E. Cummings, pers comm. 1984).

Figure 13.45 Photographs of a) part of a mandible, from above, showing a large bony swelling on the right side of the body, ante-mortem loss of right first molar with healed socket area, empty sockets where teeth have been lost post-mortem, and differential attrition of the left molars; b) dental pantomograph of jaws, including the mandible shown above, failing to give a definite cause to the swelling, and showing gross cavities in upper right molars with a cystic area periapically on upper right first molar. Also, marked attrition on left sided first molars, many empty sockets and a healed area where the lower right first molar was

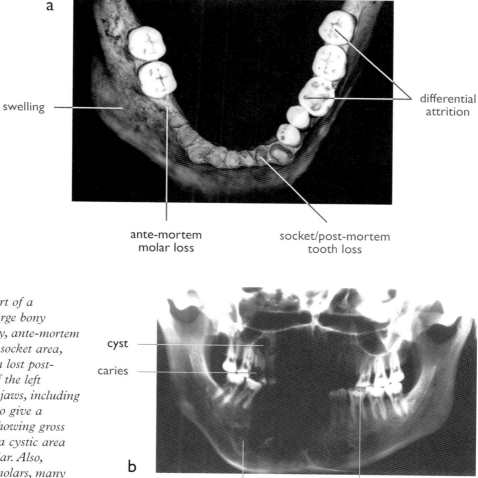

548

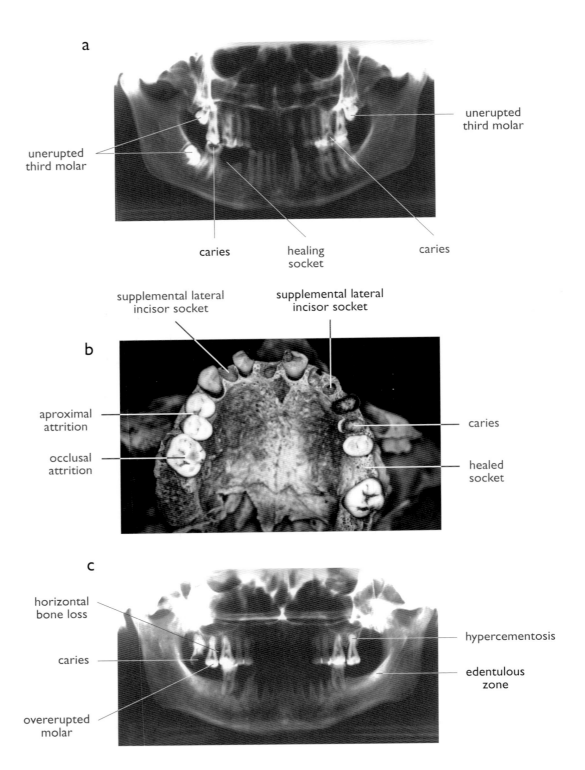

a

unerupted
third molar

unerupted
third molar

caries   healing   caries
                socket

supplemental lateral
incisor socket

supplemental lateral
incisor socket

b

aproximal
attrition

occlusal
attrition

caries

healed
socket

c

horizontal
bone loss

caries

overerupted
molar

hypercementosis

edentulous
zone

*Figure 13.46 a) dental pantomograph of jaws showing unerupted third molars, gross caries, healing socket lower right first
molar and several empty sockets; b) palate and upper dentition from occlusal aspect, showing sockets for supplemental lateral
incisors, carious teeth especially incisors and left premolars, marked attrition occlusally on right first molar and approximally
on right premolars and a healed socket where left first molar was; c) dental pantomograph showing edentulous lower molar
regions due to ante-mortem loss of molars, with over-eruption of unopposed maxillary molars, advanced horizontal bone loss
in upper jaw, hypercementosis on upper molars, gross caries and empty sockets*

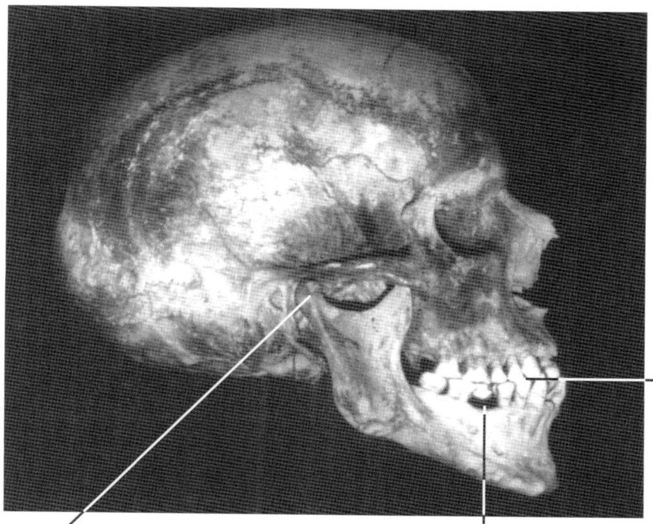

Figure 13.47 Right side of matched skull and mandible showing condyle fitting glenoid fossa, shape of mandibular ramus and good occlusion. Also, ante-mortem loss of mandibular first molar

could be found in the literature, so anatomical and clinical knowledge was pooled and suggested that the following skeletal and dental criteria were appropriate for making a match.

The skeletal criteria (Fig. 13.47) were:

1. How the mandible and skull base fitted together recreate the jaw joints (fit of the mandibular condyles into the glenoid fossae).
2. The posterior height of the mandible, measured to the top of the condyle.
3. The centreline relationships of maxilla and mandible.

The dental criteria (Fig. 13.48) were:

1. Co-ordination of the shape of the upper and lower dental arches.
2. The precise fitting together (intercuspation) of the teeth.
3. Generalised 'wear and tear' (attritional) faceting of the articulated dentition.
4. Specific faceting for individual tooth displacement.
5. Comparison of wear on upper and lower teeth.
6. Compensatory changes for irregular teeth between the jaws, such as over-eruption of unopposed teeth.
7. Comparable caries and periodontal disease patterns between the upper and lower teeth.

Each jaw was placed against a skull base to assess the fit of the condyles into the glenoid fossae, and the occlusion, until a match was found. By the end of this trial and error approach confident matching of 68 intact skulls and mandibles (eg, Fig. 13.48), and two cases of part maxillae with part mandibles had been achieved. Neither bone colour nor texture could be relied on when matching skulls and jaws as several matched pairs were of different colour or texture.

Sometimes teeth had been found close to bones during the excavation but often teeth had come out of their sockets during washing, transport and storage. By devising and applying the following guides confident relocation of many teeth within sockets was possible.

1. Observation of the empty socket shape.
2. Identification of the tooth.
3. Comparison of the shape of the socket with that of the tooth root.
4. Fit of the tooth in the socket.
5. Comparison of the amount of attrition with other teeth in the same arch.
6. Comparison of the bite level of the relocated tooth with the overall bite plane of the jaw.

7. Assessment of the fitting together (articulation) of the upper and lower dentitions in specimens with matched jaws and skulls.
8. Comparison of aspects of the tooth, regarding caries and periodontal disease, with bony evidence of oral disease at the socket.

Having tried all possible combinations of skulls, jaws, sockets and teeth there remained, unmatched, 58 skulls, 48 mandibles and 58 teeth (Table 13.8). Based on the osseous remains of skulls and jaws the maximum number of persons from whom parts could have been recovered is 179.

Comparison of the skulls with modern groups

The group of 68 matched specimens presented the same bony variation of faces and heads that we see in modern British people. Similar patterns of dental irregularity (malocclusion) are also evident. However, the shape of the dental arches in the *Mary Rose* group appeared more ideal, in general, than is seen in a late twentieth century British group. Also, the Tudor dentitions seemed to have less crowding of their teeth

Table 13.8 Numbers of skulls, jaws and teeth (and parts thereof) recovered

Parts	No.
Total of crania	126
Total of mandibles	116
Matched crania, maxillae & mandibles	68
Matched maxillae & mandibles	2
Unmatched crania	58
Unmatched mandibles	48
Unrelocated teeth	58

550

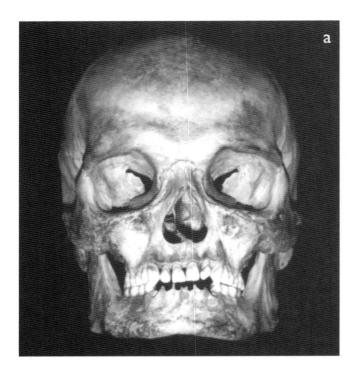

a

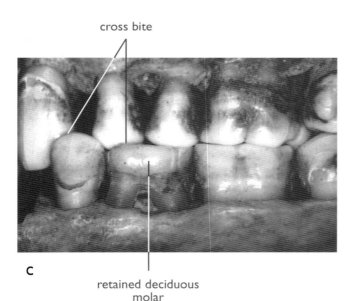

tipped molar

caries

attrition

crowding

rotated canine

cross bite

c

retained deciduous molar

than today's natural young adults, ie, people who have not had orthodontic extractions or treatment (Figs 13.45a, 13.50; see Fig. 13.49 for an explanation of the internal structure of the tooth).

The group of 68 matched, intact skulls and jaws yielded 56 specimens suitable for more detailed analysis, including radiographic examination. Having considered traditional craniometry (taking two-dimensional measurements from a three-dimensional skull), and modern, computerised three-dimensional techniques using x, y and z axis cartesian co-ordinate data (Scott 1981; Moss *et al.* 1987), it was decided to use two dimensional, radiographic cephalometry (Rakosi *et al.* 1993) for this detailed analysis because, as well as being a widely used, standardised technique, much published data from studies on other groups already existed in the literature.

Having identified which skull, jaw and teeth came from an individual, the upper and lower teeth were put together to reassemble the specimen into the bony head. Special X-ray films (cephalometric radiographs) were then taken of the reassembled specimens. Radiographs from the back to the front (postero-anterior) and right side (lateral) of the head were taken. Another technique which spreads the tooth images out in a row (dental pantomography) was used to view the teeth and surrounding bony structures. These lateral and postero-anterior cephalometric skull radiographs, and dental panto-mographs were taken of these 56 intact specimens (Figs 13.45b, 13.46b and c, 13.54, 13.55).

The lateral cephalometric radiographs were analysed geometrically on two separate occasions, with an interval of at least six weeks between each digitisation of the same film. This helped in obtaining accurate measurements. A variety of distances and angles were calculated from each radiograph using an electronic viewing box linked to a computer. These values were then compared with standard human values. If incisor teeth were missing from the specimen an estimate of the tooth position was used in the analysis. The results are given in Table 13.9, alongside the accepted, and recently

Figure 13.48 a) Full-face photograph of matched skull and mandible; b) occlusal view of mandibular dental arch showing tipping of right third molar into space created by ante-mortme loss of second molar, rotations of canines, crowding anterior to the premolar zones, gross caries and marked attrition; c) close-up of buccal teeth, including a retained deciduous lower second molar, with buccal crossbite of canines and premolars, but precise occlusion between upper and lower teeth.

Table 13.9 Comparison of *Mary Rose* skulls with Eastman Standard cephalometric data

Measure ment	*Mary Rose*		Eastman standard[1]	
	Mean	SD	Mean	SD
SNA(°)	83.6	±3.6	81	±3
SNB(°)	79.9	±4.0	78	±3
ANB(°)	3.7	±3.2	3	±3
MMPA(°)	20.8	±6.5	27	±4
FP(%)	55.6	±2.3	55	±2
UIA(°)	101.8	±8.7	109	±6
LIA(°)	90.6	±7.2	93	±6
IIA(°)	146.9	±11.1	131*	–

[1]. see MacAllister and Rock 1992 for explanation;
* by calculation

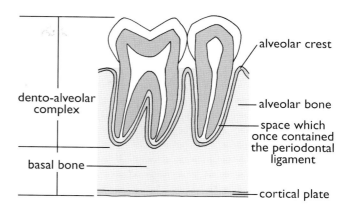

Figure 13.49 Representation of a section through a molar, premolar and jaw of one of the crew, after excavation

validated, British standard from the Eastman Hospital (MacAllister and Rock 1992).

Most of the values show the Tudor crew to be similar to modern Britons except for the vertical angle between the upper and lower jaw (mandibular-maxillary planes angle, MMPA). This angle reflects the distance from the chin to the palate. If the angle is low the chin is closer to the palate than on average and the person could have had a round face. Likewise, if the value of the angle is high, the person would tend to have a long, oval face. Statistical analysis between these groups is not possible. Although the dangers of misinterpreting the results of cephalometric analysis have been highlighted (Moyers and Bookstein 1979) it could be suggested that modern British people have longer faces than their Tudor ancestors.

Price (1939) claimed that older lifestyles led to a more natural, round, facial shape than the oval shapes of modern faces, and suggested that the rural existence, even in recent centuries, of Scottish crofters was linked to round, natural faces, and that modern, urbanised, western culture dwellers have unnatural, long faces.

In recent years atmospheric pollution has been blamed for respiratory problems, making nasal breathing difficult. A relationship has been demonstrated between difficulty in breathing through the nose, the posture of the neck and the shape of the face (Woodside and Linder-Aronson 1979). If nose

breathing is difficult the neck is extended and the mouth opened to allow mouth breathing as well. If this changed positioning of the neck and head starts in infancy, and the person grows into an adult, the upper and lower teeth slowly adapt over the years, growing together so that the bite is re-established. The jaws are therefore held further apart than they would have been if the child had been able to nose-breath. Overall with this mouth-breathing situation, the chin is further away from the palate, so the lower part of the face's height is increased and overall mouth-breathers could have longer, more oval faces than nose-breathers. Another study has shown that children with asthma and perennial rhinitis, when given intranasal corticosteroid sprays, benefited from increased nasal airway and a more normal, less extended neck posture (Wenzel *et al.* 1983). Hence, a longer face in a modern group.

It had been assumed that the *Mary Rose* group was of British stock. Many groups from the various peoples of the world have been analysed using the radiographic techniques outlined earlier but they have not been analysed using a standardised geometric system so direct comparisons are not possible for many aspects of the size and shape of the head. Care must be taken not to make false claims by unacceptable extrapolation of the data either within a particular group of X-rays or between different groups of X-rays. Also false claims about the people from whom a group of X-rays is merely a sample should not be made. However, by

Table 13.10 Comparison of cephalometric data from six racial groups

	SNA(°)	SNB(°)	ANB(°)	MMPA(°)	FP(%)	UIA(°)	LIA(°)	IIA(°)
Mary Rose	83.6	79.9	3.7	20.8	55.6	101.8	90.6	146.9
N. American Caucasian[a]	84.1	77.7	3.7	–	–	–	94.7	125.5
Saudi Arabian[b]	80.8	78.7	2.0	26.6	–	120.4	96.1	116.9
Negroid[c]	88.2	83.9	4.3	–	–	–	101.2	112.8
Indonesian[d]	84.0	78.0	6.0	31.0	–	113.0	94.0	122.0
Chinese[d]	83.8	79.9	5.0	32.0	–	109.0	90.0	129.0

[a]Riolo *et al.* 1974; [b]Jones 1987; [c]Fonseca and Klein 1978; Johnson *et al.* 1978

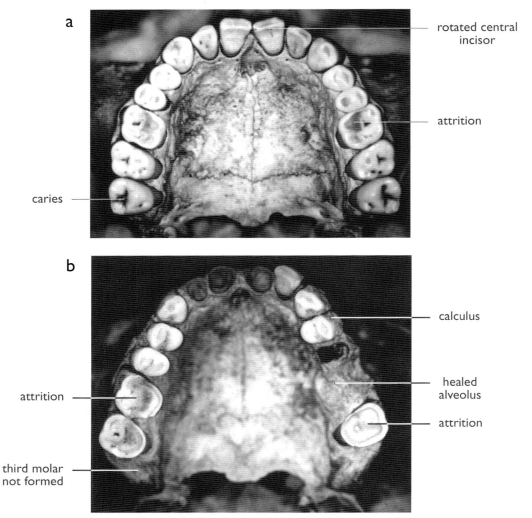

a — rotated central incisor

attrition

caries

b — calculus

healed alveolus

attrition

attrition

third molar not formed

Figure 13.50 a) Extremely good maxillary dental arch with only minimal signs of malocclusion; central incisor rotations. Attrition and caries are also shown; b) maxillary dentition from an older person than shown above. The attrition is deeper into the crowns of the teeth, especially the first molars. Heavy deposits of calculus are present on the left canine and first premolar. A healed alveolus where the left first molar was is revealed. Also, no third molars are erupted and the shape of the tuberosities suggests agenesis of the third molars.

applying a degree of common sense to the results of the *Mary Rose* analysis, a comparison with data from other studies would indicate that the crew was indeed of British caucasoid stock, rather than Chinese, Afro-caribbean or Indonesian background (Table 13.10). Preliminary Mitrochodrial DNA studies of a small sample of mandibles from the *Mary Rose* crew, and indirect evidence from artefact studies, suggest that Europeans were on board (see, for instance, discussions in Chapters 1 and 7, and Hagelberg and Frame, below). However the evidence is, at least so far, insufficient to contradict the expectation that the crew were mostly British.

Tooth decay (caries)

Tooth decay (dental caries: Figs 13.43, 13.46a, 13.50a, 13.51) is one of the few diseases which can be diagnosed with certainty even in teeth of great antiquity. It has been shown that the distribution and position of decay and cavities on teeth, the type of tooth involved and the age of the person suffering from this disease in British populations underwent no significant change over the 2000 years between the beginnings of the Iron Age (*c.* 700 BC and the Middle Ages (Moore and Corbett 1971; 1973). The majority of cavities in the ancient populations were probably secondary to alveolar bone loss which followed the severe dental attrition usual with diets of coarse physical consistency.

With poor oral care and lack of toothbrushing, food stagnated around the teeth and dental plaque accumulated. The caries process then attacked the tooth. In Iron Age, Romano-British and Anglo-Saxon populations the decay occurred along the edges of the gums (on the sides of the teeth). Not much decay set in on the biting (occlusal) surfaces because these were worn away by eating coarse and hard foods. In more

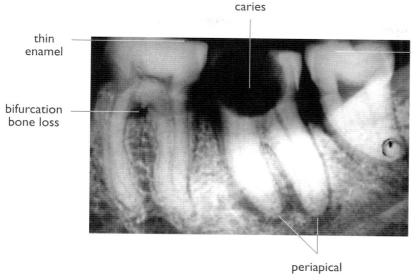

thin enamel

caries

thick enamel

bifurcation bone loss

periapical radiolucencies

Figure 13.51 Intra-oral radiograph of three molars. The tooth on the left is a first permanent molar and periodontal disease has resulted in alvolar bone resorption to the extent that the bifurcation is affected. The second molar (centre tooth) has gross coronal caries and both roots have periapical radiolucencies. The third molar, on the right, has obviously thicker enamel than the other two molars

modern populations the position of the decay sites on the tooth surfaces changed and the amount of decay suffered increased. Probably beginning in the late Middle Ages decay started to attack the occlusal surfaces and at the points of contact between adjacent teeth (Fig. 13.52). By the seventeenth century the overall prevalence of caries was considerably greater than in the earlier periods and the pattern of attack had become recognisably similar to that occuring in modern British groups (Moore and Corbett 1975).

The skeletal material recovered from the *Mary Rose* provided an opportunity to add to the knowledge of the pattern of dental caries by examining and assessing a population from the sixteenth century. The 68 matched heads and jaws and 75 parts of skulls (maxillae and mandibles) had teeth present which were suitable for examining for tooth decay.

All surfaces of the teeth were examined under a strong light with the aid of a dental probe and decay sites were recorded using a special code. Only undoubted cavities, where the probe encountered stickiness or softness, were accepted as real decay. Simply discoloured fissures were not charted as cavities. The numbers and percentages of permanent teeth present, unerupted, missing post-mortem (p-m), missing ante-mortem (a-m) and decayed are given in Table 13.11.

Cavities were classed as 'gross' when they were too large for the initial location to be decided with certainty. Thus a gross occlusal cavity would involve the whole of the occlusal surface (see Fig. 13.52) and it would almost certainly have started as a fissure cavity as no cuspal cavities were recorded. Similarly, with a gross interstitial cavity it was not possible to establish whether the initial cavity had been at the contact area or at the cemento-enamel junction. Where gross cavities extend ed onto more than one surface a cavity was scored for each surface involved. More than one cavity per surface was uncommon, occurring only in the fissures of a few molar teeth. These were counted as one cavity.

The carious lesions were charted by surface and location as follows:
1. Occlusal surface: fissure; gross
2. Interstitial surface: contact area; at or near the cemento-enamel junction (cej); gross
3. Buccal surface; fissure; cej; gross
4. Palatal and lingual surfaces; fissure; cej; gross

Very few smooth surface cavities were recorded.

It was discovered that many of the crew had a lot of tooth decay (Table 13.12). Although sophisticated dentistry has been reported in ancient peoples (Hoffmann-Axthelm 1981), no evidence of reparative dentistry, or use of artificial dental materials such as in a dental filling, was found in the teeth recovered from the wreck. The crew must have suffered with pain from tooth decay and abscesses. Although from an era before widespread consumption of sugar by Britain's inhabitants, they used honey and other decay-causing foods and drinks (Rundall 1849; Wilson 1984). Some gross cavities, seen approximally, and in the molar teeth were associated with periapical abscesses, as indicated by sinuses perforating the cortical plates of the jaws (Fig. 13.53). Evidence of this infection can be seen as

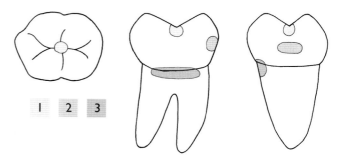

1 2 3

Figure 13.52 A illustration showing how the location of caries (decay) has changed through time. Sites 1 and 2: occlusal fissure and contact area lesions of the more modern pattern; Site 3: cervical zone caries, typical of people from more ancient times

Table 13.11 Numbers and percentages of teeth present, unerupted, missing and carious

	No. individuals	Sound	Unerupted	Missing p-m	Missing a-m	Carious	No. teeth
Matched crania & mandibles	68	674(31%)	87(4%)	1067(49%)	65(35%)	283(13%)	2176
Crania (or maxillae) only	29	173(18%)	6(<1%)	676(73%)	18(2%)	55(6%)	928
Mandibles only	46	236(16%)	15(1%)	1120(76%)	23(2%)	78(5%)	1474
Total	143	1083(24%)	108(2%)	2863(63%)	106(2%)	416(9%)	4576

dark areas around the roots of teeth on x-rays (see below).

Parts of the jaws without teeth and where no tooth socket was present effectively represent ante-mortem tooth loss (Fig. 13.46, b–c). These areas would usually have resulted from the elective extraction of a painful tooth by a barber-surgeon. However, occasionally an adult tooth fails to develop in the child's jaw so that when the deciduous (milk) tooth falls out there is no replacement and the body then fills in the socket with new bone. The absence of a tooth with no remaining socket could, therefore, be due to the congenital absence of an adult tooth, and this condition was found amongst the crew.

In some specimens (eg, Fig. 13.48b), where teeth have been lost ante-mortem, adjacent teeth have tilted into the space resulting in a typical triangular-shaped alveolar defect such as is found in modern populations following ante-mortem tooth loss.

Radiographs (Figs 13.51, 13.54) demonstrate the extent of tooth crown damage by decay and show dark areas around the tooth roots (periapical radiolucencies) which were, presumably, associated with pulp death and a resultant bony abscess of long standing. Most of the teeth lost ante-mortem were probably extracted deliberately to relieve dental pain (see Fig. 4.2 for a graphic depiction of sixteenth century tooth extraction!). Therefore, assuming that ante-mortem tooth loss was due to dental disease, it is interesting to find that 36% had lost teeth ante-mortem, 84% had caries or ante-mortem tooth loss and 13% could have suffered from painful abscesses of long standing. This means that at least 10% of the group could have been in pain from dental disease at any one time. Swellings and infections put life at risk in the days before antibiotic medicines. The socio-economic impact of this can only be speculated on (much time off work?).

Whatever the reasons for the decay in the teeth of the *Mary Rose* victims they are the earliest known group showing a modern pattern of caries, that is, occlusal fissure and enamel contact area lesions. In earlier times cavities were more common on the root surfaces exposed by peridontal destruction

Gum (periodontal) disease

All dentitions and jaws in the Tudor group show evidence of gum (periodontal) disease (Figs 13.43b, 13.46c), some to a marked extent. Heavy deposits of tartar (calculus) from both above and below the gum margins are present in many individuals. Such deposits,

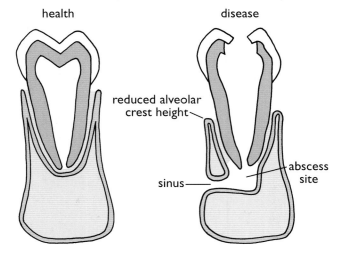 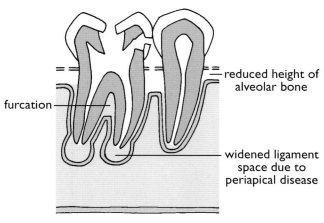

Figure 13.53 a) Illustration of a tooth that has suffered from periodontal disease, reducing the height of the alveolar crest, and from caries causing a periapical abcess resulting in a sinus perforating the cortical plate of the jaw; b) In this illustration, caries of the occlusal surface and mesial contact area of the molars has killed the pulp and the resultant periapical disease has widened the space of the periodontal ligament in the apical zones. Also, chronic periodontal disease has reduced the height of the alveolar bone supporting the tooth even at the furcation of the molar roots

Table 13.12 Carious sites on teeth

	Matched crania & mandibles	Crania (or maxillae) only	Mandibles only	Total
No. individuals	68	29	46	143
Caries: contact, fissure (smooth surface)	162(57%)	28(51%)	57(73%)	247(59%)
Caries: below contact, cej or non-fissure	68(24%)	18(33%)	7(9%)	93(22%)
Caries: gross	53(18%)	9(16%)	14(18%)	76(18%)
Total caries teeth	283	55	78	416

over a period of years, will cause generalised horizontal alveolar bone resorption and this pattern of destruction (Fig. 13.55) was seen in many specimens.

This degree of bone resorption was evidence of marked periodontal disease and frequently exposed the root furcations of teeth. Some bone contours were typical of those associated with lateral periodontal abscesses. Missing teeth induced tipping of other nearby teeth and this led to the creation of stagnation areas which, in turn, increased places where dental plaque could accumulate and start gingival disease. Perforations of the bony side wall of the jaws were present in a few specimens.

Kerr (1998) reported on periodontal disease over the 3000 years from late prehistoric to modern times in Britain. Until the *Mary Rose* crew are analysed with like methodology it can be suggested, rather than assumed, that the Tudor group fits between her medieval and seventeenth–nineteenth century groups. Kerr (1998) concluded, surprisingly, that there has been little change in the incidence of periodontal disease in Britain from late prehistoric to modern times. It is probable that we have similar periodontal health to our Tudor ancestors, a sad reflection on the lack of progress in curing gum disease in the U.K. despite the creation of the National Health Service in 1948.

Other observations

Pantomography, a special X-ray imaging technique (Figs 13.45b, 13.46, 13.54, 13.55), revealed wisdom tooth (third molar) impactions, lack of formation (agenesis) of third molars, caries, dark zones (radio-lucencies) suggestive of periapical abscess formation, and larger radiolucencies with cystic appearances.

An outstanding feature of the group was the good shape of the dental arches (Figs 13.41, bottom, 13.45a, 13.46b, 13.50a). Although many anterior teeth had been lost post-mortem the arch forms seemed more nearly ideal than those generally seen in present day white Britons. This observation agrees with the view of many anthropologists that malocclusion is linked to 'civilization' and a western lifestyle (Price 1939; Hunt 1961). Whether the arch form portrayed by the sockets reflects accurately the curvature that the tooth crowns and biting edges would have formed, or not, remains to be determined.

Another remarkable feature was the lack of crowding within the arches compared with today's population. Crowded dentitions (Fig. 13.48b), with rotated teeth, are present but the crowding tends to be anterior or posterior to the premolar zones, reflecting little premature loss of deciduous teeth. In modern children many deciduous molars are extracted because of tooth decay before they should have naturally exfoliated. The space created allows the teeth behind the gap to move forwards stealing the space into which a new adult tooth should grow. This then results in lack of space for a straight row of teeth and causes more crowding than the child should have. It seems that many modern adolescents have some crowding of their teeth because tooth decay forced them to have dental extractions.

Many other features of malocclusion have been found. Two mandibles had retained deciduous molars (Fig. 13.48c) associated with agenesis of the underlying

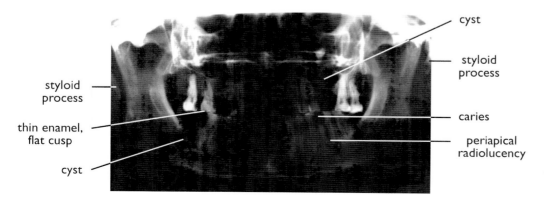

styloid process

thin enamel, flat cusp

cyst

cyst

styloid process

caries

periapical radiolucency

Figure 13.54 Dental pantomograph showing styloid processes, cystic radiolucencies where molars are missing from upper left and lower right quadrants, gross caries with a periapical radiolucency on lower left first molar, thin enamel on flattened molar and premolar cusps

556

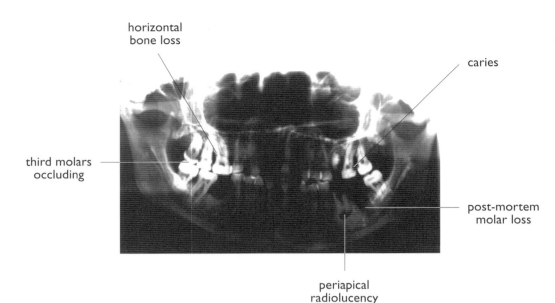

horizontal
bone loss

caries

third molars
occluding

post-mortem
molar loss

periapical
radiolucency

Figure 13.55 Dental pantomograph showing gross caries, a periapical radiolucency on lower left first molar, post-morten loss of lower left second molar and some anterior teeth, ante-mortem loss of lower right first molar with healed alveolus, severe, horizontal loss of alveolar height and third molars in occlusion

premolar. One maxilla had six incisor sockets (Fig. 13.46b), evidence of extra (supplemental) lateral incisors, well accommodated within the dental arch.

There is markedly more attrition in the *Mary Rose* group than is seen nowadays (Figs 13.45a, 13.46b, 13.48c, 13.50, 13.56) probably due to dietary differences between Tudor times and today. Assessment of the age of individuals from attrition of the teeth was not possible as there were no immature specimens to give the necessary baseline information. Until a Tudor group of known ages is found, this method of age assessment cannot be developed further. Therefore, the dentitions were divided into 'age' groups according to the amount of attrition present and this classification is given in Table 13.13. Approximately 80% of these people were mature young men, probably between 20 and 30 years (this figure agrees with that given by Stirland, above, based on a wider range of skeletal traits; Table 13.3).

In the modern human eating an ordinary diet, the dental arches are not flat. There is a gentle curve from back to front, known as the curve of Spee (Fig. 13.41, middle) and another from side to side, the curve of

Monson (Fig. 13.41, top). In primitive peoples eating coarser, unrefined diets the wear of the biting (occlusal) surfaces of the teeth over a lifetime significantly flattens these curves and can even cause a reverse curve of Monson. The teeth which erupt earliest have the greatest attrition.

Begg, in Australia, studied the dentitions of Stone Age Aborigines and formed his theory of 'attritional occlusion'. The size of a tooth reduces through progressive attrition of the occlusal and aproximal surfaces. If all the teeth in a dental arch suffer in this way a significant amount of space is created (Fig, 13.56). There is a natural tendency for teeth to migrate forwards in the mouth. So if during childhood and teenage years much wear occurs, the second adult molars move forwards leaving room behind them into which the wisdom teeth can erupt. Thus the cause of many modern people's impacted wisdom teeth could be our modern dietary habits and foods being easy to chew, causing less attrition and less space for the

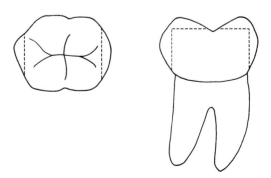

Figure 13.56 An illustration of how attrition, over a period of time, reduces the width and height, and therefore the volume, of teeth, resulting in less crowding of the dentition

Table 13.13 Classification of attrition

Primary and mixed dentitions: age estimated from teeth	
Depth of attrition	**Attrition age groups**
Immature (12–21yr): permanent dentition up to eruption of 3rd molar	0
Permanent dentition fully erupted but attrition not through enamel in any tooth	1
Attrition not exceeding exposure of areas of dentine on the cusps of any posterior teeth	2
Occlusal surfaces obliterated by attrition in one or more teeth	3
Occlusal fissures obliterated in all teeth	4
Severe attrition having destroyed most of the crowns of posterior teeth	5

Table 13.14 Numbers and percentages of skulls (or parts of skulls) within attrition groups

Attrition group	No.	%
0	8	5.6
1	7	4.9
2	70	49.0
3	48	33.6
4	8	5.6
5	2	1.4

Table 13.16 Average number of carious molars (per skull or part skull), correlated for teeth lost p-m, by location

Deck	No. skulls	Average no. carious molars
Upper	30	5.93
Main	23	6.44
Orlop	41	6.31
Hold	28	7.24

wisdom teeth, hence more impacted teeth. Consideration of the arch forms, lack of crowding and amount of attrition in the teeth of the crew of the *Mary Rose* leads one to support Begg's theory (Begg 1954).

A record was made where abcesses (periapical infections) had resulted in resorption of the outer surface of the (alveolar) bone. This, together with the dental caries information, was added to a computer record which contained other details about each skull or part, such as the location at which it was found. This latter information was obtained from the *Mary Rose* record cards for human bone. The human bone number (eg, 80H0170) of the matched skulls and both jaws, upper jaw only and lower jaw only, were recorded on each dental record. This was to see if there was a link between the disease patterns and the location in the wreck where the remains were found. In Table 13.14–16 three groups have been retained but there is no other apparent significance in this grouping. Table 13.14 gives the numbers of matched skulls and jaws and of unmatched jaws by attrition age groups. Table 13.15 divides the groups according to the decks on which they were found. The total number is less in this table than in Table 13.14 because not all remains could be precisely located within the wreck.

The amount of wear of teeth in the *Mary Rose* individuals shows that the highest number of 70 (49%) was in age group 2; age group 3 had 48 (33.6%) but there was a marked drop in groups 4 and 5. In a previous study (Moore and Corbett 1973), of 416 individuals from medieval communities, the highest number of adults was 102 (24%) in group 4, and group

5 had 49 (12%). However, it is to be expected that a fighting ship would have mainly individuals of younger age groups on board, which is in accordance with the number given in Table 13.14.

If the attrition age groups are divided according to where the individuals were found on the ship, there is a slight trend, although not statistically significant, for the younger groups to be found on the higher decks (Table 13.15), perhaps more readily available for fighting at close quarters than if they had been below decks. This lack of significance could be explained by the fact that this was one of the first ships to carry heavy guns on several decks so able-bodied men would have been positioned throughout the ship, manning the guns and fetching munitions from storage areas, not just on the open deck for fighting at close quarters. Table 13.16 relates the number of carious molar teeth per skull, or part skull, to various decks of the ship and suggests that there were more carious molars in the groups from the lower decks where, it appears from Table 13.15, the older crew members were to be found.

Concluding comment

Macroscopic examination of the cranio-facial and dental elements from the *Mary Rose* group showed similarities and differences with other groups. The great potential for using radiographs of the teeth and jaws in anthropological and sociological ways, rather than purely clinical ones, has been demonstrated. A wealth of information remains to be retrieved from further scientific study of this group.

Table 13.15 Numbers and percentages of individuals in attrition groups correlated with decks from which recovered

Attrition group	Upper		Main		Orlop		Hold	
	No.	%	No.	%	No.	%	No.	%
0	2	6.7	1	4.3	4	9.8	1	3.6
1	3	10.0	1	4.3	1	2.4	0	0
2	16	53.3	12	52.2	19	46.3	11	39.3
3	8	26.7	3	26.1	15	36.6	14	50.0
4	0	0	6	13.0	2	4.9	2	7.1
5	1	3.3	0	0	0	0	0	0

The Genetic Affinities of the *Mary Rose* Crew: DNA Analysis of the Skeletal Remains

Erika Hagelberg and Ian Frame

DNA techniques played only a limited part in the archaeology of the *Mary Rose*. A preliminary survey of genetic variation of the crew by bone DNA typing was initiated in June 2004 as this volume was reaching completion. It showed that the preservation of DNA in the human and animal skeletal remains was excellent, compared to archaeological material of similar age, and that a more extensive study would be of significant scientific interest. This section includes a brief description of molecular genetic research on human origins and variation, as well as the results of DNA analysis of the remains of nine *Mary Rose* crew members, with a discussion of their significance and future research prospects.

Maternal and paternal DNA markers

The origins of human populations can be investigated using two well-known genetic systems: the maternally inherited mitochondrial DNA and the paternally inherited Y chromosome. Mitochondrial DNA, or mtDNA for short, is a kind of DNA present in the mitochondria, cell organelles responsible for energy metabolism. In contrast to the nuclear DNA (the DNA in the nucleus of the cell, in chromosomes), which is inherited from both parents, mtDNA exhibits a maternal mode of inheritance. Mothers pass their mtDNA to both their sons and daughters, but only the daughters pass it on to their own children. MtDNA has been widely used for evolutionary and phylogenetic (family) studies because it is easier to study than nuclear DNA. In contrast to the human nuclear DNA, which consists of 3×10^9 base-pairs arranged in 23 pairs of chromosomes, the human mitochondrial genome is small, only 16,569 base-pairs in length. The first complete human mtDNA sequence was published in 1981 (Anderson *et al.* 1981), whereas it took a further two decades to determine the sequence of the entire human genome. The availability of a complete human DNA sequence permits scientists to use it as a 'reference sequence' or standard, with which sequences generated from different human samples and in different laboratories can be compared.

One further feature of mtDNA is its abundance in animal cells. For example, a typical gene present in nuclear DNA would only be found in two copies, one in each of the two paired chromosomes. In contrast, there are thousands of copies of mtDNA in each cell. The abundance of mtDNA makes it the molecule of choice in ancient DNA studies and in forensic identification, where test material is scarce or degraded (see Chapter 16). Most research on the analysis of DNA from archaeological bones has been performed using mtDNA. For example, mtDNA typing was used to infer the genetic relationships of prehistoric Pacific islanders, including native inhabitants of Easter Island (Hagelberg and Clegg 1993; Hagelberg *et al.* 1994a), and for the identification of historical persons and genocide victims (Corach *et al.* 1997; Gill *et al.* 1994).

More recently, scientists have focused increasingly on the male Y chromosome to generate a paternal perspective on human variation and evolution. The Y chromosome is much larger than the tiny mitochondrial genome, being about 60 Mb (megabases, or millions of bases) long. Scientists interested in the evolutionary history of the human Y chromosomes were initially despondent, as this chromosome is large, complicated, full of junk DNA, hard to study, and poor in genes. However, in recent years, the Y chromosome research community has identified many Y polymorphisms and managed to construct a robust phylogeny of world Y chromosomes (Jobling and Tyler-Smith 2003). Much of the progress in Y chromosome research has been stimulated by the usefulness of Y chromosome markers as forensic tools. It is a fact that most murderers and rapists are men, and there are pragmatic reasons for the establishment of Y chromosome databases. Certain markers called Y-short tandem repeats, or Y-STRs, permit the profiling of men with a high degree of resolution (Roewer *et al.* 1996). Although these markers are not as useful as the so-called biallelic markers for population studies over long historical times, due to their high mutation rate, they could be useful in projects like the *Mary Rose*, as they could help pinpoint the place of origin of the men, provided that the bone DNA is of sufficient quantity and quality to permit Y chromosome typing. (It should be noted that each male cell has only one Y chromosome, compared to about 10^4 copies of mtDNA, so it would be much more difficult to recover Y chromosomal DNA than mtDNA from very old or degraded biological remains).

Mitochondrial DNA and human history

During the past couple of decades scientists have generated thousands of partial and complete mtDNA sequences from peoples of different geographical origins. The study of mtDNA in living people has permitted scientists to infer the evolutionary history of modern human populations, told from the vantage of the female lineages. In 1987, Allan Wilson and colleagues, at the University of California in Berkeley, analysed the mtDNA of women from different geographical origins and showed that human mtDNA types were not very variable worldwide, suggesting that they had evolved recently from a common ancestor. Moreover, a phylogenetic tree of the mtDNA types appeared to be rooted in Africa, suggesting that living people trace back to a recent female ancestor who lived in Africa. This conclusion gave rise to the famed 'African Eve' or 'Mitochondrial Eve' hypothesis (Cann *et al.* 1987).

Human mtDNA is comparatively small (about 16.5 kilobases) and has only 37 genes. The DNA in the genes is called coding DNA, because it codes for a gene product such as a protein. In addition, human mtDNA has a principal non-coding region of about 1000 base-pairs, known as the hypervariable region because it contains a high proportion of the differences observed in the mtDNA of unrelated people. The characteristic differences in the patterns of variation in the non-coding and coding regions of mtDNA have been used to classify the mtDNA types of living humans into so-called mtDNA haplogroups, or clusters. The three most ancient mtDNA haplogroups (L0, L1 and L2) appear to be found in sub-Saharan Africa, where they make up the macrohaplogroup L. Macrohaplogroup L radiated to give rise to haplogroup L3 in Africa and haplogroups M and N in Europe and Asia. In Europe, most mtDNA types (>98%) belong to macrohaplogroup N, and fall into the haplogroups H, I, J, N1b, T, U, V, W and X (Mishmar *et al.* 2003; Richards *et al.* 1998). The mtDNA haplogroups exhibit a high degree of continent-specificity. For example, the mtDNA types found in native living peoples of Oceania and the New World derive from Asian types, and are quite distinct from the types found in Europe and Africa. However, African and European types are also found in living peoples of the New World as a consequence of European migrations and the introduction of African slaves.

The most relevant question for a genetic study on the human remains of the *Mary Rose* is whether it would be possible to predict the place of origin of individual crew members on the basis of their mtDNA sequence. In a limited study of a crew composed mostly of Europeans it might be hard to pinpoint individual origins, as migration and admixture throughout Europe in the past few thousand years have erased strong local genetic differences. European mtDNA haplogroups are represented in virtually all European populations surveyed to date, although their frequency varies in different populations. For example, cluster H, the most abundant European cluster, is present at a frequency of 46% in Europe at large, but only at 25% in the northern Caucasus, and it is virtually absent in the Sami (the preferred name of the nomadic Lapp people of Scandinavia and Russia) and in the Arabian peninsula (Richards *et al.* 2000). Thus, although mtDNA analysis of the *Mary Rose* crew members could serve to confirm or refute specific hypotheses concerning their origin, results based on a small sample might not be statistically meaningful.

The present study

In 1990, the successful extraction and analysis of DNA from a pig bone, part of the provisions of the *Mary Rose* crew, served to demonstrate the feasibility of typing DNA from old skeletal remains (Hagelberg and Clegg 1991; see Chapter 16). No genetic analyses of the human remains of the *Mary Rose* were instigated until fourteen years later. In May 2004, the authors received from the *Mary Rose* Trust (through Dr Michael Allen), a total of 23 human mandibles, and additional small samples of bone and teeth of a further twelve individuals, for DNA analysis. Animal bones from six

locations on the *Mary Rose* were also sent (Table 13.17). As the time available for the completion of the investigation was limited, a sub-set of nine human and two animal bones was selected for preliminary DNA typing. The human mandibles had been submitted previously for isotope analysis, though no results have been made available, and already had samples removed from them. To minimise additional destruction, a thin section of bone (c. 2g) was cut at the place at which the mandibles had been previously sampled. Gloves were worn to avoid exposure to modern DNA. Bone samples were cut with a hacksaw and the blade cleaned with 70% ethanol between samples.

Nine of the human mandibles and two animal bones (pig and cow) were tested initially. The bone samples were processed using a previously published method (Hagelberg 1994b; Hagelberg and Clegg 1991; Hagelberg *et al.* 1989). The surface of the small bone fragments was cleaned carefully by sandblasting with fine alumina grit, and the clean samples were ground to fine powder using a freezer-mill refrigerated with liquid nitrogen. DNA was extracted from 0.5g of the bone powder. A blank extraction containing all the reagents, but no bone, was performed as a control for possible DNA contamination of the extraction reagents and to monitor contamination during the extraction process. The extraction method consists of incubating the bone powder overnight in 10 ml of an extraction solution containing EDTA (ethylene diamine tetra-acetic acid, a chelating agent), proteinase K (an enzyme that breaks down proteins) and L-lauroylsarcosine (a detergent). The incubations are performed in tubes agitated continuously to prevent the bone powder settling out. Following incubation, the bone powder lysates were extracted with organic solvents, and then desalted and concentrated by dialysis centrifugation. The 0.5g portions of bone powder yielded approximately 0.3–0.4ml of a clear solution, presumably containing DNA. The bone DNA extracts and extraction control were stored in sterile tubes in a –20°C freezer, until further use.

DNA analysis

The nine human DNA extracts were analysed using PCR (polymerase chain reaction) amplification, and subsequent DNA sequencing, of a fragment of mitochondrial DNA (mtDNA). The PCR is a technique for the amplification of specific DNA fragments from DNA templates, and is particularly suitable for the analysis of very old or degraded DNA samples (see Chapter 16).

After the PCR, the amplified products were resolved by electrophoresis on a 1.2% agarose gel containing ethydium bromide, and visualised under ultraviolet light. The nine human bone extracts produced strong positive amplifications with the human-specific mtDNA

Table 13.17 List of human bones submitted for DNA analysis

Hagelberg no.	Bell no.	Archive no.	Location	Assoc-iation
1*	1	81H0021	U8	
2*	6	80H0198	M4	
3*	10	81H0169	M9	
4*	–	81H0180B	O3	FCS71
5*	17	82H0044	O8	FCS36A
6*	–	82H0071	H8	
7*	2	80H0040	U7	FCS65
8*	12	81H0256	M10	
9*	15	81H0417E	O9	FCS81
10	8	81H0014A	U8	
11	3	80H0087	M4	
12	7	80H2111	O4	
13	4	80H0093	O6	
14	16	82H0008	O7	
15	5	80H0112	H4	
16	18	82H0063	H7	FCS19A
17	14	81H0401	H10	
18	–	81H0023	M2	FCS83
19	–	81H0064	H2	FCS7
20	9	81H0105B	M10	
21	13	81H0287	O4	

*Bones from which DNA was extracted in June 2004. Hagelberg and Bell each assigned their own numbers to these samples for their respective analyses (see text)

In the case of the Mary Rose bone extracts, amplifications were performed with primers D1 and D2 specific for a 454 base-pair fragment spanning the first hypervariable region (HVRI) of human mtDNA, between position 15975 and 16429 (D1:L15996: 5'-CTC CAC CAT TAG CAC CCA AAG C-3' and D2:H16405: 5'-CGG GAT ATT GAT TTC ACG GAG GAT-3'). PCR amplifications were carried out in 25μl volumes using 1μl of bone extract, and AmpliTaq Gold DNA polymerase (Applied Biosystems), and consisted of an initial denaturation step of 95°C for 5 minutes, followed by 40 cycles of 94°C for 45 seconds, 55°C for 45 seconds and 72°C for 45 seconds, ending with a single extension step of 10 minutes at 72°C.

Unambiguous sequencing traces could be obtained, as in the example shown in Plate 68 (taken from a screen grab). The DNA sequencer uses a dye technology that produces a different colour trace for each of the four DNA nucleotides. The identification number corresponding to the individual bone sample is indicated at the top left corner of each trace, with an indication of the DNA strand (plus or minus) of the particular sequence. The vertical blue line in the centre of the trace highlights a C to T mutation at mitochondrial position 16192 in individual 80H0021. The three other individuals shown have a C at the same mitochondrial DNA site.

Results

The results are shown in Table 13.18, with the length of DNA sequence generated for each of the nine human mtDNA PCR products, the polymorphisms observed in the region sequenced, and the provisional assignment of the men to known European mtDNA haplogroups. The analyses were performed in only two weeks, and they represent a first attempt to analyse DNA from the human skeletal remains of the Mary Rose. DNA preservation was comparatively good and a fragment of mtDNA of about 450 base-pairs in length could be amplified from all nine individuals at the first attempt, a success rate of 100%. The two animal controls, extraction blank and PCR blank were free of contamination. These results are excellent, considering that DNA fragments amplified from ancient bones are typically in the order of 100–200 DNA base-pairs in length, although fragments of up to 1200 bases in length have been amplified from 70-year-old skeletal remains (Gill et al. 1994).

The amplifications were performed using just 1μl of bone extract, and this yielded sufficient PCR product for the sequencing of both DNA strands. The amount of DNA used in each amplification experiment was a tiny

primers. The two animal bone extracts failed to amplify, indicating that they were not contaminated with human DNA. The extraction control and the PCR blank (a PCR reaction tube containing all reagents but no template DNA) also produced a negative result, showing that the reagents were free of amplifyable human DNA (Fig. 13.57, taken from a screen grab).

The nine human amplification products were sequenced on a MegaBACE DNA sequencer (Amersham Biosciences), using a DYEnamic ET dye terminator kit, at the Department of Biology, University of Oslo. The sequences were checked using the Staden sequencing package, version 1.4 (Staden et al. 2000). Unfortunately, the performance of the sequencer was substandard at the time of this work, and several of the capillaries were waiting to be replaced. Nevertheless, in the hope of including at least partial results in this report, sequencing was undertaken. Both DNA strands were sequenced, using the primers D1 (L15996) and B1 (H16401: 5'- TGA TTT CAC GGA GGA TGG T-3'). Most of the PCR products yielded a readable DNA sequence for at least one of the DNA strands, and in several cases both strands were readable.

Glossary of terms relating to DNA analysis

PHYLOGENETIC TREE - A tree representing the evolutionary history of a DNA sequence, individual or species.

BIALLELIC MARKER - A genetic variant that has two alternative forms, or alleles.

CHELATING AGENT - A chemical that 'grabs' another compound. For example, the chemical EDTA used in the bone extractions binds calcium.

ELECTROPHORESIS - A technique to separate DNA (or other macromolecules) according to size and electric charge.

GLIAL CELL - The most abundant cell types in the central nervous system; supportive cells in the brain and spinal cord. Glial cells do not conduct electrical impulses (as opposed to neurons, which do); they surround neurons and provide support for and insulation between them. Glial cells are capable of extensive signaling in response to a diversity of stimuli. Bidirectional communication exists between glial cells and neurons, and between glial cells and vascular cells.

GLIAL FIBRE - Several molecules of GFAP protein (see below) bind together to form the main intermediate filament found in specialised brain cells that support functions of nerve cells in the brain and spinal cord.

GLIAL FIBRE ACIDIC PROTEIN GFAP - The protein found in the brain and spinal cord that form glial fibre

HISTOLOGY - study of the microscopic structure and function of animal (or plant) tissues, often in thin section under a microscope; ie microscopic anatomy

IMMUNOHISTOLOGY/IIMMUNOHISTOCHEMICAL ANALYSIS - microscopic study of blood related structures.

LYSATE - A solution or mixture containing the products of disintegration of tissues and cells.

sources) augurs well for a more comprehensive typing of mtDNA markers, and even Y chromosome STRs. Additional mtDNA typing will be necessary to be able to assign the individuals unambiguously to the known European mtDNA clusters. At present, only data from the first hypervariable region of mtDNA (HVR1) has been obtained but, on the basis of these data alone, it is possible to assign four of the men to haplogroup H, two to haplogroup T, one to J, one to K (a sub-group of U), and one to N. The assignment of four men to H is not secure, as the lack of polymorphisms in the HVR1 would place them either in the H, or in U cluster. H is the commonest haplogroup in Europe, as mentioned earlier, accounting for almost one half of the European mtDNAs, whereas U is found in only about 10% of Europeans. Sequencing of the second hypervariable region (HVRII) would allow the presumed assignment to H haplogroup to be confirmed, as the latter is associated with an A at mtDNA position 73, while U haplogroup has a G at the same position. The assignment of the remaining four crew members to T, J and K haplogroups is more secure, because their mtDNA HVRI sequences had polymorphisms characteristic of these clusters. The assignment of one individual to N was done on the basis of one single polymorphism, at position 16223. Again, additional information is needed to classify this person to a specific mtDNA cluster.

Our preliminary results indicate that informative mtDNA sequences survive in the human remains. The nine individuals analysed yielded sequences that are probably European. Although this is not surprising in the context of the *Mary Rose*, it is a significant step in mtDNA studies in archaeology (see Chapter 16). The small number of samples available for analysis at this time would not permit the men to be assigned to a particular place of origin with any degree of confidence, although it might be possible in a more extensive study.

proportion of the total DNA extracted from the 0.5g bone samples (which amounted typically to 300–400 µl). The good DNA yield, and the relatively high quality of DNA (when compared with other ancient DNA

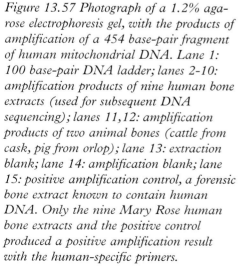
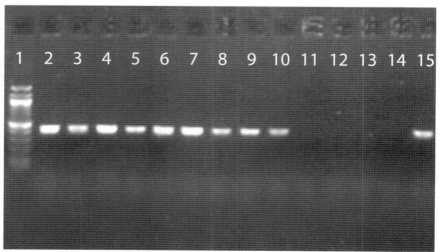

Figure 13.57 Photograph of a 1.2% agarose electrophoresis gel, with the products of amplification of a 454 base-pair fragment of human mitochondrial DNA. Lane 1: 100 base-pair DNA ladder; lanes 2-10: amplification products of nine human bone extracts (used for subsequent DNA sequencing); lanes 11,12: amplification products of two animal bones (cattle from cask, pig from orlop); lane 13: extraction blank; lane 14: amplification blank; lane 15: positive amplification control, a forensic bone extract known to contain human DNA. Only the nine Mary Rose human bone extracts and the positive control produced a positive amplification result with the human-specific primers.

Table 13.18 Mitochondrial DNA sequences of nine crew members, indicating the length of sequence read and the provisional assignment to known European mitochondrial clusters

| Reference | mtDNA position (minus 16000) | | | | | | | | | | | | | | | | | | length of sequence read | | | diagnostic polymorphisms | haplotype |
	69	126	162	163	164	168	192	207	209	213	223	224	234	274	294	296	304	311	bp	from	to		
Reference	C	T	A	A	A	C	C	A	T	G	C	T	C	G	C	C	T	T					
80H0021	.	C	.	.	.	.	T	G	.	.	.	.	.	A	T	.	C	.	349	16030	16379	16126, 16294	T
80H0198	.	.	.	.	.	.	.	.	.	.	.	.	.	.	.	.	.	.	349	16030	16379		possibly H
81H0169	.	.	.	.	.	.	.	.	.	.	.	C	.	.	.	.	.	C	349	16030	16379	16224, 16311	K
81H0180B	.	.	.	.	.	N	.	.	.	.	.	.	.	.	.	.	.	.	349	16030	16379		possibly H
82H0044	.	C	.	.	.	N	.	.	.	.	.	.	T	.	T	T	C	.	349	16030	16379	16126, 16294	T
82H0071	T	C	.	.	.	.	.	.	.	A	.	.	.	.	.	.	.	.	340	16030	16370	16069, 16126	J
80H0040	.	.	.	.	.	.	.	.	C	.	T	.	.	.	.	.	.	.	168	16200	16368		possibly H
81H0256	.	.	N	N	N	.	.	.	.	.	.	.	.	.	.	.	.	.	246	16133	16379	16223	N
81H0417E	.	.	.	.	.	.	.	.	.	.	.	.	.	.	.	.	.	.	271	16030	16301		possibly H

The sequences are aligned with the Cambridge reference sequence, with dots indicating identity with the reference sequence (Anderson *et al.* 1981). An N indicated a particular nucleotide position that could not be read clearly.

Outlook

Since the time of the successful recovery of DNA from a *Mary Rose* pig bone in 1990 (Hagelberg and Clegg 1991), ancient DNA research has had a chequered history. In the early 1990s, results of this research were met with great optimism, and there were exciting claims of the recovery of DNA from plant and animal remains of great antiquity, including insects embedded in amber and fossilised dinosaur bones (DeSalle and Grimaldi 1994; Hagelberg 1994a). In the United Kingdom several funding bodies, including the Natural Environment Research Council (NERC), the Science and Engineering Research Council (SERC) and the Wellcome Trust, established research initiatives to finance ancient DNA research and related projects in molecular archaeology. However, it became evident that some ancient DNA results were experimental artefacts caused by the amplification of modern DNA sequences (Hedges and Schweitzer 1995). Other results, like those of the DNA sequences from insects embedded in amber, could not be reproduced in other laboratories (Austin *et al.* 1997).

This led to a climate of suspicion in ancient DNA studies, and to the establishment of rigid criteria for authenticity, which are not always sensible or feasible and, in some cases, have hampered research or prevented the publication of the results of potentially useful studies. Instead, much attention has been focused on relatively few and spectacular studies performed with little regard to time or cost, like those on the recovery of DNA from Neanderthal bones (Krings *et al.* 1997), to the detriment of good quality, extensive, solid studies on historical populations.

However, basic population genetic data are of significant interest in archaeological studies, as well as helping assess the potential costs, usefulness and pitfalls of ancient DNA research. A survey of DNA survival in skeletal remains from the *Mary Rose*, part of a careful and well-conducted archaeological investigation, could help demonstrate the robustness of ancient DNA techniques. The *Mary Rose* skeletal material also provides an almost unique opportunity to investigate the genetic affinities of a historical population, and to extend ancient DNA techniques from studies of mtDNA alone, to analyses based on nuclear DNA, including Y chromosome markers and even genes for important recessive diseases.

Since this chapter was written, we have recovered DNA sequences from a further ten bone extracts, making a total of nineteen *Mary Rose* men assigned to their respective mitochondrial haplogroups.

Human Remains: Other Scientific Analyses

Michael J. Allen and Andrew Elkerton

Brain and soft tissues

Although ancient human tissue survives in a number of circumstances, its survival on waterlogged sites is not usual (O'Connor 2002, 41). Nevertheless, it is reported that unexpected survival did occur among the skeletal remains on the *Mary Rose*. The crania of a few skulls contained material thought to be brain, and the remains of spinal cord were present in a few vertebral elements (Buglass, pers. comm; Oxley pers. comm.). Because of the unexpected nature of this survival, some was lost in the washing process.

The material in the crania was pink in colour (reminiscent of blancmange) and, if not put immediately into alcohol, liquified within a matter of minutes. Nevertheless, several samples of soft tissue from crania were sent for investigation by anatomists, pathologists and a radiologist at different hospitals. Reports were received between 1982 and 1984, with mixed results (Table 13.19).

Professor G.A. Gresham, examined material from three skulls (81S1127, 81S0355 and 81S0413) and reported that: '*They contained material which had the anatomical configuration of brain tissue. Unfortunately, histological examination did not reveal any recognisable detail ... I have no doubt that these are pieces of brain.*' A second study, by J.A. Sargent (samples 81S1221 and 81S1070) stated that they: '*comprised soft, brown amorphous material*'. When these were embedded in wax, sectioned and examined very little was revealed, though there was '*some morphological suggestion of fibrous structure but there was clearly no histological evidence*'. Immunohistochemical analysis carried out at Royal Marsden Hospital on these same samples revealed the presence of glial fibre acidic protein, which is a marker for the neuroloial element of brain tissue, and it was thus concluded that this was brain. A comment from a consultant neuro-pathologist (Dr D. Brownell) also indicated that the material within 81S578 consisted of '*a grey rubbery material 4x2x1cm approx. with a somewhat wrinkled surface reminiscent of cerebral cortex*' Two other studies produced negative results (Table 13.19).

The most recent study by Dr Sonia O'Connor (Bradford University) in 2002 examined most of the available surviving material but was not able to identify anything because the submitted material was now too degraded (O'Connor, pers. comm.). In conclusion these results tend to confirm some anatomical configuration consistent with brain tissue, and the presence of brain tissue. We also note that spinal cord tissue was present in at least one vertebral column in 81H1064 (samples 81S1324/01 and 81S1325), but no examination has been conducted.

Microstructual and oxygen isotope analysis

Microstructural analysis of seventeen human teeth by Bell (1995; Chapter 16) showed very limited post-mortem diagenetic change in the skeletal material from within the main Tudor layers, and demonstrated the potential for other analyses with more direct archaeological application. Studies of the oxygen isotope ratios can provide information about the geographical location of people when alive. This information might complement that of the osteoarchaeology (Stirland above). An analytical programme to investigate this was commenced by 2000 by Dr Lynne Bell. Unfortunately neither her results nor a summary of those results were provided for publication in this volume, excepting the comment by Stirland above. It is hoped that this data will be offered for publication elsewhere.

Table 13.19 Summary of samples examined for the presence of brain tissue

Specialist	Hospital	Sample	Skull	Location	Presence/ absence of brain material
G.A. Gresham	Morbid anatomy & Histopathology, Addenbrookes	81S1127	81H0226	H4	present
		81S0355	81H0260	H9	present
		81S0413	81H0346	O4	present
J.A. Sargent	Pathology, Kettering General	81S0121	81H0459 (FCS81)	O9	no info.
		82S1070		O8	present
W.R. Timperley	Neuropathology, Royal Hallam	81S0619	81H1053	H8	absent
I.Watt & D.B. Brownell	Radiodiagnosis, Bristol Royal Infirmary	81S0578	81H0463	H8	absent
		81S0173	H2S0173	O3	absent
		82S0072	82S0072	O8	absent
		82S1070	82H0042	O8	no info

14. Provisions for Board and Lodging: the Animal and Plant Remains

Introduction
by Michael J. Allen

The acquisition of a large number of samples for environmental remains and the recovery of a well-preserved and dispersed animal bone assemblage were considerable achievements in themselves. The sampling and recovery of environmental remains was enshrined within the excavation ethos, but there would always be a dilemma as to whether to take and study a relatively small number of samples in great microscopic and chemical detail, or to study a much larger suite of samples to provide a more holistic view of life aboard the ship. The Mary Rose Trust employed the latter approach. The divers and archaeologists took many samples from interesting deposits or material, and of fragile items (see Chapter 12), both underwater, and in post-excavation.

At the time, the immense investment of time and manpower required for the processing and analysis of this large suite of samples could not have been conceived, and for many years subsequently was not wholly realised, largely because of lack of funding when the conservation of the hull and of the many thousands of recovered objects was a much more pressing concern. The processing and sorting took more than eight years (mainly 1980–88), adding up to many thousands of person days. Even today, not all of the samples have been processed or sorted, though the majority have been scanned or assessed by relevant specialists.

A team of dedicated volunteers, led by Ian Oxley (see Chapter 12) ensured that the Mary Rose Trust not only produced and processed but has analysed some of the largest and most significant assemblages of biological remains from any underwater wreck site. The fact that so many samples were taken (eg, plant remains and fish bones) has enabled a comprehensive characterisation of this aspect of the archaeological record. What follows are reports on the animal bones and plant remains that, together, provide important information about the diet of the crew, provisioning of the ship and the nature of largely decayed items such as mattresses and packing materials. A review of the historical context of these materials enables the almost unique direct comparison of evidence for foodstuffs on board, with historic records of naval provisioning at the time.

Meat and Fish: the Bone Evidence
by Jennie Coy (meat) and Sheila Hamilton-Dyer (fish) with Ian Oxley

Since the excavation of the vessel some 4071 mammal bones, including 3773 from Tudor contexts (Table 14.1), a dog skeleton and 31,793 fish bones (Table 14.7) have been recorded. Recording of the faunal elements was largely conducted in 1983-4, and reporting was completed in 2002 for this volume. This represents the most significant assemblage in Europe relating to Tudor life and living conditions. The text below largely discusses the evidence of food remains. For bones from animals living aboard see Chapter 15, and for antler objects see Chapter 8.

Origins and recovery of the animal bone assemblage

Deposition and post-deposition
The rapid sinking of the ship was followed by a number of post-depositional events, all relevant to the interpretation of the animal bones retrieved from the wreck (see Chapter 12). The ship is thought to have remained on the sea-bed exactly as it fell, sunk into the soft silts with its keel touching the natural clays. Determined attempts made immediately afterwards to refloat the ship and subsequent salvage work by early divers probably complicated the condition of the wreck and altered the position of artefacts generally and, specifically to this discussion, casks and food deposits, especially any on the Upper decks (Rule 1983b, 40–3; Gairdner and Brodie 1903–5, xx part II, 1–38). Within the surviving wreck conger eels could have taken up residence quite early on and moved artefacts that were in their way (see fish below).

The collapse of the port side and subsequent erosion by the sea dispersed more items, and layers excavated above and around the wreck contained bones that were originally on the ship. A dog skeleton lay partly inside and partly outside the Carpenters' cabin (Clutton-Brock, Chapter 15 below), and Stirland (1991, 43; Chapter 13) indicates mixing of human bones within the deck sectors. Relatively rapid burial, however, excluded oxygen from some bones, which were consequently well-preserved.

Table 14.1 Number of animal bone samples and total fragments examined

Deposit group	Total bone samples	Total bone fragments*
Tudor	178	3771
Uncertain	67	89
Recent	52	193
Unknown	11	16
Total	308	4069

* excluding fish bones, dog skeleton & red deer antler objects. See text for definition of deposit groups

Figure 14.1 Articulated fish bone embedded in silt

During many centuries on the sea-bed, silts were deposited over the wreck and busy sea traffic would have discarded material, including occasional animal bones, to mix with Tudor bones from the wreck. The post-Tudor material can, to some extent, be distinguished by criteria such as size and butchery evidence. The possibility of recognising unstratified or residual animal bone by its appearance is not unique to wreck sites but is also common in long term studies of excavated material from urban contexts where subtle differences in animal proportions and butchery techniques may be recognised.

As a result of the sinking and the post-depositional events, therefore, the food remains and any associated containers, like all other objects on the ship, were not necessarily found in the positions they originally occupied.

Unlike studies of animal bone assemblages from dryland sites, this study was not of the waste from meals disposed of in rubbish pits or scattered around an area of occupation. It was of bones of meat and fish in storage for future meals, or perhaps in preparation, that would normally have been thrown overboard after use. This, therefore, represents a collection rarely recovered under archaeological conditions. Further, many of the bones are extremely well-preserved and sometimes whole. This is, again, a rare situation for mammal bones on land and even rarer for fish bones in archaeological deposits.

Some bones were associated with Tudor containers or artefacts, and others were more isolated within layers. Most originated from either stores of pig and fish or salt beef in casks orginally positioned on the Orlop deck (see below and Rodrigues, Chapter 10). A number of other bones are considered to be Tudor by dint of their presence stratified within the grey clay layers deemed to be contemporaneous with the ship (see *AMR* Vol. 1, chapter 9 for a description of the stratigraphy of the wreck).

Other bones with less secure provenance or origin form a relatively large sample (89 fragments) from the shelly layers above the wreck which are probably largely of Tudor date and originally from the ship. The gridded recording system used during the excavation makes it possible to suggest from which area of the ship some of these might have come. A smaller number of samples, with a larger number of individual fragments (193), come from the post-Tudor (recent) layers above the wreck. Some of these could also be Tudor.

Retrieval and preparation

Good preservation of fragile organic remains was noted during excavations. Systematic environmental sampling was employed from 1981, led by Ian Oxley, and a large quantity of material was recovered: both the larger bones (mostly cattle, pig and fish) and samples of the sediments containing fish bones from within the hull.

The large fish and mammal bones were raised in their entirety, when possible with accompanying sediments. Further material was retrieved after the ship had been raised. Much of the material was placed in plastic boxes with watertight lids on the sea-bed. Sediment samples containing bone were collected in the same way.

Many cattle bones and one collection of pig bones were from casks. The casks rarely had enough structural integrity to be raised whole. Representative quantities of the interior and exterior sediments were collected, even when there appeared to be little, or no, visible difference. Other large objects, such as baskets and boxes, were often well-enough preserved to be raised intact where excavation of the contents could take place.

Several extensive deposits of animal bone were recorded. One large group of pig bones in the bow of the Orlop deck was in an excellent state of preservation because it was buried beneath a large mass of rope and sailcloth stored in the same area. It was, however, too difficult to recover whole so only a sample was retrieved for study. Elsewhere, a jumbled layer of fish bone in the stern of the Orlop deck and Hold may have been spilled from containers, and was sampled either as intact sediment (Fig. 14.1) or as buckets of sediment and bone.

Generally animal bone collections were treated as samples and given sample numbers (S) but occasionally they were recorded as artefacts in their own right and given artefact numbers (A). Objects such as chests or containers found in direct association or close proximity to bones were also recorded. Bone that was not obviously associated with other objects, nor in larger deposits, was recorded as 'isolated'.

After recovery the larger bones were washed free of salt and allowed to dry slowly at room temperature. The main method of processing sediment samples containing bone was by wet sieving, gentle disaggregation of the sediment in warm water, and washing through a series of precision sieves, the smallest with a mesh of 63 microns. Identifiable fragile items such as small bones were removed at the first convenient stage.

Methods and history of analysis

Because of the difficulties of funding, and the duration and development of the publication policy, this report has had a long gestation. Analysis was largely conducted at the English Heritage Ancient Monuments Laboratory's Faunal Remains Unit (FRU), University of Southampton. Modern comparative collections at FRU and private skeletal collections of Jennie Coy, Sheila Hamilton-Dyer and Sarah Colley were used for reference during identifications. Recording methods were the standard ones then in use, including the computer codings used in the database.

Analysis and recording of the large mammal bones from 'Tudor' and 'possibly Tudor' deposits, (ie, mainly those from secure contexts within the vessel) started in earnest in 1983–4. These were identified and recorded manually by Coy and Oxley in voluntary Saturday sessions. No computer coding or entry took place at this time as the collection was so small and the FRU computers were already fully occupied. Completion of the recording of the main bone assemblages was conducted by 1986. The report for publication was completed by Coy in 2002 with the hand written faunal 'database' transcribed for archive and future analysis to a spreadsheet package by Joyce Hamilton-Dyer. The many thousands of fish bones received a first scan from Sarah Colley, then working at FRU, and were latterly analysed by Sheila Hamilton-Dyer (1986–9), with further measurements made in 2002. In 1986 detailed recording and analysis of the fish bones and production of a computer database was undertaken by Hamilton-Dyer (1995).

The procedure for analysis of the mammal bones was unlike normal practice used for land-based sites.

Table 14.2 Fragment numbers examined from Tudor contexts

Associated with	Cattle	Pig	Sheep	Deer	Other
Galley (H5)	19	2	–	–	–
Wicker baskets	91	42	–	–	rat, fish
Dishes	6	19	2	–	fish
Other containers	26	2	–	–	fowl, rat
Main deck casks	789	–	–	–	–
Orlop deck casks	1278	2	–	–	–
Hold casks	147	2	–	–	–
Starboard Scour-pit cask	–	117	–	–	–
Orlop deck deposits	–	1199	–	–	fish*
Hold deposits	–	–	–	–	fish*
Isolated finds	15	6	2	5	rat
Total fragments	2371	1391	4	5	

* these are the main deposits of fish bones

The selection of cattle body parts for shipboard victualling (largely excluding long bones), and the immaturity of the pigs, severely restricted the number of measurements that could be obtained. Only a limited amount of comparative data of this date existed from sites excavated ashore, but the bones were compared with contemporary material from southern England. Standard measurements used by other European bone studies specialists were taken where possible. Those for mammals and birds were according to the methods of von den Driesch (1976) and those for fish according to the methods of Morales and Rosenlund (1979).

A photographic record of material *in situ* demonstrated the articulated nature of the bones, particularly in the Orlop deck pig and fish bone deposits (Fig. 14.1). This was confirmed in analysis by sections of vertebral column that obviously fitted together, and limb bones where they constituted a joint. An attempt was made to recognise vertebrae from individual animals using non-metrical criteria, minor anatomical idiosyncrasies or anomalies, or pathologies. To aid this analysis, the entire pig assemblage from the Orlop deck was spread out and checked for matching bones and recognisable individual skeletons.

Table 14.3 Distribution of animal bone fragments, Tudor contexts, by deck

	Sector											
	2	3	4	5	6	7	8	9	10	11	Total
Starboard Scourpit	–	–	–	–	–	–	117	–	–	–	117
Upper deck	–	–	–	–	–	–	2	–	–	–	2
Main deck	2	–	–	2	1	560	234	–	–	–	799
Orlop deck	1199	3	29	4	1245	15	125	–	1	fish	2621
Hold	–	–	55	98	–	46	2	–	–	fish	201
Total	1201	3	84	104	1246	621	480	0	1		3740

Fish fragments are widespread but have been omitted from totals

Glossary of terms relating to the animal bone analysis

ACETABULUM - the socket in the hip bone for the head of the upper leg bone or femur.

ADIPOCERE - a fatty or waxy substance formed during the decomposition of animal matter in the absence of air.

AVOIRDUPOIS POUND - a unit of weight equivalent to 453.6g made standard in the fourteenth century by Edward III. This pound contains 16 ounces, whereas the earlier and smaller Troy pound was divided into grains and equivalent to 372.26g. It probably still in use (see Crawforth-Hitchins, Chapter 8). Units of measurement in Europe were very complex and depended upon what commodity was being measured and where. There were hundreds of different 'pounds' in use in Europe.

AXIAL - in butchery, the division of a bone or carcase (from the anterior to the posterior) to give two symmetrical halves

BISCUIT - a kind of hard dry bread issued as part of sailors' rations

CALCANEUM - the heel bone of mammals.

CAUDAL - of or towards the tail, in fish the region of the body beyond the gut cavity (see Figure 14.13)

CENTRUM - the main body of a vertebra below the canal for the spinal cord.

EPIPHYSIS (plural epiphyses) - ends of long bones at the joints which fuse on to the main shaft of the bone at a particular age when growth in length ceases. eg, humerus upper trochanter.

GADIDAE - fish of the cod family, includes cod, haddock, ling, pollack and whiting among others.

GALLON - the imperial gallon is a measurement of volume equal to 10 imperial pounds of water = 277.27 cubic inches (4.54 litres). This makes it 8 imperial pints (see below). In Henry VII's time the standard exchequer gallon was 274.25 cubic inches but in 1545, if the old ale pint was used at the time, the gallon for measuring beer may have been a bit larger than the modern one (Whitney 1900).

GLYCAEMIC INDEX - an index of the rate at which the carbohydrate in a food substance is converted by the body into glucose

HORN CORE - the bone inside the permanent horn of hoofed animals like cattle, sheep and goats. This is sometimes preserved on archaeological sites when the horn itself has rotted away.

HUMERUS UPPER TROCHANTER - a bone process at the shoulder which fuses to the upper arm bone at a particular age.

NON-METRICAL CRITERIA - small variants in anatomy such as double instead of single holes for a blood vessel in the skull. They are usually only on one side and of no functional significance but have been used to track genetic stocks of wild mammals as they seem to be inherited.

OLECRANON PROCESS - the 'funny bone' at the elbow that fuses to the rest of the ulna at a particular age.

PELVIS - the left and right bones of the hip.

PINT - the imperial pint today is an eighth of an imperial gallon = 34.66 cubic inches (0.57 litre). It dates from the fourteenth century and is larger that the U.S. or old wine pint (28.87 cubic in.) and slightly smaller than the old customary ale pint (35.25 cubic in.). The old Scotch pint was about three times as large. Possibly the pint in use for the beer on the *Mary Rose* was more like the ale pint and just a little larger that that in use today (Whitney 1900).

POUND - see avoirdupois pound.

SUB-AXIAL - see axial, in this case the division is off-centre.

VICTUALS - Food. Pronounced by cockneys like Sam Weller in Dicken's 'Pickwick Papers' as 'wittles' and by the writer as 'vittles', the 'c' is silent. Hence victualling.

WINCHESTER PINT - is a little larger than the wine pint defined above but smaller than an ale pint and seems to have been used for measuring peas (presumably after they were soaked and cooked) (Whitney 1900).

Fragmentation and butchery evidence were recorded in more detail than usual for archaeological material of this period to aid the reconstruction of the victualling process. Planes of butchery (ie, angle of cut) in the spine were defined by comparison with the whole standing animal and given specifically defined codes (archive). The butchery planes were 'medial', for midline splitting to cut the carcases into two halves, 'horizontal' for axial chopping in the horizontal plane, and 'transverse' for chopping in the vertical plane at a right angle to these. Some oblique planes at an angle to these three were also recognised.

The domestic mammal bones present were not well-suited to either reconstructing the size of the animals or comparing them with contemporary material from land. The lack of long bones, the measurements of which are used to reconstruct withers height, and of skulls, precluded any discussion of breeds. This is difficult anyway because the definition of breeds also depends upon features not preserved, such as skin colour and shape of the soft parts.

Fish had also been subjected to butchery during preparation and the evidence for this was recorded in detail. The fish lacked heads and certain key vertebrae. Fish bone measurements were taken to aid reconstruction of sizes.

Animal bones were assigned to deposit groups, and recorded by their assigned sample or artefact numbers or groups. The number of animal bone 'samples' according to their deposit groups are presented in Table 14.1. The location and position of the main collections of animals bones are presented in Figure 14.2. This report largely concentrates on the Tudor assemblages, summarised according to association or deck (Table 14.2), but especially the 3740 bones that could be tied to a sector (Table 14.3). The proper names of the domestic species discussed below are those suggested by Clutton-Brock (1981, 196–7).

Evidence of meals

One of the most exciting contexts is the ship's kitchen or galley located in the Hold (H5) and its associated storage areas in H4 and above in O3–4. Any bones found in and around this part of the ship are likely to

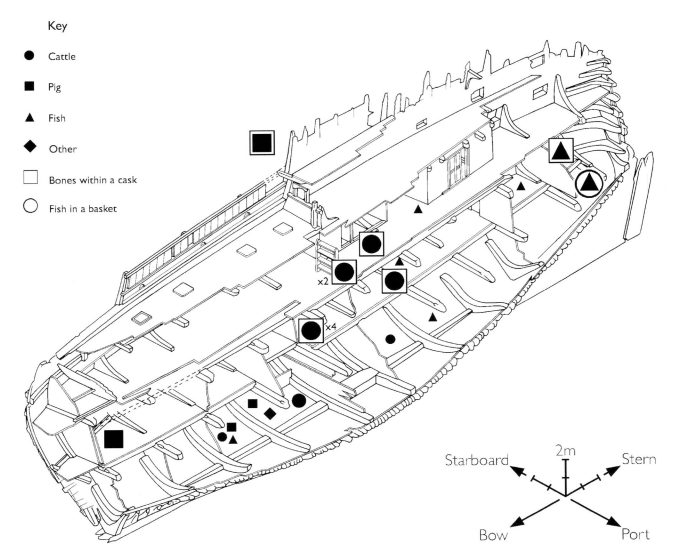

Key

● Cattle

■ Pig

▲ Fish

◆ Other

☐ Bones within a cask

○ Fish in a basket

Figure 14.2 Main distribution of mammal and fish bones

have been connected with meals. The two large cooking furnaces in the galley held large copper-alloy cauldrons used for boiling meat. They have capacities of 600 and 360 litres (Chapter 11). This type of cooking was typical of the sixteenth century (Brears 1985, 6). Billets of timber were lying ready but it is not certain whether the galley was operating on the day of the sinking though under normal circumstances it must have been in use more or less continuously. A variety of other cooking and serving vessels was found in the galley area (see Chapter 11).

The bones associated with the galley (82S100, 82S101 and 82S120) are difficult to interpret although some are unlike any found elsewhere on the ship. A matching pair of jaw fragments from domestic cattle (*Bos taurus* L.) with an erupting third molar, would today represent a two year old but in Tudor times could have been considerably older (as development was slower before cattle were improved in subsequent centuries). These are the only cattle jaws on the ship. A fragment of cattle tibia is also an unusual find for the ship.

While these might suggest that a tongue and some fresh unsalted beef was awaiting preparation the other nineteen cattle bones in the galley were not unlike those from the salt beef casks described below, and comprised butchered fragments of rib, vertebrae, scapula (shoulder blade) and pelvis. On the other hand, their particularly good preservation and whiteness is unlike the usual appearance of cask beef bones. Two pig scapula fragments were present and, like all the other pig bones on board, these are assumed to be from domestic pig (*Sus domesticus*).

Two bone contexts in H5 may have been associated with containers, one at least (82S1082) is recorded as being associated with the remains of a wicker basket (82A5102), and another (82S0116) may have been associated with a staved container. The left and right cattle temporal fragments in these contexts, along with the jaw discussed above, suggest that a whole cattle skull may have originally been on board. Fifty-three other cattle bone fragments were butchered like cask contents, and included rib sections, vertebral fragments and some butchered scapula fragments. A few were, again, unusually white and well-preserved. Also in 82S1082 was a collection of pig bones, mostly ribs but including a lower forelimb fragment and some tarsals (ankle bones). The presence of these limb extremities makes them more like the pig Orlop deposit described below than the pig bones from the single cask examined, so they may represent fresh pork or bacon, rather than salted pork.

Further bones from H4 (82S0008 and 82S0013) were originally recorded as having been associated with wicker fragments. This association cannot be verified, any such fragments having disintegrated, as they have from other contexts on the ship (A. Elkerton, pers. comm.). Of these, 30 fragments are typical beef cask butchered vertebrae and ribs but there are also some seemingly split open pelvis bones of cattle and a dozen bones from pig fore and hindquarters. The last could be either cask or fresh meat as butchery evidence and the parts represented would fit both cask and Orlop deposits of pig. One femur shaft is uncharacteristically split open.

Also recorded as a find from H5 is a fallow deer (*Dama dama*) tibia (83S0326). The rest of the venison bones (which match this one) were found above the galley on the Orlop deck. These are discussed further below.

At face value it appears that the galley area contained some unusual bones and the appearance of some of them might suggest they have gone through different processes from the cask bones discussed below. A number of interpretations are available to us.

These bones might represent higher status food than that normally given to the crew and be from food in preparation for the officers. Cow cheek, tongue (even cow brains) and fresh beef are possibilities with, additionally, a haunch of venison, fresh pork shoulder and leg (or hams), with some salt beef for good measure. The different preservation and colour noted might suggest that these are bones from meals cooked earlier rather than food awaiting preparation. There had been a banquet that day on board the *Henry Grace à Dieu*, attended by the King – perhaps some of the preparation and/or cooking for it was done on the *Mary Rose*, or else leavings from the banquet were brought on board for the benefit of the officers. This is speculation, but might help explain the unusual colour and preservation of these high status provisions.

It is also possible that this is a collection of bones from a range of locations brought together by the shifting of the heavy brick galley during sinking. Associated or articulating bones may be meat awaiting preparation and held together by tendons, rather than bones left over from stewing in cauldrons. Later post-depositional shifting is ruled out by the occurrence of some associated bones in these collections.

A difference of colour and appearance may be due to differential preservation after deposition but might distinguish boiled from unboiled meat; salted from fresh meat; or bones with meat on them from those denuded of meat. Only further study and new techniques of analysis are likely to resolve this in which detailed comparison between these bones and those from the typical salt beef casks might be profitable.

Sample 81S0617, also from the Hold (H7) look like typical salt beef cask bones, comprising butchered vertebrae, ribs, scapula fragments and a split pelvic bone (see below).

The galley areas in H4 and O3–4 contained wooden and pewter dishes and bowls and a few in O4 had bone associated with them (81A3714–16; bone 81S0500, 506, 507 and 509). These are unusual in that they include two butchered bones of domestic sheep (*Ovis aries* L.): one the bottom of a right femur (thigh bone), the other a left calcaneum (heel bone). There are also bones from cattle lower forelimb (unusual in casks so this might denote fresh meat). The rest are pig shoulder bones and butchered rib fragments which could equally well come from casks or the deposit in O2.

The origin of these bones is difficult to deduce and they may be from material which was hanging in the vicinity, conceivably even a leg of mutton and part of a forequarter of beef. Two bones from a fowl leg (81S1308), associated with a metal lid, and further fallow deer remains are discussed in the relevant sections below. Both are from O4 and both may represent the remains of high status food for the table.

Casked beef

Many of the cattle bones on the ship were associated with the remains of at least eight casks. The word 'cask' has been retained throughout this volume because 'barrel' has particular meaning in documents depending on the commodity (eg, Furlong 1999, 20–1; see

Table 14.4 Breakdown of cask contents

Cask no.	81A2610	81A2942	81A2891	81A3705	81A5923	80A1314	80A0926	81A3902	81A3346
Sample no.	81S0379	81S0411	81S0405	81S0496	81S0613	–	80S0923+	81S0533	81S0494
Sector	O6	O6	O6	O6	O8	M7	M7	M8	SS8
Meat	beef	beef	beef	beef	beef	beef	beef	beef	pork
No. frags	349	357	337	202	132	270	259	234	117
MNI	3	3	2	2	2	2	3	2	4

MNI = minimum number of individuals

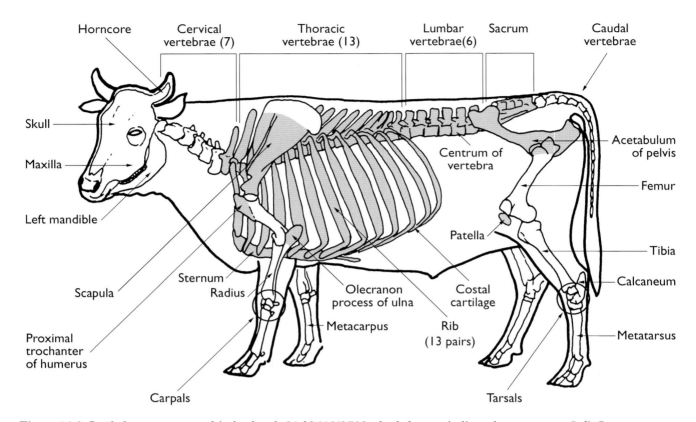

Figure 14.3 Cattle bones represented in beef cask 81A2610/2702; shaded areas indicate bones present. © J. Coy

Chapter 10). The anatomical elements of cattle represented are illustrated in Figure 14.3 and a breakdown of the main casks is given in Table 14.4. Most of the casks were also marked with Roman numerals, which may denote the amount and type of meat stored in them. The three most complete casks (81A2610, 81A2891 and 81A2942; Table 14.4), all in O6, had an estimated capacity of 27–31 imperial gallons (126–138 litres). These three casks and an incomplete one, 81A3705 (bone sample 81S496), were all found in O6, and a further cask 81A5923 was found in O8 (Table 14.4). It is noteworthy that the Orlop deck also carried other potential stores of food in the large deposits of fish and pig bones. At least three further casks were recorded on the Main deck (Table 14.4).

The casks were relatively small and of closely similar size and capacity (see Rodrigues, Chapter 10) and may have been the normal or standard size for meat, or the packed meat may have been off-loaded into these smaller casks for easier carriage. If the latter is correct then the main supplies of salt beef were elsewhere, perhaps fore and aft on racking in 'hogsheads' or 'pipes' (Furlong 1999, 34). Pithy comments in letters of the time record the return of empty casks and suggest that meat might be packed into anything watertight that was available. Meat may have been previously hung in the chain-wale in freshwater for cooling on a hot July day and for washing out excess salt prior to cooking (Rule 1983b, 141, 149; Furlong 1999, 12).

In addition to the cask contents summarised in Table 14.4, there are a number of groups of cattle bone with much smaller numbers of fragments that are also loosely associated with possible casks. In some cases very few bones are present and it is not possible to deduce whether the cask had been full, partially full or empty and, in any case, some of the containers are only represented by one or two staves.

Each of the casks held the remains from several individual cattle, and parts of the same cattle may occur in several casks. Casks seem to be made up in groups

Figure 14.4 The best preserved salt beef collection (81S0496) from cask 81A3705. © University of Southampton

Plate 50. Carved wooden panel, probably originally a ship's fitting, perhaps decorating the Captain's cabin

Plate 51. Elm nail-boarded stool, one of very few pieces of furniture on board

Plate 52 (above). Decorated chest, photographed on the sea-bed and after conservation, with details of the shield design

Plate 54 (below). Personal chest, emptied of its contents but otherwise as recovered. Note the internal compartments

Plate 53. Large fragment of wicker basket embedded in iron concretion, as recovered

Plate 55. Selection of the many surviving pewter objects

Plate 56. Pots for cooking and storage were found on the wreck

Plate 57. Many wooden eating and serving vessels were perfectly preserved

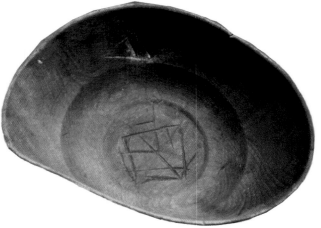

Plate 58. Reconstructed wooden drinking tankard

Plate 59. Wooden bowl with internal graffiti, possibly indicating ownership

Plate 60. Dish bearing the 'H' brand denoting official issue. © Robin Wood

Plate 61. Fine, large wooden bowl © Robin Wood

Plate 62. Selection of wooden and leather vessels associated with eating and drinking

Plate 63 (above). White slipped storage jar made in Sussex and small cooking pot (found in a chest) made in the Low Countries

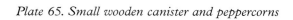

Plate 65. Small wooden canister and peppercorns

Plate 64. Pottery flask made at Martincamp in northern France. Unusually, the wicker covering has survived almost intact

Plate 66. Wine flagon. This object was found on the sea-bed rather than inside the ship and the pewter has become badly corroded (compare with Plate 55)

Plate 67. Wooden and pewter spoons. Surprisingly few spoons were found on the Mary Rose as they would have been used for eating. This may indicate that most were made of horn, which did not survive well

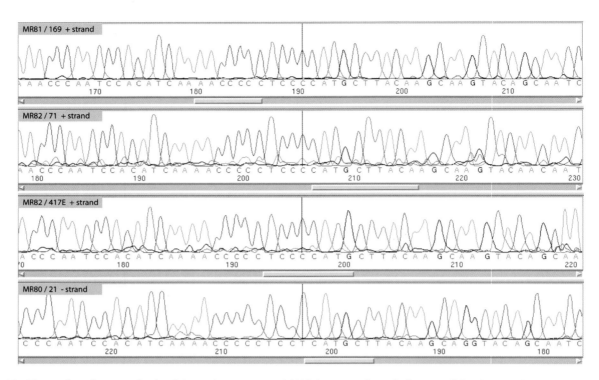

Plate 68. Examples of traces obtained from the automated DNA sequencing of nine amplification products from Mary Rose *human bone extracts (see text for explanation) © Erika Hegelberg/I. Frame*

Plate 69. Plant remains (hipnoid moss) from a sample taken from possible bedding in the Carpenters' cabin. The excavator remarked on the green colour and 'haylike' smell of the material

Plate 70. Articulated cod vertebrae
© Sheila Hamilton-Dyer

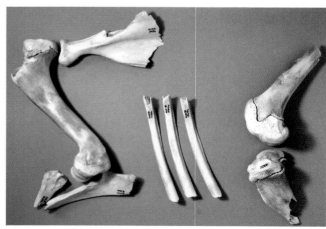

Plate 71. Articulated pig bones from cask 81A3346
© Sheila Hamilton-Dyer

Table 14.5 Anatomical elements of cattle in the three main casks in O6

Cask		81A2610			81A2942			81A 2872/ 2891/ 2916			
Bone sample			81S0379			81S0411			81S0405		
	Side	L	?	R	L	?	R	L	?	R	Total
CV3/6		–	–	–	–	–	2	–	–	–	2
CV4		–	–	–	1	–	–	1	–	–	2
CV4/5		–	–	–	–	–	1	–	–	–	1
CV5		2	–	–	4	–	2	6	–	2	16
CV6		1	–	1	2	–	2	3	–	2	11
CV7		2	–	–	–	1	–	3	–	1	7
Cervical vertebrae		–	14	–	–	9	–	–	8	1	32
TV1		1	–	2	–	–	–	1	1	2	7
TV2		1	–	–	–	–	–	–	–	–	1
TV2-5		6	–	–	3	–	3	5	–	5	22
TV7		–	–	–	1	–	1	–	–	–	2
TV6-9		7	–	4	–	–	–	4	2	2	19
TV10-12		1	–	1	–	–	–	–	1	2	5
TV12		2	–	1	–	–	1	1	–	1	6
TV13		1	–	1	1	–	1	1	–	–	5
TV12/13		–	–	–	–	–	1	–	–	–	1
Thoracic Vertebrae		–	24	–	3	33	4	3	17	2	86
Epiphyses		–	8	–	–	–	–	–	–	–	8
Rib Fragments		16	–	14	14	–	16	15	–	15	90
Rib not sided		–	114	–	–	69	–	–	46	–	229
Costal Cartilages		–	19	–	–	8	–	–	11	–	38
Sternum		–	6	–	–	6	–	–	14	–	26
LV1		–	–	–	–	–	1	1	–	–	2
LV2		–	–	–	1	–	–	1	–	–	2
LV3-6		–	–	–	4	–	2	7	–	2	15
LV6		–	–	–	–	1	–	1	–	–	2
Lumbar Vertebrae		2	2	2	–	17	–	–	5	–	28
Sacrum		1	–	–	4	–	2	2	3	1	13
Vertebral Fragments		–	18	–	–	37	–	–	18	–	73
Epiphysial Fragments		–	–	–	–	21	–	–	24	–	45
Scapula Fragments		6	25	2	4	9	2	1	11	3	63
Humerus		3	–	2	3	2	1	–	1		12
Hum Prox Ep		–	–	–	–	–	–	1	2	1	4
Ulna		3	–	1	3	–	1	2	–	–	10
Olecranon		–	–	–	1	–	–	1	–	1	3
Pelvis		2	6	2	5	18	3	6	5	4	51
Femur		–	1	–	–	–	–	2	1	–	4
Fem Prox Ep		–	–	–	–	–	–	–	–	1	1
Patella		1	–	1	1	–	1	–	–	1	5
Cattle fragments			20			24				50	94
Total		L58	257	34R	L55	255	47R	L68	220	49R	
Grand Total			349			357			337		1043
Min No Animals			3			3			2		

from the remains of several beasts. The small sample of casks (Table 14.4) restricts further interpretation. The best preserved collection from incomplete cask 81A3705 (81S0496) is shown in Figure 14.4 just as it appeared after cleaning and drying. As the cask only contained 202 bones, it may not have been full or some of its contents may have been dispersed and lost.

572

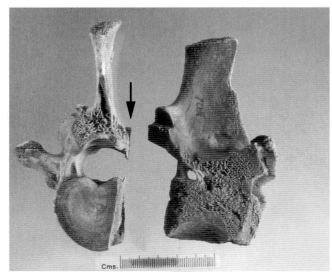

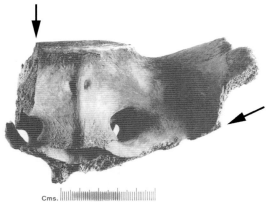

Figure 14.5 Cattle midline butchery showing offline bias; (top) lumbar vertebrae, two views; (bottom) butchered sacrum. © University of Southampton

Figure 14.6 Typical cattle butchery; (top) scapula; (middle) rib; (bottom) acetabulum of pelvis. © University of Southampton

An unusual feature of the cask contents, in contrast to assemblages from land-based sites, is that most material is from well-preserved vertebral columns and associated ribs of cattle. Normally measurement and detailed study is concentrated on the long bones. This was not possible here and therefore the 'body side' of even ribs and split vertebrae and the individual vertebra number (first thoracic, third cervical etc) was recorded where possible in order to attempt as full a reconstruction of the victualling organisation as possible.

The full anatomical listing of fragments is given in Table 14.5 and this demonstrates the consistency of fragments found; the overwhelming dominance of vertebral (backbone) remains and scarcity of limb bones; and the presence of both left and right sides of beef in all containers. This may suggest that, if these were not undisturbed salt beef cask contents, at least they were repacked meat that had not been sorted. If meat had been soaked, the pieces would need to have been taken out and shaken to remove excess salt (see regulation and organisation below).

As there are no heads, we have no evidence of the method of slaughter, but the remains do provide some information on butchery. The chopping of the bones was standardised and regular so a largescale exercise by professional butchers can be assumed. Other trades would have utilised the large quantity of by-products, such as skins, horns and offal. It would be interesting to know where the limb bones excluded from the casks ended up – perhaps in pie shops – and the location of tanneries in the vicinity of Portsmouth. We await

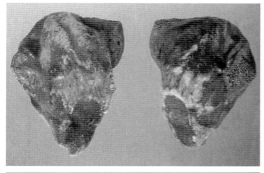

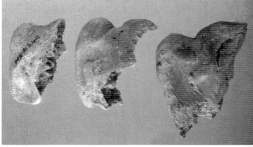

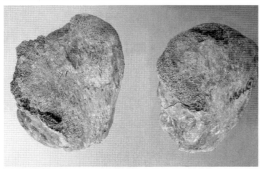

5cm

Figure 14.7 Bones pulled off during butchery of cattle; (top) left and right kneecaps (patella) from 81S0411, cask 81A2942; (middle) butchered olecranon process; (bottom) two humerus proximal trochanters, eroded.
© *University of Southampton*

excavation and analysis of faunal remains from Tudor Portsmouth to verify this.

Hanging of the whole animal and central division into sides of beef can be deduced from the appearance of the vertebrae. The increasingly off-centre nature of the midline split towards the rear of the animal on the *Mary Rose* material (Fig. 14.5) was initially assumed to be caused by the butcher starting at the neck with the weight of one side of the carcase pulling the whole carcase to one side as the splitting continued. But this is probably wrong as pictures of this time always seem to show the animals suspended by the hind legs from a 'beef tree' (Rixson 2000, 195 and see Fig. 14.27, below).

Central midline splitting of the backbone developed during the medieval period and aids cooling of the carcase (O'Connor 1984, 29). Other butchery techniques can be seen on the cattle vertebrae of the

Cattewater wreck, *c.* 1530 (Reilly 1984). Before this, division by chopping either side of the vertebral centrum can be seen, for instance, in Saxon butchery at Southampton (eg, Bourdillon 1983; 1988). In a fresh young pig midline chopping through the centra (main body of the vertebra) is not arduous and can be done by delicate chopping with a sharp knife although a saw is now normally used for cattle. The off-line nature of this 'midline' splitting is shown in Figure 14.5 showing (top) a vertebra from the lumbar region where the split has missed the vertebral canal and (bottom) butchery of the sacrum (the hip region of the backbone) where the (presumably) starting cut had been made well to one side of centre.

The effect that typical chopping of the forequarter had on the shoulder blade (scapula) is shown in Figure 14.6 (top); and that of the hindquarter on the pelvis in Figure 14.6 (bottom); and the standard way in which the heads and blades of ribs were chopped into short sections in Figure 14.6 (middle). This type of butchery is specialised: not only were standard chunks of meat produced but only the thin blade-like parts of the scapula and pelvis have been left, with the exception of the hip joint (acetabulum) itself.

The major limb bones hardly figure but any meat that was on the limbs had been pulled off and put in the casks. The evidence for this is the presence in the casks of processes from the ends of limb bones to which important tendons are attached. They are present either just as unfused bone ends (epiphyses), or those that have been chopped off with a cleaver because they were beginning to fuse and could not be wrenched or knocked off. Another case is the kneecap (patella), an important 'go-between' for muscles of the upper and lower leg. These are often in the casks although the limb bones are not (Fig. 14.7, top). Also carried in with the muscle mass are the elbow (ulna olecranon process) (Fig. 14.7, middle) and the proximal trochanter of the humerus (at the shoulder) (Fig. 14.7, bottom).

This confirms that the casks, as well as containing many chopped up blocks of trunk including pieces of backbone and ribs, must have been stocked with prime meat from the fore and hind quarters which had been efficiently, but swiftly, stripped from the limbs with a minimum of butchery cuts, leaving the major limb bones behind, denuded of meat.

Only butchered flat blade-like parts of the cattle scapula and pelvis were present and suggest the complete boning-out of major limb bones had occurred. The standardised and specialised butchery was connected both with the division into 'pieces' and the avoidance of spoilage. It would allow the brine to penetrate the relatively thin cavities of the flat bones left in, whereas it would be impossible for the salt to penetrate the major marrow-containing bones which would have been centres for putrefaction (see below).

There are occasional exceptions. Just as the presence of skull and limb bone fragments in association with the

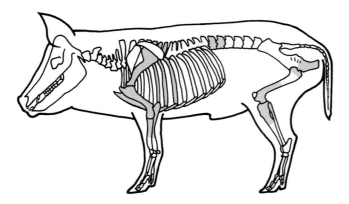

Figure 14.8 Pig bones represented in cask 81A3346; shaded areas indicate bones present. © J. Coy

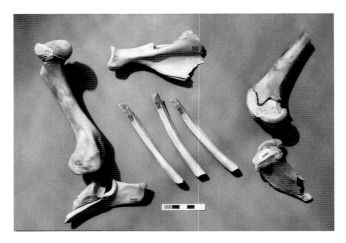

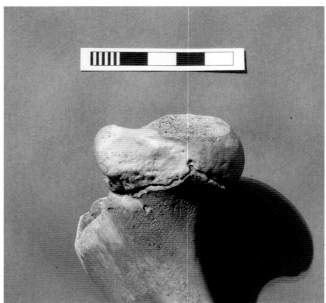

Figure 14.9 Pig bones from cask 81A3346; (top) fore-joint, knee-joint and ribs; (bottom) proximal end of butchered humerus. © Sheila Hamilton-Dyer

galley may suggest fresh rather than salt beef; so the inclusion of a limb bone fragment in a cask tells of something else: a new or inexperienced butcher, perhaps, or extreme urgency as fits the picture of victualling at this time.

The other beef bones associated with staved containers come from the Main deck in M7 and M8. Possible associations occurred in the Hold but, like that from O6 (sample 81S530), some of these putative salt beef casks may contain as little as one bone fragment.

Casked pork

The bones found in the single pork cask (81S0494 in cask 81A3346) were of domestic pig, and demonstrate butchery techniques not quite the same as those for cattle. The bones are again very well preserved and the parts of the pig skeleton represented are illustrated in Figures 14.8 and 14.9 and Table 14.6.

This single surviving cask, which presumably represents salt pork, is an important and rare find. As for cattle, there are no head bones nor limb extremities and the vertebrae and ribs present have been, respectively, split open and chopped. Unlike the cattle casks, however, there are long bones from either side of the knee and elbow joints. At least four individuals and both left and right sides are represented in the cask. As for cattle, this suggests that several casks were filled at the same time with pieces from a number of carcases.

The location of this cask is peculiar as it was in the Starboard Scourpit (SS8) at the level of the beginning of the Sterncastle. It seems to be one of a number of casks full of bones mentioned above as possibly being watered for cooking (Rule 1983b, 141 and 149; Furlong, 1999, 12). Although we cannot ever be sure what was to be eaten that Sunday, Furlong suggests that Sunday was a fish day and that this barrel of pork was soaking for Monday (Furlong 1999, 86, and see below). This may be wrong, as it seems more likely that Sunday was a pork and peas day (see below). The large deposit of pork on the Orlop deck shows that this might not

have entirely depended on salt pork from casks. If other similar casks were lashed to the sides of the ship they may have been lost, especially if they were on the port side.

Two isolated chopped ribs (81S469 and 70) in O4, and collections associated with dishes in O4 (discussed above) look similar to cask material.

Pig ribs, especially the head of the ribs, are anatomically very different from those of sheep and goats and many of those preserved have the diagnostic areas present. Where very worn or fragmentary, ribs have been designated as 'small ungulate' even though the majority are likely to be pig, being found in association with other pig bones.

Orlop deck pork store

A mass of pig bone was discovered in O2 where it was buried beneath a coil of rope and other rigging mater-

Figure 14.10 (top) diver's sketch of the disposition of pig bone in O2 (divelog 81/2/351); (bottom) pig bones and adipocere from the Orlop deposit, as recovered

Table 14.6 Anatomical elements of pig in cask 81A3346 and Orlop deposit

	SS8 Cask 81A3346, Sample 81S0494			O2 Sample 81A0175		
	L	?	R	L	?	R
Scapula	–	1	6	31	2	38
Humerus	–	–	1	32	–	30
Hum. proximal epiphysis	–	2	1	–	8	5
Ulna	–	–	1	21	–	21
Radius	–	–	1	9	–	8
Rad. distal epiphysis	–	–	–	1	–	1
Carpal	–	–	–	–	1	–
Pelvis	–	2	–	12	2	10
Femur	1	–	3	36	8	30
Fem. proximal epiphysis	–	–	1	–	15	–
Fem. distal epiphysis	2	–	2	22	–	25
Patella	1	–	1	–	14	–
Tibia	1	–	4	22	–	24
Tibia proximal epiphysis	1	–	1	14	–	19
Tibia distal epiphysis	–	–	–	–	3	–
Fibula	–	1	1	8	–	4
Tarsal	–	–	–	4	1	1
Longbone frag.	–	9	–	–	–	–
Thoracic vertebra	–	–	3	–	5	–
Lumbar vertebra	1	1	–	–	18	–
Sacrum	–	–	–	–	2	–
Vertebral frag.	–	–	–	–	1	–
Vertebral epiphysis	–	–	–	–	2	–
Rib	11	37	17	246	183	256
Sternum	–	2	–	–	4	–
Total	18L	56	43R	458L	269	472R
Grand total		117			1199	
MNI		4			30	

ials stored in the same area (Fig. 14.10, top). Only a sample (81S175) was retrieved as it was too difficult to recover completely and was not completely excavated. Burial beneath the mass of rope and sailcloth contributed to excellent preservation of this group which was covered in silt and adipocere when raised (Fig. 14.10, bottom). What was recovered represents a minimum of 30 different individuals. That is not to say the whole of their carcases were on the ship. These bones are a slightly different selection of meat from that in the single cask. Although a small sample, the casked meat suggested specialised butchery similar to that described for salt beef (above), whereas the Orlop pigs show a more normal domestic butchery of fresh pork and bacon. Later victualling accounts talk of 'quarters' (see below) which these bones may represent, and this may have been standard victualling practice even by 1545.

The bones present contrast with those in the cask (Fig. 14.11; Table 14.6). As with the cask, however, there are no head remains. The Orlop collection is dominated by well-preserved, and often whole, forelimb and hindlimb bones. Several bones of ankle and wrist were present but there were no trotters: these delicacies and the heads would have been popular wherever they were available. Vertebrae were not numerous but sufficient to show that the carcases had been halved down the midline. There were numerous ribs, some with axial cuts which would have severed them from the

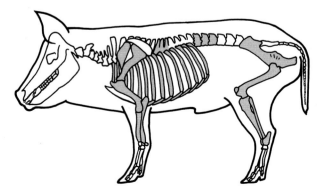

Figure 14.11 Pig bones represented in the Orlop deposit 81S0175. © J. Coy

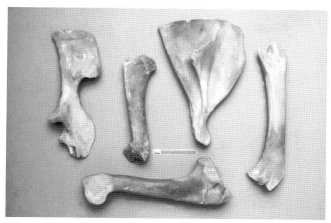

Figure 14.12 Whole bones from the Orlop pig deposit.
© *University of Southampton*

vertebral column, so it is possible that the latter was largely removed and excluded. The lack of vertebrae in this deposit is not likely to be the result of differential preservation, but we only have a small part of the pig evidence here.

Most of the bones of the shoulder, pelvic girdle, fore and hindlimbs were consistently and extensively butchered showing cuts through the shoulder, elbow, hip and knee joints. The immaturity of most of the bones hampered analysis of this butchery. Epiphyses had not fused at some joints and were often found separately. These cuts might have been within each 'ham' and have gone through the bone without severing the meat (Fig. 14.12). This would have held it together during cooking and made subsequent division into 'pieces' quicker (see below). Alternatively the meat could already have been cut into 'pieces'.

It is possible that the meat was hung up in carcase form or in bags in the bow just forward of the main Orlop galley area. A few shoulder blades had holes, which excited suggestions that the joints had been hung from hooks, but the holes look rather small for this.

Despite their occasional pathologies the pigs represented appear to have been well-built and of good size for the period, though contemporary parallels are few (see size and type of mammals below). More specialist study of this material is needed; including full analysis of the pathology present on some bones, and of some very consistent joint anomalies which may be of genetic or nutritional origin, or both.

Scattered pork, beef and mutton

Apart from the meal preparation remains, the cask contents and the Orlop pig store discussed above, there are few pig, beef and sheep bones of Tudor date (Table 14.2). A few fallow deer bones were present in O4 and are described below. Most of the remaining bones include isolated finds of, for example, cattle rib, cattle vertebrae and pig (Table 14.2). The characteristic

butchery suggests that they all originated from the casks or from the Orlop deck deposit described above.

The concentration of bones on the Main deck (M7 and M8) is mostly beef bones with staved container remains, but those in sample 82S1245–6 (M7) are associated with a bowl. They comprise two butchered cattle rib lengths typical of salt beef, but also two pig vertebral fragments. In M4 there is a fragment of possible sheep vertebra associated with a butchered cattle rib fragment.

Another 57 cattle bones, 17 pig and 7 more sheep fragments were studied from layers of 'uncertain' date, originating from the shelly layer (layer 6) over the wreck. Although many of the cattle and pig are similar to cask and Orlop finds, there are a number of atypical bones including cattle bones that have obvious sawing butchery, some extremely large pig, and some sheep (including two adult left mandibles) comparable in size to modern improved sheep. These bones are probably of mixed origin, being residual Tudor and subsequent post-Tudor material.

Among the post-Tudor layers associated with off-site, surface and backfill contexts and other isolated find places, were 128 cattle, 28 pig and 10 sheep fragments. Pig bones from O2 (81S0353) probably relate to the main pig Orlop context as their butchery is identical. Other isolated pig bones (eg, 82S1091, provenance unknown) are similar. Cattle fragments from 82S1090 and 1092 (from unknown provenances), off-site (81S1213), and from many small collections of isolated bones, are obviously originally from salt beef casks. There are a few cattle and sheep bones obviously not Tudor because of their lack of butchery and large size. One domestic fowl was also recovered (see fowl section below). Unprovenanced bones have not been completely studied but those recorded often look post-Tudor. An isolated bone of unknown date is part of a rabbit skull (see below).

Fish

Over 31,000 fish bones were recovered and recorded. Most of these are from the stern of the vessel in an area of the Orlop deck and the Hold and represent fish provisions on board (Table 14.7). These bones were in disarray, having been scattered with other items when the ship settled on the bottom, but remained within this storage area, some still in articulation. Some are associated with remains of staved containers and other objects such as a wicker basket (Table 14.8), where they may represent material removed for preparation. The small bones had to be extracted from a matrix of fine, partially hardened, silt. We can be reasonably certain that, with a few exceptions discussed below, all of the bones considered here were part of stores on the ship when she went down, rather than fish that had died and been incorporated in the deposits. This is confirmed on

Table 14.7 Fish records summarised by sector

Location	no deposits/ samples	Stored fish						possibly stored			post sinking			Total
		cod	Gadidae	conger	hake	haddock	pollack	pouting	whiting	eel	herring	sandsmelt	unident	
U7	1	1	-	-	-	-	-	-	-	-	-	-	-	1
U8	1	-	-	-	-	-	-	-	-	-	-	-	1	1
M9	1	14	-	-	-	-	-	-	-	-	-	-	230	244
O1	1	1	-	-	-	-	-	-	-	-	-	-	-	1
O7	1	7	-	-	2	-	-	-	-	-	-	-	26	35
O8	9	17	1	38	0	0	0	0	0	0	1	1	312	360
O9	1	1	-	-	-	-	-	-	-	-	-	-	-	1
O10	2	22	16	1	0	0	0	1	0	0	0	0	187	227
O11	15	891	70	114	33	13	0	20	13	4	0	0	8191	9377
H3	1	-	-	-	-	-	-	-	-	-	-	-	20	20
H4	1	162	39	-	-	-	-	-	-	-	-	-	2129	2330
H5	1	21	-	-	-	-	-	-	-	-	-	-	15	36
H8	4	26	0	13	0	0	0	0	0	0	0	0	151	190
H9	2	8	0	0	0	0	0	0	0	0	0	0	0	8
H11	7	2325	20	0	0	0	4	0	0	0	1	0	16074	18424
SS7	1	-	-	-	-	-	-	-	-	-	-	1	-	1
unknown	1	430	34	-	-	-	-	-	-	-	-	-	73	537
Total		3924	180	186	35	13	4	21	13	4	2	2	27409	31793
overall percentage		*12.34*	*0.57*	*0.59*	*0.11*	*0.04*	*0.01*	*0.07*	*0.041*	*0.01*	*0.01*	*0.01*	*86.21*	
percentage ex. unident.		*89.51*	*4.11*	*4.24*	*0.8*	*0.3*	*0.09*	*0.48*	*0.3*	*0.09*	*0.05*	*0.05*		

examination of the bones themselves.

The preservation of the fish bones is generally excellent with an amber-like appearance. Some bones are a little flaky and occasionally there is evidence of warping of some long thin bones. Some of these, such as fin rays, were broken on recovery but most bones were recovered undamaged. An exception to this is a sub-group of cod vertebrae from H4 (81S0577), which have been partially crushed but remain intact. This is not recent damage and it seems likely that a very heavy object such as one of the cannon is the cause, either at the time of the sinking or the subsequent collapse of the ship's structure.

Species present

In total 31,793 fish remains were recorded. Many thousands of these are post-cranial (ie, body parts rather than heads) elements such as fin rays, spines, vertebral fragments and ribs, etc. These small needle-like bones are difficult to identify to family level let alone species, and no attempt was made to classify them. They were, however, of gadid (cod family) morphology and are almost certainly of cod, the most frequent of the identified species. Almost all of the other skeletal elements were identified as cod (*Gadus morhua*). At 3924 bones this species accounts for 89.5% of all the bones identified to species or family and, if it is accepted that the fin rays were also of cod, then this species constituted over 90% of all of the remains (Table 14.7). The other nine species were present in only very small quantities; of these conger (*Conger conger*) is the most common at 186 bones. Eel (*Anguilla anguilla*), herring (*Clupea harengus*), haddock (*Melanogrammus aeglefinus*), hake (*Merluccius merluccius*), pollack (*Pollachius pollachius*), whiting (*Merlangius merlangus*), pouting (*Trisopterus luscus*) and sandsmelt (*Atherina presbyter*) were also identified

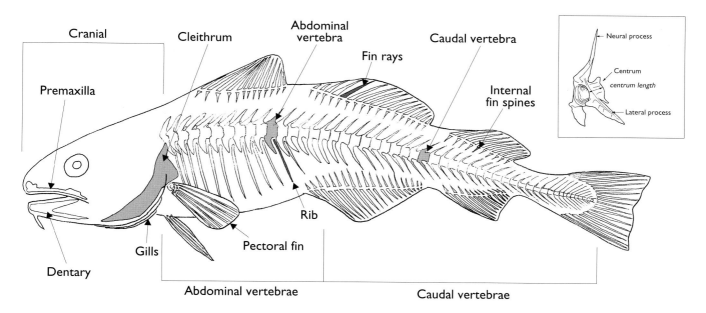

Figure 14.13 Diagrammatic skeleton of a cod indicating main bones mentioned in text. Shaded areas indicate bones present. Structure of a vertebra inset. © Sheila Hamilton-Dyer

(Table 14.7). This last species is represented by a single vertebra from O8 (82S1324) and a complete skeleton (86S0298) found in Tudor layers in the Starboard Scourpit (SS7), having presumably swum around the sunken vessel, died on the sea-bed, and been buried. It was only recovered fortuitously in a sample of sediment. A complete fresh corpse (81S0380) of a sea scorpion (*Taurulus bubalus*), was excavated from a lantern (81A2584) raised intact from the sea-bed from O11 (A. Elkerton pers. comm.), and must therefore, unlike the sandsmelt, be recent – presumably entering the lantern after excavation of much of the overlying sediment, but before its lifting two days later. The haddock, hake, pollack and conger are likely to be part of the stores by reason of position, anatomy and butchery. The few remains of eel, herring, pouting and whiting are more difficult to interpret; they may be intrusive but all are from areas that produced most of the fish bone with none found in areas with no cod remains. All are very small and could have become incorporated ashore, as contemporary contaminants during the packing and stowage of containers.

Location

The fish remains were not found scattered across the site but only in certain areas of the wreck. Most of the fish were recovered from the same areas as the other bone remains, ie, at the stern in the Hold and Orlop deck above (Table 14.7). In addition, cod bones were recovered from in and near the galley. Just a handful of bones was recovered outside these areas (and at least one of these is thought to be a labelling error). Although mainly recovered in a disarticulated state, divers had noted that some were in close association, with some vertebral columns in position. Unlike the pork and beef, some of which could definitely be associated with a particular cask, associations for fish are less clear. There is a strong possibility that some of the cod in H11 were associated with the remains of wicker basket 81A4042 and others were found near and under cask 82A1691 in O8. Certainly, cured cod and other fish were transported in casks (Table 14.8).

No cod jaws or other cranial (head) bones were recovered. There were, however, many cleithra. This is a large curved bone at the back of the head, behind the gills, and is part of the pectoral fin support (Fig. 14.13).

Table 14.8 Fish in casks, baskets and other possible containers

Association	Location	Sample	Cod	Stored fish Gadidae	Conger	Possibly stored Hake	Whiting	Unident.	Total
Cask 82A1691	O11	82S0080	62	6	5	26	–	356	455
		82S0089	29	2	25	7	–	120	183
		82S0091	5	–	38	–	–	22	65
		Total	96	8	68	33	0	498	703
?Staved container	O11	81S1289	144	–	–	–	1	1041	1186
Jug 81A5728	O11	81S1196	12	–	–	–	–	65	77
Basket 82A4042	O11	81S0099	633	–	–	–	–	4059	4692

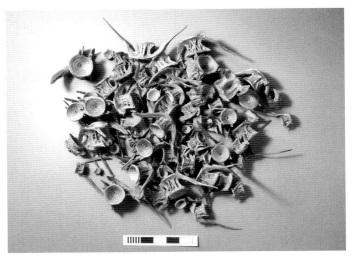

Figure 14.14 (left) Cod vertebrae and (right) fin rays etc from 82S0080. © Sheila Hamilton-Dyer

Some of the other elements of this pectoral region are also present, particularly the postcleithrum (Fig. 14.16, bottom) and scapula. The atlas (the first vertebra, next to the cranium) was also absent, along with the majority of the first five abdominal vertebrae. The caudal (tail) vertebrae dominate the assemblage, along with the bones of the fins and their internal supports (Figs 14.13, 14.14).

Butchery of cod

At least 149 of the cod bones show evidence of butchery, by way of clear cut and/or chop marks; nineteen of the probable cod bones also have marks (Table 14.9). Other bones may also have been butchered but show breaks rather than certain chop marks and have not been included.

Almost 15% (44) of the abdominal vertebrae have cut-marks. In most cases the vertebra had been chopped across the cranial side of the centrum, usually at an oblique angle (Fig. 14.15). The lateral and neural processes of the vertebrae were also sometimes

Figure 14.15 Two obliquely chopped cod vertebrae (lateral view) © Sheila Hamilton-Dyer

incomplete but it was difficult to be certain if this was deliberate butchery damage. The splitting open of the fish could well produce this type of damage. Cut-marks on the more numerous caudal vertebrae are considerably rarer at 0.7% (21). This may reflect the processing technique; after the head is removed, the abdominal vertebrae can be filleted out from the head end, with the caudal (tail) end of the column snapped off and left in the fish. At a medieval site on the north coast of Scotland the anatomical representation is reversed and butchery marks parallel those here, indicating a processing site (Barrett *et al.* 1999, 371).

Fifty-six (22.4%) of the cleithra show evidence of butchery; several of these have the cranial (anterior) portion missing. Some of the postcleithra had also been cut (28, 16.2%). These bones are part of the supporting structures of the pectoral fin, but the cleithrum projects forwards ventrally, joining the attachments for the gills. This is the most convenient place to behead a round-bodied fish, lifting the gills forward and chopping through the revealed gap. In doing so the cleithrum often receives cut-marks and may be chopped right through. Many examples were found of cleithra with the cranial tip missing, and very few of the tips were found (Fig.14.16, top) This evidence indicates that the cod had been prepared, by removal of the head at least (Tables 14.9, 14.10).

Quantity

The amount of fish originally on the ship is very difficult to estimate, not least because there are a large number of silt samples that remain unprocessed. Although large quantities of sediment were sampled in order to understand the stratigraphy and processes of deposition, even larger volumes have yet to be examined. In addition, the deeper parts of the deposit from the Orlop deck were not recovered in their entirety. Fish bones from the major deposits have, however, all been recorded and the amount of unrecorded bone is likely to be minor.

Table 14.9 Frequency of butchery marks on fish remains

Anatomy	Cod			Gadidae			Cod + Gadidae			Conger		
	cod	butchered	%	Gadidae	butchered	%	Total	Total butchered	%	conger	butchered	%
Cranium/fragment	-	-		-	-		-	-		10	2	20.0
Vomer	-	-		-	-		-	-		5	3	60.0
Parasphenoid	-	-		-	-		-	-		1	-	
Basioccipital	-	-		-	-		-	-		1	-	
Facial	-	-		-	-		-	-		23	-	
Premaxilla	-	-		-	-		-	-		3	-	
Dentary	-	-		-	-		-	-		6	1	16.7
Articular	-	-		1	-		1	-		5	-	
Angular	-	-		-	-		-	-		2	-	
Ectopterygoid	-	-		-	-		-	-		3	-	
Quadrate	-	-		-	-		-	-		2	1	50.0
Hyomandibular	-	-		1	-		1	-		2	1	50.0
Preopercular	-	-		-	-		-	-		2	-	
Opercular	-	-		-	-		-	-		3	-	
Interopercular	-	-		-	-		-	-		5	-	
Subopercular	-	-		1	-		1	-		3	-	
Ceratohyal	-	-		-	-		-	-		2	-	
Epihyal	-	-		-	-		-	-		1	-	
Branchial ray	-	-		-	-		-	-		23	-	
Branchials	1	-		-	-		1	-		3	-	
Cleithrum	250	56	22.4	78	2	2.6	328	58	17.7%	2	-	
Postcleithrum	173	28	16.2	2	-		175	28	16.0%	-	-	
Supracleithrum	1	-		1	-		1	-				
Scapula	136	-		7	-		143	-		-	-	
Coracoid	91	-		4	-		95	-		-	-	
Pelvis	1	-		-	-		1	-		-	-	
Precaudal vertebra	295	44	14.9	-	-		295	44	14.9%	45	38	84.4
Caudal vertebra	2848	21	0.7	28	1	3.6	2876	22	0.8%	15	11	73.3
Vertebra frag	113	-		27	16	59.3	140	16	11.4%	-	-	
Vertebral process	-	-		-	-		-	-		19	19	100.0
Hypural	15	-		1	-		16	-		-	-	
spines and frags	-	-		14	-		14	-		-	-	
Total	3924	149	3.8	164	19	11.6	4088	168	4.1%	186	76	40.9

NB does not include unidentified material.

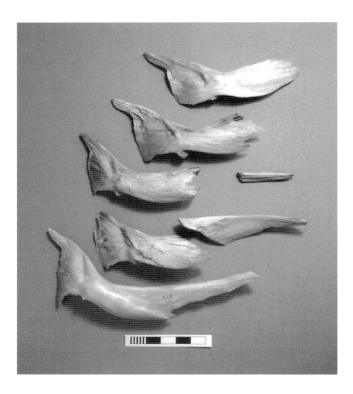

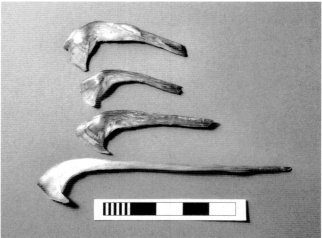

Figure 14.16 (top) Selection of butchered cod cleithra; (bottom) three chopped postcleithra. The lowest example on each photograph is a modern specimen for comparison.
© *Sheila Hamilton-Dyer*

One big question is the amount of preparation of the fish before loading. Already we have seen that the cod were all beheaded. It is possible that fish from different sources were prepared in varying ways. Some may have had all or most of the bones removed, leaving little or no evidence.

The estimation of the minimum number of cod individuals (MNI) based on cleithra is just over 100. The numbers of caudal vertebrae in cod are about 30, approximately twice the number of abdominal vertebrae. Only 295 cod abdominal vertebrae have been recovered as against 2848 caudal. This would, therefore, give minimum number estimates of 20 and 95

respectively. If boned fillets were also present these calculations could be considerable under-estimates. Modern smoked 'Finnan' haddock and salt dried cod in Britain often contain all or part of the cleithrum similar to the findings of cod here. The vertebrae, however, are usually removed except for a short section at the tail end. The cod remains from the *Mary Rose* do not have a preponderance of these small vertebrae but appear to have most of the caudal vertebrae still present.

The amounts of fish, even if it is assumed to be an under-estimate, would not have lasted a crew of 415 men more than a week at most (see discussion below).

Other fish

Haddock is represented by a single associated, and possibly articulated, group of thirteen tail vertebrae from O11 (81S0389). The whole fish would have been about 3kg fresh weight. Pollack also occurs just once; four associated (possibly articulated) abdominal vertebrae from H11 (81S0087). These represent a fish of 0.60m long. Hake was identified from three areas, two tail vertebrae from O7 (83S0338) and two groups, one of 26 and one of seven from O11 (82S0080 and 82S0089 respectively). Those from 82S0080 are almost certainly from two fish. Perhaps these odd finds of other large members of the cod family may have been included only to make up the numbers in the main consignments of cod.

Conger eel bones were recovered from three general areas, H8, O8 and O11. Unlike the cod the conger remains include head elements (Tables 14.9 and 14.10). The 76 remains from O11 could easily be the remains of a single, complete fish. The remaining 110 bones come from a minimum of four individuals. Using data provided by Fishbase (Froese and Pauly 2002), and comparisons with recent specimens of the author and the FRU, the individual from O11 is estimated to have been just over 1.2m total length and with a gutted weight of around 4kg. The other fish would have been larger, about 1.8m and weighing around 14kg gutted weight. Conger of this size are quite common in the Solent today. Originally it was thought that the conger remains might represent fish living in the wreck, since they are common inhabitants of wrecks in the Solent and elsewhere. However, the location of the remains, the presence of butchery marks, and supporting documentary evidence, show that these, like the Gadidae, were part of the stores on board.

Unlike the cod the conger had not been beheaded and the butchered remains represent all parts of the fish. Instead the conger have been cut down either side of the backbone, through the lateral processes of the vertebrae (Fig. 14.17A–D). This is presumed to be for the production of three long flat fillets from each fish for speedier preservation. The conger is a long, round-bodied fish and the central 'fillet', although including most of the vertebrae, would still have offered a

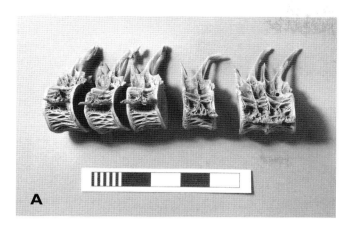

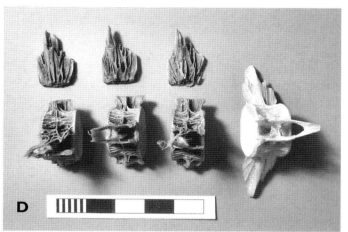

Figure 14.17 Butchery of conger eel; (A) Selection of chopped vertebrae; B) 3 chopped vertebrae, end on view; C) three lateral processes chopped off, from above; D) three processes and vertebrae chopped, from above; (E) congar eel cranium sub-axially divided. The larger, lighter coloured examples are modern specimens for comparison. © Sheila Hamilton-Dyer

worthwhile amount of flesh. Apart from the complete fish from O11, which had only one cut mark along the cranium, this sub-axial division included even the head (Fig. 14.17E).

A vertebra of a large conger recovered from late medieval deposits in Salisbury had also been split in this manner (Hamilton-Dyer 2000). These fish are likely to have been salted, as implied from the household

Table 14.10 Comparison of anatomical distribution of fish

Element	Conger Total	%	Cod Total	%	Cod + Gadidae Total	%
Cranial elements	105	56.5	1	0.03	4	0.1
Pectoral	2	1.1	651	16.6	742	18.2
Pelvic	–	0	1	0.03	1	0.02
Precaudal vertebrae	47	25.3	295	7.5	295	7.2
Caudal vertebrae	15	8.1	2848	72.6	2876	70.4
Vertebral fragments	17	9.1	113	2.9	140	3.4
Hypural and spines	–	0	15	0.4	30	0.7
Total	186		3924		4088	

accounts of Sir William Petre in 1549 (Cutting 1955, 32). Preserving conger by salting and drying was a speciality of the Channel Isles from at least the close of the twelfth century (Everard and Holt 2003, 57; Syvret and Stevens 1998, 31, see also Sources of Fish below.).

Comparison with fish remains from the *Scheurrak SO1* and Cattewater wrecks

The discovery of sixteenth century wrecks is very rare, and the analysis and publication of faunal remains from a direct parallel is very rare indeed. The wreck of a late sixteenth century merchant ship, Project *Scheurrak SO1*, off the Dutch coast does, however, provide such a comparison; six casks of cattle bones and three of fish were recovered from the Orlop deck and analysed (Zeiler 1993; Brinkhuizen 1994).

One cask contained only cod while the second investigated contained other gadids as well, namely torsk and ling/blue ling. A scan of the third cask showed it to be similar to the second. These are species not usually found round the Dutch coast; but as the cargo was wheat from the Baltic region, the fish may well also have come from there.

The anatomical distribution for both casks is similar to that for the cod on the *Mary Rose*; with almost no head elements but many from the pectoral region, vertebrae, and the small bones of the fins and supporting structures. Many of the abdominal vertebrae (at the head end of the fish) were absent. This was less frequent for fish under 0.55m. Fish lengths of the cod were estimated from measurements of vertebrae and cleithra, as being from 0.35–0.40m and up to 1.10–1.15m. The range is slightly larger than those on the *Mary Rose* and includes more of the smaller fish. Butchery marks were noted on some bones including vertebral processes and cleithra. The removal of the anterior part of this bone is very similar to that on the *Mary Rose* fish. The findings are, however, not identical

and it was concluded that these were stockfish (dried, salted), beheaded and often with the anterior part of the spinal column removed. The differences in species, size and butchery, though minor, indicate a different source for the fish from the *Mary Rose*, a finding consistent with the documentary sources.

It was estimated that the first cask was part filled and had contained at least 10 large cod, and the mixed cask at least 53 gadid fish, mostly cod. If the fish on board the *Mary Rose* represents a stored fish of equivalent type to the *Scheurrak* then it is possible that the *Mary Rose* remains represent the contents of two casks (assuming a similar standard size) together with baskets or loose stacked fish, some already taken to the galley for preparation.

Although scant mammal bone remains were recovered and published from the remnants of the Cattewater wreck, *c.* 1530 (Redknap 1984), the fish remains, as from the *Mary Rose*, were of cod and probably beheaded (Wheeler 1984), and it is suggested that these might also have been salted.

Haunches of venison

Bones of an adult fallow deer (*Dama dama*) were found in Tudor contexts in O5. These consist of what seem to be the ankle and hindlimb cannon bone (metatarsus) from the right limb (80A0951 and 80A0966) and an associated right hipbone, probably from the same limb. A right tibia (80A1019), although labelled 'surface post-Tudor', is also from O5 and probably belongs to the same limb. Figure 14.18 shows this almost complete hindlimb: the femur is missing.

A left tibia (83S0326) was recovered from the galley in H5, below O5. The left (H5) and right (O5) tibias match exactly, both being only just fused at the top and having respective total lengths of 270mm and 271mm. The left legbone in the Galley bore a lot of cuts and was probably finished with and may even have had, at this point, another function. There were originally, therefore, two haunches of what seems to have been a fallow buck on board. Such haunches would probably normally have hung from a hook in as cool and dry a place as could be found on a hot summer day. The ventilation hatch for the galley cauldrons is in O5 and it is probable that bones were displaced through this hatch during the sinking.

The introduced fallow deer, which appeared after the Norman invasion, was often a park species and was a favoured food of royalty and gentlefolk (Corbett and Harris 1991, 511; Coy and Maltby 1987, 216–7). Size alone cannot be used to distinguish it from the native roe deer (*Capreolus capreolus*) and red deer (*Cervus elaphus*). The three species overlap in dimensions and the taming and improvement of park fallow since Norman times has widened the size ranges at both ends of the spectrum. It is also possible that in the Tudor

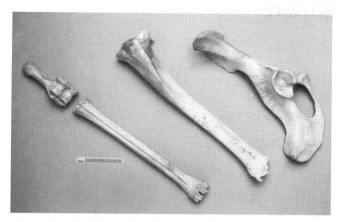

Figure 14.18 Fallow deer bones, mostly from O5. From left R. metatarsus, L. tibia, R. pelvis. © University of Southampton

period managed fallow of both sexes were sometimes castrated which provide better meat, as they were in the seventeenth century (Stringer 1977, 56).

It is necessary to rely upon a combination of size ranges and anatomical differences to identify deer bones to species, but even immature specimens can be so identified (Coy 1995, 138–9). The total length of the fully fused metatarsus was well up in the range for archaeological material (219mm in a range of 196–234mm) and compared well with the male range for modern specimens. It is outside the ranges of roe and red deer.

Other possible food species and animals present

Domestic fowl (*Gallus gallus*)

There is only evidence of one Tudor fowl (81S1308), represented by the lower end of a left drumstick or tibiotarsus and its associated lower leg (tarso-metatarsus) with an eroded spur. It was found stuck to a leaded brass lid, probably of a caulking cauldron (rather than a cooking pot) in O4 (see Chapter 8). There is no visible butchery but the foot end of the leg might have been removed during preparation or left behind after consumption. At this time, however, birds sometimes went to table with their legs attached. The bones have mature ends. These facts are somewhat contradictory; the large size suggests a male and the fusion suggests a cockerel rather than a capon; the eroded small spur, however, is more characteristic of a castrate.

The measurements put this bird above the top of the male distribution of Saxon Southampton fowl and it is larger than anything in the small medieval sample for Winchester Western Suburbs (Coy 1989, fig. 1). In the absence of any evidence for live fowl on board it is probable that this male bird was for eating, as its find location was near the galley, and it might have been a capon castrated late so that a spur had formed.

A second fowl (80A0026) is an isolated post-Tudor right tarsometatarsus of much smaller size, again with a spur, found in the area of O8.

Rabbit (*Oryctolagus cuniculus*)

A maxillary fragment of rabbit (81S0189) of unknown date was recovered from M4 amongst items of gun furniture. This need not represent food, as such a fragment might have arrived in straw or hay.

Red deer (*Cervus elaphus*)

Two worked red deer antler objects were recovered from the Carpenters' cabin (M9). These artefacts are reported in Chapter 8.

Size and type of food mammals and fish

Food mammals

For the *Mary Rose* assemblage, reconstruction of cattle and pig withers heights and animal robusticity (cf. Bourdillon 1980, 186) are precluded by the lack of cattle leg bones and the immaturity of the pigs. Few measurements of cattle bones could be taken and even where they were, they only showed that the size of the animals used was somewhat regular. The overall quali-tative impression is one of beasts of a good size, certainly larger than medieval stock from Southampton and Winchester and comparable with smaller breeds today.

Before improvements in the seventeenth and eighteenth centuries the cattle would have been slow maturing compared with those of today, reaching their preferred carcase weight at 4–5 years. Body conformation would also have been different with a heavier fat content. These beasts were nowhere near the size of the massive cattle we eat and milk today and later cattle bones found in the post-Tudor layers stand out by their larger size.

With only the evidence from a single pair of cattle jaws from a possible two year old (not associated with the salt beef remains) and the lack of limb bone fusion data, there is not the standard information on the age of the cattle that is normally found in land-based assemblages. The epiphysis evidence from the vertebrae is all we have. Many vertebrae and rib heads had unfused epiphyses but the age at which these fused in the sixteenth century may have been as late as four or five years.

It is likely that the cattle used ranged in age between two and five years. In the absence of skulls and horn cores no more can be said about their appearance or their sex although it is likely that both males and females were used.

The pigs we eat today are remarkably young. In Tudor times pigs might have grown in stature and bone maturity for as much as four years, as wild boar do

(Habermehl 1985, 106). Only a few limb bones of pig on the ship have all epiphyses fused; most have at least one end still growing and a few have both ends still growing. On this basis the pigs in the Orlop deposit probably ranged in age from less than a year old to more than three years old.

As these were mostly from skeletally immature animals it was not relevant to calculate withers heights but all bone measurements are recorded in the archive. Measurements of bone breadths were taken throughout but were frequently from bones still unfused at the other end. It is difficult to compare the data we have with archaeological assemblages, as whole bones are usually rare on archaeological sites, and many studies omit these measurements. Pig bones are often poorly preserved, eaten young and subjected to much chewing and gnawing by humans and non-humans. The pigs on the Orlop deck were, like the cattle, high up in the size ranges available for southern England.

Sheep sizes at the end of the medieval period are generally still small and the few mutton bones on the ship are characteristically small in size. Later sheep bones found in the upper layers of the excavation stand out by their larger size.

Fish

As no atlas vertebrae were found on the *Mary Rose* it is not possible to estimate the size of the cod using the method described by Enghoff (1983), nor were there any dentaries or premaxillae (Fig. 14.13) from which to estimate size following Wheeler and Jones (1976). Direct comparison of the cod bones from the *Mary Rose* with recent fish implies a total length range of 0.60–1.0m for the fresh fish, with most averaging 0.75–0.90m. The tight range is illustrated by the measurements of the centrum length of abdominal vertebrae (Fig.14.19a). Measurements of the width of the cleithra (following Brinkhuizen 1994) also indicate that most of the cod were of 0.75–0.90m total length (Fig 14.19b). After beheading, these would be reduced to approximately 0.60m, and fit quite well with the later regulations stipulating cod of 24 inches (0.61m). These estimates, although tantalisingly similar, must remain tentative as much work is still required, both in documentary research and in experimentation on modern fish.

The significance of the Mary Rose *animal bone study*

Work on the *Mary Rose* animal bones has given a new insight into the study of taphonomy in archaeology. Although the raising of the ship may have constrained further taphonomic studies, this has to be weighed against the enormous advantages of publicity for this area of archaeology, public interest, and the tremendous amount of knowledge now accumulated on the ship itself. The important decisions made during the 1970s to keep the wreck *in situ* and not to move it to shallower water for excavation were important ones for bioarchaeological studies (Rule 1983b, 210).

The deposition of the wreck and the animal bone evidence within it involved a protracted succession of processes and a complex post-depositional history as outlined above and in Chapter 12. Although this also happens in land-based archaeology, there are important differences here. First, this deposition relates to a known day in the past; secondly, the main primary depositional processes were very quick; thirdly, material which was swiftly covered was excluded from oxygen and often, therefore, extremely well-preserved. In some instances not only bone itself but some products of slow disintegration of the meat, particularly the fatty deposit known as adipocere, remained around the bones. This was especially true of the deposit of pig bones on the Orlop deck. The animal bone assemblage compares in some ways with material left by dated natural disasters, like earthquakes and volcanic eruptions, and suggests that the analysis and interpretation of shipwreck material needs to follow a different path from that of material from land-based occupation sites.

Differences in taphonomy between marine and land-based archaeology, discussed in Chapter 12 and at the beginning of this chapter, highlighted several features pertinent to the *Mary Rose*: the rapid destructive sinking phase; episodic dispersal of items; the slowly disintegrating ship; the subsequent movements and secondary depositions brought about by scouring and heavy seas; and the need to distinguish deposits of later material from bones contemporaneous with the ship by dint of their stratification in relation to the silts. Once deposited, albeit in stages, and dependent on differential waterlogging, strong currents and underwater collapse of the wreck, the archaeological artefacts are then subjected to a number of complicating post-depositional effects, for instance, conger eels live in and around them and may move things about.

Some of this is the same as conventional land-based archaeology except that the processes of silting involved are quite different. The organisms which cause breakdown and decay on the sea-bed are also different from those which work on surface and buried material on land, just as the exclusion of these organisms by oxygen-excluding silts provides different kinds of preservation in wrecks from material sealed into pits and occupation layers on land. The timescales are also quite different. Apart from the disasters, such as those mentioned above, archaeological excavations on land usually need to reconstruct more gradual processes such as the slow build-up of occupation layers or the relative speeds and types of deposition in pits and ditches.

The production of a sequential relationship of layers and linking this to a chronology, as on land-based sites (Harris 1979, 86), may not be quite so relevant to the

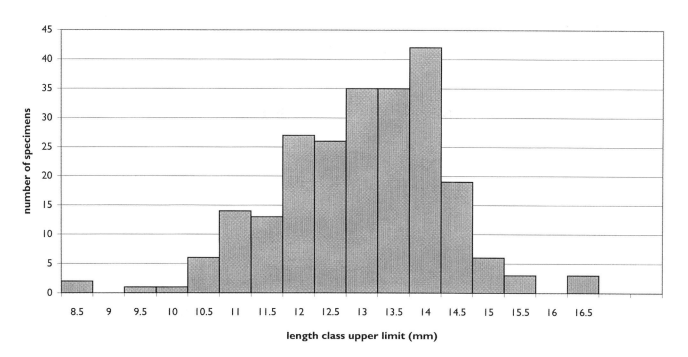

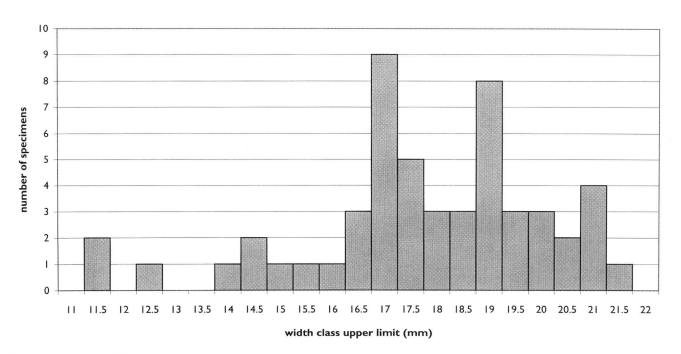

Figure 14.19 (top) Histogram of measurements of the centrum length of abdominal vertebrae; (bottom) histogram of measurements of the width of the cleithra (following Brinkhuizen 1994)

Mary Rose animal bones. Many of the bones were associated with or contained in specific structures, such as staved casks, so that they are obviously of Tudor date. However, there is a succession of less securely dated samples where the bones themselves provide an increasingly larger proportion of available evidence, culminating in some samples which are totally without associated finds and not stratified in Tudor layers, yet are below the shelly layer sealing the ship. In the case of bones recognisably Tudor in appearance, on the basis of the size of the animals or characteristic butchery, these can help to clarify the extent to which other material, both above and below this shelly layer, did, in fact, originate from the wreck.

In many ways this animal bone account is preliminary, comparable to a stratigraphic-based bone report for a land-based site written before ceramic analysis had been undertaken. Normally bone reports have to come after artefactual analysis has been completed because, whereas some objects can, to some extent, be dated by their intrinsic attributes, a bone cannot. Although the main bone material found in association with objects of Tudor date is very likely to be Tudor there are still many archaeological interpretations which can only be completed when data from the site notebooks, photographs and artefactual analysis have been thoroughly sifted. Some information from these sources may, in future, alter the conclusions above.

The measurements taken during the study of the animal bones form a useful database for future work. Not only will comparisons between this material and any future wreck studies be important but the bones themselves form a reference point for Tudor animal bone studies generally. In particular, the superb preservation of the Orlop pig deposit has provided an important insight into pigs of the time and will certainly repay further study.

Food, Packing and Plants on Board: the archaeobotanical evidence

Wendy Smith and F.J. Green
(incorporating contributions from P. Tomlinson and P. Dodd)

Background and introduction
F.J. Green

From the outset of the excavation the divers/excavators recognised the excellent state of preservation of organic materials. As a consequence, and to their credit, they instigated a programme of sampling from 1977 to 1986 that ultimately resulted in the recovery of over 6000 samples of which 287 were for archaeobotanical analysis, representing a minimum volume of 600 litres of sediment. (Sample volumes were not always recorded but typically ranged between 2 and 4 litres. Here we have used 2 litres as a minimum volume to indicate the approximate total volume of sediment sampled.) It is clear that very significant attempts were made to sample the wreck for plant and other biological remains. This report presents the results from the analysis of 112 of those samples, that was carried out in order to address the following questions:

- What plant remains occur on the *Mary Rose*?
- How might the plants identified have been used on board?

- Are certain plant remains specific to particular areas of the vessel, and does this indicate the location of definable activities or of storage areas on board?
- What lessons can be learned from the *Mary Rose* archaeobotanical study, which can be applied to future archaeobotanical analyses from shipwreck sites?

A formal rationale and research design for sampling does not appear to have been specifically or explicitly stated. This was entirely consistent with the standards prevailing on many archaeological sites excavated in the 1970s and early 1980s. In fact, the implementation of a sampling programme on an underwater site was entirely innovative at this time.

Most of the samples recovered result from observations made during excavation where it was clear that a deposit or context contained readily identifiable plant remains or other organic material. Samples were selected by the divers because the deposits looked interesting or plant remains were observed (ie, straw/hay, plums, etc).

Standard 3–4 litre samples (or 100% of the material if less than 3 litres) of observable plant matter and its surrounding sediment were collected in 10 litre containers. The cataloguing or indexing of samples as 'straw' or 'twigs' simply indicated the excavator's primary observation, quite often regardless of the sample's real content. In many cases this has led to assertions that specific contexts contained 'straw', which in some cases was not verified during the subsequent analysis of the sample. Plant material was not fully assessed or identified by archaeobotanists in the early stages of the work, and consequently myths about some botanical finds, such as the recovery of peas in pods (eg, Rule 1983b, 197), have entered the literature.

This study of sampled material, therefore, does not always provide answers to all of the obvious questions that might now be asked. However, the results clearly indicate that a wide range of plant-based food and materials were present and their sampling has further merit in suggesting advances for future programmes of research and for sampling methods on other wrecks.

Objectives of the project
The aims set in 1984 were to provide tangible evidence about the lifestyle of the crew in the early sixteenth century and the conditions that prevailed on board the ship. Establishing the range and nature of the provisions and their possible origins were major objectives. It was also considered that precise identification of wild plants, including both segetal (weeds of crops) and ruderal (weeds of waste places) species and those associated with cereal evidence, might provide information as to where the crops had originally grown. Well preserved sixteenth century cereals from daub or thatch in standing buildings were regarded as useful sources of

comparable data. It was further considered that there might be possibilities of increasing knowledge about ancient varieties of cereal or fruit crops (land-races) that had been genetically altered by traditional farming techniques. This latter objective was not of primary relevance to the research interests reported here and, therefore, remains an area for future research.

A formal assessment of the collected and stored samples in 1996 included examination of archaeo-botanical material from locations on the wreck known to have produced plant remains during excavation, but which had not been subject to any detailed exam-ination. The aims of this assessment were:

- to establish which samples were worthy of further analysis.
- to review and provide information about the collections long-term storage and curation in view of the considerable, and readily observable, degradation of some samples and plant materials.

The assessment allowed marine plants to be recognised and specifically excluded from the study of plant remains providing evidence of life on board. Details of the marine environment are presented in *AMR* Vol. 5.

The history of the plant remains study

Processing programme
A major programme of processing samples was instigated in 1979, but priorities in human resources undoubtedly lay in the recovery of objects and the structural elements of the ship. As such, the environ-mental and scientific processing and analysis programme was undertaken in a more *ad hoc* fashion (see Chapter 12 for an outline history).

Frank Green acted informally as the project's archaeobotanist, and his involvement was peripatetic and intermittent over approximately 20 years. Initial attention was placed on a programme of review, assessment and selecting material for analysis, and upon ensuring that verifiable identification of plant remains could take place. The tasks of managing and co-ordinating work on the environmental archaeological data were undertaken by Ian Oxley between 1980 and 1988, with advice from Frank Green. Oxley's tireless work in overseeing the storage and processing of the samples provided invaluable continuity; without his work this report would otherwise be significantly impoverished.

Assessment, review and selection
From 1971 until 1979 material recovered from the wreck was stored pending further examination and awaiting any archaeobotanical assessment. The majority of the samples were recovered from the 1979–1981 excavations, and immediately prior to lifting in 1982.

Ian Oxley, in conjunction with Frank Green, devised a programme of rapid inspection of the samples. Processing and sorting were undertaken by untrained, unskilled staff and volunteers who had to be trained 'on the job' and closely supervised to ensure good consistent results. Residues and sorted processed samples were periodically checked to ensure and maintain good standards.

Provisional identifications were made by Frank Green from 1982. This established the general range of species preserved on the wreck and highlighted areas of research, including the confirmation of some identifications through study at cellular level (by P. Tomlinson).

The archaeobotanical material was reviewed in 1984 by Green and colleagues (Peter Dodd, James Greig, Ian Oxley, Mark Robinson, Rob Scaife and Phillipa Tomlinson), and a number of subsidiary and specific studies were conducted. Detailed microscopic work was undertaken by Tomlinson to confirm macro-morphological identifications made by the author. The results of this work are incorporated in this report as are those of Dodd's on the plums.

In 1996–8 a formal assessment of the archaeobotanical data was conducted (by Green and Babita Sharma). Every available sample held in storage was inspected and data from previously recovered botanical material was considered. This included samples fully or partially processed, and recorded:
- the status and degree of decay of the samples,
- the quantity of material examined,
- details of disaggregation with hydrogen peroxide.

The bulk of the material examined was processed and archaeobotanical material extracted at the Mary Rose Trust, but few if any volumes were recorded. In 2002 several further samples were selected and processed for the first time (see processing) and the volumes of these samples were recorded.

In most cases the outer 50–80mm of the sample retained in 10 litre plastic containers had oxidised with a pronounced change of colour from a dark grey/black sediment to a distinctive brown colour. Where the entire sample or sub-sample had oxidised, in particular samples smaller than one litre, no further processing was undertaken.

This combination of assessment and previous reviews provided the final selection of samples for analysis that is reported below.

Storage and management of samples
Bulk samples of organic sediment and material, usually of 3–4 litres, were sampled from the sea-bed and stored in non-airtight 10 litre rigid plastic tubs with clip top lids. Samples were regularly monitored to top up their water content, but were not subject to any chemical preservation treatments. Bulk samples were stored and moved between various premises during the life of the project. Conditions varied between relatively stable environments (Old Bond Store premises 1971–1986), to those with extreme changes in temperature (former World War II air-raid shelter, 1986–2001).

590

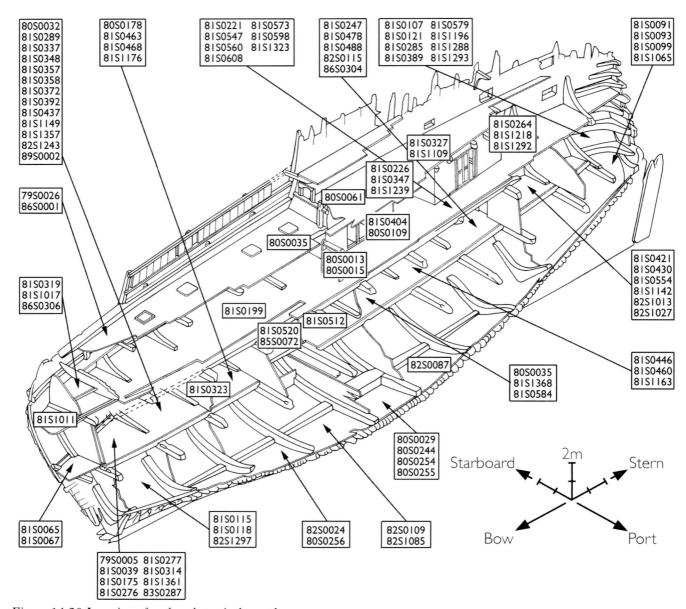

80S0032
81S0289
81S0337
81S0348
81S0357
81S0358
81S0372
81S0392
81S0437
81S1149
81S1357
82S1243
89S0002

80S0178
81S0463
81S0468
81S1176

81S0221 81S0573
81S0547 81S0598
81S0560 81S1323
81S0608

81S0247
81S0478
81S0488
82S0115
86S0304

81S0107 81S0579
81S0121 81S1196
81S0285 81S1288
81S0389 81S1293

81S0091
81S0093
81S0099
81S1065

79S0026
86S0001

81S0264
81S1218
81S1292

81S0327
81S1109

81S0226
81S0347
81S1239

80S0061

81S0404
80S0109

80S0035

80S0013
80S0015

81S0421
81S0430
81S0554
81S1142
82S1013
82S1027

81S0319
81S1017
86S0306

81S0199

81S0520
85S0072

81S0512

82S0087

81S0446
81S0460
81S1163

80S0035
81S1368
81S0584

81S0323

81S1011

80S0029
80S0244
80S0254
80S0255

81S0065
81S0067

81S0115
81S0118
82S1297

82S0024
80S0256

82S0109
82S1085

Starboard   2m   Stern

Bow   Port

79S0005 81S0277
81S0039 81S0314
81S0175 81S1361
81S0276 83S0287

Figure 14.20 Location of archaeobotanical samples

Plant and specific organic matter was stored in a wide range of other non-airtight containers. Initially they were stored in industrial methylated spirit (IMS). From 1984 some material was stored in an alcohol-glycerine formalin solution (AGF) (cf. Kenward *et al.* 1980, 8). The AGF solution was removed for the programme of identification and any botanical material extracted since 1996–7 has been stored in IMS. All the archaeobotanical material identified in this report was returned to the site archive in an AGF solution.

Unfortunately and inevitably, some of the labels had become worn or degraded and illegible which made for some difficulties during the later stages of reporting.

Processing and laboratory methods (1979–2002)
Samples were initially processed by the Mary Rose Trust, mainly from 1979 to 1986. Basic methodological information such as sample volume does not exist for many of the samples. Plant remains were largely recovered by flotation with

material collected on a 250 micron mesh sieve and transferred to containers of 50–100% IMS. Residues were water-sieved on a 250 micron mesh screen, and the archaeobotanical material was sorted from this and transferred into plastic boxes (Gardiner 2003). From 1984 some botanical material was stored in an alcohol-glycerine formalin solution (AGF).

During the assessment and re-evaluation phase (1996–8) unprocessed samples were disaggregated and the flots were collected in a 250 micron mesh sieve, and sorted. Botanical material was sorted and transferred to sample tubes and stored in IMS. The residues were washed over a 250 micron mesh sieve from which botanical and other material was removed for further examination.

In 2002 the plant remains were analysed under a low-power binocular microscope at magnifications of x15–x50. Identifications were made by comparison with material housed at the English Heritage Centre for Archaeology and Wendy Smith's personal comparative collecton. Identification

Common names for the Latin binomials used in the plant remains report and in Appendix 3

Latin Binomial	Common name	Latin binomial	Comon name
Cereals		*Cerastium* sp.	mouse-ear
Secale cereale L.	rye	*Agrostemma githago* L.	corncockle
Triticum aestivum L. type	hexaploid free-threshing wheat	Caryophyllaceae	pink family
Triticum sp.	free-threshing wheat	*Polygonum aviculare* L.	knotgrass
Cereal indeterminate.	indeterminate cereal	*Polygonum* sp./*Rumex* sp./*Carex* sp.	knotgrass/dock/sedge
Cereal/Poaceae	cereal/grass	*Polygonum* sp.	knotgrass
Clothworking plants		*Rumex* sp.	dock
Dipsacus sativus L.	fuller's teasel	*Malva* cf. *sylvestris* L.	possible common mallow
Dipsacus cf. *sativus* L - bract	possible fuller's teasel	*Viola* sp.	violet
Fibre crop		Brassicaceae	cabbage family
Cannabis sativa L.	hemp	*Brassica* sp./*Sinapsis* sp.	cabbage/mustard
Flavourings		*Agrimonia eupatoria* L.	agrimony
Humulus lupulus L.	hop	*Agrimonia* sp.	agrimony
Piper nigrum L.	pepper (black and/or white)	*Medicago lupulina* L.	black medick
Fruit		*Melilotus* sp./*Medicago* sp./*Trifolium* sp.	melilot/medick/clover
Prunus domestica s.l.	plum/greengage	cf. *Trifolium* sp.	possible clover
P. avium (L.) L./*cerasus* L.	cherry	Fabaceae? – *Vicia sativa* L.	pea family - ?common vetch
Prunus sp.	indet. plum/greengage/cherry	cf. *Chaerophyllum aureum* L.	possible golden chervil
Vitis vinifera L.	grape	cf. *Oenanthe* sp.	possible water-dropwort
Nuts		*Torilis* sp.	hedge-parsley
Juglans regia L.	walnut	*Daucus carota* L.	wild carrot
Cocus nucifera L.	coconut	cf. *Atropa bella-donna* L.	possible deadly nightshade
Corylus avellana L.	hazelnut	*Galeopsis* sp.	hemp-nettle
Tree/shrub		*Prunella vulgaris* L.	selfheal
Quercus sp.	oak	*Dipsacus* cf. *fullonum* L.	possible wild teasel
Cytisus sp.	broom	*Dipsacus* sp.	teasel
Weed/wild plant		*Carduus* sp./*Cirsium* sp.	thistle
Pteridium sp.	bracken	*Cirsium* sp.	thistle
Ranunculus acris L./*repens* L./*bulbosus* L.	meadow/creeping/bulbous buttercup	*Onopordum acanthium* L.	cotton thistle
R. flammula L. type	lesser spearwort type	*Picris* sp.	oxtongue
Ranunculus sp.	buttercup	*Sonchus* sp.	sow-thistle
Atriplex sp.	orache	*Taraxacum* sp.	dandelion
Chenopodiaceae/Caryophyllaceae	goosefoot/pink family	cf. *Achillea ptarmica* L./*millifolium* L.	possible sneezewort/yarrow
Stellaria media s.l.	common chickweed	*Anthemis cotula* L.	stinking chamomile/mayweed

criteria developed by Hall (1992) to distinguish fuller's teasel from wild teasel were used here, in addition to consulting modern comparative material.

Plant remains were categorised as follows: cereals (including both grain and chaff – which are treated separately statistically), fibre crop, fruit, flavourings, nuts, tree/shrub, clothworking plants, weed/wild plants and unidentified plants. Nomenclature for indigenous taxa follows Stace (1997) and that for economic plants follows Zohary and Hopf (2000). The traditional binomial system for cereals has been maintained here (Zohary and Hopf 2000, table 3 and table 5).

Data from samples that had been sub-divided during their original processing or sorting (Oxley 1986 and pers. comm. Frank Green) have been recombined for the purposes of this report. An Excel spreadsheet of individual results for each separate sub-sample has been placed on archive with the Mary Rose Trust.

Condition of the plant remains, location and quantification
Wendy Smith and F.J. Green

The majority of material examined was well preserved. Green even recorded that there was still a strong smell of pepper when a few of the ancient peppercorns were broken open. Items that had remained in IMS or AGF solution also clearly retained some of their original colouring, particularly the cereal grain, the grass stem fragments and moss (Plate 69). Typically, the cereal grain was red (anthocyanin pigmentation present). Stalks of what are most likely wild grasses, possibly derived from hay, were still clearly green (ie, chlorophyll still preserved). Oak leaves recovered from the Hold were still flexible even after storage in distilled water (Gardiner 2003).

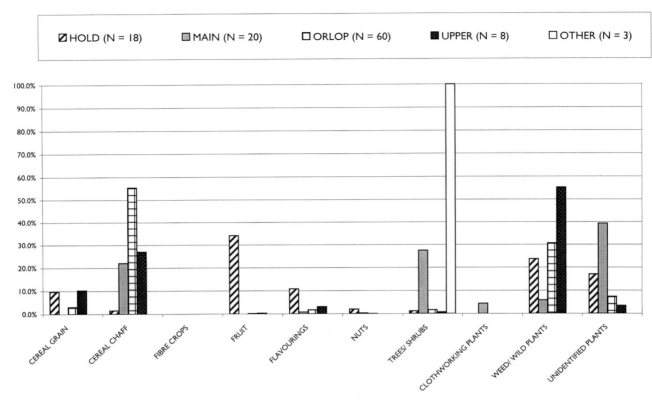

Figure 14.21 Breakdown of plant remains by deck and sector

Although the majority of material was originally stored in either IMS or AGF, approximately 25% had dried out by the time of reporting (2002). In most cases this does not appear to have affected the plant remains, however, more fragile material (such as grass caryopses) were clearly compressed or folded when dried out. Nevertheless, this only prevented accurate quantification/identification in one case and although rehydration was attempted, this was unsuccessful.

Of the total of 287 samples taken for the recovery of archaeobotanical remains, 39% (112 samples) were fully analysed, of which 106 contained plant remains (Appendix 3). The location of samples is biased (Fig. 14.20) as it is largely governed by the presence of containers (casks, baskets, chests and canisters) which might have been associated with plant matter and were recognised as such by the divers.

It was not always possible to record precise locations underwater, but nearly every sample is located to sector, if not to its direct association with a container. It was not always clear when several samples are derived from the same sector, whether these were all from the same deposit/container or from different deposits.

Despite some limitations, this is undoubtedly the most intensively sampled shipwreck to date. The general location of material is reliable, even though there was movement or mixing during sinking. It is possible, therefore, not only to define the plant contents of the ship (food, packing materials and other plants on board), but also to compare these results to those of other vessels.

In total, 5833 quantified identifications were made in addition to the unquantified material from the 112 samples studied in 2002 (Appendix 3, and archive; Fig. 14.20). The data in Appendix 3.1–3.5 only present remains studied in 2002 which are currently stored in the *Mary Rose* archive. A number of the samples previously examined by Green (1982–96) were not available for re-examination so, although they have been commented upon in this text, their identification cannot be further verified and they are not, therefore, included in the main data tables. Where they are discussed they are indicated by a★ and they are presented in Appendix 3.6. Some other finds are also no longer available for study, for example 30 plums that were defleshed for examination by Dodd, and grape skins examined by Tomlinson.

Most of the samples analysed were from the Orlop deck (57 samples, 54%). The most common plant remains are cereal chaff and weed/wild plants (Fig. 14.21), but fruit and flavourings dominate samples from the Hold and there are abundant remains of trees and shrubs throughout the Main deck (Fig. 14.21). Overall the assemblage is clearly dominated by cereal chaff (rachis, glumes and culm nodes), which account for nearly half of all the identifications recorded. Rye (*Secale cereale*) is the main cereal recorded, but small quantities of bread wheat (*Tricticum aestivum* type) were also recovered.

Table 14.11 Habitats of weeds/wild taxa indentiffed to genus or species level

	Latin binomial	Weeds of crops		Possible hay meadow taxa	Possible heath/moorland taxa	Possible free-draining soil conditions		Possible poorly drained soil conditions		Wet to dry conditions	Possible derelict ground or unshaded conditions					Possible shaded conditions				Common name
		Arable land	Cultivated ground Fields	Grassland	Acid soils Heath/moorland	Calcareous soils	Duneslack	Damp conditions	Wet places	Banks	Disturbed ground	Open ground	Rough ground	Wate ground	Wayside	Hedgerows	Scrub	Woodland	Wood clearing	
Typical crop weeds	*Stellaria media* s.l.		x									x								Common chickweed
	Agrostemma githago L.		x											x						Corncockle
	Brassica sp./*Sinapis* sp.	x												x						Cabbage/mustard
	cf. *Atropa bella-donna* L.		x											x			x	x		Possible deadly nightshade
	Dipsacus cf. *fullonum* L.			x										x				x		Possible wild teasel
	Onopordum acanthium L.			x									x	x						Cotton thistle
	Anthemis cotula L.	x				x							x	x						Stinking chamomile
	Avena sp.	x											x	x	x					Cultivated or wild oat
Typical grassland taxa	*Ranunculus acris* L./*repens* L./*bulbosus* L.			x	x	x		x	x										x	Meadow/creeping/bulbous buttercup
	Agrimonia eupatoria L.		x	x													x			agrimony
	Agrimonia sp.		x	x													x			Agrimony
	Medicago lupulina L.			x										x						Black medick
	cf. *Chaerophyllum aureum* L.			x																Possible golden chervil
	Daucus carota L. (uncultivated)			x		x								x						Carrot
	Prunella vulgaris L.			x										x					x	Selfheal
	Picris sp.			x							x		x	x						Oxtongue
	cf. *Achillea ptarmica* L./*millifolium* L.			x				x		x					x					Possible sneezewort/yarrow
Typical heath/moorland taxa	*Pteridium* sp.				x	x												x		
	Ranunculus flammula L. type							x												
	Polygonum aviculare L.										x									
	Malva cf. *sylvestris* L.												x	x						

Nomenclature and habitat information based on Stace (1997)

In addition to cereal crops, a wide range of other foodstuffs and/or economic plants has been identified. A hemp seed (*Cannabis sativa*) was recovered from one sample (81S0314C), and certainly hemp fibre was in extensive use on board (especially as rigging and other ropes and strops; see Chapter 15). Fruit remains are dominated by plum/ greengage stones (*Prunus domestica* s.l.), but also include cherry stones (*P. avium/cerasus*) and grape pips (*Vitis vinifera*). Nuts include both walnut (*Juglans regia*) and hazelnut (*Corylus avellana*), but coconut (*Cocus nucifera*) shells were also recovered. Flavourings include hop (*Humulus lupulus*) and pepper (*Piper nigrum*). The remains of trees and shrubs included oak (*Quercus* sp.) leaves, and broom (*Cytisus* sp.) leaves, stem and pods. Finally, bracts and pods of fuller's teasel (*Dipsacus sativus*) were also recovered.

Weed/wild plants account for nearly a third of all identifications. Most of the weed/wild taxa could not be attributed to a specific habitat, however crop weeds and plants typical of grassland habitats were frequently identified (Table 14.11 and see below).

Foodstuffs and seasoning

Cereal grain

Most of the cereal grain was concentrated towards the bow of the Orlop deck, especially in the galley store area of O3–4 (Fig. 14.22). Only small quantities of cereal grain were present, the majority of which was rye grain, encased within its surrounding chaff, that in many cases did not appear to be fully mature. It is unlikely that unprocessed, whole grain was stored on board. One notable absence from this assemblage is bran.

One common item of victualling would have been ship's biscuit. A great deal is known about its preparation from the seventeenth century but little is known of preparation in the early sixteenth century, although there are numerous records for provisioning (or, more usually, under-provisioning) the English fleet with biscuit at this time. No biscuit was found and, if present, then bran fragments might have been expected to survive in appreciable quantities. Several samples from staved containers and casks, which appeared to be

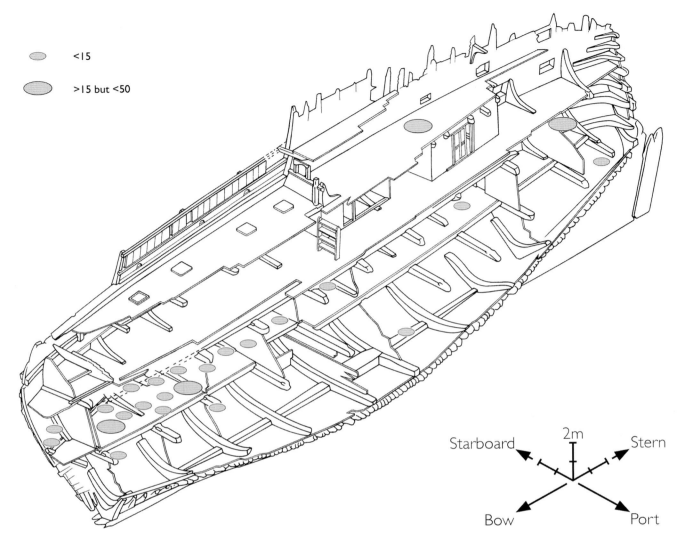

<15

>15 but <50

Starboard   2m   Stern

Bow   Port

Figure 14.22 Distribution of cereal grain

otherwise empty, were specifically examined for bran, however, none was present despite the excellent preservation of most other botanical material. Although sampling was not systematic, casks and objects were sampled. However, whether areas where bread/ biscuits/ flour was stored were sampled is not known.

There may have been no biscuit or flour on board, or it is conceivable that the samples were not taken from any of the actual storage areas of these goods. It might be assumed that the vessel, which was at war awaiting the French attack on Portsmouth Harbour, was provisioned with fresh bread. But the rapid departure of the ship may have left her without full complements of some essentials such as biscuit or bread.

Flavourings: pepper and hop
Flavourings (pepper and hop) were mainly recovered midship on the Orlop or Upper decks (Table 14.11) though pepper had the wider distribution (Orlop and Upper deck, 84 peppercorns; Main deck, 6; Hold, 27). In addition to these finds, further peppercorns* were also identified previously by Green from a sample

(80S0109/1) from the Main deck, but were not available for re-analysis in 2002. A total in excess of 650 peppercorns are recorded, of which only a proportion have been examined here (Table 14.12).

It is unclear whether both white and black pepper (white pepper simply being the peppercorn with the outer skin removed; Miller 1969, 80) were in use on board. Frank Green clearly remembers that all peppercorns he saw in the 1980s had the outer skin so taphonomic factors (possibly degradation in storage) may have resulted in the loss of the outer skin in some cases.

The recovery of pepper on several decks, including in the Hold (Table 14.12 and Appendix 3.1) suggests that, while it may have been a stored supply for the galley, most was brought on board and kept by individual crew members for their personal use as it was an expensive commodity. In addition to loose finds of pepper, it was also found in a chest (81A2099, O9) and a box (81A3065, O8) on the Orlop deck and within a basket (80A1704) in the Hold (H6). Two spice mills (presumed to be used for grinding pepper) were also recovered during excavation (see Chapter 11). In

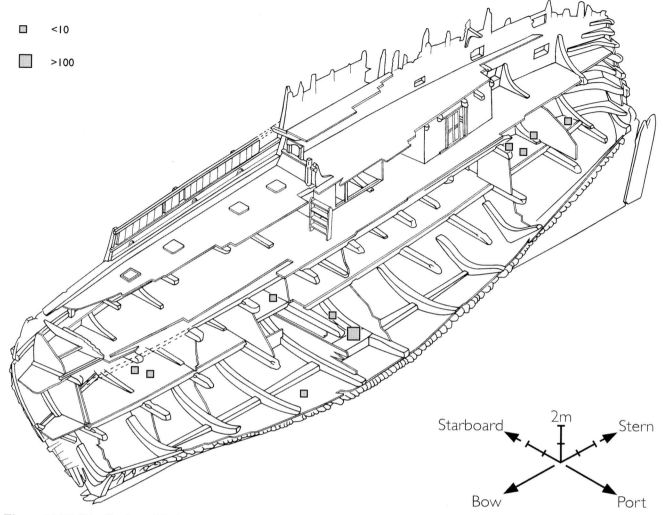

□ <10

■ >100

Starboard
2m
Stern

Bow
Port

Figure 14.23 Distribution of fruit

addition to pepper's uses as a flavouring, we can also suggest that pepper was brought on board for medicinal purposes, since peppercorns were recovered with medicinal supplies from within the Barber-surgeon's chest (see Chapter 4). Besides stimulating digestion,

Table 14.12 Records of peppercorns

Associated	Sample	Location	Count
Flask 81A2034	81S1109	U9	9
Chest 81A2099	81S0347	U9	58*
Canister 80A1561	80S0143	M7	67
Chest 80A1530	80S0109	M7	*c.*20$
Tankard 81A1392	81S0264	M9	2*
Box 81A3065	81S1163	O8	15*
Chest 81A3285	81S0479	O9	456
	81S0489	O9	4
Textile in chest 81A3285	86S0304	O9	1*
Basket 80A1784	80S0254	H6	27*
Approximate total			659

* recorded in Appendix 3.1; $ = some recorded in Appendix 3.6

pepper was considered good for constipation and urinary organs, and was also used in the treatment of gonorrhoea (Grieve 1992, 627), warts and yellow jaundice. Some early sixteenth century medicinal recipes that used pepper are given in Chapter 4.

A few hop seeds were recovered from the Orlop deck and the Hold (Appendix 3.1). The small quantities recovered suggest that they were accidental contaminants, possibly coming in with the beer (ale) in staved containers. Although the source(s) for the supply of beer (ale) are not completely known, it is clear that beer (ale) was an essential food item on board the *Mary Rose* (*AMR* Vol 1, Appendix), and a quantity of a gallon a day per man was the stated ration (see discussion below).

In a situation where the cleanliness of water was uncertain, beer or ale provided one of the safest beverages to consume:

'The processes of brewing ... produced a liquor that was not only quite sterile in itself, as far as human pathogenic organisms were concerned, but also

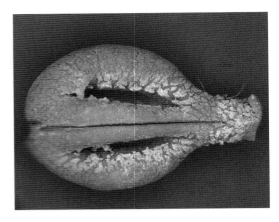

Figure 14.24 (left) Plums/greengages as recovered from basket 81A1704, (right) grape pip at x20 magnification

resisted any attempt to infect it with hostile bacteria'. (Corran 1975, 35)

Although the intoxicating effects of alcoholic beverages may be seen as a disadvantage, the process of fermentation, itself, is beneficial to health. In addition to beer being a useful source of carbohydrates, *'Fermentation is a critical food-processing method for recent and modern traditional diets, because it can boost levels of important nutrients such as essential amino acids, decreases harmful compounds, improves storage qualities, and textures'* (Samuel 1997, 580).

Hop also has medicinal uses and may have been brought on board for that purpose. Thomas Green (1824, 715) records that *'young shoots are eaten early in the spring as asparagus, and are sold under the name of hop-tops, which are said to be* [a] *diuretic, and good for the scurvy, taken by infusion'*. A decoction of fresh hops is also considered a cure for jaundice (Green 1824, 715) and as a pain killer (see Chapter 4). A hop pillow was used to relieve toothache and/or earache (Grieve 1992, 414).

Fruit

Nearly all of the fruit, predominantly plum/greengage (*Prunus domestica* s.l.) stones (Figs 14.23 and 14.24), was recovered from a single basket (80A1704) in the Hold (Appendix 3.1), with a few found on the Orlop deck (O10). Identification to the precise variety of *P. domestica* (ie, plum rather than greengage/damson) was not explored further because of the clear overlap in size range of plums and greengages observed in modern comparative material. It was also clear from historical records for 1545 (as well as preceding years) that Britain suffered several springs of bad weather, resulting in failed wheat crops. This may also have affected the size of plum/greengage fruits and their stones. In addition, very small quantities of cherries (*Prunus avium/cerasus*) and grapes/raisins (*Vitis vinifera*) were also recovered (Fig. 14.24). It is not possible, based on the seed (stone or pip), to determine if dried or fresh fruit was in use, certainly in both the cases of plums/prunes and grapes/raisins either is possible. Although it would be interesting to identify which species of cherry (or cherries) were present on board the *Mary Rose*, this was not attempted. There is some overlap in the size ranges for stones of wild (also called sweet – *Prunus avium* (L.) and dwarf (also called sour or morello – *P. cerasus* L.) cherry. Zohary and Hopf (2000, 181) provide a size range for *P. cerasus* stones of 9–13mm and report that *Prunus avium* stones typically range from 7–9mm. In addition, Stace (1997, 365) reports that the fruit (so the stone with the flesh still present) of *P. avium* ranges from 9–12mm, and potentially the stones could be slightly larger (possibly up to 10mm) based on this. Regardless, the fact that the largest recorded length for *P. avium* matches the smallest recorded length for *P. cerasus* does indicate that there is potential for overlap. The archaeological material fell into this 9–10mm range and, therefore, further identification was not pursued. Again, the poor weather conditions in 1545 may also have affected the size of wild/dwarf cherries and their stones.

The largest concentration of fruit available for study in 2002 was that found in a basket (81A1704) in H6, where 81 plum/greengage stones were recovered (records of previous work by Dodd and Green suggest that the original total count was nearer 117 stones or whole fruit). This area of the Hold is immediately adjacent to the galley. Previous work by Dodd (1983; 1986) on a selection of 30 plum stones[*] identified Catalonia plum, Mirabelle (de Nancy) plum, greengage, cherry plum and/or yellow cherry plum as the possible sub-species of *Prunus domestica* in use on board. Dodd (1986) suggests that some varieties of greengage/plum could have been ripe by the time the *Mary Rose* sailed (mid July), but this does not preclude the possibility that prunes (dried plums/greengage) were used. Certainly prunes would have been easier to store and less fragile to transport. Other plums/greengages were found with baskets 80A0963, 80A1704, 81S1142 and 81A5102 and in the Hold and on the Orlop decks.

A few grapes/raisin pips were also recovered from a basket (81A1704) in H6. It is possible, therefore, to suggest that some of the plums/greengages and grapes/raisins were galley supplies, but whether their consumption was limited to the officers is not clear.

Two grape skins★ (recorded by Green prior to 2002) were identified from a small cask (81A2959) on the Orlop deck (O10; 81S0416/2), and this was later confirmed by examination of the epidermal cell pattern (P. Tomlinson, pers. comm.). The absence of grape pips in this container may suggest that the grape skins are from the dregs of wine stored in the container, or possibly contaminants from a previous use. That they may alternatively represent verjuice – '*made from the grapes that were unripe at the end of the season [and] fermented to form a kind of sharp vinegar*' (Hagen 1995, 222) – cannot be ruled out as a possibility; however surviving records of beverages supplied to the *Mary Rose* are exclusively related to wine or beer (eg, *AMR* Vol. 1, appendix). Some of the possibly empty staved containers may also have held wine and at least one wine measure for serving the drink was recovered (see Chapter 11).

An apple (*Malus sylvestris* (L.) Mill.) pip★ (recorded by Green prior to 2002) was also present in the Hold (H11; 81S0099/4/1) associated with basket 81A4036.

Nuts

Finds of coconut, hazelnut and walnut shells were made as isolated finds throughout the vessel (Appendix 3.1). Only small quantities (ie, <3 complete nuts) were found of all three taxa. The largest concentration (1 walnut shell and 3 hazelnuts) was in H11. Two half coconut shells were found, one on the Orlop deck (85S0072) associated with basket 80A0963 (found with a plum/greengage stone), and one on the Main deck (81S1292), but as both are from post-Tudor deposits, they are not necessarily contemporary with the ship. In addition to these 'unworked' finds of coconut, half a coconut cup (77A0096) was also recovered, unstratified in the Starboard Scourpit. The archaeological context of these coconut finds remains insecure and it is not possible to claim with any certainty that they were in use on board (see Chapter 11).

Nuts do not appear be particularly abundant on board. This may relate to the season of the shipwreck; in summer supplies of the previous autumn's nuts might be limited, and it would be too early for fresh hazelnuts or walnuts.

Edible pulses: a significant absence

Although a find of a garden pea (*Pisum sativum* L.) was published (Rule 1983b, 197), none was present in material analysed and it is assumed that this was a provisional identification, during excavation or processing. The intact legume pods, which have survived, are broom (*Cytisus* sp.). Edible pulses are absent from the assemblage.

This absence is particularly significant, because the historical literature suggests that pulses (especially peas) were an important component of maritime diet in the period (below). Although preservation of edible and non-edible leguminous seeds is very rare in waterlogged conditions (Hall 1996, 636), and they tend to dissolve in water, it is possible that edible pulses were stored in areas of the ship that did not survive, or in casks that were lost or disintegrated. The Hold was not as intensively sampled for plant remains as other decks and it is possible that such foodstuffs are under-represented.

Buckwheat

A single buckwheat seed (*Fagopyrum esculentum* Moench)★ from the Orlop deck (O11) (81S0349) was recorded by Green prior to 2002 and this identification was confirmed by cellular examination by Phillipa Tomlinson. Since only a single seed was identified, it is not possible to claim that this was foodstuff on board the *Mary Rose*. It is possible that this was accidentally incorporated as a contaminant of cereal or other crops (eg, peas or beans), as buckwheat may have been growing as a result of a previous season's crop. Since no other botanical material, especially crop plants, was identified from this sample, this interpretation is hypothetical.

Recovery of foodstuffs

The recovered plant-based foodstuffs on board are limited. Certainly, the assemblage is dominated by inedible elements such as cereal chaff and weed/wild seeds (Fig. 14.21; Appendix 3.4 and 3.5). There is no evidence that livestock were kept aboard, so cereal chaff, hay, bracken and broom were not fodder (see discussions below). Foodstuffs that were present are items that could have been served whole and in a raw state (nuts or fruit) or stored whole (pepper). The majority of plant-based victuals were supplied already processed, such as bread, biscuit, flour, beer or wine – none of which was likely to survive intact or be identifiable from bulk samples. Fully processed foodstuffs would have been a realistic choice of provision. Some processed food items may simply have floated away, decayed or have been consumed by marine life.

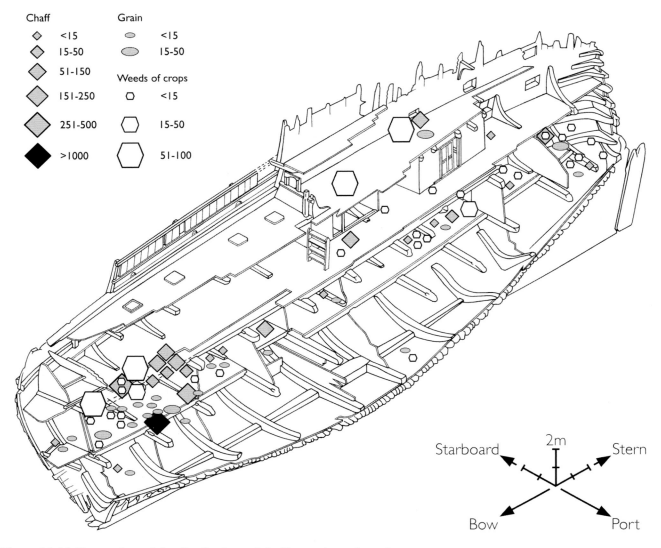

Chaff
◇ <15
◇ 15-50
◆ 51-150
◆ 151-250
◆ 251-500
◆ >1000

Grain
⬭ <15
⬬ 15-50

Weeds of crops
⬡ <15
⬡ 15-50
⬡ 51-100

Starboard 2m Stern
Bow Port

Figure 14.25 Comparison of the distributions of chaff to grain and weeds

Other plant material on board

Cereal chaff

Cereal chaff (and small quantities of cereal grain coming in with the chaff) was primarily recovered from the Orlop deck, with particularly high concentrations centred in O3 (Fig. 14.25). This suggests that cereal chaff was in use or stored, in particular, throughout the Orlop deck. It may have been used as bedding, packing or even wadding for the cannons.

Cereal chaff remains are primarily dominated by rye (*Secale cereale*). Rye has been recovered from a number of medieval sites in southern England, such as Priory Barn, Taunton, Somerset (Greig and Osborne 1984), Ower Farm and Wareham, Dorset (Carruthers 1991a; 1991b; Green 1978; Monk 1980), and Winchester and Romsey, Hampshire (Green 1984; 1991). Rye has also been recovered in a number of fifteenth–sixteenth deposits of smoke-blackened thatch from southern England, for example in Hampshire at Kings Sombourne, in Somerset at Middle Chinnock and

Crewkerne, in Wiltshire at Tisbury, and at numerous sites in Devon (Letts 1999, 52–7).

Rye crops appear to be primarily recovered from medieval sites in the Dorset and Devon area, but this may reflect the pattern and intensity of archaeological analyses in those areas. Rye recovered from Kings Sombourne, Romsey and Winchester suggests that a Hampshire source is possible. It is also conceivable that the rye chaff was imported (see below).

Hay

A large sample (*c.* 250ml) of wild grass stalks (primarily without seed heads or culm nodes and, therefore, unquantifiable) was recovered from M8 near a gun sled (81S0404). Smaller quantities were identified in samples from the Orlop deck. The absence of seed heads and culm bases (root structures) in this material strongly suggests that it was intentionally cut as hay.

The limited range of weed and wild taxa accompanying these possible hay deposits included ?clover (Fig. 14.26, left), agrimony (Fig. 14.26, right), black

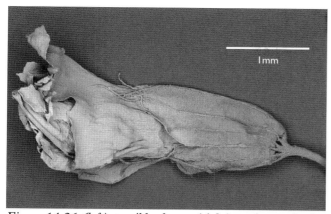 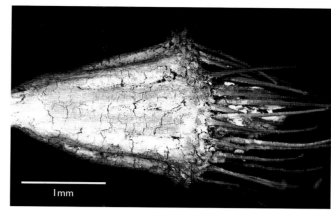

Figure 14.26 (left) possible clover; (right) agrimony, both at x 20 magnification ©English Heritage

medick, buttercup, possible golden chervil, oxtongue, selfheal, possible sneezewort/yarrow, and wild carrot, all of which occur in grassland habitats and are not particularly associated with cultivated land. This range of grassland taxa supports the interpretation that this was hay. Like cereal chaff, hay would have been useful as a bedding material and as wadding for the cannons.

Alex Naylor reported (in 1986; archive) that 'hay' was found on the two probable beds in the Carpenters' cabin (M9; see Chapters 1 and 8). These were not examined in 2002 and his first observation, on surveying the results of processing, was that the recovered plant material in twelve of the 20 sediment samples taken appeared to be hay as opposed to straw. Observations made during the processing of samples from elsewhere on the ship were that straw was the predominant component. Photographic records (Plate 69) show that this 'hay' also included hypnoid moss (ident. from photograph, P. Murphy).

Naylor reported that, in the Carpenters' cabin, the 'hay' was clearly discernible from straw in appearance, being fine and less robust, often retaining green colouring and smelling remarkably fresh. It also displayed less evidence of the fungal growth on the stems that was often visible on the straw. Hay was found in samples from the aft and, chiefly, the forward 'bed' or 'shelves' and on the decking beneath them (see Figure 12.1). The 'hay' in all of these samples was similar in texture, degree of degradation and colour. Textiles of varying types were associated with the hay, usually surviving only as tiny fragments and often compacted onto the hay, making their removal very difficult.

Although samples containing hay and textile combined were taken mainly from the forward bed, the liberal covering of hay all over the raised planking and the decking was probably caused when the cabin filled with water and dispersed everything which lay loose.

Weeds/wild plants

Most of the weeds/wild plants identified to species level (N = 199 or 12.1%) are taxa typically occurring as crop weeds, such as common chickweed, corncockle, cabbage/mustard (*Brassica* sp./*Sinapis* sp.), possible deadly nightshade (cf. *Atropa bella-donna*), ?wild teasel (*Dipsacus* cf. *fullonum*), cotton thistle (*Onopordum acanthium*), stinking chamomile (*Anthemis cotula*) and wild and/or cultivated oat (*Avena* sp.). Calcareous soils may be indicated by the presence of wild carrot (*Daucus carota*), while weed and wild taxa indicative of heavier soils include stinking chamomile (*Anthemis cotula*), and meadow/creeping/bulbous buttercup (*Ranunculus acris/ repens/bulbosus*). Those typical of damp or wet conditions include buttercup, lesser spearwort type (*Ranunculus flammula* type) and possible sneezewort/ yarrow (cf. *Achillea ptarmica/ millefolium*). Finally, pot marigold (*Calendula officinalis* L.)★ was recorded by Green from sample 81S1289/4/1; however, this sample was not available for re-analysis at the time of this study.

The weed/wild plants are primarily concentrated on the Orlop deck, especially in O2, O4, O5 and O8. Although there is a strong correlation between those typical crop weeds and the cereal grain and chaff remains (Fig. 14.25), their concentration does not always correlate with richer deposits of cereal chaff. This suggests that the weed/wild taxa not only came in as weeds of the rye crop, but are derived from a variety of sources.

Bracken

Bracken (*Pteridium* sp.) is particularly abundant in O3 (Appendix 3.4), associated with rope and textiles, where three samples have produced large quantities of bracken leaf (119, 221 and *c*. 300 leaves). Bracken has also been recovered from O4 and O6 (Appendix 3.5).

Bracken was widely used in the past for bedding or to stuff mattresses, especially since it was believed (and now has been proven) to keep down pests and parasites (Page 1988, 25). In the nineteenth century (but possibly earlier) bracken was used as a packing medium for such items as fish, cherries and potatoes (Page 1988, 26–7). Although large quantities of fish bone were recovered from the Orlop deck (Hamilton-Dyer, above; 1995), the distribution of bracken and fish does not appear to demonstrate any correspondence.

Rushes

A large quantity of rush seeds was recovered from the Upper deck (U8; Appendix 3.5). Rushes are frequently deliberately gathered as flooring material (Jones *et al.* 1991, 381); they can be used as brushes, in basketry or for thatch (Dickson and Dickson 2000, 93). The inner pith of some taxa (eg, *Juncus effusus* L.) was collected to be used as wicks.

Oak and broom

Remains of oak (leaves) and broom (stem and pods) were recovered. Large concentrations of broom (*Cytisus* sp.) stems have been recovered in samples of twigs from O2 (14 + *c.* 150 ml broom stems) and M2 (184 broom stems). Large quantities (*c.* 100 fragments) of broom stem were also found in O11 (Appendix 3.3). Some broom pods from samples taken in M2, O2 and O5 were previously identified as the native broom *Cytisus scoparius* (L) Link* (ident. P. Tomlinson), on the basis of cell structure.

Records of delivery of broom to naval vessels exist from the reign of Henry VII (eight loads cited in Oppenheim 1896b, 175) and from records in 1691 (54 faggots cited in Hattendorf *et al.* 1993, 263). Fires made from wet broom were used to disinfect ships in 1588 (Keevil *et al.* 1957, 74). Broom may have been used as a cleaning material on board – to make up brooms and brushes used for sweeping or scouring. All recorded besoms examined on board were made from hazel twigs with possible elm handles but simple bundles of broom twigs were often used as brushes at this time. Certainly, scrubbing decks seems to have been a pre-occupation in all periods – presumably to reduce accidents, and a number of leather and wooden buckets, as well as brooms and brushes, were found on the *Mary Rose* (see Chapter 8). Eighteenth century records suggest that broom was used with hot sand to cleanse decks (Keevil *et al.* 1957, 75). The larger twigs/branches recovered were probably used as fuel.

It is possible that broom was used as 'dunnage' (a springy layer of twigs and brush placed between the ship's hull and cargo as a form of packing). Evidence from Mediterranean wrecks show that thorny burnet (*Sarcopoterium spinosum* (L.)) was used for dunnage (Haldane 1993) and broom may have been used as a British equivalent.

Hemp and teasel

One fibre crop was identified on board. A single hemp seed (*Cannabis sativa*) was recovered in O2 (Appendix 3.3). Hop or hemp pollen has also been identified (Chapter 15 and *AMR* Vol. 2) and all surviving cordage is made of hemp. The ship's caulking may also have included hemp (eg, Cappers *et al.* 1998; Scaife, Chapter 15). Fuller's teasel bracts (*Dipsacus sativus*) and seed have also been recovered (Appendix 3.2), primarily from M9, near the Carpenters' cabin (at least 23 bracts

and 1 seed), and were associated with a leather textile fragment (possibly a jerkin, 81A4708).

In addition to these finds, teasel (*Dipsacus sativus*)* bracts were also recorded by Green previously from other samples (81S0573) associated with the same possible jerkin. He noted that material in sub-sample 81S0573/1 contained very fine, compressed, comminuted fibre material, which was considered to be similar to material from historic millboard.

Fuller's teasel heads are primarily used to raise the '*nap in the finishing of woollen cloth...* [or] *in the manufacture of felt*' (Hall 1992, 9). It seems unlikely that such clothworking activities were taking place on board; however, it is possible that small quantities of fuller's teasel bracts (the teeth on the teasel heads) came in with wool or felted woollen clothing (see Chapter 2).

Flax/linseed

Two capsule fragments of flax/linseed (*Linum usitatissimum* L.)* were previously identified by Green, associated with a gunshield (a firearm consisting of a small gun attached to the back of a circular iron and wood shield), on the Orlop deck (O10), and may be from linseed oil used to oil the mechanism of the gun. This only represents one plant and, therefore, is most likely an accidental incorporation into this assemblage. Flax/linseed could be a contaminant of a cereal crop; it is very rare in the pollen spectra from the ship (Chapter 15; *AMR* Vol. 2).

Charred plant remains

Only a small quantity of plant remains from the ship (0.1% of the overall assemblage) was charred. This material came from a single sample from the Carpenters' cabin (in chest 81A5783) and one from the Orlop deck (with a pewter dish 81A3310 in O4); all were unidentifiable (Appendix 3.3). The location of these charred remains does not appear to be significant.

Discussion: food, packing/bedding materials and plants on board

The assemblage appears to have been dominated by packing and/or bedding materials, rather than plant-based food supplies. Only a limited number of flavourings (pepper and hop), nuts (hazelnut, walnut and coconut) and fruit (grape, plum/greengage and cherry) were recovered. Instead of foodstuffs, plant material such as cereal chaff (primarily rye), bracken fronds and broom twigs/stems and leaves are abundant in this assemblage. These materials would have been useful for a variety of tasks on board. Seeds of weeds and/or wild plants also formed a major component of the assemblage, however, these most likely entered the deposits as contaminants of the rye chaff, hay or bracken.

Food and seasoning

The range of plant foods recovered is limited. Flavourings (pepper and hop), nuts (hazelnut, walnut and possibly coconut) and fruit (grape, plum/greengage and cherry) were largely associated with baskets or other containers. Basket 80A1704 from the Hold (H6), for instance, produced 27 peppercorns, at least 117 plums/greengages and 3 grape pips. Indeed all 91 of the plum/greengages (*P. domestica*) were from baskets or chests.

Whilst there are some sources of historical information for provisioning and victualling at sea, there is limited information from the sixteenth century. In addition, surviving documents recording victualling are often quite general, with specific foodstuffs only rarely mentioned (below and see, for instance, *AMR* Vol. 1, Appendix). Peppercorns, in particular, are recorded from other contemporaneous wrecks such as that in Studland Bay, *c.* 1520–1530 (Ladle 1993), but have also been recorded elsewhere in the world from wrecks such as the *Shinnan Gun*, Korea dating to 1266-1368 (Delgado 1997, 371–2), the Dutch East Indiaman *Kennermerland*, Scotland, 1664 (Price and Muckelroy 1977; Muckelroy 1978, fig 2.14), and the Portuguese galleon *Santissimo Sacramento*, Brazil, 1668 (Delgado 1997, 360–1).

According to the *Anthony Roll* of 1546 there were at least 415 men who needed to be fed. Of these at least 185 were soldiers and 30 were gunners, who may have only required feeding for the time spent away from the port. Based on the possible rations suggested for the *Mary Rose* (below), the daily ration per sailor would have included one pound of biscuit. In addition, twice a week, a pint of peas was included with servings of pork. On the basis of the bone evidence (above) it is clear that provision of meat and fish to the *Mary Rose* was sufficient to supply several days worth of rations. Therefore, although there is no archaeobotanical evidence, it is likely that biscuit and possibly peas may have been supplied as well.

Bedding, packing and stuffing

Bracken was recovered with unidentified textile fragments in O3 (81S0372C). The bracken could have been used as stuffing for the garment represented (see below). Cereal chaff (primarily rye) and its accompanying weeds, as well as bracken (*Pteridium* sp.), dominate in O3. Cereal chaff is also fairly abundant in O11. Fragments of broom (*Cytisus* sp.) stems are particularly concentrated in O2 and M2 – both areas that were badly damaged in the sinking. Nevertheless, the concentration of non-edible plant remains in the fore and aft of the Orlop deck and in the fore of the Main deck is worth further discussion. Certainly the Orlop deck is well represented in this analysis, with a total of 62 samples studied, which suggests that any patterning observed in the results from this deck is likely to be representative. The Orlop deck was the main storage deck with specific areas demonstrably used for the storage of specific items (see above and Chapter 10, for instance) while the Main deck was both the principal gun deck and had several cabins. The significance of the distribution of possible storage items on this deck is not clear.

The most likely use of cereal chaff on board the *Mary Rose* would have been as stuffing (eg, mattresses and shoes) and possibly as wadding for the cannons. Bracken and/or hay could also be used as stuffing, general packing materials (for food or equipment), or wadding. Broom could be either used as fuel or, indeed, used to make up brooms, or even as fresh material for stuffing or packing.

Plants with cloth and clothing

Plant remains were found in association with clothing and textiles. Bracken was recovered with textile, and rye chaff with two jerkins on the Orlop deck (81A2228 and 81A4693). Teasel bracts were also recovered with a leather fragment, possibly part of a jerkin, in M9 (81A4708). Unidentified leaves (broad leaves from either trees or shrubs) were recovered inside shoes in M2 (81A0161) and H11 (81A0890).

Two samples of rye were recovered, in both cases fewer than ten ears were present. Given the time of year and the overcrowded conditions on the *Mary Rose*, it seems unlikely that the sailors would have used rye chaff to pad their jerkins. It is possible that a small quantity of cereal chaff to be used as wadding was kept in the jerkin of a gunner in readiness for the next firing. It also is possible that mattresses were stuffed in part with cereal chaff.

Finds of leaves, chaff, teasel bracts and agrimony burrs (fruiting hypanthium; Fig. 14.26, right) with items of clothing, including shoes, may be just the incidental inclusion of plant remains, possibly brought in as sailors boarded or supplies were loaded. This is particularly true of barbed seed capsules, such as the agrimony burrs, including those found with a large sack cloth (sample 81S1302/3 with 81A1233 in O2) which could easily have become attached to clothing or cloth while on shore. In addition, Green previously identified agrimony (*Agrimonia eupatoria*)*, recovered with the same piece of sackcloth (81S1302/3). This was not available for examination in 2002.

Plant materials in the ship's construction

Several caulking samples were examined and although no plant macrofossils were recognisable, pollen evidence (see Scaife, Chapter 15) indicates that hemp (*Cannibis sativa*) and nettle (*Urtica* type) were major components of caulking. Pollen from a sample of sail cloth (81A2603) from O3 was also examined and suggest that hemp and nettle fibres were the main constituents.

Trade and supply: sources of material

Both the coconuts (if contemporary with the ship) and pepper suggest trade contacts well beyond southern England. However, it is clear that such items were regularly shipped to English ports in the sixteenth century (James 1990; Stevens and Olding 1985), and so these could have been acquired through local markets. Crops that could be grown in England were also imported from overseas. For example, there are records for the shipment of plums into Southampton in 1509–10 (James 1990).

The bracken and broom are likely to have come from sources fairly local to Portsmouth; however, the rye chaff is more problematic. Although rye is recovered occasionally from Saxon and medieval sites in southern England, it is not a particularly prevalent cereal crop in the region (Green 1984; 1991). In addition there is good evidence to suggest that the 1545 harvest (ie, the crop sown spring 1545 and harvested that autumn, after the ship sank) was not successful. Both Rogers (1866–1902, 260) and Baker (1883, 120) report that '*Wheat during the greater part of the year is at famine prices.*' It also is clear that by late 1544 prices for cereals were rising in anticipation of the poor harvest of 1545 (Rogers 1866–1902, 260). In 1539 '*the office of the King's merchant*' was established at Danzig with the intention of supplying grain in years of shortage (Davies 1965, 276). Although it is possible that the rye chaff recovered on the *Mary Rose* may have come originally from that area or elsewhere in mainland Europe, none of the weed/wild taxa recovered is exclusive to continental Europe.

Records on victualling the *Mary Rose* and other naval ships in the period (*AMR* Vol. 1, Appendix) suggest that a number of sources from London to Plymouth were utilised by the navy to supply ships. The Isle of Wight and Southampton (Hampton) are frequently mentioned as sources for supplies. In the main, records of the supply of beer and biscuit include many complaints about the shortage or lateness of supplies.

Overview

Perhaps the most significant feature of the plant remains is that it is an assemblage from a securely dated time capsule – providing a glimpse of the plants used on the *Mary Rose* and accidentally preserved by the catastrophic event of the sinking of the vessel. Moreover the waterlogged conditions ensured that the plant remains were in a good state of preservation. The assemblage is, therefore, unlike the majority of assemblages from land-based excavations that include debris accumulated over many years, and that are primarily composed of charred remains and are biased by those taxa more likely to be charred.

Expectations of what the plant materials might tell us about Tudor maritime life were greater than what

emerged in reality. Material from a trading or merchant vessel of the same period would probably have provided much greater information. Nevertheless, the archaeobotanical assemblage discussed here is unparalleled. Rather meagre assemblages have, on occasion, been recovered and studied from other underwater wrecks, though many are reported in interim form only. These included wheat, pepper and figs from the contemporaneous Studland Bay wreck *c.* 1530 (Ladle 1993), and barley husks, grape, peppercorns and stones of plum or prune from the later *Kennermerland* wreck 1664 (Price and Muckelroy 1977; Muckleroy 1978, fig 2.14).

The plant remains provide an otherwise unrecorded glimpse into the supply of plant-based materials to a Tudor vessel and a range of tantalising evidence. It is quite clear that much of the material examined was brought on board for specific use. However, analysis of this material alone does not always establish precisely how it was used. It is all too easy to dismiss interpretations of the assemblage as mundane, simply because we have recovered plant remains most likely used for packaging, bedding, stuffing and padding purposes. Nevertheless, these relatively mundane uses are what occurred on board and provide an insight into naval life in the Tudor period. However we cannot be certain that the rye straw, for instance, was used as bedding or wadding for the guns, or that broom was used for cleaning down the decks. All we can do is suggest that these are the most likely uses of such materials on board. Equally, we cannot be certain if the evidence of foodstuffs is representative of what may have been on board when the ship sank. This assemblage does, however, generate an important and otherwise unrecorded source of data that is crucial to understanding conditions on board the *Mary Rose*, and that is of relevance to other Tudor vessels.

'Flesh, Fish, Biscuit and Beer': Victuals for the Ship
Jennie Coy and Sheila Hamilton-Dyer

In terms of the evidence it has produced for the provision of food and drink to a naval warship during the sixteenth century, the *Mary Rose* is unique. The array of objects and organic food remains are of great archaeological and historical importance, not only because of their range and quantity but also because the assemblage represents the remains of a working 'kitchen' and galley store at the moment of its destruction. Consequently, although much was lost, damaged or destroyed during and after the sinking, we are able to catch glimpses of real provisions – meats, fish and other foodstuffs actually in storage or preparation – and of the items required for the storage, cooking, serving and consumption of meals. These objects are described and discussed in Chapter 11. Here we attempt to assess the animal remains from the ship against historical information on the victualling of Henry VIII's navy. Mindful of the fragmentary and incomplete nature of our evidence – both archaeological and historical – we can only offer some suggestions and possibilities.

Reconstruction of the menu

Sixteenth century information suggests that shipboard provisions would have included rations for four days in every week when 'flesh' (meat) would be served and three days of fish. Comparison of the recorded weekly shipboard rations of three centuries (Davies 1963a, 139; Maybray King 1968, 49; Anon 1731, 60; and see Rodger 1997) shows such close uniformity that it is possible to predict the weekly ration per man on the *Mary Rose* as:

> 7 pounds of biscuit
> 7 gallons of beer
> 4 pounds of beef
> 2 pounds of pork
> three-quarters of a salt fish
> 2 pints of peas
> 6 ounces of butter and
> 12 ounces of cheese

The similarity of these accounts makes it acceptable to draw on the more detailed later accounts where they seem relevant to the *Mary Rose* (note that imperial weights and measures will be used throughout this section: 1 pound (lb) = approximately 0.45kg with 16 ounces (oz) to the pound; 1 gallon = 4.5 litres and there are 8 pints to a gallon).

A discussion of Elizabethan provisioning in 1565 by Edward Baeshe gives exactly the weekly ration quoted above, but with no pork and with a weekly ration of 8lb of salt beef per man (Davies 1963a 139; 1970, 93) for the four days designated as flesh. Davies also suggests that the replacement, at the end of the seventeenth century, of half the salt beef with 2lb of salt pork might relieve the monotony, which is already triple the average meat consumption of modern Britons. At this time Edward Baeshe, having been one of the London Agents, had now been put in charge of a permanent naval victualling office (Davies 1965, 276). Similarly, in 1698, the House of Commons *Journal* relates that the food laid down for the navy included:

> *'two pounds avoirdupois of beef, killed, and made up with salt in England, of a well-fed ox, for two of the four days following, viz. Sundays, Mondays, Tuesdays and Thursdays; and for the other two of these days, one pound avoirdupois of bacon, or salted English pork of a well-fed hog and a pint of peas...'*. (Maybray King 1968, 49)

Figure 14.27 The Butcher's Shop *by Jan Victors (1620-76) showing a (very large) pig being butchered in a similar manner to those from the Mary Rose. Note that the carcase is hanging from a 'beef' tree. Bridgeman Art Library YAG23513*

As there is a quantity of pork on the *Mary Rose* we can suggest that the substitution of pork, or even pork and peas, on two days at the rate of 1lb of pork for every 2lb of beef may already have taken place when it was available (Fig. 14.27). Some confirmation of this comes from Braddock (nd), suggesting just such a substitution as early as 1522 in an account of the victualling rate for men building the dock for the *Henry Grace à Dieu* at Portsmouth (Oppenheim 1896b, 69). In this case the pound of pork was a substitute for 2lb of beef on two of the flesh days a week and accompanied by a whole pint of peas, again giving a total of two pints of peas a week.

Taking all these facts into account we can suggest how the possible rations that were provided for each man were spread through the week (Table 14.13), although we do not know which of the four flesh days were pork days on the *Mary Rose*, or that the men were given peas, butter and cheese. A single possible churn was found on board the ship (Chapter 11) but no peas have been recorded (see archaeobotanical evidence, above) despite the comment published by Rule (1983b, 197). Having the pork days on Sunday and Thursday fits later practice and spaces it out within the four given flesh days of Sunday, Monday, Tuesday and Thursday. It is only in the 1731 regulations that the week becomes less top heavy and Monday, Wednesday and Friday become non-flesh days.

The eighteenth century regulations for salt beef are very detailed and fit the *Mary Rose* material very well:

> '*The Beef provided ... is to be cut into Four Pound Pieces, and the Pork into Two Pound Pieces; and no unusual Pieces are to be put up, such as Leg Bones, Shins of Oxen, Cheeks of Hogs ...*'. (Anon 1731, 62)

Fresh meat is alluded to in 1731 (Anon 1731, 68), with fresh beef or mutton seen as essential when available, being substituted for salt beef on one day in the week and for salt pork on another. Three pounds of mutton was reckoned equivalent to 4lb of beef or 2lb of pork plus peas. By this time there had been considerable improvement of sheep compared with the position in 1545.

With considerable quantities of preserved fish on board it seems likely that Wednesday, Friday and Saturday were already days of fish, butter and cheese as observed in the menus discussed above for 1565 and 1698. The quantities of 2oz of butter and 4oz of cheese seem standard and continue in 1731 (with the addition of a pint of oatmeal but no mention of fish). Butter and cheese in these quantities is also given for the dock-builders of 1522. This seems sure enough for us to add them to the suggested rations (Table 14.13).

Fish in the menu

The amount of fish recovered, even if it is assumed to be an underestimate, would not have lasted a crew of around 400 men more than a week at most. One document of 1522 quotes a requirement of 18,000 salt fish per 3000 men for eight weeks, being one piece a day to every four men on the three fish days in the week (Gairdner and Brodie 1903–5, entry 2744).

This is actually six fish per man to last eight weeks, giving three-quarters of a fish per week, or a quarter of a fish per day. Therefore, one can deduce that, in this case, a 'piece' is the same as 'a fish'. This exactly matches the 1565 account (Davies 1970) and Braddock's dockyard workers had the same.

The observance of 'Fish days' (and Lent) is to be expected despite the reformation of the church. Old habits may have been slow to change, but the real reason for adherence was probably economic; keeping a large number of people employed, ships built and relieving the pressure on the meat supply. The household account books of Sir William Petre, Secretary of State, record stores for Lent in 1549 of:

> '*haberdine 75½ couple, ling 46½ couple, stockfish 56 couple, red herring two cades* [2 x 600 salted and smoked], *white herring [pickled] a barrel,*

Table 14.13 Possible rations per man for the *Mary Rose*

Sunday	1lb biscuit	1 gallon beer	1lb pork	1 pint peas	
Monday	"	"	2lb beef		
Tuesday	"	"	2lb beef		
Wednesday	"	"	¼ fish	2oz butter	4oz cheese
Thursday	"	"	1lb pork	1 pint peas	
Friday	"	"	¼ fish	2oz butter	4oz cheese
Saturday	"	"	¼ fish	2oz butter	4oz cheese

salted eels a barrel, salmon half a barrel and six salted congers ... '. (Cutting 1955, 30 and 71)

Presumably salt cod kept better than herrings:

> '*Spend herring first, save salt fish last: for salt fish is good when Lent is past.*'

says Thomas Tusser (1524–1580) (Cutting 1955, 32).

Herring and eel bones were almost entirely absent from the wreck despite being extremely common from archaeological sites on land, and herrings being the major fish commodity listed in the *Port and Brokage* books (eg, Studer 1913; Cobb 1961; James 1990; Locker 2000).

State letters and papers relating to the war with France of 1512–13 include lists of '*revytaylyng*' for the *Regent* for 700 men for three months. This includes '*1110 and 510 score (20) fisshe*', at two different prices, in addition to '*500 dryelinges, 300 coddes and 1,000 mud-fysshe*' (possibly small wet salted fish?). The list later quotes large numbers of fish, some '*drye fisshe*', some '*stokefisshe*', but also '*Stepping fattys for the shippe: 2 greate fattys to water fisshe in: 2s. 8d.*', ie, vats to reconstitute (steep) dried and/or salted fish (Spont 1897–8, 13–15).

These containers, whether specially made or re-using empty casks, would have been essential equipment. Salt cod must be soaked at least overnight and preferably longer and, if dried as well, the reconstitution can take more than 24 hours (Kurlansky 1998). Many sources recommend beating with a hammer to tenderise the board-like product before soaking, and a 1546 list of army victuals for Blackness includes 2380 stockfish unbeaten and 480 beaten (Turnbull 1861, 313).

In 1565 a naval victualler was contracted to supply each sailor with, amongst other things, ¾lb (400g) stockfish per week (Davies 1970). Samuel Pepys records in a contract of 1677 the provision of $\frac{1}{8}$ of a full-sized 24 inch (610mm) North Sea cod for each man on Wednesday, Friday and Saturday and gives various alternatives including ¼ haberdine of 16in (400mm) (Tanner 1920, 61). An almost identical naval

Figure 14.28 Fish butchery similar to that demonstrated by the Mary Rose *fish remains – here a header and splitter at work on cod on board ship in the late eighteenth century in the Newfoundland cod fisheries. The men are standing in casks padded with straw and covered with leather aprons to to help them maintain their balance and keep them dry. The casks were secured by ropes.* (Duhamel du Monceau 1772, vol. 2, part 2, pl. ix, fig. 2)

ration of $1/8$ of a 24in cod is recorded in the House of Commons Journal for 1698 (Maybray King 1968, 49). To date this author has insufficient evidence to tell whether this size is with or without the head, although later sources imply that the measurement is of a beheaded fish (Fig. 4.28).

Stokvis (dried salted cod) was still in use by the Royal Netherlands Navy up to World War II, with 300g being allocated per man; mustard and chutney could be eaten with it (Davidson 1979, 317).

Serving and sharing

In 1731 steeping vats carried on naval ships seem to have been housed on the upper deck as there are warnings about securing them so that they could not be washed overboard (Anon 1731, 138). On the *Mary Rose* this function may have been performed by casks full of fresh water strapped to the Sterncastle as the waist of the Upper deck would have been a busy and crowded fighting platform. It would also keep the meat cool in hot weather.

Steeping salted meat or fish would take out some of the salt by diffusion and, in the case of both salt and dry food, water would enter by osmosis into the flesh which would tenderise it, plump out the portions and help to alleviate the great thirst such a diet must have caused. There is also the possibility that rank food might be washed to make it passable for consumption if that could be got away with!

In discussing the treatment of fresh meat, eighteenth century regulations talk of it on board in 'quarters' which were to be divided in public into the '*usual mess pieces*' (Anon. 1731, 202). Quarters were a way of butchering meat that was certainly in use for mutton and pork by 1607 when the London Butchers' Company described the exact number of ribs that should be associated with forequarters and loins (Rixson 2000, 195). Further subdivision into 'mess pieces' could be what has happened to the pork on the Orlop deck and might mean that it was fresh pork ready to be eaten that day (which was a Sunday, a meat day: Table 14.13). Once divided into 'mess pieces' the fresh meat would be more prone to deterioration, especially on a summer day. Fresh pork might have been easier to obtain at short notice than hams and bacon that need more lengthy preparation.

After soaking, the food would have been boiled in one of the great cauldrons in the galley (Chapter 11). Serving the cooked meat normally required flesh hooks to pull out the cooked pieces. Such implements are illustrated in Rixson (2000, 124), but none were recovered or survived from the *Mary Rose*. Hence a custom of 'pricking for pieces', as described for later times, was probably already in existence. This aims to give a fair share for all with no special pieces going to any individual, and the sharing out of the cooked meat, like the division of fresh meat, was done in public (Anon 1731, 202). The actual size of the meat share on Tudor ships is difficult to deduce as there are other variables such as the number of meals served daily.

An extraordinary story is told of Captain Bligh in 1789, which exemplifies the extent to which seaboard victualling needed to be seen as fair. When provisions went bad or the men were actually starving, this was a potential source of great unrest. Bligh, adrift in an open boat with the rump of his crew, divided a small bird into eighteen pieces and used the 'who shall have this' method. One person pointed separately to the portions (or in our case perhaps 'pricking' for it in the cooking pot with a flesh hook) and asking aloud 'who shall have this?' while another with his back to the food names someone (Farmer 1995, 52). On shipboard, portions would presumably be allotted to a mess rather than to one individual.

The size of a mess would be the number of men who ate together and presumably shared one 'mess piece'. The word mess was even used at home at this time and Sim describes its use in courtesy books of the Tudor period where she explains that most meals were served in portions (or messes) designed to serve four people, the largest number who can conveniently share a dish (Sim 1997, 107). We cannot be certain what the typical mess size would have been on board a sixteenth century ship. Four is a commonly quoted number for a mess in many navies but on later British warships mess sizes varied depending on the size of the company and the available space for eating. By the later eighteenth century a lower limit of four was often imposed while the upper limit was likely to be determined by physical conditions. By that time messes were generally of 4–8 men, perhaps most frequently of 6 (Lavery 1987, 182). For purposes of discussion here, it will be assumed that each mess on the *Mary Rose* consisted of four men.

Jones examined references to meat in casks in State documents for 1512, 1522 and 1544. Allowing for the possible vagaries of cask size in the Tudor period (A Jones nd; Furlong 1999) we can suggest that the number of pieces might have been:

Tuns (252 gallons): 800 pieces, lasts 100 men for 2 weeks (8 flesh days)

Pipes (126 gallons): 400 pieces, lasts 100 men for 1 week (4 flesh days).

In 1522 a pipe of beef is said to contain meat from 2½ oxen and last 100 men for a week (Gairdner and Brodie 1903–5, entry 2744). The next cask size down, the hogshead, is later on stated to hold 500lb (227kg) of meat. This is very useful to know because, if a hogshead contained 200 pieces (enough for 100 men for two flesh days), then each piece would have weighed about 2½lb (1.1kg). Unfortunately there are very few instances on the *Mary Rose* where cask size and contents can be correlated, but the salt beef casks found on the ship were consistently even smaller than hogsheads, with a volume of 27–31 gallons (see Chapter 10). These might, by extrapolation, be deduced to contain 100 pieces, or enough for 100 men for one flesh day (Table 14.13).

All these calculations are based on beef and appropriate calculations will have to be done if there was only 4lb of beef a week and half that quantity of pork. The value Jones arrives at of 2½lb pieces is important, if slightly too high (see below) as the 1731 victualling accounts quoted above give 4lb pieces for beef and 2lb for pork. But confirmation of Tudor beef pieces as only 2lb is found in a contemporary account describing a shortage, where pieces which should weigh 2lb are angrily stated to be none of them more than 1½lb (*c.* 0.7kg), and some not 1lb and that every pipe contains 40–140 pieces short (Gairdner and Brodie 1903–5, 235, entry 366: 21 April 1544).

Some of the explanation for this may be shrinkage and it could be that not all Tudor personnel were as familiar with this as those in later times. Section V of the provisions section of the 1731 regulations goes into great detail about checking shrinkage of the beef in a prepared cask of brine:

> 'Every Twenty Eight Pieces of Beef, cut into Four Pound Pieces, taken out of the Cask as they rise and the Salt shaken off, are to weigh One Hundred Pounds Avoirdupois; and every Fifty-six Pieces of Pork, cut for Two Pound Pieces, and taken out and shaken in like manner, are to weigh One Hundred and Four pounds'. (Anon 1731, 62)

Theoretically they should both total 112lb (*c.* 51kg). This shows a sound practical allowance for considerable shrinkage of the pieces through the phenomenon of osmosis. This process would have the effect of liquefying the cask contents to some extent so that the pieces were swimming in brine and would rise to the surface as described. Anyone who has used salt as a preservative for organic material knows what a wet and messy process this is.

Jennifer Bourdillon of the Faunal Remains Unit calculated that, using the 1731 figures, a 4lb beef piece would average 3lb 9oz (*c.* 1.60kg) and a 2lb piece of pork 1lb 14oz (*c.* 0.65kg). On this basis the 500lb weight of a hogshead containing 200 pieces of beef would probably contain beef pieces which weighed considerably less than Jones's suggested 2½lb each, the weight of the brine probably being even more considerable than she suggests.

On the basis of the 1731 figures beef shrinks 11% compared with 6% for pork. Allowing for the greater surface area to volume ratio of the smaller pieces, the pork shows even less shrinkage than might be expected, perhaps having a denser structure to the flesh. A Tudor 2lb beef piece, because of its larger proportion of surface compared with a 1731 4lb piece might be expected to lose more than 11% and end up weighing as little as 1½lb. To check out at 2lb on board, beef pieces would have to start 3 or 4oz heavier before salting.

The size of the mess would have had an effect upon the size of the pieces but the later 4lb piece of beef fits a four man mess if there were two meat meals in the day. In Tudor times 2lb pieces of beef would have needed to double up, unless a 2lb piece was shared between two men twice a day, to give the suggested menu in Table 14.13. If pork were also in 2lb pieces, on the basis of later menu quantities, this would have provided 1lb per man with two sharing if it were all to be eaten at one sitting, or ½lb each if there were two pork meals in the day. This depends on how many meals men normally ate on board.

Tudor landsmen appear to have eaten three meals a day and sailors may have expected the same. Whether they were all fed at once or when they stood down from their duties is open to debate. Lavery states that, in the seventeenth century, all the crew took their meals together, regardless of the watches (Lavery 1987, 184).

The Tudor naval diet in its historical context

Methods for taking food on long voyages have been around since people started using boats. They often involved carrying live animals or preserving meat in imaginative ways. Salt and dried fish have a very long history and were equally in great use on land. The victualling problems facing the English navy in defending an island, or using it as a base from which to attack parts of the Continent, are somewhat different from those experienced by long-distance sailing ships or fishing fleets. With a good infrastructure ashore there would be no need to take live animals to sea, except perhaps live chickens for fresh eggs, and young animals to provide delicacies for the gentlemen. In times of war such luxuries are unlikely to have been supplied and, as discussed above, there is no evidence of livestock on board the ship (though any animals penned on the top decks would probably have been washed overboard at the sinking).

Looking in more detail at the diet of the men as suggested in Table 14.13, and imagining the effect of it on their daily lives, highlights several potential weaknesses in the diet. In some ways the *Mary Rose* diet was a healthier one than today's as it contained no obvious sources of extrinsic sugars which lead to many current medical problems; and it is unlikely that the crew suffered from obesity with all its concomitant ills. However, we are less interested in the potential long-term health of these men, and whether they would have lived to a healthy old age if they had not been drowned, than in whether this diet kept them alive from day to day and how it compared with that for other navies and seafarers of the time.

The calorific value was probably marginal. Davies calculates an estimated average daily intake of 4265 kilocalories (kcal), making allowance for the alcohol in the beer, using the Elizabethan naval diet of 1565

(which includes beef but no pork and peas). In this analysis much of the energy value would actually have come from the beer (nearly 2000 kcal a day), followed closely by the biscuit (about 1500 kcal) and then the beef (about 1000 kcal). Without the alcohol content of the beer the men could have obtained as much as 5132 kcal from this diet (Davies 1970, 93).

Morineau, in collaboration with Davies, has produced a matching calorific chart by dividing up a 1570 two month victualling for 825 men. This menu is very interesting for us as it contains pork and peas. The calorific total comes out as a little higher than Davies's menu at 4600 kcal after allowance for alcohol (Morineau 1970, 100). Using these sources and making a guess at the extent to which peas may have been involved in the *Mary Rose* menu (Table 14.13) we arrive at an average of 4725 kcal per day.

These slightly higher values, resulting from the inclusion of the more highly calorific pork in place of beef for two of the flesh days and the addition of peas, are also somewhat unbalanced in our menu as Sunday and Thursday produce a high of 5840 kcal, beef days a value of 4788 and fish and cheese days a low of 4377kcal. In later centuries the spread of the peas to four days of the week in half pint portions would have evened this out. Although these values are twice the energy recommended for today's sedentary lifestyle it was probably nowhere near enough for men labouring with sails and guns in cold, wet conditions and more would certainly have been needed in winter (COMA 1991 quoted in Saffrey and Stewart 1997, 253).

More important in modern dietary analysis than basic calorific values is the detail of ingredients. The make-up of the Tudor naval diet showed other weaknesses in this respect. Modern recommendations are that half the energy should come from carbohydrate. The effect of different carbohydrates varies according to the glycaemic index (GI), with some high GI carbohydrates, like bread, providing almost instant energy, whereas certain types of rice with a high amylose content, pasta, peas and beans have a low GI and release energy more slowly (Saffrey and Stewart 1997, 254). Without experimentation and knowing the spacing of meals, it is difficult to know how quickly the calories were used up. The best solution would have been to spread the foods through the day to sustain the men at their work. If they were only getting just enough calories, most of these would be used to maintain a suitable blood sugar level with little spare to go into store in liver and muscle.

Peas would have provided a slower digesting form of carbohydrate, as would oatmeal if used and, to some extent, the bread, if it were less well milled and therefore slower to break down than today's. Another excellent effect of the peas would come from their non-starch polysaccharide (NSP). A low NSP diet, such as a pure meat one, might result in constipation. Less soluble NSP than the mucilage from peas would really have been needed from other plant fibres to make this diet of a barely acceptable standard for health (Saffrey and Stewart 1997, 250). There is mention of beans, peas and oatmeal in a number of sixteenth century references to victualling. According to the records in the 1545 Acts of the Privy Council the army was supplied with Norfolk beans (Dasent 1890, 181). Reference to peas has been made above but in addition they are mentioned in many places including in the fifteenth century in victualling the *Sovereign* (Oppenheim 1896b, 165). Both peas and oatmeal figure in food supplied to the builders of the *Mary Rose* (Oppenheim 1896a, 73). Unfortunately, there is no surviving evidence for peas from the *Mary Rose* (see above) and there is very little evidence of bran, biscuit or flour on board.

Another potential weakness of the diet was its dependence on red meat with its potential for putrefaction in cask. According to Drummond and Wilbraham (1939, 419) there is an old popular belief that violent muscular exercise called for large amounts of red meat. Both bad meat and bad beer were problems of the time and are referred to in contemporaneous letters and accounts. As if possible food-poisoning and potential starvation were not enough, one must also consider the lowering of morale in men faced with inedible food and, even more important, drink that they depended upon for rehydration.

This leads to the next criticism of this diet: almost every ingredient, apart from the bread and beer, would have been very salty or dry. There might also have been very little water to drink. A detailed water input and output analysis for this diet is probably impossible but most adults today take in nearly half their water as food, something difficult to imagine with what we know about the *Mary Rose* diet. The hot summer of 1545 would have increased the loss of water that normally occurs from skin and lungs and this, added to extra loss from sweating during heavy work, means that these sources of water loss would probably have exceeded normal loss from urination (Saffrey and Stewart 1997, 183).

It is difficult to see how tissue water levels could be maintained under these circumstances and most body systems would have been under strain if this situation had gone on for any length of time. These men were either very tough, or expendable, or both.

Lastly the diet may have been deficient in some minerals, vitamins and trace elements. Without vegetables and milk, the diet was probably vitamin A deficient and low in anti-oxidents. The lack of fresh food suggests that vitamin C levels were so low that the men were on the edge of suffering from scurvy (Saffrey and Stewart 1997, 266–9 and see above); Stirland (Chapter 13) suggests that some of the skeletal remains showed evidence of possible scurvy and/or iron deficiency anaemia.

The eating of fish and drinking of beer may have counteracted the lack of fresh foods to some extent as these two ingredients contain important vitamin sources. Oily fish like herring are occasionally mentioned in documents and would have been valuable nutritionally, but it is not clear whether these were for victualling the men (see fish above). Rodger (1997) says four herrings per fish day could be provided instead of stockfish but, apart from a stray vertebra, none was found on the *Mary Rose*. Vegetables, fruit and milk would probably have been viewed with suspicion (Drummond and Wilbraham 1939, 148–9).

Butchered bones of cattle and pigs have been found on other wrecks from subsequent centuries and there is much documentary evidence for other navies. Morineau (1970) demonstrates the similarities in the meat-eating navies of England, Sweden, Holland and Russia, although his examples are from different centuries. The reliance on meat is not so high as in the English examples and the pea rations he suggests seem extraordinarily high for the Swedes.

An interesting example of an Italian provisioning is given for Tuscan galleys of the sixteenth century by Hémardinquer (1970). The basic rations comprised bread, wine, meat, fish or cheese, oil and vinegar and there are several mentions of pasta and vegetable items which suggests that the diet was much more varied although much of this variety was probably only enjoyed by the upper echelons.

A very full account exists of sixteenth century victualling for Spanish merchant ships in the Caribbean (K. Jarvis, pers. comm.). This specifies minutely not only the rations but how they were to be taken. Breakfast included biscuit, garlic, sardines or cheese, and wine. Meat was given on Sundays and Thursdays only and the kind is not specified. On other days fish and beans were served. The main meal was taken in the waist of the ship with each group of four men sharing a pile of biscuit and either 4lb of meat or 16 sardines, with their pot of broad beans where issued and three draughts of wine at every meal. Great stress is laid on the extent to which interesting dietary items would more than repay the owners by the happiness and loyalty of the crew (Garcia de Palacio 1587, 143).

The deficiencies in the diet eaten by the English Navy in 1545 highlighted above made it a high risk strategy in certain circumstances. In the hot summer of 1545 many of these came together. Had the *Mary Rose* survived, her men would have later suffered other setbacks and dangers. As the summer of 1545 wore on, some men in most of the ships became very ill with dysentery and the heat and bad victuals, too closely packed, were blamed (Gairdner and Brodie 1903–5 II, 2; see also Rodger 1997, 234).

Reconstructing the provisioning

The animal bones aid a reconstruction of the diet on the ship and, with the help of documentary evidence, some attempt has been made above to outline a possible weekly diet. The substitution of pork for two of the four flesh meals in the week seems already to have taken place at this time as there is evidence of salt pork. The large deposit of pork on the Orlop deck is particularly interesting as it could not have been quickly organised: the animals would need to be gathered into the markets or port, slaughtered, and hung. In the case of ham or bacon the preparation would have taken weeks.

Peas seem to be a natural complement to pork at this time. Rixson (2000, 98) points out that peas were considered to take the salt out of fatty bacon. In dietary terms the addition of any kind of pork and of peas would have added variety, calories and other dietary benefits. Preserved fish, butter and cheese were probably provided on at least three days a week. However carefully provided and used, it is suggested above that certain aspects of the diet were unsatisfactory.

The *Anthony Roll* gives a complement of 415 men so a total of 400 has been used below to work out the amounts needed for a day's ration on the ship. Using the suggested menu (Table 14.13) and the evidence from documents discussed above, it is likely that 400 men would require a daily total of 400 gallons of beer and 400lb of biscuit; for each beef day 800lb of beef would be needed; for a pork day 400lb of pork and perhaps up to 400 pints of peas; and, for a non-flesh day, 100 preserved fish, 50lb of butter and 100lb of cheese.

Without more study and some experimentation it is impossible to work out exactly how many cattle and pigs this would involve. The records of the time usually only deal in numbers. Sixteenth and seventeenth century husbandry information, where it gives carcase weights, does not tell us the age of the animals involved. We know that the age ranges of cattle and pigs represented by the bones on the *Mary Rose* was quite wide, and some of the younger pigs may have been quite small. Some references hint at 'fat cows' or 'fat oxen' or at the use by the navy of 'well-fed oxen' and 'well-fed hogs' (Maybray King 1968, 49 – though not, pehaps as well-fed as that illustrated in Fig. 14.27!) but animals before improvement would have had relatively small hindquarters and looked scraggy and small by today's standards.

However, it is interesting to put this in perspective by making some guesses even if these later prove inaccurate. Rixson explains that the carcase weight of a bovine may vary between 48% and 62% of the live weight (Rixson 2000, 3). With the omission of the main marrow bones, the percentage of meat available from a cattle carcase might be even lower than this. Given that a pipe of beef was said to contain 400 2lb 'pieces' and be made up from 2½ animals, each animal carcase would have provided 320lb of meat. Taking 40% as the carcase fraction, these animals would have had a live weight of 800lb (7 cwt; 363kg). They would have weighed only 5–6 cwt if Rixon's carcase proportions of 48–62% were used.

On the basis of 400 men the daily requirement would be 400 2lb pieces or 1 pipe, or 2½ cattle. This might be equivalent to four of the smaller casks found (if each of these contained 100 pieces as suggested earlier) or possibly more than four. The number of casks on board associated with cattle bone therefore represents only one or two days of beef if they had all been full. On this basis too, each beef day on this ship would have needed at least three cattle.

The pigs are more difficult to work out as we do not have the figures in pipes. To give an idea of what might have been involved one might take a 1612 dressed carcase weight of 140lb given for an exceptional pea-fattened pig of unknown age (Trow-Smith 1957, 251). This might represent a good example of a 'fat hog'. This probably outshone the pigs on the ship, some of whom would have weighed much less as they were only about a year old. At least three such record pigs would be needed to supply 400 men with a day's pork ration, but, in reality, it is likely that at least twice this number would have been needed. The 30 pigs represented in the Orlop deposit (if their complete carcases were there) might have provided as little as five or six pork days for 400 men.

What was actually on the menu that fatal Sunday would surely have been meat but whether this was 400lb of salt pork watering in casks on the Sterncastle; casks of beef on the Orlop and Main decks already watered and ready for cooking; or some of the Orlop deposit of pork or bacon ready to be swiftly cooked up when the action ceased for the day – we shall only discover if scientific or documentary evidence sheds more light.

Reconstruction of the victualling
Jennie Coy with Julie Gardiner

The organisation of the victualling exercise evolved with the considerable changes that occurred in naval organisation over the first half of the sixteenth century. Henry VIII's reign began with the Clerk of Ships exercising sporadic control over five ships but the rapid expansion of the navy soon led to the need for a more sophisticated system of administration. The nineteen years of peace between the second and third French wars (1525–1544) saw the creation of a variety of other offices with responsibility for running and supplying the navy and resulted in the establishment of The Council for Marine Causes in 1545 (Davies 1963b, 118; Loades 1992, 74–84; Knighton and Loades 2002). However, victualling of the King's ships did not come under a permanent official until 1550 (Davies 1965, 275). Until then it was administered by special commissioners who set the rates for the purchase of specific commodities and could also decide which brewers and bakers were to be used at the major ports. They and their agents were responsible for getting provisions to the quaysides but it was the responsibility of each ship's purser to purchase supplies and get them aboard. The purser was provided with an allowance of about 1s 3d per man per week (Loades 1992, 84; Oppenheim (1896a) suggests 18 Tudor pence per week; see Chapter 6 for a discussion of wages).

The agents were supplied, in the first place, by county purveyors who were appointed by warrant to supply given quantities of specific commodities. These were delivered to contractors in the port towns such as Portsmouth, Southampton and London, who converted them, as required, into bread and biscuit, pipes of salt beef, etc, from which the pursers obtained their supplies (Loades 1992, 85). Such a system was clearly open to considerable abuse as well as practical difficulties, especially in times of war when thousands of men in many ships needed feeding. There are many letters appealing to the King and his commissioners for the proper supply of victuals, complaining about poor quality and accusing agents and pursers alike of fraud and mishandling (see *AMR* Vol. 1, appendix for examples).

When ships were away from the channel or the southern coast, however, communications and supply lines became more problematic. But desperate cries for supplies in the letters may not always have referred to meat. Beer and bread were the staples which kept men alive, even in the absence of meat. The use of beer for hydration, rather than water, was a characteristic of the British Navy, probably a practical step because it would keep longer in a cask than water (Furlong 1999, 10).

Records for the war in 1522 during a particularly bad patch illustrate how victualling problems may be caused by basic difficulties such as a lack of wood for baking and brewing; a lack of water for brewing during a great drought; a lack of wind causing them to resort to horsemills and handmills for grinding their corn 'day and night', and mention is made in one record of having to use green corn. Much of this is for the army which, in one record, will take provisions from the *Mary Rose* if she is to be laid up. One cannot help but admire the tenacity and skill with which the suppliers worked to supply the king with the wherewithal to fight wars (Gairdner and Brodie 1903–5, 1021–46).

By June 1545, many ships of the navy were gathered in an area known as the Downs, off the coast of Kent, ready to join the transports of the army in defence of the recently captured port of Boulogne, and by mid July a substantial fleet was standing off Portsmouth (see *AMR* Vol. 1, chapter 1 for a history of the *Mary Rose*'s movements at this time).

Throughout July and August of that year, while a French force of about 25,000 menaced Portsmouth and the Isle of Wight, Davies (1963b, 264) quotes a peak figure of 140,000 English either defending the South Coast, holding Boulogne, or manning the navy. This is twice the estimated population of London at the time.

These vast numbers necessitated enormous quantities of food. Davies describes how the army coped with victualling such large numbers by having travelling mills, bakeries and breweries. In 1544 the main expedition against Boulogne included a victualling train of 2136 men and 638 waggons with 100 bakers, 100 millers and 100 brewers and assistants (Davies 1963b, 171). The transport problems for carrying this alone, let alone guns and ammunition, were massive. With a navy the problems would be different but just as complex. Victuals would have to be at the port at the same time and enough of them for increasingly long campaigns where the ships might need to be out of port for increasingly long periods. There would be no chance of 'living off the land' in any way. Ships had no choice but to return to port and the supply vessels when they ran out of food and, unlike their land-based colleagues, crew members could not easily desert if the diet was not up to scratch.

July would have been a crucial time for the supply both of beer and bread to the ships as grain supplies would have been low before the harvest. A letter of 5 August 1545, after the *Mary Rose* had sunk, notes that the harvest in Scotland was as good as that in England (Gairdner and Brodie 1903–5 I, 17). The same entry reiterates that '*if only the London and Sussex victuals were come the Lord Chamberlain would have enough to victual the fleet till October*'. The non-arrival of these longed-for victuals (in another entry described as from Rye, Dover and Thames) was said to be due to the presence of the French around the coast. All the transport of the heavy casks would have been more practical by sea at this time. A 'two month victualling' may have been empty boasting as most other contemporary reports talk of victualling the fleet for 14 days (Gairdner and Brodie 1903–5 I, 6).

Clifford Davies, in his thesis on army provisioning, gives some useful figures that set the wider scene in the 1540s (Davies 1963b). The wars of the 1540s ensured that a high military profile would have been evident at the time the *Mary Rose* sank. During Henry VIII's reign the fleet expanded from five ships in 1509 by the construction of 47 more by 1547, with another 35 ships being bought or taken. Between 1542 and 1546 twenty new ships were built.

As well as quantity there were severe problems over quality. The attempted French invasion in 1545 coincided with illness in both fleets, with the French succumbing to it just before the English. We shall never know the combination of factors which caused this – toxaemia from food poisoning and even scurvy have been suggested, and the weather that July is known to have been particularly hot which will not have helped matters. The normal diet at that time was likely to have kept people on the edge of scurvy (Davies 1963b, 280). Diet is obviously central in maintaining the immune system and resistance to disease as well as being a likely cause of disease where any long-term provisioning and mass feeding exercise is involved. In the sixteenth century food may sometimes have come under quite unwarranted suspicion just because it smelled and tasted awful. Drummond points out that, until the eighteenth century, scurvy was regarded as a putrid fever and it was considered that purer supplies of salt would be healthier for sailors as they would make the meat less likely to putrefy (Drummond and Wilbraham 1939, 311).

The animal bones from the *Mary Rose* provide evidence for a great deal of organisation but the historical records, on which we have only touched superficially, give some idea of the extent to which the supplies of food in the country must have been stretched. The complaints of rotten food, of which there are many, also show the extent to which the preservation of foods for very large numbers of men was either skimped because of the desperate times or dishonesty among the purveyors, agents or pursers, or had not yet reached adequate standards of technology. Food was packed too tight, it was put into foul casks, it leaked out and putrified. How much of this was avoidable is difficult to judge. In later accounts there are still stories of terrible food even though firm regulations were in place. That mistakes still happened and dishonesty was rife in the eighteenth century can be deduced from the firm way in which the Regulations cover complaints about the food, instructions on contracts and standard forms for surveying the leakage of beer or the number of pieces of beef or pork in a cask (Anon 1731, 182–3).

Sources of the supplies on the Mary Rose
Jennie Coy

The county purveyors, as mentioned above, may have been the principal suppliers to the special commissioners of the navy (Loades 1992, chap. 4), but what of the initial sources of supply? Studies of available sources by agricultural historians such as Fussell and Trow-Smith provide a composite picture of change and development in English agriculture, first documented from the late sixteenth century and increasing in momentum during the seventeenth and eighteenth centuries. It is frequently suggested by these commentators that this was based upon changes already in progress in some parts of the country earlier in the sixteenth century. Of note is the degree to which specialisation and movement of animals was already an issue, with recognisable local breeds often being commented upon.

Cattle from medieval times and earlier were well cared for as they were the major source of traction for ploughing and carts. Analysis of bones from archaeological sites for medieval southern England confirms Trow-Smith's view that autumn slaughter is a myth of the modern historian (Trow-Smith 1957, 182). There is evidence from documents of early in the century that some cattle fattening for food was already taking place, rather than beef supplies merely arising from the fattening of older animals not of use for other functions (Fussell 1952, 67–8).

The early dairying herds on the East Anglian fens, which later became very large, were a good source of beef. With dairying, fattening for meat was the only profitable way of using surplus males and older cows. In 1513–14 the navy victualler bought 253 fat winter-fed oxen in Lincolnshire, 322 at Wisbech, and 164 at Stamford and Peterborough (Trow-Smith 1957, 201). The increasingly extensive fenlands were already rich grazing in summer and produced hay for winter feeding. Fattening of cattle at these times also took place in the rich grazing areas of the Dorset lowlands, for example (Trow-Smith 1957, 179). At its suppression, late in the 1530s, the nunnery at Sheppey, Kent, had 132 oxen which Trow-Smith (1957, 192) suggests must have been store bullocks for fattening, presumably for the London market.

Britain was, then, primarily an agricultural country. The very large herds of animals and the extensive droving activities, whereby animals were herded to fairs and centres of population or to better grazing, in later centuries, were already starting to build up (Cornwall 1954, 77). Later in the sixteenth century there was much development of cattle droving from the southwest, Wales and Scotland but there is evidence that these areas supplied beef for the London market even earlier. Davies's statistics on victualling the army suggest that the victualling market, although sporadic, could have been a larger one than the metropolis for which the movements of these animals had developed (Trow-Smith 1957, 179).

The cheddar cheese milch industry was already in existence many centuries before (Trow-Smith 1957, 180; Dasent 1890) with cheeses being made in large oak casks. Large quantities of cheese would have been needed aboard if the menus were as the contemporary references suggest; again providing an encouragement for dairy farming.

By the seventeenth century Hampshire hogs were universally highly regarded and said to produce the best bacon. But well before this many people fattened their pigs in the great wooded areas of Hampshire where they were put in to take the acorn crop. In some accounts pigs were allowed free access to pea stacks. By 1612 some farmers were actually specialising in fattening pigs on peas and beans for the meat market (Trow-Smith 1957, 251). With most people having only a few pigs, enough for the family needs, the production of the large numbers needed for victualling in the early sixteenth century may still have depended largely on the great estates and religious houses.

In the sixteenth century it is likely that a great deal of cheese was still made from sheep's milk. Trow-Smith gives the example of Essex which still sent quantities of sheep's cheese and salted butter to London (Trow-Smith 1957, 195). Essex and Suffolk cheeses are certainly mentioned and a licence to export Essex cheese is mentioned in 1546 (Dasent 1890, 513).

The very small amount of sheep bone on the *Mary Rose* suggests that mutton was not on the menu for the men. As discussed in an earlier section, although very large numbers of unimproved sheep would have been kept, they would have been mainly for wool rather than for tender meat. There was frequent mention of their use as fresh meat for the navy in later centuries. There is also a reference in the state papers for 26 July 1545, a week after the *Mary Rose* sank, about providing more defenders for the Isle of Wight and a request for 'beefs and muttons' to be brought into the market (Gairdner and Brodie 1903–5 I, 632). Desperate measures were obviously in operation to continue the supply of meat in what might prove to be a long campaign.

It is not surprising that lamb and mutton played little part in English victualling at this time but there may already have been a market developing for meats of a better quality than the scraggy animals, unable to carry a lamb or a fleece, that previously came to the table. In our modern world it is difficult to imagine that a sheep will easily live into double figures if it can survive the winter; the mass consumption of very young sheep being a modern phenomenon.

Source of fish
Sheila Hamilton-Dyer

Although cod can be caught in considerable quantities locally in the Solent the fish are likely to have been caught or traded from many sources. An Act of Parliament in 1542 gave free entry for fish imported from Ireland, Scotland, Orkney, the Shetlands, Iceland and Newfoundland (Cutting 1955, 129). The rich cod grounds off Newfoundland had been discovered at the close of the fifteenth century and were becoming of strategic importance at the time of the *Mary Rose*. Much of this trade would have entered the major ports, including Southampton. The Port books and Brokerage accounts for Southampton, almost unique records of trade for this period, show that a considerable trade in fish, both fresh and preserved, had already been established by the preceding century. Records of saltfish and stockfish are common and include shipments from as far apart as Plymouth and Hull (Cobb 1961; Coy 1996; James 1990; Stevens and Olding 1985; Studer 1913). These documents also reveal a trade in conger, usually included in shipments of mixed fresh and preserved fish, from other British ports such as Dartmouth, Exeter, and Mudeford, as well as from the Low Countries. The salting and drying of conger had long been a major source of income in the Channel Isles and also produced revenue for the Crown (Everard and Holt 2003). By the Tudor period the Channel Isles had very close ties with Southampton (Syvet and Stevens 1988, 89) and the considerable two-way trade probably included prepared conger. While this fish species may not be much favoured in England today it is evident from the quantities being delivered to Salisbury and elsewhere (barrels, carts, hundreds or perhaps hundred-weight) that it was a regular addition to the diet in the past. It seems highly likely, therefore, that at least some of the fish stores for the *Mary Rose* were sourced through Southampton.

The animal bone and victualling evidence: a summary discussion
Jennie Coy

The animal bone evidence shows that there were rules and systems in place in 1545. A great deal of industry went into providing the best quality food that could be had on such a large scale at that time. We do not know whether *Mary Rose* was typical or was better provided for than other ships in the campaign. The provision of meat from good-sized, often young, healthy cattle and pigs; the right cuts to ensure good keeping; and the obviously centralised feeding arrangements for the men, point to a good organisation of victualling on the ship and at the port. This comes across clearly, despite the problems of food supply, which from contemporary letters often seems *ad hoc*. The potential for putrefaction of the meat was, in that hot summer especially, always a danger and illness always round the corner. International events made planning difficult (the French almost caught the English fleet unawares on the day the *Mary Rose* sank) and the sporadic nature of the campaigns meant that the thousands of men who had to be fed would rapidly use up enormous quantities of stock.

By 1590 the system was calling on the resources of England in a more organised way. Cornwall (1954, 77) refers to an entry in *Acts of the Privy Council* (1589–90, 391) showing that 150 head of Sussex oxen were driven overland for naval victualling and that, in 1590: '*This quota was only exceeded by those of Yorkshire, Lincolnshire and Somerset, all larger counties, which supplied 200 head apiece*'.

Those at the top of shipboard society would have been differently fed and there is some evidence of domestic fowl, venison, fresh beef and mutton. A letter from August 1545, from John Lee to the Vice Admiral, discusses providing 40 to 60 bullocks to '*refresh the fleet*' and biscuit and beer from London. A revealing addition to this shows that, even where officers appeared to be eating the same food, there were hidden layers of privilege. *Maison Dieu* beer and biscuit is specifically offered for the Captain and Master but the mariners, although they would like it too, '*if they had their way*', would have to do with that brought from London (Gairdner and Brodie 1903–5 II, item 265).

15. Conditions on Board: Pests, Parasites and Pollen

It is not difficult to imagine that on a loaded, armed and manned warship, space was at a premium. The decks of the *Mary Rose* must have been busy and cramped; the men living cheek by jowl. Provisions for sanitation were rudimentary. We might imagine, therefore, that conditions on board were, at best, uncomfortable and unhygienic.

Evidence for the day-to-day living conditions of the Tudor seamen can be gained from analysis of the objects and the contents of sediments mixed with them. Insect remains of several species were recovered and they indicate the types of parasite that lived in close association with man. Initial examination of plant material believed to be the padding of a mattress recovered from one of the cabins has also revealed insect remains.

Leaves and general debris processed from the sediments found on the floor timbers of the Hold area suggests that the level of cleanliness was not particularly high even in areas where food was stored and prepared. Rats must have been common on the ship though the bones of only a few specimens have been recovered.

One particular deposit of plant material has been identified as consisting of the stem fragments and pods exclusively of broom. Contemporary records indicate that this may have been intended for burning as a kind of fumigant (see, for instance, Stirland 2000, 54–5), though it may also have been a packing material (see Chapter 14). The scrubbing of decks and general attempts at cleanliness would have been daily chores (see Chapter 8) and the ship was provisioned with a variety of cleaning utensils such as brushes and buckets.

This chapter will briefly explore the limited evidence for onboard living conditions, much of which has to be inferred from the results of sampling for environmental material (see Chapter 12) and includes evidence of pollen and plants, insects and non-food animals.

Livestock and Unbooked Passengers

*The ship rat (*Rattus rattus*)*
Jennie Coy

There are a few finds of rat from various contexts in the ship. A shoulder blade, lower leg bone (tibia) and pelvis (86S0242) of a large muscular rat were associated with a bowl (80A0691) on the Upper deck in U7. In addition there is an immature tibia (79S0084) from U/M11 with no associated finds, and a similar isolated find (81S0129 from H2). Both of these are regarded as Tudor in context.

Rattus rattus is also commonly called the black house rat because of its most frequent colour and its habit of living close to humans in houses. Through this close association it has been spread by ships throughout the world and has come to be known as the ship rat. It is smaller and more slender and mouselike in appearance than the brown rat, *R. norvegicus* (often known as the common rat or sewer rat) that is widespread in Britain today. It has larger eyes, more prominent hairless ears and a longer, thinner, less scaley tail (Corbet and Harris 1991, 255–9).

Although the bones from the *Mary Rose* do not include diagnostic skull fragments they are unlikely to belong to *R. norvegicus* as this is thought to have established itself in Britain in the eighteenth century, whereas *R. rattus* is known from medieval Southampton from the thirteenth century (Bourdillon 1978, 209). Because the bones found on the ship are a good match for large comparative specimens of *R. rattus* (they are well-formed and muscular for the species) this seems a secure identification (Fig. 15.1).

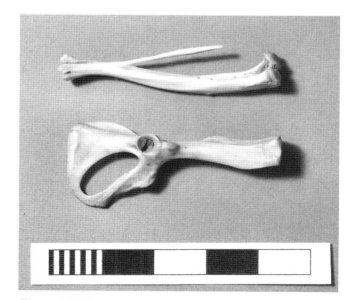

Figure 15.1 Rat bones

Black rats are agile climbers and move faster than brown rats. They could have been brought on board in hay or merchandise or made their own way on board from the quay, and they would breed on board. After her 34 years of intermittent use and idleness, *Mary Rose* could have had an indigenous population of rats that could be kept down but never eradicated. They would have spoiled or chewed any organic material, and used any fabric or fibres as bedding. Many articles on board were kept in staved containers and boxes, rather than in sacks, which may have been at least partly deliberately to prevent or minimise rat damage.

The black rat is the most dangerous of the rat species for plague transmission. The plague bacterium is a parasite of the rat flea, especially *Xenopsylla cheopis*, and it is this flea that spreads the plague. The aetiology of plague is complex. Rat fleas stick close to rats, and sufficient numbers of rodents must live close enough to humans that, on death of the rodent, the *X. cheopis* fleas move to and infect people. When rats die, a hearty rat flea can survive for up to 50 days and under certain circumstances might adapt to an alternative mammalian host (Hirst quoted in Gottfried 1978, 62).

With other pestilences around, not least dysentery, influenza, typhus, smallpox and food poisoning, the risk of plague on the *Mary Rose* would probably have paled into insignificance. It is reported that 3000 naval men died of 'plague' during the first two weeks of September 1545 (Keevil 1957) but Davies considers that this 'plague', which menaced both the French and later the English fleets, might even have been scurvy; at the time bad food was often blamed (Davies 1963b, 280).

Although there was a growing association of disease with dirt and a move to provision of proper sanitation on land (Thurley 1993, 163–77), ideas about disease were rudimentary in the sixteenth century and often related to clean air. Rats would have been considered merely a pest because of their ability to spoil food and supplies as the link with disease probably would not have been appreciated. Cats are the main predator of rats but there is no evidence of any cats on the *Mary Rose*. There was, however, at least one dog. The black rat, although it has better sight than the common brown rat, can be easier to trap as it does not have such a strong reaction to unfamiliar objects (Corbett and Harris 1991, 258).

Domestic dog *(*Canis familiaris*)*
Juliet Clutton-Brock

The skull and skeleton of a small adult dog were retrieved from an area in and around the Carpenters' cabin (M9). These were analysed and reported on in 1983. Although the bones were dispersed, only one animal is represented. Presumably, as the carcase disintegrated, the bones became disarticulated, leaving half the skeleton inside the cabin and half outside, and

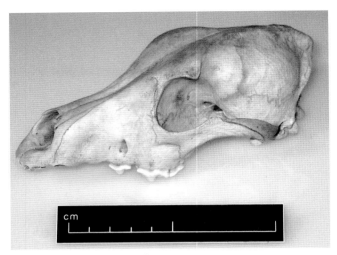

Figure 15.2 The dog skull

part of the mandible was found on the Orlop deck, just below the cabin in O9. Those bones that were found in the cabin are mostly stained very dark whilst those outside are much lighter in colour.

The distribution of the parts of the skeleton appears to be haphazard and it is not easy to determine whether the dog drowned whilst it was in the cabin or outside it (the door was slightly open). The skull (Fig. 15.2), the heaviest element, and one ramus of the mandible were both outside the sliding door of the cabin, and it could be postulated that these had moved less than other parts and that the dog died at or near the position where the skull was found. The unstained and smooth condition of the head of both humeri and the corresponding articular surfaces in the scapulae might suggest that these bones remained in articulation until retrieved. Similarly the 'clean' condition of the heads of the femurs and the acetabula in the innominate bones might suggest that the pelvis and hind limbs were articulated. However the left and right femurs were actually found in separate locations (the left in the cabin and the right one outside with the pelvis).

The skull and skeleton are almost complete with only a few teeth missing, along with a small number of vertebrae and a few foot bones. There is no penis bone and so the animal may have been a female. It was a young adult, perhaps about eighteen months to two years old based on the fusion of the skull bones and the lack of wear on the teeth. The teeth and bones are perfectly healthy except for one rib and the second left metacarpal which both have a thickening of the bone (exostoses) around their proximal ends. The teeth are relatively small and widely spaced with the first upper left premolar and the second upper molar being absent congenitally, there being no alveoli for these teeth.

The measurements show that the dog was small to medium-sized and stood about 470mm at its shoulders. The measurements of the skull and skeleton follow Harcourt (1974) and von den Driesch (1976) and are given in archive. The skull and limb bones have the average proportions of a mongrel and none of the characters that would indicate a particular breed, such as the wide muzzle and marked stop of the spaniel, or the short legs of the corgi. It is unlikely to have had a special pedigree.

The role of the dog is, obviously, uncertain. He may have been a pet or a mascot, or perhaps was brought on board to help keep down the rat population. A similar suggestion was made for the remains of a terrier-sized dog found on the wreck of the *Earl of Abergavenny* (sank 1820; Armitage 2002).

Insects

Introduction
Michael J. Allen

We can clearly divide the insect remains associated with the *Mary Rose* into two categories, of which only one is dealt with in this chapter. Those associated and contemporary with the ship are discussed here, while those subsequently associated with the wreck and its contents (eg, wood-boring insects), and relevant to its conservation are discussed by Jones in *AMR* Vol. 5.

A number of insects, insect fragments and puparia were noted during the processing of samples for plant remains. In many cases recognisable insect parts were sorted from the flots by volunteers and these were entered into the *Mary Rose* database. In other cases, insect parts were recognised by Ian Oxley or Frank Green and again these parts were extracted. Green reports that insects did not seem to be abundant, but he 'suspects that more insect remains might be found in the flots and residues' (pers. comm.). Most of these fragments were stored in Industrial Methylated Spirit (IMS), though some were freeze-dried, and a few successfully air-dried.

Various specialists visiting the *Mary Rose* commented upon these extracted items, and identified individual specimens (eg scotch broom weevil, *Apion fuscirostre*, ident. Mark Robinson, 14 October 1985). Other specimens were so well preserved and distinctive that initial identification could be made by the Mary Rose Trust (eg flea from O2) but, although cockroaches were initially reported from the assemblage, this identification does not seem to have been verified.

Dr R.C. Reay from Portsmouth Polytechnic examined a number of extracted organic remains and flots, assessing their potential and indicated the presence (or absence) and type of insect, beetle or arthropod remains (Reay 1984; Table 15.1). Although the flots and residues may contain considerable further insect remains, only those that were isolated by Reay's assessment, and that were present in the archive in 2004, were identified and reported upon by Mark Robinson. A number of items recorded by Reay (Table 15.1) could not be found (see Chapter 12).

The insects
Mark Robinson

The material examined by Dr R.C. Reay and subsequently by the present author are listed in Table 15.2. The insects provide a limited insight into conditions and activities related to the ship. One insect, the wood-boring beetle *Lyctus linearis* (powder post beetle), probably infested the structure of the ship or a wooden object. Others had been amongst commodities brought onto the ship. The grain weevil *Sitophilus granarius* can be a serious pest of stored grain and, interestingly, a fragmented seed of a cornfield weed, *Agrostemma githago* (corn cockle), was present in the same sample. This sample came from O10, one of the main stowage areas on the ship. Such remains could have represented stored grain or flour or indicate sewage. The broom weevil, *Apion fuscirostre*, was present in a pod of broom from M2/O2. Broom may have been used as dunnage (packing around stores) or as a cleaning material on board for sweeping or scouring (Chapter 14). Other insects possibly imported with plant material include *Cytilus sericeus*, a beetle which feeds on moss, and two vetch and clover-feeding weevils possibly associated with hay: *Sitona* sp. and another species of *Apion*. Finally, a photograph of a flea by Dr Reay (Fig. 15.3, left) is not sufficiently distinct for certain identification, but it resembles *Pulex irritans* (human flea: Fig. 15.3, right). The absence of oral or thoracic combs shows it not to be *Nosopsyllus fasciatus* (rat flea), *Ctenocephalides felis* (cat flea), *C. canis* (dog

Table 15.1 Insect remains recorded by Dr Reay in 1984 and not relocated for further analysis and identification

Sample	Record	Association	No. indiv.	Loca-tion
81S0566/5	insect	bed	+	M9
81S0023/6/1	insect frags	sediment	+	M1
81S0377/9	insect upper leg frags	chest 81A5783 (textile)	+	M9
81S0262	insect pupa	Orlop pork deposit	+	M9
81S0175/10.11	insect frags	pods, twigs & grass	+	O2
81S0358/1.05	insect frags		+	O3
81S0468/1/12	insect frags		+	O4
81S0520/1.5	insect frags		+	O5
81S0347/1/3	poss. moth chrysalis	chest 81A2099 (peppercorns)	1	U9
81S0421/1/7	*Diptera* (fly) pupa+ many insect frags	chest 81A2941 (fruitstones)	++	O10
81S0212/1/4	fly pupa	flowerheads	+	H3
81S0093/3/19	fly pupa	fishbones	+	H11

+ = present; ++ = many present

Table 15.2 Identified insect remains

Sample		Taxa	Common name	Association	No. indiv.	Location
Identified by Robinson (2004)						
81S0107/4/3	beetle	*Aphodius* sp.	dung beetle		1	O11
86S0293	fly puparium	*Musca domestica*	house fly	fish bones & basket	1	O11
81S0348/1.16	beetle	*Aphodius* cf. *sphacelatus*	dung beetle	flora	1	O3
81S0389/3/8	beetle	*Cytilus sericeus*		fish bones	1	O11
81S0554/7	beetle	*Lyctus linearis*	powder post beetle	fish bones	1	O10
	beetle	*Sitophilus granarius*	grain weevil		1	
81S0577/12	fly puparium	Calliphoridae indet.	blue & green bottles	fish bones	1	H4
	fly puparia	*Musca domestica*	house fly		6	
81S1289/4/3	beetle	*Apion* sp.	weevil	fish bones	1	O11
81S1300/15.1	beetle	*Sitona* sp.	weevil		1	O2
81S1300★	flea	cf. *Pulex irritans*	human flea	sackcloth 81S1233	1	O2
81S0122/1/1014★	fly puparia	*Thoracocheata zosterae*	seaweed fly	comb 81A4054	2	U9
?81S0319	beetle	*Apion fuscirostre*	broom weevil	broom pod	1	O/M2
Identified by Reay (1984)						
82S0091/4/4	beetle	indet.		fish bones	2	08
	fly puparium	*Fannia* sp	inc. latrine & lesser house fly	fish bones	1	
	fly adults	Calliphoridae or Muscidae indet	blue & green bottles		2	
	fly puparia	Calliphoridae or Muscidae indet	blue & green bottles		2+	

beetles (coleoptera), flies (Diptera), fleas (Siphonaptera) ★ = identified from photographs

flea) or *Ceratophyllus gallinae* (hen flea), which are the other fleas most likely to be found on board. While human fleas also infest pigs, it is thought most likely that this was a human flea that had presumably been brought to the ship on a crew member. The example of *Cytilus* and the *Apion* came from the store of fish in O11. The fish could have been stowed in baskets here, as a number of fragments were found, and it is possible that they were lined with moss or other plant material. The *Sitona* and the flea were associated with sackcloth and are from the rigging store in O2.

Foul organic material attracted various insects to the ship. These included the dung beetle *Aphodius* cf. *sphacelatus*, which is most usually associated with animal droppings on pasture. As there was no livestock aboard it is possible that the beetle was attracted to the ship by the smell of human sewage, otherwise it is presumed to be a stray from when the ship was in port (*Aphodius* species fly readily). There were also the puparia of flies that had been breeding in foul organic material. *Thoracochaeta zosterae* (seaweed fly: Fig. 15.4)

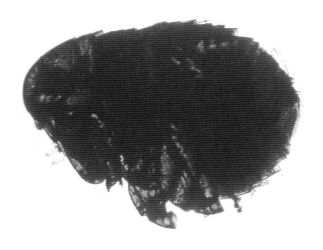
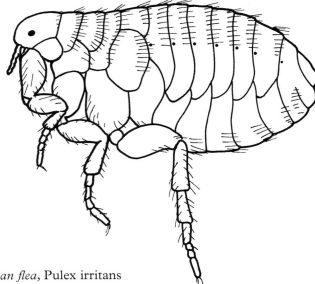

Figure 15.3 The flea (left) compared with an example of the human flea, Pulex irritans

Figure 15.4 Puparia of the seaweed fly Thoracochaeta zosterae *recovered from the teeth of a comb*

naturally occurs in rotting seaweed on the strand line but has also been recorded from many medieval and early post-medieval latrines where it fed on semi-liquid sewage. This example was found in the teeth of a comb (81A4054) in U9 not far from the possible piss-dale, whose use is apparent from its name (see Chapter 1). The genus *Fannia* includes *F. scalaris* (latrine fly), which similarly lives in semi-liquid faeces and *F. canicularis* (lesser house fly), which occurs in rotting vegetation and carrion. Two samples contained puparia of *Musca domestica* (house fly), whose larvae feed on decomposing foodstuffs, dung and carrion. Another group of flies which are often associated with decaying food products, particularly meat, the Calliphoridae (blue and green bottles) was also represented in two samples. These were all associated with fishbones.

These results from the *Mary Rose* stress the potential of palaeoentomological studies on ancient shipwrecks and the importance of more detailed studies on future excavations. Many processed samples remain to be examined from the ship and there is, therefore, the potential for recovery by paraffin flotation and extraction of many more insect remains.

A View Overboard; Pollen Analysis
Robert Scaife

Pollen analysis: a general introduction
Michael J. Allen and Robert Scaife

Pollen and spores are the reproductive gametes released by flowering and non-flowering plants (eg, ferns, liverworts and mosses) respectively. The walls of these microscopic bodies are extremely resilient and may be preserved in peat and sediments of various types. These microfossils can be extracted from the sediment and concentrated by chemical techniques in the laboratory. They are then transferred to microscope slides, where they can be examined by specialists (palynologists).

This involves identification and counting substantial numbers to obtain statistically viable data. Although seeds can often be identified to species (see Chapter 14), it is only usually possible to ascribe a pollen grain to family or morphologically similar group (eg, Poaceae: grasses or Liguliflorae: dandelion types), and quite often to genus (eg, *Quercus*: oak or *Fagus*: beech), but only exceptionally to species (eg, *Centaurea cyanus*: blue cornflower) (Dimbleby 1967, 117). The presence and quantity of pollen in sediments may be variable. Some pollen grains and spores are more robust than others and may survive better (eg, the dandelion group, *Taraxacum* and spores of ferns such as bracken: *Pteridium*). Furthermore, plants that disperse pollen by wind (anemophily) generally produce large quantities of pollen (eg, birch and pine) which may spread over long distances (kilometres), whereas insect pollinated plants (entomophilous) produce less pollen (eg, lime: *Tilia*) which is dispersed selectively and over a much more local area (metres). On archaeological sites there is also the likelihood of human introduction by crop processing, in waste food and faecal debris as well as in building materials and bedding such as mattresses and stabling.

The analysis and interpretation of pollen from archaeological deposits is, therefore, often complex (Dimbleby 1985), but can provide information about both local and wider, regional vegetation, and thus the nature of the ancient landscape. Pollen can be preserved in all kinds of archaeological deposits and its analysis is commonly employed for establishing vegetation histories and determining the role of humans in the use and modification of past landscapes. Sub-fossil pollen and spores are often preserved in waterlogged contexts such as lake and sea-bed sediments, and analysis of these is frequently undertaken by palaeo-ecologists attempting to obtain long-term vegetation and climate histories. In contrast, pollen recovered from *archaeological* deposits underwater has rarely been examined in detail (Grieg, Chapter 16), although this situation is now changing.

Unlike many other studies, the results of pollen analysis are not necessarily specific to the sampled item examined. Pollen recovered from any one location may have originated from the wider landscape. Although an item or sample from which pollen is recovered may consist of plant material that itself produces or contains pollen it, as an object, 'inhabits' that landscape and will have inadvertently trapped pollen from the wider environment through which it has passed. Thus items such as sackcloth may contain pollen relating to the material from which it is made, but also may have trapped pollen from the environment through which the sackcloth passed during its use. On the *Mary Rose* pollen may have been derived from the mainland as well as from the items actually on board. Analysis of pollen from items on the *Mary Rose* has the potential to elucidate some information about those objects or

Key

● Location of analysed pollen samples (chapter 15)

○ Location of assessed pollen samples (chapter 16)

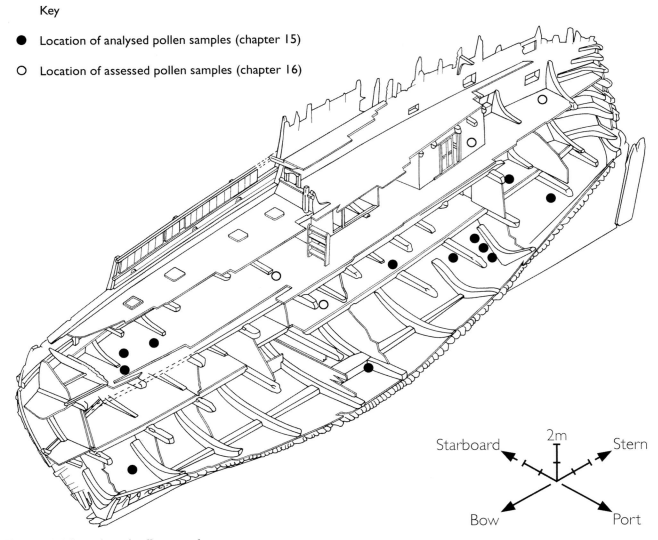

Starboard — 2m — Stern

Bow — Port

Figure 15.5 Location of pollen samples

deposits themselves and also about the vegetation in the local and wider landscape that the *Mary Rose*, her cargo and crew had inhabited and through which they had travelled.

The study
Robert Scaife

A programme of assessment of samples for the presence of pollen was established at a meeting of environmental archaeologists organised by Ian Oxley in June 1984. At the time this represented a pioneer study that has rarely been replicated since, although occasional, piecemeal work has been carried out on material from other wrecks (eg, analysis by Scaife on Hellenistic wrecks of the Mediterranean coast of Turkish; Haldane 1986). Samples were examined by James Greig and the writer. Both established that pollen was present within a range of samples (see Greig, Chapter 16). Following these assessments, no further work was pursued and the

samples were maintained in storage until the recent analysis (2002). The preliminary examinations by Greig (Chapter 16) and Scaife showed the existence particularly of *Cannabis sativa* (hemp) and cereal pollen. These were thought to have derived from hemp rope and from deck covering respectively. This report deals with more recent and detailed investigation of the original, and additional samples selected by Dr M. J. Allen, involving further preparations and larger pollen counts. A total of nineteen samples was analysed (Table 15.3), from a number of locations around the vessel (Fig. 15.5). These included samples taken from sediments associated with specific items or structures and other 'cultural' samples taken from items such as caulking, rope, textile and straw.

Method

Samples of *c.* 2ml volume were prepared in the laboratory using standard procedures for the extraction of sub-fossil pollen and spores (Moore and Webb 1978; Moore *et al.* 1991). Pollen counts of 100–300 grains per level (the pollen sum)

Table 15.3 Location and associations of pollen samples and summary of results

Pollen no.	Sample no.	Location	Material & association	Pollen summary
1	81S0153	O11	Fibrous material with brown sediment (caulking/rope) adjacent to deck beam	Pure nettle pollen (caulking/rope)
2	81S0163	H2	'Straw/hay' with soft black silt, attached to inner planking, near ballast	Some pasture types eg grasses & plantain ?(straw/hay deck covering/packing). Nettle & hemp present (rope & caulking)
3	81S0360	H11	Green-grey sand sediment adjacent to inner planking near lantern concretion	Some pasture types eg grasses & plantain
4	81S0073	M2	Soft green-black 'gunge' sediment with rope or caulking adjacent to decking at junction with starboard side Pilot's cabin	Nettle & hemp (rope & caulking)
5	81S0370	H10	Finely layered sediment of straw - soft grey clay black granular and light brown compressed organic material (?straw) - ?deck covering adjacent to inner planking, cheese cake consistency	High cereal content (?wheat/barley) & blue cornflower (straw deck covering/packing)
6	81S0326	H10	Sandwich of soft grey clay over 20mm grey sand adjacent to inner planking	Cereal pollen (?wheat/barley) (straw deck covering/packing)
7	81S0441	O8	Dark deposit or organic matter around (bilge) pump-pipe, including leather	Gunpowder and charcoal with cereal and grass pollen (including rye) - similar to 81S0120 (Greig, Chapter 16)
8	81S0092	M2	Sample of sediment with textile fragments, shoe, leather & peg, adjacent to deck planking	Cereal pollen (?wheat/barley) & some pasture types eg grasses & plantain (straw deck covering/packing). Nettle & hemp (rope & caulking)
9	81S0324	H3	Sediment within ballast	Nettle & hemp (rope & caulking), freshwater green algae
10	81S0363	H9	Sediment within ballast	Some pasture types eg grasses & plantain (straw deck covering/packing)
11	83S0307	H6	Deposit from pump-seat	Cereal pollen, and typical woodland
12	83S0342/12	H10	Sediment between frames beneath deadwood	Cereal pollen, and typical woodland
C1		Port stern hull	Caulking: between planks, lower hull	Mainly nettle
C2		Port stern hull	Caulking: under baton/lath, lower hull	No pollen
C3		Starboard hull	?Caulking: 3rd baton up starboard side between 030 & 040	Mainly nettle
C4		Starboard hull	Caulking: tar & hair under baton/lath	Mainly nettle
C5		Starboard bow (keel)	Caulking: between planks between garboard & 1st strakes under baton lath at end of baton, outboard	No pollen; probably animal fat & hair
C6		Starboard bow	Caulking: starboard side between planks	No pollen; probably animal fat & hair
S8	81A2603	O3	Sailcloth	Sailcloth made of nettle & hemp fibres
G1	81S0120	M9	Barrel contents (81A4586) (charcoal)	Little pollen – posssibly gunpowder
G2	81S0204	M5	Barrel contents (81A1071)	?
G3	80S0069	M7	Chest contents (sediment from 81A1217)	Mainly hemp or hops, much cereal pollen (straw or food remains)
G4	81S0488/4	O9	Chest contents (81A3285)	Mainly hemp or hops
G5	81S0493/3	O6	Stratified sediment at interface of hard shelly layer & soft grey lenses in Orlop deck	Little pollen

Table 15.4 Pollen data from samples 1–6

| Pollen sample | 1 | 2 | 3 | 4 | 5 | 6 |
| Sample number | 81S0153 | 81S0163 | 81S0360 | 81S0073 | 81S0370 | 81S0326 |
Sector	O11	H2	H11	M2	H10	H10
TREES AND SHRUBS						
Betula	-	7	3	9	-	1
cf.*Abies*	-	-	-	-	-	-
Pinus	-	33	1	12	3	7
Picea	-	2	-	-	-	1
Ulmus	-	3	1	2	1	3
Quercus	-	29	15	57	7	7
Tilia	-	-	-	-	-	1
Fraxinus	-	1	-	-	-	-
Carpinus betulus	-	-	-	-	-	-
Fagus sylvatica	-	-	-	7	-	-
Ilex aquifolium	-	-	-	-	-	-
Alnus	3	23	1	16	1	4
Taxus baccata	-	1	-	-	-	-
Prunus type	-	-	-	-	-	-
Hippophae rhamnoides	-	-	-	-	-	-
Corylus avellana type	1	21	16	37	11	5
Salix	-	-	-	1	-	1
Erica	-	2	-	1	-	1
Calluna	-	-	1	1	-	-
HERBS						
Ranunculus type	-	-	-	-	-	1
Papaver	-	-	-	-	2	-
Sinapis type	-	-	3	1	-	-
cf. *Hornungia* type	-	-	-	1	1	1
Dianthus type	-	-	-	-	-	-
Cerastium type	-	-	-	-	-	-
Spergula type	-	-	4	1	-	3
Chenopodium type	-	8	5	7	4	2
Fabaceae undiff.	-	-	-	-	-	-
Ononis type	-	-	-	-	-	-
Medicago type	-	-	-	-	-	-
Trifolium type	-	-	1	-	-	-
Vicia undiff.	-	-	-	-	-	-
Lathyrus type	-	-	-	-	-	-
Rosaceae undiff.	-	-	1	-	-	-
Filipendula	-	1	-	-	-	-
Sanguisorba officinalis	-	1	-	-	-	-
Apiaceae type	1	-	-	-	2	7
Euphorbia	-	-	-	-	-	-
Polygonum aviculare type	-	-	-	-	-	-
Rumex	-	1	-	-	-	-
Rumex conglomeratus type	-	-	1	1	-	-
Urtica type	198	-	-	1	-	-
Cannabis sativa	-	1	-	5	-	-
cf. *Primula* type	-	1	-	-	-	-
cf. *Lysimachia*	-	-	-	-	-	-
Symphytum type	-	1	1	-	-	-
Scrophulariaceae undiff.	-	-	1	1	-	3
Rhinanthus type	-	-	-	-	-	1
Odontites type	-	-	-	-	-	-
Mentha type	-	-	-	-	-	1
Plantago major type	-	-	-	1	-	-
Plantago lanceolata	-	1	1	7	1	-
Plantago maritima type	-	-	1	2	-	-
Plantago coronopus type	-	-	-	-	-	-
Scabiosa type	-	-	-	-	-	1
Bidens type	-	1	1	-	1	7

Pollen sample Sample number Sector	1 81S0153 O11	2 81S0163 H2	3 81S0360 H11	4 81S0073 M2	5 81S0370 H10	6 81S0326 H10
Aster type	-	-	-	-	-	-
Anthemis type	-	-	13	17	17	1
Artemisia	-	-	-	1	-	-
Centaurea scabiosa type	-	-	-	-	-	-
Centaurea nigra type	-	-	-	-	1	-
Centaurea cyanus	-	-	-	-	1	-
Lactucoideae	-	5	3	-	1	1
Poaceae	-	38	50	28	55	9
Cereal type	2	8	2	2	88	5
Secale cereale	-	-	-	-	-	-
Large *Poaceae*	-	-	-	-	-	6
Unidentified/degraded	-	1	2	3	3	4
Unidentified/exotic	-	1	1	1	2	-
MARSH/AQUATIC						
cf. *Lemna*	-	-	-	-	1	-
Typha angustifolia type	-	1	3	1	-	1
Cyperaceae	-	8	5	7	1	3
SPORES						
Pteridium aquilinum	-	6	111	30	7	2
Dryopteris type	-	9	11	6	5	9
Polypodium vulgare	-	1	1	3	-	1
Sphagnum	-	-	-	1	-	-
MISC.						
Pediastrum	-	5	5	5	-	1
Dinoflagellates	-	-	2	8	-	-
Milfordia	-	3	-	3	-	1
Pre-quaternary	-	77	60	164	4	5

where possible were made spores of ferns and miscellaneous palynomorphs (reworked ancient pollen) were also recorded. Identification and counting was carried out using an Olympus biological microscope (BH) fitted with Leitz optics. Data obtained are presented in tables (Tables 15.3 and 15.4) and diagram form (Fig. 15.6).

In the diagram the vertical arrangement of the samples is not stratigraphical as all samples are contemporaneous and are spatially distributed over the vessel (Figs 15.5 and 15.6). The diagram facilitates visual comparison of the pollen assemblages.

The percentages given where given were calculated as follows:

Sum =	% total dry land pollen (tdlp)
Marsh/aquatic =	% tdlp+sum of marsh/aquatics
Spores=	% tdlp+sum of spores
Misc.=	% tdlp+sum of misc. taxa.

Taxonomy in general follows that of Moore and Webb (1978) modified according to Bennett et al. (1994) for pollen types and Stace (1997) for plant descriptions. The pollen diagrams were plotted using Tilia and Tilia Graph. These procedures were carried out in the Department of Geography, University of Southampton.

Pollen data

The samples can be divided into those that were taken from the Solent sediments which accumulated within the vessel, and those that relate specifically to ship materials on board. The former have an admixture of pollen from both the ship and possibly the sea-bed environments. These two aspects are discussed below. Table 15.3 lists the character and position of the samples in relation to the wreck and their location is shown in Figure 15.5.

Samples (nos 3, 4, 5, 6, 11 and 12) of the sediments within the hull were taken by Ian Oxley. The initial aim (1984) was to characterise these samples and provide information on the depositional habitat and background pollen input from the regional sources. These samples have provided useful information on the pollen assemblages in sediments found at distance from the land and as such, provide useful data for

Table 15.5 Pollen data from samples 7–12

Pollen sample Sample number Sector	7 81S0441 O8	8 81S0092 H2	9 81S0324 H3	10 81S0363 H9	11 83S0307 H10	12 83S0342/12 H10
TREES AND SHRUBS						
Betula	-	3	6	1	3	9
cf. *abies*	-	-	-	-	-	1
Pinus	1	4	2	7	2	4
Picea	-	-	-	-	-	-
Ulmus	-	3	-	-	-	3
Quercus	7	29	18	25	8	40
Tilia	-	-	-	-	-	-
Fraxinus	-	-	-	-	-	-
Carpinus betulus	-	1	-	-	-	-
Fagus sylvatica	-	2	-	-	-	3
Ilex aquifolium	-	-	-	1	-	-
Alnus	-	15	6	3	1	11
Taxus baccata	-	-	-	-	-	-
Prunus type	-	1	-	-	-	-
Hippophae rhamnoides	1	-	-	-	-	-
Corylus avellana type	3	45	3	7	6	60
Salix	-	2	1	1	-	-
Erica	-	3	-	-	-	-
Calluna	1	1	-	-	-	1
HERBS						
Ranunculus type	-	9	-	-	-	-
Papaver	1	-	-	-	-	-
Sinapis type	2	1	-	4	3	1
cf. *Hornungia* type	-	-	-	-	-	1
Dianthus type	-	1	-	-	-	-
Cerastium type	-	1	-	-	-	-
Spergula type	-	-	-	-	-	-
Chenopodium type	1	8	1	-	1	2
Fabaceae undiff.	-	-	-	1	-	-
Ononis type	-	-	-	-	2	-
Medicago type	-	1	-	-	-	-
Trifolium type	-	-	-	-	-	-
Vicia undiff.	1	-	-	-	-	-
Lathyrus type	-	1	-	-	-	-
Rosaceae undiff.	1	1	-	-	-	-
Filipendula	-	-	-	-	-	-
Sanguisorba officinalis	-	-	-	-	-	-
Apiaceae type	2	1	-	-	1	1
Euphorbia	-	1	-	-	-	-
Polygonum aviculare type	-	1	-	-	-	1
Rumex	5	3	1	-	-	-
Rumex conglomeratus type	1	-	-	-	-	-
Urtica type	5	4	14	-	-	-
Cannabis sativa	5	15	27	-	-	-
cf. *Primula* type	-	-	-	-	-	-
cf. *Lysimachia*	1	-	-	-	-	-
Symphytum type	-	-	-	-	-	-
Scrophulariaceae undiff.	1	-	1	1	-	2
Rhinanthus type	-	-	-	-	1	-
Odontites type	-	-	-	-	-	-
Mentha type	-	-	-	-	-	-
Plantago major type	1	-	-	-	-	2
Plantago lanceolata	13	11	-	6	1	2
Plantago maritima type	-	1	-	-	-	1
Plantago coronopus type	1	1	-	1	-	-
Scabiosa type	-	-	-	-	-	-
Bidens type	-	3	-	1	-	-

Pollen sample	7	8	9	10	11	12
Sample number	81S0441	81S0092	81S0324	81S0363	83S0307	83S0342/12
Sector	O8	H2	H3	H9	H10	H10
Aster type	-	1	-	1	-	-
Anthemis type	5	14	-	1	1	5
Artemisia	1	-	-	1	-	-
Centaurea scabiosa type	-	1	-	-	-	-
Centaurea nigra type	-	-	-	-	-	-
Centaurea cyanus	-	-	-	-	-	-
Lactucoideae	-	-	1	1	-	-
Poaceae	108	76	14	23	6	19
Cereal type	31	38	-	9	-	30
Secale cereale	1	-	-	-	-	-
Large *poaceae*	-	-	-	-	-	1
Unidentified/degraded	1	1	-	1	1	-
Unidentified/exotic	-	-	-	-	-	-
MARSH/AQUATIC						
cf. *Lemna*	-	-	-	-	-	-
Typha angustifolia type	1	-	-	-	-	2
Cyperaceae	-	1	1	5	-	5
SPORES						
Pteridium aquilinum	4	11	1	14	3	16
Dryopteris type	-	3	3	6	1	3
Polypodium vulgare	1	-	1	-	-	1
Sphagnum	1	-	-	-	-	1
MISC.						
Pediastrum	-	-	7	5	-	7
Dinoflagellates	-	-	1	7	-	3
Milfordia	-	-	-	-	-	-
Pre-quaternary	10	41	43	54	5	192

comparison with recent studies of the Solent intertidal zone. Samples within the hull of the ship are polliniferous, relating to material on board the vessel. This is especially the case with cereal pollen and possibly wild grasses and associated weeds which probably come from floor coverings and other uses of these plants on board.

The regional vegetation
When compared with terrestrial pollen data from the region (ie, southern Hampshire), the samples 3, 4, 5, 6, 11 and 12 display pollen assemblages that are typical of woodland in the historical period that was largely dominated by oak (*Quercus*) with hazel (*Corylus*) and a scatter of other types including alder (*Alnus*), birch (*Betula*), elm (*Ulmus*), ash (*Fraxinus*), hornbeam (*Carpinus*), beech (*Fagus*), holly (*Ilex*) and lime/linden (*Tilia*) (Table 15.4 and 15.5). Holly and lime are only sporadic, individual occurrences within the samples, and are generally less well represented than wind dispersed types in the pollen assemblages as they are insect pollinated (entomophilous). These pollen elements reflect the diversity of remaining woodland types throughout the Hampshire Basin. The taphonomy

of this material may be complex; including pollen already on board adhering to items before the vessel sank, combined with that most probably derived from river sediment, discharging and deposited into the Solent subsequent to the sinking.

The marine/halophytic (salt-loving) communities
Although there is clearly evidence of typical saltmarsh plants, the pollen numbers of these types are substantially fewer than typically found in near shore/intertidal sediments of the Solent estuaries (Table 15.4 and 15.5). Studies of intertidal sediments typically show the importance of saltmarsh/halophytic communities dominated by Chenopodiaceae including glassworts, oraches and goosefoots with less well represented taxa including, for example, sea lavender (*Limonium*), sea plantain (*Plantago maritima*) and sea arrow grass (*Triglochin*). Here, values of Chenopodiaceae range from less than 1% in samples 6 and 12 to 4% in samples 2, 3 and 4. These are, therefore, considered to be small values. This may suggest that much of the non-saltmarsh pollen may indeed come from the *Mary Rose* rather than from longer distance input since higher quantities of the halophytes would

624

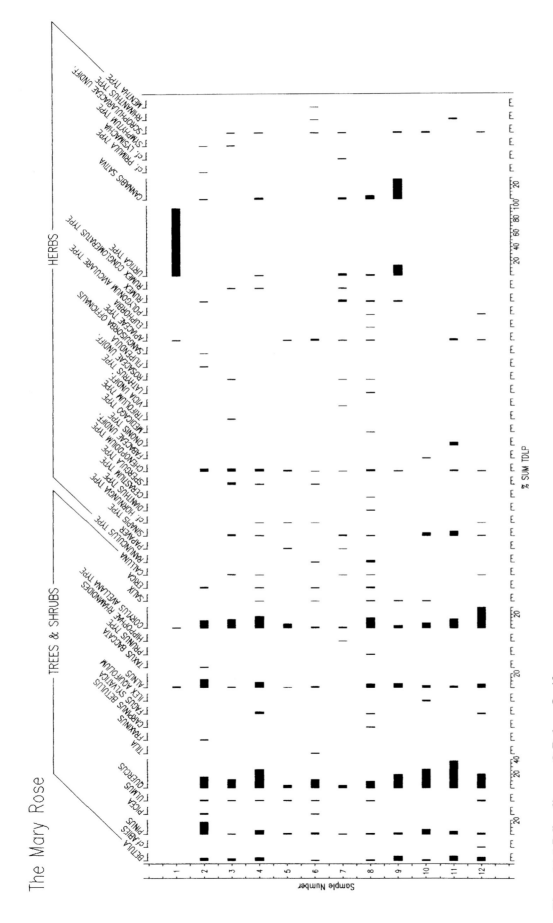

Figure 15.6 Pollen diagram © Robert Scaife

The Mary Rose

Figure 15.6 Pollen diagram (cont.) © *Robert Scaife*

also be expected if source areas were farther afield. This could be verified by taking samples of the sea-bed sediments from the wreck site.

Ship-related pollen

The diagnostic feature of these, and Greig's, samples (Chapter 16) is the substantial quantities of cereal, hemp (*Cannabis*) and nettle (*Urtica*) pollen (Tables 15.4–6). Whilst some preliminary suggestions can be made about their presence and taphonomy, it is anticipated that a fuller understanding will come when other aspects of the environmental research can be integrated (see Chapter 12).

Possible packing materials or deck coverings

Cereal pollen is especially important in samples 5 (notably high), 6, 7, 8 and 12 with lesser quantities in most of the remaining samples. Although detailed identification has not been carried out of the cereal pollen (a difficult procedure) those recorded appear to be of wheat and barley (*Triticum/Hordeum* type) with only a single grain of rye (*Secale cereale*) from sample 7. Such large numbers are rarely found in 'natural' peat sequences and are more typical of urban archaeological contexts and prehistoric grain storage pits (Iron Age). In most of these cases the cereal pollen is also associated with other pollen from weeds of disturbed, arable ground (segetals) including blue cornflower (*Centaurea cyanus*) in sample 5.

Preliminary thoughts were that these arable pollen elements are derived from straw used as deck coverings or bedding. However, three of these samples (5, 6 and 12) are from the stern area of the Hold H10, an area where there is very little 'floor' surface and the sides of the ship rise steeply. Several casks, including one containing lanterns, and a basket of fish were stored here and another possible explanation is that straw was used as packing material either inside the casks or around them in the Hold. Other sources such as faecal material and food debris are also possible. In sample 7 and to a lesser extent in samples 2, 3, 8 and 10 there is a greater importance of pasture types dominated by grasses (Poaceae) with ribwort plantain (*Plantago lanceolata*) and this may also be derived from meadow hay used for the same purposes. Sample 8 was taken from M2 and could have originated from bedding in the Pilot's cabin. Sample 7 was associated with the bilge pump (see below). Although there has been mixing of shipboard elements with the 'natural' Solent components, values of cereal pollen here are very unlikely to have come from the latter source. Their presence comes from the fact that the sediments sampled were from deposits within the hull and on the decks of the ship (Table 15.3) and are probably of cultural origin rather than from the Solent sediment.

Samples 2 and 10 are possibly pollen contents of the ships ballast.

Rope and caulking

Nettle and hemp are perhaps the most interesting pollen elements recorded here and in Greig's samples (Tables 15.4–6). Hemp is present in five of the twelve samples (samples 2, 4, 7, 8, 9) examined, with percentages up to 28% (sample 9). Sources of this are most likely to include hemp rope and fibre used in the vessels caulking. Both writers have carried out tests on hemp rope and have recovered pollen suggesting that the most likely source is the quantities of rope which would have been on board. Samples 2 and 9, from H2 and H3 respectively, come from a stowage area that contained several casks and a quantity of rigging, while samples 4 and 8 are both from M2 (sample 7, associated with the bilge pump in O8 produced only five grains each of hemp and nettle pollen).

The presence of nettle is enigmatic but its stems may also have been used for fibre. Sample 1 consisted of a fibrous deposit from the stern of the Orlop deck (O11) which contained almost pure nettle pollen (99%) and fibre. Such an abundance in one sample is exceptional. Other samples contain up to 5% pollen (sample 9). As with the hemp, the possible use of nettle may become more apparent from studies of the *in situ* fibres within the hull of the ship.

Further caulking materials

The initial examination identified one sample (sample 1; Table 15.5) which was thought to be from caulking in the planks of the ships hull. This sample contained very substantial quantities of nettle pollen. Further samples of caulking (pollen samples C1–C6) were examined to establish if nettle fibre was used in caulking. Of these, four contained substantial numbers of pollen (samples C1–3, C5–6; Table 15.6) and one had only occasional grains (sample C2). This and two other samples were devoid of pollen and appeared to be from caulking made from animal fat with hair bonding (see Ryder 1988). Those with pollen clearly consisted of plant fibre.

The pollen assemblages are clearly dominated by nettle in the three principal samples. In the case of the starboard bow and starboard keel samples (samples C3 and C5), there is also a substantial number of hemp grains. Sample C1 from the lower port hull also contained occasional hemp pollen.

Palynologically, the presence of hemp and nettle pollen can be problematic since the pollen grains of hemp, hop and nettle may be morphologically similar. Whilst it is usually possible to separate pollen of hemp from nettle, it is more difficult (or impossible in many cases) to differentiate between hop and hemp, both being Cannabinaceae. Here, however, it seems more plausible that where hemp is recorded (ie, *Cannabis*

Table 15.6 Pollen data from additional caulking samples and sailcloth

Pollen sample	C1	C2	C3	C5	C6	S8
Sample	-	-	-	-	-	81A2603
Material	caulking	caulking	caulking	caulking	caulking	Sailcloth
Location	port stern lower hull	port stern lower hull	starboard bow 3rd baton	starboard bow keel	starboard bow between planks	O3
TREES AND SHRUBS						
Betula	-	-	-	-	1	1
Pinus	-	1	-	-	-	-
Quercus	-	-	-	-	-	2
Corylus avellana type	-	1	-	-	2	-
Erica	-	-	-	-	1	1
Calluna vulgaris	-	-	-	-	1	-
HERBS						
Ranunculus type	-	-	-	-	-	3
Chenopodiaceae	-	-	-	-	-	3
Spergula type	-	-	-	-	-	1
Urtica cf dioica	150	-	61	41	83	24
Cannabis type	2	-	39	30	-	10
Cannabis/Urtica	-	-	-	-	-	4
Rumex	-	-	-	-	-	2
Plantago lancolata	-	-	-	-	2	1
Lactucoideae	-	-	-	-	1	1
Poaceae	3	-	-	-	5	31
Cyperaceae	-	-	-	-	4	1
MARSH/AQUATIC						
Dryopteris type					1	-
Sphagnum	-	-	-	-	4	-
MISC.						
Unidentified	1			1	1	5

type) we are dealing with hemp used as rope, caulking fibre and sailcloth. One further consideration is that examination of immature *Cannabis sativa* pollen shows strong resemblance to that of nettle. As far as possible, identifications here are what may be expected in 'normal' pollen assemblages following normal criteria for identification.

In the case of samples C1, C3 and C4 from the hull and keel, the pollen assemblages are dominated by nettle suggesting that this was a valued and much-used caulking fibre. Hemp in samples 3 and 5 is important with nettle probably indicating a mix of the two or possible use of hemp rope fibre. Both of these samples have little or no other pollen types indicating that we are dealing with samples which have not been contaminated by sediments surrounding the hull. Sample 6 is interesting in having a much more diverse range of pollen types/plants. This sample comes from between planks on the starboard bow in the area of the pilot's cabin in M2 and contains a moderately diverse range of plants in addition to the nettle used for caulking. Here, there are Ericaceae, *Sphagnum* moss, grasses, sedges and other plants of pasture (eg, ribwort plantain, buttercups). Whilst it is possible that these may be contaminants from the Solent sediments, it is perhaps more likely that these taxa derive from floor coverings, bedding or other extraneous material on the deck of the ship.

Sailcloth

Having identified the presence of nettle fibres, a small quantity of sailcloth was examined in an attempt to identify its make up. This had not been determined from examination of the fibres alone. Sufficient pollen was extracted to enable a pollen count to be made (sample S8; Table 15.6). Clearly, however, the taphonomy of any pollen recovered would be more complex than the caulking material since there is also the possibility of pollen impacted onto the sail and also a greater likelihood that there would be contamination from the Solent sediments. This appears to be the case although there is clear evidence that there are also elements of the make up of the sailcloth with both nettle and hemp present. It is not conclusive that the sailcloth was a mixture of the two, however, it seems probable that this was the case. The use of nettle fibre in sailmaking and for fishing nets is well known (eg, Brenchley 1919; Grieve 1931). The remaining pollen flora obtained from the sail includes sporadic records of a variety of herbs including notable numbers of grasses (Poaceae). Whether this largely pasture pollen element comes from pollen impacted onto the sails or from the sediments in which the sailcloth was recovered is, at present, conjectural.

Black gunpowder

Sample 7 (O8) proved interesting and similar to sample 81S120 described by Greig (Chapter 16). This was an extraordinarily black sooty material coming from one of the main storage areas of the ship (Chapter 10). Originally sampled as estuarine mud, this is clearly not the case and, as with Greig's sample, is probably gunpowder charcoal. A small number of pollen grains were also present and included hemp, nettle and cereal pollen, probably from sources described above.

The pump pipe

A sample (7) described as 'dark gunge' was taken from the leather valve at the end of the bilge pump recovered from O8. This rather strange deposit contained a diverse pollen assemblage dominated by herbs and especially wild grasses (Poaceae) with cereal types, plantain and some hemp. This assemblage appears to be a pasture/hay assemblage. The bilge pump could have been used on many occasions and in many locations during the life of the ship.

Ballast

Three samples provided for analysis were thought to have been ballast sediment from H3 (samples 2 and 9) and H9 (sample 10). Sample 9 is one of those noted above which has substantial quantities of hemp pollen and nettle, that have been attributed to the use of these stem fibres in rope and caulking. Quantities of rigging were found in H3, some of which may have fallen through from the main rigging store above in O3. In addition to these there is also a background element of typical woodland vegetation of the Hampshire Basin (oak and hazel) with derived pre-Quaternary spores and green algae (algal *Pediastrum*) from freshwater sources. Sample 2 contained some pasture types such as grasses and plantain. This, again, could indicate packing from casks or other stores kept in this area. Samples 2 and 9, however, contain the largest numbers of trees and shrubs in this sample suite.

Table 15.7 Pollen data from assessed samples

Object	Chest 80A1217	Staved container 81A1071	Chest 81A2385	
Location	M7	M5	O9	Common
Sample	80S0069	81S0204	81S0488/1	name
Pollen/spore				
Pteridium	–	3	1	bracken
Pediastrum	+	–	–	an alga
Pinus	1	1	1	pine
Ranunculus type	1	–	–	buttercups
Papaveraceae	1	–	–	poppy family
Cruciferae	1	–	–	cabbage family
Caryophyllaceae	+	1	–	chickweed family
Chenopodiceae	2	5	1	goosefoot family
Trifolium repens	1	–	–	white clover
T. pratense	1	–	–	red clover
Umbelliferae	2	–	–	hogweed family
Rumex	2	–	–	docks & sorrels
Urtica	7	1	1	nettles
Cannabaceae	9	–	91	?hemp
Ulmus	1	–	–	elm
Betula	+	5	–	birch
Alnus	3	3	1	alder
Corylus	4	27	–	hazel
Quercus	7	16	3	oak
Fagus	–	+	+	beech
Salix	4	–	–	willow
Ericales	–	–	1	heathers etc
Fraxinus	3	–	–	ash
Plantago lanceolata	10	–	1	ribwort plantain
Galium sp.	–	–	1	bedstraws
Artemisia	1	–	1	mugworts
Compositae (T.)	10	–	–	mayweeds etc
Centaurea nigra sp.	–	1	–	knapweed
Composite (L.)	2	1	–	hawkweeds etc
Cyperaceae	2	2	–	sedges etc
Gramineae	51	12	9	grasses
Cerealia	17	–	1	cereals
Unident.	2	4	4	

These include the highest counts of pine (*Pinus*: 16.5%) in sample 2 with oak (14.5%), alder (16%) and hazel (10%). There is also a single grain of hemp type. Whilst this assemblage may be the background pollen as described for the Solent sediments (see above), another possibility is that the pollen in this sample may have been transported within the sediments making up the ballast.

Exotics

Apart from these known elements, only a small number of non-native/exotic plants were noted. Possible fir (*Abies*: sample 12) and spruce (*Picea*: sample 2 and 6) are non-native and may have come from plantations or from long distance oceanic transport. Although there are substantial quantities of derived reworked older pollen (geological palynomorphs) present which may have been a source of these, the grains of spruce and fir were unabraded and appeared fresh by comparison. A small number of artefacts from the ship are made of these woods.

Pollen assessment of chests and containers
by James Greig

Pollen was assessed from five samples (samples G1-5, Table 15.3) in 1985 (Chapter 16), and pollen was present in three samples. Samples from chest 81A1217, staved container 81A1071 and chest 81A2385 contained pollen typical of those reported above. The assemblages (Table 15.7), contained a range of plants typical of urban sites, rather than seaside plants. Chest 81A3285 contained large quartiles of hemp, probably representing rope, cordage or canvas. Objects in this chest included aiglets, a hat, various flasks and sewing gear as well as two leather mittens that might have been used a hand protectors against rope friction burns. Staved container 81A1071 produced pollen of hazel, oak and grasses in particular, and chest 80A1217 produced a wide pollen spectra typical of the wider landscape reported above. This chest contained a quantity of fishing gear including handlines and floats

so fishing lines are an obvious possibility for the source of pollen here.

Summary

Analysis of samples from the differing contexts has produced interesting palynological assemblages and useful information about the character of the deposits associated with the hull. Perhaps the most interesting aspect is the evidence of the composition of the caulking. Other samples contain a diverse range of pollen taxa which, as discussed, come from a range of human sources and natural depositional environments which are more akin to those in urban archaeological situations. That is, pollen potentially coming from packing and possible floor coverings, bedding, human and animal faeces and waste food. What has become clear from this analysis is that pollen may be preserved in a variety of shipboard contexts. Whilst the results may appear a little esoteric within the overall scope of this volume, this represented one of the first pollen studies undertaken on samples taken from a submerged wreck. With future studies a more coherent pattern of results and a better understanding of pollen taphonomy should result and thus a better understanding of plant utilisation, that is, data which may not be available from the ship's inventories or other documentary evidence.

16. Science and the *Mary Rose*

Scientific Studies

Michael J. Allen

The *Mary Rose* produced a 'store' of materials rarely preserved on, or recovered from, land-based archaeological sites. These allowed questions to be posed, ranging from the basic level of identification ('what was this gooey mess/concretion?'), to more considered questions ('what was the type of meat flesh?', or 'what glue or resin was used to adhere or seal this object'), to others requiring complex programmes of scientific analysis. Environmental archaeologists, archaeological scientists and pure biological, environmental and medical scientists and physicists have undertaken research to help understand the living conditions on board, the nature of the stored food and diet of the crew, and the physical nature of the men. Questions were posed both by members of the Mary Rose Trust interested in examining and discovering information about the materials they had recovered, and by archaeological and 'pure' scientists wishing to realise the potential of the unusually well-preserved remains (see Chapter 12). Some analyses were conducted purely 'because the material was there'. The *Mary Rose* in turn has also provided a research pool for science itself. The materials studied have not always provided information of relevance in the interpretation of the *Mary Rose* and those who sailed in her, but their study has provided the opportunity of making significant advances in other scientific fields.

Many of the studies were undertaken at the behest of the analysts, rather than as part of any coherent analytical programme devised by the Mary Rose Trust. Some analysts were certainly offering to aid the understanding of the *Mary Rose* assemblages while others seized the opportunity of analysing materials not readily available or previously preserved. In these latter cases, the research agenda was one of testing and examining materials for the sake of *science*, rather than for interpretation of the contents of the *Mary Rose*. The *Mary Rose* assemblages have, thereby and in small ways, aided research within the separate disciplines of the physical and biological sciences; a fact few archaeological sites or assemblages can lay claim to.

There was no coherent programme of archaeological science and, although good science was undertaken, the selection of items and materials for analysis was somewhat arbitrary; as too was some of the analysis itself. These analyses were conducted by a variety of individuals and institutions, ranging from recognised scientists engaged in major programmes of work to students undertaking undergraduate and postgraduate projects (Chapter 12). We can, however, split the analyses into two main groups. First are those for which the aims and questions were driven by a desire to obtain a greater archaeological understanding of the *Mary Rose* and her contents. These were largely conducted at the behest of the Mary Rose Trust, or by archaeological scientists in pursuit of specific research aims. Secondly, there are the analyses carried for purposes of advancing archaeological science or other scientific disciplines.

This chapter presents reports and summarises a selection of some of the more significant of these studies which made use of what were, at the time, novel scientific methods, or employed the novel application of scientific methods to the largely 'palaeo-environmental' material and samples rather than to the artefacts themselves. It also includes scientific analyses used to support the interpretation of some materials presented earlier in this volume (eg, medicaments presented in Chapter 4). In the end the selection presented here is somewhat arbitrary, and is largely dependent on the level of detail and quality of results reported back to the Trust, but hopes to give a flavour of the range and significance of the archaeological science employed on materials from the *Mary Rose*. This chapter, therefore, deals with scientific methods and the application of analyses, but not with the archaeologically relevant implications or the conclusions that may have been derived; these are presented elsewhere in this volume. As a result some sections of this discourse remain necessarily technical. The reader should also note that the results of other analyses undertaken of *Mary Rose* material remain with the Mary Rose Trust archive while others have not yet been reported back or been made available for this publication.

Science for the *Mary Rose*

The preservation of the *Mary Rose* was astounding. A range organic items rarely seen before on archaeological sites was recovered. In many instances it was obvious what they were, numerous objects were so well preserved that their recognition and identification was both clear and immediate (see Chapters 2–11). In others, analyses in one form or another had to be employed to determine the basic nature of some objects, and in others to define particular substances utilised in their manufacture or use. In the 1980s a large programme of disparate scientific analyses was embarked upon (see Chapter 12). The results have aided in the identification of objects, items and substances recovered, and thus enhanced our understanding of life aboard the Tudor vessel. Some analyses were new in their application to archaeological materials, others were known by the archaeological community but had rarely been applied.

Analysis of animal fats
E. David Morgan and Michael J. Williams

Two samples of animal tissue were selected by Ian Oxley for analysis in 1985. Analysis was conducted by one of the authors (Williams 1985) when an undergraduate final-year chemistry student, supervised by Morgan, at the University of Keele. Subsequently, Morgan recalculated the composition of the samples from the original data to provide more accurate results (Morgan and Williams 2001).

One of the aims of analysis was to confirm the presence of animal fats rather than plant oils in the samples of tissue provided. Animal fats and plant oils are essentially the same; they are triglycerides of the common fatty acids. The difference is that fats contain chiefly the glycerides of the saturated fatty acids, which makes them solid at room temperature, and the oils contain more glycerides of the unsaturated acids, which makes them liquid at room temperature. Studies have shown that immersion of fat or oil in water for a long time converts them both into a material called adipocere (Fourcroy 1790), a white, waxy solid material consisting of free saturated fatty acids (reviewed by Mant 1957). The glycerol and the unsaturated acids have disappeared. The change is caused by the action of anaerobic micro-organisms (den Dooren de Jong 1961). Work has shown that 'bog butter', a material found while peat cutting in the northern and western parts of the British Isles, whatever its origin, has in the course of time also been converted into adipocere (Thornton et al. 1970; Morgan et al. 1973). Analyses of fatty materials from an tenth century AD Thule Eskimo midden near the MacKenzie Delta in Northern Canada, and from the wreck of a Basque whaling ship at Red Bay in Labrador indicated incomplete conversion to adipocere, with some of the unsaturated fatty acids still present.

Materials and methods
The samples received were preserved in industrial methylated spirit and sealed in specimen tubes. They were:

81S0175: Fat adhering to pig bones from the Orlop deck. The bones were articulated, and preserved beneath a mass

of rope and sailcloth. It is possible that the meat was originally hung up and stored in carcase form and Coy suggests that these were hams or sides of pork (Chapter 14). Remains of several dozen animal or carcases were recovered.

81S0379: Tissue from cattle bones recovered from cask 81A2610, also from the Orlop deck, are stored salt beef. A number other casks yielded animal bone, but with little or no tissue deposits surviving.

The samples were Soxhlet extracted with pure hexane (150ml) for 3 hours to extract the lipids and the residues extracted in the same way for a further 3 hours to ensure complete extraction. The solvent was removed under vacuum to leave the pure lipid fraction.

Thin-layer chromatography was used to identify the classes of compounds present in the extract. Portions of both fractions were spotted on Silica gel G plates and developed with a mixture of hexane:ether:acetic (80:20:1) and the spots developed by spraying with 60% aqueous sulphuric acid containing 1% chromic acid and heating in an oven at 180°C until sufficiently charred.

For gas chromatography, portions of the lipid extract (50mg) were dissolved in boron trifluoride-methanol complex (10ml) and the solution heated to reflux for 6 minutes, cooled and water (5ml) added. The two-phase system was extracted twice with hexane. The hexane extract containing methyl esters of the fatty acids was washed with water, dried ($MgSO_4$), and evaporated to a volume of approximately 2ml for use in chromatography. In this case the solution of methyl esters in hexane (1μl) was injected into a packed glass chromatography column (1.5m x 4 mm packed with 10% silar-10C on Gaschrom Q) in a Pye 104 Gas Chromatograph with a flame ionization detector with nitrogen gas flow of 50ml/min temperature ranged from 185 to 250°C.

Results and discussion
Qualitative analysis by thin-layer chromatography showed the presence of fatty acids, sterols and a small amount of hydrocarbon. The hydrocarbon was tentatively identified as hexadecane by gas chromatography. Unfortunately no mass spectra were available to identify the two sterols present. The quantitative analysis of the fatty acids (as their methyl esters) is given in Table 16.1

In the conversion of fats and oils to adipocere there is a loss of unsaturated acids (essentially oleic, linoleic and palmitoleic acids) and replacement of them by saturated acids of shorter chain length. So, for example, oleic acid (C:18:1) is replaced by palmitic acid (C:16:0). This process has been shown to occur in months under laboratory conditions (den Dooren de Jong 1961). Examination of Scottish bog butter showed that oleic acid had completely disappeared and there was a higher proportion of palmitic acid present than is

Table 16.1 Results of the analysis of pig fat (81S0175) and beef fat (81S0379) and ranges of recorded values

Fatty acid	Symbol	81S0175 %	Range of values for pig %*	81S0379 %	Range of values for beef tallow %#
Trideca-noic	C13:0	0.5	–	0.5	–
Myristic	C14:0	4.8	1.4–2.2	6.5	1.4–6.3
Penta-decanoic	C15:0	0.6	–	1.0	0.5–1.0
Palmitic acid	C16:0	56.9	24.0–32.0	48.6	20.0–37.0
Palmito-leic	C16:1	2.3	2.8–5.2	3.7	0.7–8.8
Hepta-decanoic	C17:0	0.8	–	1.2	0.5–2.0
Stearic	C18:0	11.8	11.0–18.0	22.1	6.0–40.0
Oleic	C18:1	22.3	31.0–46.0	16.5	26.0–50.0

* Chacko and Perkins 1965; # Spencer *et al.* 1976

usually found in butter or animal fats (Morgan *et al.* 1973).

Samples from the *Mary Rose* have quite high proportions of oleic acid still present in the meat fat of both samples. This is remarkable, and suggests that these materials have been held in an environment that was not only anaerobic (under which adipocere formation occurs), but also largely aseptic, so that the microbiological action by which adipocere is formed has not occurred. No doubt some change to adipocere occurred initially after the vessel sank, but the silt which filled the hull seems to have excluded the micro-organisms that would have altered the composition of the fat, and the complete conversion to adipocere never took place.

The actual composition of animal fat varies with the diet of the animal and the part of the body from which the fat is taken. The range of values for pig fat and beef tallow is given for comparison in Table 16.1. It is surprising how well the values found for the samples from the *Mary Rose* fit within the expected range, except for oleic acid, which is below it and for palmitic acid, which is above the range for both pig and beef. Palmitoleic acid is also low and myristic acid high for the pig sample. The only partial conversion of these animal fats to adipocere by bacterial action fits well with the remarkable state of preservation of other fragile materials preserved in the silt. The absence of the odd-numbered acids C 13:0, C 15:0, and C 17:0 from the comparison data does not mean that these acids were not present (they are always found in small quantities in animal fat), rather they were not recorded in the examples chosen. This apparent lack of bacterial action

accounts for the comparatively well-preserved state of many of the items found in the vessel.

Analysis of glue from arrows
Michael J. Allen

Scientific analyses were carried out on artefacts reported elsewhere in this series. An example is that of glue and other substances noted on the flight ends and tips of arrows (see *AMR* Vol. 3). The following is a summary extracted from archive reports by John Evans and Melvyn Card (Evans and Card 1984) of the then North East London Polytechnic.

Six samples of the glue used to attach flights to the arrow shafts were provided for analysis in 1983 (82S1280 from arrow 81A2589, part of a crate of arrows (81A2582) found in O9). It was anticipated that the glue would have a pine origin (see below). The samples were thin flakes of a pale green material with traces of a brown glue adhering to them. Typically 0.5-1.0 mg of material was taken and placed in a sterile glass vial. A small amount (approximately 200µl) of AnalaR grade chloroform/methanol (2:1 *v/v*) was added to each of the samples and the vial warmed gently to aid the dissolution of solvent soluble compounds. An aliquot (75µl) was then removed to a new vial and reduced to dryness under nitrogen. Trimethylsilylation of the dried sample was carried out using 50 p1 *N, 0-b* is (trimethylsilyl)-trifluoroacetamide and 25µl pyridine (AnalaR) was added to assist dissolution. The samples were then warmed on a hot plate at 60°C for 10 minutes before being dried under nitrogen once again. Finally the dried sample was dissolved in approximately 75µl dichloromethane.

Methods: gas chromatography and gas chromatography/mass spectrometry
Gas chromatography was carried out using a Hewlett Packard 5890 Series II instrument equipped with an on-column injector and flame ionisation detector. Data processing was carried out using dedicated Hewlett Packard 3365 Chemstation software. Gas chroma-tography/mass spectrometry was carried out using a Hewlett Packard 5972A mass selective detector in conjunction with an HP 5890 Series II GC equipped with a split-splitless injector and used in splitless mode. Data were stored and processed using HP Gl77O1AA Chemstation software.

In both cases the analytical column used was a polyimide-clad 12m x 0.22mm i.d. fused silica capillary, coated with BP-1 (SGE, UK) stationary phase (immobilised dimethyl polysiloxane, OV-1 equivalent, 0.1µm film thickness). The GC temperature program was as follows: 2 minutes isothermal hold at 50°C following injection, and then 50°–350°C at a rate of 10°C min[-1]. The final temperature was held for 8 minutes. Helium was used as the carrier gas at a

Table 16.2 Compounds identified in both a sample of glue from the *Mary Rose* arrow and in authentic beeswax

Peak	Compound
Alkanes	
1	tricosane
2	pentacosane
3	heptacosane
4	nonacosane
5	hentriacontane
6	tritriacontane
Wax esters	
7	tetracosanyl hexadecanoate
8	haxacosanyl hexadecanoate
9	octacosanyl hexadecanoate
10	tria contyl hexadecanoate
11	dotriacontyl hexadecanoate
12	tetratriacontyl hexadecanoate
Triacylglycerols	
A	C_{46} triacylglycerol
B	C_{48} triacylglycerol
C	C_{50} triacylglycerol
D	C_{52} triacylglycerol
E	C_{54} triacylglycerol

constant flow of lml min-1and a column head pressure of 25psi.

For GC/MS, samples were introduced via a splitless injector at 340 °C with a 3 minute purge time. The GC was temperature programmed from 50–340°C at 10°C min-1. The final temperature was held for 10 minutes. Helium was used as the carrier gas operating at 10 psi. The transfer line temperature was set at 340°C. Mass spectra were acquired by electron impact (EL) ionisation (70eV). Full scan mass spectra were recorded over the range *m/z* 50–700.

Results

The gas chromatograms of all six samples are virtually identical. A series of minor peaks elutes between 15 and 25 minutes, and a second, more prominent set of peaks between 28 and 41 minutes. Analysis by gas chromatography/mass spectrometry has allowed identification of these compounds as a series of odd-carbon number n-alkanes (heptacosane $C_{27}H_{56}$, being the most abundant) and a series of wax esters. Comparison with a sample of authentic beeswax shows a close match between the two. In addition, part of a homologous series of triacyiglycerides is noted eluting after the wax esters (Table 16.2). These peaks have been identified as the C_{46}, C_{48}, C_{50}, C_{52}, and C_{54} triacyiglycerides and the likely origin of these compounds is an animal fat.

Discussion

Previous analyses of organic materials from the *Mary Rose* have shown that pine pitch was used for caulking and waterproofing purposes (Evershed *et al.* 1985; Robinson *et al.* 1987). Since pine pitch has adhesive qualities as well as hydrophobic properties, it was expected that the glue used to fletch the arrows would also have a pine origin. However, the results suggest that the glue used on the *Mary Rose* arrows was a mixture of beeswax and animal fat.

The authors suggested (Evans and Card 1984) that the beeswax could have been applied first, the animal fat being added subsequently, perhaps on board the ship, or that the fat and wax could have been deliberately mixed. Fat may have been added to beeswax to alter its properties for use as a lubricant or polish (Charters *et al.* 1995) or to eke it out in the same way as animal fats such as tallow were added to beeswax in the manufacture of cheap candles (Crane 1983). It is possible that animal fat was added to the *Mary Rose* beeswax adhesive for a similar reason. Another possibility is that the triacylglycerides present do not originate from a deliberate addition of fat, but from natural oils present in the feathers used to construct the flight. It is not possible to determine the species from which the proposed fat originated as triacylglycerides are ubiquitous compounds in animal sources.

Binding
Six samples of binding from the fletching of an arrow (83S0002 from arrow 81A0429, one of a sheaf in chest 81A2582 in O9) were analysed and found to be silk. Examination also suggested that wax was put on in a series of layers. There appeared to be no extraneous matter trapped within the wax.

Arrow tips
Several samples of arrow tip were examined in a similar manner to the flight glue. These were taken from arrow 81A2506, also from O9 (samples 83S0028-9). No wax was detected, but traces of an organic substance, most probably a fish-based glue, were found.

Chemical analyses of medicines, ointments and related items
Brendan Derham

Amongst the wide range of artefacts recovered during the excavation, a wooden chest containing surgical equipment, medicine jars and a variety of wooden and pewter canisters were found in the Barber-surgeon's cabin (M7; see Fig. 1.2 for location). Many of the containers preserved residues of a range of contents and some objects bore the remains of materials impregnated with oils and other substances. Other residues and compounds were present in various locations about the ship (for instance, in a chest containing mostly hand fishing gear (80A1217) and amongst the ship's timbers). This material, especially that associated with the medicaments (Chapter 4), is the most extensive and

Table 16.3 Samples and their descriptions and locations submitted for 'chemical' analysis (see Chapter 4 for description of objects associated with the Barber-surgeon)

Object	Sample no.	Sample description	Container/object	Group
Samples from the Barber-surgeon's chest				
80A1530	3&4	Concretion: well compacted grey powder with orange streaks	Chest	3&2
80A1576	5	Loosely compact buff-brown powder	Razor	2
80A1584	6	Loosely compacted red-brown powder	Purse	2
80A1532	7&8	Contents: soft dirty white-grey powder, low density	Ointment canister	5
80A1533	9	Contents: green flake type material	Ointment canister	5
80A1535	10	Contents: orange-brown granules	Ointment canister	1
80A1537	11	Contents: grey powder	Ointment canister	4
80A1538	12	Contents: dirty white-grey powder	Ointment canister	4
80A1541	13	Contents: soft orange-brown powder, some resin	Ointment canister	4
80A1542	14	Contents: soft, buff coloured powder	Ointment canister	4
80A1551	15	Contents: grey powder	Ointment canister	1
80A1559	16	Contents: buff coloured waxy material	Medicine jar	1
80A1561	17	Contents: five seeds	Canister	6
80A1573	18	Contents: thick green slim	Medicine jar	3
80A1574	19	Contents: soft light brown to green powder, some green flakes	Medicine jar	4
80A1531	20&21	Contents: soft white powder	Ointment canister	1&5
80A1560	32	Contents: greenish brown flakes with bluish-grey lumps, bits of 'twig/leaf'	Syringe	1
80A1575	33	Contents: grey to greyish blue resin	Medicine jar	3
80A1892	37	Unguent roll: green resinous material, layered?	Bandage	7
80A1893	38	Unguent roll: thick sticky yellow-brown mass	Bandage	7
80A1894	39	Unguent roll: firm lumps black powder, white edges	Bandage	7
80A1895	40	Unguent roll: firm lumps brown powder, layered?	Bandage	7
80A1896	41	Unguent roll: firm lumps grey-black powder	Bandage	7
80A1558	42	Unguent roll: firm lumps pale green resin, layered	Bandage	7
Samples from the Barber-surgeon's cabin (M7)				
80A1629	22	Contents: soft, slightly sticky dark brown powder	Bowl	2
80A1459	23	Contents: liquid freeze-dried to light brown powder	Medicine jar	6
80A1483	24	Contents: liquid freeze-dried to green sticky lump	Medicine jar	2
80A1526	25	Contents: soft black powder	Ointment canister	3
80A1637	26	Contents: fine black powder with one very hard greenish-black lump	medicine jar	4
80A1638	27	Contents: soft pale brown powder	Ointment canister	4
80A1690	28	Contents: brown resin encrusted with buff powder	Ointment canister	3
80A1702	29	Contents: brown resin encrusted with buff powder	Ointment canister	3
80A1455	30	Contents: thin pale yellow wax or fat	Flask	6
80A1628	34	Contents: lumps of pale green powder with buff-yellow streaks	Ointment canister	2
80A1741	35	Buff material in semi-circular lump	Syringe (barrel)	2
80A1674	43	Unguent: hard pale green-buff material, red spots	Stick	7
80A1798	44	Unguent: hard brown powder	Stick	7
Samples from chest 80A1217				
80A1217	1	Concretion: a translucent viscous brown oil	chest	3
80A1217	2	Concretion: translucent orange resin encrusted with crystalline material	chest	3
Samples from objects found between the ship's timbers				
80A1863	31	Contents: soft grey powder	Canister	4
87A0013	36	Contents: liquid freeze-dried to brown powder	Ointment canister	3

Table 16.4 Basic identification of samples

Sample	Object	Context	Object type	Condition of Container	Contents	Group
1	80A1217	Chest	Chest		Degraded *Pinus/Picea* resin	3
2	80A1217	"			Marine silt & *Pinus/Picea* resin	3
3	80A1530	Barber-surgeon's chest	Chest		Degraded *Pinus/Picea* resin	3
4	80A1530	"			Marine silt/concretion	2
5	80A1576	"	Razor		Artefact corrosion complex	2
6	80A1584	"	Purse		Artefact corrosion complex	2
7	80A1532	"	Canister	Closed	Medicinal preparation	5
8	80A1532	"	Canister	Closed	Medicinal preparation	5
9	80A1533	"	Canister	Closed	Medicinal preparation	5
10	80A1535	"	Canister	Closed	Marine silt	1
11	80A1537	"	Canister	Closed	Medicinal preparation	4
12	80A1538	"	Canister	Closed	Medicinal preparation	4
13	80A1541	"	Canister	Closed	Medicinal preparation	4
14	80A1542	"	Canister	Closed	Medicinal preparation	4
15	80A1551	"	Canister	Closed	Marine silt	1
16	80A1559	"	Canister	Closed	Marine silt	1
17	80A1561	"	Canister	Closed	Peppercorns	6
18	80A1573	"	Jar	?Sealed	Degraded *Pinus/Picea* resin	3
19	80A1574	"	Jar	?Sealed	Medicinal preparation	4
20	80A1531	"	Canister	Closed	Marine sediment	1
21	80A1531	"	Canister	Closed	Medicinal preparation	5
22	80A1629	Barber-surgeon's cabin	Bowl	Open	Marine silt/concretion	2
23	80A1459		Jar	Closed	Medicinal preparation	6
24	80A1483	"	Jar	Closed	Marine silt/concretion	2
25	80A1526	"	Canister	Open	Medicinal preparation	3
26	80A1637	"	Jar	Closed	Medicinal preparation	4
27	80A1638	"	Canister	Closed	Medicinal preparation	4
28	80A1690	"	Canister	Open	Degraded *Pinus/Picea* resin	3
29	80A1702	"	Canister	Closed	Degraded *Pinus/Picea* resin	3
30	80A1455	"	Flask	Closed	Medicinal preparation	6
31	80A1863	ship's timbers	Canister	Open	Medicinal preparation	4
32	80A1560	Barber-surgeon's chest	Canister	Closed	Marine silt	1
33	80A1575	"	Jar	?Sealed	Degraded *Pinus/Picea* resin	3
34	80A1628	Barber-surgeon's cabin	Canister	?Sealed	Marine silt/concretion	2
35	80A1741	"	Syringe	?Open	Flax washer from clyster	2
36	87A0013	ship's timbers	Canister	Closed	Degraded *Pinus/Picea* resin	3
37	80A1892	Barber-surgeon's chest	Roll	Open	Degraded *Pinus/Picea* resin	7
38	80A1893	"	Roll		Medicinal preparation	7
39	80A1894	"	Roll		Medicinal preparation	7
40	80A1895	"	Roll		Degraded *Pinus/Picea* resin	7
41	80A1896	"	Roll		Medicinal preparation	7
42	80A1558	"	Roll		Medicinal preparation	7
43	80A1674	Barber-surgeon's cabin	Stick		Medicinal preparation	7
44	80A1798	"	Stick		Medicinal preparation	7

best-preserved collection recovered to date. A total of 44 'samples' was examined. These ranged in consistency from grey powders and viscous brown oils, thick green slime and resinous material to blue lumps and seeds. The samples were obtained from items associated with the Barber-surgeon's chest (80A1530), his cabin (M7), the fisherman's chest (80A1217) in M7, and from objects recovered from between the ship's timbers after

excavation (Table 16.3) Analysis was conducted to identify these materials, in particular those associated with the Barber-surgeon.

The analysis of organic residues from maritime archaeological sites has provided insights into the historical significance of natural products in the construction of ships (Evershed *et al.* 1985; Robinson *et al.* 1987; Reunanen *et al.* 1989; 1990). The medical chest from the *Mary Rose* potentially offered a rich source of information regarding historical, medical, surgical and, in particular, pharmaceutical practices of the sixteenth century (see Chapter 4). Eight of the samples (Nos 37–42) were from what were provisionally identified as unguent rolls: raw materials and compounds held in a suitable matrix and stored ready for use (Table 16.4). In several of these a spiral appearance of the structures was visible under X-ray, and enabled these, for instance, to be identified as bandages.

Analyses

Several different analytical techniques were used. Preliminary examination of the intact material was under a microscope and elemental analysis (of the percentage of the sample consisting of carbon, hydrogen and nitrogen) was undertaken to provide a general indication of the nature of the samples. The mineral elements present were identified using an X-ray fluorescence spectrometer (XRF). The results showed the intensity of emission from the sample, measured in counts per second, of X-rays at characteristic energies measured in kilo-electron volts or KeV. Identification of the individual organic compounds present was achieved using gas chromatography/mass spectrometry (GC/MS). This report presents a summary of the results in terms of the chemistry of the samples. Their archaeological interpretation is presented in Chapter 4 with full details in archive.

Sample preparation

The samples, usually 200mg each, were extracted into 5ml of solvent (dichloromethane: methanol, 3:1) and then centrifuged and the supernatant decanted. This extraction was repeated twice with fresh solvent and the extracts combined and reduced to dryness under a stream of nitrogen (Fraction A). The process was then repeated with a second solvent (methanol: water, 4:1) (Fraction B). An intractable residue, inorganic material and fragments of botanical material were left behind (Fraction C). Floating off botanical material and sand in bromoform isolated the heavy mineral content of the intractable residues. Derivatisation of the dried organic fractions was carried out using 50μLN, *0-bis* (trimethylsilyl)-trifuoroacetamide. The samples were then warmed on a hot plate at 60°C for 10 minutes before being dried under nitrogen once again. Finally the dried sample was dissolved in approximately 75μl dichloromethane prior to analysis by GC and CG-MS.

Elemental carbon, hydrogen and nitrogen (CHN) analysis

The results of CHN analysis and the C:H atomic ratio (see Table 16.5) provide an indication of the percentage of organic material present in each sample and its degree of unsaturation (low C:H ratio may indicate unsaturated organic compounds). The C:H atomic ratio

expected in organic compounds varies between approximately 1:2 in aliphatic (organic compounds where carbon and hydrogen molecules are arranged in straight or branched chains) and 1:1 in aromatic compounds. The level of nitrogen in all of the samples is very low and generally less than 0.5%. These low values suggest that the samples contain neither alkaloids nor proteinaceous matter in significant quantities. The usefulness of the elemental analysis results is restricted by the heterogeneous nature of the samples. The results however, do provide a useful qualitative screening procedure for subsequent work, serving to classify the samples into broad types.

The analyses enabled the definition of groups of materials of similar elemental composition, independent of their artefactual or typological character. The main groups were: Group 1 marine silt; Group 2 inorganic samples; Group 3a organo-mineral samples; and Group 3b organic samples. These can be further sub-divided:

Group	Sample nos	Sub-group	Sample nos
1: marine silt	10, 15, 16, 20, 32		
2: inorganic	4, 5, 6, 24, 34, 35		
3a: organo-mineral	9, 11, 12, 19, 22, 23, 25, 26, 27, 31, 39	Group 3	1–3, 18, 25, 28, 29, 33, 36
		Group 4	11–14, 19, 26, 27, 31
		Group 5	7–9, 21
3b: organic	1, 2, 3, 7, 8, 13, 14, 17, 18, 21, 28, 29, 30, 33, 36, 37, 38, 40–44	Group 6	23, 30
		Group 7	37–44

Group 1
Some samples were not analysed intensively, other than by XRF, as they were very small and consisted predominantly of 'marine silt' (details in archive; Derham 2002).

Group 2: The inorganic samples (see Table 16.5)
These had both a low CHN value (10% or less) and a C:H ratio well outside the range 1:1–2, hence they could be identified as being essentially inorganic. The XRF analysis demonstrated the presence of predominantly silica, calcium and iron. Sample 4 comprised a concretion matrix produced by the interaction of an amorphous corroding ferrous metal object with marine salts and silts including mineral sulphur (North and MacLeod 1987). The inorganic nature of the samples was confirmed by the analyses of the solvent extracts. Of these, some samples associated with the purse, razor (samples 5, 6 and 34) and pewter canister contained only mineral sulphur (S8). Examination of the semicircular 'wad' of fibres from inside the pewter syringe (sample 35) demonstrated that this had been made from flax fibres (*Linum*

Table 16.5 Results of CHN elemental analysis (sample 17 not analysed)

Object no.	Object	Sample	Group	%C	%N	%H	%C/ 12.011	%H/ 1.008	C:H Ratio	CHN %
Inorganic samples (Group 2)										
80A1530	concretion	4	2	10.18	0.04	0.21	0.85	0.21	0.2	10
80A1576	powder with razor	5	2	1.11	0.12	0.93	0.09	0.92	10	2
80A1584	powder with purse	6	2	1.40	0.04	1.62	0.12	1.60	14	3
80A1483	jar contents	24	2	0.96	0.00	0.65	0.08	0.64	8	2
80A1628	canister contents	34	2	1.06	0.09	0.75	0.09	0.74	8	2
80A1741	syringe washer	35	2	1.60	0.05	0.77	0.13	0.76	6	2
Organo-mineral samples (Group 3a)										
80A1637	jar contents	26	4	4.35	0.32	1.39	0.36	1.38	4	6
80A1638	canister contents	27	4	12.20	0.07	2.57	1.02	2.55	3	15
80A1533	canister contents	9	5	19.59	0.86	3.66	1.63	3.63	2	24
80A1537	canister contents	11	4	35.89	0.10	5.30	2.99	5.26	2	41
80A1538	canister contents	12	4	28.49	0.13	4.98	2.37	4.94	2	34
80A1574	jar contents	19	4	2.79	0.05	0.36	0.23	0.35	2	3
80A1629	bowl contents	22	2	2.66	0.03	0.38	0.22	0.38	2	3
80A1459	jar contents	23	6	19.66	0.45	3.67	1.64	3.64	2	24
80A1526	canister contents	25	3	25.12	0.19	3.46	2.09	3.43	2	29
80A1863	canister contents	31	4	17.42	0.18	2.78	1.45	2.75	2	20
80A1894	unguent roll	39	7	26.79	0.18	3.21	2.23	3.18	1	30
Organic samples (Group 3b)										
80A1217	concretion/resin	1	3	64.08	0.00	8.22	5.33	8.16	2	72
80A1217	concretion/resin	2	3	75.15	0.00	8.96	6.26	8.89	1	84
80A1530	concretion	3	3	50.73	0.13	6.33	4.22	6.28	1	57
80A1532	canister contents	7	5	60.83	0.47	9.90	5.06	9.82	2	71
80A1532	canister contents	8	5	58.69	1.03	9.57	4.89	9.49	2	69
80A1541	canister contents	13	4	72.18	0.30	9.73	6.01	9.66	2	82
80A1542	canister contents	14	4	58.01	0.74	7.99	4.83	7.92	2	67
80A1561	peppercorns	17		-	-	-	-	-	-	-
80A1573	jar contents	18	3	81.42	0.06	11.48	6.78	11.39	2	93
80A1531	canister contents	21	5	63.72	0.08	10.85	5.30	10.76	2	75
80A1690	canister contents	28	3	75.04	0.14	9.08	6.25	9.01	1	84
80A1702	canister contents	29	3	89.54	0.24	10.51	7.46	10.43	1	100
80A1455	flask contents	30	6	68.72	0.02	11.39	5.72	11.30	2	80
80A1575	jar contents	33	3	48.52	0.08	5.85	4.04	5.80	1	54
87A0013	canister contents	36	3	54.31	0.81	5.74	4.52	5.69	1	61
80A1892	unguent roll	37	7	71.89	0.18	10.22	5.98	10.14	2	82
80A1893	unguent roll	38	7	76.80	0.03	10.32	6.39	10.24	2	87
80A1895	unguent roll	40	7	56.00	0.14	8.29	4.66	8.22	2	64
80A1896	unguent roll	41	7	53.93	0.19	8.48	4.49	8.41	2	63
80A1558	unguent roll	42	7	71.49	0.32	10.43	5.95	10.34	2	82
80A1674	unguent stick	43	7	75.84	0.13	10.26	6.31	10.17	2	86
80A1798	unguent stick	44	7	70.30	0.09	11.00	5.85	10.91	2	81

usitatissimum) as demonstrated by Trease and Evans (1996, 198-9). XRF analysis of the sample identified the presence of tin corrosion compounds that had been leached out from the pewter.

Group 3a: The organo-mineral samples (see Table 16.5)
Eleven samples were identified with a C:H ratio close to 1:1–2 and an intermediate CHN value between 3% and 50%. These consisted mainly of inorganic material dispersed within an organic matrix. In six of these samples (11, 19, 22, 23, 31 and 39) the analysis of the intractable residues by XRF identified only silica, calcium and iron, the main components of marine silt. The organic fraction of most of these samples consisted of material indistinguishable from the lipids extracted from the silt filling the ship. In five of the samples, however, from wooden canisters (samples 9, 12, 25, 27) and a pottery jar (sample 26), the proportion of marine silt within the inorganic fraction was small. The contents of the inorganic fraction of these were dominated by distinct metallic compounds that had been deliberately blended with the organic material. The organic fraction of these five samples was also completely different from the background silt.

Group 3b: the organic samples (Table 16.5)
This comprised the remaining 22 samples with a C:H ratio within the range 1:1–2 and a high CHN value of >50%. They are similar to Group 3a except that only a minor component of them is inorganic.

The organo-mineral and organic groups
The chemical composition of the organic matrices divides the 'organo-mineral' (Group 3a) and 'organic' (Group 3b) samples into five further groups (see Tables 16.4 and 16.5). Group 3 encompasses those samples that consist predominantly of diterpenes (resins). The samples in Group 4 contain mainly beeswax esters although, frequently, other materials are also present. Group 5 consists of samples dominated by triacylglycerols (fats), and Group 6 contains anomalous samples that do not really fit in any of the other groups. The seventh group (Group 7) represents those samples that were part of resinous artefacts, such as the 'unguent rolls' (ie, resin and flax fibres), as opposed to the contents of containers.

Group 3, predominantly diterpenes (resins)
The fraction A extracts consist of mainly abietane- and pimarane- based diterpenoids (Fig. 16.1A), and low levels of common fatty acids (C16:0 and C18:0), a mixture similar in composition to Pinaceae oleoresins; the viscous protective exudates secreted by pine (*Pinus*) and spruce (*Picea*) in response to damage. The major European sources of resin are pine and spruce, are very similar in composition and cannot readily be distinguished. The extraction of resin from pine and spruce

trees has traditionally been achieved by two distinct methods (Coppen *et al.* 1984).

The first method, destructive distillation of bark and branches as a product of the timber and charcoal industry, produces pine tar or pitch. The second method consist of bleeding oleoresin from live trees; pine trees are naturally abundant in oleoresin and can exude up to 3kg per year in response to damage to the bark. The extracted oleoresin may then be fractionated by distillation to form two distinct products. The material that is distilled off is termed oil or spirit of turpentine and contains mainly volatile monoterpenes (Mills and White 1994, 83–92). The solid residuum left behind by the distillation process is termed rosin or colophony and consists mainly of diterpenoids and fatty acids. Dry distilling the rosin decarboxylates the diterpenoids producing what is termed rosin spirit or oil.

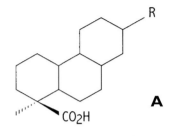

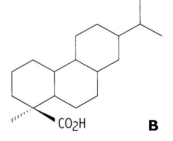

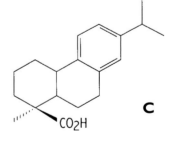

Once diterpenoids (Fig 16.1A), in particular abietic acid, become exposed to the external environment they are subject to a wide range of degradative processes. The two main steps are the removal of reactive or functional groups ie, –COOH, and degradation by either oxidation or reduction depending upon the environmental conditions.

The degradation of natural pinaceae resins occurs via two distinct processes. The first is microbially mediated in anaerobic sediments which form significant

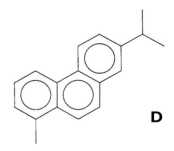

Figure 16.1 Structure of various chemicals found in samples of medicaments A) Diterpenoids; B) Tetrahydroabiatic acid; C) Dehydroabiatic acid; D) Retene

quantities of tetrahydroabietic acid (Fig. 16.1B) (Reunanen *et al.* 1989; 1990). The presence of a significant proportion of tetrahydroabietic acid (THA) in samples is, therefore, indicative of extensive post-depositional microbial degradation. The second process is degradation in aerobic conditions and results in the formation of dehydroabiaetic acid (Fig 16.1C) and several oxygenated derivatives but no tetrahydroabiaetc acid (Beck *et al.* 1994).

Several samples (1, 18, 28, 29, 33 and 36) contain particularly high proportions of defunctionalised diterpenes, over 50% peak area, the presence of THA indicating that the degradation occurred after the sinking of the ship. These samples have been degraded beyond being of much archaeological significance.

The presence of dehydroabietic acid and defunctionalised abietanes in samples 2, 3 and 25 is indicative of the aerobic ageing and degradation of pine and spruce resins. Dehydro- and dihydroabietic acids dominate the composition of the samples. These two resin acids and the defunctionalised diterpenes such as retene (Fig. 16.1D) constitute over 50% of the samples. The analysis demonstrates that these samples appear to be *Pinus/Picea* oleoresins that have been heavily degraded before deposition, not surprising as samples 2 and 3 consisted of a sediment in the bottom of the Barber-surgeon's (80A1530) and so-called fisherman's (80A1217) chests respectively (Table 16.4).

Analysis of the organic fraction of sample 25 (found in poplar canister 80 A 1526) demonstrates that the sample consists predominantly of defunctionalised diterpenes and unesterified dehydroabietic acid. The absence of any THA implies that the defunctionalisation occurred before deposition, ie, during the preparation of the material. This may have been a deliberate action to convert a viscous resin into a more mobile rosin oil by deliberately heating to break off the acidic (-COOH) groups. Analysis of the inorganic fraction shows that the main component is based on a mercury compound, with smaller lead peaks also present. The results suggest that sample 25 is a bled *Pinus/Picea* oleoresin, that had been 'dry distilled' to produce a rosin oil, and then blended with either metallic mercury or a mercury salt.

Group 4, mainly wax esters
These samples contain beeswax esters and terpenoids. In samples 11, 12, 14, 26, 27 and 31 diterpenoids are present, whilst in samples 13 and 19 both di- and triterpenoids are present. The GC/MS analysis of the extracts demonstrates a very limited range of free fatty acids, palmitic, oleic and stearic acid. Samples 12 and 31 also contain 10-hydroxystearic acid, a degradation product of oleic acid. The detection of homologous series of *n*-alkanes (with a clear odd over even preponderance), even carbon number long chain alcohols and, in samples 11, 12, 26 and 27, the presence of intact wax esters in the range C40–C52 indicates that

beeswax is present (Heron *et al.* 1994). The presence of 14- and 15-hydroxy-substituted hexadecanoic acid wax esters was also detected (samples 12, 13 and 27), and the presence of these compounds has been closely associated with unrefined beeswax (Tulloch 1971).

Samples 11, 12 and 27 also contain diterpenes in low levels. Nissenbaum (1992) has reported the presence of diterpenes blended with beeswax from an Egyptian mummy. The samples here imply that beeswax had become contaminated or tainted with a pine rosin.

Three samples (12, 26 and 27) contain significant quantities of distinctive inorganic components. This can be explained as the deliberate addition of an inorganic based component to an organic matrix of beeswax and pine resin. Sample 12 contained lead, while samples 26 and 27 both contain mineral sulphur with copper and zinc respectively. Sample 27 from a canister (Table 16.3) was a viscous material, with the mineral sulphur and zinc dispersed within a waxy ointment. In contrast, mineral sulphur, copper, beeswax and pine oleoresin were present in sample 26. Curiously this sample was recovered from a ceramic jar (Table 16.3), and some form of liquid, such as an oil, must have originally been present. The particularly low percentage of organic material demonstrated by the CHN value obtained for samples 26 and 27 (Table 16.5) may imply that most of the material has been lost.

Samples 11 and 12 are more complex. The presence of a plant sterol in both indicates that a plant oil was also present, although the associated fatty acids and acylglycerols upon which it was based are now heavily degraded. The identification of the sterol as cyclolaudenol is, however, not totally reliable. A mass spectrum of the trimethylsilyl (TMS) derivative of cyclolaudenol has never been published. It is therefore only possible to compare the TMS derivative of the putative cyclolaudenol with that of an isomer 24-methylenecycloartenol.

The sterol 4,4,14-trimethyl 9,19-cycloergosten-3-ol or methylene-cycloartenol may occur as two isomers, in which a double bond is present either at carbon 24 or 25. The 24 isomer is an intermediate in the biosynthesis of common phytosterols and, therefore, the sterol would only ever be present in minute quantities (Misso and Goad 1983). The sterol in question is present at such a high level implies that it is the methylenecycloart-25-enol commonly termed cyclolaudenol. The plant oil may, therefore, be poppy seed oil (*Papaver*; Bentley *et al.* 1955).

In addition, unbranched odd carbon number mono-ketones (C31, C33:1, C33, C35 and C37) were present in sample 11 (Table 16.5), and the epicuticle of higher plants is frequently rich in these long chain aliphatic compounds (Evershed *et al.* 1991). Subsequent work by Evershed *et al.* (1994; 1995) demonstrated that long-chain ketones (C31, C33, C35), both saturated and mono-unsaturated, could also be formed by the thermal free-radical decarboxylation and condensation of fatty acids. The ambiguities regarding identifying the source of the ketones in sample 11 remain unresolved, although condensation during heating remains the most likely explanation. Samples 11 and 12, therefore, appear to consist of beeswax dispersed in a heat-treated plant oil possibly derived from poppy seeds.

Several of the samples in this group (13, 14, 19, 26 and 31) contain significant quantities of terpene based compounds. The proportion detected here would indicate that it was a significant component of the pharmaceutical preparation. In samples 14, 26 and 31 the organic material is diterpene based, with some evidence of beeswax present. The absence of any THA indicates that the samples have not been degraded after deposition. The high level of defunctionalised diterpenoids, ie, dehydroabietane, nor-abietatriene and retene in sample 14 indicates that the resin may have first been thermally degraded to produce a rosin oil; the sample consisting of beeswax blended with rosin oil. In contrast, the predominance of intact dehydroabietic acids in samples 26 and 31 suggest that the diterpenoids had not been heavily degraded either before or after deposition. Samples 26 and 31 from canisters 80A1637 and 80A1863 appear, therefore, to have contained beeswax blended with *Pinus/Picea* oleoresin, with mineral copper and sulphur being added to sample 26. It is also possible that a mobile component was also originally present to give a more liquid consistency to the contents of jar 80A1637.

The vast majority of the residue from poplar canister 80A1541 (sample 13) consists of compounds of *Pinus/Picea* oleoresin. The major compound identified is nor-abietatriene. The large proportion of a defunctionalised diterpene indicates the resin has undergone intensive degradation. It contains a small proportion (7% peak area) of tetrahydroabietic acid as opposed to the dehydroabietic acid present (16% peak area) which indicates that post-depositional degradation is only slight. It is possible to deduce that the original material had been thermally degraded to produce a more mobile rosin oil. Several triterpenes, including boswellic acid, and a range of wax esters, hydrocarbons and long chain alcohols were also detected. This suggests that the sample is representative of the rosin fraction of a *Pinus/Picea* oleoresin that was dry distilled to produce a rosin oil, which was blended with frankincense and beeswax.

Elemental analysis of sample 19 from stoneware jar 80A1574 in the Barber-surgeon's chest indicates that it is predominantly inorganic (Table 16.5). The intractable residue recovered (Fraction C) demonstrates only marine silt, but analysis of Fraction A demonstrated that palmitic, stearic and the diterpenoid acids characteristic of the rosin fraction of a tapped *Pinus/Picea* oleoresin were present. That the sample contained tetrahydroabietic acid (29% peak area) indicates that the rosin has undergone extensive post-depositional reductive degradation.

Also present in the sample is a group of triterpenoids, amongst them the ß-boswellic acid from frankincense (*Boswellia* spp.; Khalid 1983). This sample is representative of the rosin fraction of *Pinus/Picea* oleoresin blended with frankincense. The obvious extensive diagenesis (ie, post-depositional changes) and the fact that the sample was from a jar suggests that a liquid dilutent must also have been present originally.

Group 5, dominated by triacylglycerols (fats)
The triacylglycerols present dominate the organic fractions in this group. The intractable residue consists of a fine, soft, calcium-based powder. Although it may be soluble minerals deposited from seawater, it could also represent the deliberate addition of a finely powdered gypsum.

GC/MS analysis of the organic extracts from poplar canister 80A1531 (samples 20 and 21) showed that diacyl- and triacylglycerols are present, these compounds indicating some form of fat or oil. Also present were both short straight-chain fatty acids (ie, dodecanoic), and odd carbon number fatty acids (ie, pentadecanoic) that are usually associated with bacterial metabolism (Gunstone *et al.* 1994, 11–12). The presence of multi-branched hexadecanoic acid (ie, 7,11,15-trimethylpalmitic acid and 3,7,11,15-tetramethylpalmitic acid) implies that the fatty acids are a product of the bacterial metabolites present in ruminant fat such as butter or tallow. This is supported by the presence of the animal-derived sterol, cholesterol in the sample.

Two samples were examined from the poplar canister 80A1532 (samples 7 and 8). Neither has cholesterol, but both contain acylglycerols, 7,11,15-trimethylpalmitic acid and nonanoic and nonandioic acids. Sample 8 also contains octanoic and octandioic acid. The presence of very short chain fatty acids, especially when part of a triacylglycerol, has frequently been associated with ruminant fat. A homologous series of wax esters was detected but only in sample 7. This suggests that the samples contain butter or tallow blended with beeswax.

Sample 9 from poplar canister 80A1533 is dominated by triacylglycerols and fatty acids including 7,11,15-trimethylpalmitic acid in the organic extract. The main XRF peaks from the intractable residue are from lead with much smaller marine silt and copper peaks present. This sample consists of a lead compound dispersed in a ruminant fat such as butter or tallow.

Group 6, miscellany
Sample 23 was from an earthenware jar (80A1459) that had been open to the elements and therefore the analysis constitutes a rather tenuous identification. The intractable residue is a fine brown powder, and analysis identifies it as a calcium compound, probably calcium sulphate. Analysis of the organic components demonstrate that the only diterpene detected was

dehydroabietic acid present merely at a trace level. The presence of low levels of pentadecanoic and 7,11,15-trimethylpalmitic acid may indicate that some ruminant fat may have been present. The presence of two plant sterols, β-sitosterol and possibly cyclolaudenol, is intriguing. Only the common fern (*Polypodium vulgare*) contains these two sterols together in significant quantities (Goad and Goodwin 1972, 113–98). The sample may possibly be representative of a plant oil (fern root) dispersed in a ruminant liquid fat, possibly milk.

A sample from pewter flask 80A1455 was examined (sample 30). It can be assumed that the flask was designed to contain a free-flowing liquid. The results of XRF analysis indicate the presence of predominantly tin and some copper (ie, the pewter). The small size of the inorganic fraction, only 4μm (Table 16.5), is also consistent with corrosion of the pewter flask. The organic components are mainly common fatty acids, although some are present as the methyl esters rather than free fatty acids. The presence of fatty acid methyl esters in natural lipids and oils is uncommon (Kolattukudy 1976, 243–4). The formation of these esters may occur, however, by refluxing organic acids with alcohol and an acid catalyst; the type of conditions that occur during the extraction and distillation of volatile oils. This sample, therefore, may be a product or by-product of the processing of crude material. It is impossible, however, to identify the original contents with any degree of certainty.

Group 7, resinous artefacts with flax and fibre
Of this group of eight samples, six contained flax fibres (37–42) and two of these (40 and 42) had a spiral appearance in cross-section in X-ray photographs. The samples appear to be a medicated ointment applied to linen bandages which were then rolled up, the whole preparation then having set solid. The preponderance of tetrahydroabietic acid and degraded diterpenes in the organic components of samples 37 and 39 implies that they have been extensively degraded since deposition. In contrast, the six other samples contain no tetrahydroabietic acid, although the composition of a significant proportion (>20%) of samples 38, 39 and 41 could not be identified. Sample 38 predominantly consists of dehydroabietic acid and defunctionalised diterpenoids, implying that a pine or spruce resin had been thermally degraded to make a more mobile rosin oil, blended with other compounds and applied to the bandage. Within sample 39 undegraded diterpenoids are present as the methyl ester rather than the free acid. This implies that it is based on 'tar', the volatile degradation products from the pyrolysis of pine or spruce wood, rather than a bled resin. Samples 40 and 41 had been heavily degraded. Sample 42, similar in composition to samples 43 and 44, represents colophony that has been applied to a linen bandage (see Chapter 4 for an explanation).

Samples 43 and 44 do not contain any flax fibres and were not bandage rolls. The original material did not appear to have any form of container and yet had retained the appearance of a rigid stick. The material appears to have been a solid resin at the time of deposition. Bled pine or spruce resin that has had the volatile monoterpenes removed forms hard resin blocks termed colophony. The samples themselves consist of undegraded diterpenoids with only very low levels of fatty acids and alkanes present, analytical results that are compatible with colophony.

Human remains

Various limited analytical programmes were undertaken on human remains (brain and soft tissues) in an attempt to identify the surviving material and these are summarised in Chapter 13. A programme of oxygen isotope ratio analysis to provide information of the geographical origin of some of the crew was commenced by Lynne Bell in 2000. Although the analysis has essentially been completed (L. Bell pers. comm.), neither the results or a summary of them were provided for this publication. It is assumed that this information will be published by Bell at a later date; other work by Lynne Bell is summarised below.

Other science

Numerous other studies were also undertaken. These included analysis of trace metals in arrow fletchings (Janaway), other chemical and XRF etc analysis conducted by students under the auspices of the late Dr John Evans at North East London Polytechnic, now the University of East London, and biological and sedimentological analyses largely carried out by staff and students at Portsmouth Polytechnic College, now Portsmouth University. The quality and relevance of these studies are variable and most can be accessed at the Mary Rose Trust.

The *Mary Rose* as a Source of Scientific Study

In many cases the unique preservation and known date of the site provided an important scientific resource to enable basic research and advances in other archaeological scientific fields. Amongst the reports here are some of the first trials (in 1985) to examine for the presence of pollen from underwater sites using standard methods, the use of known-age samples to verify radiocarbon methodologies, and the discovery that mtDNA survives in archaeological material.

Palynological trials
James Greig

Five samples were examined in 1984/5 by James Greig for the presence of pollen (see Table 15.7, above). At the time this was novel, as pollen had rarely been sought from underwater archaeological contexts and no work had been published from previously excavated British wrecks. Thus this trial aimed to show if pollen was preserved on the *Mary Rose*, which might be of value to wider understanding of the ship (see Chapter 15), and provide clues to its applicability as an analytical tool in other wreck and submarine studies. This application was initially reported in November 1985 (Greig 1985). At the same time, samples were prepared by Robert Scaife, who subsequently (2000–4) undertook analysis of selected samples (see Chapter 12). His results are presented in Chapter 15 and *AMR* Vol. 2.

Trials
Assessment of samples from the *Mary Rose* showed that pollen is preserved and that its analysis could be usefully employed technique on the *Mary Rose* (see Chapter 15; Table 15.7). The pollen types present are largely those also found on urban archaeological sites, without any characteristic sign of seaside plants. So the first indications are that the pollen mostly relates to what was on board ship and not to the marine sediment within which it came to rest and be buried. The main characteristic of the pollen spectra is the large amount of Cannabaceae pollen in two samples (80S0069 and 81S0488/1). This pollen type represents either hemp or hops, and products containing either might have been found on the ship. The former is far more likely given the amount of cordage and canvas (this word is derived from the French word for hemp) used in the rigging. Rope from the *Mary Rose* has been analysed for its pollen content and was found to contain large amounts of Cannabaceae pollen.

Sample S69 also contained a significant amount of cereal pollen, which could have come from straw or cereal food remains. The rest of the pollen covers a wide range of habitats, such as arable and weedy grassland, without any indication of whether it is significant, or whether the pollen was simply present on the various objects when they were brought on board.

These first results were quite encouraging. Pollen analysis can show up some features of a sample of material not evident from other studies, and the samples need only be quite small. The best understanding is obtained when pollen results are considered together with results from the study of larger plant remains such as seeds, etc.

Also examined were samples from 81S0120 (cask 81A4586l), in M9 which contained fine black material, possibly charcoal, so this may have been gunpowder or its ingredients. Sample 81S0493/3 was from a sediment layer in O6 and contained only a little pollen.

In 1985 this work was ground-breaking in establishing, for the first time in British archaeology, the preservation of pollen relating to archaeological deposits rather than purely marine environments from an underwater archaeological site.

Absolute dating on the Mary Rose

Absolute dating of the sinking of the *Mary Rose* is not required as this date is precisely known from historical documents. However, the known date, combined with the presence of short-lived organic materials such as pig bones and plant materials from mattresses or floor coverings, provided an unparalleled opportunity for research valid to the science of radiocarbon dating and 'validating' methods and results especially at the younger end of its range. Dendrochronology, on the other hand, was employed in an attempt to differentiate different phases of rebuilding and refitting of the ship; a level of precision not possible for radiocarbon dating. This was undertaken to compare timbers from key sections of the ship (Bridge and Dobbs 1996) and is discussed in detail in *AMR* Vol. 2.

Radiocarbon dating of short-lived organic material from the *Mary Rose*
Robert E. M. Hedges

Radiocarbon dating depends on the fact that living material is composed of carbon (there are some exceptions) which comes from the carbon dioxide in the atmosphere. This comes about by the photosynthesis of CO_2 by plants, which is then carried up the food chain into animal bone. Atmospheric carbon dioxide contains a small amount of radiocarbon, generated in the stratosphere by cosmic rays. Living, actively metabolising creatures, therefore, all have the same level of carbon dioxide, but once they die (or rather cease to replace their tissues) the level of radiocarbon falls at a uniform rate determined by its 'half-life'. In the time elapsed since the *Mary Rose*'s capsize, about 4% of the radiocarbon content of the animals and plants that were alive then has disappeared (through radioactive disintegration).

The Research Laboratory for Archaeology in Oxford carried out several radiocarbon dates on material from the *Mary Rose*. These were predicated on that fact that the historical date of death of the pig bones and plant materials was known. Therefore, for the laboratory, the measurements were undertaken largely as a check on the method being used for sample preparation and measurement at the time (early 1980s).

Six samples were measured (Table 16.6); five on pig bones from the food store in O4 and one on a sample of 'straw' from an unrecorded location, but almost certainly from the 'bed' in the Carpenters' cabin in M9. The method involves extracting and purifying the protein, collagen, which makes up 20% of a fresh bone

Table 16.6 Radiocarbon determinations

Material	Lab. no.	Result BP	cal AD	Reference
Pig rib	OxA-424	300±60	1450–1800	1
Straw	OxA-514	290±70	1440–1810	2
Pig rib	OxA-793	360±80	1410–1800	3
Pig rib	OxA-825	310±80	1430–1810	3
Pig femur	OxA-988	265±45	1480–1800	4
Pig femur	OxA-1106	350±60	1440–1650	5

Combined value for 6 dates is 304±25 (cal AD 1490–1650)
References: 1. *Archaeometry* 27 (1985), 242; 2. *Archaeometry* 28 (1986), 117; 3. *Archaeometry* 28 (1986), 208; 4. *Archaeometry* 29 (1987), 126; *Archaeometry* 29 (1987), 289

(and, because of the excellent preservation of organic material in the burial site, still amounted to about 20% for the 450 year old material). It can be seen from the table (Table 16.6) that a fairly consistent set of results was achieved (Fig. 16.2) over a quite wide period of time, and that the average age corresponds very satisfactorily with the historical age. Some additional comments and explanations can also be made.

First, it must be noted that the 'result BP' (that is, in 'radiocarbon years before present') requires to be 'calibrated' to a calendrical date. This is because the radiocarbon level in the atmosphere has fluctuated as a result of fluctuations in the sun's activity (which affects cosmic rays). The effect of calibration is usually to reduce the accuracy of the final date but, in any case, the agreement can also be regarded as a confirmation that calibration at this point of time is valid. Secondly, short-lived material was chosen because longer lived material would contain a radiocarbon 'signal' from the time it was formed (eg, the date of a sample of wood is the date of when that particular ring was grown rather than when the tree was felled). This could make a difference of 20–40 years or more. Thirdly, it is

interesting to see errors of 50–80 years being quoted; present operation now (2004) produces errors of about 30 years or less (emphasising the need for careful sample selection and for careful calibration).

Finally, although not mentioned here because the method was scarcely available at the time, there is also the possibility of isotopic change to both radiocarbon and to another isotope of carbon in collagen. This would be particularly apparent if the pigs had been fed on material containing fish residues, and it would also have made a serious difference in the date. At this point in time, however, we can confirm that the pigs were given a purely terrestrial diet, and we do not need to worry about the fact that the consumption of fish would have lead to an erroneous radiocarbon date.

In summary, these dates, produced early in the career of the Oxford Radiocarbon Laboratory, have demonstrated that radiocarbon dating was directly and accurately applicable to surviving material from the wreck. If we had not already known the date of the disaster, they would have been able to recover it for us, albeit within a range of uncertainty.

DNA History and the Mary Rose
Erika Hagelberg

In 1990, the analysis of DNA from a pig bone (pig femur 81S0175C), part of the provisions of the *Mary Rose* crew, became a benchmark in the field of ancient DNA typing. This seemingly modest achievement, greeted by amusing news headlines, such as '*Pig brings in the bacon for DNA*' (Connor 1991) helped to prove the important principle that original DNA sequences could be recovered from bones that were hundreds of years old. Shortly afterwards, bone DNA typing was admitted for the first time in a court of law as evidence in a murder case, and the same techniques were used to

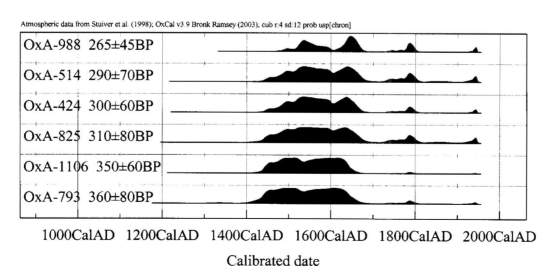

Figure 16.2 Oxcal distribution of radiocarbon dates

644

help identify the skeletal remains of the Nazi physician Josef Mengele and several members of the Romanov family. The scientific methods used in these cases are now used routinely by police forces around the world. Since the publication of the *Mary Rose* pig results in 1991, bone DNA typing has been applied successfully in archaeology, anthropology, and palaeontology, for example in the analysis of Neanderthal bones. Although the history and results of this analysis have been published in the relevant scientific journals, it is summarised here because of its relevance to the *Mary Rose* and because its archaeological significance has not previously been presented to an archaeological audience.

The field of human molecular genetics

The rapid development of molecular genetics has had a great impact on many areas, including medicine, forensic identification and food production. Molecular techniques have also provided important new tools for biological research, in fields as diverse as evolutionary and population biology, ecology and conservation. The genetic material of living organisms, deoxyribonucleic acid, or DNA for short, consists of two chains of nucleic acid bases (A, C, G and T) on a sugar-phosphate backbone. The bulk of the DNA is present in the nucleus of the cell, in structures called chromosomes. Humans have 23 pairs of chromosomes, of which 22 pairs are called autosomes, and the remaining pair are the sex chromosomes (of which women have two X chromosomes, and men an X and a Y chromosome). The chromosomal DNA is inherited from both parents, following a shuffling process called recombination. Women can pass either of their X chromosomes to their children. When a man passes his Y chromosome to a child, the resulting offspring is a male (XY), but if he passes on his X chromosome, the child is female (XX).

The two strands that make up a DNA molecule are twisted around each other to form a double helix. The pairing of the nucleotide bases is complementary, an A always pairing with a T, and a G with a C. During replication (the copying of DNA), the two complementary strands unwind, and each can serve as a template to make a copy of its partner, to produce two identical copies of the original DNA molecule. Although elucidation of the structure of DNA in 1953 helped explain its function as the genetic material (Watson and Crick 1953), it took scientists more than a decade to determine the genetic code, the precise way in which the linear sequence of the DNA building blocks encodes biological information.

Throughout the 1960s and 1970s, scientists developed techniques to manipulate and study DNA. Recombinant DNA methods seek to reproduce in a test-tube the processes that occur in biological cells, including the cutting and copying of DNA by means of specific enzymes, such as restriction enzymes and DNA polymerases, respectively. Using sophisticated techno-

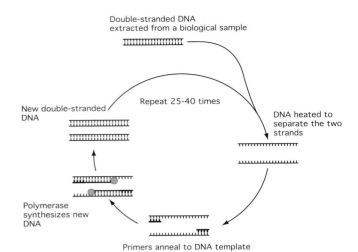

Figure 16.3 The polymerase chain reaction (PCR), a method for the amplification of a specific DNA sequence, is used for the analysis of materials that contain very little or degraded DNA. DNA extracted from biological materials, such as bones or mummified remains, is initially heated to separate its two complementary strands. The reaction is then cooled to allow two 'primers' to bind at positions flanking the DNA segment to be amplified. A DNA polymerase enzyme begins to copy the template DNA at the primer binding site by incorporating nucleotides present in the reaction, creating an identical copy of the original template sequence. The process is repeated 25–40 times, resulting in a huge number of copies of the original sequence.

logy, the entire human genome of 3×10^9 base-pairs was sequenced recently by an international consortium of laboratories (Lander *et al.* 2001).

The genomes of two human beings are very similar, but also have points of difference, reflected in the phenotypic uniqueness of each person. Only identical twins have identical genomes. Some of the differences between people are individual-specific, but some are characteristic of family or ethnic background, and can be used as genetic markers. These markers can be exploited by forensic scientists interested in human identification, or by population biologists interested in the affinities of human populations. By the mid-1980s, scientists had started to use molecular biology techniques for forensic identification (Jeffreys *et al.* 1985). Also in the mid-1980s, DNA markers began to be used in studies of the evolutionary relationships of present-day human populations (Wainscoat *et al.* 1986). A huge amount of genetic information on living human populations is now available, and these data are used increasingly to shed light on human history.

However, it is worth noting that the study of human genetic variation pre-dates molecular biology techniques. In the pre-DNA era scientists relied on blood groups and enzymes, the so-called classical genetic markers. A substantial amount of genetic information on human populations was generated throughout the twentieth century using these markers, and compiled by Luca Cavalli-Sforza and his colleagues in their monumental work *The History and Geography of Human Genes* (Cavalli-Sforza *et al.* 1994). Despite their usefulness, blood markers have limitations because their analysis requires blood samples, which are not always easy to collect and store, and many exhibit low levels of polymorphism (variability). In contrast, many DNA markers are highly polymorphic, and can be typed using different DNA sources including hair, saliva, old bloodstains and bone. The advantages of DNA techniques make them ideal for the study of degraded organic remains such as archaeological materials.

Ancient DNA studies

Ancient DNA studies have attracted considerable attention from the scientific community, the news media and the public. More than a decade ago, this field of research was illustrated dramatically in the popular film *Jurassic Park*. In the story, scientists recovered DNA from dinosaur blood ingested by insects preserved in Cretaceous amber and used it to bring dinosaurs back to life. This fantastic story was loosely based on real work on the molecular analysis of DNA from ancient biological remains and museum specimens. In real life, scientists have claimed to extract DNA from insects entombed in amber, although not from dinosaur blood ingested by insects (see DeSalle and Grimaldi 1994, for a review of studies on 'very old DNA').

Ancient DNA studies span only the past two decades. As molecular biology techniques improved during the 1970s and early 1980s, scientists began to speculate on the possibility of recovering DNA from the preserved remains of extinct animals. The first successful attempt was by Russell Higuchi, Allan Wilson and colleagues at the University of California at Berkeley. In their 1984 paper, these scientists described the extraction of DNA from the preserved skin and connective tissue of a quagga kept at a museum in Germany (Higuchi *et al.* 1984). The specimen was over a century old, and its tissues contained very little DNA. Most of the DNA extracted was of micro-organisms, and only a small percentage was original quagga DNA. The scientists used a technique called cloning to multiply the extracted DNA. Cloning involves the introduction of foreign DNA (in this case quagga DNA) into a rapidly growing organism such as a bacterium. As the bacteria reproduce and multiply their own DNA, the foreign DNA is copied as well, until enough DNA is produced for its sequence, to be determined. The extinct quagga DNA sequence was compared with sequences obtained from present-day members of the horse family, and was shown to be identical to that of the zebra, indicating a very close relationship between the two animal species.

Shortly afterwards, the first study was published on the DNA of an ancient human, a predynastic Egyptian mummy (Pääbo 1985). Although the result simply demonstrated that a little original human DNA had survived for thousands of years in mummified tissue, it was greeted with enthusiasm because it suggested that old DNA might help shed light on the origins of ancient individuals and civilisations. At the time, the potential applications of this finding seemed almost limitless. Unfortunately, it was evident that old DNA was usually very damaged, and that the technical difficulties in the analysis of ancient DNA would limit its applicability. Ancient DNA threatened to remain a scientific curiosity (Jeffreys 1984).

This outlook changed after the development of a new and powerful molecular biology technique, the polymerase chain reaction, or PCR for short (Saiki *et al.* 1985). The PCR allows the amplification, or copying, of DNA sequences from biological samples containing very little or severely degraded DNA (Fig. 16.3). Instead of using bacteria to multiply the DNA, as in cloning, which is cumbersome and non-specific, specific pieces of the DNA can be targeted. The PCR became the method of choice in ancient DNA studies (although several years later some ancient DNA researchers started to advocate again the use of cloning).

The first article on the PCR amplification and sequencing of ancient human DNA was published in 1988 (Pääbo *et al.* 1988). DNA segments were amplified from a piece of brain tissue preserved in a 7000 year old skeleton recovered from a peat bog in Florida, and shown to contain two population markers found also in present-day Amerindians. This result confirmed the potential usefulness of genetic studies on ancient human populations, provided soft tissue is available for DNA analysis.

DNA from skeletal remains

At the time of publication of the first amplified ancient human sequence in 1988, scientists believed that DNA did not persist in skeletal remains. A comprehensive review of forensic anthropology methods stated that DNA typing of a cadaver was impossible unless soft tissue remained on the skeleton, as it was thought that bone itself would be useless for DNA analysis (Isçan 1988). This contention was proved incorrect when human bones ranging from 300 years to 5000 years old were shown to contain amplifiable human DNA (Hagelberg *et al.* 1989). The successful amplification of bone DNA attracted the attention of the scientific community and of forensic experts and police authorities interested in the potential application of bone DNA typing in human identification. However, news of the recovery of DNA from bones was also greeted with scepticism. Critics suggested that the bone DNA sequences could be artefacts caused by the inadvertent amplification of modern DNA sequences. The very sensitivity of the PCR, which permits tiny amounts of DNA to be recovered, is also a potential source of error, because any available target DNA can be amplified, regardless of whether it is original DNA from the sample or contamination from an extraneous DNA source. Human DNA is the main source of contamination of ancient materials because human beings handle the remains, reagents and equipment. The main constituent of house dust, shed human skin, is probably a richer source of human DNA than many ancient human mummified remains or bones.

At a meeting of participants of the Biomolecular Palaeontology Initiative of NERC (Natural Environment Research Council) in Glasgow in 1990, Svante Pääbo, the first scientist to recover DNA from mummified human remains, described an attempt to recover DNA from a bone extract of the extinct New Zealand moa, that had yielded a human DNA sequence rather than a bird-like sequence. Pääbo argued for caution in the interpretation of DNA analyses performed on skeletal material, suggesting that the results might be due to contamination.

DNA from the *Mary Rose* pig bone

One way to overcome these objections was to demonstrate that the DNA extracted from bones made sense, for example that DNA extracted from animal bones corresponded to the correct species. The author analysed a pig bone (femur 81S0175, from the pig store in O2) from the *Mary Rose*, kindly provided by the Radiocarbon Accelerator Laboratory at the University of Oxford, together with human bones from different contexts (Fig. 16.4). A small amount of each bone, less than one gramme, was powdered in a freezer mill, and the powder was extracted in a solution containing a detergent, an enzyme for breaking down protein, and high levels of salt, the same way as described in Hagelberg *et al.* (1989). After incubation for several hours, the solutions were extracted with organic solvents to remove the protein and then desalted and concentrated. The resulting solution, it was hoped, would contain the DNA from the bones. The DNA samples were subsequently used for PCR amplification, targeting a specific piece of a mitochondrial DNA gene.

Mitochondrial DNA, or mtDNA for short, is used frequently in ancient DNA research. Mitochondria are the energy-producing organelles inside cells, and each cell contains thousands of copies of usually identical mtDNA copies, inherited from the mother. As mtDNA is so abundant in cells, there is a much better chance of retrieving mtDNA sequences than chromosomal DNA from degraded biological samples. The chromosomal DNA, present in the cell nucleus, has typically only two copies of each particular gene, one inherited from the mother and one from the father (see also Chapter 13).

To compare the DNA amplified from the human and the pig bones, a mitochondrial gene called *cytochrome b* was selected. A similar form of the gene is present in all animals, although the exact sequence varies from species to species. It was hoped that it would

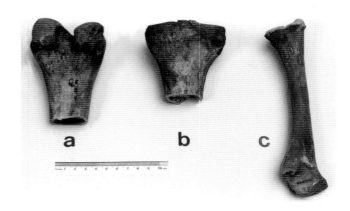

Figure 16.4. Three bone specimens from which DNA was recovered in 1990. (a) Human femur fragment, dated 750+80 years BP, from the medieval cemetery in Abingdon, Oxfordshire; (b) human tibia fragment from a mass grave in Argentina; (c) pig bone from O2 of the Mary Rose *(from Hagelberg and Clegg 1991).*

be possible to recover and sequence a piece of the *cytochrome b* gene from the *Mary Rose* pig bone, and compare it to the human *cytochrome b* gene, to discover whether the amplified DNA fragment was from a pig or the result of contamination, most likely from human DNA.

The amplification primers used in the *Mary Rose* pig study were designed to recognise a 375 base-pair portion of the *cytochrome b* sequence of many different animals, including pigs and humans (Kocher *et al.* 1989). Figure 16.5 shows the DNA sequence of the fragment of the *cytochrome b* gene of pigs and humans, indicating the differences between the two forms of the gene in the portion amplified by the primers.

The DNA sequence amplified from the pig bone was determined by a manual sequencing technique (Sanger *et al.* 1977), which involves labelling the DNA with a radioactive isotope and reading the sequence from an X-ray film (Fig. 16.6). The sequence was clearly that of a pig and not human, as would have been the case if the pig sample had been contaminated by human DNA. The results of this study were published as part of a larger study (Hagelberg and Clegg 1991). Although the *Mary Rose* pig bone was not the first bone from which DNA was extracted, it helped to prove the basic contention that DNA could be extracted from old bones.

Applications of the analysis of DNA from bone

Many studies on ancient bone DNA have been carried out since the publication of the *Mary Rose* pig results. There have been many refinements in PCR technology, and today most sequencing is done with automatic sequencers that make the *Mary Rose* pig sequence look antediluvian (compare Figure 16.6 of this section with the results of automatic sequencing of *Mary Rose* human DNA, performed fourteen years later). How-

```
primer L14841    AAAAAGCTTCCATCCAACATCTCAGCATGATGAAA──────▶
human            CTCCCCACCCCATCCAACATCTCCGCATGATGAAACTTCGGCTCACTCCTTGGCGCCTGC
pig              CTCCCAGCCCCCTCAAACATCTCATCATGATGAAACTTCGGTTCCCTCTTAGGCATCTGC

human            CTGATCCTCCAAATCACCACAGGACTATTCCTAGCCATGCACTACTCACCAGACGCCTCA
pig              CTAATCTTGCAAATCCTAACAGGCCTGTTCTTAGCAATACATTACACATCAGACACAACA

human            ACCGCCTTTTCATCAATCGCCCACATCACTCGAGACGTAAATTATGGCTGAATCATCCGC
pig              ACAGCTTTCTCATCAGTTACACACATTTGTCGAGACGTAAATTACGGATGAGTTATTCGC

human            TACCTTCACGCCAATGGCGCCTCAATATTCTTTATCTGCCTCTTCCTACACATCGGGCGA
pig              TATCTACATGCAAACGGAGCATCCATATTCTTTATTTGCCTATTCATCCACGTAGGCCGA

human            GGCCTATATTACGGATCATTTCTCTACTCAGAAACCTGAAACATCGGCATTATCCTCCTG
pig              GGTCTATACTACGGATCCTATATATTCCTAGAAACATGAAACATTGGAGTAGTCCTACTA

primer H15149                                      ◀──────TGAGGACAAATATCATTC
human            CTTGCAACTATAGCAACAGCCTTCATAGGCTATGTCCTCCCGTGAGGCCAAATATCATTC
pig              TTTACCGTTATAGCAACAGCCTTCATAGGCTACGTCCTGCCCTGAGGACAAATATCATTC

primer H15149    TGAGGGGCTGCAGTTT
human            TGAGGGGCCACAGTAA
pig              TGAGGAGCTACGGTCA
```

Figure 16.5. Alignment of the published sequences of the human and pig mitochondrial DNA cytochrome b genes, showing the positions at which the two sequences differ from each other.

ever, many DNA extraction techniques have remained remarkably constant, as the main problem in the study of ancient DNA is not how to get DNA out of the tissues in the first place, but how to avoid contamination by modern DNA.

The techniques for bone DNA typing were originally developed for the study of archaeological bones, and much of the early funding came from science-based archaeology and palaeontology research initiatives. The research discussed here was funded by the NERC Special Topic in Biomolecular Palaeontology. Interestingly, the most significant applications of the initial work were in the field of forensic identification. Even before the pig bone work had been completed, police departments were requesting help to identify missing individuals using DNA. Sir Alec Jeffreys (the inventor of DNA fingerprinting) and the author used bone DNA typing to identify skeletal remains thought to be those of a missing Cardiff teenager, Karen Price. In 1991, the results of this analysis were accepted as evidence in the trial of the men accused of her murder. This was the first case where bone DNA typing and a kind of DNA called microsatellite DNA were accepted as evidence in a court of law, and the first case in Europe where PCR was used (Hagelberg et al. 1991). The same techniques were used for the identification of the skeleton of the Nazi physician Josef Mengele (Jeffreys et al. 1992) and the remains of the family of the last Tsar of Russia (Gill et al. 1994). Methods originally developed by scientists in university research laboratories were soon adopted by professional forensic scientists, and eventually found their way into routine forensic casework. Bone DNA typing has also been used for the identification of the victims of mass disasters and genocide (for example, Holland et al. 1993; Corach et al. 1997).

Problems and opportunities of ancient DNA

Despite the potential usefulness of bone DNA typing for the study of human prehistory, the techniques have been applied in comparatively few studies. In many cases, the problem of contamination has been insurmountable. The techniques have been applied with good results to the study of the phylogenetic relationships of extinct animal species (for example, Hagelberg et al. 1994b; Cooper et al. 2001). Among the best-known studies involving human bones are those on the origins of the Polynesian and Native American populations (Hagelberg and Clegg 1993, Hagelberg et al. 1994a; Stone and Stoneking 1993; 1999; Lalueza-Fox 1996).

The most publicised application of bone DNA typing has been in the study of the origins of our own species. In 1997, scientists in Germany announced the recovery of a mtDNA sequence from a bone fragment from the original Neanderthal type specimen (Krings et al. 1997). The sequence differed sufficiently from that of living humans to suggest that the archaic individual had not contributed to the gene pool of anatomical modern humans. Additional Neanderthal sequences have been published (Ovchinnikov et al. 2000, Krings et al. 2000). These molecular data have fuelled debates about the origins of our species as they purport to provide definite evidence of the 'Out of Africa'

648

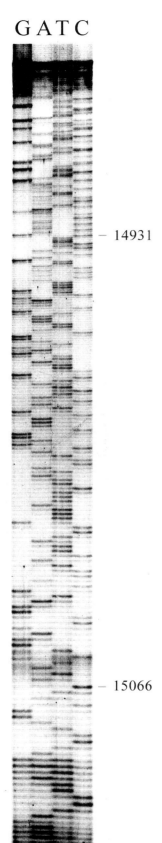

G A T C

— 14931

— 15066

Figure 16.6. Direct sequencing of a fragment of the mitochondrial cyto-chrome b gene, amplified from an extract of a Mary Rose pig bone (from Hagelberg and Clegg 1991)

hypothesis of human origins. Some scientists believe that although the Neanderthal sequences seem to fall outside the range of variation of modern humans, the DNA results alone are not enough to consign Neanderthals to a separate biological species (Relethford 2001). Despite these differences in opinion, there is little doubt that the results themselves can help us build new models to interpret the past. It is evident that ancient DNA sequences have much to contribute to our knowledge of the evolutionary history of past human and animal populations, to complement information gained from other fields of research.

Sadly, ancient DNA research has been hampered by the problems of contamination. Some early results could not be reproduced, and differences of opinion led some scientists to argue for a strict set of criteria for ancient DNA studies. After the publication of the first Neanderthal study, Ryk Ward and Chris Stringer suggested the implementation of standards for ancient DNA research, with little discussion whether these standards were appropriate in all studies (Ward and Stringer 1997). The standards consisted of:

1.   Determination of the extent of amino acid degradation in the ancient tissue.
2.   Determination of the number of intact DNA molecules remaining in the tissue extract.
3.   Cloning of the PCR products and sequencing of each clone.
4.   Replication of the study in a different laboratory.

In the intervening time, there has been a trend towards tightening of the requirements of ancient DNA studies, and this author believes this has stifled innovation. The adherence of imposed and inflexible rules for scientific investigations seems of doubtful merit. It is frequently hard to publish ancient DNA data, and approaches deviating from the 'standard' are labelled unorthodox, or described in rather emotive terms (eg, *Ancient DNA: Do it right or not at all*, Cooper and Poinar 2000). The load imposed by 'verification' has made much ancient DNA research too expensive for many laboratories, and concentrated research and funding in a few selected centres.

Twenty years after the publication of the first ancient DNA study (Higuchi *et al.* 1984), and 15 years after it was shown that DNA survived in old bones, ancient DNA is once again in danger of becoming nothing more than a scientific curiosity restricted to a few high-profile studies. However, our recent results on human DNA of crew members of the *Mary Rose* (Chapter 13) demonstrate that ancient DNA techniques are robust and have a potential that is still waiting to be exploited.

Other analyses
Michael J. Allen

Microstructural analysis of bone
Microstructural analysis was conducted on samples of human bone by Lynne Bell as a part of her doctoral research (Bell 1995). This examined diagenetic (or post-mortem) changes to the physical microstructure of the bone. The aims of this examination were to assess the extent of post-mortem marine-type changes from various locations within the wreck, and to determine any relationships between the extent of post-mortem attack and the length of time and depth of burial. The information below is abstracted and summarised from her thesis after cross-referencing with the *Mary Rose* archive (original archive numbering and contextual information is not provided in the thesis).

Materials and methods
Seventeen mandibles and maxillae were examined, including samples from all decks and from differing locations and depths of burial (see below, and Fig. 16.7).

In each case, a single tooth and accompanying socket was removed from the mandible or maxilla by

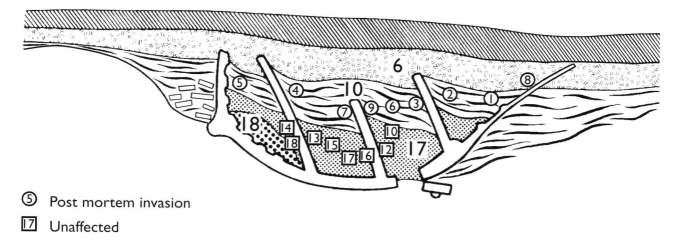

⑤ Post mortem invasion

⑰ Unaffected

Figure 16.7 Location of the human jawbones examined for microstructual changes

cutting the tooth and socket free using a wet, diamond-edged circular saw. Each section was then rinsed in tepid tap water and allowed to dry. The sections were in methylmethacrylate and 5% (by volume) styrene, placed in a 32°C oven and removed after the monomer had polymerised to polymethylemethacrylate (PMMA). The methacrylate nonomer had been prepared by the 'flash distil' method described by Boyde *et al.* (1992). Embedded specimens were cut in a longitudinal section buccolingually using an Isomet-11-1180 circular saw, and polished using graded abrasives and finished with 1μm diamond abrasive on a rotary lap. Each block face received a coating of carbon in vacuum and was mounted on an aluminium stub. The specimens were examined using a Cambridge Steroscan S4-10 SEM (operated in BSE mode working at 20 kV beam voltage).

Diagenetic changes

Examination showed that all hard tissues, except enamel, had undergone quite radical diagenetic change. The alveolar bone (see Chapter 13) was extensively affected, while the enamel, whether covered by calculus or not, appeared unaffected. In striking contrast to the enamel the dentine was observed to have undergone significant diagenetic change to its microstructure, and this change was different to other samples recovered from terrestrial sites and buried in soil (Bell 1995; Bell *et al.* 1991). The attack was peripheral and possibly short-lived. The dentine was primarily attacked at the cervical margin where the enamel was partially undermined for a short distance. The full spread of this post-mortem attack appeared to have been limited and only affected the root dentine to a level above the alveolar crest. Invading micro-organisms appeared less affected by the collagenous network of the dentine. The cementum, unlike soil buried examples from land sites, seemed hardly affected by diagenesis as a result of its location mostly within the preserved joint space (Bell *et al.* 1991; Bell 1995). However, the small amount that

was affected, in a band horizontally above the alveola crest, showed tunnelling similar to that seen in bone and dentine.

SEM imaging (BSE images) of the dental and supporting bony tissue could detect and record changes that had occurred in the mineral density and morphology of the specimens. All of the hard tissues other than enamel underwent some diagenetic change to microstructure, and the microstructure of each calcified connective tissue influenced the pattern of diagenesis. Sampling protocols for biochemical and mtDNA extrication studies could gain considerable benefit from identifying and microscopically locating the distribution of diagenesis before the sampling of bone or dentine. Rather than considering diagenesis as a contaminating factor also, it represents a resource for understanding taphonomic processes at the microscopic level.

The nature and degree of changes relating to burial and location

Microstructural post-mortem alteration to skeletal remains by tunnelling or microboring recorded in marine samples are connected to microbial fouling. By examining the nature and degree of post-mortem attack, an assessment of the degree of alteration in relation to the length of time and depth of burial could be made.

The embedded, uncoated blocks of tooth and bony tissue section were dry mounted and examined under a Lasertec 1LM11 confocal reflection microscope (CRM) using a helium neon light source. This allowed identification of tissue morphology and characterisation of post-mortem alteration shown by slight micro-topographical relief created by polishing. The lasertec's integrated software enabled accurate measurements of x, y and z dimensions within 0.25μm (Jones *et al.* 1992).

All measured data were recorded without reference to the location of the sampled jaws within the wreck. The distribution of post-mortem tubule invasion was

Table 16.7 Human mandibles examined for diagentic changes and invasion

Bone group no.	Mandible no.	Sample no.	Bell analysis no.	Location	Context	Grade	Condition
80H0087	*81/14A*	*8*	*54*	U8	6	B3	pm
80H0093	*80/21*	*1*	*53*	U8	10	B3	pm
80H0040 (FCS 65)	*80/40*	*2*	*52*	U7	10	B1	pm
80H0112	*80/87*	*3*	*57*	M4	10	B2	pm
–	*80H0093*	*4*	*64*	O6	10	B3	pm
81H0417E	*80/112*	*5*	*68*	H4	10	B3	pm
80H0198	*80/198(x2)*	*6*	*58*	M4	10	B1	pm
81H0169	*80/11I*	*7*	*62*	O4	10	B2	pm
81H1058 (FCS71)	81/1058	*9*	*55*	H8	10	B3	pm
–	*81H0023*	11	61	M2	10	–	–
80H211I	*81/169*	*10*	*59*	M9	17	O	u
81H0014A	*81/256*	12	60	M10	17	O	u
–	81/257	13	63	O4	17	O	u
82H0063	*81/401(x2)*	14	*70*	H10	17	B3	pm
81H0401 (FCS81)	*81/417E*	15	67	O9	17	B1	pm
81H0256	*82/8*	*16*	*65*	O7	17	O	u
81H0287 (FCS36)	*82/44*	*17*	*66*	O8	17	O	u
(FCS19)	82/63	*18*	*69*	H7	17	O	u

B= bilateral; O = unaffected; pm = post-mortem invasion; u = unaffected; FCS = fairly complete skeleton. Items in italics were selected by Bell for examination of isotopes but no results have been made available for this publication (see Chapter 12)

recorded in terms of total morphology and distribution, maximum ingress, and maximum tubule diameter at eight different sites on each specimen. The levels of ingress were assessed and allocated three ranges:

grade 1= slight ie < 100mm
grade 2 = moderate ie $\leq$100–<200mm
grade 3 = deep ie $\geq$200mm – pulp cavity

Total distribution of invasive tunnelling was recorded as unaffected (O) or bilateral (B).

Presence or absence of invasion of the periodontal joint (PDJ) was also assessed. All of this information was recorded against the location and burial of the items. The distribution of change varied in terms of invasive depth and distribution but was always peripheral leaving the periodontal joint unaffected. The enamel and calculus was unaffected, but was undermined by microborings. The diameter of tunnels ranged between *c*. 5 and 19μm (to the nearest 0.5 μm). Within this range, two distinct groups were distinguished: 5–8μm and 11–19μm, with commonest tunnel

(84%) falling with the smaller group. When the levels of invasion were recorded (Table 16.7) and plotted against their recovered location and degree of burial (Fig. 16.7) a clear pattern emerges.

Most of the sample group from the lower sediments in the ship (mainly 17; referred to in Bell 1975 as the 'first' or 'initial' Tudor layer) exhibited no postmortem alteration, presumably being rapidly buried and sealed in an inert environment (Fig. 16.7). Only two specimens were affected by post-mortem tunnelling, 17 (from a mid-silt layer (17) on the Orlop deck) and 15 (which has doubtful provenance). All specimens in the 'second Tudor layer' (10) were affected by postmortem tunnelling. No specimens were examined from the modern sea-bed.

This study demonstrated for the first time that there was a relationship between microstructural postmortem change and stratigraphy. The lower silts, which represent a period of rapid silting, accumulated in probably only a few months (see Chapter 12). The lack of post-mortem changes in specimens from this layer suggests that the sea-bed conditions within the wreck immediately after sinking were not conducive to the endolithic micro-organisms responsible for tunnelling, and that burial was rapid. The swift accumulation of the lower silts elegantly illustrates the preservation properties of rapid silting

The fine grey clay and seaweed lenses overlying the initial silting inside the hull (layer 10) formed over a longer period of time and were subject to inwash, local deflation, and redistribution. Collapse of the superstructure would open up the site to more light, heat, increased current-borne fauna and detritus. Skeletal material would have provided an ideal substrate for many endoliths, and it seemed likely that silt-sensitive polychaete, thraustochrid or algal micro-organisms were responsible for most of the tunnelling.

PART 3: LOOKING TO THE FUTURE

17. Concluding Comments and Avenues for Future Research

Julie Gardiner and Michael J. Allen

The wreck of the *Mary Rose* has produced an unprecedented assemblage of sixteenth century objects. As the preceding chapters have demonstrated, the range and sheer quantity of items recovered is breathtaking, even leaving aside all the ship's fittings, rigging, ordnance and weaponry relating to the operation and fighting of the ship herself that are discussed elsewhere in this series. The exceptional preservation of organic materials has provided unparalleled opportunities for the study of many classes of wooden, leather and textile objects that are normally rare survivals on archaeological sites. It has also enabled us to gain valuable insights into the provisioning of the vessel and provided some idea of the general conditions experienced by the men on board. We have learnt much about the crew themselves, both from their physical remains and from the many personal objects they brought on board.

Because of the sudden and unexpected nature of the sinking, the ship went down with most of her contents and nearly all her crew. Despite the displacement of many items and subsequent disintegration of a large part of the structure, a great many became trapped by rapidly accumulated silts. Unusually in archaeology, therefore, we can be certain that the majority of finds from the 'site' were associated in use at a specific date – July 1545. This fact is of immense importance as it lies on the cusp between the late medieval and early post-medieval periods and has implications for the interpretation of all archaeological assemblages (and many historical records) of the time from southern England and beyond, challenging some previously held assumptions and confirming others.

In this final chapter we will briefly review some of the major aspects of life and death on board the ship that have been demonstrated, or touched upon, by analysis of objects, environmental material and human remains and suggest some areas for future research. It is, however, fair to say that every aspect of the *Mary Rose* assemblages will benefit from further study – both in their own right and in terms of the wider implications of this unique collection. The sum of the collection is undoubtedly greater than its parts and there are many years of study yet to come. Its specific composition, as the contents of a functioning warship, mean that all

items are, to a greater or lesser extent, inter-related, but there are several major topics that present themselves for consideration.

Use of Space and the Operation of the Ship

Volumes 2 and 3 of this series (on the structure of the ship and the ordnance respectively) deal at length with the overall operation of the vessel, both as a ship and, more specifically, as a fighting unit. Here we remind ourselves of some of the more domestic arrangements.

The chaos of the sinking belies an underlying organisation of space and activity that is, of course, paramount to the effective loading and use of any ship. Here, space was at a premium and the primary function as a heavily armed gunship dictated the principal use of the various decks. The men were obliged to live and work around the distribution of weapons and related supplies in what were already cramped and austere conditions.

There is a distinct lack of furniture aboard the *Mary Rose* – not entirely unsurprising given her function, though we might, perhaps have expected more in the way of stools and tables from the remains of officers cabins at least. Apart from fixtures and fittings such as sleeping platforms (the word 'bed' hardly seems to apply to these basic board constructions), only a handful of stools and benches have been recovered and one of these seems to have had a specific function as a treatment table in the Barber-surgeon's cabin (Chapter 9). The cabins themselves are few and have only been recognised on the Main deck. Of these, two were occupied by the Barber-surgeon and probably his surgery and another by the Carpenters. The last seems to have been an officer's cabin, in the bow of the ship, though its association with the ship's pilot(s) (in litt.) now seems to be rather spurious. We may assume that the missing port side of the ship was a mirror image of the starboard, which provides for a similar number of cabins on that side of the Main deck (this is suggested also by the positioning of guns and gunports; see *AMR* Vol. 3.). A concentration of gunnery equipment may suggest that the cabin matching the Carpenters' was occupied by a Master Gunner (A. Hildred & P. Marsden, pers. comm.: see *AMR* Vols 2 and 3).

Overall, however, this tells us rather little about the location of cabins or their inhabitants. We might expect at least a Captain's cabin and several for his retinue and ship's officers but it is likely that these would have been high up in the bow and stern of the ship – the areas that survive least well. There are some hints at the presence of at least one such cabin in the bow in the form of fragments of decorated oak panels that might have adorned the walls (Chapter 9). The distribution of loose objects that could indicate the presence of higher status individuals and cabins does not show any specific concentration in the area of the destroyed bow, however, though there are a number of personal chests in the stern that seem likely to have belonged to officers. A more detailed analysis of the distribution of objects might yield further information in future.

That the crew in general had their living accommodation mostly in the stern, beneath the Castle deck, has been confirmed by the detailed study of the distribution and association of objects, with a concentration of personal and 'domestic' items in the aft part of the Upper deck, along with a large number of chests (Chapters 3, 10). Many chests were lockable and some were probably of continental manufacture, and there is some correlation here with the presence of higher status objects (within the context of the ship) such as books, jewellery, pewter plates, pocket sundials and gold coins. Chests also carried supplies and served a secondary function as benches.

The Upper deck also carried guns and the men must have eaten and slept around them, using whatever space they could find. An outline analysis of the available space on the Upper and Main decks suggests that it would not have been possible to feed all the men below decks at one time, though available historical evidence, albeit a little later in date, suggests that the men were fed in one 'sitting' rather than by watch, assuming, of course, that a watch system was in operation (Chapter 11). However, someone had to man the ship! Similarly, it is difficult to calculate how many off-duty men could have found room to sleep at any one time, in the absence of hammocks, that were not yet available. If a double watch system was employed then up to 200 men could have been off-duty at any time and potentially asleep. Such a number could certainly not have been accommodated on the gundecks alone. The logistics of such basic aspects of life aboard require much fuller investigation and this will probably need to be addressed through much wider study of (mostly later) historical and naval records.

The analysis of surviving items relating to the feeding of the crew demonstrates that vessels used for eating and drinking were widely distributed on the ship, presumably indicating where they were used, while those involved in the preparation and serving of food were mostly in storage in and around the ship's galley and in its associated storage areas in the Hold and on the Orlop deck.

There was no room for untidiness on the ship and both the Hold and Orlop decks were used principally for the stowage of supplies. Analysis of the overall contents of these decks has demonstrated more of the organisation involved (Chapter 10). Most of the many casks carrying supplies disintegrated, their contents spilled or lost. Apart from the obvious concentration of food-related items in and around the galley, we can see some patterning in the location of casks of meat and fish; barrels of pitch and tar were stored in the Hold, forward of the galley; and those containing lanterns and tallow in the stern, but there are some frustrating omissions. Where, for instance, was the ship's powder store? The *Anthony Roll* (1546) states that 27 barrels of gunpowder were issued to the ship but the only cask that has provided a sample of probable gunpowder was in the Hold, alarmingly close to the furnaces of the galley! Circumstantial evidence suggests that powder may have been stored in the stern of the Orlop

Figure 17.1 The Mary Rose *as she appears in the* Anthony Roll *of 1546*

deck, along with the flammable tallow and incendiary devices. As the furthest part of the ship from the galley that was not also a gundeck, this would seem to be the most sensible location (see *AMR* Vol. 3).

Further analysis is bound to provide more detailed evidence for the organisation of stowage on the ship. For instance, no full analysis of all the casks has yet been possible. This would require the laying out of well over 3000 individual elements (most of which remain in wet storage) in order to match and piece together the original objects. While this is unlikely to tell us directly much more about their contents, there is already sufficient evidence to suggest that casks of different size, shape and construction/finishing held specific contents (Chapter 10). In combination with study of the incised marks on the casks, documentary evidence and the distribution of different types/sizes, much more could be gleaned about both the provisioning of the ship and stowage methods. Other related areas of study include, for instance, work on the detailed associations between objects (see below), on the question of access between decks and areas and how they affected both the loading and handling of supplies and on the analysis of, as yet unprocessed, environmental samples (Chapter 12).

The *Mary Rose* spent most of her working life in waters relatively close to home, but she was provided with the most up-to-date navigation equipment and, presumably, more than one skilled pilot (at least one of whom, ironically, could well have been French). The instruments recovered confirm the use of traditional devices such as the log-reel and sounding lines, but also includes several 'state of the art' compasses, chart sticks and dividers, all at an early date compared with previously known examples (Chapter 7). As such, this is an extremely important assemblage for the history of navigation and will provide much food for thought for experts in that field.

Other skilled non-combatants and crew vital to the operation of the ship were its carpenters (Chapter 8). It is not known how many carpenters were typically engaged on board ships of this time but the quantity and range of tools suggest that there may have been at least six aboard the *Mary Rose* when she sank. One of the cabins on the Main deck was full of woodworking tools and several chests were found inside

Figure 17.2 The Mary Rose *as she is today*

the cabin and stacked just outside it. At least one of these seems to have been part of the official issue of the ship but most included personal objects too and seem to be the personal tool chests of the men involved. One of the carpenters should have been specifically appointed to the ship and the presence of monogramed pewter vessels in the cabin certainly points towards there being an officer amongst them. Again, the importance of this assemblage for the future study of the history of woodworking tools and the role of the ship's carpenter cannot be overstressed.

Many other questions about the internal organisation of the ship remain to be answered. We will probably never be able to say much more about the internal structure and use of the bow, Castle and Upper decks but there is a good deal more that can be attempted elsewhere. For instance, we have only been able to suggest in outline how the men were fed. We have seen that the logistics are complicated, with cooking facilities in the Hold and the men probably eating on the Main deck and above with, apparently, only one (or two if there was also one on the port side) narrow ladders for communication. It seems unlikely that these companionways would have been adequate for the job so the question of how meals were served and physically transported round the ship is certainly a topic for further consideration – were they hoisted up through the hatches, perhaps, or could they simply be handed up from one deck to another? Indeed, the whole subject of movement and access around the ship needs much further examination as there are few recorded companionways and many obstacles (including hatchways, stanchions, low decks and poor lighting). tThese would have had implications not only for the everyday activities of the men but also on major considerations such as the loading and arranging of

supplies, the installation of heavy iron and bronze guns, and the operation of the ship during an engagement.

Provisioning the Ship

It was only in years after the sinking of the *Mary Rose* that good order was brought to the supply of provisions to the burgeoning navy, and not until later centuries that provisioning or victualling yards became permanent features of the major ports in England. Although there were established and regulated sources of supply in the first half of the sixteenth century, the organisation of provisioning seems to have been somewhat haphazard and open to considerable corruption and abuse, particularly with regard to victuals (Chapter 14). The documentary sources are full of complaints about the food and ale (or, more often, the lack thereof).

Most consumables were provided, to warships at least, salted, cured or dried, rather than 'on the hoof' or fresh. Fresh food was a rarity and the menu, which was regulated, was monotonous and lacking in many nutrients and vitamins. The few instances of fresh fruit found on board suggest individual supply. The freshness of water could not be guaranteed so beer and wine were the staple liquids. It is possible that bread was baked on board (the reproduction of one of the *Mary Rose*'s galley furnaces produces excellent bread) but more likely, for short campaigns at least, that bread and biscuit were supplied from shore – but that is an interesting area for further historical research. Unfortunately, while animal bone has survived very well on the wreck, evidence for other foodstuffs has not and we are left with a rather biased picture of an already restricted diet (Chapter 14).

In addition to information pertaining to diet and provisioning, the animal bones provide a well preserved assemblage of known date from which further analysis of the size, robusticity and morphology of animals will undoubtedly aid in the understanding of breeding and husbandry and of butchery practices. Pioneering analysis of a pig bone from the *Mary Rose* (Chapter 16) proved that ancient DNA can survive under some preservational circumstances. Analysis of DNA from animal bone and plant remains, such as the plums and rye grains recovered (Chapter 12), may, by comparison with modern samples, provide clues as to the breeds and varieties that were in use at the time. It may be possible to establish if varieties of staple food plants, such as cereals, are the same as those cultivated today or are no longer cultivated, or even extinct, and to identify sources for foodstuffs that are likely to have included imported ingredients.

It is difficult to determine what proportion of the many categories of 'domestic' object found on the ship were official issue and what personal belongings. As stated above, the chests of woodworking tools seem to have been the toolkits of individual carpenters, as we might predict, but at least one collection of tools was found in a chest that was almost certainly official issue. There are nineteen similar chests that are of simple, crate-like construction, with or without lids, and these seem certain to have contained supplies. Some specifically contained arrows and longbows and there are others whose original contents are not known for certain. There is no reason to suggest that any of the crates contained other than official supplies, though we do not know what most of those were.

Other categories of non-ordnance related objects that could have been supplied include clothing, in the form of uniforms and shoes at least, galley equipment, serving and eating/drinking vessels and general equipment such as shovels, brushes and brooms (Chapters 2, 11, 8). Although there are quite a large number of clothing fragments, there is no evidence for the presence of uniforms. However, the survival of cloth is very variable and probably very specific to the circumstances in which the garment was buried, so absence of evidence here should not be taken as evidence of absence. There is some suggestion of the provision of footwear – a sack of shoes, not all of them in pairs, was found in storage on the Orlop deck and some shoes have Roman numerals incised on the soles that are suggestive of official tally marks (Chapter 2). Most of the crew seem to have worn simple, low-cut slip-on shoes, which were often subject to much wear and tear.

Official marks occur on a wide variety of items from the *Mary Rose*. Some of these marks are well known: the 'H' brand for Henry VIII, for example, and the broad arrow. These occur on, for instance, cask components, gun carriages, wooden bowls and dishes, copper-alloy vessels, various articles of weaponry and tools. A great many other markings occur, ranging from personal marks of ownership, such as the 'GC' initials of the Vice Admiral, George Carew, on his pewter dinner service, and makers'/privy marks, such as those found on other pewter objects, through religious devices and good luck symbols to complex, apparently indecipherable graffiti such as occur widely on items like wooden bowls. Close inspection of many of these marks has shown that they incorporate the figure '4' (a good luck symbol) and/or the broad arrow design and many resemble merchants' marks. It seems likely that, in the case of the wooden bowls, officially issued items were incised with individually recognisable patterns and treated as personal objects (Chapter 11). There are a number of published studies of merchants' marks and there are official records of pewterers' and other makers' marks. All the marks on *Mary Rose* objects deserve much fuller, comparative, study than has yet been possible in order to investigate their meaning and origin and help in understanding the supply of material to the ship.

Welfare

The *Mary Rose*'s Barber-surgeon had a chest in his cabin that is a real Pandora's box. It was raised full and intact and was found to contain an array of surgical instruments, jars, glass bottles and wooden canisters of ointments and medicaments. Other medical equipment was found in the cabin itself, along with more personal items, some stamped with the initials 'WE' and 'BWE'. Although only the handles of most of the instruments survive this is a very important find as it represents a 'closed' assemblage of known date that can be compared with historical sources and illustrations, very few other such instruments having survived at all. The contents of jars and wooden canisters have long since degraded but chemical analysis of residues within them was able to identify some basic ingredients that could be compared favourably with known recipes for medicines and ointments (Chapters 4, 16).

The Barber-surgeon offered a grooming service – his equipment included razors and combs – and the regular sweeping of decks would have been routine, but there was very little provision for hygiene and pests of all kinds are likely to have inhabited the ship. Rats were present and would have been an unavoidable part of the ship's company; their voracious appetites would have necessitated the storage of anything edible or chewable in casks and chests. The threat they posed as a direct health hazard is unlikely to have been appreciated, as would that of a variety of other pests, such as fleas, latrine flies and bluebottles, whose presence was probably considered to be mere nuisance (Chapter 15). Only a small number of environmental samples has been processed for the recovery of insect remains but they demonstrate the great potential for survival of these delicate fragments. Many more are available for study that could provide valuable and more detailed information about living conditions.

The Crew

The *Mary Rose* sank with catastrophic loss of life, but out of that tragedy has come the opportunity to study in detail the skeletal remains of about half the crew (Chapter 13). This represents the only large sample for the Tudor period available for study in England.

Many illnesses and injuries leave marks on the skeleton. The possibilities for serious injury at sea were legion; many went untreated while methods of treatment were, in any case, generally crude and frequently brutal (Chapter 4). Diseases such as rickets and scurvy were endemic, arthritis and tooth decay were common, as was syphilis. Other common ailments of the time, such as food poisoning and gonorrhoea, and injuries that did not involve the bones or major muscle attachments, would not be detectable from skeletal remains but were equally rife.

Examination of the surviving human remains (Chapter 13) suggests that the crew of the *Mary Rose* were, on the whole, a reasonably healthy lot, with few 'out of the ordinary' conditions for the time but plenty of tooth decay and relate problems – but they were mostly very young men, some were only boys, and their histories are unknown. A few particularly nasty injuries were apparent, which would have had permanent repercussions for the individuals concerned but most of which happened well before death rather than being its cause. Unusual features of some skeletons points to those individuals being archers and gunners. The remains of probably one entire gun crew, drowned at their station, have been identified. Preliminary DNA results suggest that not all the crew were British, a fact that ties in with various historical records for the period. In some cases, shoes had been modified to accommodate foot injuries or conditions such as bunions. The human remains were examined in detail in the 1980s. Analytical and forensic techniques have advanced considerably in recent years and there is much further analysis that could now be undertaken. The DNA studies are currently ongoing.

Fragments of clothing, examples of fastenings, laces and sewing kits were found inside chests. We may assume that spare clothing and shoes were brought aboard and that some spare time was spent in darning and patching, a topic of perhaps rather mundane nature that would benefit form further study, and surviving woollen garments show considerable evidence of repairs (Chapters 2, 3).

Other items that each man is almost certain to have had, and probably kept about his person, were a sharp knife that could be used for a variety of purposes, a comb and a spoon for eating (forks were not used at this time). Many examples of the first two have been recovered but very few spoons, suggesting that they were made of horn that has not survived. Many of the knives were found within decorated boxwood sheaths, presumably whittled during idle moments, providing the only known assemblage of these individual, personal objects (Chapter 3) that certainly deserve more detailed analysis. Such idle moments could also be occupied with hand-fishing or playing a variety of games. The men are unlikely to have played for money. Historical records tell us that the crew would have been paid on return from campaign and this seems to be borne out by the comparatively small amount of money found on board. Coins, including gold coins, were generally found in very small individual quantities, often kept in leather purses in locked chests. One chest, stored on the Orlop deck, held a considerable sum and may have been that of, or used by, the ship's purser (Chapter 6).

Music was a feature of the ship – whether purely for the entertainment of the officers, for general enjoyment or to accompany regular tasks cannot be determined but, as with so many of the *Mary Rose* assemblages, there is an unprecedented collection of early sixteenth century instruments on board, including the first known surviving example of a specific type of woodwind instrument called a douçaine or still shawm (Chapter 5). The importance of this ensemble to the future study of both the history of musical instruments and musicology cannot be over-emphasised.

Also of considerable wider significance is the presence of a number of religious items, mostly stowed away in chests (Chapter 3). Several paternosters or rosaries, book covers probably from prayer books and a few individual pieces such as a casket panel and token, are evidence of the spiritual concerns of crew members. The significance of these objects, apart from their intrinsic rarity, is that they all relate to the Catholic church and occur here after Henry VIII's break with Rome. They provide a fascinating, if enigmatic, insight into the men's attitude to the religious upheaval of the times: a topic that is bound to prove of great further interest to archaeologists and historians alike.

Science and Technology

Chapter 16 illustrates how certain items from the *Mary Rose* have already contributed to the development and application of scientific methods above and beyond study of the ship herself. There is no doubt that many more opportunities for the application of 'pure' science will present themselves and, to this end, it is vital that the assemblages are curated and maintained for the benefit of future generations. The material archive contains a many processed samples in which reside items, such as insects, that would warrant much more detailed study. The research here has only touched the surface; the stored processed samples have huge potential for further physical and chemical research, and for DNA and other studies. There will be many, as yet, unformulated questions and untried methodologies that will seek to draw on them.

Volume 5 of this series demonstrates the importance of the conservation work carried out on the hull and her contents and the contribution made to the development of conservation science. The many different materials and classes of object provide opportunities for research into the histories of various branches of technology and materials science. Analysis of metals using a wide range of techniques has already contributed significantly to discussion on the development of, for instance, iron technology and the uses of different forms of iron for different purposes. Metallurgical analysis is providing insights into the actual composition of pewter used in objects of different classes – compositions that were supposed to be strictly regulated – and of copper-based alloys used for the manufacture of various categories of object. For non-metal objects, the technology involved in the manufacture of, for instance, leather bottles and shoes, turned wooden vessels and musical instruments has been explored. The last 20 years or so of scientific analysis has, however, marked only the beginning of what is possible and the publication of these volumes will undoubtedly stimulate the desire for much further work in many fields not directly connected with the understanding of the *Mary Rose* herself.

Spatial Analysis of the Ship

An important aspect of the excavation of the *Mary Rose* was the use of the DSM survey method (see Chapter 1 and *AMR* Vol. 1) to provide three-dimensional survey of key items in relation to one another and to the structure of the ship. Many hundreds of DSM measurements were taken throughout the wreck. Unfortunately, a lack of computer facilities and funding has meant that the full results have still not been processed and the finds plotted accurately. This has led to difficulties in understanding the precise location of and associations between objects in the absence of any conventional site planning. The processing of this data should be a priority for future analysis in order that the spatial analysis of the ship and her contents can be fully achieved.

Closing the Chapter

This volume, like the others in this series on the archaeology of the *Mary Rose*, has only begun to scratch the surface of an understanding of life and death aboard this great ship. The size and range of the assemblage and the peculiar circumstances of its depositional history and preservation have dictated that much primary effort has gone into the conservation and basic recording of the many thousands of objects and timbers. It is only in the last few years that in-depth analysis and wider research have been possible for many classes of material. Conservation is ongoing and there remain many items in wet storage that it has not yet been possible to examine in detail and that that are so-far classed as 'unidentified'. Many fragmentary objects, especially those of leather and textile, also remain to be examined in detail. The first 20 years or so of conservation and investigation have served to highlight just how little we really know about many aspects of life in Tudor England, let alone on board a warship. As happens so often in archaeological research, the work has posed more questions than it has yet answered, and opened many more avenues for research than it has so far been possible to explore.

The publication of these volumes serves to close the first chapter in the analysis of the *Mary Rose*, both as an archaeological site and as a functioning warship. Here we can only demonstrate the state of our knowledge up to the present time (Spring 2005) and much work remains to be done. It is certain that the publication will stimulate interest in all aspects of the ship and her contents, and in individuals and interested groups ranging from the most eminent of scholars to the youngest of schoolchildren. Now begins the rest of the story.

Appendices

Appendix 1: Contents of all chests

CHEST 81A1555. (F058) TYPE 1.1/1. M9. POPLAR
In jumble of chests outside Carpenters' cabin. Large concreted area at one end causing chest to disintegrate. Small box standing upright in corner. Max length 1190mm

UNIDENTIFIED	81A4539-40
UNIDENTIFIED	81A4547-8
CONCRETION	81A4781
NAIL	81A1545
BOX,TOOL-?	81A1754
AXE (HANDLE)	81A4866/1-5
AXE (HANDLE)	81A4538
BUNG+CHAIN	81A1546
ADZE	81A1544
AUGER	81A4780
PLANE,STEMMED PLOUGH	81A1542
PLANE,CORNER ROUND	81A4537
PLANE,JOINTING-	81A1537
PLANE,MOULDING-	81A1538
PLANE,MOULDING-	81A4869
PLANE,REBATE-	81A4175/1-2
PLANE,REBATE-	81A4868
PLANE,SMOOTHING-	81A4867
PLANE,TRYING-	81A1543
CAULKING-MALLET	81A4865
HANDLE?	81A1427
TAMPION	81A1426
KNIFE-SHEATH	81A1428
PLANE,MOULDING-	81A1425
PLANE,ROUND-	81A1440
PLANE,SNIPE-BILL-	81A1424

CHEST 81A5967. (F131) TYPE 1.1/1. M9. POPLAR
Found inside Carpenters' Cabin. Chest itself damaged and largely filled with concretion with wooden handles protruding. 1140x480x400mm

UNIDENTIFIED	81A3707
UNIDENTIFIED	81A3875
UNIDENTIFIED	81A3878
UNIDENTIFIED	81A4848
UNIDENTIFIED	81A4851-2
UNIDENTIFIED	81A4856
BOWL, WOOD	81A5988
STOPPER?	81A3697
FRAME?	81A4482
STRAP	81A5973
LINSTOCK	81A3872
LINSTOCK?	81A4479
BY-KNIFE	81A3828
BILL	81A3787
KNIFE	81A4779
INGOT?, LEAD (SHIP'S FITTING)	81A4850
INGOT?, LEAD (SHIP'S FITTING)	81A4858
METAL-SHEET	81A4855
METAL-SHEET	81A4857
PICK?	81A4864
TINDER-BOX?	81A3874/1-3

HANDLE (AXE)	81A3869
HANDLE	81A3873
HANDLE (BRACE)	81A4859
HANDLE	81A5975
HANDLE (AXE/ADZE)	81A5976
HANDLE (AXE/ADZE)	81A5977
HANDLE (AXE/ADZE)	81A5978
HANDLE	81A5982
AUGER (HANDLE)	81A3827
AUGER (HANDLE)	81A3870
BRACE	81A4481
AXE/ADZE HANDLE	81A5984
MALLET	81A5974
PLANE,SMOOTHING-	81A4849
PLANE,TRYING-	81A3706
RULER	81A4483
RULER	81A4853
RULER	81A4854
FID	81A4480

CHEST 82A0894. (F187) TYPE 1.1/1. 010. ASH/POPLAR
Collapsed and incomplete, lid missing. 1300x460x410mm

UNIDENTIFIED	82A0878
ANKLE-BOOT	82A5012-3
ANKLE-BOOT	82A0877
SHOES (pair)	82A0877
PLATTER, WOOD	82A0834
FLASK, LEATHER	82A5009/1-4
TRENCHER?	82A0879
ARROW(S)	82A5004/1-9
COMB	82A5010
KNIFE?	82A5005
SHIVES	82A0826-31
SHIVE	82A5011
SPILES	82A0818-25
SPILE+SHIVE	82A0832/1-2
SPILE+SHIVE	82A0833/1-2
SPILE+SHIVE	82A0880/1-2

ARROW CHEST 80A0726. (BX02) TYPE 1.1/2.1 U7/8. ELM
Almost complete, lidded and full. Broken open, one end crushed. 1920x400x340mm

SHERD, CERAMIC	80A1867
ARROWS	80A0764/001-268

ARROW CHEST 81A2398. (F036) TYPE 1.1/2.1 09. ELM Lidded and full of arrows though crushed at one end. Rope handles found inside. 1935x385x340mm	
ARROW	81A4285
ARROW	81A4289
ARROW	81A4294
ARROW(S)	81A2415/1-29
ARROW(S)	81A2416-7
ARROW(S)	81A2418/1-24
ARROW(S)	81A2419/1-28
ARROW(S)	81A2420-1
ARROW(S)	81A2422/1-25
ARROW(S)	81A2423/1-30
ARROW(S)	81A2424/1-24
ARROW(S)	81A2425/1-36
ARROW(S)	81A2426/1-19
ARROW(S)	81A2427/1-27
ARROW(S)	81A2428/1-25
ARROW(S)	81A2429/1-24
ARROW(S)	81A2430
ARROW(S)	81A2443/1-19
ARROW(S)	81A2444/1-14
ARROW(S)	81A2445/1-14
ARROW(S)	81A2446/1-20
ARROW(S)	81A2447/1-18
ARROW(S)	81A2448/1-19
ARROW(S)	81A2449/1-63
ARROW(S)	81A2450/1-22
ARROW(S)	81A2451/1-36
ARROW(S)	81A2452/1-28
ARROW(S)	81A2453/1-30
ARROW(S)	81A2454/1-27
ARROW(S)	81A2455/1-23
ARROW(S)	81A2456/1-18
ARROW(S)	81A2457/1-26
ARROW(S)	81A2458/1-27
ARROW(S)	81A2459/1-24
ARROW(S)	81A2460
ARROW(S)	81A2461/1-29
ARROW(S)	81A2462/1-29
ARROW(S)	81A2463/1-25
ARROW(S)	81A2464
ARROW(S)	81A2465/1-24
ARROW(S)	81A2466/1-24
ARROW(S)	81A2467/1-17
ARROW(S)	81A2468/1-17
ARROW(S)	81A2471/1-21
ARROW(S)	81A2472/1-55
ARROW(S)	81A2473/1-24
ARROW(S)	81A2474/1-44
ARROW(S)	81A2475/1-24
ARROW(S)	81A2476/1-24
ARROW(S)	81A2477/1-14
ARROW(S)	81A4298

ARROW CHEST 81A2582. (F029) TYPE 1.1/2.1. 09. ELM Recovered intact but damaged, standing on end. Incised III on one side. 1935x380x365rnm	
ARROW	81A4299
ARROW-SHEAF	81A2489/1-19
ARROW-SHEAF	81A2490/1-31
ARROW-SHEAF	81A2491/1-26
ARROW-SHEAF	81A2492/1-21
ARROW-SHEAF	81A2493/1-23
ARROW-SHEAF	81A2494/1-22
ARROW-SHEAF	81A2495/1-30
ARROW-SHEAF	81A2496/1-29
ARROW-SHEAF	81A2497/1-42
ARROW-SHEAF	81A2498/1-23
ARROW-SHEAF	81A2499/1-22
ARROW-SHEAF	81A2500/1-20
ARROW-SHEAF	81A2501/1-28
ARROW-SHEAF	81A2502/1-21
ARROW-SHEAF	81A2504/1-28
ARROW-SHEAF	81A2506/1-31
ARROW-SHEAF	81A2507/1-26
ARROW-SHEAF	81A2508/1-28
ARROW-SHEAF	81A2509/1-23
ARROW-SHEAF	81A2510/1-79
ARROW-SHEAF	81A2511/1-23
ARROW-SHEAF	81A2512/1-29
ARROW-SHEAF	81A2513/1-27
ARROW-SHEAF	81A2514
ARROW-SHEAF	81A2515/1-27
ARROW-SHEAF	81A2518
ARROW-SHEAF	81A2519/1-38
ARROW-SHEAF	81A2520/1-39
ARROW-SHEAF	81A2556/1-23
ARROW-SHEAF	81A2559/1-36
ARROW-SHEAF	81A2560
ARROW-SHEAF	81A2561/1-34
ARROW-SHEAF	81A2562/1-28
ARROW-SHEAF	81A2563/1-38
ARROW-SHEAF	81A2564/1-31
ARROW(S)	81A2440
ARROW(S)	81A2546/1-113
ARROW(S)	81A2557/1-108
ARROW(S)	81A2558/1-99
ARROW(S)	81A2565
ARROW(S)	81A2566/1-75
ARROW(S)	81A2567/1-136
ARROW(S)	81A2568/1-18
ARROW(S)	81A2588
ARROW(S)	81A2589/1-88
ARROW(S)	81A4293

ARROW CHEST 81A5638. (F169) TYPE 1.1/2.1 08. ELM
Lidded. Complete but broken open and partially empty but arrows lying around. 1885x340x364mm

ARROW	81A5616
ARROW(S)	81A3910/1-49
STAVED-CONTAINER	81A6700

ARROW CHEST 82A1761. (F201) TYPE 1.1/2.1. H9. ELM
Lidless. Found upside down over barrels. One end empty of arrows, other contained arrows. Bucket and staved container probably fell into chest. 1890x345x365mm

ARROW	82A4428/1-2
ARROW	82A4429/1-2
ARROW	82A4430/1-2
ARROW	82A4431
ARROW	82A4432/1-2
ARROW	82A4461
ARROW	82A4497/1-2
ARROW-SHEAF	82A1887/1-49
ARROW-SHEAF	82A1888/1-55
ARROW-SHEAF	82A1889
ARROW-SHEAF	82A1890
ARROW-SHEAF	82A1891
ARROW-SHEAF	82A1892
ARROW(S)	82A1703
ARROW(S)	82A1755
ARROW(S)	82A1756
ARROW(S)	82A1757
ARROW(S)	82A2023
STAVED-CONTAINER	82A1728
BUCKET	82A1758

LONGBOW CHEST 81A1862. (F028) TYPE 1.1/2.2 09. ELM
Recovered intact, full of longbows. 2250x360x280mm

LONGBOWS	81A1597-1620
LONGBOW	81A1622
LONGBOWS	81A1638-48
LONGBOWS	81A1654-7
LONGBOW	81A1767

LONGBOW CHEST 81A3927. (F159) TYPE 1.1/2.2 08. ELM
Complete, lidded chest. Had broken open and partially collapsed but contained full complement of 50 bows. 2240x330x310mm

UNIDENTIFIED	81A3978
LONGBOWS	81A3928-77

CHEST 80A1504. (PERS2) TYPE 2.1. M4. ELM
Broken open. Incomplete. 1155x375x380mm

UNIDENTIFIED	80A1505
CLOTHING FRAG?, LEATHER	80A1509
JETTON	80A1854
JETTON	80A1859
DISH, WOOD	80A1520
POUCH	80A2009
FLOAT	80A1502

CHEST 81A0153. (F004) TYPE 2.1. U10. OAK
Base and front fragments. 640x876x305-335mm. Gun frag. and weight 4021 adjacent to chest

UNIDENTIFIED	81A6714
CANISTER,OINTMENT-	79A0765
COMPASS	79A0766/1-2
DIVIDERS	81A0084
DIVIDERS	81A0085
GUN, ?SWIVEL, MUZZLE FRAG.	81A0154
WEIGHT	81A4020
WEIGHT	81A4021
UNIDENTIFIED("THING")	81A0806
UNIDENTIFIED	81A6783
AIGLET	81A4039
AIGLET(S)	81A0801/1-2
SHOE	81A0731
RIAL/ROSE-NOBLE	81A1007
COIN(S)	81A0796/1-3
STRAP	81A0797
COMPASS	81A0802/1-5
SCABBARD	81A0795
SCABBARD	81A0808
SCABBARD	81A6782
SWORD	81A0718/1-4
SWORD	81A0719
SWORD?	81A0688
SHOT	81A0798
PURSE-HANGER	81A0689
SUNDIAL	81A0730/1-3
KNIFE+SHEATH	81A0793/1-2

CHEST 81A1415. (F027) TYPE 2.1. M9. ELM
Complete? 1000x350x320mm

FLASK, LEATHER	81A1214/1-2
HANDLE	81A0880
BRUSH?	81A1322
COMB	81A1320
MANICURE-SET?	81A4130
MIRROR?	81A4139
RAZOR	81A1315
AXE (HANDLE)	81A1321
TOOL-HOLDER	81A0879
TOOL-HOLDER	81A1317
HANDLE, CHISEL	81A1316
SAW (HANDLE)	81A1314
RULER	81A1319

THIMBLE-RING	81A4600
WHETSTONE	81A4129

CHEST 81A1337. (F044) TYPE 2.1. M9. BEECH
Found in jumble of chests outside Carpenters' cabin. Standing on end, appeared to have been smashed open by large wooden plank. 1260x465x395mm

CONCRETION	81A1155
?BOBBIN	81A1157
UNIDENTIFIED(S)	81A1225
UNIDENTIFIED	81A6781
UNIDENTIFIED	81A6845
TALLY-STICK(S)	81A1224
PEPPERMILL	81A1219/1-2
METAL-WASTE	81A1226
SAND-GLASS	81A1172/1-6
KNIFE?	81A1218
METAL-SHEET	81A1150
NAIL	81A1246
THIMBLE-RING	81A1280
THREAD	81A1305
LINSTOCK	81A1332
TAMPION	81A1329
PUMP-VALVE	81A1335/1-2

CHEST 81A1429. (F042) TYPE 2.1. M9. OAK
Very fine chest with handles recovered from outside Carpenters' cabin. Complete. Front decorated with crest with 14 grooves either side. 942x373x367mm

UNIDENTIFIED	81A4220
AIGLET(S)	81A4214/1-3
SHOE(S)	81A1353/1-2
COIN, SILVER	81A1349
COIN, SILVER	81A4213
COIN, SILVER	81A4215
COIN(S), SILVER	81A4425
HANDLE	81A1799
LINSTOCK	81A1753
PRIMING-WIRE	81A1291
BY-KNIFE	81A4324
BY-KNIFE	81A6955
KIDNEY-DAGGER	81A1304
BOOK	81A1350/1-3
BOOK?	81A4218
CALL (BOSUN'S)	81A4172
CALL (BOSUN'S)	81A4226
PENDANT+RING+SIGNET-RING	81A1347/1-3
PIN	81A1348
DICE	81A4204-9
KNIFE	81A4219
KNIFE?	81A4227
KNIFE(S)?	81A4325/1-4
ROPE	81A4225
HANDLE	81A1121
HANDLE, CHISEL	81A1292
HANDLE, CHISEL	81A4222
AUGER (HANDLE)	81A1800

SAW (HANDLE)	81A1132
WEIGHT	81A4221
THIMBLE-RING	81A4211
THIMBLE-RING	81A4249
WHETSTONE	81A1798
WHETSTONE	81A4210
NETTING?	81A4728

CHEST 81A3825. (F130) TYPE 2.1. M9. ELM/POPLAR
Found upside down, complete but base collapsed into chest. 995x458x365mm

UNIDENTIFIED	81A4474
UNIDENTIFIED	81A4469-70
AIGLET	81A4466
AIGLET(S)	81A4471/1-2
BRAID	81A4465
THREAD	81A4467
SHOT, LEAD	81A4468
KNIFE	81A4473
WHETSTONE	81A4464

CHEST 80A1217. (FISH) TYPE 2.2. M7. ELM
Damaged, side fallen in. 970x330x350mm

UNIDENTIFIED	80A1220/1-2
UNIDENTIFIED	80A1233/1-3
UNIDENTIFIED	80A1234/1-3
BOWL, WOOD	80A1222/1-28
COOKING-POT, CERAMIC	80A1225
FLASK, LEATHER	80A1223/1-27
BY-KNIFE?	80A1221/1-2
DISGORGER?	80A1230
FLOAT	80A1229
FLOAT	80A1939
FLOAT?	80A1219
FLOAT?	80A1890
HANDLINE	80A1227/1-3
HANDLINE	80A1228/1-4
WEIGHT, FISHING	80A1231
WEIGHT, FISHING	80A1870
COMB	80A1236
KNIFE	80A1232/1-2
KNIFE-SHEATH	80A1237
KNIFE(S)+SHEATH	80A1218/1-2

CHEST 81A1328. (F043) TYPE 2.2. M9. ELM/OAK
Found in jumble of chests outside Carpenters' cabin. Complete but one side collapsed inwards. Lid decorated with circles containing stylised flowers. 965x355x340mm

UNIDENTIFIED("THINGS")	81A1022-3
UNIDENTIFIED	81A1047
UNIDENTIFIED("THING")	81A1048/1-2
UNIDENTIFIED	81A1067
UNIDENTIFIED	81A1052
HANDLE?	81A1042
HANDLE?	81A1045
HANDGUN-BOLT(S)	81A1093/1-11
FLOAT	81A1046

COMB	81A4234
BOOK	81A1062
INK-POT?	81A1054
KNIFE	81A1065
BASKET	81A1055
BOX	81A1049
BRUSH	81A1061/1-2
HANDLE+A395	81A1043
HANDLE	81A1044
HAMMER?	81A1041
PLANE,MOULDING-	81A1039
PLANE,MOULDING-	81A1040
BALANCE?	81A1053
WHETSTONE	81A1066
ANTLER (WORKED)	81S1272
BRACKET FUNGUS	81S1275

CHEST 80A1413. (PERS1) TYPE 2.3. 04. PINE
Found almost complete. Internal compartment. Graffiti on end. 1350x382x455mm

UNIDENTIFIED	80A1840
UNIDENTIFIED	80A1860
AIGLET	80A1850
AIGLETS	80A1871-4
BUTTON?	80A1383
SHOES (pair)	80A1401/1-2
SHELL	80A1848
COIN(S)+CLASP?, SILVER	80A2087
FLASK, LEATHER	80A1852
STRAP(S)	80A1846/1-2
STRIP(S)	80A1945
SHOT-MOULD	80A1847/1-4
SCABBARD	80A1851
SWORD	80A1405/1-3
SWORD	80A1838
COMB	80A1370
COMB	80A1382
COMB	80A1839
COMB	80A1841
COMB-CASE	80A1949
BEAD(S)	80A1845
PENDANT	80A1849
DIE	80A1956
KNIFE	80A1369
PIN	80A1388

CHEST 81A2941. (F109) TYPE 2.3. 010. PINE
Excellent condition. Complete. Small shelves or compartments at either end. Battened lid. 1360x380x385mm

UNIDENTIFIED	81A2980
AIGLET(S)	81A4353
SHOES (pair)	81A2978/1-2
RIBBON	81A4751
SCABBARD	81A2977
SWORD	81A2979/1-2
BEAD(S)+BRAID+RIBBON+UNID.	81A6841/1-3

DIE	81A2986
PATERNOSTER	81A2985/1-29
KEY? = SMALL CONCRETED FRAGS	81A2982

CHEST 81A0045. (F001) TYPE 2.4. M2. ELM
Complete dovetailed chest with handle and internal lidded compartment. 1350x430x410mm. Pouch found lying on top of compass box. V. degraded fabric in main chest and compartment

AIGLET	81A6832
AIGLET(S)	81A4001/1-8
AIGLET(S)	81A6831/1-2
AIGLET(S)	81A6833/1-2
COIN	81A4002
COMPASS	81A0071
POUCH	81A0072/1-3
KNIFE-SHEATH	81A0069
HANDLE FOR SMALL ADZE	81A4003

BARBER-SURGEON'S CHEST 80A1530. (BB/SG) TYPE 2.4. M7. BEECH/ELM/WALNUT
Complete, dovetailed, elm handles and beech battons. Internal compartment. 1330x485x460

BUCKLE+STRAP	80A1612/1-2
SHOE	80A1571
COIN(S)	80A1861
COIN(S)	83A0004
BOWL, WOOD	80A1562
BOWL, WOOD	80A1536
BOTTLE, GLASS	80A1540
BOTTLE, GLASS	80A1565
BOTTLE,FEEDING, WOOD	80A1555
CANISTER, WOOD	80A1561/1-2
CANISTER, WOOD	80A1567/1-2
CANISTER, PEWTER	80A1582/1-2
CANISTERS,OINTMENT-, WOOD	80A1531-8
CANISTER,OINTMENT-, WOOD	80A1541/1-2
CANISTER,OINTMENT-, WOOD	80A1542/1-2
CANISTER,OINTMENT-, WOOD	80A1551/1-2
JUG, CERAMIC	80A1534
JUG,MEDICINE-, CERAMIC	80A1559/1-2
JUG,MEDICINE-, CERAMIC	80A1573-5
JUG,MEDICINE-, CERAMIC	80A1637
JUG,MEDICINE-, CERAMIC	80A1662
?BANDAGE ROLL	80A1558
?BANDAGE ROLL	80A1892-6
EAR-SCOOP	80A1577
HANDLE	80A1539
HANDLE	80A1563
HANDLE	80A1566
HANDLE	80A1579
HANDLE	80A1580
HANDLE	80A1917
HANDLE	80A1919
HANDLE	80A1920
HANDLE, SAW	80A1578
SYRINGE	80A1560
TREPAN?	80A1581

TREPAN?	80A1585
TREPAN?	80A1918
SPATULA	80A1557
SPATULA	80A1587
SPATULA	80A1915
SPATULA	80A1927
SPATULA?	80A2063
STRAP	80A1608
WHISTLE?	80A1586
CASE?	80A1564
PURSE	80A1584
COMB	80A1572
RAZOR	80A1570
RAZOR	80A1576/1-2
RAZOR	80A1921-5
KNIFE	80A1588
WHETSTONE	80A1569

CHEST 81A2035. (F041) TYPE 2.4. M10. ELM
Standing upright. Virtually complete but broken open. Internal compartment. Cooking pot in one end of chest, Rest at other end. 1090x0380x325mm

UNIDENTIFIED	81A1994
UNIDENTIFIED("THING")	81A2191
SHOE	81A1682–3
JETTON	81A1903
JAR, CERAMIC	81A2103/1-25
WRISTGUARD	81A2192
COMB	81A2190
RAZOR	81A2101/1-2
LINE-ADJUSTER (RIGGING)	81A2104
WHETSTONE	81A2102

CHEST 81A2573. (F118) TYPE 2.4. M8. ELM/OAK/POPLAR
Fragmentary. Internal compartment. Smashed open against gun carriage wheel. 1275x490x500mm

UNIDENTIFIED	81A2697-8
UNIDENTIFIED	81A2837
UNIDENTIFIED	81A4271
UNIDENTIFIED	81A4819
UNIDENTIFIED	81A4821
AIGLET	81A4268
AIGLET	81A4818
AIGLET(S)	81A4448/1-2
SHOE	81A4274
SHOE	81A4449
TALLY-STICK?	81A4266
COIN? SILVER	81A4265
COIN(S), SILVER	81A4264
COIN(S), SILVER	81A4920
HANDLE	81A6887
?CASKET PANEL	81A2851
KIDNEY-DAGGER?	81A4261
POUCH	81A2685
WEIGHT? (FISHING)	81A4269
WEIGHT? (FISHING)	81A4270

SEAL	81A4262
SIGNET	81A4267
DIE	81A4263
BRUSH	81A2696/1-2
BRACE	81A4820
PLANE-BLANK?	81A4447
SPOKESHAVE?	81A2673
THIMBLE-RING	81A2857
WHETSTONE	81A2856
SHOE	81A2700
UNIDENTIFIED	81A2854
HANDLE	81A4288
COMB	81A4287
RING	81A2042
WEIGHT	81A2699

CHEST 81A2706. (F126) TYPE 2.4. 05. ELM/OAK
Broken open, poor condition. Internal compartment and handle. 970x340x285mm

WRISTGUARD	81A2845
WEIGHTS	81A2843-4

CHEST 81A5783. (F128) TYPE 2.4. M9. ELM/WALNUT
Standing on end against Upper deck planks. Intact, contents excavated on shore. 1140x455x385mm

UNIDENTIFIED	81A5819
UNIDENTIFIED	81A5821
UNIDENTIFIED	81A5825
COIN+RING(S)	81A4394
PLATE, PEWTER	81A5823
PLATE, PEWTER	81A5827
PLATE, PEWTER	81A6849
PLATE, PEWTER	81A6850
ARROW	81A5829
WRISTGUARD	81A5826
?CLOTHES FASTENING	81A4392/1-6
?CLOTHES FASTENING	81A4393/1-5
SHOT, LEAD	81A4432
POUCH	81A5818/1-11
BOOK	81A5817
DICE	81A4391/1-2
SUNDIAL+CASE	81A5681/1-2
KNIFE	81A5828
CABLE	81A5815
CHALK-LINE-REEL(LONG-)	81A5686
GIMLET?	81A5820
GIMLET?	81A5824
WEIGHT	81A4431
WEIGHTS	81A4433-4
TANKARD, PEWTER	81A5654

BENCH CHEST 81A0917. (F020) TYPE 3.1. M4/5. OAK
Complete, found standing on end. 1125x397x??mm

UNIDENTIFIED	81A0907
AIGLET+LACE	81A4318
SHOE(S)	81A4108/1-2
SHOE(S)	81A4109/1-2
SHOE(S)	81A4112/1-2
HAT	81A0904/1-3
FLASK, PEWTER	81A0906
CANDLE-SNUFFER?	81A0905
BOOK	81A0895
BOOK	81A4116
BEAD	81A4319
BOX?	81A0910/1-2
BOX?	81A4113
BOX?	81A4114
BRUSH	81A0903
BALANCE-CASE	81A4107

BENCH CHEST 81A2099. (F110) TYPE 3.1. U9. POPLAR
Small and in poor condition, wood very soft. Corners split open and contents spilling out. Contents in good condition. Appears to have been neatly packed. Surviving dimensions 665x250x260mm

UNIDENTIFIED	81A4157
UNIDENTIFIED("THING")	81A4301-2
AIGLET	81A4382
AIGLET(S)	81A2015
SHOE	81A4375
SHOE(S)	81A2016
BALANCE-CASE	81A2012/2+
BALANCE,COIN-	81A2012/1+
WEIGHTS	81A2012/3.1-4
COIN, SILVER	81A2196
FLASK, LEATHER	81A2034
KIDNEY-DAGGER?	81A4380
FLOAT?	81A2017
FLOAT?	81A4303
COMB	81A2010-11
COMB	81A4304
STAVED-CONTAINER(UNID)	81A4376/1-13
OCTAGONAL DISC, WOOD	81A2013

BENCH CHEST 81A0882. (F026) TYPE 3.2. M10. OAK
Found open with shoe inside. Back, end, front and lid. 650x273mm

SHOES (pair)	81A0883/1-2

BENCH CHEST 81A0923. (F025) TYPE 3.2. M10. OAK
Found on side outside Carpenter's cabin. Broken open. 1 end, lid and sides + part of compartment. 970x895mm

PLATE, PEWTER	81A0877
LINSTOCK	81A0837/1-2
PRIMING-WIRE	81A0835
BOOK	81A4131
BOOK	81A4143
KNIFE	81A4877
BOX	81A4875/1-3
SAW	81A0878

BENCH CHEST 81A5843. (BX15) TYPE 3.2. 010. ELM/OAK
Virtually complete. Internal compartment. Found upside down with base displaced. 1040x460x575mm

AIGLET	81A4630
AIGLET	81A4634
COINS: ANGELS	81A4616-20
HALF-ANGEL	81A4621
COINS: HALF-SOVEREIGNS	81A4615-19
COIN, SILVER	81A4622
COIN, SILVER	81A4623
COIN, SILVER	81A4626
COIN, SILVER	81A4628
COIN, SILVER	81A4629
COIN, SILVER	81A4633
COIN, SILVER	81A4635
COIN(S), SILVER	81A4624
COIN(S), SILVER	81A4625
THREAD	81A4632
GUN-SHIELD	81A4642-5
KNIFE	81A4631
PIN	81A4627
TINDER-BOX?	82A0070/1-3

BENCH CHEST 82A0942. (F186) TYPE 3.2. 010. ELM
Recovered complete but in fragile condition. 1125x425x390mm

UNIDENTIFIED	82A0947
UNIDENTIFIED	82A0967/1-2
UNIDENTIFIED("THING")	82A0969
AIGLETS	82A5002-3
BOOT (THIGH)	82A5014/1-2
SHOE	82A0845
BRAID	82A5000
WRISTGUARD	82A0943
DAGGER-SHEATH	82A0970
INSET-SHOT	82A0799
COMB	82A0945
KNIFE	82A5001
BESOM	82A0946

CHEST 81A3285. (F146) TYPE 3.3. 09. OAK	
Complete, dovetailed. Lid has overlapping battens on each edge. Internal compartment with peppercorns. Two flasks together at one end. 850x318x300	
UNIDENTIFIED	81A6785
UNIDENTIFIED	81A6800-2
AIGLET	81A6786
AIGLET	81A6790
AIGLET(S)	81A3295
AIGLET(S)	81A6787/1-2
AIGLET(S)	81A6789/1-5
AIGLET(S)	81A6793/1-2
MITTEN	81A3292
MITTEN	81A3293
HAT	81A3291
FLASK, GLASS	81A3287
FLASK, CERAMIC	81A3288
PEPPERMILL	81A3290
KNIFE+SHEATH	81A3294/1-2
RULER	81A3307
NEEDLE/PIN?	81A6792
PIN	81A6788
PIN	81A6791
PIN	81A6794
THIMBLE-RING	81A6784

Broken chests and fragments from U9 (F021/22)

CHEST 81A4360. ELM. Back only. 500x365mm	
CHEST 81A4585. ELM. Side with nails. Dovetailed?	
CHEST 81A1136. ELM/WALNUT. Side frags	
CHEST 81A1161. TYPE 2.1. U9. ELM. Front. 735x345mm	
CHEST 81A1188. TYPE 2.4. U9. ELM. End, dovetailed. 402x215mm	
CHEST 81A1352. ELM. Side frag	
UNIDENTIFIED	81A1199
UNIDENTIFIED	81A4124
UNIDENTIFIED	81A4417
UNIDENTIFIED	81A4885/1-6
UNIDENTIFIED TEXTILE	81A4333
AIGLET	81A4286
AIGLETS	81A4886-8
SHOE	81A1331
SHOE	81A4125
SHOE	81A4305/1-2
SHOE	81A6947
SHOES (pair)	81A6942/1-2
SHOES (pair)	81A6943/1-2
ANKLE-BOOTS (pair)	81A4259
ANKLE-BOOTS (pair)	81A4305
HAT	81A4706/1-3
COIN, SILVER	81A0913
COIN, SILVER	81A1095
JAR, CERAMIC	81A1144
HANDLE	81A1346
RIBBON	81A1223
STRAP	81A1446

ARROW	81A1139
ARROW-SPACER	81A1341
ARROW(S)	81A1340
TAMPION	81A1345
BY-KNIFE	81A1437
KIDNEY-DAGGER	81A1422
SCABBARD	81A1421
BILL	81A1351
CHAIN-MAIL?	81A1436
POUCH	81A1194/1-7
COMB	81A4654
KNIVES	81A1438-9
KNIFE+SHEATH	81A1135/1-3
CORDAGE	81A1197
BOBBIN	81A1433
BOBBIN	81A4334/1-2
UNIDENTIFIED	81A4580-4
?JERKIN	81A4362
SHOE	81A4259
SHOE	81A6943
SHOE	81A6944
SHOE	81A6947
SHOE(S)	81A4578/1-2
SHOE(S)	81A6942/1-2
BOWL, WOOD	81A4359
ARROW(S)	81A4357
ARROW(S)	81A4579
BILL?	81A4358
COMB	81A4655
BATTEN	81A4583

Chests and chest fragments with dubious associations

CHEST 80A0476. (BX04) TYPE 1.1/2.1 U7/8. ELM	
Arrow type chest. Broken, unlidded, empty but one longbow beside. 1900x350x335mm	
LONGBOW	80A0473

CHEST 82A0842. (F190) TYPE 1.1/1. H7. POPLAR	
Base, handle and a few other frags only, very crumbly when recovered. Arrows not certainly associated (chest too short). 700x300mm	
ARROW(S)	82A0843

CHEST 81A1327. (F024) TYPE 1.1/1. M9/10. ELM	
Unlidded; end and side fragments. 1214x425mm. Empty but closely associated with:	
KIDNEY-DAGGER	81A0818
COMB	81A0816
STAVED-CONTAINER	81A0819

CHEST 81A1681. (BX10) TYPE 1.1/1. 03. ELM	
Disintegrated. 1259x380x385mm	
ASH-BOX?	81A3922/1-5

CHEST 81A3824. (F158) TYPE 1.1/2.2. 08. ELM
Longbow type chest, lidless, one end missing. Empty of longbows, contents probably fell in. 2880x330x350mm

SHOE	81A4738
KNIFE-SHEATH	81A3276
LINE	81A4737

CHEST 80A0602. (BX05) TYPE 1.1/2.2 U7/8. ELM
Longbow type. Chest sprung open and incomplete, unlidded though 'spare' lid nearby. Items may have fallen in. 2192x350x278mm

UNIDENTIFIED	80A0606/1-4
SHOE	80A0604/1-2
ARROW	80A0607
BILL	80A0603/1-2

CHEST 81A1325. (F059) TYPE 1.1/2.2 U9. ELM
Longbow type chest with no lid. Some longbows nearby. Objects in chest probably fell in. 1910x285x304mm

UNIDENTIFIED	81A6858
ANKLE-BOOT	81A4750/1-3

CHEST 81A3088. (F136) TYPE 2.4. 09. WALNUT
Badly damaged. Lidless, Internal compartment. Scabbard-hanger beside chest. 995x295x347mm

SCABBARD-HANGER?	81A3089

BENCH CHEST 81A1302. (F058) TYPE 3.1. U9. ELM
Broken open and incomplete. Contents spilled so associations not definite. 830x365x320mm

SHOES (pair)	81A4313/1-2
STRAP+UNIDENTIFIED	81A1703
COMB	81A1704
CORDAGE	81A4314
CABLE	81A1303/1-3

BENCH CHEST 81A4879. (BX13) TYPE 3.3. 01. OAK
Lid, front and side frags. Decorated with panels incised with diagonal lines in a variety of patterns 730x370mm

TINDER-BOX?	81A5922

CHEST 78A0110. (BX01) ?H1/2. ASH
Side fragments only

COMB	78A0082
KNIFE-SHEATH	78A0055

CHEST 80A1320. (BX07) U6. OAK
Lid only

BATTEN	80A1321
HANDLE	81A0265/1-6
LANTERN	81A0236/1-7

CHEST 81A0717. U9. WALNUT
Handle of chest only

BRUSH	81A0692
THIMBLE,FINGER-	81A0805
UNIDENTIFIED	81A0806
UNIDENTIFIED	81A6783
AIGLET	81A4039
AIGLET(S)	81A0801/1-2
SHOE	81A0731
RIAL/ROSE-NOBLE	81A1007
COIN(S)	81A0796/1-3
STRAP	81A0797
COMPASS	81A0802/1-5
SCABBARD	81A0795
SCABBARD	81A0808
SCABBARD	81A6782
SWORD	81A0718/1-4
SWORD	81A0719
SWORD?	81A0688
SHOT	81A0798
PURSE-HANGER	81A0689
SUNDIAL	81A0730/1-3
KNIFE+SHEATH	81A0793/1-2

CHEST 81A2399. M10. OAK
Handle only

TAMPION	81A1928

CHEST? 81A3708. M9. OAK
Handle only

WHETSTONE	81A4472

CHEST 81A4164. U10. OAK
Poss. compartment from chest

SHOT, STONE	81A1955-6

Empty chests and chest fragments

CHEST 82A1877. TYPE 1.1/1. H/05. ELM/OAK/ POPLAR. Lidded. Incomplete. 1250x410x420mm

CHEST 81A0608. TYPE 1.1/1. 01. POPLAR. Base & end frags. prob. Max. 990x375mm

CHEST 81A3907. TYPE 2.2. 06. ELM/OAK/PINE. Found front down against Orlop deck. Broken but complete. Traces of red and white paint on one end, white paint and red circle on other. 765x305x245mm

CHEST 77A0114. TYPE 3.3. H1. OAK. End

CHEST 78A0617. ?U10. OAK. End, seems to be Type 3

CHEST 77A0450. H1. OAK. End frags

CHEST 78A0057. Frag. (missing)

CHEST 78A0618. U10. ELM. Side frag

CHEST 78A0638. ?. POPLAR. Frag. Part of front with lock plate. Max 550x250mm

CHEST 78A0640. ?. POPLAR. End

CHEST 78A0642. ?. OAK. Compartment

CHEST 79A0099A. U6/7. OAK. back/front frag with rebate for compartment

CHEST 79A1345. M/U11. OAK. Side frags

CHEST 80A1044. U8. ELM. Lid only with nail-holes 1940x415mm - ?arrow chest

CHEST 80A1172. U8. ELM. Lid only frags, max 1420x340mm - ?longbow chest

CHEST 80A1506. M4. OAK. Handle

CHEST 81A1094. M9. ELM. Handle

CHEST 81A1108. M9. ASH. Handle

CHEST 81A1272. U9. ELM. End

CHEST 81A1931. H9. SPRUCE. Side

CHEST 81A2246. M10. OAK. Handle

CHEST 81A2252. O6. ELM. End with dovetails

CHEST 81A2990. O9. WALNUT. Handle

CHEST 81A3100. O9. WALNUT. End

CHEST 81A6798. O3. ELM. End frag. with nail-holes

CHEST 81A6843. U10. ELM. End

CHEST 81A6853. M10. ?. Side frag.

CHEST 81A6937. M10. OAK. Base. Could be base to 81A0923. 950x170mm

CHEST 82A0004. SS8. WALNUT. Side frag with dovetails

CHEST 82A1272. U9. ELM. End

CHEST 82A1611. O8. ELM. Lid, arrow chest?

CHEST 82A2044. M9. POPLAR. End

CHEST 82A4739. ? ELM. Lid

CHEST 83A0122. M7. POPLAR. lid and side frags. Apparently found associated with Barber-surgeon's chest

CHEST 83A0700. ? ELM. Back

CHEST 90A0114. SS2/3. ELM. Side

Appendix 2: Catalogue of textile fragments

Obj. no.	Location	Fibre	Weave	Nap	Count sys 1 per cm	Count sys 2 per cm	Ply sys 1	Ply sys 2	Ply spin	Spin sys 1	Spin sys 2	Yarn Dia sys 1 mm	Yarn Dia sys 2 mm	Max Length mm	Max Width mm	Selve	Cut edge	Hem	Seam	Stitches	Classification
79A0776	U4	Wool	Plain	0	14	15	1	1		S	S	0.75-1	0.75	202	70	n	y	n	n	y	
79A1247	U4	Wool	2/1 Twill	0	4	3	1	1		S	S	2.16	2.24	148	97	n	n	n	n	n	frag
80A0295	O5	Wool	Plain	1	9	?	1	1		Z	?	1	?	102	40	n	y	y	n	y	frag
80A1410	O4	Wool	2/2 Twill	0	30	?	1	1		S	S	0.3	?	38	15	n	y	y	n	y	frag
		Wool	Plain	0	4	3	1	1		Z	Z	2	2	217	240	y	n	n	n	n	frag
		Wool	Plain	0	7	7	1	1		S	Z	1	1	211	186	y	n	n	n	n	frag
		Wool	Plain	0	8	6	1	1		S	Z	0.6	1.2	53	87	n	n	n	n	n	frag
		Wool	Plain	0	6	4	1	1		S	Z	1.2	1.6	97	82	?	?	?	?	n	frag
80A1725	M4	Wool	Plain	2	7	7	1	1		?	?	1	1	110	122	n	?	?	?	?	frag
		Wool	Plain	0	?	?	1	1		?	?	?	?	338	145	?	n	n	n	n	frag
		Wool	Plain	0	?	?	1	1		?	?	?	?	217	157	y	y	y	n	y	Garment
80A1856	M7	Silk	Plain	0	54	24	1	1		S	S	0.2	0.1	60	31	n	y	y	n	y	frag B.S Hat lining
		Velvet	Plain	0	45	?	1	1		Z	?	0.2	0.1	32	10	n	y	y	n	y	frag B.S Hat lining
80A1972	M7	Wool	2/2 Twill	0	16	14	1	1		S	S	0.5-0.6	0.5	104	80	n	y	n	n	y	frag
		Wool	2/2 Twill	0	16	14	1	1		S	S	0.5-0.6	0.5	100	60	n	y	n	n	y	frag
		Wool	2/2 Twill	0	12	10	1	1		S	S	1	0.75-1.25	115	145	n	n	n	n	n	Sacking
81A0161	U9	Wool	Plain	2	5	4	1	1		S	S	1	1.25	140	65	n	n	n	n	n	Sacking
		Wool	Plain	1	10	10	1	1		S	Z	0.75	0.75	100	65	n	y	n	n	n	frags
81A0904	M4	Silk	Plain	0	46.8	25.4	1	1		S	S	0.25	0.25	674	13.5	y	n	n	n	n	Hat ribbon
81A0973	M10	Silk	Plain	0	42.6	28.2	1	1		S	S	0.2	0.3	1079	34	y	n	n	n	n	Ribbon
81A1233	O9	Wool	Plain	0	4	3	2	2	Z	S	S	1	1	1620	1100	y	n	n	n	n	Sacking+V186
81A1237	O2	Wool	2/2 Twill	1	20	18	1	1		S	S	0.5	0.5	240	56	n	y	n	n	y	Gusset
		Wool	2/2 Twill	2	20	18	1	1		S	S	0.5	0.5	164	112	n	y	n	n	y	Gusset
		Wool	2/2 Twill	1			1	1						237	110	n	y	n	n	y	Gusset and patch.
81A1394	H2	Wool	Plain	0	4	3	2	2	S	Z	Z		0.75-1	90	100						Sackcloth
81A2480	O3	Wool	Plain	1	8	8	1	1		S	S	1	0.75-1	610	487						
		Wool	Plain	1	8	8	1	1		S	S	1	1	610	505						
		Wool	Plain	1	8	8	1	1		S	S	1	1	550	300	n	y	y	y	y	Cloth jerkin
		Wool	Plain	1	8	7	1	1		S	S	1	1	420	130.5	n	y	y	n	y	"
		Wool	Plain	1	12	12	1	1		S	S	0.5	0.75	430	376	n	y	n	n	y	"

Obj. no.	Location	Fibre	Weave	Nap	Count sys 1 per cm	Count sys 2 per cm	Ply sys 1	Ply sys 2	Ply spin	Spin sys 1	Spin sys 2	Yarn Dia sys 1 mm	Yarn Dia sys 2 mm	Max Length mm	Max Width mm	Selve edge	Cut edge	Hem	Seam	Stitches	Classification
81A2480	O3	Wool	Plain	1	7	7	1	1		S	S	0.6	0.6-0.7	45	4	n	y	y	n	y	"
		Wool	Plain	1	7	7	1	1		S	S	0.6	0.6-0.7	310	130	n	y	y	n	y	"
		Wool	Plain	1	12	10	1	1		S	S	0.75	0.75	245	520	n	y	n	n	y	"
		Wool	Plain	1	12	10	1	1		S	S	0.5	0.75	375	325	n	y	y	n	y	"
		Wool	Plain	1	12	10	1	1		S	S	0.5	0.75	570	632	n	y	y	n	y	"
		Wool	Plain	1	7	7	1	1		S	S	1	0.75-1	350	360.5	n	y	y	n	y	"
81A2539	O3	Wool	Plain	1	3	3.5	2	2	S	Z	Z	2.5	2	98	195	n	y	y	n	n	cut frag with shoes
		Wool	Plain	2	4	4	1	1		Z	Z	2	2	70	135	n	n	n	n	n	"
		Wool	Plain	0	10	10	1	1		Z	Z	1	1	47	38	n	n	n	n	n	"
81A2544	O3	Wool	Plain	2	12	8	1	1		S	S	1	1-1.25	110	70	n	y	y	y	y	?garment
		Wool	2/2 Twill	2	12	8	1	1		S	S	0.75	1	245	127	n	y	n	n	y	"
		Wool	2/2 Twill	0	20	18	1	1		S	S	0.4	0.5	83	37	n	y	y	y	y	"
		Wool	2/2 Twill	0	20	18	1	1		S	S	0.5	0.5	182	38	n	y	y	n	y	"
		Wool	Plain	0	10	8	1	1		S	S	1	1	293	132	n	y	y	n	y	"
		Wool	Plain	0	8	8	1	1		S	S	1	1	174	110	n	y	n	y	y	"
		Wool	Plain	0	10	8	1	1		Z	S	0.75-1	1	106	103	n	y	y	n	y	"
		Wool	Plain	0	9	8	1	1		S	S	0.75-1	1	196	204	n	y	y	y	y	"
81A2880	O3	Wool	Plain	0	6	7	1	1		S	Z	1	1	474	260	n	y	n	n	y	?garment
81A2888	O3	Wool	Plain	0	8	8	1	1		S	S	0.7-1	0.7-1	138	55	n	y	n	n	y	frag
		Wool	Plain	0	6	6	1	1		S	S	1.5	1.5	220	85	n	y	n	n	y	cord
		Wool	Plain	2	8	6	1	1		Z	Z	0.75	1	313	586	n	y	n	n	y	cloth jerkin
		Wool	Plain	2	8	6	1	1		Z	S	0.75-1	1	313	586	n	y	y	y	y	"
		Wool	Plain	2	8	6	1	1		S	Z	1.2-1.3	1.2	369	163	n	y	n	n	y	"
		Wool	Plain	2	8	6	1	1		S	S	1	1.2-1.3	250	175	n	y	n	n	y	"
		Wool	Plain	1	8	6	1	1		Z	S	1.5	1	250	150	n	y	y	n	y	"
		Wool	Plain	1	8	6	1	1		S	Z	0.75	1	242	177	n	y	y	n	y	"
		Wool	Plain	1	8	6	1	1		S	Z	0.75	1	127	56	n	y	y	n	n	"
		Wool	Plain	2	8	6	1	1		S	Z	0.75	0.75-1	477	410	n	y	y	n	y	"
		Wool	Plain	2	8	6	1	1		S	Z	0.75-1	1	470	425	n	y	n	n	y	"
81A2911	O3	Plant	Plain	0	4	3	2	2	S	S	Z	2	2.4	785	375	n	n	n	n	n	frag
		Wool	Plain	0	3	3	2	2	S	S	Z	2.27	2.5	266	135	n	n	y	n	n	frag
		Wool	Plain	0	4	3	2	2	S	S	Z	2.4	1.8	225	227	n	n	y	n	n	frag
		Wool	Plain	0	4	3	2	2	S	S	Z	1.75	2	420	281	y	n	y	n	n	frag+V6
		Wool	2/1 Twill	0	3	3	1	1		S	Z	3.5	3	129	110	n	n	n	n	n	frag
		Plant	Plain	2	4	3	2	2	S	Z	S	2	2.3	192	152	n	n	n	n	n	frag

Obj. no.	Location	Fibre	Weave	Nap	Count sys 1 per cm	Count sys 2 per cm	Ply sys 1	Ply sys 2	Ply spin	Spin sys 1	Spin sys 2	Yarn Dia sys 1 mm	Yarn Dia sys 2 mm	Max Length mm	Max Width mm	Selve	Cut edge	Hem	Seam	Stitches	Classification
81A2911	O3	Wool	Plain	0	8	6	1	1		Z	S	1	1	285	70	n	n	n	n	n	frag
81A2995	H4	Wool	Plain	0	8	6	1	1		Z	S	1	1	308	66	n	n	n	n	n	frag
81A4090	H2	Wool	Plain	2	8	10	1	1		S	S	0.75-1	0.75	632	312	y	y	y	n	y	Hose frag
		Wool	Plain	2	8	6	1	1		S	S	0.75	1	98	90	n	y	y	n	n	frag
		Wool	Plain	2	8	6	1	1		S	S	0.75	1	147	90	n	y	y	n	n	frag
81A4141	H2	Wool	2/2 Twill	1	11	11	1	1		S	S	0.6	0.4-0.5	82	100	n	y	y	n	n	frag
		Wool	Plain	0	4	3	2	2	S	S	Z	2	2	240	277	n	n	n	n	n	Sackcloth
		Plant	?		4	3	2	2	S	Z	Z	2	2.1	175	204	n	n	n	n	n	"
		Wool	Plain	0	4	3	2	2	S	Z	Z	2	2.4	1067	567	n	n	n	n	n	"
81A4258	O3	Wool	Plain	2	8	8	1	1		S	S	0.75-1	1	192	288	y	y	n	n	y	Cloth jerkin
		Wool	Plain	2	8	8	1	1		S	S	0.75-1	1	240	101	n	y	y	y	y	"
		Wool	Plain	1	8	8	1	1		S	S	1	0.75-1	267	343	n	y	y	y	y	"
		Wool	Plain	1	8	8	1	1		S	S	1	0.75-1	444	417	n	y	n	n	y	"
		Wool	Plain	2	8	8	1	1		S	S	1	1	645	316	n	y	y	n	y	"
		Wool	Plain	1	8	8	1	1		S	S	0.75-1	1	245	10	n	y	y	n	y	Cord
		Wool	Plain	2	8	8	1	1		?	S	1	1	220	7	n	y	y	n	y	Cord
		Wool	Plain	1	7	7	1	1		?	?	1	?	140	9	n	y	n	n	y	Cord
		Wool	Plain	1	8	8	1	1		S	S	?	1	120	9	n	y	n	n	y	Cord
		Wool	Plain	1	8	7	1	1		?	S	1	1	111	9	n	y	n	n	y	Cord
		Wool	Plain	1	?	?	1	1		S	S	1	?	93	8	n	y	n	n	y	Cord
		Wool	Plain	1	8	8	1	1		?	S	?	1	455	9	n	y	n	n	y	Cord
		Wool	Plain	1	8	8	1	1		S	?	1	?	47	16	n	y	n	n	y	Cord
		Wool	Plain	1	8	8	1	1		?	?	?	1	46	10	n	y	n	n	y	Cord
		Wool	Plain	1	8	8	1	1		S	S	1	1	275	9	n	y	n	n	y	Cord
81A4292	M9	Wool	Plain	1	14		1	1		Z	S	1.5	1.5	130	97	n	y	n	n	y	frag
81A4744	O2	Wool	Plain	2	14	14	1	1		S	Z	0.5-0.75	0.5	642	140	n	y	n	n	y	?garment
81A4307	H3	Wool	2/2 Twill	1	20	18	1	1		S	S	0.5	0.5	100	21	n	y	y	n	y	frag
		Wool	2/2 Twill	1	20	18	1	1		S	S	0.5	0.5	50	10	n	y	n	n	y	frag
		Wool	2/2 Twill	1	20	18	1	1		S	S	0.5	0.5	49	19	n	n	n	n	n	frag
		Wool	2/2 Twill	1	20	18	1	1		S	S	0.5	0.5	29	30	n	y	n	n	y	frag
		Wool	2/2 Twill	2	20	18	1	1		S	S	0.5	0.5	30	14	n	y	n	n	y	frag
		Wool	2/2 Twill	2	20	18	1	1		S	S	0.5	0.5	129	97	n	y	y	n	y	frag
		Wool	2/2 Twill	1	20	18	1	1		S	S	0.5	0.5	72	45	n	y	n	y	y	frag
		Wool	2/2 Twill	1	20	18	1	1		S	S	0.5	0.5	43	45	n	y	n	n	y	frag
		Wool	2/2 Twill	2	20	18	1	1		S	S	0.5	0.5	60	46	n	y	n	n	y	frag

Obj. no.	Location	Fibre	Weave	Nap	Count sys 1 per cm	Count sys 2 per cm	Ply sys 1	Ply sys 2	Ply spin	Spin sys 1	Spin sys 2	Yarn Dia sys 1 mm	Yarn Dia sys 2 mm	Max Length mm	Max Width mm	Selve	Cut edge	Hem	Seam	Stitches	Classification
81A4307	H3	Wool	2/2 Twill	0	20	18	1	1		S	S	0.5	0.5	204	160	n	y	n	n	y	Garment
		Wool	2/2 Twill	1	20	24?	1	1		S	S	0.5-0.75	0.5	185	148	n	y	n	n	y	Garment
		Wool	2/2 Twill	1	24	20?	1	1		S	S	0.5	0.5	155	43	n	y	n	y	y	Garment
		Wool	2/2 Twill	1	20	22	1	1		S	S	0.5	0.5	95	102	n	y	n	n	y	Garment
		Wool	Plain	2	20	?	1	1		S	Z	0.5-0.75	0.75	164	73	y	y	n	n	y	Garment
		Wool	2/2 Twill	2	20	?	1	1		S	S	0.25-0.5	0.5	164	73	y	y	n	n	y	Garment
		Wool	2/2 Twill	2	20	20	1	1		S	S	0.5	0.5	105	45	n	y	n	n	y	Gusset.
		Wool	Plain	0	8	6	1	1		S	Z	0.75	1	171	105	n	y	n	n	n	frag
		Wool	Plain	2	8	6	1	1		S?	S?	1	0.75-1	133	192	n	y	n	y	y	frag
		Wool	Plain	2	8	6	1	1		S?	S?	0.75-1	1	240	191	n	y	n	n	y	frag
81A4336	O3	Wool	2/2 Twill	1	6	6	1	1		Z	S	1.3-1.5	1.5	300	295	n	y	n	n	n	frag
81A4338	O3	Wool	2/2 Twill	1	10	10	1	1		S	S	0.5	0.6	230	115	n	y	n	y	y	Shoe Lining
	O3	Wool	2/2 Twill	1	12	10	1	1		S	S	0.4-0.5	0.6			n	y	n	n	y	Shoe Lining
81A4340	O3	Wool	?											240	72						Shoe Lining
81A4343	O3	Wool	Plain	2	10	10	1	1		S	S	0.7	0.6-0.7	305	87	n	y	n	y	y	Shoe Lining
		Wool	Plain	2	8	8	1	1		S	S	0.7	0.7	288	195	n	y	y	n	y	Shoe Lining
		Wool	Plain	2	8	8	1	1		S	S	0.7	0.7	160	103	n	y	y	n	y	Shoe Lining
81A4351	H3	Wool	Plain	2	4	4	1	1		S?	S?	1.9	2	73	70	n	n	n	n	n	frag
		Wool	Plain	1	4	3	2	2	S	S	Z	2	2.1	70	50	n	n	n	n	n	frag
		Wool	Plain	1	4	3	2	2	S	S	Z	2	2	60	50	n	n	n	n	n	frag
81A4371	O4	Wool	2/2 Twill	1	8	8	1	1		Z	S	0.5-1	1-1.25	251	177	y	n	n	n	n	frag with tassel
81A4400	O9	Silk	2/1 Twill	0	42	36-8	1	1		?	?	0.1	0.1	320	30	n	y	y	y	y	Ribbon
		Silk	2/1 Twill	0	42	36-8	1	1		?	?	0.1	0.1	306	36	n	y	y	y	y	Ribbon
81A4402	O9	Silk	Plain	0	36	34	1	1		S	Z	0.2	0.2-0.3	725	33	y	n	y	y	y	Braid
		Silk	Plain	0	36	34	1	1		S	Z	0.2	0.2-0.3	900	34	y	n	y	y	y	Braid
81A4404	O9	Silk	2/1 Twill	0	60	28	1	1		None	None	0.1	0.1	92	155	n	y	n	y	y	Trimming
81A4405	O9	Silk	Plain	0	31	27	1	1		Z	Z	0.1	0.2	135	17	n	y	y	n	n	Ribbon
81A4406	O9	Wool	2/2 Twill	1	20	18	1	1		S	S	0.3	0.2-0.3	57	34	n	y	n	n	n	frag
		Wool	2/2 Twill	0	14	12	1	1		S	S	0.5	0.25	60	13	y	y	n	n	n	frag
81A4412	O9	Silk	Plain	0	c.40	43	1	1		S	?	0.1-0.2	0.2	450	4	n	n	n	n	n	Braid
		Silk	Plain	0	40	43	1	1		S	?	0.1-0.2	0.2	505	4	y	n	n	n	n	Braid

Obj. no.	Location	Fibre	Weave	Nap	Count sys 1 per cm	Count sys 2 per cm	Ply sys 1	Ply sys 2	Ply spin	Spin sys 1	Spin sys 2	Yarn Dia sys 1 mm	Yarn Dia sys 2 mm	Max Length mm	Max Width mm	Selve	Cut edge	Hem	Seam	Stitches	Classification
81A4412	O9	Silk	Plain	0	40	43	1	1		S	?	0.1-0.2	0.2	346	4	y	n	n	n	n	Braid
		Silk	Plain	0	40	43	1	1		S	?	0.1-0.2	0.2	185	4	y	n	n	n	n	Braid
81A4574	O3	Wool	2/2 Twill	1	12	12	1	1		S	S	0.25	0.25	250	53	n	y	y	y	y	cut skirt frag
		Wool	2/2 Twill	1	12	12	1	1		S	S	0.25	0.25	127	48	n	y	y	n	y	frag
		Wool	2/2 Twill	1	12	12	1	1		S	S	0.5	0.5	157	50	n	y	y	y	y	frag
		Wool	2/2 Twill	1	11	10	1	1		S	S	0.5	0.5-0.7	427	145	n	y	y	y	y	Garment
		Wool	2/2 Twill	1	11	11	1	1		S	S	0.5	0.5-0.6	154	140	n	y	y	y	y	Garment
		Wool	Plain	1	10	10	1	1		S	S	0.5	0.5	445	52	n	y	y	y	y	frag
		Wool	Plain	2	10	10	1	1		S	S	0.5	0.5	338	49	n	y	y	y	y	frag
		Wool	Plain	1	10	10	1	1		S	S	0.5	0.5-0.6	358	49	n	y	y	y	y	frag
		Wool	Plain	1	11	10	1	1		S	S	0.5	0.5	464	50	n	y	y	n	y	frag
		Wool	Plain	0	12	10	1	1		S	S	0.5	0.5	165	48	n	y	y	n	y	frag
		Wool	2/2 Twill	2	12	10	1	1		S	S	0.6-0.7	0.7	190	7	n	y	n	n	y	Cord
		Wool	2/2 Twill	1	12	10	1	1		S	S	0.6-0.7	0.6-0.7	345	155	n	y	y	y	y	Garment
		Wool	2/2 Twill	1	12	10	1	1		S	S	0.6-0.7	0.6-0.7	407	170	n	y	y	y	y	Garment
		Wool	2/2 Twill	1	12	10	1	1		S	S	0.6-0.7	0.6-0.7	587	246	n	y	y	y	y	Garment
81A4589	O3	Wool	Plain	1	8	8	1	1		S	S	1	1	277	97	n	y	n	n	n	frag
		Plant	Plain	0	20	14	1	1		S	Z	0.5	0.4	129	7	y	y	y	y	y	Cord
81A4681	O3	Wool	Plain	0	7	7	1	1		?	?	1	0.75-1	170	240	n	y	y	y	y	Aiglets & laces
81A4692	O9	Wool	2/2 Twill	0	12	10	1	1		S	S	0.5-0.7	0.5-0.7	112	83	n	n	n	n	n	frag
		Wool	2/2 Twill	0	14	8	1	1		S	S	0.25-0.5	0.5	167	28	n	y	n	n	y	frag
81A4693	O3	Wool	Plain	1	5	5	1	1		S	S	1.5	1.25	205	192	n	y	n	n	y	Cloth jerkin
		Plant	Plain	0	18	15	1	1		?	?	0.2	0.2	46	50	n	n	n	n	n	"
		Wool	Plain	0	8	8	1	1		S	S	0.5	0.5	32	46	n	n	n	n	n	"
		Wool	2/2 Twill	0	5	5	1	1		S	Z	1.5	1	48	33	n	n	n	n	n	"
		Wool	?	0	24	?	1	1		?	?	?	0.33	40	23.5	n	n	n	n	n	"
		Wool	Plain	1	6	5	1	1		S	S	1.25	1.25	52	18	n	y	n	n	y	Button
		Wool	Plain	1	6	5	1	1		S	S	1.25	1.25	52	16	n	y	n	n	y	Button
		Wool	Plain	1	6	5	1	1		S	S	1.25	1.25	54	18	n	y	n	n	y	Button
		Wool	Plain	0	8	8	1	1		S	S	0.75	0.6-0.7	140	80	n	n	y	n	y	Yellow Check
		Wool	Plain	0	8	8	1	1		S	S	0.7	0.7	140	80	n	y	y	n	n	Red Check

Obj. no.	Location	Fibre	Weave	Nap	Count sys 1 per cm	Count sys 2 per cm	Ply sys 1	Ply sys 2	Ply spin	Spin sys 1	Spin sys 2	Yarn Dia sys 1 mm	Yarn Dia sys 2 mm	Max Length mm	Max Width mm	Selve	Cut edge	Hem	Seam	Stitches	Classification
81A4693	O3	Wool	Plain	0	8	8	1	1		S	S	0.7-1	0.7-1	147	111	n	n	n	n	n	Red Yellow Check
		Wool	Plain	2	6	6	1	1		S	Z	0.8-1.3	1-1.5	60	37	n	n	n	n	n	"
81A4694		Wool	?	2	10	?	1	1		?	?	?	0.5	75	42.5	n	n	n	n	n	"
	O3	Plant	Plain	0	8	8	1	1		?	?	1	1.25	192	70	n	y	y	n	y	"
		Plant	Plain	0	8	8	1	1		?	?	1	1.25	100	70	n	n	n	n	n	frag
		Plant	Plain	0	8	8	1	1		?	?	1	1.25	100	38	n	n	y	n	n	frag
		Plant	Plain	0	8	8	1	1		?	?	1	1.25	114	35	n	n	y	n	n	frag
		Plant	Plain	0	8	8	1	1		?	?	1	1.25	115	140	n	n	y	n	n	frag
81A4699	H6	Silk	Threads	0			2	2	S			0.1	0.3	220	20	n	n	n	n	n	Threads
81A4706	U9	Silk	Plain	0	52	36	1	1		S	Z	0.2	0.2	177	22	y	n	y	n	n	Hat ribbon
		Silk	Plain	0	52	36	1	1		S	Z	0.2	0.2	55	12	y	n	y	n	n	Ribbon
81A4748	O2	Wool	Plain	1	8	6	1	1		S	S	1	1.25	215	260	n	y	y	n	y	Garment
		Wool	Plain	0	6	6	1	1		S	S	1	1	245	186	n	y	y	n	y	Garment
		Wool	Plain	0	9	9	1	1		S	S	0.75	0.75	?	148	n	n	n	n	?	frag
		Wool	2/2 Twill	0	12	8	1	1		Z	Z	3-4.0	2-3.5	126	21	n	n	n	n	?	frag
		Wool	Plain	0	3	2	2	1		Z	Z	2	2	140	130	n	n	n	n	n	frag
		Wool	Plain	0	4	3	2	2		Z	Z	2	2	600	195	n	n	n	n	n	frag
		Wool	Plain	0	4	3	2	2		Z	Z	2	2	400	425	n	y	n	n	y	Folded edges & aiglets
		Wool	Plain	1	6	6	1	2		S	S	1	0.75-1.25	430	340	n	y	y	n	y	Garment
		Wool	Plain	1	6	6	1	1		S	S	1-1.25	0.75-1	320	245	n	y	n	n	y	Garment
		Wool	Plain	1	4	3	1	1		S	S	1	0.75	269	139	n	n	y	n	n	frag
		Plant	Plain	0	4	3	2	2	S	Z		2.3	2	120	65	n	n	n	n	n	frag
		Plant	Plain	0	6	6	2	2	S	S	S	2.5	1.75	402	330	n	n	n	n	n	frag
81A4922	M2	Linen	Threads	0			2	2	S	S	S	0.25	0.25	300	0.4-Q550.5	n	n	n	n	n	Thread from leather garment
81A6781	M9	Wool	Plain	1	8	8	1	1		S	S	1-1.25	1.1-1.25	15	8	n	n	n	n	n	frag
81A6921	H4	Wool	Plain	1	12	8	1	1		Z	Z	0.5	0.75-1	354	140	n	y	n	n	y	Hose
		Wool	Plain	1	8	8	1	1		Z	Z	1	0.75-1	62	75	n	y	y	n	n	Hose
81A6945	O3	Wool	Plain	1	12	10	1	1		Z	?	0.3-0.5	0.5-0.75	290	138	n	y	y	n	y	Shoe Lining
		Wool	Plain	1	12	10	1	1		S	S	0.3	0.5	157	131	n	y	y	n	y	Shoe Lining
82A2065	O9	Wool	Plain	0	4	3	2	2	S	Z	Z	2	2.5	63	95	n	n	n	n	y	Sackcloth
		Wool	Plain	0	4	3	2	2		Z	Z	2	2.5	39	30	n	n	n	n	n	"
		Plant	Plain	0	4	3	2	2	S	Z	Z	2	1.8	379	250	n	n	n	n	n	frags & sacking
		Plant	Plain	0	9	8	1	1		Z	S	1	1	152	181	n	y	n	n	n	"
82A2155	O9	Wool	Plain	0	4	3	2	2	S	S	Z	2	2	560	?	y	n	n	n	n	frag with weaving faults
82A2260	O9	Wool	Plain	1	8	8	1	1		Z	Z	0.5-1	0.5-1	118	75	n	y	n	n	n	frag
82A4744	O9	Wool	Plain	1	14	14	1	1		S	Z	0.3	0.3	150	195	n	y	n	n	y	Garment
		Wool	Plain	1	14	14	1	1		S	Z	0.3	0.3	67.7	53	y	n	y	n	n	Garment
82A5000	O10	Silk	Satin	0	60	48	1	1		S	Z	0.4	0.3	66.2	18.2	n	y	y	n	n	frag
		Silk	?	1	62	28	1	1		S	Z	0.12	0.1	520	12.5	n	y	y	n	y	Braid

Appendix 3: Plant remains

Appendix 3.1:   Fruit, flavourings and nuts associated with baskets and boxes

Appendix 3.2:   Rye chaff and teasel bracts/achenes associated with jerkins

Appendix 3.3:   Remains of trees/shrubs, especially broom

Appendix 3.4:   Cereal grain and chaff

Appendix 3.5:   Samples primarily containing remains of weeds/wild plants

Appendix 3.6   Plant remains recorded prior to 2002, mentioned in text

Appendix 3.1 Fruit, flavourings and nuts associated with baskets and boxes

Location	O5 basket 80A0963	O9 basket 82A2264	O10 basket frags in 81A2941	H5 basket 82A5102	H6 basket (fruit) 80A1704	H6 basket (fruit) 80A1704	H6 basket (fruit) 80A1704	H11 basket 81A4036
Associated with/from								
Feature Number			F109	F211				F16
Context Number	10	17	44	(17/18)	17	17	17	10
Sample No	85S0072	82S0115C	81S1142	82S1085C	80S0244	80S0254	80S0255	81S0099/4.1
Volume (L. - unless otherwise indicated)		2.5 L						
Seeds per litre		17.6						
CEREALS								
Secale cereale L. - lemma	-	16	-	-	-	-	-	-
Secale cereale L. - rachis	-	11	-	-	-	-	-	-
Cereal/ POACEAE - caryopsis	-	2	-	-	-	-	-	-
Cereal/ POACEAE - culm node	-	1	-	-	-	-	-	-
Cereal/ POACEAE – straw	-	(+)	-	-	-	-	-	-
FLAVOURINGS								
Humulus lupulus L.	-	-	-	-	-	-	-	1
Piper nigrum L.	-	-	-	-	-	27	-	-
cf. *Piper nigrum* L.	-	-	-	-	-	-	-	-
FRUIT								
Prunus domestica s.l.	1	-	1	2	81	-	-	-
Prunus avium (L.) L./ *cerasus* L.	-	-	-	-	-	-	-	-
Prunus sp.	-	-	-	-	-	-	-	-
Vitis vinifera L.	-	-	-	-	-	-	3	-
NUTS								
Juglans regia L. – nutshell	-	-	-	-	-	-	-	-
Cocus nucifera L.	1	-	-	-	-	-	-	-
Corylus avellana L. - nutshell	-	-	-	-	-	-	-	-
TREE/ SHRUB								
Quercus sp. (leaf)	-	-	-	-	-	-	-	-
cf. *Quercus* sp. (leaf)	-	-	-	-	-	-	-	-
Cytisus sp. - leaf/ stem	-	-	-	-	-	-	-	-
WEED/ WILD PLANTS								
Pteridium sp. – leaves	-	7	-	-	-	-	-	-
Ranunculus acris L./ *repens* L./ *bulbosus* L.	-	-	-	-	-	-	-	2
Ranunculus sp.	-	-	-	-	-	-	-	-
cf. *Ranunculus* sp.	-	-	-	-	-	-	-	-
Atriplex sp.	-	-	-	-	-	-	-	2
cf. *Agrostemma githago* L.	-	-	-	-	-	-	-	-
CARYOPHYLLACEAE - unident seed coat frags	-	-	-	-	-	-	-	-
Polygonum sp./ *Rumex* sp./ *Carex* sp. – intern. strct.	-	-	-	-	-	-	-	-
Malva cf. *sylvestris* L.	-	-	-	-	-	-	-	1
Brassica sp./ *Sinapis* sp.	-	-	-	-	-	-	-	2
cf. *Trifolium* sp. - type calyx	-	-	-	-	-	-	-	-
FABACEAE – unidentified pod	-	1	-	-	-	-	-	-
cf. *Oenanthe* sp.	-	-	-	-	-	-	-	-
Prunella vulgaris L.	-	-	-	-	-	-	-	-
cf. *Dipsacus* sp. - bract	-	-	-	-	-	-	-	-
Carduus sp./ Cirsium sp.	-	-	-	-	-	-	-	-
Cirsium sp.	-	-	-	-	-	-	-	-
Onopordum acanthium L.	-	-	-	-	-	-	-	-
Anthemis cotula L.	-	-	-	-	-	-	-	-
cf. ASTERACEAE	-	-	-	-	-	-	-	-
Avena sp.	-	-	-	-	-	-	-	-
cf. *Avena* sp.	-	1	-	-	-	-	-	-
POACEAE - culm node	-	1	-	-	-	-	-	-
POACEAE - unident large grass caryopsis	-	-	-	-	-	-	-	-
POACEAE - unident rachis	-	2	-	-	-	-	-	-
POACEAE - unident small grass caryopsis	-	-	-	-	-	-	-	-
cf. POACEAE - unident small grass caryopsis	-	-	-	-	-	-	-	-
UNIDENTIFIED PLANTS								
Unident - Bryophyte	-	-	-	-	-	-	-	-
Unident - calyx	-	-	-	-	-	-	-	-
Unident - fruit/ seed	-	-	-	-	-	-	-	-
Unident - leaf	-	2	-	-	-	-	-	-
Unident - leaf (? marine)	-	-	-	-	-	-	-	-
Unident - leaf/ calyx	-	-	-	-	-	-	-	-
Unident - leaf/ grass	-	-	-	-	-	-	-	-
Unident - plant fibre	-	-	-	-	-	-	-	-
Unident - plant fragment	-	-	-	-	1	-	-	-
Unident - root/ tuber	-	-	-	-	-	-	-	-
Unident - seed	-	-	-	-	-	-	-	-
Unident - seed coat	-	-	-	-	-	-	-	-
Unident - seed/ bud	-	-	-	-	-	-	-	-
Unident - stalk	-	-	-	-	-	-	-	-
Unident - stalk (? marine)	-	-	-	-	-	-	-	-
Unident - stem	-	-	-	-	-	-	-	-
Unident - wood fragments	-	-	-	-	-	-	-	-
Total number of quantified identifications	2	44	1	2	82	27	3	8

H11 basket 81A4036 F16 10 81S099AC 0.01 2500.0	U9 chest 81A2099 F110 39 81S0347/1 0.5 L 120.0	O9 in chest upper sed. 81A3285 F146 52 81S0478/02 2 L 0.5	O9 in chest lower sed. 81A3285 (*P) F146 52 81S0488C	M7 barber surg chest in cabin 80A1530 BB/SG 24 80S0109/1.2	M9 at bottom of chest 81A5783 F128 55 81S0598C 208 L (?4 L) 1.4	M9 in chest 81A5783 F128 55 81S0608C	O9 (textiles) in chest 81A3285 F146 52 86S0304C 3.8 L 2.1	O10 (under shoe) in chest 81A2941 F109 44 81S0421C
-	-	-	-	-	-	-	-	-
2	-	-	-	-	-	-	-	-
-	-	-	-	-	-	-	-	-
-	-	-	-	-	(++)	-	-	-
-	58	-	-	3	-	-	1	-
-	-	-	-	1	-	-	-	-
-	-	-	-	-	-	-	-	4
-	-	-	-	-	-	-	-	-
-	-	-	-	-	-	-	-	-
-	-	-	-	-	-	-	-	-
-	-	-	-	-	-	-	-	-
-	-	-	-	-	1	-	-	-
-	-	-	-	-	-	3	-	-
-	-	-	-	-	-	1	-	-
-	-	-	-	-	-	-	-	-
-	-	-	-	-	-	-	-	-
9	-	-	-	-	-	-	-	-
-	-	-	-	-	-	-	-	-
-	-	-	-	-	-	-	-	-
1	-	-	-	-	-	-	-	-
-	-	-	-	-	-	-	-	-
-	-	-	-	-	-	-	-	-
1	-	-	-	-	-	-	-	-
-	-	-	-	-	-	-	-	-
-	-	-	-	-	-	-	-	-
1	-	-	-	-	-	-	-	-
-	-	-	-	-	1	-	-	-
-	-	-	-	-	-	-	-	-
-	-	-	-	-	-	-	-	-
1	-	-	-	-	-	-	-	-
-	-	-	-	-	-	-	-	-
-	-	-	-	-	-	-	-	-
2	-	-	-	-	-	-	-	-
-	-	-	-	-	-	-	-	-
-	-	-	-	-	-	-	1	-
-	-	-	-	-	-	-	-	-
-	-	-	-	-	-	-	2	-
-	-	-	-	-	-	-	-	-
3	-	-	-	-	-	-	-	-
-	2	-	-	-	2	-	-	-
-	-	-	-	-	-	-	-	-
-	-	-	2	-	2	-	-	2
-	-	1	2	-	11	-	1	-
-	-	-	1	-	-	-	1	-
-	-	-	-	-	2	-	1	-
-	-	-	1	-	5 (& 8 ch)	-	-	1
1	-	-	-	-	-	-	-	-
1	-	-	-	-	1	-	-	-
3	-	-	-	-	-	-	-	-
-	-	-	-	-	-	-	-	1
-	-	-	-	-	1	-	2	-
-	-	-	-	-	1	-	-	-
-	-	-	-	-	5	-	-	-
-	-	-	-	-	248	-	-	-
25	60	1	6	4	288	4	8	17

	O8 inside box 81A3065	O10 chest 82A0942	O3 concre-tion on gun	O11 fishbone	H11 fishbone	M9 serving tankard 81A1392	U9 flask 81A2034	O7 marine sediment	U3	M10	H4
Feature Number	BX06	F186		F16	F16	F69	F110			(1/2)	10
Context Number	17	17		57	57	17	17	17			
Sample No.	81S1163C	82S1013	89S0002	81S0389C	81S0093C	81S0264/2	81S1109	81S0584	86S0001/3	81S1292	80S0256
CEREALS											
Secale cereale L. - lemma	-	-	-	-	-	-	-	-	-	-	-
Secale cereale L. - rachis	-	-	-	-	-	-	-	-	-	-	-
Cereal/ POACEAE - caryopsis	-	-	-	-	-	-	-	-	-	-	-
Cereal/ POACEAE - culm node	-	-	-	-	-	-	-	-	-	-	-
Cereal/ POACEAE – straw	-	-	-	-	-	-	-	-	-	-	-
FLAVOURINGS											
Humulus lupulus L.	-	-	-	2	-	-	-	1	-	-	-
Piper nigrum L.	11	-	-	-	-	2	9	-	-	-	-
cf. Piper nigrum L.	4	-	-	-	-	-	-	-	-	-	-
FRUIT											
Prunus domestica s.l.	-	2	-	-	-	-	-	-	-	-	-
Prunus avium (L.) L./ cerasus L.	-	-	-	-	2	-	-	-	1	-	-
Prunus sp.	-	-	1	-	-	-	-	-	-	-	-
Vitis vinifera L.	-	-	-	-	-	-	-	-	-	-	-
NUTS											
Juglans regia L. – nutshell	-	-	-	-	1	-	-	-	-	-	1
Cocus nucifera L.	-	-	-	-	-	-	-	-	-	1	-
Corylus avellana L. - nutshell	-	-	1	-	3	-	-	-	-	-	-
TREE/ SHRUB											
Quercus sp. (leaf)	-	-	-	-	2	-	-	-	-	-	-
cf. Quercus sp. (leaf)	-	-	-	-	-	-	-	-	-	-	-
Cytisus sp. - leaf/ stem	1	-	-	-	-	-	-	-	-	-	-
WEED/ WILD PLANTS											
Pteridium sp. – leaves	-	-	-	-	-	-	-	-	-	-	-
Ranunculus acris L./ repens L./ bulbosus L.	-	-	-	2	-	-	-	-	-	-	-
Ranunculus flammula L. type	-	-	-	-	-	-	-	-	-	-	-
Ranunculus sp.	-	-	-	2	-	-	-	-	-	-	-
cf. Ranunculus sp.	-	-	-	1	-	-	-	-	-	-	-
Atriplex sp.	-	-	-	3	-	-	-	-	-	-	-
cf. Agrostemma githago L.	-	-	-	1	-	-	-	-	-	-	-
Polygonum sp./ Rumex sp./ Carex sp. – intern. strct.	-	-	-	-	-	-	-	-	-	-	-
Malva cf. sylvestris L.	-	-	-	-	-	-	-	-	-	-	-
Brassica sp./ Sinapis sp.	-	-	-	-	-	-	-	-	-	-	-
cf. Trifolium sp. - type calyx	-	-	-	-	-	-	-	-	-	-	-
FABACEAE - ???? Vicia sativa L.	-	-	-	-	-	-	-	-	-	-	-
FABACEAE – unidentified pod	-	-	-	1	2	-	-	-	-	-	-
cf. Oenanthe sp.	-	-	1	-	-	-	-	-	-	-	-
Prunella vulgaris L.	-	-	-	-	-	-	-	-	-	-	-
cf. Dipsacus sp. - bract	-	-	-	-	-	-	-	-	-	-	-
Carduus sp./ Cirsium sp.	-	-	-	1	-	-	-	-	-	-	-
Cirsium sp.	-	-	-	-	-	-	-	1	-	-	-
Onopordum acanthium L.	-	-	-	3	-	-	-	-	-	-	-
Anthemis cotula L.	-	-	-	-	-	-	-	-	-	-	-
cf. ASTERACEAE	-	-	-	1	-	-	-	-	-	-	-
Avena sp.	-	-	-	-	-	-	-	-	-	-	-
cf. Avena sp.	-	-	-	-	-	-	-	-	-	-	-
POACEAE - culm node	-	-	-	-	-	-	-	-	-	-	-
POACEAE - unident large grass caryopsis	-	-	-	-	1	-	-	-	-	-	-
POACEAE - unident rachis	-	-	-	-	-	-	-	-	-	-	-
POACEAE - unident small grass caryopsis	-	-	-	-	-	-	-	1	-	-	-
cf. POACEAE - unident small grass caryopsis	-	-	-	-	-	-	-	1	-	-	-
UNIDENTIFIED PLANTS											
Unident - Bryophyte	-	-	-	-	-	-	-	-	-	-	-
Unident - calyx	-	-	-	1	-	-	-	-	-	-	-
Unident - fruit/ seed	1	-	-	-	-	-	-	-	-	-	-
Unident - leaf	1	-	-	-	7	-	-	-	-	-	-
Unident - leaf (? marine)	-	-	-	-	-	-	-	-	-	-	-
Unident - leaf/ calyx	-	-	-	-	9	-	-	1	-	-	-
Unident - leaf/ grass	-	-	-	-	-	-	-	-	-	-	-
Unident - plant fibre	-	-	-	-	-	-	-	-	-	-	-
Unident - plant fragment	-	-	-	-	-	-	-	-	-	-	-
Unident - root/ tuber	-	-	-	-	-	-	-	-	-	-	-
Unident - seed	2	-	-	-	1	-	-	-	-	-	-
Unident - seed coat	-	-	-	-	-	-	-	-	-	-	-
Unident - seed/ bud	-	-	-	-	-	-	-	-	-	-	-
Unident - stalk	-	-	-	-	-	-	-	-	-	-	-
Unident - stalk (? marine)	-	-	-	-	-	-	-	-	-	-	-
Unident - stem	-	-	-	-	-	-	-	-	-	-	-
Unident - wood fragments	-	-	-	-	-	-	-	-	-	-	-
Total number of quantified identifications	20	2	3	18	28	2	9	5	1	1	1

Appendix 3.2 Rye chaff and teasel bracts/achenes associated with jerkins

Location Associated with/from	M9 cask & leather ?jerkin 81A4708	M9 leather ?jerkin 81A4708	O2 textile 81A4475	O3 jerkin 81A4693	O8 next to pump +fish/ textile
Feature Number				F86	
Context Number	38	38	10	(10/27)	17
Sample No.	81S0547C	81S0573C	83S0287	81S1357	81S0460C
Volume (L. - unless otherwise indicated)	1.3 L	3 L			
Seeds per litre	34.6	2.3			
CEREALS					
Secale cereale L. - lemma	-	-	-	72	-
Secale cereale L. - rachis	-	-	-	36	-
Triticum aestivum L. type - rachis segment	-	-	-	-	1
CLOTHWORKING PLANTS					
Dipsacus sativus L.	1	1	-	-	-
Dipsacus sativus L.- bract	23	-	-	-	1
Dipsacus cf. *sativus* L. - bract	5	4	-	-	-
TREE/ SHRUB					
Cytisus sp. - leaf/ stem	-	-	(+)	-	-
WEED/ WILD PLANTS					
Pteridium sp. – leaves	-	-	-	-	-
Agrostemma githago L.	-	-	-	-	3
Agrimonia eupatoria L.	-	-	-	-	10
Agrimonia sp.	-	-	-	-	2
Torilis sp.	-	-	11	-	-
Dipsacus cf. *fullonum* L. - bract (immature)	16	-	-	-	-
Dipsacus sp.	-	2	-	-	-
Cirsium sp.	-	-	1	-	-
Avena sp.	-	-	-	-	4
POACEAE – culm node	-	-	2	-	-
UNIDENTIFIED PLANTS					
Unident – bark	-	-	1	-	-
Unident – stalk (? marine)	-	-	-	-	1
Unident – twigs	-	-	5	-	-
Unident – wood fragments	-	-	1	-	-
Total number of quantified identifications	45	7	21	108	22

Appendix 3.3 Remains of trees/shrubs, especially broom

Location Associated with/from	M2 twigs, broom	O2 twigs, broom	H11 in shoe 81A0890	O4 pewter dishes 81A3310	O11 fishbone
Feature Number	F65	F65		F156	F16
Context Number	17	10	6	17	17
Sample No.	81S0319C	81S0314C	81S1065/1. 3	81S1176C	81S1288C
Volume (L. – unless otherwise indicated)	21.8g	7		0.25 L	
Seeds per litre	9.7	25.4		36.0	
CEREALS					
Cereal - cf. rachis node	-	-	-	-	1
Cereal/ POACEAE - caryopsis	-	30	-	-	-
Cereal/ POACEAE – straw	-	(+)	-	-	-
FIBRE CROP					
Cannabis sativa L.	-	1	-	-	-
TREE/ SHRUB					
Cytisus sp. - leaf/ stem	184	14 (& 150 ml)	-	-	(+++)
Cytisus sp. – pods	15	37	-	1	2
cf. *Cytisus* – seeds	-	-	-	-	-
cf. *Cytisus* sp. – calyx	2	1	-	-	-
cf. *Cytisus* sp. – twigs	3	-	-	1	-
WEED/ WILD PLANTS					
Pteridium sp. – leaves	-	5	-	-	-
Ranunculus acris L./ *repens* L./ *bulbosus* L.	-	-	-	-	1
Atriplex sp.	-	-	-	1	5
cf. *Atriplex* sp.	-	-	-	-	1
Stellaria media s.l.	-	-	-	-	1
CARYOPHYLLA- CEAE - unident seed coat frags	-	-	-	-	5
Polygonum sp.	-	-	-	-	1
cf. *Polygonum* sp.	-	-	-	-	1
cf. *Trifolium* sp. - type calyx	-	-	-	-	5
FABACEAE – unidentified pod	-	5	-	-	cf. 1
Torilis sp.	-	1	-	-	-
Taraxacum sp.	-	-	-	-	1
Juncus sp.	1	-	-	-	-
Avena sp. – spikelet fork (rachilla)	-	1	-	-	-
UNIDENTIFIED PLANTS					
Unident – Bryophyte	-	-	-	-	4
Unident – bud	2	1	-	-	-
Unident - bud/ calyx	-	2	-	-	5
Unident – calyx	2	-	-	-	-
Unident – flowerhead	1	-	-	-	-
Unident – leaf	-	92	1	-	3
Unident – plant fibre	-	-	-	5	-
Unident – plant fragment	1	-	-	(2 ch)	-
Unident – possible flower	-	-	-	-	1
Unident – seed	-	2	-	1	2
Total number of quantified identifications	211	178	1	11	40

Appendix 3.4 Cereal grain and chaff concentrations

Location Associated with/from	U9 cask 81A1847	O3 cask 81A2251	O3 cask	O3 beneath cask 81A2251	O3 staved container 81A2228	H4 casks 82A0077 /0082/0086	M7 basket frgs	O3 textile (thread) 81A4523
Feature Number		F105	F105	F 105	F19	F180	80A1530	F(65/83)
Context Number	17	10	17	10	17	17	10	(18/21)
Sample No.	81S0327C	81S0337C	81S0348C	81S0358C	81S1149	82S0024C	80S0115/2	81S0289C
Volume (L. - unless otherwise indicated)			8.27 L	1.53 L		2 L		2 (& 10g)
Seeds per litre			c. 43.7	126.1		9.5		7.5
CEREALS								
Secale cereale L. – grain	30	-	-	2	-	-	-	-
Secale cereale L. – lemma	-	726	68	93	22	-	58	-
Secale cereale L. – rachis	78	440	44	68	12	-	110	4
cf. Secale cereale L. - caryopsis	-	-	-	1	-	-	-	-
cf. Secale cereale L. - lemma	-	-	-	-	-	-	-	-
cf. Secale cereale L. – rachis	-	-	5	-	-	-	-	-
Triticum aestivum L type – glume	-	-	-	-	-	-	-	-
Triticum aestivum L. type - rachis segment	-	-	-	-	-	-	-	-
Triticum sp. - free-threshing rachis node	1	-	-	-	-	-	-	-
Triticum sp. - rachis node	-	-	-	-	-	-	-	-
Cereal - indeterminate rachis node	-	-	-	-	-	-	-	-
Cereal - cf. bran	-	-	-	-	-	-	-	-
Cereal - cf. grain	-	-	-	-	-	-	-	-
Cereal/ POACEAE – caryopsis	-	-	-	-	-	10	-	1
Cereal/ POACEAE - culm base	-	-	-	-	-	-	-	1
Cereal/POACEAE - culm node	-	-	1	1	-	-	-	5
Cereal/ POACEAE – straw	-	-	-	(+)	-	-	-	(+)
cf. Cereal/ POACEAE – caryopsis	-	-	3	-	-	-	-	-
TREE/ SHRUB								
Cytisus sp. - leaf/ stem	(+)	-	-	-	-	-	-	-
Cytisus sp. - pods	1	6	1	-	-	-	-	-
WEED/ WILD PLANTS								
Pteridium sp. – leaves	1	-	c. 221	-	-	-	-	-
Pteridium sp. – stem	-	-	4	-	-	-	-	-
Ranunculus acris L./ repens L./ bulbosus L.	1	-	-	-	-	-	-	-
Atriplex sp.	-	-	-	-	-	-	-	-
CHENOPODIACEAE/ CARYOPHYLLACEAE – unidentified internal structure	-	-	-	-	-	-	-	-
Agrostemma githago L.	-	-	-	-	-	-	-	-
CARYOPHYLLACEAE - unident seed coat frags	-	-	-	-	-	-	-	-
Rumex sp. - achene	-	-	-	-	-	-	-	-
Rumex sp. – tepal (perianth)	-	-	6	-	-	-	-	-
Rumex sp. - turbucle	-	-	2	-	-	-	-	-
Malva cf. sylvestris L.	-	-	1	-	-	-	-	-
Brassica sp./ Sinapis sp.	-	-	-	-	-	-	-	1
cf. Trifolium sp. - flowers	-	-	-	-	-	-	-	-
FABACEAE – unidentified pod	-	-	3	-	-	5	-	-
cf. FABACEAE – tendril	-	-	-	-	-	-	-	-
cf. FABACEAE – unidentified pod	-	-	-	-	-	-	-	-
cf. FABACEAE - unidentified seed	-	-	-	-	-	-	-	-
Galeopsis sp.	-	-	-	-	-	-	-	-
Picris sp.	1	-	-	-	-	-	-	-
Sonchus sp.	-	-	-	-	-	-	-	1
Anthemis cotula L.	55	-	-	11	-	-	-	-
cf. Anthemis cotula L.	1	-	-	-	-	-	-	-
Carex sp. - 3 sided	-	-	-	-	-	-	-	-
cf. Carex sp. - 3 sided	-	-	1	-	-	-	-	-
Avena sp. – spikelet fork (rachilla)	-	-	-	13	-	-	-	1
POACEAE - unident large grass caryopsis	-	-	1	1	-	-	-	1
POACEAE - unident small grass caryopsis	1	-	-	-	-	-	-	-
cf. POACEAE - unident large grass caryopsis	-	-	-	-	-	-	-	-
cf. POACEAE - unident small grass caryopsis	-	-	-	-	-	-	-	-
UNIDENTIFIED PLANTS								
Unident - bark	-	-	-	-	-	-	-	-
Unident - Bryophyte	-	-	-	-	-	-	-	-
Unident - leaf	-	-	-	-	-	3	-	-
Unident - leaf/ calyx	-	-	-	-	-	-	-	-
Unident - plant fibre	-	-	-	-	-	-	-	-
Unident - possible flower	-	-	-	-	-	-	-	-
Unident - seed	-	-	-	-	-	-	-	-
Unident - seed coat	-	-	-	-	-	-	-	-
Unident – stalk	-	-	-	1	-	-	-	-
Unident – stem	-	-	-	2	-	1	-	-
Total number of quantified identifications	170	1172	c. 361	193	34	19	168	15

H2 textile/ sack cloth 81A4141	H2 textile/ sack cloth 81A4141	O3 fastening aiglets 81A4681	O3 rope 80A2021	O1 next to spoked wheel 81A8402	H7 hay/packing wooden bowl 82A5056	O3	O3/ O4 galley	O5
F10/18 81S0115/1.1.2	F10/18 81S0118C 8	17 81S0392/01.04 2 L	80S0032C 1	10 81S0067/2 2	17 82S0087C	17 81S0437C 4 L	21 81S0323C 16.5 L	21/17 81S0520C 1 L
1.5	1.5	26.0	663.0	7.5		31.0	4.2	109.0
-	-	-	6	-	-	.	-	-
-	-	29	236	2	-	82	-	62
-	-	17	198	6	-	41	-	44
-	-	-	-	-	-	-	2	-
-	-	-	-	-	-	-	1	-
-	-	-	6	-	-	-	-	-
-	-	-	10	-	-	-	18	-
-	-	-	-	-	-	-	-	-
-	-	-	-	-	-	-	1	-
-	-	-	3	-	-	-	4	-
-	-	-	-	-	-	-	1	-
-	-	-	-	-	-	1	-	-
-	2	2	41	1	11	-	5	1
-	-	-	-	-	-	-	-	-
4	-	-	17	1	-	-	5	-
-	-	-	-	-	-	(+)	(+)	-
-	-	-	-	-	-	-	1	-
-	-	-	-	-	-	-	-	-
-	-	-	-	-	-	-	-	-
-	-	-	119	-	5	-	-	-
-	-	-	4	-	-	-	-	-
-	-	-	-	-	-	-	-	-
-	1	-	-	-	-	-	-	-
-	-	-	2	-	-	-	-	-
-	-	-	-	-	1	-	-	-
-	-	-	-	-	-	-	1	-
-	-	-	-	-	3	-	3	-
-	-	-	1	-	3	-	10	-
-	-	-	2	-	-	-	1	-
-	-	-	-	-	1	-	-	-
-	-	-	-	-	-	-	-	-
-	2	-	-	1	1	-	-	-
-	-	-	-	1	-	-	-	2
-	-	-	1	-	-	-	-	-
-	-	1	-	-	-	-	-	-
-	-	-	3	-	-	-	-	-
-	-	-	-	-	1	-	-	-
-	-	-	-	-	-	-	-	-
-	-	-	-	-	1	-	-	-
-	-	1	8	-	6	-	7	-
-	-	-	-	-	-	-	-	-
-	-	-	-	-	-	-	3	-
-	-	-	-	-	-	-	-	-
-	1	1	1	1	-	-	-	-
-	-	1	-	-	1	-	-	-
-	-	-	-	-	1	-	-	-
-	-	-	-	-	-	-	1	-
-	-	-	1	-	-	-	-	-
-	-	-	1	-	-	-	-	-
-	-	-	-	-	-	-	2	-
-	-	-	1	-	-	-	-	-
-	5	-	-	-	-	-	-	-
-	-	-	-	-	-	-	1	-
-	1	-	1	-	2	-	2	-
-	-	-	-	1	-	-	-	-
-	-	-	1	1	-	-	-	-
-	-	-	-	-	-	-	-	-
4	12	52	663	15	37	124	70	109

Appendix 3.5 Samples primarily containing remains of weeds/wild plants

Location Associated with/from	U3 timber	U7 next to wood plate 80A0728	U8 chopping block 80A1143	U9 sewing bobbin 81A4333	U9 weapons	M1 scabbard	M2 shoe 81A0161	M2 in chest 81A0045
Feature Number				F 22	F9	F11		F1(81)
Context Number	17		10	17	10	16	10	10
Sample No.	79S0026	80S0035/1	80S0061	81S0226/3.2	81S1239	81S1011	81S1017	86S0306C
Volume (L. – unless otherwise indicated)		1	2					3.5 L
Seeds per litre		1.0	54.0					0.3
CEREALS								
Secale cereale L. - lemma	-	-	-	-	-	-	-	-
Secale cereale L. - rachis	-	-	-	-	-	-	-	-
Triticum aestivum L type - glume	-	-	-	-	-	-	-	-
Triticum aestivum L. type - rachis segment	-	-	-	-	-	-	-	-
Triticum sp. - free-threshing rachis node	-	-	-	-	-	-	-	-
Triticum sp. – grain	-	-	-	-	-	-	-	-
Cereal/ POACEAE - caryopsis	-	-	-	-	-	-	-	-
Cereal/ POACEAE - culm node	-	-	-	-	-	-	-	-
Cereal/ POACEAE - glume	-	-	-	-	-	-	-	-
Cereal/ POACEAE – indet. chaff	-	-	-	-	-	-	-	-
Cereal/ POACEAE – straw	-	-	-	-	-	-	-	-
cf. Cereal/ POACEAE - caryopsis	-	-	-	-	-	-	-	-
TREE/ SHRUB								
Quercus sp. (leaf)	-	-	-	-	-	1	-	1
cf. *Quercus* sp. (leaf)	-	-	-	-	1	-	-	-
Cytisus sp. – pods	-	-	-	-	-	-	-	-
cf. *Cytisus* – seeds	-	-	-	-	-	-	-	-
WEED/ WILD PLANTS								
Pteridium sp. – leaves	-	-	-	-	-	-	-	-
Pteridium sp. – stem	-	-	-	-	-	-	-	-
Ranunculus acris L./ *repens* L./ *bulbosus* L.	-	-	1	-	-	-	-	-
Ranunculus flammula L. type	-	-	23	-	-	-	-	-
cf. *Ranunculus flammula* L. type	-	-	1	-	-	-	-	-
Atriplex sp.	-	-	-	-	-	-	-	-
cf. *Atriplex* sp.	-	-	-	-	-	-	-	-
Stellaria media s.l.	-	-	1	-	-	-	-	-
Cerastium sp.	-	-	-	-	-	-	-	-
Polygonum aviculare L.	-	-	-	-	-	-	-	-
Rumex sp. - achene	-	-	-	-	-	-	-	-
Rumex sp. – tepal (perianth)	-	-	-	-	-	-	-	-
Rumex sp. - turbucle	-	-	-	-	-	-	-	-
cf. *Rumex* - turbucle	-	-	-	-	-	-	-	-
Viola sp.	-	-	-	-	-	-	-	-
BRASSICACEAE - unident	-	-	-	-	-	-	-	-
Agrimonia sp.	-	-	-	-	-	-	-	-
Vicia hirsuta L. Gray - pods	-	-	-	-	-	-	-	-
Medicago lupulina L.	-	-	-	-	-	-	-	-
Melilotus sp./ *Medicago* sp./*Trifolium* sp.	-	-	-	-	-	-	-	-
cf. *Trifolium* sp. - flowers	-	-	-	-	-	-	-	-
cf. *Trifolium* sp. - type calyx	-	-	-	-	-	-	-	-
FABACEAE - ???? *Vicia sativa* L.	-	-	-	-	-	-	-	-
FABACEAE – unidentified pod	-	-	-	-	-	-	-	-
cf. FABACEAE – tendril	-	-	-	-	-	-	-	-
cf. FABACEAE - unidentified seed	-	-	-	-	-	-	-	-
cf. *Chaerophyllum aureum* L.	-	-	-	-	-	-	-	-
cf. *Atropa bella-donna* L.	-	-	-	-	-	-	-	-
Prunella vulgaris L.	-	-	-	-	-	-	-	-
Onopordum acanthium L.	-	-	-	-	-	-	-	-
Sonchus sp.	-	-	-	-	-	-	-	-
cf. *Achillea ptarmica* L./ *millefolium* L.	-	-	-	-	-	-	-	-
Anthemis cotula L.	-	-	-	-	-	-	-	-
ASTERACEAE - *Picris* type	-	-	-	-	-	-	-	-
cf. ASTERACEAE	-	-	1	-	-	-	-	-
Juncus sp.	-	-	65	-	-	-	-	-
cf. *Juncus* sp.	-	-	-	-	-	-	-	-
Carex sp. - 2 sided	-	-	3	-	-	-	-	-
Carex sp. - 3 sided	-	-	2	-	-	-	-	-
cf. *Carex* sp. - 3 sided	-	-	-	-	-	-	-	-
Lolium sp.	-	-	-	-	-	-	-	-
cf. *Lolium* sp.	-	-	-	-	-	-	-	-
Avena sp. – spikelet fork (rachilla)	-	-	-	-	-	-	-	-
POACEAE - culm node	-	-	-	-	-	-	-	-
POACEAE - unident large grass caryopsis	-	-	5	-	-	-	-	-
POACEAE - unident small grass caryopsis	-	-	-	-	-	-	-	-
POACEAE - unidentified complete heads	-	-	-	-	-	-	-	-
POACEAE - unidentified incomplete head (florets counted)	-	-	-	-	-	-	-	-
POACEAE - grass stalks	-	-	-	-	-	-	-	-
cf. POACEAE – unident large grass caryopsis	-	-	-	-	-	-	-	-
cf. POACEAE – unident small grass caryopsis	-	-	-	-	-	-	-	-
UNIDENTIFIED PLANTS								
Unident – bark	-	1	-	-	-	-	-	-
Unident – Bryophyte	-	-	-	-	-	-	-	-
Unident – calyx	-	-	-	-	-	-	-	-
Unident – flowerhead	-	-	-	-	-	-	-	-
Unident – leaf	-	-	-	-	-	-	3	-
Unident - leaf (? marine)	-	-	-	-	-	-	-	-

M5 in cask 81A1071	M7 under chest in Cu bowl 80A1629	M8 (gun sled)	M9 next top chest nr Carpenters' Cabin	M9 Carpenters' cabin next to bed (matress)	M9	M10 gun carriage	O2 rigging cordage 81A4809	O2 rigging block 79A0156
F48	BB/SG 80A1530	F143	F44			F30	F19	
(10/17) 81S0199 2	10 80S0113	17 81S0404C 0.25 L	17 81S0221	38 81S0560/2.7 2.5 L	76 82S1323	17 81S1218	17 81S0277/7	17 79S0005C 2.5
4.0		80.0		2.4				43.2
-	-	-	-	-	-	-	-	-
-	-	-	-	-	-	-	-	-
-	-	-	-	-	-	-	-	-
-	-	-	-	-	-	-	-	-
-	-	-	-	-	-	-	-	1
-	-	-	-	-	-	-	-	-
-	-	-	-	-	-	-	1	2
-	-	-	-	-	-	-	-	-
-	-	-	-	-	-	-	-	6
-	-	-	-	-	-	-	-	-
-	-	-	-	-	-	-	-	-
-	-	-	1	-	1	-	-	-
-	-	-	-	-	-	1	-	-
-	-	-	-	-	-	-	-	-
-	-	-	-	-	-	-	-	-
-	-	-	-	1	-	-	-	-
-	-	-	-	-	-	-	-	-
-	-	-	-	-	-	-	-	-
-	-	-	-	-	-	-	-	-
-	-	-	-	-	-	-	-	-
-	-	-	-	-	-	-	-	-
-	-	-	-	-	-	-	-	-
-	-	-	-	-	-	-	-	-
-	-	-	-	-	-	-	-	-
-	-	-	-	-	-	-	-	16
-	-	-	-	3	-	-	-	61
-	-	-	-	-	-	-	-	19
-	-	-	-	-	-	-	-	-
-	-	-	-	-	-	-	-	-
-	-	-	-	-	-	-	-	-
-	-	-	-	-	-	-	-	-
-	-	-	-	-	-	-	-	-
-	-	-	-	-	-	-	-	-
-	-	-	-	-	-	-	-	-
-	-	-	-	-	-	-	-	-
-	-	-	-	-	-	-	-	-
-	-	-	-	-	-	-	-	-
-	-	-	-	-	-	-	-	-
-	-	-	-	-	-	-	1	-
-	-	-	-	-	-	-	-	-
-	-	-	-	-	-	-	-	-
-	-	-	-	-	-	-	-	-
-	-	-	-	1	-	-	-	-
-	-	-	-	-	-	-	-	-
-	-	-	-	-	-	-	-	-
-	-	6	-	-	-	-	-	-
-	-	-	-	-	-	-	-	-
-	-	-	-	-	-	-	-	-
-	-	2	-	-	-	-	-	-
-	-	c. 250 ml	-	-	-	-	-	-
-	-	-	-	-	-	-	-	1
-	-	-	-	-	-	-	-	-
-	-	-	-	-	-	-	-	-
1	-	-	-	1	-	-	-	-
-	-	-	-	-	-	-	-	-
-	-	-	-	-	-	-	-	1
1	1	-	-	-	-	-	-	-
1	-	-	-	-	-	-	-	-

Location Associated with/from	U3 timber	U7 next to wood plate 80A0728	U8 chopping block 80A1143	U9 sewing bobbin 81A4333	U9 weapons	M1 scabbard	M2 shoe 81A0161	M2 in chest 81A0045
Feature Number				F 22	F9	F11		F1(81)
Context Number	17		10	17	10	16	10	10
Sample No.	79S0026	80S0035/1	80S0061	81S0226/3.2	81S1239	81S1011	81S1017	86S0306C
Volume (L. – unless otherwise indicated)		1	2					3.5 L
Seeds per litre		1.0	54.0					0.3
Unident - leaf/ grass	-	-	-	-	-	-	-	(+)
Unident - plant fibre	-	-	-	-	-	-	-	-
Unident - plant fragment	-	-	-	-	-	-	-	-
Unident - root plate	-	-	-	3	-	-	-	-
Unident - seed	-	-	6	-	-	-	-	-
Unident - seed coat	-	-	-	-	-	-	-	-
Unident - seed coat/ calyx	-	-	-	-	-	-	-	-
Unident - stalk	-	-	-	-	-	-	-	-
Unident - stalk (? marine)	-	-	-	-	-	-	-	-
Unident - stem	-	-	-	-	-	-	-	-
Unident – thorn	-	-	-	-	-	-	-	-
Unident - thorny calyx	-	-	-	-	-	-	-	-
Unident – twigs	20 ml	-	-	-	-	-	-	-
Unident - wood fragments	-	-	-	-	-	-	-	-
Total number of quantified identifications	+	1	108	3	1	1	3	1

M5 in cask 81A1071	M7 under chest in Cu bowl 80A1629	M8 (gun sled)	M9 next top chest nr Carpenters' Cabin	M9 Carpenters' cabin next to bed (matress)	M9	M10 gun carriage	O2 rigging cordage 81A4809	O2 rigging block 79A0156
F48	BB/SG 80A1530	F143	F44			F30	F19	
(10/17) 81S0199 2	10 80S0113	17 81S0404C 0.25 L	17 81S0221	38 81S0560/2.7 2.5 L	76 82S1323	17 81S1218	17 81S0277/7	17 79S0005C 2.5
4.0		80.0		2.4				43.2
-	-	-	-	-	-	-	-	1
-	-	-	-	-	-	-	-	-
1	-	-	-	-	-	-	-	-
-	-	-	-	-	-	-	-	-
-	-	-	-	-	-	-	-	-
-	-	-	-	-	-	-	-	-
4	-	-	-	-	-	-	-	-
-	-	-	-	-	-	-	-	-
-	-	-	-	-	-	-	-	-
-	-	-	-	-	-	-	-	-
-	-	-	-	-	-	-	-	-
-	-	-	-	-	-	-	-	-
8	1	8	1	6	1	1	2	108

	O2	O2	O2	O3	O2	O3	O3	O4
Location **Associated with/from**	und. sailcloth (rope+bone) 81A4416		(bone) 81A4184	textile	textile	with textile	next to cask 81A2251	in chest 80A1413
Feature Number	F19A					F19	F105	Pers 1
Context Number	10	21	17	17	10	17	10	30
Sample No.	81S0175/10.12	81S0039C	81S0276/1.6	81S0357C	81S1361	81S0372C	82S1243	80S0178
Volume (L. - unless otherwise indicated)		2		2.25 L		0.25		
Seeds per litre		6.0		57.3		c. 1244		
CEREALS								
Secale cereale L. - lemma	-	-	-	-	-	-	-	-
Secale cereale L. - rachis	-	-	-	-	-	-	-	-
Triticum aestivum L type - glume	-	-	-	-	-	-	-	-
Triticum aestivum L. type - rachis segment	-	-	-	-	-	-	-	-
Triticum sp. - free-threshing rachis node	-	-	-	-	-	-	-	-
Triticum sp. - grain	-	-	-	-	-	-	-	-
Cereal/ POACEAE - caryopsis	-	-	-	-	-	-	-	-
Cereal/ POACEAE - culm node	-	-	-	-	-	-	-	-
Cereal/ POACEAE - glume	-	-	-	-	-	-	-	-
Cereal/ POACEAE – indet. chaff	-	-	-	-	-	-	-	-
Cereal/ POACEAE – straw	-	-	-	-	-	-	-	-
cf. Cereal/ POACEAE - caryopsis	-	-	-	1	-	-	-	-
TREE/ SHRUB								
Quercus sp. (leaf)	-	-	-	-	-	-	-	-
cf. Quercus sp. (leaf)	-	-	-	-	-	-	-	-
Cytisus sp. - pods	-	-	-	-	-	-	1	-
cf. Cytisus - seeds	-	-	-	-	-	-	-	-
WEED/ WILD PLANTS								
Pteridium sp. – leaves	-	-	-	-	-	c. 300	-	-
Pteridium sp. – stem	-	-	-	-	-	1	-	-
Ranunculus acris L./ repens L./ bulbosus L.	-	-	-	3	-	-	-	-
Ranunculus flammula L. type	-	-	-	-	-	-	-	-
cf. Ranunculus flammula L. type	-	-	-	-	-	-	-	-
Atriplex sp.	1	-	-	-	-	-	-	-
cf. Atriplex sp.	-	-	-	-	-	-	-	-
Stellaria media s.l.	-	-	-	-	-	-	-	-
Cerastium sp.	-	-	-	3	-	-	-	-
Polygonum aviculare L.	-	-	-	-	-	-	-	-
Rumex sp. - achene	-	-	-	-	-	-	-	-
Rumex sp. – tepal (perianth)	-	-	-	-	-	-	-	-
Rumex sp. - turbucle	-	-	-	-	-	-	-	-
cf. Rumex - turbucle	-	-	-	-	-	-	-	-
Viola sp.	-	-	-	-	-	-	-	-
BRASSICACEAE - unident	-	-	-	-	-	-	-	-
Agrimonia sp.	-	-	-	-	-	-	-	-
Vicia hirsuta L. Gray - pods	-	-	-	-	-	-	-	-
Medicago lupulina L.	-	-	-	1	-	-	-	-
Melilotus sp./ Medicago sp./ Trifolium sp.	-	-	-	18	-	-	-	-
cf. Trifolium sp. - flowers	-	-	-	36	-	-	-	-
cf. Trifolium sp. - type calyx	-	-	-	-	-	-	-	-
FABACEAE - ???? Vicia sativa L.	-	-	-	-	-	3	-	-
FABACEAE – unidentified pod	-	-	-	-	-	4	-	-
cf. FABACEAE – tendril	-	-	-	-	-	-	-	-
cf. FABACEAE - unidentified seed	-	-	-	-	-	-	-	-
cf. Chaerophyllum aureum L.	1	-	-	-	-	-	-	-
cf. Atropa bella-donna L.	-	-	-	-	-	-	-	-
Prunella vulgaris L.	-	-	-	-	-	-	-	-
Onopordum acanthium L.	1	-	-	-	-	-	-	-
Sonchus sp.	-	-	-	3	-	-	-	-
cf. Achillea ptarmica L./ millefolium L.	-	-	-	3	-	-	-	-
Anthemis cotula L.	-	-	4	-	-	-	-	-
ASTERACEAE - Picris type	-	-	-	-	-	-	-	-
cf. ASTERACEAE	-	-	-	-	-	-	-	-
Juncus sp.	-	-	-	-	-	-	-	-
cf. Juncus sp.	-	-	-	-	-	-	-	-
Carex sp. - 2 sided	-	-	-	-	-	-	-	-
Carex sp. - 3 sided	-	-	-	-	-	-	-	-
cf. Carex sp. - 3 sided	-	-	-	-	-	-	-	-
Lolium sp.	-	-	-	34	-	-	-	-
cf. Lolium sp.	-	-	-	1	-	-	-	-
Avena sp.	-	-	-	-	-	-	-	-
Avena sp. - spikelet fork (rachilla)	-	-	-	-	-	-	-	-
POACEAE - culm node	-	-	-	1	-	-	-	-
POACEAE - unident large grass caryopsis	-	-	1	-	-	-	-	-
POACEAE - unident small grass caryopsis	-	-	1	2	-	-	-	-
POACEAE - unidentified complete heads	-	-	-	3	-	-	-	-
POACEAE - unidentified incomplete head (florets counted)	-	-	-	-	-	-	-	-
POACEAE - grass stalks	-	-	-	-	-	-	-	-
cf. POACEAE - unident large grass caryopsis	-	-	-	-	-	-	-	-
cf. POACEAE - unident small grass caryopsis	-	-	-	3	-	-	-	-
UNIDENTIFIED PLANTS								
Unident – bark	-	-	-	-	-	-	-	-
Unident – Bryophyte	-	-	-	-	-	-	-	-
Unident – bud	-	-	-	-	-	-	-	-
Unident – calyx	-	-	-	-	-	-	-	-
Unident – flowerhead	-	-	-	15	-	-	-	-
Unident – leaf	-	11	-	-	1	-	-	1

O4	O4	O6	O7	O8	O9	?O9 scour	O10	O10
oak table	mallet 81A3240		basket/ container	concreted pump +fish/ textile	concretion		in chest 81A2941	F16 = fishbone
F152			F167		F21		F109	F16
49	50	17	17	17	17	(6/8)	44	57
81S0463C	81S0468C	81S0512/02	81S1368	81S0446C	81S0247C	81S1097C	81S0430C	81S0554/9
	0.042 L	2 L	0.25 L		4		0.002 L	
4047.6	31.5	8.0			10.0		2500.0	
-	-	6	-	-	-	-	-	-
-	-	5	-	-	-	-	-	-
-	1	-	-	-	-	-	-	-
-	3	-	-	-	-	-	-	-
-	-	-	-	-	-	-	-	-
1	-	-	-	-	-	-	-	-
8	1	1	-	-	-	-	-	-
1	-	-	-	-	-	-	-	-
-	-	-	-	-	-	-	-	-
-	-	-	-	-	1	-	-	-
-	-	-	-	-	-	-	1	-
-	-	-	-	-	-	-	-	-
-	-	-	2	-	-	-	-	-
-	-	-	-	-	-	-	-	-
-	-	-	-	-	-	-	-	-
-	-	-	-	-	-	-	-	-
-	140	50	-	-	-	-	-	-
-	5	1	-	-	-	-	-	-
-	-	-	-	-	-	-	-	1
-	-	-	-	-	-	-	-	-
-	-	-	-	-	-	-	-	-
-	-	-	-	1	-	-	-	4
-	-	-	-	-	-	-	-	1
-	-	-	-	-	-	-	-	1
-	-	-	-	-	-	-	-	-
-	-	-	-	-	-	-	-	-
-	1	-	-	-	-	-	-	-
6	3	-	-	-	-	-	-	11
-	1	-	-	-	-	-	-	-
1	1	-	-	-	-	-	-	-
-	-	-	-	-	-	-	-	-
2	-	-	-	-	-	-	-	-
-	-	-	-	3	-	-	-	-
-	-	2	-	-	-	-	-	-
-	-	-	-	-	-	-	-	-
-	-	-	-	-	-	-	-	-
-	2	-	-	-	-	-	-	-
-	-	-	-	-	-	-	-	-
1	2	-	-	-	-	-	-	-
-	1	-	-	-	-	-	-	-
-	-	-	-	-	-	-	-	-
-	-	-	-	-	-	-	-	-
1	-	-	-	-	-	-	-	-
-	-	-	-	-	-	-	-	-
-	-	-	-	-	-	-	-	-
-	-	-	-	-	-	-	-	-
-	-	-	-	-	4	-	-	-
1	-	-	-	-	-	-	-	-
-	-	-	-	-	-	-	-	-
-	-	-	-	-	-	-	-	-
-	-	-	-	-	-	-	-	-
-	-	-	-	-	-	-	-	-
-	-	-	-	-	-	-	-	-
-	-	-	-	-	-	-	-	-
-	-	-	-	-	-	-	1	-
-	-	-	-	-	29	-	-	-
2	-	-	-	-	-	-	-	-
-	-	-	-	-	-	-	-	-
-	-	-	-	-	-	-	-	-
-	-	-	-	-	-	-	-	-
-	-	-	-	-	-	-	-	-
-	-	-	-	-	-	-	-	-
-	-	-	-	-	-	-	-	-
-	-	-	-	-	-	-	-	-
-	-	-	-	-	-	-	-	-
-	-	-	-	-	1	1	-	1
-	-	-	-	-	1	1	-	1

	O2	O2	O2	O3	O2	O3	O3	O4
Location								
Associated with/from	und. sailcloth (rope+bone) 81A4416		(bone) 81A4184	textile	textile	with textile	next to cask 81A2251	in chest 80A1413
Feature Number	F19A					F19	F105	Pers 1
Context Number	10	21	17	17	10	17	10	30
Sample No.	81S0175/10.12	81S0039C	81S0276/1.6	81S0357C	81S1361	81S0372C	82S1243	80S0178
Volume (L. - unless otherwise indicated)		2		2.25 L		0.25		
Seeds per litre		6.0		57.3		c. 1244		
Unident - leaf (? marine)	-	-	-	-	-	-	-	-
Unident - leaf/ grass	-	-	1	-	-	-	-	-
Unident - plant fibre	-	-	-	-	-	-	-	1
Unident - plant fragment	-	1	-	1	-	-	-	-
Unident - root plate	-	-	-	-	-	-	-	-
Unident – seed	-	-	-	1	-	-	-	-
Unident - seed coat	-	-	-	-	-	-	-	-
Unident - seed coat/ calyx	-	-	-	-	-	-	-	-
Unident – stalk	-	-	-	-	-	-	-	-
Unident - stalk (? marine)	-	-	-	-	-	-	-	-
Unident – stem	-	-	-	-	-	3	-	-
Unident – thorn	-	-	-	-	-	-	-	-
Unident - thorny calyx	-	-	-	-	-	-	-	-
Unident – twigs	-	-	-	-	-	-	-	6
Unident - wood fragments	-	-	-	-	-	-	-	-
Total number of quantified identifications	3	12	7	129	1	c. 311	1	8

O4	O4	O6	O7	O8	O9	?O9 scour	O10	O10
oak table	mallet 81A3240		basket/ container	concreted pump +fish/ textile	concretion		in chest 81A2941	F16 = fishbone
F152			F167		F21		F109	F16
49	50	17	17	17	17	(6/8)	44	57
81S0463C	81S0468C	81S0512/02	81S1368	81S0446C	81S0247C	81S1097C	81S0430C	81S0554/9
	0.042 L	2 L	0.25 L		4		0.002 L	
	4047.6	31.5	8.0		10.0		2500.0	
-	-	-	-	-	-	-	-	-
-	-	-	-	-	-	-	-	-
-	-	-	-	2	-	-	3	2
-	-	-	-	-	-	-	-	-
1	1	-	-	-	-	-	-	-
-	-	-	-	-	4	-	-	1
-	7	-	-	-	-	-	-	-
-	-	-	-	-	-	-	-	-
1	-	-	-	-	1	-	-	-
-	1	-	-	-	-	-	-	-
-	-	-	-	1	-	-	-	-
-	-	-	-	-	-	-	-	-
-	-	-	-	-	-	-	-	-
26	170	63	2	7	40	1	5	24

692

Location	O10	O11	O11	O11	O11	O11
Associated with/from	concretion & sediment	Raeren stonew'e mug 81A5728	fishbone + mixed	fishbone	fishbone	fishbone
Feature Number			F16		F16	
Context Number	17	(17/25)	57	17	10	57
Sample No.	82S1027	81S1196/5	81S0107C	81S0285/4.3	81S0121/04.01	81S0579C
Volume (L. - unless otherwise indicated)						
Seeds per litre						
CEREALS						
Secale cereale L. - lemma	-	-	-	-	-	-
Secale cereale L. - rachis	-	-	-	-	-	-
Triticum aestivum L type - glume	-	-	-	-	-	-
Triticum aestivum L. type - rachis segment	-	-	-	-	-	-
Triticum sp. - free-threshing rachis node	-	-	-	-	-	-
Triticum sp. - grain	-	-	-	-	-	-
Cereal/ POACEAE - caryopsis	-	-	-	-	-	-
Cereal/ POACEAE - culm node	-	-	-	-	-	-
Cereal/ POACEAE – glume	-	-	-	-	-	-
Cereal/ POACEAE – indet. chaff	-	-	-	-	-	-
Cereal/ POACEAE – straw	-	-	-	-	-	-
cf. Cereal/ POACEAE - caryopsis	-	-	-	-	-	-
TREE/ SHRUB						
Quercus sp. (leaf)	-	-	-	-	-	-
cf. *Quercus* sp. (leaf)	-	-	-	-	-	-
Cytisus sp. - pods	-	-	-	-	-	-
cf. *Cytisus* - seeds	-	-	-	-	-	-
WEED/ WILD PLANTS						
Pteridium sp. – leaves	-	-	-	-	-	-
Pteridium sp. – stem	-	-	-	-	-	-
Ranunculus acris L./ *repens* L./ *bulbosus* L.	-	-	-	-	-	-
Ranunculus flammula L. type	-	-	-	-	-	-
cf. *Ranunculus flammula* L. type	-	-	-	-	-	-
Atriplex sp.	4	-	-	4	5	11
cf. *Atriplex* sp.	-	-	-	-	-	1
Stellaria media s.l.	-	-	-	-	-	-
Cerastium sp.	-	-	-	-	-	-
Polygonum aviculare L.	-	1	-	-	-	1
Rumex sp. - achene	-	-	-	-	-	-
Rumex sp. – tepal (perianth)	-	-	-	-	-	-
Rumex sp. - turbucle	-	-	-	-	-	-
cf. *Rumex* - turbucle	-	-	-	-	-	-
Viola sp.	-	-	-	-	-	1
BRASSICACEAE - unident	-	-	-	-	-	-
Agrimonia sp.	-	-	-	-	-	-
Vicia hirsuta L. Gray - pods	-	-	-	-	-	-
Medicago lupulina L.	-	-	-	-	-	-
Melilotus sp./ *Medicago* sp./ *Trifolium* sp.	-	-	-	-	-	-
cf. *Trifolium* sp. - flowers	-	-	-	-	-	-
cf. *Trifolium* sp. - type calyx	-	-	-	-	-	-
FABACEAE - ???? *Vicia sativa* L.	-	-	-	-	-	-
FABACEAE – unidentified pod	-	-	-	-	-	-
cf. FABACEAE – tendril	-	-	-	-	-	-
cf. FABACEAE - unidentified seed	-	-	-	-	-	-
cf. *Chaerophyllum aureum* L.	-	-	-	-	-	-
cf. *Atropa bella-donna* L.	-	-	-	-	-	-
Prunella vulgaris L.	-	-	-	-	-	1
Onopordum acanthium L.	-	-	-	-	-	-
Sonchus sp.	-	-	-	-	-	-
cf. *Achillea ptarmica* L./ *millefolium* L.	-	-	-	-	-	-
Anthemis cotula L.	-	-	-	-	-	-
ASTERACEAE - *Picris* type	-	-	-	-	-	-
cf. ASTERACEAE	1	-	-	-	-	-
Juncus sp.	-	-	-	-	-	-
cf. *Juncus* sp.	-	-	1	-	-	-
Carex sp. - 2 sided	-	-	-	-	-	-
Carex sp. - 3 sided	-	1	-	-	-	-
cf. *Carex* sp. - 3 sided	-	-	-	-	-	-
Lolium sp.	-	-	-	-	-	-
cf. *Lolium* sp.	-	-	-	-	-	-
Avena sp.	-	-	-	-	-	-
Avena sp. – spikelet fork (rachilla)	-	-	-	-	-	-
POACEAE - culm node	-	-	-	-	-	-
POACEAE - unident large grass caryopsis	-	-	-	-	-	-
POACEAE - unident small grass caryopsis	-	-	-	-	-	-
POACEAE - unidentified complete heads	-	-	-	-	-	-
POACEAE - unidentified incomplete head (florets counted)	-	-	-	-	-	-
POACEAE - grass stalks	-	-	-	-	-	-
cf. POACEAE - unident large grass caryopsis	-	-	-	-	-	-
cf. POACEAE - unident small grass caryopsis	-	-	-	-	-	-
UNIDENTIFIED PLANTS						
Unident – bark	-	-	-	-	-	-
Unident – Bryophyte	-	1	-	-	-	-
Unident – calyx	-	-	-	-	-	1
Unident – flowerhead	-	-	-	-	-	-
Unident - leaf	-	-	-	-	-	-
Unident - leaf (? marine)	-	-	-	-	-	-
Unident - leaf/ grass	-	-	-	-	-	-

O11	BB metal-sheet	H2 pitch/tar cask 81A1001	H6 ballast	H9 adhering to arrow in chest	H/O5 in cauldron 82A2340	H11 next s'board frames (fishbone)	O1 beneath gun carriage axil 81A8425	PS2	SS8 leather bucket 82A0095
17 81S1293	72 82S1078/1	F33 (10/25) 82S1297	18 80S0029	F201 17 82S1262C	F209 18 82S0109	F16 10 81S0091/4.3	10 81S0065/1 ?4 L	8 77S0006/2	60 82S1005
							4.3		
-	-	-	-	-	-	-	-	-	-
-	-	-	-	-	-	-	-	-	-
-	-	-	-	-	-	-	-	-	-
-	-	-	-	-	-	-	-	-	-
-	-	-	-	-	-	-	-	-	-
-	-	-	-	-	-	-	2	-	-
-	-	-	-	-	-	-	-	-	-
-	-	-	-	-	-	-	-	-	-
-	-	-	-	-	-	-	-	-	-
-	-	-	-	-	-	-	-	-	-
-	-	-	-	-	-	-	-	-	-
1	1	-	1	-	-	-	-	-	-
-	-	-	-	-	-	-	-	1	1
-	-	-	-	-	-	-	2	-	-
-	-	-	-	-	-	-	4	-	-
-	-	-	-	-	-	-	-	-	-
-	-	-	-	-	-	-	-	-	-
-	-	-	-	-	1	-	-	-	-
-	-	-	-	-	-	-	-	-	-
-	-	-	-	-	-	-	-	-	-
-	-	-	-	-	-	2	-	-	-
-	-	-	-	-	-	-	-	-	-
-	-	-	-	-	-	-	-	-	-
-	-	-	-	-	-	-	-	-	-
-	-	-	-	-	-	-	1	-	-
-	-	-	-	-	-	-	4	-	-
-	-	-	-	-	-	-	1	-	-
-	-	-	-	-	-	-	-	-	-
-	-	-	-	-	-	-	-	-	-
-	-	-	-	-	-	-	-	-	-
-	-	-	-	-	-	-	-	-	-
-	-	-	-	-	-	-	-	-	-
-	-	-	-	-	-	-	-	-	-
-	-	-	-	-	-	-	-	-	-
-	-	-	-	-	-	-	1	-	-
-	-	-	-	-	-	-	-	-	-
-	-	-	-	-	-	-	-	-	-
-	-	-	-	-	-	-	-	-	-
-	-	-	-	-	-	-	-	-	-
-	-	-	-	-	-	-	-	-	-
-	-	-	-	-	-	-	-	-	-
-	-	-	-	-	-	-	-	-	-
-	-	-	-	-	-	-	-	-	-
-	-	-	-	-	-	-	-	-	-
-	-	-	-	-	-	-	-	-	-
-	-	-	-	-	-	-	-	-	-
-	-	-	-	-	-	-	-	-	-
-	-	-	-	-	-	-	-	-	-
-	-	-	-	-	-	-	-	-	-
-	-	-	-	-	-	-	-	-	-
-	-	-	-	-	-	-	-	-	-
-	-	-	-	-	-	-	-	-	-
-	-	-	-	-	-	-	-	-	-
-	-	-	-	-	-	-	-	-	-
-	-	-	-	-	-	-	-	-	-
-	-	-	-	-	-	-	-	-	-
-	-	-	-	-	-	1	1	-	-
-	-	-	-	-	-	-	-	-	-
-	-	1	-	3	-	-	-	-	-
-	-	-	-	-	-	-	-	-	-
-	-	-	-	-	-	-	-	-	-

Location Associated with/from	O10 concret- ion & sediment	O11 Raeren stonew'e mug 81A5728	O11 fishbone + mixed	O11 fishbone	O11 fishbone	O11 fishbone
Feature Number			F16		F16	
Context Number	17	(17/25)	57	17	10	57
Sample No.	82S1027	81S1196/5	81S0107C	81S0285/4.3	81S0121/04.01	81S0579C
Volume (L. - unless otherwise indicated)						
Seeds per litre						
Unident - plant fibre	-	-	-	-	-	-
Unident - plant fragment	-	2	9	-	-	-
Unident – possible flower	-	-	-	-	-	-
Unident - root plate	-	-	-	-	-	-
Unident – seed	-	1	-	-	-	-
Unident - seed coat	-	-	-	-	-	-
Unident - seed coat/ calyx	-	-	-	-	-	-
Unident – stalk	-	-	-	-	-	-
Unident - stalk (? marine)	-	-	5	-	-	-
Unident – stem	-	-	-	-	-	-
Unident – thorn	-	-	-	-	-	-
Unident – thorny calyx	-	-	-	-	-	-
Unident – twigs	-	-	-	-	-	-
Unident - wood fragments	-	-	57	-	-	-
Total number of quantified identifications	5	6	72	4	5	16

O11	BB metal-sheet	H2 pitch/tar cask 81A1001	H6 ballast	H9 adhering to arrow in chest	H/O5 in cauldron 82A2340	H11 next s'board frames (fishbone)	O1 beneath gun carriage axil 81A8425	PS2	SS8 leather bucket 82A0095
17 81S1293	72 82S1078/1	F33 (10/25) 82S1297	18 80S0029	F201 17 82S1262C	F209 18 82S0109	F16 10 81S0091/4.3	10 81S0065/1 ?4 L	8 77S0006/2	60 82S1005
							4.3		
-	-	-	-	-	-	-	-	-	-
-	-	-	-	-	-	-	-	-	-
-	-	-	-	-	-	-	-	-	-
-	-	-	-	-	-	-	-	-	-
-	-	-	-	-	-	-	1	-	-
-	-	-	-	-	-	-	-	-	-
-	-	-	-	-	-	-	-	-	-
-	-	-	-	-	-	-	-	-	-
-	-	-	-	-	-	-	-	-	-
1	1	1	1	3	1	3	17	1	1

Appendix 3.6 Plant remains recorded prior to 2002, mentioned in text

Location	M7 Barber-surgeon's chest in cabin 80A1530	H11 Basket 81A4036	M9 With jerkin (cloth) 81A4708	O2 Sackcloth 81A1233	O10 Gunshield	O10 In staved container 81A2959	O11	O11 Fish bones	H6 Basket (fruit) 80A1704
Associated with/from Feature Number	BB/SG	F16				F135		F16	
Context Number		10	38						17
Sample No.	80S0109/1	81S0099/4/1	81S0573 and 81S0573/3/2	81S1302/3	81S0581/8	81S0416/2	81S0349/5 or 81S0349/6	81S1289/4/1	80S244/1
CEREALS									
Fagopyrum esculentum Moench seed	-	-	-	-	-	-	1	-	-
CLOTHWORKING PLANTS									
Dipsacus sativus L.- bract	-	-	+++	-	-	-	-	-	-
FLAVOURINGS									
Piper nigrum L.	c. 15-20	-	-	-	-	-	-	-	3
FRUIT									
Prunus domestica s.l.	-	-	-	-	-	-	-	-	30-56
Vitis vinifera L. – skins -	-	-	-	-	-	2 skins	-	-	-
Malus sylvestris L. pip	-	1	-	-	-	-	-	-	-
TREE/ SHRUB									
Cytisus scoparius pods	-	-	-	-	-	-	-	+	-
WEED/ WILD PLANTS									
Linum usitatissimum L. – capsules	-	-	-	-	2	-	-	-	-
Calendula officinalis L	-	-	-	-	-	-	-	+	-
Agrimonia eupatoria – burrs	-	-	-	≥ 3	-	-	-	-	-
Total number of quantified identifications									

Bibliography

Adams, I.H. & Fortune, G. (eds), 1980. *Alexander Lindsay, a Rutter of the Scottish Seas Circa 1540*. Greenwich: National Maritime Museum Maritime Monograph and Report 44

Adams, J. & Harris, E., 1997. Sea Venture. In J. Delgado (ed.), *Encyclopaedia of Underwater and Maritime Archaeology*, 365–6. London: British Museum Press

Adams, J. & Rule, N., 1990. DSM – an evaluation of a three-dimensional method of survey on underwater sites. In R. Reinders (ed.), *Sheeparchaeologie: prioriteiten en lopend onderzoek. Proceedings of the Glavimans Symposia 1986 and 1988*. Rijksdienst Ijsselmeerspolders, Flevobericht 322

Admiralty Manual of Seamanship, 1864. London: HMSO

Alburger. M.A., 2000. 'The fiddle in fyst': bowed stringed instruments from the *Mary Rose*. *Galpin Society Journal* 53, 12–24

Alcega, J., de., 1589. *Tailors Pattern Book* (trans. J. Pain & C. Bainton (1979). Bedford: Carlton

Allan, J.P., 1983. Some post-medieval documentary evidence for the trade in ceramics. In P. Davey & R. Hodges (eds) 1983, *Ceramics and Trade*, 37–45. Sheffield: University of Sheffield

Allan, J.P., 1984. *Medieval and Post-Medieval Finds from Exeter 1971–1980*. Exeter: Exeter Archaeological Report 3

Anderson, R. and Anderson, R.C., 1926. *The Sailing Ship. Six Thousand Years of History*. New York: Bonanza (1963 reprint)

Anderson, S., Bankier, A.T., Barrell, B.G., Bruijn, M.H. de, Coulson, A.R., Drouin, J., Eperon, I.C., Nierlich, D.P., Roe, B.A., Sanger, F., Schreier, P.H., Smith, A.J.H., Staden, R. & Young, I.G., 1981. Sequence and organization of the human mitochondrial genome. *Nature* 290, 457–65

Anon., 1540. *Ordonnances sur le Faict des Monnoyes, Estat & Regle des Officiers d'icelles*. Paris

Anon., 1633. *Ordonnantie des Coninghs op het general regelement van sijne Munte*. Antwerp

Anon., 1731. *Regulations and Instructions Relating to his Majesty's Service at Sea*

Arbeau, T., 1588. *Orchésographie*. Langres (facsimile edition, Geneva: Minkoff 1972)

Archibald, E.H.H., 1987. *The Fighting Ship of the Royal Navy AD 897–1984*. New York: Military Press

Archibald, M.M. (ed.), 1975. Medieval and modern coin hoards: British and Irish. *Coin Hoards* 1, 87–108

Archibald, M.M., 1983. Coinage in Andrew Halyburton's Ledger. In C.N.L. Brooke, I. Stewart, J.G. Pollard & T.R. Volk (eds), *Studies in Numismatic Method Presented to Philip Grierson*, 263–301. Cambridge: University Press

Armitage, P.L., 1989. Ship rats, salted meat and tortoises: selected aspects of maritime life in the 'Great Age of Sail' (1500–1800s). *Bermuda Journal of Archaeology and Maritime History* 1, 143–59

Armitage, P.L., 2002. Study of the animal bones. In E. Cummings, *The Wreck of the English East Indiaman Earl of Abergavenny*. London: MIBEC Enterprises, CD Rom

Arnold, J., 1985. *Patterns of Fashion, the Cut and the Construction of Clothes for Men and Women* c. *1560–1620*. London: Routledge

Ashelford, J., 1996. *The Art of Dress, Clothes and Society*. London: Abrams

Aston, M., 1993. *The King's Bedpost. Reformation and Iconography in a Tudor Group Portrait*. Cambridge Mass.: University Press

Austin, J.J., Ross, A.J., Smith, A.B., Fortey, R.A. & Thomas, R.H., 1997. Problems of reproducibility – does geologically ancient DNA survive in amber-preserved insects? *Proceedings of the Royal Society of London, Series B, Biological Sciences* 264, 467–74

Backhouse, J., 1989. *The Luttrell Psalter*. London: British Library

Baines, A., 1950. Fifteenth-century instruments in Tinctoris's *De Inventione et Usu Musicae*. *Galpin Society Journal* 3, 19–26

Baker, T.H., 1883. *Records of the Seasons, Prices of agriculture Produce and Phenomena observed in the British Isles*. London, Simpkin Marshall and Co.

Banester, J., 1588. *A Compendious Chyrugerie*. London

Barbour, P.L. (ed.), 1986. *The Complete Works of Captain John Smith, vol. III*. Chapel Hill, North Carolina: University of North Carolina Press

Barfoot, A., 1959. *Discovering Costume*. London: University Press

Barnard, F.P., 1916. *The Casting Counter and the Gaming Board*. Oxford

Barnet, P., 1997. *Images in Ivory. Precious Objects of the Gothic Age*. Detroit: Institute of Arts/Princeton University Press

Barrett, J. & Yonge, C.M., 1958. *Collins Pocket Guide to the Sea Shore*. London: Collins (1985 reprint)

Barrett J., Nicholson R. & Cerón-Cerrasco, R., 1999. Archaeo-ichthyological evidence for long-term socio-economic trends in northern Scotland: 3500 BC to AD 1500. *Journal of Archaeological Science* 26, 353–88

Bartels, M., Haan, A. de, Jansen, H. & Verhelst, E., 1995. *Archeologisch Onderzoek aan de Achterweg te Teil*. Teil: Archeologie in Teil 1

Bartlett, C. & Embleton, G., 1995. *English Longbowman 1330–1515*. London: Osprey Military Warrior Series 11

Barton, K.J., 1979. *Medieval Sussex Pottery*. London: Phillimore

Basketmaker's Association 1956. *The National List of Basic Wage Rates in the Basketry Industry 1956: list of basket specifications*. Basketmaker's Association (1989 reprint)

Bass, W. M., 1971. *Human Osteology: a laboratory and field guide to the human skeleton*. Columbia, Missouri (2nd edn)

Bauner, L., 1992. The fashionable sex 1100–1600 and male clothing. *History Today* 42, 37–44

Beck, C.W., Stewart, D.R. & Stout, E.C., 1994. Appendix D. Analysis of naval stores from the Late-Roman ship. *Journal of Roman Archaeology*, Supplementary series 13, 109–21

Begg, P.R., 1954. Stone Age Man's dentition. *American Journal of Orthodonics and Dentofacial Orthopedics* 40, 298–312, 373–83, 462–75, 517–31

Beigbeder, O., 1965. *Ivory: pleasures and treasures*. London: Weidenfield & Nicholson

Bell, L.S., 1995. *Post Mortem Microstructural Change to the Skeleton*. University College, London: unpublished. PhD Thesis

Bell, L.S., Boyde, A. & Jones, S.J., 1991. Diagenetic alteration to teeth *in situ* by backscattered electron imaging. *Scanning* 13, 173–83

Bell. R.C., 1980. *Discovering Old Board Games*. Aylesbury: Shire

Bennett, K.D., Whittington, G. and Edwards, K.J., 1994. Recent plant nomenclatural changes and pollen morphology in the British Isles. *Quaternary Newsletter* 73, 1–6

Beresford, M & Hurst, J., 1990. *Wharram Percy. Deserted Medieval Village*. New Haven & London: Yale University Press

Berg van den, W.S. (ed.), 1917. *Antidotarium Nicolai 1530* (facsimile edition, Leiden)

Besly, E.M., 1997. Coinage from post-medieval wrecks. In Redknap (ed.) 1997, 137–41

Bettley, T.S., 1985/6. *Analysis of Sediments from the Mary Rose*. University of Leicester: unpublished undergraduate project

Beuningen, H.J.E., van, Koldeweij, A.M. & Kicken, D., 2001. *Heilig en Profaan 2. 1200 Laatmiddeleeuwe Insignes uit Openbare en Particuliere Collecties*. Rotterdam: Rotterdam Papers 12

Biddle, M., 1990. *Artefacts from Medieval Winchester: object and economy in medieval Winchester*. Winchester: Winchester Studies 7

Biggs, N., 1996. *Verification Marks on Weights, the Administrative Background*. Llanfyllin

Biggs, N. & Withers, P., 2000. *Lead Weights, the David Rogers Collection*. Llanfyllin

Bingeman, J., 1985. Interim report on artefacts recovered from *Invincible* (1758) between 1978 and 1984. *International Journal of Nautical Archaeology* 14(3) 191–210

Blackmore, H.L., 1976. *The Armories of the Tower of London*. London: HMSO

Blair J. & Blair C, 1991. Copper alloys. In J. Blair & N. Ramsay (eds), *English Medieval Industries*, 81–106. London: Hambledon

Bonfield, K., 1997. *The Analysis and Interpretation of Lipid Residues Associated with Prehistoric Pottery: Pitfalls and Potentials*. Bradford University: unpublished PhD thesis

Bosmans, W., 1991. *Eenhandsfluit en Trom in de Lage Landen*. Peer: Alamire

Bourdillon, J., 1978. The animal bone. In J.S.F. Walker, Excavations in medieval tenements on the Quilters' Vault in Southampton, *Proceedings of the Hampshire Field Club and Archaeological Society* 35, 207–12

Bourdillon, J., 1980. Town life and animal husbandry in the Southampton area, as suggested by the excavated bones. *Proceedings of the Hampshire Field Club and Archaeological Society* 36, 181–91

Bourdillon, J., 1983. *Animal Bones in an Urban Environment, with Specific Reference to the Faunal Remains from Saxon Southampton*. University of Southampton: unpublished MPhil Thesis

Bourdillon, J., 1988. Countryside and town: the animal resources of Saxon Southampton. In D. Hooke (ed.), *Anglo-Saxon Settlements*, 177–88. Oxford: Blackwell

Bourne, W., 1574. *A Regiment for the Sea*. Cambridge (reprint 1963, ed. E.G.R. Taylor)

Boyd, P., 1982. *Interim Report on Aspects of the Sedimentary History of the Wreck Site of the* Mary Rose. Portsmouth: Mary Rose Trust, unpublished archive report

Boyde, A., Howell, P.G.T., Bromage, T.G., Elliot, J.C., Riggs, C.M., Bell, L.S., Kneissell, M., Reid, S.A., Jayasinghe, J.A.P. & Jones, S.J., 1992. Application of mineral quantification of bone by histogram analysis of back scattered electron imaging. In H. Slavkin & P. Proce (eds), *Chemistry and Biology of Mineralized Tissues*, 47–61. London: Excerpta Medica

Boylston, A., Novak, S., Sutherland, T., Holst, M. & Coughlan, J., 1997. Burials from the Battle of Towton. *Royal Armouries Yearbook* 2, 36–9

Braat, J., Gawrovski, J.H.G., Kist, J.B., Put, A.E.D.M. van de & Sigmond, J.P. (eds) 1988. *Behouden uit het Behouden Huys: catalogus van de voorwerpen van de Barentsexpeditie (1596), gevonden op Nova Zembla*, Amsterdam: De Bataafsche Leeuw

Braddock, N., nd. *Victualling rates for Henry the Eighth's Fleet*. Portsmouth: The Mary Rose Project Paper 1

Bradfield, N., 1958. *Historical Costumes of England from the Eleventh to Twentieth Century*. London: George Harrrap

Bradley, C., n.d.. *Preliminary analysis of the staved container remains recovered from the 1981 underwater excavations at Red Bay*. Ottawa: Parks Canada Microfiche Report 260

Brears, P., 1985. *Food and Cooking in 16th Century Britain*. London: Historic Buildings & Monuments Commission for England

Brenchley, W.E., 1919. The uses of weeds and wild plants. *Science Programs* 15(53), 128–9

Bridge, M.C. & Dobbs, C.T.C., 1996. Tree-ring studies on the Tudor warship Mary Rose. In J.S. Dean, D.M. Meko &

T.W. Swetnam (eds), *Tree Rings, Environment and Humanity*, 491-6, *Radiocarbon* Special Issue

Brinkhuizen D.C., 1994. Some notes on fish remains from the late 16th century merchant vessel *Scheurrak SO1*. In W. van Neer (ed.), Fish exploitation in the past. *Proceedings of the 7th Meeting of the ICAZ Fish Remains Working Group*, 197–205. *Annales du Musée Royal de l'Afrique Centrale* 274

British Museum, 1924. *A Guide to the Medieval Antiquities and Objects of Later Date in the Department of British and Medieval Antiquities*. London: British Museum Press

Britton, F., 1987. *London Delftware*. London: Horne

Broadwater, J., 1995. In the shadow of wooden walls: naval transports during the American War of Independence. In M. Bound (ed.), *The Archaeology of Ships of War* 58–63. London: Anthony Nelson

Brown, D.H., 1986. The pottery. In J. Oxley, *Excavations at Southampton Castle*, 85–108. Southampton: Southampton Archaeology Monograph 3

Brown, D.H., 1998. Documentary sources as evidence for the exchange and consumption of pottery in 15th century Southampton. *Acta das 2.as Jornadas de Ceramica Medieval e Pos-Medieval – Metodos e Resultados para o sue Estudo*, 429–38

Brown, D.H, 2002. *Pottery in Medieval Southampton c. 1066–1510*. York: Southampton Archaeology Monograph 8, Council for British Archaeology Research Report 133

Brown, D.H. & Thomson, R.G., 1996. Later medieval pottery of the Beauvaisis found in Southampton. *Groupe de Recherches et d'Etudes de la Ceramique du Beauvaisis Bulletin* 18, 37–60

Brown, W.R., 1991. *The Stuart Legacy, English Art 1603–1714*. Birmingham Alabama: Birmingham Museum of Art

Brownsword, R. and Pitt, E.E.H., 1990. An analytical study of pewterware from the *Mary Rose*. *Journal of the Pewter Society* 7(4), 109–25

Brunschweig, H., 1525. *The Noble Experience of the Warke of Surgerie*

Brunschweig, J., 1497. *Book of Surgery*

Buckland, K., 1979. The Monmouth Cap. *Costume* 13, 23–37

Buckland, K., 2001–2. Daily molested, vexed and troubled, the true making of woollen cloth. *Text* 29, 20–4

Burden, B., 1983. *The Hold and its Contents*. Portsmouth: Mary Rose Trust internal report

Burford E.J., 2001. *The Bishop's Brothels*. London: Trafalgar (2nd edn)

Burwash, D., 1969. *English Merchant Shipping 1460–1540*. Newton Abbot: David & Charles

Butcher, M., 1995. *Willow Work*. Canterbury: Mickle Print

Butler, R. & Green, C., 2003. *Bronze Cooking Vessels and their Founders 1350–1830*. Honiton

Byrne, M. St Clare, 1981. *The Lisle Letters*. Chicago: University Press

Calendar of Letter Books Preserved Among the Archives of the Corporation of the City of London 1275–1498 (1899–1912)

Calicó, F., Calicó, X. & Trigo, J., 1988. *Monedas Españolas desde Fernando e Isabel a Juan Carlos I, Años: 1474 a 1988*. Barcelona (7th edn)

Cann, R.L., Stoneking, M. & Wilson, A.C., 1987. Mitochondrial DNA and human evolution. *Nature* 325, 31–6

Caple, C., 1985. The pins and wire from site S. In Cunningham, C.S. & Drury, P.J., *Post-medieval Sites and their Pottery*, 47–50. London: Council for British Archaeology Research Report 54

Cappers, R.J.T., Mook-Kamps, E., Bottema, S., Zanten, B.O. van & Vlierman, K., 1998. The analayis of caulking material in the study of shipbuilding technology. *Palaeohistoria* 39/40, 577–90

Carlin, M., 1996. *Medieval Southwark*. London: Hambledon Press

Carruthers, W.J. 1991a. The charred plant remains. In P.A. Harding, L. Mepham & R.J.C Smith, The excavations of the 12th–13th century deposits at Howard's Lane, Wareham. *Proceedings of the Dorset Natural History & Archaeology Society* 117, 86–90

Carruthers, W.J. 1991b. Carbonised plant remains. In P.W. Cox & C M Hearne, *Redeemed from the Heath: the archaeology of the Wytch Farm Oilfield (1987–90)*, 203–9 Tables 71–82 mf. E8-F13. Dorchester: Dorset Natural History & Archaeological Society Monograph 9

Cavalli-Sforza, L.L., Menozzi, P. & Piazza, A., 1994. *The History and Geography of Human Genes*. Princeton: University Press

Chacko, G.K. & Perkins, E.G., 1965. Anatomical variation in fatty acid composition and triglyceride distribution in animal depot fat. *Journal of the American Oil Chemists Society* 42, 1121–4

Champness, R., 1966. *The Worshipfull Company of Turners of London*. London: Lindley Jones & Brother

Charleston, R.J., 1972. The vessel glass from Rosedale and Hutton. In Crossley & Aberg 1972, 128–50

Charleston, R.J., 1984. The glass. In Allan 1984, 258–78

Charters, S., Evershed, R.P., Blinkhorn, P.W, & Denham, V., 1995. Evidence for the mixing of fats and waxes in archaeological contexts. *Archaeometry* 37(1), 113–27

Chinnery, V., 1979. *Oak Furniture – The British Tradition*. Woodbridge: Baron Publishing

Christie's, 1988, *Gold and Silver of the* Atocha *and* Santa Margarita. *Sale catalogue*, 14–15 June 1988. New York: Christie's

Clifford, H.M., 2004. *A Treasured Inheritance; 600 Years of Oxford College Silver*. Oxford: Ashmolean Museum

Clifton, G., 1995. *Directory of British Scientific Instrument Makers 1550–1851*. London: Zwemmer

Clutton-Brock, J., 1981. *Domesticated Animals from Early Times*. London: British Museum Natural History/ Heinemann

Coad J.G. & Streeten, A.D.F., 1982. Excavations at Castle Acre Castle, Norfolk, 1972–77. Country House and Castle of the Norman Earls of Surrey. *Archaeological Journal* 139, 138–301

Cobb, H.S. (ed.), 1961. *The Local Port Book of Southampton 1439–40*. Southampton: University Press

Cockburn, W., 1896. *An Account of the Nature, Causes, Symptoms and Cure of the Distempers that are Incident to Seafaring People*. London

Cogne, J. 1974. Le Massif Armoricain. In J. Debelmas, J (ed.), *Geologie de la France* 1, 105–61

Collinson, R., 1867. *The Three Voyages of Martin Frobisher* (facsimile, New York)

Committee on the Medical Aspects of Food Policy (COMA), 1991. *Dietary Reference Values for Food, Energy and Nutrients for the UK*. Norwich: HMSO

Connor, R.D., 1987. *The Weights and Measures of England*. London: HMSO

Connor, S., 1991. Pig brings home the bacon on DNA. *Independent on Sunday* 24 March

Coppen, J.J.W., Greenhalgh, P. and Smith, A.E., 1984. *Gum Naval Stores: an industrial profile of turpentine and rosin production from pine resin*. Tropical Development and Industrial Research Inst. ODA

Coo, J. de 1969. *Museum Mayer van den Bergh. Catalogus 2. Beeldhouwkunst, Plaketten, Antiek*. Antwerp

Cooper, A., Lalueza-Fox, C., Anderson, S., Rambaut, A., Austin, J. & Ward, R., 2001. Complete mitochondrial genome sequences of two extinct moas clarify ratite evolution. *Nature* 409, 704–7

Cooper, A. & Poinar, H.N., 2000. Ancient DNA: do it right or not at all. *Science* 289, 1139

Corach, D., Sala, A., Penacino, G., Iannucci, N., Bernardi, P., Doretti, M., Fondebrider, L., Ginarte, A., Inchaurregui, A., Somigliana, C., Turner, S. & Hagelberg, E., 1997. Additional approaches to DNA typing of skeletal remains: the search for 'missing' persons killed during the last dictatorship in Argentina. *Electrophoresis* 18, 1608–12

Corbett, G.B. & Harris S. (eds), 1991. *The Handbook of British Mammals*. Oxford: Blackwell Scientific (3rd edn)

Cornwall, J., 1954. Farming in Sussex 1560–1640. *Sussex Archaeological Collections* 92, 48–92

Corran, H.S., 1975. *A History of Brewing*. Newton Abbot & London: David & Charles

Cotterell, H.H., 1929. *Old Pewter: its makers and marks*. London: Batsford

Cotton, B., 1990. *The English Regional Chair*. Antiques Collectors Club

Cowgill, J., Neergaard, M. de & Griffiths, N., 1987. *Knives and Scabbards*. London: Medieval Finds from Excavations in London 1

Cowham, M., 2004. *A Dial in Your Poke: a book of portable sundials*. Cambridge: privately printed

Cox, M.L., 1911. Inventory of the Arundel Collection. *Burlington* 19, 323–25

Coy, J., 1989. The provision of fowls and fish for towns. In D. Serjeantson & T. Waldron (eds), *Diet and Crafts in Towns*, 25–40. Oxford: British Archaeological Report 199

Coy, J.P., 1995. The animal bones. In P.J. Fasham & G. Keevil, *Brighton Hill South (Hatch Warren)*, 132–9. Salisbury: Wessex Archaeology Report 7

Coy J.P., 1996. Medieval records versus excavation results – examples from southern England. *Archaeofauna* 5, 55–63

Coy, J. & Maltby, M., 1987. Archaeozoology in Wessex. In H.C.M.Keeley (ed.), *Environmental Archaeology: a regional review vol. 2*, 204–51. London: Historic Buildings & Monuments Commission for England Occasional Paper 1

Crane, E., 1983. *The Archaeology of Beekeeping*. London: Duckworth

Credit Communal Belgique, 1984. *Catalogue Tresors sur Table – Exposition du Credit Communal Belgique*. Brussels: Crédit Communal

Crédit Communal, 1985. *Trésors de l'Armada, Catalogue of Exhibition organised by Ulster Museum at Brussels, 30.10.85–26.1.86*. Brussels: Crédit Communal

Croft, R.A., 1987. *Graffiti Gaming Boards*. Finds Research Group 700–1700. Datasheet 6

Crossley, D.W. & Aberg, F.A., 1972. Sixteenth century glass-making in Yorkshire at furnaces in Hutton and Rosedale, North Riding 1968–1971, *Post-Medieval Archaeology* 6, 107–59

Crowfoot, E., Pritchard, F. & Staniland, K., 1992. *Textiles and Clothing c. 1150–c. 1450*. Medieval Finds from Excavations in London 4 (revised edn)

Crummy, N., 1988. *The Post-Roman Small finds from Excavations in Colchester 1971–85*. Colchester: Colchester Archaeological Report 5

Culley M., 1985 *The 'Shell Layer' in the* Mary Rose. Portsmouth: Mary Rose Trust, unpublished report

Cunnington, P. & Lucus, C., 1967. *Occupational Costume in England*. London: Adam Charles Black. W.J. Mackay

Cunnington, W.C., Cunnington, P. & Beard, C., 1960. *A Dictionary of English Costume 900–1900*. London: Adam & Charles

Cutting, C.L., 1955. *Fish Saving. A History of Fish Processing from Ancient to Modern Times*. London: Hill

Dahlig, E., 1994. A sixteenth-century Polish fiddle from Plock. *Galpin Society Journal* 27, 111–22

Dalton, O.M., 1912. *Catalogue of the Finger Rings. Early Christian, Byzantine, Teutonic, Medieval and Later*. London: British Museum Press

Dasent, J.R. (ed.), 1890. *Acts of the Privy Council of King Henry VIII*, New Series Vol 1, A.D. 1542–1547. London: HMSO

Dassow, M., 1984. *A Preliminary Investigation of Sedimentary Characteristics Within the* Mary Rose *and their Relation to the Structural Degradation of the Ship*. Portsmouth Polytechnic: unpublished Post-gradutate project

Davenport, T.G. & Burns, R., 1995. A sixteenth century wreck off the Island of Alderney. In M. Bound (ed.), *The Archaeology of Ships of War*. Oxford: International Maritime Archaeology Series 1

Davidson, A., 1979. *North Atlantic Seafood*. London: Macmillan

Davies, C.S.L., 1963a. Les rations alimentaires de l'armée et de la marine anglaises au XVIe siècle. *Annales (Economies, Societes, Civilisations)* 18, 139–41

Davies, C.S.L., 1963b. *Supply Services of English Armed Forces 1509–1550*. University of Oxford: unpublished Ph.D. Thesis

700

Davies, C.S.L., 1964. Provisions for the armies 1509–1560, a study in the effectiveness of early Tudor government. *Economic History Review* 17, 234–48

Davies, C.S.L., 1965. The administration of the Royal Navy under Henry VIII: the origins of the navy board. *English Historical Review* 80, 268–88

Davies, C.S.L., 1970. Les rations alimentaires de l'armee et de la marine anglaises au XVIe siecle. In Hémardinquer J-J. (ed.), *Pour une Histoire de l'Alimentation*, 93–5. Paris: Cahiers des Annales

Davis, S., 1989. *Sixteenth century footwear from Red Bay.* Manuscript on file Archaeological Division, Parks Service, Environment Canada, Ottawa, December 1989

Davis, S., 1991. Textiles, fibers and mats recovered from the *San Juan. Textile Conservation Newsletter* 2, 6–10

Davis, S., 1997. Piecing together the past: footwear and other artefacts from the wreck of a 16th-century Spanish Basque galleon. In Redknap (ed.) 1997, 110–20

Dean, M., Ferrari, B., Oxley, I., Redknap, M. & Watson, K., 1995. *Archaeology Underwater; the NAS Guide to Principles and Practice.* Portsmouth: Nautical Archaeological Society

Delgado, J.P. (ed.), 1997. *The British Museum Encyclopaedia of Underwater and Marine Archaeology.* London: British Museum Press

Delgado, J.P., 2001. *Lost Warships: an archaeological tour of war at sea.* London: Conway Maritime

DeSalle, R. & Grimaldi, D., 1994. Very old DNA. *Current Opinions in Genetics and Development* 4, 810–15

Derham, B., 2002. *Provision for Injury and Illness.* Portsmouth: Mary Rose Trust unpublished archive report

Dexel ,W., 1943. *Holzgerat und Holzform.* Berlin

Dickson, C. & Dickson, J.H. 2000. *Plants and People in Ancient Scotland.* Stroud: Tempus

Dieudonné, A., 1925. *Manuel des Poids Monétaires.* Paris

Dimbleby, G.W., 1967. *Plants and Archaeology.* London: John Baker

Dimbleby, G.W., 1985. *The Palynology of Archaeological Sites.* London: Academic Press

Dionis, P., 1710. *Course of Chirurgical Operations*

Dixon, P., 1994. *The Reading Lathe.* Newport: Cross

Dobbs, C.T.C. & Price, R.A., 1991. The *Kennermerland* site, an interim report. The sixth and seventh seasons 1984 & 1987, the identification of five golf clubs. *International Journal of Nautical Archaeology* 20(2), 111–22

Dobson J. & Milnes Walker R., 1979. *Barbers & Barbers Surgeons of London.* Oxford: Blackwell Scientific

Dodd, P. 1983. Horticultural treasures from the Mary Rose. *The Garden* 108(5), 203–5

Dodd, P., 1986. *The Identification of Fruitstones Recovered from the* Mary Rose. Portsmouth: Mary Rose Trust, unpublished manuscript

Dooren de Jong, L.E. den, 1961. On the formation of adipocere from fats. *Antonie van Lewenhoek Journal of Microbiology and Serology* 27, 337–61

Drey, R.E.A., 1978. *Apothecary Jars.* London: Faber & Faber

Driesch, A. von den, 1976. *A Guide to the Measurement of Animal Bones from Archaeological Sites.* Harvard University: Peabody Museum Bulletin 1

Drummond, J.C. & Wilbraham, A., 1939. *The Englishman's Food.* London: Jonathan Cape

Dubbe, B., 1998. British contacts with the pewterer's trade in the Low Countries, *De Tinkoerier* 6(2), 8–12

Duff, E. Gordon, 1905. *Century of the British Book Trade.* London: Bibliographical Society

Duffy, E., 1992. *The Stripping of the Altars. Traditional Religion in England 1400–1580.* New Haven & London: Yale University Press

Duhamel du Monceau, H-L., 1772. *Traité Général des Pesches.* Paris

Duplessy, J., 1988. *Les Monnaies Françaises Royales de Hugues Capet à Louis XVI (987–1793), Tome I: Hugues Capet–Louis XII.* Paris-Maastricht

Duplessy, J., 1989. *Les Monnaies Françaises Royales de Hugues Capet à Louis XVI (987–1793), Tome II: François 1er–Louis XVI.* Paris-Maastricht

D'Urfey., T., 1719–20. *Wit and Mirth or Pills to Purge Melancholy – An Odd Collection of Songs*

Dyer, G.P., 1997. Thomas Graham's copper survey of 1857. *British Numismatic Journal* 66, 60–6

Easton, T., 1999. 'Spiritual middens' and 'scribed and painted symbols'. In Olver, P. (ed.) *The Encyclopaedia of Vernacula Architecture of the World.* Cambridge: University Press

Edlin, H.L. 1949. *Woodland Crafts in Britan.* London: Batsford

Egan, G., 1991. Beads, in Egan & Pritchard 1991, 305–17

Egan, G., 1994. *Lead Cloth Seals and Related Items in the British Museum.* London: British Museum Occasional Paper 93

Egan, G., 1997a. Dice, *Finds Research Group* 700–1700 Datasheet 23

Egan, G., 1997b. Children's pastimes in past time – medieval toys found in the British Isles (with observations on some excavated dice. In G. de Boe & F. Verhaeghe (eds), *Material Culture in Medieval Europe*, 413–21. Zellick: Papers of the 'Medieval Europe Brugge 1997' 413–21

Egan, G., 1998. *The Medieval Household, Medieval finds from excavations in London.* London: Museum of London

Egan, G., 2005. *Material Culture in London in an Age of Transition: Tudor and Stuart period finds c. 1450–1700 from Excavations at Riverside Sites in Southwark.* London: Museum of London Archaeological Service Monograph 19

Egan, G. & Pritchard , F., 1991. *Dress Accessories c. 1150–c. 1450.* London: Medieval Finds from Excavations in London

Elmhirst, T., 1959. *English Merchants' Marks.* London: Harleian Society (CD facsimile, CD Archive Books Project)

Enghoff, I.B., 1983. Size distribution of cod (*Gadus morhua* L.) and whiting (*Merlangius merlangus* L.) (Pisces Gadidae) from a mesolithic settlement at Vedbaek, North Zealand, Denmark. Vidensk. *Meddr dansk naturh. Foren.* 144, 83–97

Ernesto, R., 1995. *L'Universo della Pharmaecopoeia – Plant Medicinale* (facsimile)

Evans, J., 1872. On a hoard of English gold coins found at St Albans. *Numismatic Chronicle* 2nd ser 12, 186–98

Evans, J. & Card, M., 1984. *Analysis of Glue from the* Mary Rose *Livery Arrows*. North-East London Polytechnic: unpublished report

Evan-Thomas, O., 1932. *Domestic Utensils of Wood*. Hartford: Stobard Davies (1992 reprint)

Evershed R.P., Jerman, K. & Eglington, G., 1985. A Pine Wood Origin for Pitch from the Mary Rose. *Nature* 314, 528–30

Everard J.A. & Holt J.C., 2003. *Jersey 1204: the forging of an island community*. London, Thames & Hudson

Evershed, R.P., Heron, C. & Goad, L.J., 1991. Epicuticular wax components preserved in Potsherds as chemical indicators of leafy vegetables in ancient diets. *Antiquity* 65, 540–4

Evershed, R.P., Arnot, K.I., Collister, J., Eglington, G. & Charters, S., 1994. Application of isotope ratio monitoring gas chromatography-mass spectrometry to the analysis of organic residues of archaeological origin. *Analyst* 119, 909–14

Evershed, R.P., Stott, A.W., Raven, A., Dudd, S.N., Charters, S. & Leyden A., 1995. Formation of long-chain ketones in ancient pottery vessels by pyrolysis of acyl lipids. *Tetrahedron Letters* 36(48), 8875–8

Falke, O. von, 1917. *De Sammlung Richard von Kaufmann, Berlin III*. Berlin

Farmer, T., 1995. Who shall have this? Letter to *New Scientist* 29 July 1995

Finnegan, M., 1978. Non-metric variation of the infracranial skeleton. *Journal of Anatomy* 125, 23–37

Finlay J.M., 2002. Some British medieval copper-alloy mortars, *Journal of the Antique Metalware Society* 10, 22–8

Fioravanti, 1565. *Specchio Universale*

Fioreto, V., Boylston, A. and Knusel, C. (eds), 2000. *Blood Red Roses: the archaeology of a mass grave from the Battle of Towton AD 1461*. Oxford: Oxbow

Firth, A., 2002. *Managing Archaeology Underwater: a theoretical, historical and comparative perspective on society and its submerged past*. Oxford: British Archaeological Report S1055

Flanagan, L., 1988. *Ireland's Armada Legacy*. Gloucester: Sutton

Fairclough, G.J., 1979. *St Andrews Street 1976*. Plymouth: Plymouth Museum Archaeological Series 2

Floud, R., Wachter, K. & Gregory, A., 1990. *Height, Health and History: nutritional status in the U.K., 1750–1980*. Cambridge: Cambridge Studies in Population, Economy and Society in Past Times

Fonseca, R.J. & Klein, W.D., 1978, A cephalometric evaluation of American Negro Women. *American Journal of Orthodonics and Dentofacial Orthopedics* 73(2), 152–60

Forbes T.R., 1984. *Thomas Palmer's Admirable Secrets of Physick and Chirurgery*. Yale: University Press

Fourcroy, A.F., 1790. Memoire sur les differens états des cadavres, trouvé dans les fouilles du Cimetière des Innocens en 1786 et 1787. *Annales de Chimie* 5, 154–85

Fox, R. & Barton, K.J., 1986. Excavations at Oyster Street, Portsmouth, Hampshire, 1968–71. *Post-Medieval Archaeology* 20, 31–255

Foy, D. & Sennequier, G., 1989. *À Travers le Verre du Moyen Age à la Renaissance*. Musee et Monuments Departementaux de la Seine-Maritime

Friel, I., 1995. *The Good Ship: ships, Shipbuilding and technology in England 1200–1520*. London: British Museum Press

Froese R. & Pauly D. (eds). 2002 *Fishbase*, World Wide Web electronic publication www.fishbase.org May 2002

Frutiger, A., 1978. *Signs and Symbols: their design and meaning*. London; Ebury Press (trans. 1998)

Furlong, D., 1999. *Tudor Victuals and Naval Barrels*. Unpublished MA dissertation, University of Southampton

Fussell, G.E., 1952. Four centuries of farming systems in Sussex 1500–1900. *Sussex Archaeological Collections* 90, 60–101

Gadd, J., 1995. Some European guilds and their marking practices. *Journal of the Pewter Society* 10(1), 1–19

Gaimster, D., 1997. *German Stoneware 1200—1900*. London: British Museum Press

Gaimster, D., 2003. Great sites: the Mary Rose. *British Archaeology* 71, 14–19

Gaimster, D., Hayward, M., Mitchell, D. and Parker, K., 2002. Tudor silver-gilt dress-hooks: a new class of treasure find in England. *Antiquaries Journal* 82, 157–96

Gairdner, J., & Brodie, R.H., 1903–5. *Calendar of Letters and Papers Foreign and Domestic of the Reign of Henry VIII, Vol XX, Parts I and II* (Kraus Reprint, Vaduz, 1965)

Gale, T., 1563. *Certain Workes of Chirurgerie*

Garcia de Palacio, D., 1587. *Nautical Instructions*. Bisbee, Arizona: Terrenate Associates (trans J. Barkston 1986)

Gardiner, J., 2003. Appendix 2: Processing and storage of environmental samples and materials. In Jones, M., *For Future Generations; conservation of a Tudor maritime collection*, 134–5. Portsmouth: Mary Rose Trust, The Archaeology of the Mary Rose 5

Gelder, H.E. van & Hoc, M., 1960. *Les Monnaies des Pays-Bas Bourguignons et Espanols 1434–1713*. Amsterdam

Gent, R. van., 1999. Magnetic declination for 1550. http://www.phys.uu.nl/~vgent/magdec/ magdec.htm

Gerard, J., 1975. *The Herbal or Historie of Plants 1597*. New York: Dover Press (facsimile)

Gersdorff, H. von, 1517. *Feldbuch der Wundartzney*

Gill, P., Ivanov, P.L., Kimpton, C., Piercy, R., Benson, N., Tully, G., Evett, I., Hagelberg, E. & Sullivan, K., 1994. Identification of the remains of the Romanov family by DNA analysis. *Nature Genetics* 6, 130–5

Girling, A.F., 1964. *English Merchants' Marks; A field survey of marks made by merchants and tradesmen in England between 1400 and 1700*. London: Oxford University Press

Goad, L.J. & Goodwin, T.W., 1972. The biosynthesis of plant sterols. In L. Reinhold & Y. Liwschitz (eds), *Progress in Phytochemistry*, 113–98. London: Academic

Goodall A.R., 1981. *Medieval Industries*. London: Council for British Archaeology Research Report 40

Goodall, I.H., 1990. Part 2: objects and economy in Medieval Winchester. In Biddle, M. (ed.), *Artefacts from Medieval Winchester*. Oxford: University Press

Goodman, W.L., 1964. *The History of Woodworking Tools*. London: G. Bell & Sons

Goodman, W.L., 1993. *British Planemakers*. London: Astragal

Gottfried R.S., 1978. *Epidemic Disease in Fifteenth Century England*. Leicester: University Press

Gouk, P., 1988. *The Ivory Sundials of Nuremberg 1500–1700*. Cambridge: Whipple Museum

Grant, A., 1991. *Grenville*. Appledore: North Devon Museum Trust

Granville, R., 1895. *The History of the Granville Family*. Exeter

Greber, J.M., 1956. *Geschichte des Hobels*. Zürich

Green. E.M., 2001. *Is Tudor London Trendy? Tudor Textiles from London: Cloth Clothing and Status*. University of Bradford: unpublished undergraduate dissertation

Green, F.J., 1978. Botanical remains. In R.A. Chalker & M.A. Gale, Excavations in East Street, Wareham. *Proceedings of the Dorset Natural History and Archaeology Society* 100, 125

Green, F.J., 1984. The archaeological and documentary evidence for plants from the medieval period in England. In W. van Zeist & W.A. Casparie (eds), *Plants and Ancient Man: studies in palaeoethnobotany*, 99–114. Rotterdam: A.A. Balkema

Green, F.J., 1991. Landscape archaeology in Hampshire: the Saxon plant remains. In J. Renfrew (ed.), *New Light on Early Farming: recent developments in palaeoethnobotany*, 363–77. Edinburgh: University Press

Green, J.N., (ed.), 1977. *The VOC Jacht Vergulde Draeck wrecked Western Australia 1656*. Oxford: British Archaeological Report S36

Green, T., 1824. *The Universal Herbal: botanical, medical and agricultural dictionary*. London: Caxton (2nd edn)

Grenier, R., 1988. Basque whalers in the New World. The Red Bay wrecks. In G. F. Bass (ed.), *Ships and Shipwrecks of the Americas*, 69–84. London: Thames & Hudson

Greig, J., 1985. *Palynological trials (18th November 1985)*. Portsmouth: Mary Rose Trust unpublished report

Greig, J. & Osborne, P. 1984. Plant and insect remains at Taunton Priory. In P. Leach (ed.), *The Archaeology of Taunton*, 160–7. Gloucester: Western Archaeological Trust Monograph 8

Grieve, M., 1992. *A Modern Herbal: the medicinal, culinary, cosmetic and economic properties, cultivation and folklore of herbs, grasses, fungi, shrubs and trees with all their modern scientific uses*. London: Tiger (3rd edn)

Gunstone, F.D., Harwood, J.L. & Padley, F.B., 1994. *The Lipid Handbook*. London: Chapman & Hall

Gutierrez, A., 2000. *Mediterranean Pottery in Wessex Households*. Oxford: British Archaeological Report 306

Habermehl, K-H., 1985. *Altersbestimmung bei Wild- und Pelztieren*. Hamburg & Berlin: Paul Parey (2nd edn)

Hagelberg, E., 1994a. Ancient DNA studies. *Evolutionary Anthropology* 2, 199–207

Hagelberg, E., 1994b. Mitochondrial DNA from ancient bone. In B. Herrmann & S. Hummel (eds), *Ancient DNA*, 195–204. New York: Springer

Hagelberg, E. & Clegg, J.B., 1991. Isolation and characterization of DNA from archaeological bone. *Proceedings of the Royal Society of London, Series B, Biological Sciences* 244, 45–50

Hagelberg, E. & Clegg, J.B., 1993. Genetic polymorphisms in prehistoric Pacific islanders determined by analysis of ancient bone DNA. *Proceedings of the Royal Society of London, Series B, Biological Sciences* 252, 163–70

Hagelberg, E., Sykes, B. & Hedges, R., 1989. Ancient bone DNA amplified. *Nature* 342, 485

Hagelberg, E., Gray, I.C. & Jeffreys, A.J., 1991. Identification of the skeletal remains of a murder victim by DNA analysis. *Nature* 352, 427–9

Hagelberg, E., Quevedo, S., Turbon, D. & Clegg. J.B., 1994a. DNA from ancient Easter Islanders. *Nature* 369, 25–6

Hagelberg, E., Thomas, M.G., Cook, Jr. C.E., Sher, A.V., Baryshnikov, G.F. & Lister, A.M., 1994b. DNA from ancient mammoth bones. *Nature* 370, 333–4

Hagen, A., 1995. *A Second Handbook of Anglo-Saxon Food and Drink: production and distribution*. Hockwold cum Wilton: Anglo-Saxon Books

Haldane, C., 1986. Archaeobotany underwater. *Circaea* 4, 11–12

Haldane, C., 1991. Recovery and analysis of plant remains from some Mediterranean shipwreck sites. In J. Renfrew (ed.), *New Light on Early Farming; recent development in palaeoethnobotany*, 213–23. Edinburgh: University Press

Haldane, C., 1993. Direct evidence for organic cargoes in the Late Bronze Age. *World Archaeology* 24(3), 348–60

Hall, A., 1992. The last teasel factory in Britain, and some observations on teasel (*Dipsacus fullonum* L. and *D. sativus* (L.) Hockeny) remains from archaeological deposits. *Circaea* 9(1), 9–15

Hall, A., 1996. A survey of palaeobotanical evidence for dyeing and mordanting from British archaeological excavations. *Quaternary Science Review* 15, 635–40

Hall, J., 1994. *Illustrated Dictionary of Symbols in Eastern and Western Art*. London: John Murray

Hamilton-Dyer, S., 1995. Fish in Tudor naval diet – with reference to the *Mary Rose*. *Archaeofauna* 4, 27–32

Hamilton-Dyer, S., 2000. The faunal remains. In M. Rawlings, Excavations at Ivy Street and Brown Street, Salisbury, 1994. *Wiltshire Archaeological and Natural History Magazine* 93, 45–51

Harcourt, R.A., 1974. The dog in prehistoric and early historic Britain. *Journal of Archaeological Science* 1(2), 151–75

Hardy, R., 1995. *Longbow: a social and military history*. Sparkford: Patrick Stevens

Harris, E.C., 1979. *Principles of Archaeological Stratigraphy*. London: Academic Press

Harvey, J.M., nd. *Report on Dye Analysis on Fabric from Coif from Surgeon's Cabin*. Portsmouth: unpublished report for Mary Rose Trust

Hatcher, J. & Barker, T.C., 1974. *A History of British Pewter*. London: Longman

Hattendorf, J.B, Knight, R.J.B., Pearsall, A.W.H., Rodger, N.A.M. & Hill, G. (eds), 1993. *British Naval Documents 1204–1960*. Aldershot: Navy Records Society Publication 131

Hayward, H. (ed.), 1965. *World Furniture*. London: Paul Hamlyn

Heath, C., 1804. *Historical and Descriptive Accounts of the Ancient and Present State of the Town of Monmouth*. Privately printed

Hedges, S.B. & Schweitzer, M.H., 1995. Detecting dinosaur DNA. *Science* 268, 1191–2

Hémardinquer J.-J., 1970. Sur les Galeres de Toscane au XVIe Siecle. In Hémardinquer J-J. (ed.), *Pour une Histoire de l'Alimentation*, 85–92. Paris: Cahiers des Annales

Henig, M., 1976. The small finds. In G. Lambrick & H. Woods, Excavations on the second site of the Dominican Priory, Oxford, *Oxoniensia* 41, 213–22

Herald, J., 1981. *Renaissance Dress in Italy 1400–1500*. London: The History of Dress

Hero, M., 1533. *Schachtafelen der Gesuntheit*. Strasburg

Heron, C.P., Nemcek, N. & Bonfield, K.M., 1994. The chemistry of Neolithic beeswax. *Naturwissenschaften* 81, 266–9

Higton, H., 2001. *Sundials: an illustrated history of portable dials*. London: Philip Wilson

Higuchi, R., Bowman, B., Freiberger, M., Ryder, O.A. & Wilson, A.C., 1984. DNA sequences from the quagga, an extinct member of the horse family. *Nature* 312, 282–4

Hildred, A.,1997. The material culture of the Mary Rose (1545) as a fighting vessel: the uses of wood. In Redknap (ed.) 1997, 51–72

HMSO, 1970. *An Inventory of the Navigation and Astronomy Collections in the National Maritime Museum*. Norwich: HMSO

Hobson, G.D., 1940. *English Bindings 1490–1940 in the Library of J.R. Abbey*. London: Privately Printed

Hoffmann-Axthelm, W., 1981. *History of Dentistry*. Chicago: Quintessence

Holland, M. M., Fisher, D. L., Mitchell, L.G., Rodriquez, W.C., Canik, J.J., Merril, C.R. & Weedn, V.W., 1993. Mitochondrial DNA sequence analysis of human skeletal remains: identification of remains from the Vietnam War. *Journal of Forensic Sciences* 38, 542–3

Holman, R.G., 1975. The Dartmouth, a British frigate wrecked of Mull, 1690: culinary and related items. *International Journal of Nautical Archaeology* 4(2), 253–65

Holme, Randle III., 1649–88. *An Academie of Armory. A Store House of Armory & Blazon, Containeing all thinges Borne in Coates of Armes Both Forreign and Domestick, With the termes of Art used in each Science... Which treateth of all sorts of Working Tooles, of Chyrurgions Instruments, of Houses and Churches, of Weapons of Warr, &c. Volume 2*. London: The Roxburghe Club (1905 reproduction, ed. I.H. Jeayes)

Holmes, G.F., nd. *Sewing Thimbles*. Oxford: Finds Research Group 700–1700 Datasheet 9

Homer, F., 1995. Pewter in a Somerset church. *Pewter Society Journal* 10(1), 19–22

Hornsby, P.G., Weinstein, R. & Homer, F., 1989. *Pewter: a celebration of the craft 1200–1700*. London: Museum of London

Horsley, J.E., 1978. *Tools of the Maritime trades*. Newton Abbott: David & Charles

Houben, G.M.M., 1998. *Coin-weightmakers*. Zwolle

Howard, M., 1996. Coopers and cask in the whaling trade 1800–1850, *Mariner's Mirror* 82, 436–50

Hulst, R., 1987. Casks as a packing material: an archaeological typology and a historical reconstruction. In Gawronski, J.H.G. (ed), *V.O.C. ship* Amsterdam. Amsterdam: VOC-ship Amsterdam Foundation

Hunt, E.E., 1961. Malocclusion and civilisation. *American Journal of Orthodonics and Dentofacial Orthopedics* 47(6), 406–22

Hunt, T., 1994. *Popular Medicine in 13th Century England*. D.S. Brevier

Hurst, J.G., Neal, D.S., & Beuningen, H.J.E. van, 1986. *Pottery Produced and Traded in North-West Europe 1350–1650*. Rotterdam: Rotterdam Papers 6

Ickowicz, P., 1993. Martincamp Ware: a problem of attribution. *Medieval Ceramics* 17, 51–60

Işcan, M.Y., 1988. Rise of forensic anthropology. *Yearbook of Physical Anthropology* 31, 203–30

Işcan, M.Y., Loth, S.R. & Wright, R.K., 1984. Age estimation from the rib by phase analysis: white males. *Journal of Forensic Sciences* 29, 1094–104

James T.B., 1990. *The Port Book of Southampton 1509–10*. Southampton: Southampton Records Series 32 & 33

Janssen, H.L.,1983. Bewerkt been. In H.L. Janssen (ed.), *Van Bos tot Stad. Opgravingen in 's-Hertogenbosch*. 's-Hertogenbosch

Jeffreys, A.J., 1984. Raising the dead and buried. *Nature* 312, 198

Jeffreys, A.J., Allen, M.J., Hagelberg, E. & Sonnberg, A., 1992. Identification of the skeletal remains of Josef Mengele by DNA analysis. *Forensic Science International* 56, 65–76

Jeffreys, A.J., Wilson, V. & Thein, S.L., 1985. Individual-specific 'fingerprints' of human DNA. *Nature* 316, 76–9

Jenkinson, H., 1911. Exchequer tallies. *Archaeologia* 62, 367–80

Jenkinson, H., 1925. Medieval tallies, public and private. *Archaeologia* 74, 289–351

Jennings, S., 1981. *Eighteen Centuries of Pottery from Norwich*. Norwich: East Anglain Archaeology 13

Jerman, K.,1984. *A Study of Tars and Pitches From Ancient Ships*. Unpublished Thesis, University of Bristol

Jobling, M.A. & Tyler-Smith, C., 2003. The human Y chromosome: an evolutionary marker comes of age. *Nature Reviews Genetics* 4, 598–612

Johnson, J.J., Soetamat, A. & Winoto N., 1978. A comparison of some features of the Indonesian Occlusion with those of two other ethnic groups. *British Journal of Orthodontics* 5, 183–8

Jones, A., nd. *The 16th century diet*. Portsmouth: Mary Rose Trust unpublished report/typescript

Jones, G., Straker, V. & Davis, A., 1991. Early medieval plant use and ecology. In A.G. Vince (ed.), *Aspects of Saxon and Norman London 2: Finds and Environmental Evidence*, 347–85. London: London and Middlesex Archaeological Society Special Paper 12

Jones, M.L.,1999. A checklist of woodwind instruments marked !! *Galpin Society Journal* 52, 243–80

704

Jones, S.J., Boyde, A., Piper, K. & Komiya, S., 1992. Confocal microscopic mapping of osteoclastic resorption. *Microscopy & Analysis* 18-20

Jones, W.B., 1987. Malocclusion and facial types in a group of Saudi Arabian patients referred for orthodontic treatment; a preliminary study, *British Journal of Orthodontics* 14, 143–6

Jupp, E.B. & Pocock, W.W., 1887. *Historical Account of the Worshipful Company of Carpenters*. London: Pickering & Chatto (2nd edn)

Kapandji, I.A., 1983. *The Physiology of the Joints: annotated diagrams of the mechanics of the human joints: vol. 2, lower limb*. Edinburgh: Churchill Livingstone (2nd end)

Keary, C.F., 1878. Bisham Treasure Trove. *Numismatic Chronicle* 2nd series 18, 304–6

Keene, D., 1990, Wooden vessels. In M. Biddle (ed.), *Object and Economy in Medieval Winchester*, 959–66. Oxford: Clarendon Press

Keevil, J.J., Coulter, J.L.S. & Lloyd, C.C., 1957. *Medicine and the Navy, 1220–1900, Vol. 1*. Edinburgh & London: Livingstone

Keevil J.J., 1963. *Medicine and the Navy 1200–1900, Vol I*. Baltimore: Williams & Wilkins

Kemp. P., 1970. *The British Sailor*. London: Dent

Kenchington, T.J., Carter, J.A. & Rice, E.L. 1989. The indispensability of non-artifactual data in underwater archaeology. In J. Barto Arnold III (ed.), *Underwater Archaeology Proceedings from the Society for Historical Archaeology Conference 1989*, 111–20. Baltimore

Kenward, H.K., Hall, A.R. & Jones, A.K.G. 1980. A tested set of techniques for the extraction of plant and animal macrofossils from waterlogged archaeological deposits. *Science and Archaeology* 22, 3–15

Kerr, N.W., 1998. The prevalence and natural history of periodontal diseasde in Britain from prehistoric to modern times. *British Dental Journal* 185(10), 527–35

Kert, F., 1981. *1981 Trench Report*. Portsmouth: Mary Rose Trust unpublished report

Keynes G. (ed.), 1951. *The Apologie and Treatise of Ambroise Pare*. London: Falcon

Keys, L., 1998. Wooden vessels. In Egan 1998, 210–12

Khalid, S.A., 1983. Chemistry of the Burseraceae. In P.G. Waterman & M.F. Grundon (eds), *Chemistry and Chemical Taxonomy of the Rutales*, 281–99. London: Academic

Kilby, K., 1971. *The Cooper and his Trade*. London: John Baker

Knell, D., 1997. Tudor Furniture from the *Mary Rose*. *Regional Furniture* 1997, 62–79

Knight, J., 1994. Excavations at Montgomery Castle part III. The finds: other than metalwork. *Archaeologia Cambrensis* 143, 139–203

Knighton, C.S. & Loades, D., 2000. *The Anthony Roll*. London: Ashgate for the Navy Records Society

Knighton, C.S. & Loades, D., 2002. *Letters from the* Mary Rose. Stroud: Sutton

Kocher, T. D., Thomas, W.K., Meyer, A., Edwards, S.V., Pääbo, S., Villablanca, F.X. & Wilson, A.C., 1989. Dynamics of mitochondrial DNA evolution in animals: amplification and sequencing with conserved primers. *Proceedings of the National Academy of Sciences of the United States of America* 86, 6196–200

Kolattukudy, P.E., 1976. *Chemistry and Biochemistry of Natural Waxes*. Oxford: Elsevier

Koller, Galerie, 1979. *The Ernest Brummer Collection. Medieval, Renaissance and Baroque Art Vol. 1*. Zurich

Krings, M., Stone, A., Schmitz, R.W., Krainitzki, H., Stoneking, M. & Paabo. S., 1997. Neandertal DNA sequences and the origin of modern humans. *Cell* 90, 19–30

Krings, M., Capelli, C., Tschentscher, F., Geisert, H., Meyer, S., Haeseler, A. von, Grossschmidt, K., Possnert, G., Paunovic, M. & Pääbo, S., 2000. A view of Neandertal genetic diversity. *Nature Genetics* 26, 144–6

Krogman, W.M., 1973. The Human Skeleton in Forensic Medicine. Springfield, Illinois: Charles Thomas

Krueger, I., 1990. Glasspiegel im mittelalter:Fakten, Funde und Fragen. *Bonner Jahrbüch* 190, 233–319

Kunitz, S.J., 1987. Making a long story short: a note on men's height and mortality in England from the first through the 19th centuries. *Medical History* 31, 269–80

Kurlansky M., 1998. *Cod: a biography of the fish that changed the world*. London: Jonathan Cape

Ladle, L., 1993. *The Studland Bay Wreck; a Spanish shipwreck of the Dorset Coast*. Poole: Poole Museum Heritage Series 1

Lalueza Fox, C., 1996. Mitochondrial DNA Haplogroups in Four Tribes from Tierra del Fuego-Patagonia: Inferences about the Peopling of the Americas. *Human Biology* 68, 853–71

Lander, E. S., Linton, L.M., Birren, B., Nusbaum, C., Zody, M.C., Baldwin, J., Devon, K., Dewar, K., Doyle, M., FitzHugh, W, (and 245 others). 2001. Initial sequencing and analysis of the human genome. *Nature* 409, 860–921

Lasocki, D. with Prior, R., 1995. *The Bassanos: Venetian musicians and instrument makers in England, 1531–1665*. Aldershot: Scolar

Lavagne, F., 1981. *Balanciers Etalonneurs, Leurs Marques – Leurs Poinçons*. Montpelliers

Lavery, B., 1987. *The Arming and Fitting of English Ships of War, 1600–1815*. London: Conway History of Sail

Lavery, B., 1988. *The Royal Navy's first* Invincible. Portsmouth: Invincible Conservations (1744–1758) Ltd

Lawson, W., 1986, The boatswain's call: its role in the European maritime tradition. In *Second Conference of the ICTM Study Group on Music Archaeology 1, General Studies*, 131–40. Stockholm: Royal Swedish Academy of Music

Letts, J.B., 1999. *Smoke-Blackened Thatch (SBT): A new Source of Late Medieval Plant Remains from Southern England*. London & Reading: Ancient Monuments Laboratory (English Heritage), Department of Agricultural Botany & the Rural History Centre, University of Reading

Levi, J., 1998. *Treen for the Table*. Antique Collectors Club

Liberson, F., 1937. Os acromiale – a contested anomaly. *Journal of Bone and Joint Surgery* 19, 683–9

Lightbown, R.W., 1992. *Mediaeval European Jewellery*. London: Victoria & Albert Museum

Lissaman, A.J. & Martin S.J., 1983. *Principles of Engineering Production*. London: Hodder & Stoughton

Loades D., 1992. *The Tudor Navy*. London: Scholar Press

Loewen, B., 1992. *Change and Diversity within Traditional Cooperage Technology*. Material History Review/Revue d'Histoire de la Culture Matérialle 36

Loewen, B., 1999. *The Casks from* La Belle *and the Rochefort Arsenal, c. 1684*. Austin, Texas: unpublished report for Texas Historical Commission

Locker, A., 2000. *The Role of Stored Fish in England 900–1750 AD; the evidence from historical and archaeological data*. Unpublished PhD Thesis, University of Southampton

Longhurst, M.H., 1929. *Catalogue of Carvings in Ivory*. London: Board of Education

Longmate, N., 1989. *Defending the Island*. London: Hutchinson

Lorenz, F. & Hubert, A., 1993. *A Guide to Worldwide Cowries*. Wiesbaden

Lovell, J., 1999. Roger's Hill Farm burial, near Bere Regis. In C.M. Hearne, & V. Birbeck, *A35 Tolpuddle to Puddletown Bypass DBFO, Dorset, 1996–8*, 89–96. Salisbury: Wessex Archaeology Report 15

Luzi, R., Mancini, C., Mazzucato, O. & Romagnoli, M., 1992. *Ceramics of the Apothecary and of Love*. Italy: TusciArt Editrice

MacAllister, M.J. & Rock, W.P., 1992. The Eastman Standard Incisor Angulations: are they still appropriate? *British Journal of Orthodontics* 19, 55–8

MacCulloch, D., 1994. New spotlights on the English Reformation. *Journal of Ecclesiastical History* 45(2), 319–24

MacGregor, A., 1985. *Bone, Antler, Ivory & Horn. The Technology of Skeletal Materials Since the Roman Period*. London

McBride, P., 1976. The *Dartmouth*, a British frigate wrecked off Mull 1690: 3. The guns. *International Journal of Nautical Archaeology* 5(3), 189–200

McCarthy, M.R. & Brooks, C.M., 1988. *Medieval Pottery in Britain AD 900–1600*. Leicester: University Press

McEwan, C., 1997. Whistling vessels from pre-Hispanic Peru. In I. Freestone and D. Gaimster (eds), *Pottery in the Making. World Ceramic Traditions*, 177–81. London: British Museum Press

McKee, A., 1982. *How we Found the* Mary Rose. London: Souvenir

McMillan, N.F., 1968. *British Shells*. London: Frederick Warne & Co

Magedans, J.F.C., 1987. The identification of vegetable material: tobacco from the '*Amsterdam*'. In J.H. Gawronski (ed.), *Annual Report of the VOC-Ship Amsterdam Foundation* 1986, 88–92. Amsterdam

Mainwaring, G.E., 1923. Boatswain's whistles or calls. *Mariners Mirror* 9(11), 342

Maire, J., 1990. Le Marais-vert à Strasbourg et le travail de l'os. In *Vivre au Moyen Age: 30 ans d'archéologie médiévale en Alsace*, 79–80. Strasbourg

Mann, D.L. & Littke, N., 1989. Shoulder injuries in archery. *Canadian Journal of Sports Science* 14, 85–92

Mant, A.K., 1957. Adipocere – a review. *Journal of Forensic Medicine* 4, 18–35

Manual of Seamanship, 1915. London: HMSO

Margeson, S., 1993. *Norwich Households. Medieval and Post-Medieval Finds from Norwich Survey Excavations 1977–78*. Norwich: East Anglian Archaeology 58

Marly, D. de, 1986. *Working Dress, a History of Occupational Clothing*. London: Batsford

Marsden, P., 1972. The wreck of the Dutch East Indiaman Amsterdam near Hastings, 1749: an interim report. *International Journal of Nautical Archaeology* 1, 73–96

Marsden, P. and Lyon, D., 1977. A wreck believed to be the warship Anne, lost in 1690. *International Journal of Nautical Archaeology* 6(1), 9–20

Martin, C.J.M., 1975. *Full Fathom Five. Wrecks of the Spanish Armada*. London: Chatto & Windus

Martin, C.J.M., 1978. The Dartmouth, a British frigate wrecked off Mull, 1690: 5. The ship. *International Journal of Nautical Archaeology* 7(1), 29–58

Martin, C.J.M, 1997. Ships as integrated artefacts. In M. Redknap (ed.), 1997, 1–13

Martin, P.F. de C., 1977. The *Dartmouth*, a British Frigate wrecked off Mull, 1690: 4. The clay pipes. *International Journal of Nautical Archaeology* 6(3), 219–23

Martindale, W., 1941. *The Extra Pharmacopoia*. London: Pharmaceutical Society of Great Britain (22nd edn)

Mathewson, R. Duncan III, 1986. *Treasure of the* Atocha. *Sixteen Dramatic Years in Search of the Historic Wreck*. London: Sidgwick & Jackson

Matthews, L.G. & Green, H.J.M., 1969. Post-medieval pottery of the Inns of Court. *Post-Medieval Archaeology* 3, 1–17

Maurice, K., 1968. *Von Uhren und Automaten*. Munich: Das Messen der Zeit

Maybray King, H., 1968. *Before Hansard*. London: Dent

Mead, V.K., 1977. Evidence for the manufacture of amber beads in the City of London in the 14th–15th century. *Transactions of the London & Middlesex Archaeological Society* 28, 211–4

Melendez, B., 1958. *Mapa Geologico de Espana y Portugal* (explicacion geologica). Madrid

Meyer, O., Bourgeau, L., Coxall, D.J. & Meyer, N., 1979. *Archéologie Urbaine a Saint–Denis*, not paginated. Saint-Denis

Micklethwaite, J.T., 1982, On the indoor games of school boys in the Middle Ages. *Archaeological Journal* 49, 319–28

Miles, A.E.W., 1994. Non-union of the epiphysis of the acromion in the skeletal remains of a Scottish population of ca. 1700. *International Journal of Osteoarchaeology* 4, 149–3

Miller, J.I. 1969. *The Spice Trade of the Roman Empire: 29 B.C. to A.D. 641*. Oxford: Clarendon Press (1998 reprint)

Mills, J.S. & White, R., 1994. *The Organic Chemistry of Museum Objects*. London: Butterworth-Heinemann

Mishmar, D., Ruiz-Pesini, E., Golik, P., Macaulay, V., Clark, A.G., Hosseini, S., Brandon, M., Easley, K., Chen, E., Brown, M.D., Sukernik, R.I., Olckers, A. & Wallace, D.C., 2003. Natural selection shaped regional mtDNA variation in humans. *Proceedings of the National Academy of Sciences of the United States of America* 100, 171–6

Misso, N.L.A. & Goad, L.J., 1983. The synthesis of 24-methylenecycloartenol, cyclosadol and cyclolaudenol by a cell free preparation from Zea mays shoots. *Phytochemistry* 22(11), 2473–9

Monk, M., 1980. Seed evidence. In D.A. Hinton & R. Hodges (eds), Excavations at Wareham, 1974–5. *Proceedings of the Dorset Natural History and Archaeology Society* 99, 77

Montagu, J., 1976. *Making Early Percussion Instruments.* Oxford: University Press

Montagu, J., 1997. Was the tabor pipe always as we know it? *Galpin Society Journal* 50, 16–30

Montagu, J., 2002. *Timpani and Percussion.* New Haven & London: Yale University Press

Montagu, J. & Montagu, G., 1998. *Minstrels and Angels: carvings of musicians in English medieval churches.* Berkeley: Fallen Leaf Press

Moore, P.D. & Webb, J.A., 1978. *An Illustrated Guide to Pollen Analysis.* London: Hodder and Stoughton

Moore, P.D., Webb, J.A. & Collinson, M.E., 1991. *Pollen Analysis.* Oxford: Blackwell Scientific (2nd edn)

Moore, S., 1999. *Cutlery for the Table.* Hallamshire Press

Moore, W.J. & Corbett, M.E., 1971. The distribution of dental caries in ancient British populations. I. Anglo-Saxon period. *Caries Research* 5, 151–68

Moore, W.J. & Corbett, M.E., 1973. The distribution of dental caries in ancient British populations. II. Iron Age, Romano-British and mediaeval periods. *Caries Research* 7, 139–53

Moore, W.J. & Corbett, M.E., 1975. The distribution of dental caries in ancient British populations. III. The 17th century. *Caries Research* 9, 163–75

Morales, A. & Rosenlund, K., 1979. *Fish Bone Measurements.* Copenhagen: Steenstrupia

Morgan, E.D., Cornford, C., Pollock, D.R.J. & Isaacson, P., 1973. The transformation of fatty material buried in soil. *Science and Archaeology* 10, 9–10

Morgan, E.D. & Williams, M.J., 2001. *Analysis of two samples of meat fat recovered from the warship 'Mary Rose'.* Portsmouth: Mary Rose Trust Archive MS

Morineau, M., 1970. Marines du Nord (Angleterre, Hollande, Suede et Russie) Conclusions. In Hémardinquer J-J. (ed.), *Pour une Histoire de l'Alimentation*, 100–5. Paris: Cahiers des Annales

Morris, C., 1993, various contributions. In Margeson 1993

Morris, C., 2000. *Craft, Industry and Everyday Life: Wood and Woodworking in Anglo-Scandinavian and Medieval York.* York: Council for British Archaeology, Archaeology of York Fascicule 17/13

Moss, J.P., Linney, A.D., Grindrod, S.R., Arridge, S.R. & Clifton, J.S., 1987. Three dimensional visualisation of the face and skull using computerised tomography and laser scanning techniques. *European Journal of Orthodontics* 9, 247–53

Mould, Q., 1993. *The leather from the Studland Bay wreck.* Unpublished report for the Borough of Poole Museum Services

Moulin, D. de, 1988. *A History of Surgery with Emphasis on the Netherlands.* Dordrecht: Nijhoff

Moyers, R.E. & Bookstein, F.L., 1979. The inappropriateness of conventional cephalometrics. *American Journal of Orthodontics and Dentofacial Orthopedics* 75(6), 599–617

Muckelroy, K., 1978. *Maritime Archaeology.* Cambridge: New Studies in Archaeology

Müller, U., 1996. *Holzfunde aus Freiburg und Konstanz.* Stuttgart

Multhauf, R., 1956. The significance of distillation in Renaissance medical chemistry. *Bulletin of the History of Medicine* 30, 329–46

Munday, J., 1978. Heads and tails: the necessary seating. In P.G.W. Annis (ed.), Ingrid *and Other Studies*, 125–40. London: National Maritime Museum Monograph 36

Myers, H.W., 1983. The *Mary Rose* 'shawm'. *Early Music* 11(3), 358–60

Nadolski, D., 1987. *Old Household Pewterware.* Teaneck, New Jersey: Holmes & Meier

Natanson, J., 1951. *Gothic Ivories of the 13th and 14th Centuries.* London: Alec Tiranti

Nelson, A., 2001. *The Tudor Navy.* Chatham: Conway Maritime

Nevinson, J.L. 1978. The dress of citizens of London 1540–1640. In J. Bird, H. Chapman & J. Clark (eds), *Collectanea Londinensia*, 265–80. London: London and Middlesex Archaeological Society Special Paper

Neyland, R.S. & Schröder, B., 1996. *A Late Seventeenth Century Dutch Freighter Wrecked on the Zuiderzee.* Amersfoort: Nederlands Instituut voor Scheeps- en onderwater Archeologie/ROB (NISA) Excavation Report 20

Nissenbaum, A., 1992. Molecular archaeology: organic geochemistry of Egyptian mummies. *Journal of Archaeological Science* 19, 1–6

North, J.J., 1991. *English Hammered Coinage. Volume 2: Edward I to Charles II, 1272–1662.* London: Spink (3rd edn)

North, N.A. & MacLeod, I.D., 1987. Corrosion of metals. In C. Pearson (ed.), *Conservation of Marine Archaeological Objects*, 68–98. London: Butterworth

Northover, J.P., 2002. *Compositions of copper alloy, pewter and lead artefacts from the* Mary Rose. Portsmouth: Mary Rose Trust, unpublished report

Okey, T., 1907. *The Art of Basket-Making.* Basketmaker's Association (1986 reprint)

O'Connor, S., 2002. Brain pseudomorphs; grey matter, grey sediments, and grey literature. In K. Dobney & T. O'Connor (eds), *Bones and the Man; studies in honour of Don Brothwell*, 41–50. Oxford: Oxbow

O'Connor, T. P., 1984. *Selected Groups of Bones from Skeldergate and Walmgate.* York: Archaeology of York Fascicule 15/1

Oexle, J., 1985, Würfel- und Paternoster-hersteller im Mittelalter. In D. Plank (ed.), *Der Keltenfürst von Höchdorf: Methoden und Ergebnisse der Landesarchäologie, Katalog zur Austellung, Stuttgart Kunstgebäude, 14 Aug. bis 13 Okt. 1985 (Stuttgart, 1985)*, 455–62, 484–89. Stuttgart

Ogden, M., 1971. *The Cyrurgie of Guy de Chauliac (1260–1320)*. Oxford: Early English Text Society & Oxford University Press (facsimile)

Oldham, B., 1958. *Blind Panels of English Binders*. Cambridge: University Press

Oman C.C., 1930. *Catalogue of Rings. Victoria & Albert Museum, Department of Metalwork*. London: Victoria & Albert Museum

Oman, C.C., 1965. *English Silversmiths' Work Civil and Domestic: an introduction*. London: Victoria & Albert Museum

Oppenheim, M., 1896a. *Naval Accounts and Inventories of the Reign of Henry VIII 1485–8 and 1496–7*. London: Navy Records Society 8

Oppenheim, M., 1896b. *History of the Royal Navy and of Merchant Shipping in Relation to the Navy (from 1509 to 1660)*. London: Bodley Head/Shoe String Press (1961 reprint)

Ortner, D.J. & Eriksen, M.F., 1997. Bone changes in the human skull probably resulting from scurvy in infancy and childhood. *International Journal of Osteoarchaeology* 7, 212–20

Ortner, D.J., Kimmerle, E.H. & Diez, M., 1999. Probable evidence of scurvy in subadults from archaeological sites in Peru. *American Journal of Physical Anthropology* 108, 321–31

Ovchinnikov, I. V., Götherström, A., Romanova, G.P., Kharitonov, V.M., Lidén, K. & Goodwin, W., 2000. Molecular analysis of Neanderthal DNA from the northern Caucasus. *Nature* 404, 490–3

Oxley, I., 1984. Non-artefactual materials from underwater sites. *International Journal of Nautical Archaeology* 13(4), 337–8

Oxley, I., 1986. *Labelling of Samples and Sample Components*. Portsmouth: Mary Rose Trust, unpublished manuscript

Oxley, I., 1991. Environmental sampling underwater. In J.M. Coles & D.M. Goodburn (eds), *Wet Site Excavation and Survey*, 36–40. Exeter: WARP

Pääbo, S., 1985. Molecular cloning of Ancient Egyptian mummy DNA. *Nature* 314, 644–5

Pääbo, S., Gifford, J.A. & Wilson, A.C., 1988. Mitochondrial DNA sequences from a 7000-year-old brain. *Nucleic Acids Research* 16, 9775–87

Page, C.N., 1988. *Ferns: their habitats in the British and Irish landscape*. London: Collins

Palmer, F., 1983. Musical instruments from the *Mary Rose*: a report on work in progress. *Early Music* 11(1), 53–9

Palmer, R., 1985. Pharmacy in the Republic of Venice in the 16th century. In A. Wear, R.K. French & I.M. Lonie (eds), *The Medical Renaissance in the 16th Century*, 100–17. Cambridge: University Press.

Peacock, D.P.S., 1969. A contribution to the study of Glastonbury ware from south-western Britain. *Antiquaries Journal* 49, 41–61

Pearce, J.E., 1992. *Border Wares. Post-Medieval Pottery in London, 1500–1700, Volume 1*. London: Museum of London & HMSO

Pellenc-Turcat, F., 1993. Les icônes de la Slava Rossii: technologies, typologies, catalogue sommaire et comparaisons, 1–57. *Travaux Scientifiques du Parc National de Port-Cros* 15

Pelling, M., 1982. Occupational diversity of the Barber Surgeons of Norwich 1550–1640. *Bulletin of the History of Medicine* 56, 484–511

Pettegree, A., 1986. *Foreign Protestant Communities in Sixteenth Century London*. Oxford: University Press

Phillips, C.R., 1992. *Six Galleons for the King of Spain. Imperial Defence in the Early Seventeenth Century*. Baltimore: John Hopkins University Press

Philips, T., 1839. The life of Sir Peter Carew, of Mohun Ottery, co. Devon. *Archaeologia* 28, 96–151

Pinto, E., 1969. *Treen and Other Wooden Bygones*. London: G. Bell & Sons

Pitt, E., 1989. *Short Report on the Analysis of Non Ferrous Based Alloy Artefacts Salvaged from the* Mary Rose. Coventry: Coventry Polytechnic, unpublished report

Planche, J. Robertson, 1876. *Cyclopedia of Costume*

Platt, C. & Coleman-Smith, R., 1975. *Excavations in Medieval Southampton 1953–69, Vol. 2. The Finds*. Leicester: University Press

Potter, E.C., 1992. On being interested in the extreme. *Journal of the Royal Society of New South Wales* 125, 79–81

Poynter, F.N.L., 1948. *The Selected Writings of William Clowes (1544–1604)*. London: Harvey Blythe

Prentice, R., 1994. *A Celebration of the Sea. The Decorative Arts Collections of the National Maritime Museum*. London: HMSO

Prentice, R., 1997. Striking ships' bells. *Maritime Heritage* 12, 51–5

Prentice, R., 1998. Buoy, gun and keel: the boatswain's call. *Maritime Heritage* 13, 30–1

Price, R. & Muckelroy, K., 1974. The second season of work on the *Kennermerland* site, 1973: an interim report. *International Journal of Nautical Archaeology* 3(2), 257–68

Price, R. & Muckelroy, K., 1977. The *Kennermerland* site: the third and fourth seasons 1974 and 1976, an interim report. *International Journal of Nautical Archaeology* 6(3), 187–218

Price, R. & Muckelroy, K., 1979. The *Kennermerland* site, the fifth season, 1978, an interim report. *International Journal of Nautical Archaeology* 8(4), 311–20

Price, R., Muckelroy, K. & Willies, L., 1980. The *Kennermerland* site; a report on the lead ingots. *International Journal of Nautical Archaeology* 9(1), 7–25

Price, W.A., 1939. *Nutrition and Physical Degeneration. A Comparison of Primitive and Modern Diets and their Effects*. New York: North Wind

Provoyeur, P., 1994. Les arts de la table, les bijoux et les objets de dévotion. In D. Carré, J.-P. Desroches & F. Goddio (eds), *Le San Diego. Un Trésor sous la Mer*, 258–97. Paris

Pryor, F. and Taylor, M., 1993. Use, re-use, or pre-use? Aspects of the interpretation of ancient wood. In Coles, J., Fenwick, V. and Hutchinson, G. (eds), *A Spirit of Enquiry, essays for Ted Wright*, 81–6. Exeter: WARP

Rackham, O., 1976. *Trees and Woodland in the British Landscape*. London: Dent

Rakosi, R., Jonas, I. & Graber, T.M., 1993. *Color Atlas of Dental Medicine, Orthodontic Diagnosis*, 179–205, New York: Thieme Medical

Rastall, W., 1588. *A Collection in English of the Statutes now in force, from the beginning of Magna Charta ... until the ende of the Session of Parliament holden in the 28 Yeare ofthe reigne of ... Queene Elizabeth*

Reade, B. 1951. *The Dominance of Spain 1550–1660*. London: Harrap. Costume of the Western World 3(4)

Reay, R., 1984. *Results of Insect Examination*. Portsmouth: Portsmouth Polytechnic unpublished typscript for the Mary Rose Trust

Redknap, M., 1984. *The Cattewater Wreck: the investigation of an armed vessel of the sixteenth century*. Oxford: British Archaeological Report 131

Redknap, M., (ed.), 1997. *Artefacts from Wrecks. Dated Assemblages from the Late Middle Ages to the Industrial Revolution*. Oxford: Oxbow Monograph 84

Redknap, M. & Besly, E., 1997. Wreck de Mer and dispersed wreck sites: the case of the Ann Francis (1583). In Redknap (ed.) 1997, 191–207

Reilly, K., 1984. The bones. In Redknap 1984, 88–92

Relethford, J.H., 2001. Absence of regional affinities of Neandertal DNA with living humans does not reject multiregional evolution. *American Journal of Physical Anthropology* 115, 95–8

Remnant, M., 1986. *English Bowed Instruments from Anglo-Saxon to Tudor Times*. Oxford: Clarendon

Resnick, D. & Niwayama, G., 1981. *Diagnosis of Bone and Joint Disorders*. Philadelphia: Saunders

Reunanen, M., Ekman, R. & Heinonen, M., 1989. Analysis of Finnish pine tar and tar from the wreck of frigate St. Nikolai. *Holzforschung* 43, 33–9

Reunanen, M., Ekman, R. & Heinonen, M., 1990. Long-term alteration of pine tar in a marine environment. *Holzforschung* 44, 277–8

Richards, M., 1997. Form, function, ownership: a study of chests from Henry VIII's warship *Mary Rose*, 1545. In Redknap (ed.) 1997, 87–98

Richards, M.B., Macaulay, V.A., Bandelt, H.J. & Sykes, B.C., 1998. Phylogeography of mitochondrial DNA in western Europe. *Annals of Human Genetics* 62, 241–60

Richards, M., Macaulay, V., Hickey, E., Vega, E., Sykes, B., Guida, V., Rengo, C., Sellitto, D., Cruciani, F., Kivisild, T., et al. 2000. Tracing European founder lineages in the Near Eastern mtDNA pool. *American Journal of Human Genetics* 67, 1251–76

Richers, R.H., 1983. *Elm*. Cambridge: University Press

Riley, H.T. 1868. *Memorials of London Life*. London: Longman

Riolo, M.L., Moyers, R.E., McNamara, J.A. & Hunter, W.S., 1974. *An Atlas of Craniofacial Growth*. Ann Arbor, Michigan: University Press

Ritz, G., 1975, Der Rosenkranz. In *500 Jahre Rosenkranz, 1475–1975: Kunst und Frömmigkeit im Spätmittelalter und ihr Weiterleben*, 51–101. Cologne

Rixson, D., 2000. *The History of Meat Trading*. Nottingham: University Press

Robinson, N., Evershed R.P., Higgs W.J., Jerman, K. & Eglinton,G., 1987. Proof of a pine wood origin for pitch from Tudor (*Mary Rose*) and Etruscan shipwrecks: application of analytical chemistry in archaeology. *Analyst* 112(5), 637–44

Roberts, E. & Parker, K., 1992. *Southampton Probate Inventories 1447–1575 (2 Vols)*. Southampton: University Press, Southampton Records Series 34–5

Rocacher, J., 1980. Les mouliers de Rocamadour. *Bulletin de la Société des Etudes du Lot (Oct–Dec)*, 284–92

Rodger, N.A.M., 1997. *The Safeguard of the Sea: a naval history of Britain, Volume 1: 660–1649*. London: Harper Collins

Rodrigues, J., 2001. *Staved Containers from the Wreck of the Mary Rose (1545)*. University of Southampton: unpublished MA dissertation.

Rodríguez-Salgado, M.J. et al., 1989. *Armada 1588–1988. The Official Catalogue*. London: National Maritime Museum

Rodwell, K. & Bell, R., 2004. Acton Court. *The Evolution of an Early Tudor Courtier's House*. London: English Heritage

Roewer, L., Kayser, M., Dieltjes, P., Nagy, M., Bakker, E., Krawczak, M. & Knijff, P. de, 1996. Analysis of molecular variance (AMOVA) of Y-chromosome-specific microsatellites in two closely related human populations. *Human Molecular Genetics* 5, 1029–33

Rogers, J. & Waldron, T., 1995. *A Field Guide to Joint Diseases in Archaeology*. Chichester: Wiley

Rogers, J.E.T. 1866–1902. *History of Agriculture and Prices in England 1259–1793*. Oxford, Clarendon Press (1963 reprint)

Ross, L., 1980. *16th-century Spanish Basque Coopering Technology: a report of the staved containers found in 1978–79 on the wreck of the whaling galleon San Juan, sunk in Red Bay, Labrador, AD 1565*. Ottawa: Manuscript Report number 408, Parks Canada

Rouyer, J. & Hutcher, E., 1858. *Histoire du Jeton au Moyen Age*. Paris

Rowlands, J., 1985. *Holbein. The Paintings of Hans Holbein the Younger. Complete Edition*. Oxford: Phaidon

Rowse., A.L., 1937. *Sir Richard Grenville of the* Revenge. London: Jonathan Cape

Ruempol, A.P.E. & Dongen A.G.E. van, 1991. *Pre-industrial Utensils*. Rotterdam: Museum Boymans van Beuningen

Rule, M., 1982. *The* Mary Rose: *the Excavation and Raising of Henry VIII's Flagship*. London: Conway Maritime Press

Rule, M., 1983a. The search for the *Mary Rose. National Geographic* 163, 654–75

Rule, M., 1983b. *The* Mary Rose, *the Excavation and Raising of Henry VIII's Flagship*. London: Conway Maritime Press (2nd edn)

Rule, N., 1989. The Direct Survey Method (DSM) of underwater survey and its application underwater. *International Journal of Nautical Archaeology* 18, 157–62

Rule, N., 1995. Some techniques for cost-effective three-dimensional mapping of underwater sites. In J. Wilcock & K. Lockyear (eds), *Computer Applications and Quantitative*

Methods in Archaeology 1993, 51–6. Oxford: British Archaeological Report S589

Rundall, T. (ed.), 1849. Voyages towards the North West. *Hakluyt Society Publication* 5, 232

Russell, H., n.d. Rule holders and joggle sticks?. *The Mortice and Tenon* 3, unnumbered pages

Rutt, R. 1987. *A History of Hand Knitting.* London:Batsford

Ryder, M.L., 1984. Wools and textiles in the *Mary Rose*, a Six-teenth century English warship. *Journal of Archaeological Science* 11, 337–443

Ryder, M.L., 1988. Animal hair in medieval ship caulking throws light on livestock types. *Environmental Archaeology* 2, 61–6

Sachs, H. & Amman, J., 1568 *The Book of Trades (Ständebuch).* New York: Dover Publications (1973 facsimile)

Saffrey, J. & Stewart, M. (eds), 1997. *Maintaining the Whole.* Milton Keynes: Open University Human Biology and Health Book 3

Saiki, R.K., Scharf, S., Faloona, F., Mullis, K.B., Horn, G.T., Erlich, H.A. & Arnheim, N., 1985. Enzymatic amplification of beta-globin genomic sequences and restriction site analysis for diagnosis of sickle cell anemia. *Science* 230, 1350–4

Salaman, R.A., 1976, *Dictionary of Tools: used in the woodworking and allied trades* c. *1700–1970.* London: Macmillan

Samuel, D., 1997. Cereal foods and nutrition in ancient Egypt. *Nutrition* 13(6), 579–80

Sanger, F., Nicklen, S. & Coulson, A.R., 1977. DNA sequencing with chain-terminating inhibitors. *Proceedings of the National Academy of Sciences of the United States of America* 74, 5463–7

Scammell, G.V., 1970, Manning the English merchant service in the sixteenth century. *Mariner's Mirror* 56, 151–4

Scarisbrick, D., 1995. *Tudor and Jacobean Jewellery.* London: Tate

Schmidt-Thomé, P., 1985. Hölzernes Alltagesgeschirr und Spiele aus einer mittelalterlichen Abfallgrube in Freiburg. *In Der Keltenfürst von Hochdorf. Methoden und Ergebnisse der Lanesarchäologie, Katalog zur Austellung Stuttgart, 14 Aug.–13 Okt 1985*, 462–71, 490–5. Stuttgart

Schlosser, Julius von, 1920. *Die Sammlung Alter Musikinstrumente.* Vienna: Anton Schroll (1974 facsimile Georg Olms, Hildesheim)

Schuck, M., 1992. Horn-, Geweih- und Knochenverarbeitung. In *Stadtluft, Hirsebrei und Bettelmönch. Die Stadt um 1300*, 416–17. Zürich

Scott, P.J., 1981. The Reflex Plotters: measurement without photographs. *Photogrammetric Record* 10(58), 435–46

Sharman, I.M., 1981. Vitamin requirements of the human body. In J. Watt, E.J. Freeman & W.F. Bynum (eds), *Starving Sailors*, 17–26. London: National Maritime Museum

Sichel, M., 1977. *Tudors and Elizabethans.* London: Batsford

Sim, A., 1997. *Food and Feast in Tudor England.* Gloucester: Sutton

Simpson, A., 1961. *The Wealth of the Gentry, 1540–1660.* Cambridge: University Press

Simpson, K. & Knight, B., 1985. *Forensic Medicine.* London: Edward Arnold

Smith, A.H., 1952. *New College Oxford and its Buildings.* Oxford: New College

Smith, J., 1627, *A Sea Grammar.* London

Smith, K.G.V., 1986. *A Manual of Forensic Entomology.* London: British Museum Natural History

Smith, R., 1816. *Key to the Manufacturers of Sheffield.* Sheffield

Spencer, B., 1985. Fifteenth-century collar of SS and hoard of false dice with their container, from the Museum of London. *Antiquaries Journal* 65, 449–53

Spencer, B., 1990, *Pilgrim Souvenirs and Secular Badges.* Salisbury: Salisbury Museum Medieval Catalogue Part 2

Spencer, B., 1998. *Pilgrim Souvenirs and Secular Badges.* London: Medieval Finds from Excavations in London 7

Spencer, G.F, Herb, S.F. & Gorminsky, P.J., 1976. Fatty acid composition as a basis for identification of commercial fats and oils. *Journal of the American Oil Chemists Society* 53, 94–6

Spitzers, T.A., 1997. Late medieval bone-bead production: socio-economic aspects on the basis of material from Constance, Germany. In G. de Boe & F. Verhaeghe (eds), *Material Culture in Medieval Europe*, 147–54. Zellick: Papers of the 'Medieval Europe Brugge 1997' conference 7

Spont, A., 1897–8. *Letters and Papers Relating to the War with France 1512–1514.* London: Navy Records Society 10

Stace, C., 1997. *New Flora of the British Isles.* Cambridge: University Press (2nd edn)

Staden, R., Beal, K.F. & Bonfield. J.K., 2000. The Staden package, 1998. *Methods in Molecular Biology* 132, 115–30

Staniforth, M., 1987. The casks from the wreck of the William Salthouse. *Australian Historical Archaeology* 5, 21–8

Staniland, K., 1993. *London Bodies, The Changing Shape of Londoners from Prehistoric Times to the Present Day.* London: Museum of London

Staniland, K., 1997. Getting there, got it: archaeological textiles and tailoring in London, 1330–1580. In D. Gaimster & P. Stamper (eds), *The Age of Transition. The Archaeology of English Culture 1400–1600*, 239–48. Oxford: Society for Medieval Archaeology Monograph 15

Stannard J., 1971. Hans von Gersdorff, *Pharmacy in History* 13, 55-65

Stannard, J., 1972. Botanical Nomenclature in Gersdorff's *Feldtbuch.* In Debus, G. (ed.), *Science, Medicine and Society in the Renaissance*, 87–103, New York: Science History Publishers

Starkey, D. (ed.), 1991. Henry VIII. *A European Court in England.* London: Collins & Brown

Starkey, D., (ed.), 1998. *The Inventory of King Henry VIII. The Transcript.* London: Society of Antiquaries of London

Starnes, D. & Leake, C.D., 1945. *Profitable and Necessarie Booke of Observations by William Clowes.* New York: Scholars' Facsimiles and Reprints

Steane, J.M. & Foreman, M., 1991. The archaeology of medieval fishing tackle. In G.L. Good, R.H. Jones & M.W. Ponsford (eds), *Waterfront Archaeology*, 88–101. London: Council for British Archaeology Research Report 74

Stenuit, R., 1978, The sunken treasure of St Helena. *National Geographic* 154(4), 562–76

Stevens, K.F. & Olding, T.E. (eds), 1985. *The Brokage Books of Southampton for 1477–8 and 1527–8.* Southampton: Southampton Records Series 28

Stewart, I. J., 1988. Note on the Tabula set. In T. Darvill, Excavations on the site of the early Norman castle at Gloucester, 1983–84. *Medieval Archaeology* 32, 31–2

Stewart, R.G., 1980. *The* Mary Rose *1971–1979: an environmental Statement.* Portsmouth: Mary Rose Trust, upublished report

Steinbock, R.T., 1976. *Paleopathological Diagnosis and Interpretation: bone diseases in ancient human populations.* Springfield, Illinois: Charles Thomas

Sterling, J.C., Meyers, M.C., Chesshir, W. & Calvo, R.D., 1995. Os acromiale in a baseball catcher. *Medicine and Science in Sports and Exercise* 27, 795–9

Still, G.F., 1931. *The History of Paediatrics.* London: Oxford University Press

Stirland, A., 1984. A possible correlation between os acromiale and occupation in the burials from the *Mary Rose. Proceedings of the 5th European Meeting of the Paleopathology Association*, 327–34

Stirland, A., 1991. Diagnosis of occupationally related paleopathology: can it be done?. In D.J. Ortner & A.C. Aufderheide (eds), *Human Paleopathology: current syntheses and future options*, 40–7. Washington: Smithsonian

Stirland, A.J., 1992. *Asymmetry and Activity-Related Change in Selected Bones of the Human Male Skeleton.* Unpublished Ph.D Thesis, University College London

Stirland, A.J., 1993. Asymmetry and activity-related change in the male humerus. *International Journal of Osteoarchaeology* 3, 105–13

Stirland, A.J., 1996. Femoral non-metric traits reconsidered. *Anthropologie* 24, 249–52

Stirland, A., 2000. *Raising the Dead. The Skeleton Crew of King Henry VIII's Great Ship, the* Mary Rose. Chichester: Wiley

Stirland, A., 2005. *Raising the Dead. The Skeleton Crew of King Henry VIII's Great Ship, the* Mary Rose. Stroud: Tempus (revised edn)

Stirland A.J. & Waldron T., 1997. Evidence of activity related markers on the vertebrae of the crew of the *Mary Rose. Journal of Archaeological Science* 24, 329–35

Stone, A.C. & Stoneking, M., 1993. Ancient DNA from a pre-Columbian Amerindian population. *American Journal of Physical Anthropology* 92, 463–71

Stone, A.C. & Stoneking, M., 1999. Analysis of ancient DNA from a prehistoric Amerindian cemetery. *Philosophical Transactions of the Royal Society, London, Series B, Biological Science* 354, 153–9

Stone, A.C., Milner, G.R., Pääbo, S., & Stoncking, M., 1996. Sex determinaton of ancient skeletons using DNA. *American Journal of Physical Anthropology* 99, 231–8

Strayer, J.R. (ed.), 1988. *Dictionary of the Middle Ages Vol. II.* New York: Scribner

Stringer, A., 1977. *The Experienced Huntsman.* Belfast: Blackstaff Press (first published 1714, repinted edn, ed. J. Fairley)

Strutt, J., 1801. *The Sports and Pastimes of the People of England*

Studer, P., 1913. *The Port Books of Southampton: accounts of Robert Florys, water bailiff and receiver of petty customs A.D. 1427–1430.* Southampton: Southampton Records Society

Surtees Society, 1914. *York Memorandum Book 1482*

Suchey, J.M. & Brooks, S.T., 1988. Skeletal age determination based on the male os pubis. *Presentation to the 12th International Congress of Anthropological and Ethnological Sciences.* Zagreb

Swann, J., 2001. *History of Footwear in Norway, Sweden and Finland. Prehistory to 1950.* Stockholm

Syvret M. & Stevens J., 1998. *Balleine's History of Jersey.* Chichester: Phillimore

Tanner, J.R., 1920. *Samuel Pepys and the Royal Navy.* Cambridge: University Press

Taylor, E.G.R., 1971. *The Haven-Finding Art: a history of navigation from Odysseus to Captain Cook.* London: Hollis & Carter (2nd edn)

Taylor, E.G.R., 1954. *The Mathematical Practitioners of Tudor and Stuart England.* Cambridge: University Press

Taylor, G., 1968. *Silver.* London: Pelican (1986 reprint)

Taylor, G. & Scarisbrick, D., 1978. *Finger Rings from Ancient Egypt to the Present Day.* Oxford: Ashmolean Museum

Taylor, M., 1992. Flag Fen: the wood. *Antiquity* 66, 476–98

Thomas, D.H., 1991. *St Catherines. An Island in Time.* Georgia: Georgia History & Culture Series

Thomas, C., Sloane, B. & Phillpotts, C., 1996. *Excavations at the Priory and Hospital of St Mary Spital.* London: Museum of London Archaeology Service

Thomas, M., 1972. *Mary Thomas's Knitting Book.* New York: Dover

Thornton, M.D., Morgan, E.D. & Cerolia, F., 1970. The composition of bog butter. *Science and Archaeology* 2/3, 20–4

Throckmorton, P., 1987. *The Sea Remembers.* London: Chancellor

Thurley, S., 1993. *The Royal Palaces of Tudor England: Architecture and Court Life 1460–1547.* London & New Haven: Yale University Press

Tierra, M., 1998. *The Way of Herbs.* New York: Pocket

Townend, P., 1988. Bone working industry. In P. Hinton (ed.), *Excavations in Southwark 1973–76. Lambeth 1973–79, 408 & 411–12.* London: London & Middlesex Archaeological Society/Surrey Archaeological Society Joint Paper 3

Trease, G.E. & Evans, W.C., 1996. *A Textbook of Pharmacognosy.* London: Bailliere, Tindall & Cassell

Treasure Trove Reviewing Committe, 1988. *Annual Report 1996–97.* London

Trevelyan, G.M. 1947. *English Social History: a survey of six centuries Chaucer to Queen Victoria.* London: Oxford University Press

Trotter, M., 1970. Estimation of stature from intact long limb bones. In T.D. Stewart (ed.), *Personal Identification in Mass Disasters*, 71–8. Washington D.C.: Smithsonian

Trow-Smith, R., 1957. *A History of British Livestock Husbandry to 1700.* London: Routledge & Kegan Paul

Tulloch, A.P., 1971. Beeswax: structure of the esters and their component hydroxy acids and diols. *Chemistry and Physics of Lipids* 6, 235–65

Turnbull, W.B., 1861. *Calendar of State Papers, Foreign Series, of the reign of Edward VI, 1547–53*. London: Longman

Turnau, I., 1991. (ed). *History of Hand Knitting Before Mass Production*. Warsaw: Institute of the History of Material Culture (trans A. Szonert)

Turner, W., 1965. *Libellus de re Herbaris 1538 and A Gardener's Herbal 1548*. London: Ray Society (facsimile)

Ubelaker, D.H., 1984. *Human Skeletal Remains: excavation, analysis, interpretation*. Washington D.C.: Smithsonian

Urdang, G., 1944 (ed.). *Pharmacopoeia Londinensis 1618*. Madison: Wisconsis State History Society (facsimile)

Vernier, R., (ed.), 1994. *Le Barbier-Chirurgien Vol II*. Brussels

Vernier, R., (ed.), 1999. *L'Exposition 'Le Barbier-Chirurgien' instruments des Chirurgie Vol III – Brussels 1994*. Brussels: Editiones du Cabinet d'Expertises

Verster, A.J.G., 1957. *Old European Pewter*. Amsterdam

Vigo, G. da [John de], 1543. *The Most Excellent Workes of Chirurgerye*

Wainscoat, J. S., Hill, A.V., Boyce, A.L., Flint, J., Hernandez, M., Thein, S.L., Old, J.M., Lynch, J.R., Falusi, A.G., Weatherall, D.J. & Clegg, J.B., 1986. Evolutionary relationships of human populations from an analysis of nuclear DNA polymorphisms. *Nature* 319, 491–3

Wakely, J., 1996. Limits to interpretation of skeletal trauma – two cases from medieval Abingdon. *International Journal of Osteoarchaeology* 6, 76–83

Wakely, J., Manchester, K. & Roberts, C., 1991. Scanning Electron Microscopy of rib lesions. *International Journal of Osteoarchaeology* 1, 185–9

Waldron, T., 1994. *Counting the Dead. The Epidemiology of Skeletal Populations*. Chichester: Wiley

Waldron, T., 1998. A note on the estimation of height from long bone measurements. *International Journal of Osteoarchaeology* 8, 75–7

Walker, P., 1982. The tools available to the mediaeval woodworker. In McGrail, S. (ed.), *Woodworking Techniques Before 1500*. Oxford: British Archaeological Report S129

Walton, P. & Eastwood, G., 1988. *A Brief Guide to the Cataloguing of Archaeological Textiles*. York: York Archaeological Trust

Ward, C., 2001. The Sadana Island shipwreck; an eighteenth century ad merchant man off the Red Sea coast of Egypt, *World Archaeology* 32(2), 368–82

Ward, R. & Stringer, C., 1997. A molecular handle on the Neanderthals. *Nature* 388, 225–6

Waters, D.W., 1958. *The Art of Navigation in England in Elizabethan and Early Stuart Times*. London: Hollis & Carter

Waters, D.W., 1967. *The Rutters of the Sea. The Sailing Directions of Pierre Garcie. A Study of the First English and French Sailing Directions*. New Haven & London: Yale University Press

Watson, J.D. & Crick, F.H., 1953. Molecular structure of nucleic acids; a structure for deoxyribose nucleic acid. *Nature* 171, 737–8

Watt, Sir J., 1981. Some consequences of nutritional disorders in eighteenth century British circumnavigations. In J. Watt, E.J. Freeman & W.F. Bynum (eds), *Starving Sailors*, 51–71. London: National Maritime Museum

Watt, Sir J., 1983. Surgeon's of the *Mary Rose*. *Mariner's Mirror* 69, 3–19

Watt Sir J. 1994. The *Mary Rose* and Tudor surgery. *Journal Royal Naval Medical Services* 80, 156–65

Waugh, N., 1964. *The Cut of Men's Clothes 1600–1900*. London: Faber & Faber

Weinstein, R., 2005. Early pewter with an English provenance. *Journal of the Pewter Society* Autumn 2005, 2–6

Weinstein, R., forthcoming. The origins of the crowned rose symbol on pewter. *Journal of the Pewter Society* (2006)

Welch, C., 1902. *History of the Worshipful Company of Pewterers of the City of London*. London

Wells, F.A., 1972. *The British Hosiery and Knitwear Industry: its history and organisation*. Newton Abbot: David & Charles

Wendrich, W. 1991. *Who is Afraid of Basketry? A Guide to Recording Basketry and Cordage for Archaeologists and Ethnograhpers*. Leiden: Centre for Non-Western Studies, Leiden University

Wenzel, A., Henriksen, J. & Melsen, B., 1983. Nasal respiratory resistance and head posture: Effect of intranasal corticosteroid (Budesonide) in children with asthma and perennial rhinitis. *American Journal of Orthodontics* 84, 422–6

Wheeler, A., 1984. The fish bones. In Redknap 1984, 93

Wheeler, A. & Jones, A.K.G., 1976. Fish remains. In A. Rogerson (ed.), *Excavations on Fullers Hill, Great Yarmouth*. Dereham: East Anglian Archaeol 2, 131–245

Whitlock, P. 1985. The boatswain's call: an updating. *Mariner's Mirror* 71(1), 167–8

Whitney, W.D., 1900. *The Century Dictionary*. London & New York: The Times

Williams, D.F., 1983. Petrology of ceramics. In D.R.C. Kempe & A.P. Harvey (eds), *The Petrology of Archaeological Artefacts*, 301–29. Oxford

Williams, M.J., 1985. *An Investigation of the Minor Constituents of Fatty Materials from a 1000-year-old Thule Eskimo site: II; an Investigation of the Decomposition of Food Remains Retrieved from the Wreck of the* Mary Rose. Department of Chemistry, University of Keele, unpublished project (in Mary Rose Trust archive)

Williams, N., 1971. *Henry VIII and his Court*. New York: Macmillan

Willmott, H., 2002. *Early Post-Medieval Vessel Glass in England c. 1500–1670*. York: Council for British Archaeology Research Report 132

Wilson, C.A., 1984. *Food and Drink in Britain from the Stone Age to Modern Times*. Harmondsworth: Penguin

Wilson, E., 1987. The debate of carpenter's tools. *Review of English Studies* 38, 445–70

Wilson, P., 2001. The Mary Rose fiddles. *Newsletter of the British Violin Making Association* 25, 16–25

Windisch-Graetz, F., 1983. *Möbel Europas* (Vol. I – Romanik-Gotik). Munich

Wingood, A., Wingood, M. & Adams, J., 1986. Sea Venture. *The Tempest Wreck*. Hamilton: Island Press

Winkler, L., (ed.) 1934. *Das Dispensatorium des Valerius Cordus 1546*. Innsbruck (facsimile)

Winston-Allen, A., 1997. *Stories of the Rose. The Making of the Rosary in the Middle Ages*. Pennsylvania: University Press

Withers, P. & Withers, B., 1993. *British Coin Weights*. Llanfyllin

Wittop Koning, D.A. & Houben, G.M.M., 2000. *Jaar Gewichten in de Nederlanden, Lochem, 1980*

Wood, A.B., 1919. The Lord Admiral's whistle. *Mariner's Mirror* 5, 58

Wood, R., in press. *The Wooden Bowl*. Ammanford: Stobart Davies

Woodall, J. 1617. *The Surgeon's Mate 1617*. London: Kingsmead (facsimile 1978).

Woodbury, R.S., 1961. *History of the Lathe to 1850*. Cleveland, Ohio: Society for the History of Technology

Woodfield, C., 1981. Finds from the Free Grammar School at the Whitefriars, Coventry, *c.* 1545–*c.* 1557/8. *Post-Medieval Archaeology* 15, 81–159

Woodhead, P., 1996. *Sylloge of Coins of the British Isles 47: Herbert Schneider Collection Part I, English Gold Coins and their Imitiations* 1257–1603. London: Spink

Woodside, D.G. & Linder-Aronson, S., 1979. The channelization of upper and lower anterior face heights compared to population standard in males between ages 6 to 20 years. *European Journal of Orthodontics* 1, 25–40

Wright, D., 1983. *The Complete Book of Baskets and Basketry*. Newton Abbot: David & Charles (2nd edn)

Wyss, M., 1991, Ein Spielbrett des 12. Jahrhunderts aus Saint-Denis (Frankreich). In A. Kluge-Pinsker, *Schach und Trictrac. Zeugnisse mittelalterlicher Spielfreude in Salischer Zeit*, 58–61. Römisch-Germanisches Zentralmuseum Monographien Bd 30

Yarwood, D., 1952. *English Costume from the Second Century B.C. to 1952*. London: Batsford

Yarwood, D., 1961. *English Costume from the Second Century BC to 1960*. London: Batsford

Youings, J., 1984. *Sixteenth-Century England*. London: Penguin

Zekert, O. (ed.), 1938. *Dispensatorium – Pro Pharmacopoeis Viennensibus 1570* (facsimile, Berlin)

Zimmerman L.M. & Veith, I., 1961. *Great Ideas in the History of Surgery*. Baltimore: Williams & Wilkins

Zeiler, J.T., 1993. Zes Vaten Rundvlees uit het Scheepswrak *Scheurrak SO1*, Project SO1. *Tussentijdse Rapportage* 10. Alphen aan den Rijn

Zohary, D. & Hopf, M., 2000. *Domestication of Plants in the Old World: the origin and spread of cultivated plants in West Asia, Europe, and the Nile Valley*. Oxford: Clarendon Press (2nd edn)

Index

by Barbara Hird

NOTE: References in italics denote illustrations.

Aachen, Germany 225
Aberafan Sands, South Wales 292
access around ship 13, 15, 655–6
accessories *see* bags, leather; pouches, leather; purses, leather
accounting, tally sticks for 334, *335*
action, ship in 16–17, 293–4, 297
activity and occupation *see* under human remains
adipocere 567, 586, 631–2
adzes 295, 305, *305*
    'stirrup' 295, *306*, 307
age of crew
    dental evidence 519–20, 556–7
    youth 12, 174, 516, 519–20, 657
agrimony burrs *599*, 601
ague (malarial fever) 174, 180
aiglets 18, 25, 56, 65, 94–5, *94*
    in chests 24, 25, *26*, 95, 109
    with laces 94–5, *98*, 99
    with leather jerkins 25, 38
    with shoes 65, 79
Alcega, Juan de 20, 48
alcohol-glycerine formalin solution (AGF) 507, 590, 591
Altarnum, Cornwall 244, *248*
alumino-silicate sediments 511
Amati violin, Ashmolean Museum, Oxford 243, 244
Amerindian populations; ancient DNA 645, 647
amputation 178, *179*, 181, *211*, 212, 377
Amsterdam wreck 409, 414, 501, 503
anaemia, iron deficiency 525–6, *525*, *526*, 608
anaerobic conditions 18, 501, 511
angels, bone casket panel carved with 16, 123–6, *124*, 127, 658, Pl. 17
animal remains *see* bone, animal; fats, animal
Ann Francis wreck 126, 292
Anne wreck 503
anodynes 181
Anthony Roll (1546) 11

archery equipment 390–1, 534
    cask contents not listed 409
    crew 519, 533, 601, 609
    picture of ship 1, 1–2, *654*
antler objects 319
Antwerp, Belgium
    pewter mark (rose) 490
    pharmaceutical trade 224
    pottery 192
    trade with London 225
apothecary's balance, supposed 258, 508
apple pip 15, 597
archaeobotany *see* plant remains
archers and archery 2, 11, 17, 390–1, 533–8
    jerkins 25–6, 27, 45–7, *47*
    number on ship 519, 533–5
    specialist war bow men 175, 529, 533–8, 544, 657
    see also arrows; bracers; longbows
archive record cards 6, *7*
Armada wrecks 126, 292, 423
armour 26, 41, 101, 528
army, victualling of 604, 608, 610
arrow-shaped marks 296, 490, 493, 496, 656
    on boatswain's call *287*, *288*, 288
    on bowls *447*, 448, 481, *481*
    on bucket 365
    on casks 140, 419
    on flagons *437*, 439, *451*, 452, 490
    on shoes 91–2
    on shovels, with letters 349
    on tankards *451*, 452, 490, 493
    on trestle *379*, 380
arrows 11, 534
    binding 633
    chests 656, 389–90; location 2, 13, 17, 27, 385, *388*
    glues 632–3
    trace metals in fletchings 641
    wounds 176, 531, *533*
    see also archers and archery
arthritis 528, 532, 541, 657

ash boxes 370–1, *370*
augers 295–6, 297, 299–301, *300*
axes 295–6, 304–5, *305*

backgammon 15, 134
see also Tables set
badge, token or icon of Virgin Mary, lead 16, 109, 126–7, *126*, 658
Baeshe, Edward 603, *603*
bags, leather 107, *108*, 109, 244
    stoppers or lids for 371–3, *372*
balances and balance cases *see* scales
Ballad of the Caps 32, 33
ballast 2, 13, 511
    pollen analysis 619, 626, 628
bandages 189, 207, *208*, 211, 219
    chemical analysis 219, 221, 222–3, 634, 636, 637
banquet on *Henry Grace à Dieu* 19, 441, 443, 569
Barber-surgeon 11, 171–2
    assistant 11, 15, 154, 172
    Book of Trades on 196, 216, *217*
    cabin 2, *2*, 13, 14–15, 171, 189– 225, 653
    chest 14–15, 171, 189, *190*, 225, 393, 394, 397, Pl. 26
    contents of cabin and chest 14–15, 189–218, Pls 27–30; scientific analyses 633–41; *see also* benches; buckles; canisters; medical and shaving equipment; medicaments; peppercorns; pewter objects; pottery; purses, leather; tankards; wallet; whistles
    fragments of second chest 216
    marks on items in cabin 200, *201*, *201*, 460, *491*; initials 11, 37, 200–1, *202* *203*, 225, 439–40, *439*, *492*, 493, 657
    origin of items used by 224–5
    role and status 11, 37, 171–2, 189, 657
    shaving and grooming service and

equipment 11, 15, 154, 156–7, 171, 172, 189, 216–18, *216–18*, 657; *see also* ear-scoops; whet-stones
    training 171–2
    see also caps (silk); benches; medical and shaving equipment; medicaments; medicine
Barber-Surgeons, Company of 36–7, 171, 175, 224, Pl. 25
Barbers, Company of 171
Barents, Willem; *Nova Zembla* 269, 273
barrels *see* casks
baskets 400–8, *403–7*, Pl. 54
    cleft wood and willow 402, 407
    distribution and functions 407–8, *407*, 348, 385; Barber-surgeon's equipment 216; carpenters' tools 13, 297, 299, 305, 308–9, 310, 312, *503*; foodstuffs 15, 385, 407–8, 566, *568*, 579, 594, 595, 596–7, 601; pins 329
    fitched 402, 406, *406*, 407
    general styles 401–4
    glossary of terms 403
    handles 404, *404*
    large rectangular 402, 405–6, *405–6*, *407*, 408
    oval *403*, 404, 407, *407*; lidded, with plait border 402, 404–5, *404*, 407
    round-based 402–3, *403*, 407, *407*
    unusual 404-7
Bassano family (musical instrument makers) 228, 233, *237*
Bayeux Tapestry 425, 483
beads Pl. 14
    see also paternosters
bedding 13, 598, 599, 600, 601, Pl. 69
    insect remains in 613
    pollen analysis 626
    see also mattresses
beds 13, 15, 296, 382, 653
beef *see* cattle bones and beef
'beef tree', butcher's 573, *603*
beer 15, 595–6, 656
    Maison Dieu for officers 612
    and hydration 608, 610
    nutritional value 595–6, 607, 608, 610
    rations 523, 595, 603, 604, 609
    safety 15, 422, 524, 595–6, 608, 610
    storage 385, 422
    supply 610, 656
beeswax in glue on arrows 633
beetles
    Cytilus sericeus 615, 616
    dung 616
    powder post 615, 616
bell, ship's 281, 284, *285*
bellows 369–70, *370*

belts, leather 20, 100
bench-chests 394–6, *394–7*, 397
    see also purser (chest)
benches 13, 653
    Barber-surgeon's treatment 14, 171, *177*, 214, 377, *378*, 653
    chests function as 15, 376, 394–6, 654
Bermuda; wreck of *Sea Venture* 293
besoms 600
bilge pump 13
    pollen from 619, 626, 628
bills (weapons) *see* pikes and bills
binnacles 266, 267
biscuit 593–4, 601, 603, 604, 609, 656
black dye 34, 36
blanket 296
bleeding 180, 214
    bowl for 189, 200–1, *202*
blood groups 644–5
blue- and greenbottles 616, 617, 657
boatswains 11, 227, 262
    calls 227, 281, *282*, 284–92, *286–9*, *291*
bobbins, sewing 327–8, *328*
bog butter, Scottish 631–2
bone, animal 501, 514, 564–88
    adipocere 567, 586, 631–2
    in bowls and dishes 566, 569, 577
    in casks 385, 566, *568*, 569; *see also* under cattle bones and beef; pig bones and pork
    distribution 385, 565, 566, 567, *568*
    glossary of terms 567
    meals, evidence of 567–9
    methods and history of analysis 505–6, 514, 566–7
    numbers 564, 565
    origins and recovery 564–7
    post-Tudor 565
    preservation 564, 568, 569
    recording system 6, 565, *565*, 566, 567
    retrieval and preparation 506, 565–6, *565*
    from shelly layer 565, 577
    significance of study 586–8
    size, robusticity and morphology of animals 585–6, 656
    taphonomy 564–5, 586–8
    see also butchery; cattle bones and beef; deer, fallow; dog skeleton; fowl, domestic; pig bones and pork; rabbit (bones); rats
bone, human *see* human remains
bone objects
    knife handles 145, 148, 152
    see also casket panel; dice; domino; ear-scoops; manicure or toilet sets; paternosters

bonnet, *see* coif, Barber-surgeon's
Book of Trades 196, 216, *217*, 303, 352, 353, *376*, *377*
book mark or paper knife 128, *129*, 132
books 13, 16, 127–32, *128–32*, Pl. 15
    adapted covers: balance case 131, 260–1, *261*; sundial case 130, 131, 167, 168, *169*, 261
    clasps 128, *128*, 129–30, *129*, *130*, *132*, 261, *261*
    paper fragments 127, 128, *128*
    with pouch 109
    prayer 16, 117, 127, *130*, 131, *131*, 132, 658
    ribbons 128, 130, *131*, *132*, 132
boots
    ankle 72–4, *73*, *74*, *75*, 82–4
        associated finds 25, 83; human remains 22, 23, 25, 83, 84
        in chests 24, 25, *26*, 83, 84
        comparable finds elsewhere *85*, 85–6
        construction 72, *73*, 86
        distribution 83, *84*
        number 18
        in sack on Orlop deck 79, 83, 84
        textile elements 86
        types 73–4, *74*, *75*, 82–4; buckled 73–4, *75*, 83, 84, 85, *85*, 100; laced 73, *74*, 74, 83, 84, *85*
    thigh 74, 76–8, *76*, *77*, *78*, 84–5
        buckled 76–7, *78*, 86, 100
        comparable finds elsewhere 85–6
        distribution *84*
        number 18
        as officers' property 27
        straight-legged 74, 76, *76*, *77*, 84–5, 86
        straps 74, 76, *76*
        straw insulation *88*, 88
        textile elements *76*, 76, 86, 87–8
        turn-welted 61
Bos, Cornelis *228*, 248–9
bottles
    glass, Barber-surgeon's 189, 192–3, *193*, 225, Pl. 28
    leather 215, *215*, 424, 428–9, *448*, 454–6, *454–6*, 458
    pottery 424, 462, 464, 467–9, *468*, 476, Pl. 64
    wooden feeding- 189, *212*, 212–14
Bourne, William; *A Regiment for the Sea* 265, 266, 276
bow, fiddle 227, 229, 247–8, *247–8*
Bowcastle *2*, 2, 15, 17
bowls
    animal bones with 569, 577
    copper-alloy, Barber-surgeon's 204–5, *205*, 216–17, *216*, *217*; pitch/tar 14, 320, *320*, *321*, Pl. 48

marks 11, 446, *447*, 448, 449, 481, *481*, 493, *494*, 496, 497, 656, (Ny Coep) 11, 446, *447*, 448, 493
pewter 424, 448–9, *448*; Barber-surgeon's porringer or bleeding bowl 189, 200–1, *202*
pottery 464, 467, 474, 476, 477
wooden 15, 426, 480–4, *481–3*, 489, Pls 57, 59, 61; Barber-surgeon's 189, 205, 207, *207*, 225; distribution 385, *441*, 447–8, 483; as drinking vessels 15, 483, *483*, 497; food preparation or serving 385, *483*, 483–4; marks 446, 447, *448*, 481, *481*, 493, *494*, 497, 656, Pl. 59, (Ny Coep) 11, 446, *447*, 448, 493; 'messing' items 424, 446–8, *446–7*, Pl. 61; paint on 482–3
boxes, small wooden 397–8, *398–401*
cylindrical, holding metal clasps *97*, 97, 99, *398*, 400
distribution 398, *401*
peppercorns in 595
with razors, Barber-surgeon's 398
recording system 5
for scales 131, 258, *258*, 260–1, *261*
tinder boxes 398
use against rats 614, 657
bracers, archers' 100, 103, 534
braces, carpenters' 295–6, 301–3, *301*, Pl. 44
bracken 599, 601, 602
bracket fungus 319, 514
braids 18, 20, *35*, 36, 105–6, *106*
see also ribbons
brain tissue, human 501, 510, 514, 516, 563
brands on woodware 358, 359, 419, 482
see also 'H' mark
bread 523, 594, 607, 610, 656
breeches 18, 19, 20, *49*, 50, 56, 58
Bristol
Apprentice Register 240
export of caps to Iceland 33
Greyfriars; wooden bowl 484
broom 507, 514, 593, 600, 602, Appx 3.3
broom weevil in 615, 616
distribution 510
misidentified as peas in pod 508, 588, 597
uses 600, 601, 613
brooms 15, 353, 353–6, 656
brothels 174
Browne, John (Master of *Mary Rose*) 11, 262
Brueghel, Pieter
The Blind Leading the Blind 19, *19*
The Peasant and the Birdnester 99, *99*

The Peasant Dance 85, 86
The Triumph of Death 135
The Wedding Feast 426
Brunschwig, Hieronymus
Compounds 181, 182, 185–6
Liber de arte distillandi de simplicibus 185–6, 223
The Noble Experience of the Warke of Surgerie 171–2, 175–6, 217, 224
brushes 353–5, *354–6*
broom twigs used as 600, 601
grooming 218, *219*, 354
paintbrush type 353, 355, *355*, *356*
shaving, possible *156*, 156, 355
sweeping and scrubbing 15, 353–6, *354–6*, 613, 656, Pl. 47
see also brooms
buckets
distribution 15, 348, 359, 363, 366, 385, 613
leather 15, 359–67, *359–62*, *364–5*, Pl. 47; arrow-mark 365; caulking 320; distribution 15, 359, *359*, 363, 366
wooden staved 15, 356, 357–8, *357*, 359; incised lines on base 357, *357*, 359; possible mess bucket 357, *357*, 424, 440; T?Brown branded, possibly post-Tudor 358, 359
buckles
copper-alloy 20, 99–105, *100*, *101*, *104*
and armour 101
in chests 24, 25, *26*; Barber-surgeon's 100, 102, 103, 189, 214
clothing associated with 25
decoration 100, *104*
distribution 25, 100, *105*
footwear with: ankle boots 73–4, *75*, 83, 84, 85, *85*, 100; shoes 25, *69*, 70, *71*, *72*, *85*, 86, 100, 101; thigh boots 76–7, *78*, 86, 100
metallurgy 103, 105
military and civilian 99–103
number 18
types *100*, 100, *101*
iron 18, 99, 100, 101, 103
buckwheat 597
building of *Mary Rose* 12, 303, 349, 350, 608
bullet wounds 175
bungs/plugs 295, 371, *371*
cork, for stoneware jars 190, *191*, 192, 225, 471–2
wooden, for costrel neck/funnel 488, *488*
bunions 92, 657

burns and scalds 179
butchery
fish 567, 580, *580*, 581, 582–4, *582–3*, *605*
meat 567, 569, 572–4, *572–4*, *603*, 605, 656
butter 523–4, 603, 604, 609
buttonholes in leather jerkins 38, 41, *42*, *43*, 47, 48, 96, 97
buttons 18, 94, *95*, 96–7, *96*
in chest 24, *26*
of cloth jerkin 55
of leather jerkins 25, 38, 40, *96*, 97; on flap of inside pocket 20, 38, 39, *39*, 47, *47*
silk 39, 40, *95*, *96*, 96–7, 113
silk-covered leather, possible 39, 48, *95*, 97
wool *95*, 96, 97
butts, archery 531, 533–4

cabins 2, *2*, 13–15, 653–4
beds in 13, 15, 296, 653
see also under Barber-surgeon; carpenters; gunners; pilots
cables 2, 385
device on flagon 493
see also rope
calls 11, 284–92, *286–9*, *291*, Pl. 41
see also whistles
candle holders 13, 343, 346, *347*
candle snuffer, possible 347, *348*
candles 13, 343
casks of 13, 410, 417, 421
religious use 124, 125–6
candlesticks 346–7, *347*
canisters
pewter, Barber-surgeon's 189, 199, *200*, 423, 424, 460
wooden, Barber-surgeon's 189, 193–9, *194–5*, *197*, 199, 398–400, 657, Pls 30, 65; *Book of Trades* illustration 196, *217*; contents 220–1, 222, 592, 595; distribution *401*; grooved decoration 196, 197, 489; imports from Germany 198, 225; manufacture 196–9, *197*; paint traces 196, 199; turning groups 195, 197–8, *199*, 481, 487
wooden, not in Barber-surgeon's cabin 400
cannon motif on flagon *437*, 438, 439, *495*, Pl. 62
cape or collar, cloth jerkin with 18, 20, 27, 50–1, *51*, 53
caps and hats 31–7
distribution *26*
silk: Barber-surgeon's velvet coif 27, 30, 31, 35–7, *35*, 171, 215–16, 225, Pl. 3; satin with ribbons 25,

36, *37*, 37, 396
  silk linings 20, 24, *30*, *33*, *34*, 34–5,
    Pl. 4
  woollen 18, 31–5, *33*, *34*
carbohydrate in diet 607
carbon/hydrogen/nitrogen (CHN) analysis 222, 636–41
Carew, Sir George, Vice Admiral 11, 12,
  19, 291
  pewter tableware 15, 424, 440–1,
    442, 444–5, 490, *491–2*, 493, 656
Carew, Sir Peter 519
carpenters 11, 293–319
  cabin and area 2, *2*, 13–14, 296–7,
    653
    baskets of tools 13, 297, 299,
      305, 308–9, 310, 312, *503*
    beds and bedding *503*, 504, 599
    chests 13, 14, 294–5, 296, 297–9,
      392, 393, 394, 397; official
      tool crate 299, 655, 656; personal 13, 124–5, 127, 329,
      391, 391–2, 655, 656, Pls
      52–3, (tools in) 13, 294–5,
      297, 298, 299, (other items)
      96, 113, 116, 117, 121, 123,
      124–5, 127, 250, 262, 329
    organic remains *503*, 504, 599,
      600
    tools 294–6, 299–319, 655, Pl.
      46; assemblage 294–6, *296*;
      unfinished 14, 293, 296; *see
      also* individual types
    twisted-wire loops 96
  contemporary illustrations *303*, 317,
    318
  furniture made by 377, *377*, 380–1,
    380–1
  on *Henry Grace à Dieu* 299
  injuries 175
  number 293, 297, 299, 655
  officer amongst 13, 392, 394, 655
  repair damage to ship in action 293–
    4, 297
  travel and life ashore 297, 339–40
  working on Orlop deck at time of
    sinking 14, 96, 293, 297, 310–11,
    317, 337
  Worshipful Company of; privy marks
    296
cases 227, 232
  see also fleam case and under combs;
    dividers; fiddles; scales; shawm,
    still; sundials, pocket; tabor
casket panel, bone 16, 123–6, *124*, 127,
  658, Pl. 17
casks 13, 409–21
  on *Amsterdam* 414
  cask-related activities on board 419
  condition of components 409, 411

construction 412–15, *413–15*, 419
distribution 2, 13, 348, 385, 419–21,
  568, 654; *see also under individual
  decks and* Hold
fish processers standing in *605*
future research potential 655
gaming boards incised on 15, 133,
  135, *138*, 139–40, 410, 418
hoops 317, 319, 356, 409, 411, 414
markings/style 140, 419, *420*, 655
with original contents 415–18
Red Bay wreck 409, 413, 414, 415,
  419, 421
repair 317, 319, 415
reuse of staves 357
sample 409, 410–11
sizes 418–19
steeping vats 385, 410, 418, 421,
  422, 566, *568*, 569, 574, 604,
  605, 606, 609
tubs made from 358
use against rats 657
on *William Salthouse* 421
see also spiles and/or shives and under
  bone, animal; candles; cattle
  bones and beef; fish; fruit; gunpowder; pig bones and pork;
  pitch/tar; tallow; tampions; wine
Castle Acre, Norfolk 135–6, 139
Castle Hedingham, Essex 291, 292
castles, ship's 15, 17
  see also Bowcastle; Sterncastle
casts, bandage 222–3
cats, absence of 614
Cattewater wreck 503, 573, 584
cattle bones and beef
  analysis of fat adhering to 631–2
  anatomical elements 568, 568–9,
    570, 571, 572
  beef in diet 15, 523, 603–4
  butchery 569, 572–4, *572–3*, 605
  casks of salt beef 385, 410, 417, 421,
    565, 566, *568*, 569–74, *570*,
    572–3, 606
  distribution 13, 385, 566, *568*, 574,
    577, 654
  fresh beef 568, 569, 604, 605, 612
  limb meat taken off bones 573, *573*
  scattered 566, 577
  size of pieces 604, 606–7
  size 585, 609
  sources of supplies 611
  unusually white and well–preserved
    568, 569
  watering before cooking 570, 574
cauldrons 424, *428–30*, 429–31
  large, from galley furnaces 12–13,
    17, 422, *423*, 424, 425, *428*, 429,
    431, 568, 605
  small: cooking 424, *429–30*, 431,

432, *432*, *433*, 493; pitch/tar 14,
  320, *320*, 321, *322*
caulking 175, 299, 319–23
  equipment 14, 294–5, 299, 319–23,
    320–4, Pl. 48
  materials 600, 601; pollen analysis
    619, 626–7, 629
cautery, hot iron 175, 178, *179*
  iron for 208, *208*, 211
cephalometric data 550–2
cereals 589, 591, 592, 593–4, 656, Appx
  3.4
  chaff 592, 593, 598, *598*, 599, 601,
    602, Appx 3.4
  common names 591
  distribution 592, *594*, *598*, 598
  pollen analysis 618, 619, 621, 623,
    625, 626, 628
  supply 588–9, 602
  see also weeds (crop)
chafing dish, copper-alloy 203–4, *205*,
  211, 219, 225
chain mail 26, 42, 95
chalk line reels 295, *302*, 303, *303*
chamber pot, pewter 16, 154, 157, 161–
  2, *164*, 423
Chamberlayn, Thomas (pewterer) 440,
  442, 490, *491*
Channel Islands 200, 584
charred plant remains 600
chart sticks 11, 264, *265*, 266–7, 271–3,
  272, 655
Chauliac, Guy of 172, 181
cheese 523–4, 603, 604, 609, 611–12
chemical analyses
  of medicaments 219–24, 514, 633–
    41, 657
  see also CHN analysis; isotopes,
    chemical
Chenopodiaceae 620, 622, 623
cherry stones 15, 593, 596, 601
chests 387–97, Appx 1, Pls 52–3
  as benches 15, 376, 394–6, 654
  construction 387–8
  contents by chest Appx 1
  continental manufacture 393–4, 654
  decoration 391–2, *391–2*, 396, 397,
    Pl. 52
  distribution 2, 13, 15, 385, *386*, *388*,
    390, *394*, 654
  dovetailed 124–5, 133, 225, 390,
    393, 393–4, 397
  effect of sinking 13, 14, 297
  handles 388, *389*
  locks 391, 654
  marks 391–2, *391*, Pl. 52
  paint, traces of 392–3
  pollen analysis of contents 619, 628,
    629
  raising with contents intact 6, 504

recording system 5
types/contents 387, 388–96, Appx 1
Type 1, storage 396–7, 388–91, *388–9*, 656; in carpenters' cabin 299, 655, 656; *see also* under arrows; longbows
Type 2, personal *390*, 391–4, *391–3*, 397, 654, Pls 52–3; *see also* under Barber-surgeon; carpenters; pilots
Type 3, bench-chests 394–6, *394–7*, 397; *see also* purser
children in crew 12, 520, 657
chisels/files
carpenters' 295–6, 297, 307–8, *308*
surgical 189, 211, 212
turners' use 197, *197*
CHN (carbon/hydrogen/nitrogen) analysis 222, 636–41
chopping block 14, 379, *379*
chromatography 514, 631–2, 632–3
churn, possible 424, 460, *460*, 603
clasps
copper-alloy, on books and balance case 128, *128*, 129–30, *129*, *130*, *132*, 261, *261*
pewter alloy, for clothing 18, 19, 94, *97*, 97, 99, 398, Pl. 10
classification of finds 6–9, 502
Clinton, Edward Fiennes de, Lord High Admiral 291–2, *291*
cloak, compass 18, 20, 27, 50–1, *51*, 53
clothing 18–106, 657
assemblages 18–31
associated artefacts 25–6, 27; *see also* under jerkins (leather)
bracken stuffing 601
in chests 23–5, *26*, 26, 35, 79, *82*, *83*, 83, 84
colours 20; black 34, 36; dyes 20, 34, 36, 514; leather 41; red 41, *96*, 96–7; silk *96*, 96–7; wool 27, 28, 34, 48, 50, 54, 55, 56, 58
fastenings 94–106; *see also* button-holes; buttons; clasps; lace-holes; laces; loops, twisted-wire
fibres and fabrics 28–31
laws on 19, 32–3
leather 20, 28, 31; *see also* jerkins
occupation and status 18, 19, 26–7
preservation 18
provision 19–20, 656
range 20
recording methods 27–8
repairs 16, 20, 41, 48, 657
typical Tudor 19, *19*
see also braids; breeches; caps and hats; cloak, compass; footwear; hose; human remains (clothing associated with); jerkins; mittens;

ribbons; sleeves; sock or 'scogger'
clothworking plants 591, 592, 600
see also dyes; teasels
Clowes, William 208, 211, 219
cockroaches 615
coconut shells 593, 597, 602
cups 458, 597
cod Pl. 70
butchery 580, *580*, 581, *582*
distribution 578, 579
keeping qualities of salted 604
Newfoundland onboard processing *605*
Scheurrak SO1 compared 584
see also fish (salt and dried)
Coep, Ny *see* Cop or Coep, Ny
coif, Barber-surgeon's velvet 27, 30, 31, 35–7, *35*, 171, 215–16, 225, Pl. 3
coins and jettons 15, 250–7, Pls 33–4
as charms 250
in chests 15, 189, 214, 250, *251*, *253*, 254, 255, 254, 261; possible purser's chest 11, *252*, 253, 255, 262, 396, 397, 657
corrosion and concretion 250, 253–4
distribution on ship 15, 250, *251*, *253*, 254–5, *256*
gold 250–3, *251*, *252*, Pls 33–4; Edward IV 250–1, *252*; Henry VII 250, 251, *252*; Henry VIII 251–2, *252*, 253; international currency 262–3; unworn *252*, 253; value 262; weights for 259–60, *258*, *259*
human remains associated with 250, 254–5
and pay 255, 261–2
post-Tudor 255–6
in pouches/purses 15, 109, 214, 250, 254, 255, 261, 657
silver 250, 253–5, *253*, *257*; Ferdinand and Isabella of Spain 255, 262; Henry VIII 254–5; impression in empty balance case 260, *261*
see also scales
colander, copper-alloy 424, *427*, 433
Colchester, Essex 95, 96
Cole, Humphrey; navigational compendium *280*, 281
Cologne, Germany 120, 224, 225
column samples 504–5, *505*
combs 16, 154, *154*, 156–9, *157–9*, Pls 6, 21
in Barber-surgeon's chest 15, 16, 189, 218, 657
cases *157*, 159, *160*
distribution 15, 156–7, *157*
ivory 156, *158*
with jerkins 25, 27, 41, 43, Pl. 6

personal 15, 16, 25, 27, 41, 43, 83, 157, 657
in pouches 109
seaweed fly on 616, 617
commissioners for victualling 180, 609
communication equipment 281–92, Pl. 41
distribution 281, *282*, 284, 286, 288
see also bell; calls; sandglasses
companionways 13, 15, 655–6
compass, carpenter's wooden 273, *294*, 295, 312, *312*
compass-drawn circles on chests 392, *392*
compasses, navigation 11, 264, 267–71, *267–71*, 655, Pl. 36
distribution *265*, 266, *266*, 268, 270
possibly privately-owned 264, 266, 268, 270
in sundials 163–4, 165, *166*, 169–70, *170*
compendium, navigational *280*, 281
computation, jettons used for 256–7
concretion 41, 212, *212*, 250, 253–4, 296
condiment holders 424, *457*, 458–60
see also peppermills
conditions on board 613–29
see also insects; living accommodation; pollen analysis; rats; sanitation
conger eels
butchered, in stores 578, 579, 581, 582–4, *583*
disturbance of wreck by live 564, 586
context numbers 5, 10
cook, possible *see* Cop or Coep, Ny
cooking, serving and eating vessels and utensils 13, 422–98, 654
assemblage 423–9
condiment holders and other flasks 424, *457*, 458–60
cooking vessels 13, 385, *427*, 429–34
eating and drinking vessels 13, *424*, 448–58
'messing' items 424, 434, 440–8, *441–7*
official issue or personal possession 489–96, *491–2*, *494–5*, 656
serving vessels and utensils 13, 385, *426*, 434–40, 497, 605–7, 656, Pl. 57
storage vessels 424, *459*, 460–2
see also individual types of vessels and utensils
cooking pots
copper-alloy 425; cauldron, tripod, or flesh pot 424, 432, *432*, *433*; reused as pitch-pot 321, *323*
distribution 13, 385, *427*
pottery 424, 462, 464, 466, *466*,

469–70, *470*, 474–5, 476, 477, Pl. 63
cooking vessels 13, 385, *427*, 429–34
  see also cauldrons; colander; cooking pots; mortars; skimmer
cooperage 412–13, 419, 427
  white 356–9, *357*, 427
Coopers' Company; 'H' brand 419, 429, 490
Cop or Coep, Ny, possible cook 11, 428, 446, *447*, 448, 493
Copland, Robert; *The Rutter of the Sea* 264, 277, 279, 280
copper-alloy objects
  metallurgical analysis 658
  see also aiglets; bowls; buckles; candle snuffer; candlesticks; cauldrons; chafing dish; colander; cooking pots; cooking vessels; dividers; jettons; kettle, hanging; locks; loops, twisted-wire; mortars; paternosters; pendants; pins; purse-hangers; scales; skimmer; spigot; syringes; thimbles; weights; whistles
coral paternoster bead 117, *122*, 123
cordage, hemp 600
cords, silk
  garment-related 20
  on horn inkpot 132, *133*
  of paternoster 117, *122*, 123
  of pomander 161, *163*
  for scales, lost 259
cork jar stoppers 190, *191*, 192, 225, 471–2
cornflower, blue 619, 626
Cornwall, Duchy of; rose stamp 199, *200*
corrosion of metal objects 1, 250, 501, 512
  see also concretion
costrels
  neck of leather 454, 488, *488*, 489
  pottery 464, 467, *471*, 472, 473, *474*, 475, 476, 477; Iberian Red Micaceous ware 192, *192*
counters, gaming 133, 134, *135*, *136*, 140, *141*, 657
courtiers, possible presence on ship 19
Coventry, Warwickshire; Whitefriars 120, 138
Cowdray House murals and engraving 20, 516
cowrie shell 263
crabs 511
crater, impact 509, 510, 511
Crepidula fornicata (slipper limpet) 513
crew 11–12, 657–8
  composition 11–12, 544
  size 515, 519, 601, 609
  see also age of crew; archers and archery; Barber-surgeon; boatswains; carpenters; Cop or Coep, Ny; foreigners in crew; gunners; health of crew; human remains; living accommodation; officers; pilots; purser; survivors of sinking
Cromwell, Thomas (Earl of Essex) 125, 382
crosses
  marks in form of saltire *451*, 493
  pendants 16, *115*, *125*, 126
culverin, large bronze 540, 543
Cytilus sericeus (beetle) 615, 616

daggers, kidney 26, 42, 83
Danzig (Gdansk, Poland) 290, 602
Dartmouth wreck 503
databases 9–10
date of assemblage 501, 653
dating, absolute 642–3
Deane, John and Charles 255, 478
deck surfaces 15, 16, 600, 613, 626, 657
deer, fallow 569, 577, 584–5, *585*, 612
dehydration 608, 610
Deliverance (ship) 293
dendrochronology 642
dentistry 181, 514, 544–57
  age, evidence on 519–20, 556–7
  attrition *547–8*, *550*, 552, 556, *556–7*
  caries (decay) 546, *546*, 552–4, *553*, *555*, *556*, *557*, 657
  cephalometric data 550–2
  condition of bone and teeth 544–7, *546*, *547*, 549, 555
  dental arches 549, 555
  extra (supplemental) lateral incisors *548*, 556
  extraction of teeth 172, *173*, 181, 554
  lack of crowding 549–50, 555
  microstructural analysis 563, 648–50
  number of individuals 549
  oxygen isotope analysis 12, 544
  pantomography 555, *555*, *556*
  parts of tooth *546*
  periapical radiolucencies and abscesses 553–4, *553*, 555, *555*, *556*, 557
  periodontal disease 546, 554–5, *546*, *548*
  pterygoid hamulus *546*
  relocation of loose teeth in sockets 549
  retained deciduous molars *550*, 555
  skull bones *545*
  skull-mandible matching 517, 547–9, *549–50*
  skulls compared with modern groups 549–52
  third molars unerupted or unformed 546, *546*, *548*, 552, 555, *556–7*

tooth loss 546, *546*, *547*, *548*
dice, bone 15, 109, 133, *135*, *137*, 137–9
dice shaker, leather 134, *136*
diet 15–16, 514, 603–5, 607–8
  and health 172, 523–6, *523–6*, 543, 595–6, 607–8, 610, 656; deficiency diseases *see* anaemia; osteomalacia; rickets; scurvy; *see also* dysentery; food-poisoning
  menu 15, 603–5
  and nutrition 182, 543, 595–6, 607, 608, 610
  officers' and men's 612
  for the sick 182
  see also individual foodstuffs and food and drink; victualling
dinner on *Henry Grace à Dieu* 19, 441, 443, 569
direct survey method (DSM) 5, 658
disabilities, physical 175, 176, 178
discharge from active service 175, 176, 178
discs
  copper-alloy, possible jetton 257
  leather, from tabor case 232
  silk-covered leather 39, 48, *95*, 97
  wooden octagonal, possible mirror frames 374, *374*
disease 12, 614, 657
  diet-related 172, 174, 180; *see also* anaemia; dysentery; food-poisoning; osteomalacia; rickets; scurvy
  fevers 174, 180
  in French and English fleets 12, 174, 608, 610, 614
  infectious 180, 526, *527*; *see also* tuberculosis; venereal disease
  periodontal 546, 554–5, *546*, *548*
  suppurative, ears and jaw joints 544
  see also jaundice; Perthe's disease; plague
disgorgers, wooden 143–4, *143*
dishes
  animal bones in 566, 569, 574
  pewter 423, 424, 444, 445; distribution *441*; marks 201, *203*, 444, 445, *495*, 495–6; standards and weights 425
  wooden 15, 484–7, *485*, *487*, Pl. 57; assemblage 426; distribution *441*, 447; 'messing' items 424, 445, *445*, 447
dislocation of limbs 177, 178
dividers 11, 264, 273–4, *273*, 655, Pls 38–9
  case 266, *273*, 274
  distribution *265*, 266, 270
DNA studies 508, 516, 557–62, 643–8, Pl. 68
  ancient DNA 645, 647–8

contamination 646, 647, 648
  forensic use 643–4, 647
  glossary of terms 561
  Mary Rose studies 514, 557–62, 643–8; human remains 552, 559–61, 645–6, 647, 657; pig bone 559, 646, *646*, 647, 656; plant remains 656
  microstructural analysis as aid 649
  mitochondrial DNA 12, 508, 514, 558–9, 646
  outlook 561, 562
  polymerase chain reaction (PCR) amplification 559, *644*, 645, 646
  principles 644–5
  Y chromosome research 558, 561
dog skeleton 13, 16, 564, 614–15, *614*
domino, bone 135, 140, 141
Doture, Martin (bookbinder and stationer) 131, Pl. 15
doublets *see* jerkins
douçaine *see* shawm, still
drinking vessels
  bowls as 15, 483, *483*, 497
  see also bottles (wooden feeding-); mug; tankards
drugs *see* medicaments
drumstick 226, 227, 232
DSM (direct survey method) 5, 658
Dudley, John *see* Lisle, Viscount
dulcina 239, 240
  see also shawm, still
dunnage, broom as 600
Dutch East India Company 272, 273–4
dyes 20, 34, 36, 514
dysentery 174, 180, 524–5, 608, 614

ear-scoops, bone or ivory
  Barber-surgeon's 15, 16, 154, 161, 189, 196, 218, *219*
  distribution 154, *157*, 161
  individual 154, 161, *161*
Earl of Abergavenny wreck 547, 615
eating *see* diet; food and drink; meals, organisation of
eating and drinking vessels 424, 426, 448–58
  distribution *448*
  official supply 426, 656; personalising of woodware 428, 446, *447*, 448, 449–50, *449*, 481–2, *481–2*, 493, *494–5*, 496, 497, 656
  see also bottles; bowls; coconut shells (cups); costrels; dishes; flasks; mug; platters; spoons; tankards
eels 578, 579, 604
  see also conger eels
eel grass (*Zostera*) 508, 512
embroidery on leather pouches
  silk 16, 107–11, *110–11*, 117

silver thread 109, 110, *111*
environmental data 501–14, 564–629
  aims of analysis 508
  on *Amsterdam* wreck 501, 503
  artefact-associated samples 507
  bias of assemblage 509
  in carpenters' cabin *503*, 504, 599, 600
  data acquisition 501–14
  DNA analysis 508
  flotation 506, 507
  numbering of samples, items and components 506
  and philosophy of excavation 501–3
  post-excavation history 505–8
  processing of samples 506, 507, *506–8*
  redefinition of methods 501
  sampling programme 5–6, 501–2, 503–4, 564
  sea-bed environment, processes and effects of 511–13
  and taphonomy 508–10, *509*, 511–13
  see also bone, animal; isotopes, chemical; plant remains; pollen analysis
ergot poisoning (St Anthony's Fire) 174
erysipelas 174
Evstafii wreck 127
excavation methods 3–6

Faber, Felix 267, 289
farming techniques, genetic alteration of varieties by 589
fastenings 94–106, 657
  see also aiglets; buckles; buttonholes; buttons; clasps; laces; loops, twisted-wire
fats, animal 501, 514, 631–2
  adipocere 567, *575*, 586, 631–2
  in caulking 619, 626
  in glue 633
FCS (Fairly Complete Skeletons) 517–19, *539*
feature numbers 5
feeding-bottle, wooden *212*, 212–14
felting *see* fulling and felting
fern oil (*Polypody* root extract) 192, 220, 222, 472
Feversham, HMS 250
fiddles 16, *228*, 229–30, 242–7, *243–7*, Pl. 31
  bag, leather 244
  case 226, 227, 229, 244, *245*, 249
  contemporary parallels *228*, 230, 248–9
  general description *228*, 229–30
  location *226*, 227, 244
  reproduction *243*, 244, *246*, 248

see also bow, fiddle
Fioravanti, Leonardo; *Specchio Universale* 193, 208, 216
fir pollen 628–9
fire sticks 316
fish
  fresh 15–16, 141; *see also* fishing gear
  post-sinking sand-smelt 578, 579
  salt and dried 514, 577–84
    anatomical parts 579–80, 581, 584
    articulated *565*, 566, 577, 579, Pl. 70
    in baskets 407–8, 566, *568*, 579
    butchery 567, 580, *580*, 581, 582–4, *582–3*, 605
    in casks 13, 410, 417, 421, 565, 579; steeping vats 604, 605
    Cattewater wreck 584
    in diet 15–16, 141, 523, 603, 604–5, 607, 608
    in dishes 566
    distribution 13, 385, 566, *568*, 577, 578, 579–80, 605, 654
    insects associated with 616, 617
    on Orlop deck *565*, 566, 577, 578, 579, 616, 617
    personal storage 385
    photographic record *565*, 566
    processing of finds 506–7
    quantity 580, 582, 609
    on *Scheurrak SO1* wreck 584
    significance of study 586–8
    size/type of food fish 586, 587
    sources of supplies 612
    state of preservation 578
    vitamin content 608
  see also individual fish, especially cod; conger eels; eels
fishing gear 2, 15–16, 141–4, *142–3*, 657, Pl. 22
Fishmonger's Company 55
flagons 424, 435–9, *435–7*, 439
  distribution 2, 435, 439
  pewter 423, 424, 428, 435–9, *435–6*, *439*, Pl. 66; marks *435*, 437–8, *491*, 493, *495*
  wooden 15, 427–8, 439; marks and inscriptions *437*, 438, 439, 493, *495*, 496, Pl. 62; *see also* tankards (gallon serving)
flasks
  glass 424, *459*, 460–1, *461*
  distribution *448*, 459
  leather 424, *448*, *453–4*, 454, 456, *456*
  pewter 423, 424, *458*, 459, 459–60, 595; Barber-surgeon's 189, 199–200, *201*, 429, Pl. 29
  see also bottles

flax/linseed 600
fleam case, possible 196, *213*, 214
fleas 16, 157, 508, 615–16, *616*, 657
flies
    house 616, 617
    latrine 16, 616, 617, 657
    puparia 615, 616, *617*
    seaweed 616–17, *617*
floats, fishing 142–3, *143*
flotation methods 506, 507
food and drink
    bias of assemblage 656
    origin 588–9
    plant foodstuffs 588–9, 593–7, 600, 601
    putrescence 524, 608, 612, 614, 616, 617, 657
    rations 523–4, 595, 601, 603, 604, 609
    serving and sharing 15, 424, 462, *463*, 496, 605–7, 655–6; vessels and utensils 385, 426, 434–40, 497, 605–7, 656, Pl. 57
    size of portions 604, 606–7
    storage 16, 385, 420–1, 422, 424, *459*, 460–2; *see also* baskets; casks; sacks
    supply *see* victualling
    see also diet; eating and drinking vessels; meals, organisation of
food-poisoning 174, 180, 524, 608, 610–11, 612, 614, 657
foot conditions 92–4, *92*, *93*
footwear 59–94
    alterations and repairs 16, 20, 61, 88–9, *89*
    anachronisms 86–7
    comparable finds elsewhere *85*, 85–6
    constructions 59–65, 78–9
    distribution *21*, 79, *82*, 83, *83*, *84*
    hose associated with *88*, 88
    materials and stuffing 87–8
    officers' 27, 82, 86, 87–8; *see also* boots (thigh)
    quantity recovered 18, 78
    recording 28, 59
    in sack on Orlop deck 18, 20, 25, 58, 79, 83, 84, 408, 409, 656
    styles found 79
    textile components 18, 19, 25, 58, *76*, 76, 86, *87*, 87–8, 94
    see also boots; hose; shoes; sock or scogger
forceps, surgical 208, *208*
foreigners in crew 12
    DNA 12, 127, 516, 552, 657
    Flemish survivor 12, 174
    isotope analysis 174, 544
    possible French pilot 12, 266, 655

fossa
    Allen's 521–2
    hypotrochanteric 521–2
fowl, domestic 566, 569, 585, 612
fractures 174, 176–8, *177*, 526–31, *528–33*, 544
    avulsion 529, *530*
    closed 176–8, *177*
    disability from 176, 178
    nasal 528, *528*
    and occupation 529, 544
    open 178
    of skull 176, *177*, 531, *532*, *533*, 544
    treatments available 172, 174, 178
fragile items; designation as 'samples' 503, 564
France 12
    disease in fleet 12, 174, 608, 610, 614
    pilots from 12, 266, 655
frankincense 220, 221, 222
Freiburg, Germany 135, 483
fringe, woven leather, on willow rod 374–5, *375*
Frobisher, Sir Martin 182, *291*, 292
fruit 182, 507, 524, 589, 591, 593, *595–6*, 596–7, Appx 3.1
    cask of wine or 15, 385, 410, 417–18, 421, 597
    distribution 592, *595*, 596, 597, 601
    individual supply 656
    see also apple pip; cherry stones; grapes/raisins; plums/prunes/greengages
Fuchs, Leonhart; *De Historia Stirpium* 185, 188
fuel
    broom as 600, 601
    logs 12, 385, 422
fulling and felting 29, 30, 31–2, 35, 55
fumigant, broom as 613
fungi
    bracket 319, 514
    'red heart' infection in wood 484
funnels, wooden
    staved 352, 356, 358–9
    turned 454, 488, *488*
furnaces, galley 422, *423*, 497
    see also cauldrons (large)
furniture 376–83
    boarded construction 377, *377*, 380–1, *380–1*, Pl. 51
    chests as 15, 376, 394–6, 654
    dovetailed-board construction 377
    fox-wedging 379–80
    framed-panel construction 377, 381–3, *382*
    scarcity 13, 15, 497, 653
    rails 382–3
    staked-leg (wedged construction)

376, *376*, 377–80, *378–9*
    see also beds; benches; chopping block; panelling, decorative oak; stand, folding; stools; trestles
future research 651–8

Gabryll Royall (ship) 12
Gadidae 578, 579, 581, 582, 584
    see also cod
Gale, Thomas; *Certaine Works of Chirurgerie* 171, *172*, 223
galley 12–13, 422, *423*, 496, 654
    animal bones 566, 567–9
    area on Orlop deck 12–13, 385, 422
    human remains 17, *515*
    location and layout 422, *423*
    shifts at sinking 17, 569
    storage 12, 13, 385, 422, 496
    see also ash boxes; bellows; cauldrons (large); furnaces
gaming equipment 15, 133–41
    boards, incised on wood 15, *135*, 657; on cask head 15, 133, *135*, *138*, 139–40, 410, 418; on wooden equipment 133–4, *135*, *138*, *139*, 139–40
    see also counters, gaming; dice; dice shaker; Tables set
Garcie, Pierre; *Le Routier de la Mer*, Copland's translation of 264, 277, 279, 280
garnet in pendant 125, 126
gauds (religious beads) 117, 120
gavels, possible 368–9, *369*
GC-MS (Gas Chromatography-Mass spectrometry) 222, 632–3, 636
genetics
    human molecular 643–8; classical markers 644–5
    plant varieties 589
    see also DNA studies
Germany
    folding stool 381
    manufactures from 190, *191*, 192, 196, 198, 224–5; Nuremberg 163–4, 168, 170, 256–7, 274, 329, 330
    see also Hanse merchants; pottery; *and individual places*
Gersdorff, Hans von; *Feldbuch der Wundartzney* 171, *177*, 178, *179*, 181
Giglio, Italy; wreck 311
gimlets 295, 299, 303–4, *304*
ginger root, false identification of 508
Girona wreck 126, 292
glass objects
    assemblage 424, 429
    flasks/bottles 424, 460–1, *461*
    phials and bottles, Barber-surgeon's 189, 192–3, *193*, 225, Pl. 28

glues 632–3
glycaemic index 607
Gokstad ship; incised merels board 139
gold finger ring 113, *114*, 116
gonorrhoea 174, 181, 205, 657
graffiti on lanterns 343, *347*
El Gran Grifon wreck 126
grapes/raisins 15, 182, 514, 601
    pips 593, 596, *596*, 597
    skins 15, 592, 597
grasses 619, 621, 623, 625, 628
gratuities for disabled seamen 175
greengages *see* plums/prunes/ green-
    gages
grenade, possible incendiary 467
Grenville, Roger (Master of *Mary Rose*)
    11
gribble 510, 512
grinding wheel and mount 13–14, 294,
    295, 340–1, *341*, 385
Grocers' Company 332
grooming items 16, 153–62, *156–64*,
    354, 657, Pl. 20
    see also individual items
gun carriages 2, 16, 349
gun wadding 510, 598, 601
gundecks 2, 3, 13, 15, 16
    ammunition storage 385
    buckets by gun positions 359, 363,
        366
    living accommodation 13, 15, 496,
        497–8, 654
gunners
    gun crew 11, 17, 26–7, 538–41, 544,
        657
    injuries 174–5
    master 127, 396, 397, 653–4
    pay 262
gunnery techniques, new 12, 293–4, 297
gunpowder
    casks 385, 410, 415–16
    flasks 26, 27, 41
    location of stores 13, 17, 27, 385,
        654–5
    pollen analysis 619, 628
    sieving of 352
guns 2, 3, 13, 15, 16, 540, *543*
gunshields 101, 385
    mark resembling man holding *437*,
        438, 439, *495*, Pl. 62

'H' marks
    brands on woodware: Coopers'
        Company mark 419, 428, 490;
        on 'messing' items 443, 445, *445*,
        447; of official issue 296, 487,
        496, 656, Pl. 60; on staved wood-
        ware 428, 439, 490; on turned
        woodware 426, 445, *445*, *447*,
        447–8, 482, 487, *487*, 490, Pl. 60

incised on casks 419
    on pewter measures 428
    stamped on metal *329*, 330; crowned
        331, 332
    verification mark *331*, 332, 419, 428,
        490
haddock 578, 579, 582
hair in caulking 619, 626
hairbrushes 354
hake 578, 579, 582
halters for boatswain's calls 285, *286–8*,
    Pl. 41
hammers
    handles of iron-headed 295–6, 297,
        305, 306
    see also marks
hammocks 382
hand-line frames, fishing 15, 141, *142*
hand protector, leather 373, *373*
handles, wooden 1
    adze 295, 305, *305*, *306*, 307
    axe 295, 304–5, *305*
    basketry 404, *404*
    brush 218, *219*
    chisel/file 295, 297, 307–8, *308*
    hammers, iron-headed 295–6, 297,
        305, 306
    knife 145–7, *146–8*, 148, 149, 152,
        155, 320
    mallet 295, 310
    personal marks on 295–6, 307, *308*
    razor 217, *218*
    saw 297, 316–17, *317*
    surgical instruments 189, 208–12,
        210–12, 214, *215*, 224–5
    tang-holed 307–8, *308*
    unidentified types 295, 308–9
    whittle tang type 211–12, *210–12*
handles, rope
    chests 388, *389*
    staved buckets 356, 359
Hanse merchants 225
Harry, health of crew of 174
harvest, poor 596, 602, 610
Hastings Manuscript *277*, 278
hatches 13, 15
hats *see* caps and hats
hay 13, 296, *503*, 598–9, 601, 626
hazel twig besoms 600
hazelnut 593, 597
head injuries 176, *177*, 531, *532*, *533*,
    544
heads (lavatories) 16, 153
heads, 'Romayne', designs using 131–2,
    168, 261, *261*, 383
health of crew 174–5
    diet and 172, 523–6, *523–6*, 543,
        595–6, 607–8, 610, 656; deficien-
        cy diseases *see* anaemia; osteo-
        malacia; rickets; scurvy

human remains as evidence 543, 657
    see also dentistry; disease; fractures;
        injuries; medicine; pathology
hearing, measuring range of 214
Hedingham, Norfolk 291, 292
helmets 531
hemp 18, 593, 600, 601, 618, 619, 620,
    622, 626–7, 628
Henry VIII, King
    at banquet on *Henry Grace à Dieu* 19,
        441, 443, 569
    and Barber Surgeons' Company 36–
        7, 171, Pl. 25
    Carew receives whistle from 291
    clothing for crew of *Mary Rose* 19
    gaming 136–7, 140
    Holbein's representations 36–7, 86,
        Pl. 25
    Inventories 136–7, 290
    and mathematics 274
    musicians at coronation 240
    naval construction programme 11–
        12, 265
    psalter written for *228*, 229–30
    religious reform, and popular recep-
        tion 16, 120, 123, 125–6, 126–7,
        656, 658
    Sumptuary Laws 290–1
    wardrobe and clothing accounts 19,
        240
    and whistles 290–1
Henry Grace à Dieu (ship) 12, 299, 603
    banquet for King on 19, 441, 443,
        569
Herald of Free Enterprise, sinking of 515
herbs 620–1, 622–3, 624–5, 626, 628
hernias 172, 179–80
herring 523, 578, 579, 604
Holbein, Hans
    caps in portraits by 31, *32*
    cartoon of Henry VIII 86
    Henry VIII and the Barber Surgeons
        36–7, 171, Pl. 25
    Portrait of a Man with a Lute 292
    Thomas Cromwell 382
    Unknown young man at his office desk
        132
Hold 2, *2*, 3, 12–13
    animal and fish bones 566, 567–9,
        568, 574, 577, 578, 579, 584
    cleanliness 613
    heating of pitch/tar for caulking 320
    human remains 22, 23, 27
    musical instruments *226*, 227, 244
    plant remains 592, 594, 601
    stowage 12, 13, 384, *384*, 385, 422,
        567–9, 654–5; in baskets *407*,
        407–8, 597; in casks 27, 419–20,
        421; distribution of chests *386*
    see also ballast; bilge pump; galley

Holme, Randle III; *An Academie of Armory* 377–8, *379*, *381*
hook tool, turners' use of 481
hooks, iron and wooden 350, 352, *352*
hoops, wooden, of staved containers 317, 319, 356, 409, 411, 414
hops 593, 595–6, 601, 619
horn objects
    inkpot 132, *133*
    'lights' in lanterns 343
hose
    cut 18, 19, 20, 22, 50, 56, *57*, 58, 88, *88*
    trunk *99*, 99
House of Commons Journal (1698) 603, 605
housekeeping equipment
    general tools and equipment 15, 348–71
    weaving and sewing 323–30, *328–9*, Pl. 43
    weights and measures 330–6
    see also individual types
Howard, Sir Edward 262, 291
Howard, Lord Thomas, High Admiral 419
hull; sampling during cleaning 504, *504*
human remains 501, 514, 515–63
    activity and occupation 26–7, 521, 532–41, 543–4, 657; archers 175, 529, 533–8, 544, 657; boatswain 288; gun crew 11, 17, 26–7, 538–41, 544, 657; purser 542–3, *543*
    age at death 12, 174, 516, 519–20, 556–7, 657
    brain tissue 501, 510, 514, 516, 563
    clothing associated with 18, 20, 21–3, *21*, 26–7, 42–5, *45*, *46*; footwear 25, 79, 82, 83, 85
    condition 516–17, 532–3, 544–7, *546*, *547*, 549, 555
    disarticulation 509, 510, 511
    distribution in ship 17, *515*, 516
    DNA analysis 552, 559–61, 645–6, 647, 657
    entheses 517, *517*, 537, 543
    enthesophytes 537–8, *537*, *538*
    extoses in trochateric fossa 521–2
    FCS (Fairly Complete Skeletons) 517–19, *539*
    glossary of terms 522
    inca bones 543, 544, *544*, *547*
    iron oxide staining 517
    mandibles 545, *547*, 648–50
    matching into individuals 516–19, *516–18*
    microstructural analysis 563, 648–50
    Norwich cemetery compared 521, 522, 533, 536–7, 539–40
    noses 528, *528*, 544–5

numbers of individuals 519
os acromiale 533, *534*, 536, 537, 538
oxygen isotope ratio analysis 544, 563, 641
pairs, bones occurring in 519
preservation 516–17, 532–3
processing 506, 516
recording system 6, 516
skeletal morphology 521–3; *see also* inca bones above
skeleton, parts of *518*
skulls *see* dentistry
soft tissue 501, 510, 514, 516, 563
stature 519–20
taphonomy 511, 516, *516*, *517*, 648–50
see also disease; fractures; health; injuries; pathology; wounds
Hutton, Yorkshire; glassmaking site 193, 461
hydration and dehydration 608, 610
hygiene 16, 153–62, 156–64, 657, Pl. 20

Iceland 33, 612
IHS motif on pouch 16, 109, 110, *111*, 117
illness *see* disease; fractures; injuries; pathology
illustration of ship, *Anthony Roll* 1, 1–2, *654*
impact crater in sea-bed 509, 510, 511
impressment of crews 12
IMS *see* methylated spirits, industrial
inca bones 543, 544, *544*, *547*
injuries 174–5, 657
    see also burns and scalds; dislocation of limbs; fractures; hernias; wounds
inkpots 13, 127, 132–3, *133*, 467, 477
inscriptions *see* graffiti; marks, privy; religion and religious items (inscriptions and devices)
insects 16, 514, 613, 615–17, *616–17*, 657
    potential for further recovery 617, 657
    processing 506, 507, 615, 617, 657
inventories
    of Henry VIII 136–7, 290
    of *Mary Rose* (1514) 264, 268, 277, 281, 408, 490
Invincible wreck 444, 503
Ireland, import of fish from 612
iron objects 658
    buckle 18, 99, 100, 101, 103
    corrosion and concretion 1, 99, 103, 296, 308
    hooks 350, 352, *352*
    nails 321
    pot, indicated by black stain 296

iron oxide staining on human remains 517
isotopes, chemical, in human remains 12, 508, 514, 544, 563, 641
Italy; naval provisioning 608
ivory objects
    comb 156, 157, *158*
    earscoop 218, *219*

jackets *see* jerkins
jars, pottery 464, 469, 464, 472, 464, 466–7, *466–7*, *471*, 472–3, *473*, 474, 475–6, 477, Pls 56, 63
    chemical analysis of contents 220, 222
    cork bungs 190, *191*, 192, 225, 471–2
jaundice 174, 180
jerkins
    cloth 18, 19, 20, 48–55, Pl. 5
        buttons 55
        centre-fastening 48, *53*, *54*, 55
        collars 48
        colour 27, 48, 48, 50, 54, 55
        with compass cloak 18, 20, 27, 50–1, *51*, 53
        cross-over 48–50, *49*, *50*
        decoration 48, 48, 54, *54*, 55
        location 27
        raised naps 48, 50, 51, 54
        style and assembly 48
        tunic style 48, *52*, *54*, 54–5
    leather 19–20, 37–48, Pl. 6
        archer's 25–6, 27, 45–7, *47*
        associated items: aiglets 25, 38; ankle boots 25; archery equipment 25–6; armour 26, 41, 42; buckles 25; buttons 25, 38, 39, *39*, 47, *47*, 48, 95, *96*, 97; coins 25; combs 25, 27, 41, 43, Pl. 6; fuller's teasel 600, 601; pouches 25, 42; powder flasks 26, 27, 41; shoes 25, 42; spoon 42; sundials 27, 41, 168; textile fragments 25; tokens 25; weapons 25–6, 42
        buttonholes 38, 41, *42*, *43*, *47*, 48, *96*, 97
        collars *39*, 40–1, 46
        concretion 41
        crosses sewn onto 20, 27, 41–2, *42*, *43*
        cross-over 25, 37, 38, *39*, 44
        decoration 37, 41, 44; applied 20, 27, 41–2, *42*, *43*, 45; incised 26, 41, 45–7, *46*, *47*
        distribution *21*, 22, 23, 26–7, 44
        examples 41–8
        front-fastening 37–8, *39*, 41,

42–5, *45, 46*

human remains associated with *21*, 22, 23, 26–7, 42–5, *45, 46*

inside pocket 37, 39–40, *39*, 47–8, *47*

lace-holes 38, 41, 42, 43, *46, 46*, 99

leather types 44

number 18, 37

padded 528

reconstructable 38, *39, 40*

recording 28

red 41

reinforcement and repair 20, 41, 48

reversible 39–40, *47*, 48

seam types 38, *38*

second, worn under one with crosses 20, 42

side-fastening 26, 37, 38, *39*, 44, *45–7, 47*

sleeves *39*, 40

small, with inside pocket 37, 39–40, *39*, 47–8, *47*

straps 26

style and assembly 37–41

summary table 44

thread types 38

jettons 256–7, *256, 257*, 435, 437–8

jewellery 15, 113–17, *114–16*

whistles as 290–2, *291*

see also pendants; pins (silver, dress); rings, finger

joggle stick 295, 297, 310–11, *310*

John of Grenewyche (ship) 12

joiners' work, framed–panel construction 377, 381–3, *382*

jugs, pottery 469, 475, 476, 477

Barber-surgeon's: Low Countries tin-glazed, miniature 192, *192*, 464, 470, 477, Pl. 27; Raeren stoneware 190, *191*, 192, 464, 471–2, *471*, 477

Kateryn Pledmore (ship) 426

kelps 512

Kennemerland wreck 503, 601, 602

Ketel, Cornelius *291*, 292

kettle, hanging 424, *430*, 431

Kinnagoe Bay; *La Trinidad Valencera* wreck 126, 325, 343, 488

knife holder, leather 147, 368, *369*

knife sheaths 16, 144, 147–53, *149–51*, 153–5, 657, Pl. 19

distribution 145, *145*, 148

incised personal mark 151, *151*

with knives 144, *145*, 147–8, *149*, 150, 152

knitting 29, 30, 31–5, 58–9, *58*

knives 144–53, *144–51, 153–5*

distribution 145, *145*, 147, 148

handles 145–7, *146–8*, 148, 149, 152, *155*, 320, Pl. 16

incised marks of ownership 146, *146*

paper 128, *129*, 132

personal 15, 83, 145, *146*, 146, 497, 657

scale tang *144*, 144–5, *145, 147*, 149

in sheaths 144, *145*, 147–8, *149*, 150, 152

surgical 189, 208, *208, 209*, 211

whittle tang *144*, 144–5, 145, *146*, 149

see also knife holder; knife sheaths

knots in log-line 277

Korea; *Shinnan Gun* wreck 601

La Belle wreck 409

lace-holes

in hose fragment 99

in leather jerkins 38, 41, 42, 43, 46, *46*, 99

laces 94, *98, 99*, 99, 657

aiglets with 94–5, *98*, 99

breeches with 56

hose *99*, 99

jerkin 38

knives attached by 150

leather, linen and woollen 99

shoes with 25, 65, 79, 99

silk 18, 79, *98, 99*, 99

with woollen fragments 25

see also under boots (ankle; types, laced)

ladders between decks 13, 15, 655–6

ladles, wooden 424, 440, *440*, 488, *488*

Lailey, George, of Bucklebury, Berkshire (turner) 481, 488

lanterns 13, *342*, 343, *344–7*, 385, 654, Pl. 40

lathes 196–9, *197*, 479–80, *479*

latrine fly 16, 616, 617, 657

lavatories, areas used as 153–4

see also piss-dale

laws

on clothing 19, 32–3

on pastimes 137

Protection of Wrecks Act (1973) 9, 503

Sumptuary 19, 120, 290–1

layout of ship 1–3

lead-based compounds, medicinal 220, 221, 222, 223

lead objects *see* badge, token or icon; plumb-bob; sounding leads; weights

leather and leather objects Pl. 62

preservation 18

sources, thickness and quality 31

skived 60

types 31, 87

see also bags; belts; books; boots;

bottles; buckets; buttons; cases; clothing; combs (cases); costrels; dice shaker; discs; fiddles (bag; case); flasks; footwear; fringe; hand protector; jerkins; knife holder; laces; mittens; pouches, purses; shawm (case); shoes; straps; sundials, pocket (case); tabor (case); thong; tool holders; trousse; wallet

leaves, shoes stuffed with 601

legislation *see* laws

Legros, E (tabor pipe maker) 228, 233, *234*

leisure time 15, 657–8

levelling of site 513

lice 16, 157, 181

life assemblage 501

life on board 12–16

see also conditions on board; living accommodation

lighting equipment 13, 343–7, *344–8*, Pl. 40

see also candles; lanterns

limpet, slipper 513

linen fragments 18, 19, 20, 28

decorative tape 48, 55

linenfold panelling 3, 383, *383*, 385, 654

linstocks 385

Lisle, John (Master of *Harry*) 174

Lisle, Viscount (John Dudley), Lord High Admiral of the Fleet; pewter 441, 443, *491, 492*, 493

living accommodation 2, 3, 13, 15, 496, 497–8, 654

see also cabins; meals, organisation of; sleeping arrangements

location references 5

locks 109, 112, 391, 654

log-reel 264, *265*, 266, 270, 276–7, *276*, 655, Pl. 37

London

aiglets 94

buckles 100, 101

combs 157, 159

continental merchants 225

dice manufacture 138

hose 58

leather mitten 55

Lord Mayor's Day (1616) 55

paternoster production 120

pewter 199–200, *200*, 213, 423, 440

pottery 468, 469

pouches 112

privy marks on cooking pots 432

skimmer 432

stirrup adze blade 307–8, *308*

sundials 168

tally sticks 334

thimbles 330

twisted-wire loops 96
weaves of woollen textiles 30
whistles 290
woodware, turned 196, 207
SITES
Abbots Lane, Southwark 196
Baynard's House, Queen Victoria St. 196
Borough High St. Southwark 138
Cannon Street 199–200, *200*
Dowgate Ward, the Steelyard 225
Eldon Street 469
Finsbury 58
Guy's Hospital, Southwark 423
St Bartholomew's Hospital 175
St Mary Spital, Hospital at 207
Southwark, and military supply 425
Thames foreshore 168, 213, 290, 423, 440
Wapping High St 55
Windgoose Lane 225
Worship Street 168
longbows 11, 17, 390–1, 534
chests 2, 390–1, 656; distribution 2, 13, 27, 385, *388*
see also archers and archery
loom, fiddle 325–7, *325–7*
loops, twisted-wire 18, *94*, 95–6
Luttrell Psalter 136, 426, 432

magdaleones (medicated bandages) 219
magnetic variation 268
Main deck 2, *2*, 13
guns 13, 16
human remains 22, 23, *515*, 538; gun crew 11, 17, 26–7, 538–41, 544, 657
plant remains 592, 594, 600
stowage 13, 385, 390–1, 420, 421, 422, 566, *568*, 574; in baskets *407*, 408; casks 385, 420, 421, 422, 566, *568*, 574, 578; chests 24, *26*, *386*, 390–1
weapons 13, 16, 385, 390–1
see also cabins
maintenance equipment 348–71
weaving and sewing 323–30, *328–9*, Pl. 43
see also caulking
maker's marks *see* marks, privy
malarial fever 174, 180
Malines (Mechelen), Belgium
glass bottle 193
ship's bell made in 284, *285*
mallets
carpenters' 295, 297, *309*, 309–10
caulking 294–5, 320, *320*, 321, 323, *324*, Pl. 48
handles 295, 310
miniature 109, 368–9, *369*

surgical *209*, 214, *215*
malnutrition 523–6, *523–6*, 543, 608, 656
diseases of, *see* anaemia; osteomalacia; rickets; scurvy
manicure or toilet sets 154, 157
bone 159, 161, *161*
wooden 159, *162*
marking gauge, carpenter's 294, 295, 311–12, *311*
marks, privy 489–96, *491–2*, *494–5*
makers' 490–3, *491*
official 490, *491*; *see also* arrow-shaped marks; 'H' marks
owners' *492*, 493; brands for items in common ownership 419, 482; incised on knives and sheaths *146*, 146, *151*, 151; personalising of official issue woodware 428, 446, *447*, 448, 449–50, *449*, 481–2, *481–2*, 493, *494–5*, 496, 497, 656, Pl. 59
protective and religious devices 493–4, (*see also* Alpha; figure 4; Trinity; Virgin Mary below)
verification, on weights/measures *331*, 332, 428
MARKS
acorn 166, *166*, 169
Alpha *442*, 494
B 419
BWE or RWE (on Barber-surgeon's property) 439–40, *439*, *492*, 493, 657
cable device 493
cannon or man carrying gunshield *437*, 438, 439, *495*, Pl. 62
of Carpenters' Company 296
cross, saltire *451*, 493
crowned 10-rayed flower or star 259
dolphin and cross 438
figure 4, marks based on 201, 202, *203*, *204*, 214, 493, 494, *494*, *495*, 495–6, 656
fleur-de-lis *449*, 449, 490, *491*
GC (Sir George Carew) 15, 440–1, *442*, 444–5, 490, *491–2*, 493, 656
GD *492*
GI 133, 134, 449, *492*, 655
HB 13, 445, *492*, 655
HR 419
IR 166, 169
IS 449
J and E *451*, 493, *495*
Legros, E (E:LEGROS) 228, 233, *234*
lion rampant, possibly Duchy of Cornwall 424, 460, *491*
Lisle family 441, 443, *491*, *492*, 493
M 166, 169

man walking with branch in left hand 200, *201*, 460, *491*
MM or MA, on mortar 433, *433*
monk, tonsured *435*, *495*, 495
Ny Coep or Cop, coek 11, 428, 446, *447*, 448, 493
of Pewterers' Company 490
of pewterer's hammer 201, 423–4, 445, 490, *491*
rose 199, *200*; crowned 423, 490
swan 201, *491*
T?Brown brand 358, 359
TC (Thomas Chamberlayn) 440–1, *442*, 490, *491*
Trinity symbols *433*, 438, 453, 493, *494*
of Virgin Mary 16, *433*, 440–1, 444, 453, 493, *494*
W *158*, 159, 217, 419, 446; *Virgo Virginum* 440–1, 444, 453, 493
WE 37, 200–1, 202, 203, 225, 439–40, *439*, *492*, 493, 657
X, XI 446
‼, 'double plume' or 'rabbit's foot' 228, 233, *237*
see also arrow-shaped marks; 'H' marks; religion and religious items (inscriptions and devices); and under individual types of object
Mary (royal yacht) 162
Mary, Virgin
badge, token or icon, lead 16, 125–6, 126–7, *126*
scratched motifs of 16, *433*, 440–1, 444, 453, 493, *494*
Mary Magdalen, depictions of 196, 198
mass spectrometry 222, 632–3, 636
Massey, Edward; mechanical log 276
masters, ship's 262, 266
of *Mary Rose* 11
masts 1, 3
mattresses 13, 296, 511, 598, 599, 600, 601, 613
meals, organisation of 13, 15, 496–8, 607
apportioning of food 424, 462, *463*, 496, 605–6, 655–6
location 13, 15, 496, 497–8, 654
see also messes
measuring devices 334–6
see also rules, wooden; tally sticks
meat 523
sharing 496, 605–6
size of pieces 604, 606–7
see also cattles bones and beef; pig bones and pork; mutton; venison
Mechelen *see* Malines
medical and shaving equipment 2, 14–15, 176, *176*, *177*, 189–25

see also bandages; bottles (glass; wooden feeding-); bowls (copper alloy; wooden); canisters; chafing dish; chisel; ear-scoops; flasks; knives (surgical); mallets (surgical); mortars; needles, surgeon's; probe, surgical; razors; saws (amputation); screw-elevator, surgical; spatulas; spoons; surgical instruments, turned handles from; syringes

medicaments 182–9, 219–24, 471–2, 657

   anaesthesia and anodynes 181

   chemical analysis 219–24, 514, 633–41, 657

   hop *seeds* 596

   mineral-based 220–1, 222, 223

   painkillers and soporifics 181, 223, 596

   peppercorns 595

   plant oils and resins 192, 220–1, 222, 223, 472

   purges 16

   simples and compounds 175, 180–1, 182–9, 192

   trade 224

   see also bandages

medicine 171–225, 657

   anatomical knowledge 171

   conditions encountered 174–5

   diet for the sick 182

   in England 172–4

   practitioners 171–4; *see also* Barber-surgeon; Barber Surgeons, Company of

   surgical and medical care 175–81

   see also amputation; cautery; dentistry; disease; fractures; health of crew; injuries; medical and shaving equipment; medicaments; parasites; pathology; wounds

Mengele, Josef 644, 647

mercenaries 174

Merchant Adventurers' Company 225

mercury 214, 220, 222

merels board, incised on cask end 15, 133, *138*, 139, 140

mess tags 434, 496

messes 15, 496, 497, 605–6

messing items 422, 424, 426, 440–8, *441–7*, 496

   distribution *441*

   mess tags 434, 496

   staved wooden bucket 357, *357*, 424, 440

metallurgical analysis 103, 105, 658

metals, preservation of 99, 103, 321

   see also concretion; corrosion

methylated spirit, industrial (IMS) 507, 590, 591, 615

microstructural analysis of bone 563, 648–50

mirrors, possible 156, 374, *374*

mites 16

mittens, leather 18, 20, 55, *56*, 396

mollusca, marine 513

money 250–63

   cowrie shell 263

   scales and weights for 257–61

   see also coins and jettons

Morbus Gallicus (venereal syphilis) 174, 180

More, Sir Thomas 274

mortar graters *see* peppermills

mortars, copper-alloy

   Barber-surgeon's pestle and 202–3, *204*, 211

   cooking 202–3, 424, *427*, 432–3, *433*

mortise gauge 311

moss 13, 507, Pl. 69

moth chrysalis, possible 615

mothballing of *Mary Rose* 11, 614

movement around ship 13, 15, 655–6

mtDNA (mitochondrial DNA) *see* DNA studies

mug, Raeren stoneware 424, 452, 462, 464, 472, *473*, *474*, *477*

musical instruments 15, 16, 226–49, 657–8

   distribution 15, *226*, 227

   see also bow, fiddle; drumstick; fiddles; shawm, still; tabor; tabor beater; tabor pipes

mutton, fresh 604, 612

nail-cleaners/tooth-picks 154

navigation 11, 12, 15, 264–81, 655, Pls 36–9

   charts 266–7, 271–3, *272*, 655

   distribution of instruments 2, 3, 15, *265*, 266, 276

   log, use of 266, 276–7

   master's role 266

   pilot's role 264–7

   supposed device for (*see* gaming board) 133–4, *135*, *139*, 140

   written sailing directions 264–5, 272

   see also chart sticks; compasses, navigation; compendium, navigational; dividers; log-reel; pilots; protractors; rutters; sounding leads and lines; tide calculator

navies

   Henry VIII's creation of Royal 11–12, 265

   provisioning of other nations' 605, 608

   victualling 602–12

Navy Board 265

Neanderthal DNA 647–8

needle case, possible 327–8, *328*, 329

needles, surgeon's 207–8, *207*, 211

Nelson, Horatio (Viscount Nelson) 181

Netherlands

   naval provisioning 605, 608

   pharmaceutical trade 224

   pottery from 192

   surgical equipment exported 224–5

   see also Antwerp; Bruges; pottery (Low Countries); and individual artists

netting, anti-boarding 2, 16–17, 509, 516

nettle 601, 619, 620, 622, 624, 626–7, 628

Newfoundland fisheries *605*, 612

nibs, quill 127, 132, *134*

nine men's morris *see* merels

nomenclature and citations 10

non-starch polysaccharide (NSP) 607–8

Northumberland wreck 431

Norwich, Norfolk 138, 140, 329, 330, 432

   human remains from medieval cemetery 521, 522, 533, 536–7, 539–40

Nova Zembla (Barents' ship) 269, 273

NSP (non-starch polysaccharide) 607–8

Nuestra Señora de Atocha wreck 123

numbering of objects 6

numerals on sundials, form of 169, *170*

Nuremberg, Germany

   manufacturing: jettons 256–7; sundials 163–4, 168, *170*, 274; thimbles 329, 330

   pharmaceutical trade 224

   sumptuary laws 120

nutrition 182, 543, 595–6, 607–8, 610

   malnutrition 523–6, *523–6*, 543, 608, 656; diseases of *see* anaemia; osteomalacia; rickets; scurvy

nuts 15, 591, 592, 593, 597, Appx 3.1

Ny Cop or Coep *see* Cop or Coep, Ny

oak leaves 507, 591, 593, 600

oatmeal 604, 607, 608

objects-centred approach 501, 502–3

occupations

   clothing and 26–7, 32, 33

   see also human remains (activity and occupation)

officers 11, 12

   cabins 15, 654

   carpenter 13, 392, 394, 655

   chests 654

   footwear 27, 82, 86, 87–8; *see also* boots (thigh)

   victualling 15, 612

see also Barber-surgeon; Carew, Sir George; gunners (master); masters, ship's; pilots
olive jars 424, 462, 464, 471, 472, 475, 477
olive oil 471, 477
open-area excavation 4, *4*
ordinary, *Mary Rose* in 11, 614
organic materials
    insects associated with foul 615, 616–17
    lenses in sediments 512
    preservation 6, 501, 524, 653
    see also individual types
Orkney, import of fish from 612
Orlop deck 2, *2*
    carpenter's tools 14, 96, 293, 297, 310–11, 317, 337
    galley area 12–13, 385, 422
    insects 616, 617
    plant remains 592, 599, 600, 601
    stowage 2, *3*, 12, 13, 384, *384*, 385, 654–5; archery equipment 27, 385, 390–1; in baskets 385, *407*, 407, 408, 579; in casks 385, 419–20, 420–1, 565, 566, *568*, 569, 570–4, 579, 631–2; distribution of chests 385, *386*; fish bones in layer in stern 565, *565*; footwear in sack 18, 20, 25, 58, 79, 83, 84, 408, 409, 656; pork deposit in bow 385, 565, 566, *568*, 574–7, *575–7*, 586, 588, 609, 631–2
    target for enemy guns 297
ornaments and jewellery 113–17, 114–15
os acromiale 533, *534*, 536, 537, 538
osteoarthritis 528, 532, 541, 657
osteomalacia 180, 524, *524*, *525*, 526
ownership
    official issue or personal possession? 489–96, *491–2*, *494–5*, 656
    personalising of official issue woodware 428, 446, *447*, 448, 449–50, *449*, 481–2, *481–2*, 493, *494–5*, 496, 497, 656
    see also marks, privy
oxygen isotope analysis 12, 563, 641
    see also isotopes, chemical
oysters and oyster spat 511, 512, 513

packing materials 598, 599, 600, 601, 613, 626
paint, objects with traces of
    leather: bottles 454; tabor 231, *231*
    wooden: bowl 482–3; chest 392–3; ointment canisters 196, 199
paintbrushes 353, 355, *355*, *356*
palm, sail 373, *373*
palynology *see* pollen analysis

panel, bone casket 16, 123–6, *124*, 127, 658, Pl. 17
panelling, decorative oak 3, 383, *383*, 385, 654, Pl. 50
pantomography 555, *555*, *556*
paper 127, *128*, 128
paper knife 128, *129*, 132
parasites 16, 181, 613
Paré, Ambroise 171, 175, 176, 178, 179, 181, 182
Parliament
    House of Commons Journal (1698) 603, 605
    Protection of Wrecks Act (1973) 9, 503
pastimes, legislation on 137
pasture types 619
paternosters 16, 117–23, *118–19*, *121–2*, 658
    bone 117, *118*, 123
    brass 117, *122*, 123
    coral 117, *122*, 123
    human remains associated 121
    medallions attached to 126
    in pouch 109, 123
    silver bead 117, *122*, 123
    stone 117, *122*, 123
    wood 117, *119*, *121*, 123
pathology 516, 523–32
    archers' 175, 529, 533–8
    malnutrition and 523–6, *523–6*
    osteoarthritis 528, 532, 541
    osteomalacia 524, *524*, *525*, 526
    vertebral 539–41, *539–41*
    see also dentistry; disease; foot conditions; fractures; injuries; os acromiale; rickets; scurvy
Patience (ship) 293
pay 12, 171, 174, 255, 261–2, 266
PCR (polymerase chain reaction) amplification of DNA 559, *644*, 645, 646
pear-shaped buttons and purse-hanger 113
peas 15, 524, 601, 603, 604, 607–8, 609
    in pod; broom misidentified as 508, 588, 597
pendants
    copper-alloy 116, *116*, 117, Pls 11, 13
    silver cruciform 16, *115*, *125*, 126
pensions 175
peppercorns 507, 524, 591, 593, 594–5, 601, Pl. 65
    in personal chests 15, 395, 396; Barber-surgeon's 221, 222, 223, 595
peppermills 15, 396, 424, *457*, 458–9, 489, 594
    textile wrapping 408, 409, 459
Pepys, Samuel 604

personal possessions 2–3, 15, 107–70, Pl. 2
    see also bags; books; chamber pot; fishing gear; gaming equipment; grooming items; jewellery; knife sheaths; knives; marks, privy (owners'); peppermills; pomanders; pouches, leather; purses, leather; religion and religious items; sundials, pocket; writing equipment
Perthes disease, bilateral 542–3, *543*
pests and parasites 16, 181, 613, 657
Peter Pomegranate (ship) 299
Petre, Sir William 583–4, 604
petrology of whetstones 337–40
pewter objects Pl. 55
    Barber-surgeon's 189, 199–202, *201–3*, 221, 222, 444, *491*, 423; *see also* syringes
    carpenter's monogrammed 13, 655
    class of owners 478, 655
    composition and provenance 423–4
    cooking assemblage 423–5; *see also individual items*
    dating 423
    European 200, 423–4, 437–8
    garnish (full service) *see under* Carew, Sir George
    metallurgical analysis 658
    privy marks 13, 423–4, *442*, 460, 490–3, *491–2*, 494, 495–6; on Barber-surgeon's property 200–1, *202–3*, 444, *491*, *492*, 493; *see also under* Carew, Sir George; Lisle, Viscount
    standards and weights for flatware 423, 424–5
    see also bowls; canisters; chamber pot; clasps; dishes; flagons; flasks; platters; porringers; pottle/ potel; saucers; spoons; syringes; tankards; trenchers; wine measure
Pewterers' Company 423, 440, 441, 490
pharmaceuticals *see* medicaments
phials or bottles, Barber-surgeon's glass 189, 192–3, *193*, 225, Pl. 28
philosophy of excavation 501–3
photography 6, *565*, 566
pig bones and pork 574–7, *574–7*, Pl. 71
    age at death 609
    anatomical elements present 576–7
    butchery 574, *574*, 576–7
    casks 565, 566, 574, *574*, 606; in rigging 385, 410, 418, 421, 422, 566, *568*, 569, 574, 606, 609
    in diet, with peas 15, 601, 603–4, 607, 608–9
    distribution 566, 568, *568*, 569, 574, 577, 654

DNA analysis 559, 646, *646*, 647, 656
fat adhering to 586, 631–2
feed contained no fish residues 643
fresh pork or bacon 569
matching of skeletons 566
Orlop deck deposit 385, 565, 566, *568*, 574–7, *575–7*, 586, 588, 609, 631–2
quantity needed daily 609
radicarbon dating 642–3
scapula fragments 568
scattered 577
size of animals 585–6, 609
size of pieces 604, 606, 607
sources of supplies 611
watering before cooking 385, 410, 418, 421, 422, *566*, 568, 569, 574, 606, 609
pikes and bills 2, 17, 26, 42
pilots 11, 264–7, 655
cabin, so-called 2, *2*, 15, 266, 268, 653
chest with navigational instruments 15, *265*, 266, 394, 397
foreign, possibly French 12, 266, 655
pay 262, 266
pins
copper-alloy 328, *328*, 329, 398
silver: dress *115*, 116, 117; sewing 329
pipkins, pottery 466, *466*, 474–5, 477
piss-dale 16, 153–4, 617
pitch/tar
casks of 13, 14, 320, 323, 385, 410, 416–17, *416*, Pl. 48
chromatography 514
iron nails preserved in 321
leather buckets sealed with 366
location of stores 13, 14, 385, 654
origin of supplies 323
pot for 14, 320, *320*, 321, *323*, Pl. 48
tankards lined with *451*, 452
see also caulking
plague 174, 180, 614
planes 295, 297, 312–16, *314–16*, Pl. 49
unfinished blank 296, 316
plant remains 501, 514, 588–602, Appx 3
assessment, review and selection 589
charred 600
colouring 591
common names 591
condition of remains 591–2
dating secure 602
DNA analysis 656
farming techniques and genetic alteration 589
foodstuffs and seasonings 593–7, 600, 601

incorrect earlier identifications 508, 588, 597
insects in 613
location of samples *590*, 592
objectives of project 588–9
preservation 591, 602
processing programme 507, 589–91
quantification 592–3
sampling 588, *590*
textiles associated with 601
trade and supply 602
types by deck and sector 592
value of assemblage 602
see also bedding; caulking; cereals; fruit; packing materials; pollen analysis; weeds; and individual plants
plantains 619, 620, 622, 626, 628
plaque on femoral neck 521–2
plasters, surgical 219, 223, 224
platters
distribution *441*
pewter 424, 440–1, *441–2*, 443; marks 440–1, *442*, 443, *491–2*, 494
wooden 15, 424, 426, 440, *441*, 443, 484–7, *485*, *487*; marks 419, 443
Plock, Poland; fiddle-like artefact 242, 244
plugs *see* bungs/plugs
plumb-bob, lead *333*, 334
plums/prunes/greengages 15, 182, 385, 407–8, 592, 593, 596–7, *596*, 601, 602
analysis 506, 514, 656
pollack 578, 579, 582
pollen analysis 514, 617–29
exotics, fir and spruce 628–9
general introduction to 617–18
location and associations of samples and summary of results *618*, 619
marine/halophytic plants 623, 626
marsh/aquatic types 621, 623, 625
method 618, 621
packing materials/deck coverings 626
palynological pilot studies 506, 508, 642
pollen data 620–6
pollen diagram *624–5*
in sediments 619, 620, 623, 626
ship-related pollen 626–9
spores 621, 623, 625, 628
in staved container 628, 629
and regional vegetation 623, 626
see also individual plants and types of plant and under ballast; bedding; bilge pump; caulking; chests; gunpowder; rope; sailcloth
polymerase chain reaction (PCR) amplification of DNA 559, *644*, 645, 646

polypody root extract 192, 220, 222, 472
pomanders 157, 161, *163*, 168
pork *see* pig bones and pork
porringers, pewter, Barber-surgeon's 189, 200–1, *202*
Port books and Brokerage accounts 604, 612
port side of ship, collapse of 512, 564
porthole with shutter 13, 296
Portsmouth, Hampshire
building of ship in 12, 303, 349, 350, 608
dysentery outbreak (1545) 524
Oyster Street; pottery 466
Portugal
pottery 192
silver whistles 289
post-Tudor period
finds 255–6, 346–7, 358, 359
salvage operations 255, 478
sea-bed environment 513, 579; *see also* shelly layer
pottery 424, 429, 462–78, Pl. 56
Barber-surgeon's *see* Raeren stoneware (jars; jugs); Low Countries (tin-glazed) below
catalogue 476–7
cooking and serving vessels 424, *427*, 429, Pl. 63
see also cooking pots; costrels
dating 464
distribution 2, 429, *448*, 464, *465*
petrological analysis 464
vessel types 463–4
WARES 463–4
English
local 464, 466–7, *466–7*, 474–5, 476, 478
Surrey Whiteware or Border Ware 464, 467, 476, 477, 478, Pl. 56
Sussex blackware 466–7, *466–7*, 476, 478, Pls 56, 63
French 464, 467–9, *468*, 476, 478
Beauvais/Martincamp 464, 467–9, *468*, 475, 476, 477, 478
Breton 464, 469, 476, 477, 478
Loire–type 464, *468*, 469, 475, 476, 478
Saintonge 464, 469, 476, 478
German
Bartmann jug or Bellarmine 478
Raeren stoneware 478; jars 189, 190, *191*, 192, 225, 464, 471–2, *471*, 474, 477; jugs 464, 471–2, *471*, 477; mug 424, 452, 462, 464, 472, *473*, 474, 477
Iberian 464, 472–4, *473*, 475, 477
Red Micaceous ware 192, 192,

464, 472, 477, *471*, 472–3, 478
    Seville 464, 472, 477, 478
    tinglazed 464, 474, 477
    uncertain source 464, 473–4, *473*, 477
    Valencian 464, 474, 477, 478
  Low Countries 464, 466, 468, 469–70, *470*, 475, 476–7, 478, Pl. 63
    tin-glazed (maiolica) 192, *192*, 464, 470, 477, Pl. 27
  unknown
    Breton/Galicia 464, 474
    tin-glazed 464, 474, 477
  see also bottles; bowls; cooking pots; costrels; grenade; inkpots; jars; jugs; mug; olive jars; pipkins; storage vessels (pottery)
pottle or potel, pewter 428, *436*, 438
pouches, leather 107–12, *110–12*
  associated finds 109; human remains 111; leather jerkins 25, 42
  contents 109, 123, 126, 138; coins 15, 109, 250, 254, 255, 261, 657
  distribution 15, 107–8, 109, 214
  embroidered 16, 107–11, *110–11*, 117
  see also purses, leather
poultices 219, 223
pouting 578, 579
powder flasks 26, 27, 41
Pox, French (venereal syphilis) 174, 180
Poyntz family 36, 290
Praetorius, Michael; *Syntagma Musicum* 233, 236
prayer books *see under* books
preservation
  bone 501, 516–17, 564, 568, 569
  fish 578
  human remains 501, 510, 516–17, 532–3, 563
  leather 18
  metals 99, 103, 321
  organic materials 6, 501, 524, 653
  plant remains 591, 602
  rope and rigging 3, 18
  textiles 18
  woodware 478–9
pricker, wooden 374
'pricking for pieces' (sharing of meat) 496, 605–6
prisoners of war 12
privy marks *see* marks, privy
probes, surgical 189, 208, 211
Protection of Wrecks Act (1973) 9, 503
protective devices *see* marks (protective and religious devices)
protractors 265, 274–5, *275*
  slate 274–5, *275*, Pl. 39
  wooden 275, *275*

provisioning 12, 514, 594, 608–9, 656
  see also victualling
psalter, Latin, of Henry VIII 228, 229–30
pump, bilge 13
  pollen from 619, 626, 628
punishment, injuries from 181
purges 16, 181
purse-hangers, copper alloy 112–13, *112*
purser 11, 180, 542–3, *543*, 609–10, 657
  chest possibly belonging to 11, *252*, 253, 255, 262, 396, 397, 657
purses, leather 15, 657
  Barber-surgeon's 112, *112*, 214
  see also pouches, leather
purveyors, county 610, 611

quills
  holder 368, *369*
  nibs 127, 132, 134

rabbits
  bones 585
  fur lining in shoe 31, 82, 87–8
radicarbon dating 642–3
rails, oak 382–3
rations 523–4, 601, 603
rats 16, 181, 566, 613–14, *613*, 615, 657
razors 154, 156, 157, 657
  Barber-surgeon's 15, 16, 154, *157*, 189, *209*, 217, *218*, 398
recording system 3–10
  archive record cards 6, *7*
  classification of finds 6–9
  databases 9–10
  open–area excavation 4, *4*
  sectors 5, *5*
  trenches 3–5, *4*, *5*
recovery methods 5–6
recreational objects *see* games and gaming; musical instruments
Red Bay, Labrador; *San Juan* wreck
  binnacle 267
  casks 409, 413, 414, 415, 419, 421
  fatty materials 631
  footwear 85, 88
  incised gaming/counting board 140
  mess tub 358
red textiles 41, *96*, 96–7
red heart (fungal infection) 484
reels *see* chalk line reels; log-reel
Regent (ship) 604
religion and religious items 16, 117–27, 658
  candles in devotion 124, 125–6
  Henry VIII's reforms, and popular reception 16, 120, 123, 125–6, 126–7, 656, 658
  inscriptions and devices 16, 109, 110, *111*, 117, 125–6, 126–7, *130*, *131*, 131–2; 167, 168, *169*,

261, *261*, 433, *433*, *437*, 438, 439, 440–1, 444, *451*, *453*, 493–4, *494*, *495*, 656, Pl. 62
  see also badge, token or icon of Virgin Mary; books (prayer); casket panel; crosses; pater-nosters
repairs
  brass pitch/tar bowl 320, *321*
  carpenter working on Orlop deck at sinking 14, 96, 293, 310–11, 317, 337
  casks 317, 319, 415
  clothing 16, 20, 41, 48, 657
  to ship in action 293–4, 297
  shoes 16, 20, 61, 89, *89*
  wooden wedges to repair ship 349
  woodware 487–8, *487*
  see also caulking; sewing equipment
respiratory conditions 180, 526, *527*
ribbons, silk 18, 20, 25, *30*
  books with 128, 130, 131, *132*, 132
  caps with 32, *33*, *34*, 35
  halters for boatswain's calls 285, *286–8*, Pl. 41
  see also braids
rickets 180, *523*, 524, 526, 657
rigging
  preservation 3
  steeping vats strapped to 385, 410, 418, 421, 422, 566, *568*, 569, 574, 605, 606, 609
  stowage 2, 13, 385
rigging block, unfinished 14, 293, *294*, 311
rings, finger 109, 113–17, *114–16*
  signet *115*, 116–17, Pl. 12
rod, willow, with woven leather fringe 374–5, *375*
Romanov family; DNA identification 644, 647
'Romayne' heads 131–2, 168, 261, *261*, 383
rope
  handles 356, 359, 388, *389*
  end of woven strop 327, *327*
  Orlop deck deposit 2, 127, 385
  pollen analysis 619, 626
  preservation 3, 18
  see also rigging
rosaries *see* paternosters
Royal Armouries, Leeds 100, 101
Royal George wreck 87
rules, wooden 294, 295, 297, 334–6, *335*, 367–8
rushes 600
Russia
  naval provisioning 608
  objects of piety on ships 127
  rutters 264–5, 272
  Hastings Manuscript *277*, 278

rye
   chaff 593, 598, 601, 602, Appx 3.2
   grain 592, 593, 656

sacks 15, 29, 18, 385, 408–9, 614
   of footwear, on Orlop deck 18, 20,
      25, 58, 79, 83, 84, 408, 409, 656
   insects associated with 616
   peppermill with fragment of 408,
      409, 459
sail palm 373, *373*
sailcloth 18
   pollen analysis 601, 619, 627–8
St Anthony's Fire (ergot poisoning) 174
Saint Denis, Paris 120, 135
Salisbury, Wiltshire 139, 583
salvage operations
   16th century 3, 564
   19th century, by Deanes 255, 478
sampling programme 503–4, 505, 564,
   588
   recording system 5–6
stratigraphy 504–5, *505*
San Diego wreck 123
San Juan wreck see Red Bay, Labrador
sandglasses 11, 264, 266, 270, 281–4,
   282–4
sand-smelt 578, 579
sanitation 16, 153–4, 161–2, 164
   piss-dale 16, 153–4, 617
   see also chamber pot
Santa Margarita wreck 292
Santissimo Sacramento wreck 601
saucers
   pewter 424, 444–5, *444*, *491–2*
   Barber-surgeon's 201–2, *203*, 444,
      491
   distribution *441*, 444
   marks: crowned pewterer's hammer
      444–5, 445; HB 13, 445, *492*;
      swan 201, *203*, *491*
   wooden *441*
sawing horse, stool or trestle 14, 295,
   297, 317, *318*
saws
   amputation 189, 208, *209*, *211*, 212
   carpenter's 295–6, 316–17, *317*
scabbards, leather sword 26, 161, 163
scales 257–61, 262–3
   copper-alloy, for coins; in box
      257–60, *258–9*, 395, 508, Pl. 35;
      empty leather balance case 131,
      260–1, *261*
   wooden 424, *459*, 462, *463*, 489
   see also weights
Scanning Electron Microscopy 27
Scheurrak SO1 wreck 272, 584
scientific studies 630–50
   data acquisition 501–14
   glues 632–3

medicines, ointments and related
   items 219–24, 633–41, 657
   for sake of *Mary Rose* project 630–41
   for sake of science 630, 641–50, 658
   see also chemical analyses; CHN
      analysis; chromatography; den-
      drochronology; DNA studies;
      fats, animal; microstructural
      analysis of bone; plant remains;
      pollen analysis; radiocarbon
      dating
scogger, possible 18, 22, 58–9, *58*
scourpits 510, 511–12
   pig bones in Starboard 566, *568*,
      569, 574
   recording system 4, *4*, 5, *5*
   sand-smelt in Starboard 578, 579
screw-elevator, surgical 176, 177, 189,
   208, *208*, 212, *212*
scurvy 174, 180, 524, 596, 614, 657
   naval diet and 174, 608, 610, 611
   pathology 524–6, *525–6*
sea scorpion, recent 579
Sea Venture (ship) 293
sea-bed environment 511–13
seal matrix, boxwood 109, 127, 133, *134*
'seaweed', material identified as 512
seaweed fly 616–17, *617*
sediments 5–6, 510, 511–13, 514
   pollen analysis 619, 620, 623, 626
   see also shelly layer
sewing
   equipment 16, 105, 327–30, *328–9*,
      657, Pls42–3
   stitching methods 38, *38*, 63, *63*, 66,
      68, *69*, 70, *70*
Shakespeare, William 40
   Birthplace, Stratford-upon-Avon
      392, 396
sharpening tools 336–41
   see also grinding wheel; whetstones
shaving and grooming items 11, 15, 16,
   154, 156–7, 171, 172, 189, 216–18,
   216–18, 355, 657, Pl. 20
   see also combs; ear–scoops; whet-
      stones
shawm, still 228, *229*, 230, 236–41,
   239–41, 657–8, Pl. 32
   case *226*, 227, 236, 242
   consonance in pitch with tabor pipes
      230, 241
   incomplete range, and solution 228,
      240
   location *226*, 227
   importance 228, 657–8
sheaths *see* knife sheaths
sheep 569, 577, 586, 611–12
sheepskin 31, 41, 87
shelly layer 510, 513, 565, 577, 619
Shinnan Gun wreck 601

shipbuilding 11–12, 293
   Henry Grace à Dieu 603
   Mary Rose 12, 303, 349, 350, 608
shirts, linen 19
shoes 19, 59–72
   buckled 25, *69*, 70, *71*, 72, *85*, 86,
      100, 101
   cereal chaff stuffing 601
   in chests 24, 25, *26*, 79, *82*, *83*
   comparable finds elsewhere 85–6
   construction 59–65
   cut down from taller examples 88
   decoration 89–90, *90*; slashing 68,
      68, *69*, 80, *80*, 89–90, *90*, Pl. 8;
      stitching *66*, 68, *68*, *69*, 70, *70*
   distribution *21*, 79, *82*, *83*
   early medieval 87
   high-throated 18, 79–81, *80*, *81*, *83*,
      85–6
   human remains associated with *21*,
      22, 23, 25, 79, 82
   incised and inscribed marks 20, *91*,
      91–2, 656
   jerkins associated with 25, 42
   with laces or aiglets 25, 65, 79, 99
   leaf-stuffed 601
   linings: rabbit fur 82, 87–8; textile
      18, 19, 25, 58, 86, *87*, 87–8, 94
   low-cut slip-on 18, 27, 70, *72*, 72,
      81–2, *81*, *83*, *85*, 85–67, 656, Pl.
      7; very low-cut fashionable 27,
      82, 86, 87–8
   modified for foot conditions 92–4,
      92, *93*, 657
   mules 80–1, *92*
   official issue 91–2, 656
   repairs 16, 20, 61, 89, *89*
   reuse of parts 88, 88–9
   sackful on Orlop deck 18, 20, 25, 58,
      79, 408, 409, 656
   sizing, possible marks *91*, 91–2
   skiving 60
   suede *87*, 87–8, 89
   turnshoes 61, *61*, *62*, 85
   turn-welted 61, *62*
   types (1–4) 65–72
   wear patterns, abnormal 93–4
   welted 59–61, *59*, *60*, 85
   see also boots
shore excavations 6, 504
shot 2, 109, 385
shovels, wooden 348–9, *349*, 385, 656
shrapnel wounds 174–5
shutter, porthole 13, 296
sickness *see* disease; health of crew;
   medicine
sieves 352, *353*, 358–9
signet ring 115, 116–17, Pl. 12
silk
   arrow binding 633

checked and striped 35
laces 18, 79, *98, 99*, 99
preservation 18
quantity 20
red *96*, 96–7
weaves 29, 30–1
thread attached to sounding lines 279
threads associated with skeleton 23
see also braids; buttons; caps and hats; cords, silk; discs (silk-covered leather); embroidery; ribbons
silts *see* sediments
silver objects *see* calls; rings, finger; paternosters; pendants; pins
silver thread embroidery 109, 110, *111*
simples and compounds, medicinal 175, 180–1, 182–9, 192
sinking of *Mary Rose* 16–17
and chests 13, 14, 297
crew trapped by netting 2, 17, 509, 516
immediate attempts to refloat ship 564
impact crater 509, 510, 511
survivors 17
violence and speed 17, 297, 509, 510, 516, 569
skantyllyon (marking gauge) 311
skimmer, copper alloy 424, *427, 431*, 432
skulls, human *see under* dentistry; fractures
slate protractor, possible 274–5, *275*
slates, navigational recording 274–5, *275*
Slava Rossii wreck 127
sleeping arrangements 13, 15, 653, 654
see also bedding; beds; mattresses
sleeves 18, 20, 23, 40, 50
knitted (scogger), possible 18, 22, 58–9, *58*
Sleipner (recovery ship) 6, 504
slipper limpet (*Crepidula fornicata*) 513
Smith, Captain John; *A Sea Grammar* 266, 278
soap, possible 446, 448
social stratification 15, 18, 19, 478, 612
see also officers
sock or scogger 18, 22, 58–9, *58*
soft tissue, human 501, 510, 514, 516, 563
sounding leads and lines 11, 264, *265*, 266, 270, 272, 277–9, *277–8*, 655
Southampton
combs 157
decline 174
domino tiles 140
foodstuffs, trade in 602, 612
tally sticks 334
wooden bowls 482
Sovereign (ship) 608

space and activity, organisation of 653–6, 658
Spasmadraps see bandages
spatulas, Barber-surgeon's 189, 207
Spert, Thomas (Master of *Mary Rose*) 11
spice/peppermills *see* peppermills
spigot, copper-alloy 373
spiles and/or shives 385, 389, 424, *459*, 461–2, *462*
splints 176, 177
spoke shaves 295, 296, 317, 319, *319*
spoons
distribution *448*
as personal possessions 15, 42, 109, *449*, 449–50, 657
pewter 424, *448*, 449–50, *449*, Pl. 67; fleur-de-lis mark *449*, 449, 490, *491*
wooden 15, 42, 109, 424, *448*, 449–50, *449*, Pls57, 67; Barber-surgeon's *212*, 213; owners' marks *449*, 449–50
spores 621, 623, 625, 628
spruce pollen 628–9
staining
black, indicating iron object 296
iron oxide, on human remains 517
stamps *see* marks, privy
stand, folding wooden 376, 381–2, *382*
stature, human 519–20
staved wooden items *see* wooden vessels and containers, staved
steelyard poises, lead 330–1, *330, 333*
Sterncastle *2*, 2, *3*, 15, 17
steeping vats strapped to 385, 410, 418, 421, 422, 566, *568*, 569, 574, 605, 606, 609
Stirling Castle wreck 431, 441, 444
stitching methods 38, *38*, 63, *63*, *66*, 68, 69, 70, *70*
stone objects *see* whetstones
stones, decorative and semi-precious 117, *122*, 123, *125*, 126
stools 653
boarded 380–1, *380, 381*, Pl. 51
four-legged 377–8, *378, 379*
stoppers or lids 295
cork 190, 191, 192, 225, 471–2
wooden 295, 371–3, *372*, 488, *488*
storage vessels for foodstuffs 424, *459*, 460–2
stowage 16, 384–421, 422, 654–5
main areas 2–3, *3*, 12, 13, *384*, 384–7; *see also under* Hold; Main deck; Orlop deck
see also individual commodities and basketry; boxes, small wooden; canisters; casks; chests; sacks
straps, leather 26, 100, 103, 189, 214
Strasbourg, France 120, 224

Stratford-upon-Avon, Warwickshire; Shakespeare's Birthplace 392, 396
stratigraphy 10, 565, 577
and microstructural post-mortem change 650
sampling 504–5, *505*
see also sediments; shelly layer
straw *503*, 507, 588, 599, *605*
pollen analysis 619, 626
radicarbon dating 642–3
thigh boots stuffed with *88*, 88
strops, 'sword-matting' 325–7, *326–7*
structure of ship *2*, 2–3
Studland Bay wreck, Dorset 88, 601, 602
styptics 211, 219
Sumptuary Laws 19, 120, 290–1
sundials, pocket 162–70, *165–7, 169–70*, Pls 23–4, 39
case, reused book cover 130, 131, 167, 168, *169*, 261, Pl. 24
in chests 167–8
compasses in 163–4, *165, 166*, 169–70, *170*
distribution 167–8
with human remains 168
with leather jerkins 27, 41, 168
letters on gnomons 166, *166*, 169
magnetic declination marks 163–4, 165, *166*, 169–70, 170
numerals 169, 170
place of manufacture 163–4; Nuremberg 163–4, 168, 170, 274
in pouch 109
supply *see* provisioning; victualling
Surgeons, Fellowship of 171
surgical instruments, turned handles from 189, 208–12, *210–12*, 214, *215*, 224–5
survivors of sinking 12, 17, 174
Sviatoï Nikolaï wreck 127
Swan wreck 431
Sweden; naval provisioning 608
Switzerland 168, 174
'sword-matting' (strops) 325–7, *326–7*
swords 26, 216
Symson, Robert (surgeon on *Mary Rose*) 11
syphilis, venereal 174, 180, 526, 657
syringes 189, *202*, 205, *206*, 208, *208*, 423

Tables set 133, 134–7, *135, 136*, 137, Pl. 18
tableware
Carew's 15, 424, 440–1, *442*, 444, 445, 490, *491–2*, 493, 656
Lisle's 441, 443, *491, 492*, 493
see also individual types and woodware, turned

tabor 16, *226*, 227–8, 230–2, *231–2*
  case *226*, 227, 232, 233
    playing of 15, 227–8, *228–9*, 229–30
tabor beater *226*, 227, 232, 233
tabor pipes 16, 227–8, *228–9*, 229–30, 233–6, *234–8*
  location *226*, 227
  length 227–8, *228–9*, 233
    marked E:LEGROS 228, 233, *234–5*, 236; probable tabor beater stored inside 232, 233
    marked !! 228, 233, *235*, 236, *237–8*
    playing of 227–8, *228–9*, 229–30, 241
    unmarked pipe 233, *235*, 236, *236–7*
tabula *see* Tables set
tailoring patterns 20, 48
tallow 385, 410, 417, 654
  candles of 343
tally sticks 109, 295, 334, 335
tampions, cask of 385, 410, 417, 421
tankards
  pewter 423, 424, *448*, 450–1, *450*
  staved wooden 424, 427–8, 450, *451*, 452, Pl. 58
  Barber-surgeon's 214, 225, *451*, 495
  distribution 15, *448*
  gallon serving 15, 117, 385, 427
  marks 214, 428, *451*, 452, 493, *495*, 496; Ny Coep/Cop 11, 428, 493
  pitch or waxy lining 428, *451*, 452
taphonomy 508–13
  animal bone 564–5, 586–8
  human remains 516, *516*, *517*, 648–50
  marine/land-based differences 586–8
teasels 591, 593, 600, 601, Appx 3.2
teeth *see* dentistry
teredo worm 510, 512
textiles 28–31, Appx 2
  assemblage 20, 31
  associated finds: bracken 599, 601; buckles 25; footwear 18, 19, 25, 58, *76*, 76, 86, *87*, 87–8, 94; laces 25; plant remains 599, 601
  weave types 28–31, *28*, *29*
  see also dyes; linen; sacks; sailcloth; sewing; silk; wool
thimbles 109, 328, 329–30, *329*, Pl. 42
thong, leather, attached to plumb-bob 334
thread, sewing 38, 88
thrums, woollen 33
tide calculator *265*, 266, *275*, 279–81, *280*
Tiel, Netherlands 123, 140
timber, measure for thickness of 310–11, *310*
timepieces *see* sandglasses; sundials,

pocket
tin alloy *see* pewter
Tinctoris, Johannes; *De Inventione et Usu Musicae* 228, 239, 240
tinder boxes 398
tobacco leaves on *Amsterdam* 501
toilet items 154, 156–62, 156–63
  see also combs; earscoops; toilet sets
toilet sets 154, 157
  bone 159, 161, *161*
  wooden 159, *162*
tokens 25
  of Virgin Mary 16, 109, 126–7, *126*, 658
tonnage of *Mary Rose* 12
tool holders
  leather 368, *369*
  wooden 14, 295, 297, 367–8, *367*
tools
  carpenters' 2, 13, 293–319, 655, Pl. 46; assemblage 294–6, *296*; basketful in cabin 13, 297, 299, 305, 308–9, 310, 312, *503*; in chests and crates 297, 385, 389, 391; on Orlop deck 14, 96, 293, 297, 310–11, 317, 337; unfinished 14, 293, 296; *see also* adzes; augers; axes; braces; chalk line reels; compass, measuring; gimlets; hammers; joggle stick; mallets; marking gauge; planes; sawing horse; saws; spoke shaves
  concretion of iron parts 296, 308
  general 348–56, *350–6*
  personal marks 295–6, 307, *308*
  sharpening 336–41
  see also individual types
tooth-picks 154
Towton, N. Yorkshire; battle 516, 538
travel, crew members' 339–40
treatment bench, Barber-surgeon's 14, 171, 177, 214, 377, *378*, 653
tree of life symbols 493
trees and shrubs 591, 592, 593, Appx 3.3
  pollen analysis 620, 622, 623, 624, 625, 628–9
trenchers
  pewter 444
  wooden 424, *441*, *443*, 443–4
trenches 3–5, *4*, *5*
trepan *see* screw-elevator, surgical
trestles 13, 137, 379–80, *379*, *381*
La Trinidad Valencera wreck 126, 325, 343, 488
Trinity, symbols of *433*, *453*, 493, *494*
troughs, wooden 424, 434–5, *434–5*
trousse, possible 368, *369*
tuberculosis 180, 526, *527*
tubs, wooden staved 15, 356, 358, 359, Pl. 47

turning *see* woodware, turned
tweezers 154
twybill, absence of 295
Tysill, Edmund (fl.1513, metalworker) 425, 431

unguents 219, 224
unguent rolls *see* bandages
uniform, possible 19–20, 656
Upper deck 2–3, *2*, 15
  anti-boarding netting 2, 16–17, 509, 516
  baskets *407*, 407, 408
  casks 420, 421
  chests 385, *386*
  clothing 24, *26*, 25, 82–3, 84, 96; with human remains 22, 23, 25; leather jerkins 41–2, *43*, *43*, *45*, 44
  guns 15, 16
  plant remains 592, 594, 600

Vasa (ship) 86, 250, 383
vegetables in shipboard diet 524
velvet *see* caps and hats
venereal disease 174, 180–1, 205, 526, 657
venison 569, 577, 584–5, *585*, 612
Vergulde Draeck wreck 123
verjuice 597
Vesalius, Andreas 171, *209*
victualling 180, 602–12, 656
  army 604, 608, 610
  and crew's efficiency 607–8
  menu 15, 603–5
  officers' 612
  organisation 180, 609–11, 612, 656
  problems of quality 610–11, 656
  quantities 608–9, 610
  rations 523–4, 603, 609–10
  records 602
  sources of supplies 611–12
  see also food and drink
Vigo, Giovanni (John) da
  Antidotarie 182
  Compounds and Simples 182, 183–5, 186–9
  The Most Excellent Workes of Chirurgerye 172, 175, 176, 178, 179, 180–1
Virgin Mary *see* Mary, Virgin
vitamin deficiencies 524, 608

wadding, gun 510, 598, 601
wallet, Barber-surgeon's wood-stiffened leather 189, *213*, 214
walnuts 593, 597
Warrior, HMS 426
watch system 281–4, 654
wax candles 343

waxy substance for waterproofing 428
weapons 2, 15, 17, 25–6, 385
    wounds from cutting 175, 175–6
    see also arrows; grenade; guns; long-bows; pikes and bills; swords
weather 12, 596, 602, 608, 610
weaving 28–31, 323–7
    weave types of textiles 28–31, *28, 29*
    weaving equipment 325–7, *325–7*
webbing strops 325–7, *326–7*
wedges, wooden 296, 349–50, *350–1*
weeds 588–9, *599*, 599–600, Appx 3.5
    common names 591
    crop *598*, 598, *599*, 599, 602, 615, 619, 626
    distribution 592, 599
    grassland 598–9
    habitats by genus or species 593
    pollen analysis 620–1, 622–3
weevils 16, 615, 616
weights 330–4, *330–3*
    copper-alloy *331*, 332, 334; coin 257, 259–60, *258, 259*, Pl. 35; fishing 141–2, 143
    lead 109, *331*, 332, *333*, 334; fishing 141–2, 143; steelyard poises 330–1, *330, 333*
    trade weights 332
    Troy 332, 334
    verification stamps *331*, 332
    see also scales
welfare 657
wheat, bread 592
wheels
    repair of 317, 319, *319*
    spare gun carriage 385
whetstones 337–40, *338*, Pl. 45
    Barber-surgeon's 13, 189, *208*, 217, 337, 339
    carpenters' 13, 294, 295
    cases 340, *340*, Pl. 45
whistles 227
    Barber-surgeon's 189, 214
    see also calls
whiting 578, 579
wicker
    vessels covered with: ceramic 424, 462, 464, 467–9, *468*, 476, Pl. 64; glass 424, 460–1, *461*
    see also baskets
William Salthouse wreck 409, 421
willow rod with woven leather fringe

374–5, *375*
Winchester, Hampshire 145, 330, 343, 482, 598
wine 656
    possible casks 15, 385, 410, 417–18, 421, 597
    wine measure, pewter 15, 385, 424, 439–40, *439*, 492, 597
Witte Leeuw wreck 292
Wolin, Poland 143–4
Wolsey, Cardinal Thomas, Archbishop of York 419
wooden objects *see* bottles (wooden feeding-); bowls; boxes, small wooden; bungs/plugs; candle holders; candlestick; canisters; combs; compass, carpenter's wooden; discs (wooden octagonal); disgorgers; dishes; dividers (case); fiddle case; flagons; floats, fishing; funnels, wooden; gaming equipment (counters); hand-line frames, fishing; handles; hooks; knife sheaths; ladles; log-reel; mallets; manicure or toilet sets; mess tag; 'messing' items; needles, surgeon's; panelling, decorated oak; plank; pomanders; pricker; protractors; rod; shawm, still (case); shovels; spatulas; spoons; stoppers; tabor (case); tankards, staved wooden; tide calculator; tool holders; trenchers; troughs; weighing scales, wooden; whetstones (cases); wooden vessels and containers, staved; woodware, turned
wooden vessels and containers, staved 385, Pl. 62
    inscriptions and incised marks 357, *357*, 359, 419, *437*, 438, 439, *495*, 655, Pl. 62
    large container 424, *459*, 460, *460*
    pollen analysis 628, 629
    rat-proof 614
    reuse of parts 356, 359
    white cooperage 356–9, *357*, 427
    see also casks; buckets (wooden staved); flagons; funnels; tankards; tubs
woodware, turned 424, 426, 478–89, Pls 57, 59–61
    choice of timber 489
    class of users 15, 478
    conservatism of design 481, 485

decoration 480–1, 489
fungal infection ('red heart') 484
imports 489
lathes: bow 479; pole 479–80, *479*
marks 481–2, *481–2*, 493, *494–5*, 496; H brands 426, 482, *487*, 487
preservation 478–9
repairs 487–8, *487*
turning groups 481, 485–7, 489
turning technology 479–80, 484, 488, 489
    see also bowls; canisters; dishes; feeding-bottle; funnels; ladles; peppermills; platters; weighing scales
woollen textiles 28–30, Pl. 9
    colours 27, 28, 34, 48, 50, 5–6, 58
    fleece types 28
    fragments 15; with leather jerkins 25; with sounding lines 279
    fulling and felting 29, 30, 31–2, 35, 55
    laces 99
    preservation 18
    quantity 20, 31
    raised naps 29, 30, 31–2, 48, 50, 51, 54
    weave types 28–30, *28, 29*, 31, Pl. 9
    see also caps and hats; breeches; buttons; hose; jerkins (cloth); knitting; sacks; shoes (linings, textile); sleeves; sock or scogger
worms
    intestinal 181
    marine 510, 512
wounds 175–6, 205, *206*, 223, 531, *533*
writing equipment *see* inkpots; quills; seal matrix

X–ray fluorescence spectrometry (XRF) 222, 636

Yarmouth Roads wreck 437–8
Yonge, Henry (surgeon on *Mary Rose*) 11
York 33, 334, 488
Yorktown, USA; wreck sites 411

Zeebrugge, Belgium; *Herald of Free Enterprise* sinking 515

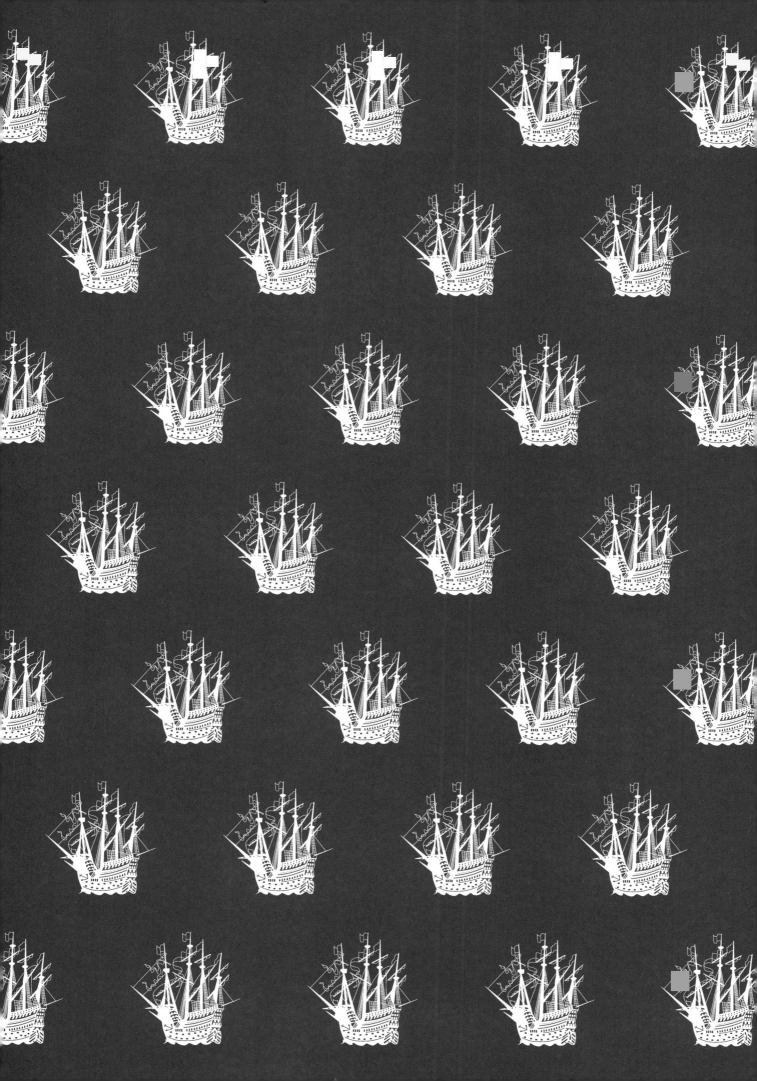

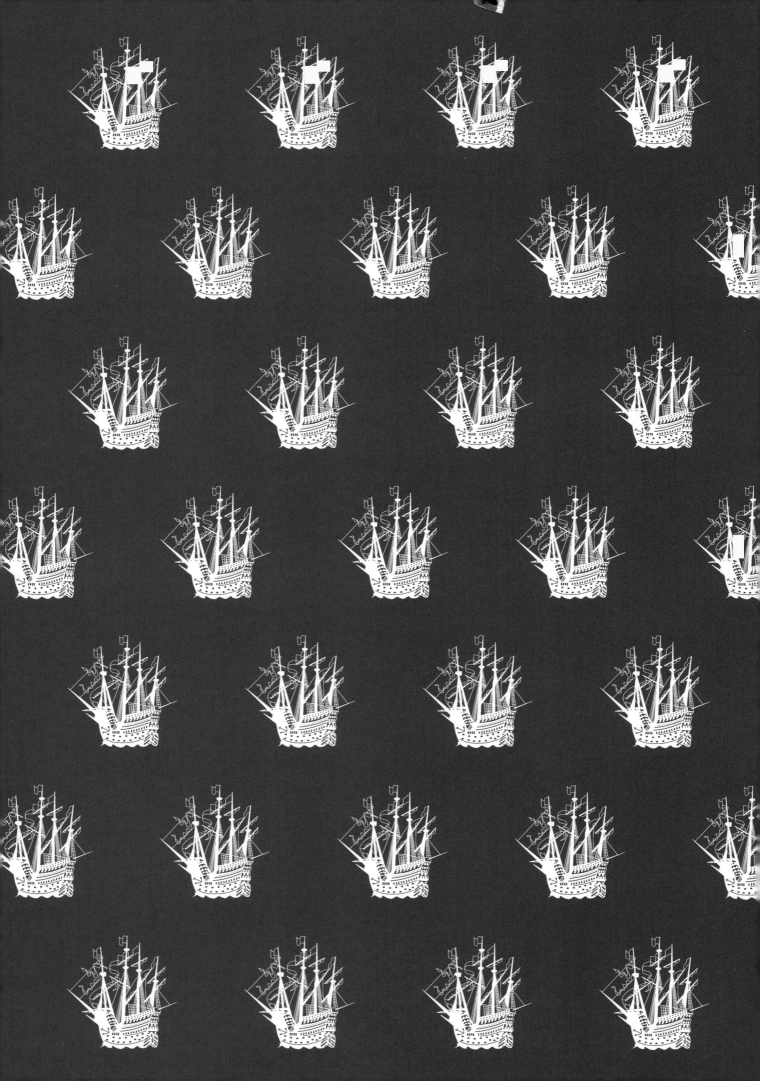